International Banking

The Addison-Wesley Series in Finance

International Banking
TEXT AND CASES

Jane E. Hughes
Brandeis University

Scott B. MacDonald
Aladdin Capital Holdings, Inc.

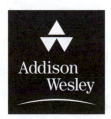

Addison
Wesley

Boston San Francisco New York
London Toronto Sydney Tokyo Singapore Madrid
Mexico City Munich Paris Cape Town Hong Kong Montreal

Editor in Chief: Denise Clinton
Acquisitions Editor: Donna Battista
Editorial Assistant: Amy Gembala
Marketing Manager: Adrienne D'Ambrosio
Managing Editor: James Rigney
Production Supervisor: Katherine Watson
Design Manager: Regina Hagen
Art Styling: Meredith Nightingale
Cover Design: Susan Carsten Raymond
Cover Art: © 2002 PhotoDisc
Text Design, Electronic Page Makeup, and Project Coordination: Electronic Publishing
    Services Inc., NYC
Manufacturing Manager: Hugh Crawford

Library of Congress Cataloging-in-Publication Data

Hughes, Jane E. (Jane Elizabeth)

International banking : text & cases / Jane Hughes, Scott MacDonald.
    p. cm.

Includes bibliographical references and index.

ISBN 0-201-63535-6

1. Banks and banking, International. I. MacDonald, Scott B. II. Title.

HG3881 .H834 2002

332.15--dc21

2001018867

Please visit our website at www.aw.com

ISBN 0-201-63535-6

1 2 3 4 5 6 7 8 9 10—MA—05 04 03 02 01

BRIEF CONTENTS

CONTENTS

PREFACE

International banking is a key component of the global economy. As an economic activity, it is central to the flow of capital around the world through the provision of loans, the supply of financial advice, and its involvement in securities markets. The role of banks has been and continues to be shaped by a number of mega-trends—the globalization of financial markets, the rise of nonbank competitors, the ongoing evolution and implementation of new technologies, and deregulation and disintermediation (i.e., the movement away from the middleman role played by banks between depositors and lenders).

Those banks that have opted to go international—that is, to extend their business across national boundaries and into the larger world in search of new customers and profits—find a pressing need to be more innovative. They must also be able to reconsider traditional ways of competing and be willing and flexible in their commitment to finding solutions to new challenges, such as marketing their services and products in multiple foreign markets, striking alliances with institutions in new markets, or developing secure e-banking service systems.

The purpose of this book is to provide a straightforward approach to understanding international banking. While the literatures on international banking, finance, and economics are extensive, the universe of basic textbooks on international banking is more limited. Indeed, the task of compiling a basic text on international banking is difficult, considering the fields of study that such an endeavor cuts across. Whereas money and banking are often taught as part of economics, foreign exchange trading and international banking are usually part of a business school curriculum. Depending on one's academic standing, international banking has different meanings, and any text that seeks to cover the subject matter must be holistic by its very nature.

The professional lens through which this particular book was initially visualized and written derived from the teaching of international banking at a university (Brandeis University) and considerable experience working for commercial banks (including Bankers Trust, Manufacturers Hanover Trust, and three regional banks), a banking regulatory agency (the Office of the Comptroller of the Currency), two investment banking firms on Wall Street (Credit Suisse First Boston and Donaldson, Lufkin & Jenrette), and a fixed income hedge fund. The authors brought the sum of those experiences into the defining of international banking and how such a text should read. It should be of use to those wishing to understand international banking, answering the fundamental questions and creating an awareness of the key issues.

Beyond identifying and defining key issues in international banking, the authors also seek to provide a theme for the book. We believe that international banking is in a state of tremendous change, reflected by an upswing in mergers and acquisitions within the banking sector, cross-border alliances between banks (often done through swaps in equity share ownership), and mergers and alliances across business sectors (such as between banking and insurance). In the year 2000 alone we witnessed multi-billion-dollar deals that brought about the acquisition by Chase Manhattan Bank of J.P. Morgan & Co.; the purchase by Citigroup of Associates (a large finance company); Union Bank of Switzerland's acquisition of Paine Webber; Goldman Sachs & Co.'s purchase of market maker Spear, Leeds & Kellogg; and Credit Suisse's takeover of Donaldson, Lufkin & Jenrette. Also evident are the rise of nonbank financial institutions actively engaged in many of the same areas where banks were traditionally dominant; deregulation of financial service sectors; and the growing trend toward disintermediation. These forces pose a challenge to the practice of international banking and augur substantial metamorphoses ahead.

The primary forces behind the change dynamic in international banking are technological innovations, acting in tandem with the globalization of markets. For example, before the 1990s bankers were not deeply concerned with the spread of the Internet. By the end of the 1990s all banks were linked by e-mail and racing to develop e-banking facilities to tie into the multibillion-dollar e-business sector. With Internet usage estimated at over 200 million users worldwide in 2000 and with rapid increases in usage expected in Asia and Latin America, no major international bank can afford to ignore e-banking or leave the field entirely to bank and nonbank competitors. Consequently, as we take the reader through the chapters of our book, we convey the message that international banking is a dynamic business, in which change is a constant feature, forcing bankers to adapt or be left behind in the highly competitive stampede to reach the commanding heights of the global economy. To complement our chapters, we have added seven case studies, which provide an in-depth examination of particular issues. These case studies are from the Harvard Business School, Richard K. Ivey School of Business, and EAP—European School of Management, and we are thankful for their permission. It should also be noted that teaching notes are available through Harvard, Ivey, and EAP.

The book seeks to address two audiences, not mutually exclusive. The first audience is the university circuit, either at the advanced undergraduate or the graduate level. The second audience is that of professionals in international finance who wish for a basic overview of international banking and an update on major trends in the industry.

The authors take full responsibility for the material in the book, but wish to thank the following who gave of their time to provide constructive criticism. These include Professor Albert L. Gastmann, Professor Emeritus, Trinity College, Hartford, Connecticut; Leon S. Tarrant, formerly a Senior Bank Examiner and the Chairman of the Interagency Country Risk Exposure Review Committee (ICERC) in Washington, D.C.; Matt Burnell, Senior Finance Company and Bank Analyst in the Fixed Income Research Department at Merrill Lynch (who was kind enough to provide data on a number of banking systems during the course of a busy day); Allerton Smith, Bank Analyst and Director of Investment Grade Fixed Income Research (rated as one of the top banking analysts by Institutional Investor magazine for close to ten years) at Credit Suisse First Boston; Professor Barry Rosen of Baruch College in New York City (who was good enough to suffer through a couple of chapters and provided useful criticism); Keith Rabin, President of KWR International; and Jon Hartzell, formerly Deputy Comptroller at the Office of the Comptroller of the Currency and now at Dresdner Bank. We also greatly appreciate the hard work and efforts of our reviewers, in particular, Gunter Dufey of the University of Michigan; Patrick A. Groenendijk of Vrije Universiteit Amsterdam; Laurent L. Jacque of Tufts University; Kurt Jesswein of Murray State University; Lawrence W. Lovik of Troy State University; Timothy A. Manuel of the University of Montana; Yoon S. Park of George Washington University; Joe Peek of Boston College; E. N. Roussakis of Florida International University; Sudhir Singh of Frostburg State University; Stephanie A. M. Smith of Texas A&M International University; Leo A. van Eerden of Rotterdam School of Management; and Michael C. Walker of the University of Cincinnati. Dean Peter Petri and other faculty and staff members of Brandeis University Graduate School in International Economics and Finance provided support and assistance at critical points along the way. Thanks are also extended to the library staffs at Trinity College, the Business Library of the City of New York, Sarah Woolf at Pine Manor College Library, the White Plains Public Library, and to the graduate research assistants at Brandeis University who helped in so many ways. Finally, the authors extend their appreciation to those individuals at Addison–Wesley who went through the long and sometimes frustrating birthing of this book.

Jane E. Hughes

Scott B. MacDonald

PART ONE

AN OUTLINE
OF INTERNATIONAL
BANKING

CHAPTER 1

INTRODUCTION

Everyone knows a little bit about banking. Indeed, most people in the industrialized countries of North America, Europe, and the Asia-Pacific region have put their money in banks, have mortgages, and have, on occasion, cursed the slowness of standing in line waiting for a teller. Now more of those curses are reserved for the slowness of the Internet service or their home computers. In the last two decades of the twentieth century, banking—and for the purposes of our study, international banking—has undergone massive changes in how business is conducted, the products offered, and the customer base as well as in who competes in the area of international finance. International money, capital, and securities markets have expanded rapidly. Banks play a pivotal role in each of these areas, making it incumbent on us to better understand the role that international banks play in the global economy.

This need for understanding gains in urgency as we expect the trends driving change in international finance to continue and accelerate in the early decades of the twenty-first century. Indeed, the changes that have rocked international banking since the 1980s have involved billions of dollars and have directly affected the health of the global economy. The debt crisis that hit Latin America and parts of Central and Eastern Europe, Africa, and Asia in the 1980s lost the banks more than $200 billion, and there have been 127 systemic bank crises in ninety-four countries during the past twenty-five years. (A systemic crisis is one in which large chunks of the banking capital in a country are wiped out.) Moreover, the 1997–98 financial crisis in Asia and its aftermath, which hit Russia and Brazil, reminded many people of the significant influence of banks and their management in the shaping of our daily lives. Perhaps "weiji," noting crisis of change, best captures the sense of what is taking place in international banking. *Weiji* denotes that both danger and opportunity are possible in the face of change. To achieve profit, effective risk management is essential. Bankers and other financial actors, after all, are caught up in what economist Joseph Schumpeter referred to as "the perennial gale of creative destruction."

This is a book about international banking, a vast subject. International banking is when a bank in one country undertakes activities that involve it in some form of business (loans, advice, securities issuance) in another country. International banks are those institutions heavily engaged in international business. Not all banks are international banks nor do they want to be, considering the often higher level of risk attached to developing markets outside of one's home turf. Our focus is on the forces that are shaping international banking—in particular, globalization, innovation, and technological change. These forces have had and continue to have a major impact on the evolution of the central **intermediary** role (middleman function) played by banks throughout history, from the traditional intermediation between borrowers and lenders to the more complex intermediation as risk managers.

International banking has a long and interesting history, with the modern business of extending credit beginning with the Italian merchant banks in the late Middle Ages. Throughout the evolution of international banking, there has been a close and essential relationship with business. The former helps intermediate for the latter in what has been an ever-expanding network of trade and commercial relationships. Indeed, the globalization of business, which has accelerated in past decades, has made the ability to obtain credit around the planet critical to conducting daily operations. At the same time, what is meant by international banking has changed considerably since the Italian merchant-bankers began to extend credit in the late Middle Ages. Banks have made a substantial transformation from the days of the Italian city-states to the dawn of the twenty-first century, when nonbank financial institutions play a major role and banks are in the midst of a major consolidation.

The Approach of the Book

The approach taken by this book borrows from the academic fields of finance, macroeconomics, strategic management, and public policy. Since the 1980s, the international banking industry has become one of the most dynamic and changing sectors in the global economy. In a simplistic sense, our vision of international banking is that of a constantly evolving field, driven by a number of variables the most significant of which are the globalization of financial markets, the emergence of new competitors, the deregulation process, and the application of technological innovations. The combination of these factors has resulted in reduced profit margins, increased competition (both within the banking world as well as from nonbank financial institutions), disintermediation of traditional banking (the movement away from the role of bankers as financial middlemen, replaced by direct interaction between the source of capital and those who need capital), ongoing product and process innovation, fundamental transformations in regulatory frameworks, and changes in the structure of banking. These changes provide a significant challenge to bank management as the new century begins. Bank management is forced to come up with solutions by formulating new product and client portfolios, by internationalizing strategy on mergers and acquisitions, and by creating better lines of communication in global networks. All of this, of course, is done with an eye to making profits.

To this view of international banking should be added three more points, which are reflected in the following chapters. One is historical, one is economic, and the last is structural. Although most finance and banking courses give scant treatment of the historical development of international banking, much can be learned from the successes and follies of the past. Moreover, the evolution of civilization is reflected in the evolution and growing sophistication of international banking. The expansion of trade around the planet has certainly been a stimulus to the globalization of banking as well as at least a superficial application of common banking practices and structures. Although the role of international banks should not be overstated, they have been active agents for the economic transition of Central and Eastern Europe from command economies to more market-oriented systems.

The second factor to be discussed is economic in nature—soft infrastructure. With the fast pace of technological innovation and the breakdown in geographical barriers to business development, soft infrastructure looms as a critical factor for international banking in the twenty-first century. We define soft infrastructure as the following: a high-tech skilled pool of workers, preferably with English, Japanese, French, or German language skills; a pleasant living environment, ranging from personal safety to taxi drivers conversant in an international language; and strong public institutions that uphold the rule of law and can deal with such matters as bankruptcy and honoring of contracts in a fair and fast fashion. Consequently, international banks must increasingly take into consideration the development of their human capital. Failure to see to soft infrastructure issues impinges on the bank's bottom line.

The third and last factor is structural. The lines between commercial banks, investment banks, and universal banks are increasingly blurred, even though commercial and investment banks still have distinct skill sets and cultures. However, there is a convergence in what these institutions offer and in the structures of these institutional models. This is increasingly the case in the United States, where firewalls created under the Glass-Steagall Act of 1934, which separated commercial and investment banking, have been dismantled. The same differences that were established in Japan are also falling by the wayside. The convergence in banking models is far from complete, but clearly in motion. The key drivers in this are the fall in bank profits during the early and mid-1990s and the diversification into other market activities, ranging from mergers and acquisitions to real estate.

This process of structural convergence in international banking has seen its problems. The concomitant deregulation that occurred also opened the door to areas of business activity that carry higher risks. This was mirrored in the real estate market problems that hit Scandinavian, U.S., and French banks in the late 1980s and early 1990s. Credit Lyonnais's troubled saga in the 1990s is another example of the dangers of diversification; this bank overexpanded in many directions in the 1980s, leading to a series of bailouts by the French government.[1]

These three factors indicate that international banking will continue to change throughout the twenty-first century. Competition and innovation remain as the core forces determining the pressing need to stay one step ahead of rival firms—be they universal banks, commercial banks, financial arms of major corporations (such as GE Capital), or insurance companies.

Outline of the Book

This book provides a primer on international banking. It is accessible to the general reader as well as to the student of finance who wants a comprehensive treatment of the subject. There are fifteen chapters broken into three overarching sections. The first part of the book focuses on definitions, a history of international banking, and a comparative view of the world's major banking systems, encompassing the United States, Japan, Europe, and key emerging market countries, such as Mexico, India, South Africa, and Indonesia. The approach in the first part of the book is historical and comparative, grounding the reader in the historical framework in which today's international banks function, while also underscoring that international banks operate under different guidelines stemming from their initial domicile.

The second part of the book focuses on the structure and functions of the international bank. Subject matter includes structure and functions of the global commercial banks, international investment banking, international retail and private banking, offshore financial centers, and the role of banks in the foreign exchange markets. The third part of the book covers risk management, obviously a key concern in a world characterized by money laundering scams and other financial fraud, sovereign debt defaults, and increasing international competition. Topics include modern risk management techniques, such as value at risk (VAR), supervision and regulation, international financial fraud, and emerging issues in international banking.

In several chapters, we have included a case study. Each detailed case reinforces the discussion in the particular chapter. We have also provided a glossary of international banking terms and a list of subject-related websites.

Defining Our Terms

International banking is often perceived as the more racy and exciting cousin to plain old domestic banking. After all, how can making loans to a student, local construction company, or retailer compete with the glamour of providing the necessary credit for the construction of railways in Tsarist Russia, the building of the Panama Canal, and financing of much of Hong Kong's impressive skyline? Historically, international banking certainly had a high degree of cachet as the domain of the rich, the well-born, and the talented, those with access to and influence with the movers and shakers of the day. The names of the Warburgs, Rothschilds, and Morgans evoke the age of bank houses with strong and colorful personalities at the helm, presiding over the international flow of credit as it helped shape national destinies from Argentina and Canada in the Americas to China and Thailand in Asia.

While the glamour of memorable families in international banking was a factor in the nineteenth and twentieth centuries, the business has evolved considerably and the network of who is involved has radically changed. Financing is no longer the purview of a few closeted and powerful individuals; rather, it is generally characterized by armies of investment bankers, credit committees, and regulators. Large numbers of analysts and complicated quantitative models have replaced a whisper in the ear from a finance minister or judging a loan on the basis of character. Giant corporations, such as Hong Kong Shanghai Bank (HSBC), Deutsche Bank, and Chase J.P. Morgan Bank, span the globe, employ tens of thousands of people, and are engaged in a wide range of businesses that are active around the clock. Some of these business activities fit our traditional view of international banking, but others entail significant changes in how the industry is evolving.

The place to start is by defining the word *bank*. The technical term *bancus* emerged only in the Middle Ages and was a Latin translation of the ancient Greek word *trapeza,* which referred to a bench or table where a professional banker displayed his monies and records. Through time, the concept of a bank evolved; banks came to be seen as institutions that take deposits and make loans, with the major source of income derived from interest charged on those loans. In a sense, banks came to play the role of intermediaries, functioning as the middlemen between depositors and borrowers. Banks are in the business to make a profit and differ from other kinds of financial firms in that they offer deposit and loan products.

Money and credit are the commodities that banks use as their stock in trade. Money was traditionally a tangible item made from gold, silver, and copper, which over time became central to humankind's ability to trade, run national economies, and acquire wealth. Credit, while similar to money, is intangible and represents a unit of monetary value that can be traded in the form of a loan agreement, an electronic transfer from one bank to another, or a letter of credit used to facilitate trade. Both money and credit are central to the idea of a bank. Without them, banks would have no purpose.

We have made reference to the intermediary function of banks, which is based on *information costs*. In looking at these terms, perhaps the best way to provide adequate definitions is to ask the following question: Why do borrowers and lenders need a bank to act as a middleman? The answer is twofold: borrowers and lenders have different liquidity preferences; and the existence of information costs undermines the ability of a potential lender to locate the most appropriate borrower. Consequently, there is a role for an intermediary to deal with *search, verification, monitoring, and enforcement costs. Search costs* occur when transactors (those conducting the financial transaction on the behalf of the transactees) and transactees (those needing banking services such as letters of credit) have to search for and obtain information about, select, meet, and negotiate with another party to reach a mutually acceptable contract. This may take more time and money than nonbank institutions wish to invest, especially when banks often have privileged information if prospective borrowers hold accounts at the bank. *Verification costs* exist because it must be ascertained that the information provided by the potential borrower is accurate. *Monitoring costs* relate to the next stage once the loan is negotiated; the activities of the borrower must be followed to differentiate between legitimate and unsound reasons for a borrower missing a payment. Finally, *enforcement costs* pertain to the role of the bank as the agent to enforce the contract or seek compensation if there is a breach of the contract.

Directly related to the concept of information costs is the critical term of **risk management.** Because banks are institutions actively engaged in profit maximization, they face the risks inherent in any such activities. It is a banker's job to manage risk, not avoid it. While risks arise from such things as political interference, technological glitches, and acts of God, risk management pertains to those potential problems arising from the banks' function as an intermediary. The following constitute some of the risks confronting the international banker:

- **Credit risk,** the danger that a borrower defaults on a debt obligation

- **Liquidity and funding risk,** the threat of insufficient liquidity on the part of the bank for normal operating requirements
- **Settlement/payment risk,** which is created when one party of a deal pays money or delivers assets before receiving its own cash or assets, hence exposing itself to a potential loss and interest rate risk
- **Interest rate risk,** the risk that arises from mismatches in both the volume and maturity of interest-sensitive assets, liabilities, and off–balance sheet items
- **Market or price risk,** the exposure of banks to losses due to market or price fluctuations in well-defined markets
- **Foreign exchange or currency risk,** the exposure of banks to fluctuations in foreign exchange rates that affect positions held in a particular currency for a customer or the bank
- **Sovereign risk,** in which the political or economic conditions in a particular country threaten to interrupt repayment of loans or other debt obligations
- **Operating risk,** arising from losses caused by fraud, failure of internal control, or unexpected expenses, as in the case of lawsuits

Equally important to the working of a bank (i.e., the handling of information costs and risk management) are the ideas of trust and confidence. The actual word *credit* comes from the Latin *credere,* meaning trust. There must be trust that it ultimately has value that will be honored. In turn, the users of credit must have confidence that the banking institution with which they are conducting business has the necessary resources to honor claims brought to it.

Related to the ideas of money, credit, trust, and confidence is the rule of law. The rule of law upholds the concept that a contract is a contract and that obligations must be met or the consequences will be paid at the hands of the authorities. Along these lines, the law is not arbitrary, but impartial in the sense that no person or no single institution is above the law. The regulatory authorities function as referees, enforcing the rules, not as participants in the game. In international banking the rule of law is essential because of the cross-border operational risk that is inherent in the business. A country that has well-specified and enforceable laws pertaining to international finance is a far more attractive place to conduct business than a setting where laws are not clear, transparency and disclosure are weak, and the authorities are arbitrary.

While banks were traditionally deposit-taking institutions, this definition does not capture all the lines of business in which they have become involved. The United States and Japan opted throughout much of the twentieth century to make a division between deposit-taking institutions active in commercial banking (i.e., making loans) and investment banks (involved in securities underwriting), a situation that was to change in the twenty-first century. Most major banking systems, however, are defined as being universal in nature. A universal bank functions as a deposit-taking institution and also provides other services, such as securities underwriting, project finance, insurance, and advice on mergers and acquisitions and privatization. Universal banks have, in fact, been referred to as financial supermarkets. The trend is increasingly toward the development of financial supermarkets, as reflected by the end of Glass-Steagall legislation in the United States in 1999, which had divided commercial and investment banking. Indeed, the Financial Services Modernization Act of 1999 was passed by the U.S. Congress to allow combinations of banks, securities, and insurance firms, putting U.S. banks on the same competitive footing as their overseas competitors. The trend toward universality of banking services is also underscored by the merging of investment banking, insurance, and commercial banking operations as seen in the merger of Travelers Insurance, Salomon Smith Barney, and Citibank in the late 1990s.

Two additional factors need to be considered to complete our definition of international banking—the impact of technology, and globalization. Advances in technology have been a major force in revolutionizing how international banking is conducted. In particular, breakthroughs in communications have helped establish a global business grid characterized by a 24-hour flow of credit, around-the-clock cross-border financial transactions, and an ongoing stream of information. The intermix of technology and capital flows central to international banking is evident in such institutions as CHIPS (the Clearing House Interbank Payment Systems) and SWIFT (Society for Worldwide Interbank Financial Telecommunications), which electronically process billions of dollars of international payments daily for major international banks. Technology also has automated the settlement of checks, the transfer of large sums, and foreign exchange transactions. Considering that the fax machine, the Internet, and e-mail have become central to daily business, international banking has certainly come a long way from the days when the Rothschilds used carrier pigeons to communicate with their banker colleagues during the siege of Paris in the Franco-Prussian War.

Globalization and technological change have also opened the door to new challenges in international banking. In a globalized market, countries and corporations have become dependent on international capital markets for credit. In good times, this means a ready pool of capital for development, which helps improve the national standard of living, upgrade infrastructure, and enhance productivity. In bad times, it means a drying up of the global capital pool. Such a credit crunch, combined with underdeveloped local credit markets, can be devastating to national development goals while sparking bank failures, corporate bankruptcies, and rising unemployment. The Latin American debt crisis in the 1980s and the Asian Contagion of 1997–98 exemplify this negative side of globalization.

Another problem area related to globalization is the spread of financial fraud, in particular, money laundering. The more rapid the ability to transmit and receive money and credit, the more difficult it is for regulatory and law enforcement agencies to deal with the illicit flow of funds and practices. Every day, international criminal organizations seek to launder their ill-gotten profits through a number of offshore financial centers, while seeking new means to facilitate the washing of dirty money into clean and more investable legal tender and assets. Bankers, therefore, are under acute pressure to know their customer, and if they do not, they can be heavily penalized in a number of countries. All this affects the costs of international banking and raises the risks of conducting cross-border transactions.

International banking is no longer a business that can be easily defined—not that it ever was. Therefore, we are left with a broad-gauged definition that centers on cross-border lending, supplemented by the facilitation of financing in the forms of debt (bonds) and equity (stocks). Additionally, other forms of international finance—foreign exchange trading, exotic products such as derivatives (part of which is often called financial engineering), and advisory services—round out what falls under the most encompassing umbrella of what constitutes an international bank. It is equally important to underscore that international banking is an ever-changing business, especially in recent decades as it has become a more globalized industry.

Suggested Readings

Canals, Jordi. *Universal Banking: International Comparisons and Theoretical Perspectives.* New York: Oxford University Press, 1997.

Edwards, Burt, "The History and Future of Credit." Burt Edwards, editor, *Credit Management Handbook,* pp. 3–14. Aldershot, UK: Gower, 1997.

Hayes, Samuel L., and Philip M. Hubbard. *Investment Banking: A Tale of Three Cities.* Boston: Harvard Business School Press, 1990.

Hefferman, Shelagh. *Modern Banking in Theory and Practice.* New York: John Wiley and Sons, 1996.

Smith, Roy C., and Ingo Walter. *Global Banking.* New York: Oxford University Press, 1997.

Note

1. Credit Lyonnais was in the 1980s one of the world's largest banks. Based in France, it expanded aggressively overseas, including in Europe, the United States, and Asia. The bank's rapid expansion, however, was accomplished with little consideration of the creditworthiness of many loans and projects. By the early 1990s, Credit Lyonnais was in deep trouble and was forced to turn to the French government for a rescue. Considering that the bank was already owned by the French government, this raised questions within the European Union over competition policy, unfair practices, and the role of the state in the economy. After more than one massive infusion of French government assistance (at the cost of French taxpayers), Credit Lyonnais returned to some degree of creditworthiness in the late 1990s.

CHAPTER 2

A BRIEF HISTORY
OF INTERNATIONAL BANKING

The history of international banking starts with the "banks" of antiquity, moves to the rise of the Italian merchant-bankers in the late Middle Ages, and swings through to the rise of first Antwerp and Amsterdam, then London, and finally New York as major international financial centers. Throughout this lengthy period there was an evolution of the banking industry that encompassed improvements in accounting, the transfers of payments, services rendered, and the uses of technology. Although bankers have often been depicted as cold-blooded and calculating creatures, their services have played a significant role in the development of the global economy, in particular in the areas of trade, industrial development, and infrastructure.

International banking has been and still is closely linked to the development of world trade, the process of urbanization, and the rise of the nation-state. For world trade to develop, credit was needed, especially for long-distance commerce. As Europe, North America, and parts of Asia became sufficiently urbanized, a critical mass of people and goods helped create greater demand for credit. Essential to the development of an international banking system capable of functioning as a financial intermediary for peoples in cities around the Earth, the nation-state eventually provided the fundamentals: rule of law, political stability, and large-scale economies with depth and scope to support major international banking hubs, such as New York, London, and Tokyo. One last point to emphasize is that the modern international banking system has roots in the European banking system, though other regions have made their own contributions to the field.

Early Banking

No one knows the precise moment that banking started. The world did not go to bed one night and wake the next day to find bankers scurrying to work. One of the earliest references to the banking profession or to the practices conducted by bankers is the Code of Hammurabi. Drawn up by King Hammurabi, the founder of the Babylonian Empire (1728–1686 B.C.), the Code contains around 150 paragraphs that pertain to loans, interest, pledges, and guarantees. Economic histori-

THE END OF "HIGH" FINANCE

Ron Chernow

It's easy to picture J. Pierpont Morgan snarling in the afterlife as he contemplates his bank's sale to Chase Manhattan. That his august firm should be swallowed up by a respectable but plebeian bank that issues mortgages and car loans, along with its corporate business, would seem anathema to such an old-school banker. After all, the House of Morgan imported into America the wholesale banking formula patented by the Rothschilds in Europe; an exclusive focus on sovereign states, blue-chip companies and wealthy individuals.

Morgan CEO Douglas "Sandy" Warner III must have shuddered at the thought of how Pierpont would have reacted to the sale of his bank. What Morgan executive wanted to end the most illustrious saga in American finance? And yet, in all fairness to Sandy Warner, his defeat may have been a noble failure rather than a shameful one. For it was an excessive homage to the past, rather than a reckless defiance of it, that finally proved the bank's undoing.

Fall from Grace

To chart Morgan's dizzying fall from grace, one need only glance back at the late 1980s, when this Rolls Royce of banking seemed elegantly invincible. In my rather breathless preface to "The House of Morgan" (1980), I quoted analysts who extolled the bank as "first in quality by any measure you can think of" and "for many the perfect bank." Morgan boasted the largest market capitalization of any American bank and was more expensive to buy than Citicorp. By contrast, before the recent run-up in J.P. Morgan stock inspired by merger rumors, the bank was valued by investors at a paltry one-tenth of Sandy Weill's colossal Citigroup. The bank found itself stuck in a spot insupportable for any self-respecting Morgan veteran: the middle tier of Wall Street firms.

The Morgan bank didn't founder from complacency. In the 1980s, Lew Preston, the urbane but hard-charging chairman, observed that Morgan's traditional corporate clients were abandoning wholesale lending and defecting to the capital markets. He foresaw, with great prescience, a financial system revolving around stocks and bonds, not loans. In an audacious move that profoundly shook the genteel Morgan culture, he decided to recreate the commercial bank as an investment bank. The only other commercial bank even remotely that far-sighted was Bankers Trust, while Citicorp, Chase, Chemical, et al, languished in the stodgy byways of commercial banking.

The stumbling block to this ambitious strategy was the Glass-Steagall Act of 1934, which severed the old House of Morgan into the commercial bank of J.P. Morgan & Co. and the investment bank spin-off Morgan Stanley.

(continued)

Bestowing its blessing on Preston's strategy, the Federal Reserve Board granted a special dispensation to J.P. Morgan that allowed it to engage in limited underwriting long before the Glass-Steagall's repeal. With this head start, J.P. Morgan seemed poised to emerge as the model for the new universal banks that would dominate American finance. How could it have squandered that precious lead when its strategic vision was so unerring?

Source: Wall Street Journal, September 14, 2000

ans surmise that bank operations by temples and great landowners had become prevalent enough that King Hammurabi felt compelled to establish standard rules of procedure.[1]

The next major development in the history of banking was the creation of money. The Chinese probably invented money, but it was the Lydians in ancient Anatolia (modern-day Turkey) who get the credit in the West. Being a trade-oriented people, their idea was that a standardized unit of commerce would simplify transactions. Between 640 and 630 B.C. the Lydians began to mint the first coins, which were made from electrum, a naturally occurring mixture of gold and silver. The use of coins soon caught on, and the surrounding city-states and kingdoms followed suit.

Although what we describe as banking was still rudimentary, the creation of money and improved means of sea travel helped spread trade throughout the early Mediterranean world as well as among the Mediterranean, Indian Ocean, and the Far East. Although our knowledge of Greco-Roman banking is not extensive, it is believed that the oft-mentioned coin dealers, deposit-and-transfer bankers, silversmiths and collectors, money changers, and inspectors of currency fulfilled many of the functions of international bankers.[2] There was also a clear link to trade—most of these early "bankers" raised their surplus capital from trade.

The Roman Empire at its zenith in the first century A.D. controlled most of Western Europe and the Mediterranean basin and much of the Middle East. The Pax Romana ("Roman peace") translated into a sharp reduction in piracy, the construction of roads and ports linking the far-flung parts of the empire to the center, and the standardization of law. With law more formalized and predictable, a Roman banking system functioned, though it was to remain relatively rudimentary. The Romans, like the Greeks before them, also made use of money: it provided a fluid medium for trade and helped advance new ideas in the realm of finance—people began to borrow to buy, and speculation emerged. The development of international banking, however, took a step backward with the fall of the Roman Empire in the fifth century.

Prospects for international banking improved in the early eleventh century. The survival of the Byzantine Empire and trade and war with the Islamic states in the Middle East and North Africa put pressures on Western Europe to move beyond localized trade. The process of "opening up" was first noticeable in Italy's ports, which had easy access to the Levant (contemporary Lebanon, Syria, and Israel) and its exotic goods. The Crusades (1095–1272) were a major impetus for the development of trade, especially as a number of Frankish states were established in the Levant, hence expanding Western Europe's cultural and trade horizons. Although the Knights Templar, an order of warrior monks with holdings throughout Europe and the Middle East, were probably the first to develop an international banking network, it was the Italians who pioneered early international banking. Geographically located in a strategic position between Western Europe and the Levant, the Italians became actively engaged in ferrying Crusaders to the Holy Land and returning with Eastern goods. The emergence of the Italian city-states as commercial and banking powers was furthered by the coining of the florin in Florence in 1252 and the ducat in Venice a few years later, as these instruments were used in trade and were usually the currency accepted in loans. From Italy, the "commercial revolution" spread to the rest of Europe.

The Trade Fair

A new phenomenon, the trade fair, helped spread the commercial revolution as well as create demand for cross-border credit. While the Italians were important to the flow of trade in the Mediterranean, it was in the Flemish cities of the north that the first staple of medieval European international trade, wool, was discovered. By 1050 the first internal trade routes developed, linking Flanders across Europe to northern Italy, where merchants bought Flemish cloth to trade with the Byzantine Empire or Islamic states. One offshoot of this new activity was the emergence of trade fairs, which provided safe and convenient meeting places between northern and southern Europe.

The system of credit was what made the trade fairs work. Credit was used in settling large cross-border transactions without the physical expense and risk of transporting coined or uncoined bullion. In a world with weak central authorities, bandits were an everyday factor in conducting trade from one location to another. Credit worked in the trade fair system because of the rule of law that supported it as well as a healthy dose of self-regulation. Contracts made at one fair were valid and could be enforced anywhere in the system, especially as the participants in the fairs created their own legal system for the settlement and arbitration of crimes.

While the trade fairs were important for the development of international trade in Europe, the Italians remained central to the advancement of international banking. The merchants of Genoa, Milan, Venice, and Florence established some of the first banks in the modern world, introduced the practice of double-entry bookkeeping, and established one of the first international banking networks. The Italians were the early innovators, as it was their exchange banks that led to the creation of commercial credit and to the clearance of client obligations by book transfer, something that bankers in Genoa were doing at the close of the twelfth century. By clearance, we mean the movement of client obligations that were deposited or the movement of funds for the payment of goods in the opposite direction. Genoa was also one of the first states to attempt to found a public bank.

By the thirteenth century, clearance was apparently a standard function of exchange banking throughout the Mediterranean region. Only in the fourteenth century did northern money changers adopt the techniques of deposit and transfer banking pioneered and carried across the Alps by the Italians. During this broad historical period, three distinctive types of banks emerged:

1. Institutions providing foreign exchange services (called exchange banks) and accepting deposits and extending loans for local businesses. (A bill of exchange is a financial instrument representing an amount of credit extended by one business to another for a short period of time. The lender draws up a bill of exchange for a specified sum of money payable at a given future date, and the borrower signifies agreement to pay the amount indicated by signing [accepting] the bill.)

2. Large merchant banks combining foreign trade with dealings in bills of exchange used in financing international commerce.

3. Pawn banks that extended credit to consumers, secured by liens on personal assets.

Another critical development included the emergence of maritime insurance underwriting, which allowed another means of commercial risk diversification. In all of this, the Italian city-states, in particular, Florence, Genoa, and Venice, were on the cutting edge. The Italians maintained a leading role in international banking through the fourteenth and fifteenth centuries, but competition steadily grew as northern Europe's economic structure became more dynamic and patterns of trade changed.

The Expansion of International Banking

In the period between 1350 and 1600, international banking took a considerable leap forward. First under the dominance of the Italians, who introduced deposit-and-transfer banking and bills-of-exchange banking, and followed by the Germans, Flemish, and Dutch, international banking became a recognized profession, maintaining its close linkage to trade. Consequently, it is important to note that the creation of negotiable credit instruments paralleled the shift in mercantile power from the Mediterranean to the Atlantic, or from the Italians to the Dutch and English. After the Portuguese explorer Vasco da Gama discovered a sea route to India at the close of the fifteenth century, the dominance of the Italian city-states in European trade declined. The new passage to the Spice Islands bypassed the Venetians and Genoese as well as the Ottomans and elevated the fortunes of the Atlantic peoples, first the Portuguese and Spanish and over time the Dutch and English. Although the Italians remained a force in international banking through the sixteenth century with the likes of the House of Medici, the center for international finance moved from Bruges to Antwerp and then to Amsterdam.

THE MEDICIS OF FLORENCE

One of the best-known names in early international banking was that of the Medicis of Florence. Beginning as farmers and evolving into merchants and bankers, this clan became one of Europe's most powerful families, spanning the period from the mid-1300s to 1748. Led by Giovanni Medici in the early 1400s and then by Cosimo, the Tuscan clan gradually expanded its banking operations beyond the confines of Florence, opening branches in Milan, Geneva, Bruges, Ancona, Pisa, London, and Avignon. The branch in Rome handled the pope's account. In Florence, the Medici bank took deposits from rich Florentines, which could be withdrawn on due notice (between three months and a year) and earned interest of around 10 percent a year. The Medicis also came to rule Florence, reflecting the powerful combination of finance and political power. This mixture came in handy in 1452 when Naples and Venice were at war with Florence. Faced with a double threat, Cosimo called in the debts from these two enemy cities, making it impossible to continue fighting, which was often conducted by costly mercenaries.

The Medici star was at its highest under Lorenzo the Magnificent (1449–1492), the grandson of Cosimo. Lorenzo was regarded as the epitome of the Renaissance man—he was the ruler of Florence, a poet, scholar, and patron of the arts, as well as a banker. Such fame, however, had a price. Under Lorenzo the Medicis lent money to Edward IV of England during the Wars of the Roses. This was costly to the bank as the English king could not repay all his loans, forcing the bank to close its London branch. The Medicis were also actively engaged in the politics of the Roman Catholic Church, for which they gained a certain fame for underhanded measures. The Medicis were sophisticated bankers, taking every opportunity to eliminate competitors.

The Medici star waned in the 1500s when Florence was invaded several times, and by the sixteenth century, the House was helped out of bankruptcy by the Fuggers, an important southern German banking house. By the 1700s, the House of Medici was a pale shadow of itself, but it had left its name in the history of international banking.

From Antwerp to Amsterdam

Antwerp became Europe's financial hub in the early 1500s. Antwerp's central position as the entrepôt for trade between the Baltic, the Atlantic, and the Spice Islands in Asia was confirmed when the first Portuguese ship laden with pepper and cinnamon pulled into its docks in 1501. More significantly, Antwerp had one of the only two world bourses (stock markets) in the sixteenth century, where capital and

THE FUGGERS

One of the most prominent German banking families in the late Middle Ages was the Fuggers, often referred to as the bankers to the Hapsburgs. In the late fifteenth century, the Fuggers emerged as a powerful merchant family in the city of Augsburg. In 1487, Jakob Fugger loaned Sigismund, the archduke of Tyrol, 20,000 ducats. As a security to the loan, the Hapsburg lord gave Jakob control of the most productive of the Schwarz silver mines and the revenues of the entire province of the Tyrol. Silver was in high demand for fine ornaments and as the second negotiable currency after gold. Control of such resources was both profitable and added to the Fuggers' financial power. Another loan to Sigismund in 1488 gave the Fuggers the management of silver production in its entirety. When Maximilian followed Sigismund as archduke of Tyrol in 1490, he inherited the relationship with the Fuggers, which he promptly used in 1491 with a new loan needed to finance his wars consolidating the Hapsburg holdings. Maximilian became emperor of the Holy Roman Empire in 1493, providing the Fuggers with a powerful friend as well as a needy client.

By 1508, the Fuggers had spread all over Europe, with investments in textiles, pepper, real estate, and silver and copper mining. They were also involved in helping to finance expeditions to the Americas. Their extensive international network also allowed them to provide another service to the Hapsburgs, whose empire was fragmented throughout the continent. As the vassal states paid money to the Hapsburgs, they provided payment in multiple European currencies, and the movement of such payments was slow and fraught with dangers. Consequently, it was easier to rely on the Fuggers, who could get their money to Augsburg in as little as two weeks by means of bills of exchange. Simply stated, the Fugger agent in Antwerp received the money due in exchange for a written credit note, which could be moved with haste to Germany and exchanged for cash in Augsburg against Fugger assets.

The fortunes of the Fuggers, however, became closely tied with the actions of their major borrower. Under Charles V, who followed Maximilian, the heavy costs of fighting wars against the Ottomans, the French, and Protestants in Germany put imperial finances under considerable strain. Although the Fuggers believed that they were overextended to the Hapsburgs, they reluctantly continued to provide credit. The Fuggers were particularly shaken when Philip II of Spain declared bankruptcy in 1577, and their fortunes declined forthwith.

credit were available to royal borrowers on an ongoing basis in return for guaranteed tax revenue or other promises of repayment. As Randall Germain noted: "The rise of Antwerp, and particularly its bourse, signaled a shift in the structure of public financing that mirrored the expansion of both the resources available to sovereigns (American bullion and revenue from the granting of lucrative trading monopolies) and the imperial demands which they assumed."[3]

Antwerp attracted a wide range of international bankers. The Germans, such as the Fuggers and Welsers, were major players, though the Italians were also well represented. Throughout much of the sixteenth century, Antwerp thrived, with Asian goods brought by the Portuguese pouring into its harbor, bound for Germany, the Baltic region, and England; and German and Hungarian silver and copper pouring out. Large trading expeditions set sail from the city, financed by Fugger and Welser loans. Antwerp's golden age in financial history came to an end in the 1580s, when religious strife between Protestants and Catholics resulted in war in the Low Lands (what is today known as Belgium and the Netherlands). Unfortunately, Antwerp was sucked into the conflict with its sizable Protestant minority, who incurred the wrath of the devoutly Catholic Spanish Hapsburg ruler Philip II. In 1585, Spanish troops sacked Antwerp, an event that did great, lasting damage to the city's role in international finance.

Banking in the sixteenth century was not without its risks. While the large German and Italian houses lent to royalty throughout Europe, repayment of loans could be difficult. Backing the wrong side in a war could result, for example, in the death of the borrower and the conquest of his territory by a hostile force. Equally dangerous, the major royal families could and did overstretch their fiscal resources, often leading to default. This was exemplified when Philip II of Spain declared bankruptcy in 1557. In the aftermath of that event, the great German finance houses were badly shaken.

As Antwerp declined, Amsterdam rose to prominence as the world's financial center. In the 1500s the Dutch came to dominate the carrying trade in the Baltic and were active in Spain and Portugal. The struggle with Spain in the late sixteenth century caused the Dutch to turn to the larger world for trading opportunities. This provided them with the impetus to establish their own empire, ultimately gaining control of New Amsterdam (New York), what is today Indonesia, a number of Caribbean islands and Suriname, and for brief periods, parts of Brazil and the west coast of Africa.

The Dutch instigated profound changes in finance in the early seventeenth century. Despite ongoing national security concerns posed by the Spanish, French, and German princes, by 1600 Dutch independence was relatively secure, providing a degree of domestic political stability essential for the flowering of commerce and trade. This created a need for a more sophisticated financial infrastructure. By 1602, the Dutch had established organized markets for trading in financial instruments. They founded the Amsterdam Exchange Bank in 1609, and the Amsterdam Stock Exchange opened its doors in 1611. In the background to these developments, the Dutch also developed a relatively sound banking system, which clearly made them the envy of the rest of Europe, in particular, the English. The Dutch remained a dominant force in international finance throughout much of the seventeenth century, with funds from the small maritime nation finding their way into the economic development of England and France. Their financial dominance, however, gave way to that of the British in the nineteenth century.

The Emergence of London

Although the British had been a part of Europe's emerging international credit system as early as 1260, when the Italians had opened shop on what came to be known as Lombard Street in London, periodic political turmoil precluded the rise of the British capital as an important banking center. This was to change in the eighteenth and nineteenth centuries, especially after the defeat of Napoleon in 1814. Critical for the development of a modern banking system and influenced by the Dutch experience, the British introduced a central bank, the Bank of England, in 1694. Known as the Old Lady of Threadneedle Street, this institution was owned by private holders but represented the government's interest in maintaining control over the nation's finances, which entailed some supervision of the banks. The Bank of England was to gain in importance through the 1700s and into the 1800s, eventually taking deposits and issuing paper money, which came to be called pounds. With sound fiscal policies, the establishment of a national debt, relative political stability, strong economic growth stimulated by the gaining momentum of the Industrial Revolution, and the expansion of trade, Britain was ready to assume the role of the world's banker after the defeat of Napoleon. In essence, the close working relationship between the Bank of England and other parts of the government and the private sector banks meant that few savings lay idle and the combined financial resources of the economy were fully tapped.

While the British state played an important role in fostering the development of its financial system, the private sector's role was equally important. The London banks were closely linked to trade, and most of the major institutions that held sway in the nineteenth century had their roots in merchant activities. Schroders, for example, was established in London during the Napoleonic wars by Johann Heinrich Schroder, who was a member of a well-known and wealthy North German merchant family involved in the trade of wine, coffee, sugar, salmon, herring, lemons, rye, and cloth. Barings Brothers was involved in the drapery business.

Important to the involvement of the merchant banks in trade was their heavy involvement in the working of the gold standard and commitment to free trade. Britain was the most powerful country in the nineteenth century, especially after the defeat of the mercantilist French by 1815. Consequently, the British imposed a free trade system on the global economy. A linchpin to the free trade system was the international acceptance of the gold standard. This meant that the global financial and trade system was established on the concept that national currencies were related to the international price of gold, which was set by the British. Consequently, the London bullion market was where most of the newly minted gold came into the international market, and London was where the connection between gold and credit was the strongest.

Within this system, the British merchant banks played a key role, financing foreign trade, bringing new bond offerings to market, and assisting their clients in making sound investments. An additional advantage for the British banks was their ability to issue long-term bonds and loans, which provided them with a competitive advantage over other financial houses in Paris, Frankfurt, Hamburg, Berlin (after 1870), Vienna, and New York. British banks, therefore, were active in financ-

THE ROTHSCHILDS

L ike the Medicis and Fuggers, the Rothschilds represented the marriage of banking and political power. As a banking family still active in global markets, the Rothschilds had their beginnings in the Jewish ghetto of Frankfurt, Germany, in the mid-1700s. Mayer Amschel Rothschild began by dealing in cloth and old coins, but over time he extended this to money changing and discounting bills for the Landgrave of Hesse-Cassel. Mayer, like many Jews of his time, was prohibited from owning land or pursuing other pursuits such as crafts, hence turning many to financial services and related trades. As his business gradually grew, he sent his five sons to Paris, Vienna, Naples, London, and Frankfurt, where they formed the basis of the Rothschild international network.

The Rothschilds were quick to grasp that superior information could mean the difference between massive profits and losses. Consequently, they constructed their own international intelligence network, with fast packets, agents, carrier pigeons, and couriers. Their emerging importance as the bankers to European governments also provided them with additional access to information. The Napoleonic period was particularly good for them, as they became actively involved in smuggling. After 1815 they were in a good position to provide financing for reparations, the initial loans of the Belgian Kingdom, and the boom in railway construction.

Although the Naples, Frankfurt, and Vienna branches declined, the London and Paris branches of the family did well, joining the upper classes of both countries, and continuing to conduct their business. Rothschild continues to be an active international bank, with a holding company in Switzerland and a major bank in London.

ing the industrial and infrastructure development of much of the Americas, continental Europe, and the British colonies in Africa and Asia. For most Latin American countries, London was the key financial center, and the vast bulk of their loans was in pounds. (See Table 2.1.) The London merchant banks dominated what came to be referred to as haute finance, becoming the primary mechanism that facilitated the flow of capital from areas of surplus to areas of demand.

London's merchant banks were supplemented by the existence of joint-stock banks, like the Westminster and the National. These institutions took deposits from the growing number of small savers, lending money cautiously but profitably. They were owned by anonymous shareholders and were run by professional managers. The joint-stock banks had their roots in the provincial banks that were held by local landed families, many of them Quakers. The Quakers as a persecuted but industrious minority had created a tradition of mutual trust and financial prudence. The last joint-stock bank to be created was Barclays, which was a federation of Quaker banks.

TABLE 2.1 Foreign Loans to Latin American Governments, 1850–1875

Country	Total No. of Loans	Nominal Value (Br. £ thousands)	Purpose (%) Military	Purpose (%) Public Works	Purpose (%) Refinance
Argentina	7	13,488	20	68	11
Bolivia	1	1,700	—	100	—
Brazil	8	23,467	30	13	57
Chile	7	8,502	37	51	12
Colombia	2	2,200	—	9	91
Costa Rica	3	3,400	—	100	—
Ecuador	1	1,824	—	—	100
Guatemala	2	650	—	77	23
Haiti	1	1,458	—	—	100
Honduras	4	5,590	—	98	2
Mexico	2	16,960	70	—	30
Paraguay	2	3,000	—	80	20
Peru	7	51,840	10	45	45
Santo Domingo	1	757	—	100	—
Uruguay	1	3,500	—	—	100
Venezuela	2	2,500	—	30	70
Total	51	140,836			

Source: Carlos Marichal, *A Century of Debt Crises in Latin America: From Independence to the Great Depression, 1820–1930* (Princeton, N.J.: Princeton University Press, 1989), p. 80.

The British-dominated international banking system was not without its periodic defaults and financial panics. The flow of bank loans into Latin America, the United States, and some of the lesser-developed European countries, such as Greece and Turkey (then the Ottoman Empire), carried considerable country risk. Other factors weighed heavily on making loans in the developing world for Europe's international bankers during the nineteenth and early twentieth centuries, as amply demonstrated by Table 2.2.

The Rise of American Banks

The emergence of U.S. banking in a significant fashion came between 1890 and 1920. This was a period when the American economy underwent a profound structural change from being rural, agrarian, and self-sufficient to being industrialized, urban, and market-oriented. With these transformations, banks became more significant as the major financial intermediaries; in particular, their role expanded considerably as they were active in putting together massive deals that led to the rapid

TABLE 2.2 Selected Crises, 1875–1914

Country of Origin (Year)	Description	Cause
Turkey (1875)	Debt default	Fiscal deficits were funded by foreign borrowing that eventually could not be sustained.
Peru (1876)	Debt default	Falling guano exports and stagnation of other revenues combined with increasing fiscal deficits to generate a crisis.
Egypt (1876)	Debt default	Increased foreign borrowing to finance consumption led to unsustainable debt growth.
Argentina (1890)	Debt crisis and institutional failure	Argentina's inability to meet debt-service payments led to the bail-out of Barings Brothers.
United States (1873)	Financial crisis	Bank runs and failures and fears about U.S. commitment to gold parity followed by a stock market crash.
Greece (1893)	Debt default	Increased borrowing to finance consumption led to unsustainable debt growth.
United States (1894–96)	Speculative attack	Speculation against the U.S. gold standard parity followed the Sherman Act (1890) and increasing fiscal deficits.
Brazil (1898)	Debt default	A 64% decline in coffee prices over the preceding five years generated an external crisis.
United States (1907)	Financial crisis	Banking panic and suspension of cash payments followed interest rate hikes and bank failures.
Canada (1907)	Speculative attack/banking crisis	High interest rates in Canada (in response to hikes in the United States) led to excessive credit expansion that generated speculation against the Canadian dollar.
Brazil (1914)	Debt default	A sharp decline in coffee prices in the preceding two years generated a debt crisis.

Source: International Monetary Fund, *International Capital Markets: Developments, Prospects, and Key Policy Issues* (Washington, D.C.: International Monetary Fund, November 1997), p. 238.

centralization of many businesses.[4] The bankers acted as both principal (borrower) and agent (named by members of a multibank syndicate to protect the interests of the participating banks in administering a loan to a foreign or domestic borrower) in many deals on Wall Street. In doing so they helped rationalize industry into sizable holding companies. These holding companies gathered considerable power, leading the populist wing of American politics to rail against the emergence of the plutocrats and their money trusts.

Like much of American business during this period, the banks organized themselves into holding companies. Consequently, through their subsidiaries they were able to become involved in the securities industry, even though in theory they were expected to remain apart from this industry. This was not the case, as many banks provided loans to brokers trading on the market.

The rise of U.S. banking was supported in part by the development of a functioning central bank system. Prior to 1913–14, the United States lacked a central bank. Two efforts to produce a central bank had failed in the early days of the Republic. This meant that the private banking sector had developed without the supervision of a central bank. Consequently, the boom-bust cycles of U.S. business were much more pronounced. With no central institution to modify interest rates or use moral suasion on bankers to provide credit, bankers had a tendency to provide too much credit during the boom and too little credit during the bust, hence aggravating the situation. There were major banking panics in 1873 and 1893 and severe problems in 1884 and 1890.[5] The financial panic of 1907, in particular, confirmed to many that a central bank was needed to establish a more prudent banking system. By 1913, the Federal Reserve system was established with the help of private bankers, such as the Warburgs.

In the aftermath of World War II, American banks became the dominant players in the international game for very obvious reasons. The U.S. economy was the world's largest and had survived the war intact. In fact, U.S. industry rapidly expanded overseas due to the weak condition of Europe and Japan, both heavily damaged by the war. For the banks, the expansion of U.S. industry meant growth in services provided, ranging from trade finance to lending for the development of manufacturing industries. At the same time, U.S. banks became important sources of private capital for the reconstruction of Europe.

Bretton Woods and Its Institutions

In the aftermath of the Great Depression and World War II (1939–1945), the leadership of the surviving powers, in particular, the United States and the United Kingdom, pushed for the creation of a new order in the international economy. The weakness of international monetary institutions following World War I was seen as contributing to the world depression in the late 1920s and 1930s and facilitating the emergence of a regime like Nazi Germany that placed emphasis on economic self-sufficiency over international trade and cooperation. If such a turn of events was to be avoided in the future, it was essential to establish a new international economic order, founded on institutions oriented to providing the necessary coordination of monetary policy among the major economies.

At the Bretton Woods Conference held in 1944, the broad overarching concepts of the new international monetary order were established. Central to the emerging

J. P. MORGAN

Without a doubt, John Pierpont Morgan (1837–1913) was one of the most influential figures in the rise of U.S. banking. Born in 1837 in Hartford, Connecticut, Morgan began his career as a finance and investment agent for his father in New York City. In that capacity he developed a familiarity with finance in both the United States and the United Kingdom, then the world's dominant political and economic power. In 1871, he established the banking house of Drexel, Morgan & Co. Twenty-four years later it was renamed J.P. Morgan & Co., which it was to remain until the firm's purchase by Chase Manhattan in 2000.

Through the offices of J.P. Morgan and other banks, credit was extended to a hungry and growing U.S. corporate sector, especially following the U.S. Civil War. Following the financial crash in 1893, Morgan became active in railroads, reorganizing several rail lines in the eastern United States. He also marketed U.S. government securities on a large scale. In 1889, he entered the field of industrial consolidation, forming the United States Steel Corporation, which became the first billion-dollar corporation in the world. He also had a hand in setting up International Harvester and General Electric. His involvement in the restructuring of the U.S. corporate world was guided by his interest in imposing a measure of order on the turbulent economic development of the United States. He preferred to have large stable systems rather than boom-bust cycles, a result of the wasteful and speculative recklessness of unchecked competition.

Although Morgan was sometimes depicted as one of the "robber barons" of the Gilded Age, he was a firm believer in the development of a more stable U.S. financial system. During the second half of the nineteenth century, the U.S. banking system was plagued by a number of banking panics (see Table 2.2). In 1895, Morgan came to the rescue of the U.S. government, which had run out of gold, raising $65 million for the Treasury and making certain that it remained as a reserve. In 1907, a failed effort to corner the copper market on Wall Street spiraled into a major financial crisis. The U.S. government lacked a central bank and was forced to turn to Morgan for help. Through his good offices, Morgan spearheaded a major private sector rescue effort, helping to restore confidence in the banking system. His actions also helped the argument in favor of a central bank. In 1912–13, the Federal Reserve system was established to function as a central bank for the United States.

Morgan died in Rome in 1913, at the age of seventy-six. As one of his biographers, Jean Strause commented on the scope and significance of Morgan's career: "He had organized giant railroad systems and corporate 'trusts,' presided over a massive transfer of wealth from Europe to the United States, and at a time when America had no central bank, acted as monitor of its capital markets and lender of last resort."[1]

---

[1]Jean Strause, *Morgan, American Financier* (New York: Random House, 1999), ix.

Bretton Woods system were the International Monetary Fund (IMF), the World Bank, and the General Agreement on Tariffs and Trade (GATT). Influenced by the two major architects of the postwar monetary system, John Maynard Keynes of the United Kingdom and Harry Dexter White of the United States, the IMF was the linchpin of the new regime. Its primary mission was to promote international monetary cooperation by establishing and maintaining exchange rate stability. The IMF was also to facilitate the expansion and balanced growth of international trade and provide confidence to members by making available the IMF's resources (with conditionalities), hence allowing members to correct maladjustments in their balance of payments without resorting to measures detrimental to national or international economic order. The combined effect of the IMF was to help shorten the duration of and lessen the degree of disequilibrium in the international balance of payments.

The World Bank's role initially was to provide long-term loans for reconstruction following the end of World War II. It was also to provide loans for economic development of the newly independent nations in Africa, Asia, and the Caribbean as well as the older and more established republics in Latin America. Over time, the World Bank extended technical expertise to developing economies. As for the GATT, the other element of the Bretton Woods system, its role was to promote a free international trading system through tariff reduction and nondiscrimination. Over time, the GATT evolved into the World Trade Organization (WTO).

The Bretton Woods system worked as long as one nation was willing to bear the burden of providing the world a reserve currency backed by gold. The United States was willing to do this through the late 1940s and into the 1950s. In the 1960s, pressures mounted on the U.S. economy and there was a growing reluctance to shoulder the burden, especially as the United States was running consecutive current account balance-of-payments deficits, was dealing with inflationary pressures, and had to finance a growing involvement in Vietnam. In 1971, the Nixon administration took the U.S. dollar off the gold standard, an action that brought the Bretton Woods system to an end. Although the formal idea of the Bretton Woods system is regarded as having ended in 1971, many of the institutions created by the system, such as the IMF and World Bank, continue to function. Moreover, the idea of the need for international policy coordination was not discarded, as the Group of Seven (G–7) countries (the United States, Japan, Germany, the United Kingdom, France, Canada, and Italy) came to meet regularly to discuss international economic policy issues.

The Eurocurrency and Eurobond Markets

One of the most significant developments in international banking in the postwar period was the development of the **eurodollar** and **eurobond** markets, sometimes referred to as the **eurocurrency** market. Eurocurrencies are currencies held outside their home country; thus, eurodollars are dollars on deposit outside the United States. Simply stated, the eurodollar market is an international money market focused on short-term credit flows, while the eurobond market is an international capital market dealing with long-term bonds (debt). The development of these two markets was interrelated and mirrored both the structure of Cold War politics and international economics.

The eurodollar market emerged in the late 1940s and 1950s when large amounts of U.S. dollars ended up outside the United States. This included deposits of dollars in U.S. bank branches located outside the United States. The explosion of U.S. business around the planet meant that U.S. dollars flowed almost everywhere, making the greenback the legal tender of international trade. As large multinational corporations headquartered in the United States built factories in Germany, France, or Spain, paid their foreign workers, or purchased raw materials, U.S. currency remained outside of the United States. At the same time, efforts to reconstruct Europe's economy, like the Marshall Plan, resulted in public dollar flows into European nations. Although some dollars were repatriated, the offshore pool gradually expanded.

U.S. dollars also stayed outside of the country because of the Cold War. As the great divides of the Cold War became evident, a number of Communist countries, such as China, decided not to repatriate their dollar earnings to the United States, instead putting them in deposits in carefully selected banks in Europe. In the Cold War environment, Communist governments feared that they would be cut off from U.S. dollar deposits in the States, which would create problems in their trade with other nations. Consequently, another stream of U.S. dollars was created outside the borders of the United States. It is vital to underscore that though the Communist pool of dollars was important, the U.S. dollars that remained in Western Europe were far more substantial and formed the real foundation for the development of the eurodollar market.

The eurodollar market emerged in 1957, and its roots were largely political. Prior to 1957 the foreign dollar deposit market was perceived as little more than an appendage to the U.S. money market. This changed with the Suez Crisis. In 1956, the United Kingdom and France, together with Israel, launched an attack on Egypt, which was threatening to nationalize the Suez Canal. The United Kingdom, the former colonial power over Egypt, refused to accept this. Although the British, French, and Israelis were able to seize control of the Suez Canal, the United States, together with the Soviet Union, refused to go along. This caused a crisis for the British government. Within a short period of time, the British pound came under pressure from speculative attacks. In 1957, the British government took the fateful action of prohibiting the use of pounds sterling in trade credits between nonresidents. As a result, British and other international banks turned to the dollar to use as trade credits. In turn, this led to the active solicitation of dollar deposits by banks in Western Europe.

While the eurodollar market emerged in a significant fashion in the late 1950s, the eurobond market—that is, the issuing of bonds outside of the United States in eurodollars—developed in the early 1960s. In 1963, Autostrade, an Italian toll road authority, issued the first eurobond, worth $15 million. This was the first debt issued in dollars outside of the United States. As Europe was regaining its economic strength and the United States was beginning to feel the costs of being a superpower, there was some concern about the large amounts of U.S. currency effectively outside of U.S. monetary control. In 1963, the U.S. government, in an effort to reduce the dollar outflow, imposed an interest equalization tax which sought to dissuade foreign governments and corporations from borrowing in U.S. bond markets. Moreover, the U.S. Commerce Department ruled that U.S. companies investing abroad had to raise money outside of the United States. Consequently, many U.S. corporations turned to the eurobond market to raise capital. Further stimulus for the development of the eurobond market came from U.S. efforts to contain inflation in the 1966–1969 period. Facing tight money practices at home, U.S. banks were able to tap the eurodollar market.

Development of the eurodollar market at this time was significant for the following reasons. First and foremost, the market served as a source of short-term funds for the trade financing activities of international banks. Second, the eurocurrency market facilitated foreign exchange transactions by banks and provided short-term money market trading opportunities. Third, international banks used the market as an outlet for placing surplus funds temporarily at attractive yields. Fourth, the eurocurrency interbank market became the central mechanism to channel flows of international funds among banks. Significantly, that gave birth to the **London Interbank Offered Rate** or **LIBOR,** which became one of the most important international interest rates.[6] The eurocurrency market also provided an outlet for the recycled petrodollars in the early 1970s.

The eurobond market emerged in the 1960s and 1970s as a major alternative to issuing debt in the United States. From 1963 to 1983, $266 billion worth of eurobonds were issued. For any major international bank, ranging from the big U.S. institutions to German, British, and French banks, the eurobond market was an important element in remaining competitive. This was easier, in some respects, for European banks as they were universal by nature and not constrained by legislation such as Glass-Steagall, which prohibited U.S. commercial banks from involvement in securities.

The eurobond market's development also stimulated the development of two new institutions, Euroclear and CEDEL. Both are clearing houses for eurobonds; the former was established in 1968 by Morgan Guaranty and later became independent, and the latter was created in 1970 by a group of European banks active in eurobond trading.

By the early 1990s, the eurobond market had developed into a more mature market. (See Table 2.3.) Although it is a virtually unregulated market, it remains

TABLE 2.3 A Maturing Eurobond Market, Volume of New Issues (US$ billions)						
	1990	*1991*	*1992*	*1993*	*1994*	*1995*
U.S. Bonds, Total	$418.71	$670.04	$976.10	$1225.40	$792.7	$756.5
International Bonds	224.86	267.40	342.13	482.70	485.2	385.1
Of which, Eurobonds are	159.19	228.02	265.79	388.00	425.9	322.4

Sources: Securities Data Corporation, IFR, and Smith and Walter, *Global Banking*, p. 244.

subject to self-imposed standards of practice. Usually listed on the Luxembourg or London stock exchanges, the issues are normally made subject to British law. The confidence in the eurobond market is underpinned by two factors: both the London and Luxembourg stock exchanges have their own specific disclosure requirements, and minimum standards are set by the Association of International Bond Dealers (AIBD), which is a nongovernmental industry association. These self-regulating bodies have helped maintain a high level of confidence in the smooth functioning of the eurobond market and make it an attractive option for companies and governments in need of financing in international debt markets.

The Expansion of International Banking

International banking grew in the 1960s and 1970s, with U.S. institutions dominating as they were rapidly expanding into foreign markets. (See Table 2.4.) The hike in oil prices in the early 1970s meant that petrodollars—that is, dollars generated by enhanced oil revenues through the largely Middle Eastern hydrocarbon producers—required recycling. U.S. and European banks became active agents in this process, by taking Saudi and Kuwaiti oil profits as deposits and quickly lending them to countries in Asia, Latin America, and Africa. This recycling of petrodollars reduced potential inflationary pressures in the United States and Europe as well as meeting the growing demand for credit from countries such as Argentina, Brazil, Mexico, Turkey, and Poland.

Competition among international banks became increasingly intense as American, German, Japanese, French, and Canadian bankers slugged it out to lead large syndications extending billions of dollars. By the late 1970s there was too much credit being funneled into the developing world as bankers sought to maintain high margins of profit. Despite problems with external debt obligations by Poland, Zaire, and Turkey, international bankers continued to pour money into Latin America. However, in August 1982, the Mexican government informed its international bankers

---

TABLE 2.4 International Operations of U.S. Banks, 1960–1975 (US$ billions)

	1960	1964	1965	1967	1969	1970	1973	1975
Foreign Loans from U.S. Offices	$4.2	$9.4	$9.7	$9.8	$9.3	$9.7	$17.2	$30.5
No. of Banks with Foreign Branches	8	11	13	15	53	79	125	126
No. of Foreign Branches	131	181	211	295	459	536	699	762
Assets of Foreign Branches	3.5	6.9	9.1	15.7	41.1	52.6	118.0	176.5

Source: Yoon S. Park and Jack Zwick, *International Banking in Theory and Practice* (Reading, Mass.: Addison-Wesley Publishing Company, 1985), p. 27.

that it was unable to meet its debt repayments, an action that was followed by a series of defaults throughout the rest of Latin America and the Philippines and Nigeria. While Latin America was plunged into the "lost decade," international banks experienced profound problems with debt reschedulings, forced new lendings, and ultimately debt write-offs. The developing world's debt crisis also reduced the number of banks actively engaged in international activities, especially in the United States.

In the mid-1980s, U.S. dominance gradually underwent a decline as European and Japanese institutions grew and became more competitive. The development of the eurocurrency markets helped recast European banks as tough global competitors, while the depreciation in the U.S. dollar in the middle and late 1980s aided the international expansion of Japanese banks. Japanese banks, long closely linked to major corporations in Japan for which they were the main source of funds, became major international players. U.S. banks declined dramatically in terms of the international pecking order—at least in terms of asset size. In 1974, U.S. banks counted for five of the largest banks in the world, with BankAmerica Corp., Citicorp, and Chase Manhattan Bank coming in first, second, and third.[7] By 1997, there were no U.S. banks in the top ten, which were dominated by Japanese and European institutions, with Chase Manhattan Bank being number eighteen, followed by Citicorp at twenty-one. (See Table 2.5.)

Moreover, the 1980s deregulation of the U.S. banking system led to domestic problems, such as the savings and loans banking crisis. By the 1990s, U.S. banks had restructured, and they reemerged as more competitive institutions. Changes in legislation in the United States also helped, providing commercial banks with the opportunity to move in a more pronounced fashion into the securities business.

Banking in the 1990s

By the end of the 1990s, international banking was dominated by large institutions, primarily in the most developed economies—the United States, Japan, Germany, the United Kingdom, France, Italy, and Canada. Although national boundaries continue to have some relevance, the major trends defining international banking are consolidation within national frontiers, cross-border mergers, and the ongoing shift to universal banking. We briefly define the last-mentioned as the ability to offer the full range of financial services including commercial banking as well as securities issuance and trading and the selling of insurance products, all under one roof. The continuing onslaught of new technology means that financial markets are truly global and instantaneous. This has meant that international banks have to invest, develop, and implement new technologies to remain competitive. Related to this trend is the rise of nonbank financial institutions, such as insurance companies, pension funds, and asset management firms, all of which provide alternative sources of credit. International banks, therefore, must consider how to compete with or how to own such institutions. This has led to proposed bank regulation changes in a number of countries, including the United States, Australia, and Canada. Indeed, in late 1999, the United States removed several Depression-era prohibitions on universal banking.

TABLE 2.5 Top Twenty-Five World Banking Companies in Total Assets as of December 31, 1997

Rank/Bank	City	Total Assets (US$ billions)
1. Bank of Tokyo-Mitsubishi Ltd.	Tokyo	$691.9
2. Deutsche Bank AG	Frankfurt	580.0
3. Sumitomo Bank Ltd.	Osaka	483.7
4. Credit Suisse Group	Zurich	473.8
5. HSBC Holdings, Plc.	London	471.0
6. Dai-Ichi Kangyo Bank, Ltd.	Tokyo	433.1
7. Sanwa Bank Ltd.	Osaka	428.0
8. Credit Agricole Mutual	Paris	419.7
9. Fuji Bank Ltd.	Tokyo	414.2
10. ABN AMRO Bank N.V.	Amsterdam	412.8
11. Societe-Generale	Paris	410.8
12. Sakura Bank Ltd.	Tokyo	399.5
13. Union Bank of Switzerland	Zurich	395.1
14. Norin Chunkin Bank	Tokyo	392.6
15. Barclays Bank Plc.	London	385.9
16. Dresdner Bank	Frankfurt	371.4
17. Industrial Bank of Japan, Ltd.	Tokyo	370.0
18. Chase Manhattan Corp.	New York	365.5
19. Banque Nationale de Paris	Paris	339.6
20. Westdeutsche Landesbank Girozentrale	Dusseldorf	335.8
21. Citicorp	New York	311.0
22. ING Bank	Amsterdam	307.6
23. NatWest Group	London	304.9
24. Swiss Bank Corporation	Basel	300.2
25. Commerzbank	Frankfurt	286.9

Source: The Wall Street Journal Almanac 1999 (New York: Ballantine Books, 1999), p. 189.

International banking in the 1990s also has a geographical dimension. The largest and most powerful international banks are located in the industrialized northern countries, namely in North America, Japan, and Western Europe. In this, cities still play a critical role, in particular, New York, London, and Tokyo. Saskia Sassen noted that in 1997, twenty-five cities controlled 83 percent of the world's equities under institutional management and accounted for roughly half of global market capitalization (around $20.9 trillion).[8] Of these, New York, London, and Tokyo together held a third of the world's institutionally managed equities and accounted for 58 percent of the global foreign exchange market. In the emerging market countries, São Paulo and Mumbai (Bombay) have emerged as players in international capital markets.

Another trend evident in the late 1990s was the globalization of the market for financial services. Deregulation of capital markets in both the developed and developing groups of countries since the 1980s has resulted in a system allowing a much freer flow of capital, spearheaded by investors in the more economically developed parts of the planet, wealthy individuals from developing countries, investment banks looking for profits, and governments with a need to find financing for infrastructure.[9] The new mantra for economic development is liberalization, privatization, and deregulation. The driving forces in this process were the end of the Communist bloc, marked by the collapse of the Soviet Union in 1991, the adoption of market-oriented economic strategies by many countries in Asia and Latin America that had previously pursued more statist-oriented programs, and an explosion in international trade. Asia's long growth spurt, beginning in the 1980s and lasting until 1997, also pushed the globalization of capital markets.

While globalization brought new opportunities and rewards, it also brought new risks. At roughly the same time that President George Bush proclaimed a "new world order," the process of consecutive disorders afflicted global finance. As Ethan B. Kapstein noted in the November 1998 issue of *Current History:* "Beginning with the exchange rate shocks that rocked Western Europe in 1992 and 1993, the world has experienced banking and currency crises in Mexico in 1994–95, East Asia in 1997–98, and Russia and Latin America in August 1998."[10] Brazil was threatened again in early 1999 with a similar meltdown, indicating that the globalized market and free flow of capital carried the risk of contagion that was both rapid and deadly.

For international banks, the 1990s were a decade of massive change typified by consolidation, the introduction of new technology, intense competition from other financial institutions, and a widening of the parameters of risk. While many international bankers continued to shift away from taking deposits and making loans to fee-income business (i.e., underwriting, consulting, and leasing), the margins of profitability shrank, pushing the banks and their competitors into riskier areas of business, in particular, high-yield bonds (the junk market) and emerging markets. Consequently, by the beginning of the 2000s, international banking is once again in the process of reinventing itself. Like the Italian and German bankers in the period between the thirteenth and sixteenth centuries, a new world order is being formed, which will test the skill and prudence of the banker in practicing his or her craft in a volatile world. No doubt the bankers that extended credit to President Suharto in Indonesia experienced the same sickening feeling in their stomachs when that regime fell in 1998, as did the German and Italian bankers who provided loans to Charles the Bold, duke of Burgundy, when he was killed in combat in 1477.

Questions

1. Who were the first people to develop modern banking techniques?
2. What was the contribution of the Fuggers to international banking?
3. What is the eurobond market, and how did it develop? What is a eurodollar?
4. What was the Bretton Woods system? How did it function, and what, if anything, has replaced it?
5. How did the system of international banking evolve, starting with the Italians and eventually ending up with the Americans as the dominant force? What is the structure of international banking today? Are U.S. banking institutions still dominant, or have banks from other countries become competitive?
6. International banking has gone through several crises. What has been the cause of these crises, such as in the cases of Latin America in the 1980s or of Asia in the late 1990s?

Notes

1. Roger Orsingher, *Banks of the World* (New York: Walker and Company, 1967), p. x.
2. Robert S. Lopez, "The Dawn of Medieval Banking", in the Center for Medieval and Renaissance Studies, University of California, Los Angeles, editors, *The Dawn of Modern Banking* (New Haven, Conn.: Yale University Press, 1979), p. 2.
3. Randall Germain, *The International Organization of Credit* (Cambridge, UK: Cambridge University Press, 1997), p. 36.
4. Charles R. Geisst, *Wall Street: A History* (New York: Oxford University Press, 1997), p. 127.
5. For a comprehensive discussion about U.S. bank panics, see Elmus Wicker, *Banking Panics of the Gilded Age* (New York: Cambridge University Press, 2000).
6. Yoon S. Park and Jack Zwick, *International Banking in Theory and Practice* (Reading, Mass: Addison-Wesley Publishing, 1985), p. 55.
7. Data from *The New York Times*, July 15, 1995.
8. Saskia Sassen, "Global Financial Centers," *Foreign Affairs* (January/February 1999), p. 77.
9. As Peter Warburton notes: "The excursion into the realm of financial fantasy has taken place gradually since the mid-1980s. The pace and variety of innovations in the global financial system have been so remarkable that there has scarcely been enough time to catalogue them, let alone analyse them.... Access to personal and business credit has burgeoned, financial activities have been de-regulated and a host of new financial instruments have been developed." *Debt and Delusion: Central Bank Follies that Threaten Economic Disaster* (London: Penguin Press, 1999), p. 3.
10. Ethan B. Kapstein, "Global Rules for Global Finance," *Current History* (November 1998), p. 355.

CHAPTER 3

BANKING SYSTEMS
AROUND THE WORLD

As the adjacent article in *The Economist* depicts, international finance is characterized by considerable change. There is a decided move toward convergence in what banks, insurance companies, and other nonbank financial institutions offer in terms of services.[1] Competition is keen and likely to get keener still among banks and between banks and nonbank financial institutions. In this matrix of increasing international competition and convergence, technology is one major factor, as is globalization: both break down geographical as well as functional barriers. At the same time, these trends hardly mean that banks will disappear from the map. They will remain as central players in financial disintermediation, especially as financial innovation, globalization, and deregulation are likely to continue to restructure markets and create ongoing demand for services. Consequently, it remains important to have an understanding of what the word *bank* means around the world. Although considerable similarities exist between the banks of the United States, Japan, the United Kingdom, Germany, and France, there are differences that reflect a variety of historical and functional evolutions.

It can be stated that one commonality that almost every nation on the planet shares is the existence of banks. Even at the height of the Cold War, Communist nations operated banks and used them in the allocation of credit or in international payments. Yet not all banks are created equal. Some banks are far more internationally oriented than others; some are very limited in their functions and products offered; and some banks have no or little interest in international banking. The large federated (universal) banks in Europe, such as Union Bank of Switzerland, Deutsche Bank, and Banco Santander Central Hispano, operate with very different business objectives than savings and cooperative banks in Germany, France, and Austria, savings banks in Spain and Norway, UK mortgage lenders, or Swiss cantonal banks. Although the trend toward globalization is breaking down some of these differences, there is likely to remain a divide between those institutions actively engaged in international banking and those with a strong local orientation. Citigroup, Inc. offers a wider range of financial services around the planet, while People's Bank is largely limited to the state of Connecticut in the United States.

One clarification in defining international banking at the beginning of the twenty-first century is that the *universal model* is clearly dominant. Although the U.S. and Japanese systems sought to separate commercial and investment bank-

THE NEW FINANCIERS

The business of financing large companies is converging with the business of insuring them.

This June, a brave American power firm invested in electricity supply in Colombia. Raising finance for the venture was always going to be hard, since project-finance lending to Latin America had all but dried up. So the company borrowed in two tranches: it hired Bank of America to arrange a senior loan, and an outfit called Centre to arrange, as well as guarantee, a subordinated loan. The structure inspired enough confidence for other banks to join. In July, Centre was at it again, this time backing a risky loan to help Alterra, America's largest nursing-home operator, to buy 20 homes for Alzheimer's victims. The Centre financed the purchase of aeroplanes by Canadian Airlines and, in August, a management buy-out in Britain. Who are these enterprising bankers? Not, in fact, bankers at all, but part of Zurich, a giant Swiss insurance company.

Putting Colombian power plants to one side, consider Mickey Mouse in Japan. Like thousands of companies that straddle fault-lines in, say, Turkey or California, Tokyo Disneyland had to buy earthquake insurance this year. It arranged the cover not through an insurance company but through Goldman Sachs, a blue-chip Wall Street investment bank. With Goldman Sachs' help, Disney issued $200m worth of bonds—on the understanding that if there is an earthquake, it will not pay them back.

Insurers doubling as banks, banks acting like insurers—it has a familiar ring to it. But this is deceptive. So far "convergence" has been a buzzword only for retail banks, with bricks-and-mortar branches, and retail insurers peddling home insurance or pension annuities. In boardrooms, this trend is referred to either in French, as bancassurance, or in German, as Allfinanz, and has already spawned mega-mergers such as that in America between Citibank and Travelers to form Citigroup last year. But the real convergence may be that under way at the wholesale end of the finance business.

Source: The Economist, September 4, 1999, p. 69.

ing in the 1930s and 1940s respectively, universal banking gradually crept into the banking system, with the walls separating commercial and investment banking activities being consistently eroded. Table 3.1 provides an idea of the different universal banking systems in the late 1990s.

In this chapter we provide a comparative view of banking around the world. We have divided banks into two broad groups, those within the OECD (Organization for Economic Cooperation and Development) group of countries and those within emerging markets. OECD countries include those with the most developed

---

TABLE 3.1 Universal Banking in the Late 1990s

- Fully integrated financial services: banking, securities, insurance, and other services
- Germany: banking, insurance, mortgage, and securities
- France: banking, insurance (sold through bank branches), and securities
- United Kingdom: securities and insurance (by a bank)
- United States: banking, securities, and insurance (by a holding company)
- Canada: banking and securities (by a bank)

---

economies in the world, including the United States, Japan, Germany, Italy, France, and the United Kingdom as well as the Netherlands, Finland, and Korea. Although these terms are not exact, they serve as a rough dividing line between more developed banking systems and banking systems that are less mature and open to greater risk. At the same time, OECD banks are certainly not exempt from market volatility and crisis. Most OECD banking systems underwent profound crises in the second half of the twentieth century. Moreover, a small number of OECD countries, such as Mexico, are also regarded as being still in the emerging market category despite their achievement of membership.

We provide brief surveys of the banking systems in the United States, Japan, France, the United Kingdom, and Germany in the OECD category. Our OECD selections (minus Mexico) were made on the fact that the five countries constitute the five largest economies on the planet and, hence, carry considerable weight in international banking. (See Table 3.2.)

In the emerging markets category, we have selected Mexico (an OECD member), India, Indonesia, China, South Africa, Hungary, and Russia. Our selections were based on geographical range (China, India, and Indonesia are representative of Asia, South Africa of Africa, Mexico of Latin America, and Hungary and Russia of Central and Eastern Europe). We underscore that the changes occurring in the more developed economies representative of the OECD countries are also in motion in emerging market economies. Banking systems throughout Asia, Latin America, Central and Eastern Europe, and parts of the Middle East and Africa are rushing to mature into mirror images of their counterparts in OECD countries. Generally speaking, this process is in its early stages, as the Asian financial crisis of 1997–98 demonstrated.

OECD Banking Systems

The Organization for Economic Cooperation and Development (OECD) was established in the postwar era by the most economically developed countries to conduct

economic research and help provide a policy framework for economic development. Over time, the OECD came to be regarded as the club of industrialized
nations. Membership was seen as a badge of success for countries that reached a
certain level of economic development. By the 1990s, membership had expanded
beyond the major G–7 economies of the United States, Japan, Germany, France,
Italy, United Kingdom, and Canada and other Western European nations to encompass Mexico, South Korea, Poland, the Czech Republic, and Hungary. Consequently, the term *OECD country* reflects a higher level of economic development
and a more sophisticated banking system. For the purposes of this chapter, it refers
to the most economically developed set of countries in the global economy.

In the twentieth century there was a marked divergence between the United
States and Japan, which demarcated commercial and investment banking activities in their countries, vis-à-vis the European and Canadian banking regimes that
remained wedded to universal banking. Universal banking comes out of the European tradition and allows banks to provide, under one roof, a wide range of financial services, such as the taking of deposits, making loans and underwriting, and
in some cases, insurance. In a sense, universal banks are one-stop financial supermarkets. The creation of fully universal banks in the image of their European counterparts in the United States and Japan has yet to occur. Yet globalization will
continue to dictate change and an ongoing homogenization of banking systems.
Over time, the *Allfinanz* or *bancassurance* model is likely to dominate even in the
United States and Japan. The merger of Citibank and Travelers Insurance to form
Citigroup in the late 1990s demonstrates that this process is already well under
way. Moreover, the 1999 repeal of the federal Glass-Steagall Act effectively
reopens the door to universal banking in the United States.

The United States

Banking commenced in the United States in the 1780s along universal lines as a
rather loosely supervised business through the nineteenth century. Charters prior
to the 1860s were obtained from state governments, which allowed banks to issue
currency. At the same time, much of the trade finance and investment financing
came from British banks and British and Dutch investors. In 1912–13, the United
States established a central bank, the Federal Reserve, partially due to concerns
about recurrent banking crises. Such a crisis occurred with the Great Depression
in 1929, which carried on through the 1930s and functioned as the stimulus for a
major restructuring of U.S. banking.

In the midst of the Great Depression, in 1934, the Glass-Steagall Act was
passed by the U.S. Congress and signed into law. The Glass-Steagall Act effectively
separated commercial and investment banking, prohibiting the former to participate
in or possess its own security firms. It also provided for the implementation of a
deposit insurance system (the Federal Deposit Insurance Corporation, or FDIC) to
guarantee that deposit holders would receive a certain sum if their bank failed.

The reasons for the radical restructuring of the U.S. financial industry
included the 1929 stock market crash, the banks' involvement in the securities
industry, and the seemingly inherent conflict of interest and abuses in traditional

TABLE 3.2 Top Twenty-Five Arrangers of All International Syndicated Loans[1]

	1998	
Rank/Bank	Amount (US$ billions)	Issues
1. Bank of America	$200.6	1,673
2. Chase Manhattan	200.5	1,246
3. Citigroup	132.4	745
4. J.P. Morgan	92.0	353
5. Deutsche Bank	71.7	651
6. Bank One	55.3	552
7. Barclays	40.6	248
8. ABN AMRO	37.9	420
9. Bank of New York	31.6	248
10. First Union	30.3	474
11. Credit Suisse First Boston	26.2	240
12. Bank of Nova Scotia	25.1	274
13. Toronto-Dominion	23.6	205
14. BankBoston	22.5	353
15. Warburg Dillion Read	21.6	127
16. CIBC	20.8	305
17. Bank of Montreal	20.5	159
18. SG	20.0	296
19. Fleet Financial	19.9	435
20. Royal Bank of Canada	17.6	113
21. HSBC	16.5	142
22. Credit Lyonnais	16.2	172
23. Greenwich NatWest	15.9	158
24. Banque Nationale de Paris	14.9	141
25. Lehman Brothers	13.5	114

(continued)

financial intermediation and in activities related to financial asset transactions. Additionally, a number of interest groups were active in lobbying Congress to restrict the activities of banks. U.S. public opinion was also a factor, as many Americans were suspicious of any concentration of economic power.

Despite the emotions of the day that pointed many an accusing figure at the banker, considerable evidence exists indicating that the involvement of banks in the securities business was not the cause of the Great Depression. In a well-documented study by E. H. White, it was discovered that bank failures affected only 4 out of a total of 62 banks that had subsidiaries specializing in the trading of financial assets and 11 out of 145 banks that operated directly on the stock market.[2]

TABLE 3.2 Top Twenty-Five Arrangers of All International Syndicated
Loans *(continued)*

1999

Rank/Bank	Amount (US$ billions)	Issues
1. Chase Manhattan	$109.3	607
2. Bank of America	103.9	74
3. Citigroup	70.3	366
4. Bank One	33.4	302
5. Deutsche Bank	28.9	240
6. Barclays	25.0	138
7. J.P. Morgan	20.8	105
8. Bank of New York	19.0	128
9. ABN AMRO	18.8	204
10. Credit Suisse First Boston	15.1	112
11. First Union	14.1	254
12. Bank of Nova Scotia	13.6	147
13. Commerzbank	12.5	94
14. Banque Nationale de Paris	11.5	105
15. HSBC	11.3	95
16. CIBC	10.4	162
17. SG	10.0	122
18. Toronto-Dominion	9.1	110
19. WestLB	9.1	81
20. BankBoston	8.8	149
21. Fleet Financial	8.8	190
22. Dresdner Bank	8.2	108
23. Warburg Dillon Read	8.0	44
24. Royal Bank of Scotland	7.6	32
25. Paribas	7.4	78

Source: Capital Data Loanware, as in *Euromoney,* September 1999, p. 139.
[1]Loans that are organized by a lead bank, with a supporting group of banks providing the rest of the loan. The syndicate is the entire group of banks.

Glass-Steagall was later modified by the Section 20 Amendment, which permitted U.S. banks to have subsidiaries with limited powers to undertake securities operations, granted there were adequate firewalls (i.e., an intentional separation of the two activities, complete with a refusal to share sensitive information between them, which could provide an unfair advantage in the form of insider information) between the operations of the commercial bank and securities firm. Glass-Steagall and related laws were repealed in 1999. Under the new legislation, the Financial Services Modernization Act of 1999, banks can now participate freely in the securities and insurance businesses. The legislation will more easily enable financial companies to offer corporate clients a full range of services from loans to investment bank services and insurance. For American consumers, it opens the door to financial supermarkets that offer an array of services, much akin to the European *bancassurance* idea.

U.S. commercial banks are allowed to provide deposit-taking services and make residential real estate loans, agricultural loans, and loans to other financial institutions. Until the 1999 repeal of Glass-Steagall, they could not directly act as an underwriter and dealer in corporate securities, but they were allowed to offer securities brokerage services, provide trust services, or act as a dealer in U.S. government and municipal securities. Moreover, most major U.S. banks have created holding companies that provide greater scope of action in the conduct of nonbank financial services through separate subsidiaries.[3] In 1994, thirty-five subsidiaries of bank holding companies were operating with Federal Reserve approval to underwrite and deal in certain bank-ineligible securities.[4] In these circumstances, these subsidiaries are supervised by both the Federal Reserve and the Securities Exchange Commission. The Fed examiners have a mandate to ensure that adequate firewalls and internal controls are in place for Section 20 subsidiaries (subsidiaries of commercial banks permitted limited powers to undertake security operations) to prevent prohibited intercompany transactions and transfers of assets between the subsidiary broker-dealer and the affiliated insured commercial bank.

The U.S. banking system is converging into a community of commercial banks. Thrift and savings banks (initially established to meet the needs of small savers and provide services geared for savings) continue to exist, but in declining numbers. The vast bulk of banking assets are with the nation's commercial banks. There are a little more than 2,500 nationally chartered banks and still more state-chartered banks, pushing the total number of banks to around 7,000. New York City remains the undisputed financial and banking hub of the United States as well as of the global economy, providing the headquarters address for Citigroup and Chase Manhattan. At the same time, the breakdown of barriers against interstate banking has allowed a considerable degree of consolidation, much of it outside of New York City. (See Table 3.3.) This is amply reflected by the pending merger of Charlotte-based NationsBank and San Francisco–based Bank of America, as well as the merger of Fleet and Bank of Boston into Fleet Boston.

The U.S. bank regulatory system is divided into a number of bodies, each with their own particular mandate, yet working in tandem with each other. The Office of the Comptroller of the Currency (OCC) is the primary bank supervisory agency for nationally chartered banks. In 1998, it had a staff of over 1,800 bank examiners performing the statutorily required regular on-site examinations of more than 2,500 banks subject to its supervision. The OCC is attached to the Treasury Department, but it operates with a high degree of autonomy. The Comptroller, for example, is a presidential appointee.

The OCC works with the Federal Reserve Board, which has authority over bank holding companies. State-chartered banks are supervised by state bank supervisory agencies, while their holding companies fall under the jurisdiction of the Federal Reserve Board. The Office of Thrift Supervision is responsible for savings and loan associations and savings banks. In addition, banks are subject to the supervision of the Federal Deposit Insurance Corporation (FDIC) and various commit-

TABLE 3.3 Top Ten U.S. Commercial Banks as of September 30, 2000

Rank/Bank	City	Total Assets (US$ billions)
1. Bank of America	San Francisco, CA	607.1
2. Citibank	New York, NY	369.0
3. Chase Manhattan Bank	New York, NY	346.2
4. First Union Bank	Charlotte, NC	227.8
5. Morgan Guaranty	New York, NY	178.3
6. Fleet National Bank	Providence, RI	161.7
7. Wells Fargo Bank	San Francisco, CA	103.2
8. Bank One	Chicago, IL	98.1
9. Suntrust Bank	Atlanta, GA	97.4
10. HSBC	Buffalo, NY	84.0

Source: Federal Reserve Board, Web Site, data as of September 20, 2000.

tees of the U.S. Congress. One example of intergovernmental cooperation is the Interagency Country Exposure Review Committee (ICERC), which supervises the foreign loan exposure of U.S. banks and has the power to mandate reserve requirements (capital set aside for the provision of bad loans). ICERC membership is composed of the OCC, the FDIC, and the Federal Reserve. Moreover, there is interagency cooperation in the securities area with the Securities Exchange Commission (SEC). Under the 1999 repeal of the Glass-Steagall Act, it was agreed that the Treasury Department (including the OCC) and the Federal Reserve will share supervision of new financial conglomerates while the SEC will continue to oversee securities subsidiaries.

Foreign banks operating in the United States fall under the jurisdiction of federal and state authorities and are expected to comply with the statutes and laws to which U.S. banks must adhere. In theory, foreign banks are given a level playing field with their U.S. counterparts. In the past this has led to certain problems, considering that most European and Canadian banks have been universal in nature as opposed to the breakdown in U.S. finance between commercial and investment banking. U.S. financial authorities had problems with the idea of allowing a Dutch bank, for example, to come into the U.S. market and sell insurance products as well as securities all under the same roof, while their U.S. counterparts were prohibited from selling insurance and could only have a securities business wing if it was in a special subsidiary of the bank holding company and contained by internal firewalls. Consequently, there were often bilateral negotiations between the United States and other countries, such as the Netherlands, Germany, and France, over exactly which powers their banks could and could not exercise in the domestic U.S. market. With the demise of Glass-Steagall and related legislation in 1999, some of the complications related to foreign bank supervision were removed. Concerns remain, however, with other issues as to how U.S. banks are treated in foreign countries, the primary concern being whether U.S. banks are allowed to compete on a level playing field or are discriminated against.

Japan

Japan's banking system is one of the most important in the global economy, with its banks dominating the top ranks of banks in asset size throughout the first half of the 1990s before experiencing a precipitous decline in the latter part of the decade. Although undergoing substantial changes at the end of the 1990s, Japanese banks still play an important international role, providing finance for Japanese multinational corporations and loans to governments and corporations throughout much of Asia, Latin America, and Central and Eastern Europe. Japan's banking system is divided between commercial and investment banks; most of these are referred to as city banks, of which there are nine. The most significant of these are Bank of Tokyo-Mitsubishi, Sumitomo Mitsubishi Banking Corporation (a merger of Sumitomo Bank and Sakura Bank), and the Mizuho Financial Group (a three-way merger of Dai-Ichi Kangyo Bank, Fuji Bank, and Industrial Bank of Japan). As a group, the city banks generally conduct operations nationwide. They accounted for around 46 percent of all lending and 31 percent of all deposits in 2000.[5] Major trends facing the city banks include the pressing need to follow through with announced mergers and create cohesive banking cultures, the implementation of the necessary technology (including the unification of computer systems in merger situations), and how to contend with both nonbank and foreign bank competition. All of this points to the need to restructure with an eye to enhancing profitability and developing a credit culture that better understands risk.

There are also 119 regional banks (as of year-end 2000), broken down into the traditional regional banks and the former Sogo banks. As a group, the traditional regional banks are smaller than their city bank counterparts, are based in each one of Japan's sixty-four prefectures, and usually conduct the majority of their operations within that prefecture. Consequently, they are tied to the local economy, which has meant heavy lending to the troubled real estate, construction, and retail sectors. A small number expanded beyond their prefectures and grew their international operations. The former Sogo banks are smaller than the traditional regional banks and form a second tier of regional banks. They were originally established under the Sogo Bank Law after World War II and were mutually owned institutions specializing in banking activities for small and medium-sized enterprises. As a group (including the former Sogo banks), regional banks accounted for 30 percent of all lending and 31 percent of all lending at year-end 2000.

In the early 2000s, the regional banks are facing tough decisions. Economic conditions have remained difficult in nonmetropolitan regions, with a high number of bankruptcies and with 2000 seeing a record number of corporate failures. The major trends facing regional banks are deteriorating balance sheets due to unreserved bad assets (owing to weak economic growth and difficult corporate conditions), long-term concerns over profitability, and the related issue of leading Japanese banks increasingly encroaching on the mid-sized blue-chip corporate loan markets of regional banks. The cost of adopting new technology is also an issue. Regional banks need to implement radical structural reform to solve their problems.

Rounding out the picture are specialized banks, including state-owned institutions like the Postal Bank, the Japan Development Bank, the Small Business Corporation, trust banks, and Shinkin banks. The Shinkin banks were established under the Shinkin Bank Law of 1951 and are small cooperative institutions focusing on deposit and lending activities with members (generally small, locally oriented companies and individuals). The Zenshinren Bank plays the role of central bank for the 390 Shinkin institutions, which serve their 8.5 million medium and small business and individual members. Zenshinren's position in this ¥100 trillion (US$1 trillion) cooperative system provides it with a large and stable funding base.[6] Another major institution is the Norinchukin Bank, which functions as the central bank for agricultural, fishing, and forestry cooperative federations throughout Japan. In 2000, it was estimated that Norinchukin had ¥49.8 trillion in assets.

It is important to distinguish that the city banks are largely the most active international players, though some regional banks have also developed international businesses. Equally important is that Japan's banks traditionally have focused on short-term lending and in attracting deposits, as opposed to the specialized institutions that were created for long-term lending and trust activities. These short- and long-term divisions of labor, however, are disappearing as Japanese banks are undergoing a considerable restructuring in the late 1990s and early 2000s.

Japan's banking system was initially universal in nature, following the European model, in particular the German model that encouraged designated banks to fund industrial development and have heavy involvement with a particular conglomerate.[7] The central bank played a broad, sometimes unofficial role of developing specialized institutions that provided financing for specific purposes, such as agriculture, industry, housing, and exports. Following Japan's defeat at the end of World War II, it was occupied by the United States. During the U.S. occupation (1945–1952) the universal model was discarded. U.S. occupation authorities, inspired by the Glass-Steagall Act in their homeland, imposed mirror-image legislation on the Japanese in Article 65. Throughout most of the postwar era, Japanese banking was thus divided between city and regional banks, such as Sakura Bank and Sanwa Bank, and investment banks, such as Nomura.

Although Japanese banks were subject to Glass-Steagall-like restrictions, they maintained their main bank characteristics, functioning as the key financial institutions for a cluster of related businesses, sometimes referred to as **keiretsu**. This meant that within one business group, such as the Sumitomo Group, there would be a bank, trust, insurance, leasing, investment bank, and real estate companies, cemented by cross-firm shareholdings. (See Table 3.4.) This system worked well when Japan was a developing economy seeking to catch up with the West. It did not, however, function well when Japan reached a postindustrial stage of development, requiring it to contend with globalization and the need to move away from traditional short-term lending operations. Equally important, this system of close linkages left a legacy of a weak credit culture in which banks gave little concern to credit risk in making loans. Asset growth was in some ways more important than

TABLE 3.4 Two Japanese Banks and Their *"Keiretsu"* in 1989

Sumitomo Group

Banks	Sumitomo Bank
	Sumitomo Trust
	Kansai Bank
	Mie Bank
Insurance	Sumitomo Marine & Fire
	Sumitomo Life
Leasing	Sumisho Lease
	SB General Leasing
Investment Bank	Daiwa Securities
Real Estate	Meiko Securities
	Sumitomo Realty & Development

Mitsubishi Group

Banks	Mitsubishi Bank
	Mitisubishi Trust
	Nippon Trust
	Hachijuni Bank
	Shinwa Bank
Insurance	Tokyo Marine & Fire
	Meiji Mutual Life
	Misshin Fire & Marine
Leasing	Diamond Leasing
Consumer Finance	Diamond Credit
Investment Banks	Nikko Securities
	Ryoko Securities
Real Estate	Misubishi Estate

Source: *The Economist,* March 25, 1989, p. 92.

profitability. The bubble economy in the late 1980s only made this worse when the crash came in the early 1990s.

In the 1990s measures were taken to dismantle the barriers imposed under Article 65. In April 1994, Japan introduced the Financial System Reform Act, which allows banks and securities firms to enter each other's business through newly created subsidiaries or acquisition of existing entities.[8] Other legislation has sought to deepen the reform process, opening up Japanese financial markets to a "Big Bang" by 2002. (See Table 3.5.)

Considering the serious nature of Japan's recession in the late 1990s, after a decade of low economic growth (on average), ballooning fiscal deficits, a growing public sector debt, and an increasing number of corporate failures, the changes occurring in the banking system are likely to be far-ranging. The fail-

TABLE 3.5 Top Ten Japanese Banks, 1998

Rank/Bank	City	Asset Size (US$ billions)
1. Bank of Tokyo-Mitsubishi	Tokyo	$656.45
2. Sumitomo Bank	Osaka-shi	464.8
3. Dai-Ichi Kangyo Bank	Tokyo	419.1
4. Sanwa Bank	Osaka-shi	415.88
5. Fuji Bank	Tokyo	399.13
6. Sakura Bank	Tokyo	385.7
7. Norinchukin Bank	Tokyo	381.06
8. Industrial Bank of Japan	Tokyo	356.2
9. Tokai Bank	Nagoya-shi	251.5
10. Long-Term Credit Bank of Japan	Tokyo	195.9

Source: The Banker, January 1999.

ure of Hokkaido Takushoku, a city bank, in 1997, followed by the collapse of Yamaichi Securities, one of Japan's so-called Big Four brokerages, signaled that the current restructuring was going to be tough and extensive. This message was reinforced by the subsequent nationalization of two other troubled banks, Nippon Credit Bank and Long-Term Credit Bank. The asset quality of Japanese banks remains problematic, with official estimates putting bad debts at around ¥70 trillion ($623 billion).

Prior to the latest wave of reforms, Japanese banks played a key role in an economy that was largely resistant to the idea of transparency. Relations between large corporations and their banks were close, with the latter holding large amounts of shares in the particular company. Indeed, most major corporations had one bank with which they had a particularly close relationship. These main banks were largely city banks and were the financial institutions that carried out the largest share of the company's financial transactions. Lending to the same company, in a sense, ensured the bank a healthy balance sheet. From the standpoint of many Japanese corporations, the relationship with the banks meant there was an unwillingness to issue significant amounts of new equity to outsiders. Unfortunately, this reinforced their dependence on bank financing, creating a situation in which Japan became overbanked relative to the size of its economy and population. Moreover, this state of affairs contributed to overly high levels of debt within the corporate sector and did little to further develop Japanese capital markets. Change came in the 1990s when Japanese companies found bad-debt-burdened banks unable to provide them the financing they required. The situation became more complicated when the banks were forced to sell corporate shares in order to bolster their balance sheets. Consequently, by the late 1990s, when the economy dipped into another recession, both the country's corporate and banking sectors came under considerable pressure to change. That pressure remained constant into the next decade as the economic recovery was fragile and large-scale

TOKYO REGAINS ITS PLACE AS A FINANCE HUB
Robert Steiner

Tokyo—Tokyo is a boom town again for foreign securities companies and banks, less than a decade after many began turning their attention to Asia's other markets.

Nine years ago, Jarett Wait left his job as a bond trader in Japan, soon to be followed by many other foreign bankers and brokers who decided that Japan's moment in the sun was over. In November, however, Lehman Brothers Inc. moved him and five currency traders to Japan from Hong Kong and told Mr. Wait to turn Tokyo into Lehman's new bond and foreign-exchange hub for Asia.

J.P. Morgan & Co.'s Asia unit moved eight derivatives traders to Tokyo from Hong Kong and London in January to help it profit from Japan's financial restructuring. And Chase Manhattan Corp. put together a mergers-and-acquisitions team two months ago here to help Japanese companies sell units they no longer need, and is planning an expansion into other fee-based services here.

Source: Wall Street Journal, May 29, 1997.

corporate bankruptcies, as in the construction and retail sectors, remained causes of concern to bank health.

Reforms are seeking to modify Japan's cross-shareholding structure, increase investor confidence in corporate governance, allow banks to help promote venture capitalism, and permit banks to market investment trusts (institutions established to pool funds for investment). The overall intention of bank reform in Japan is to transform the role of banks from being deposit-taking institutions with equity holding in major borrowers, to that of modern banks more in line and competitive with their European and North American counterparts. Reform also means moving away from the division of short- and long-term lines of lending and a decline in specialized lending institutions. This last trend was underscored by the collapse of the Long-Term Credit Bank (LTCB) in 1998.

LTCB was once one of Japan's largest and most prestigious specialized banks. Mandated to make long-term loans to Japanese industry, it helped to finance much of the country's rapid recovery and economic resurgence after World War II. LTCB, however, made extensive speculative loans in the 1980s, many of them in the real estate sector. Like many other banks, LTCB saw a large portion of these loans unpaid in the economic slowdown in the early 1990s. It was caught with a heavy load of nonperforming loans, which became increasingly onerous throughout the decade. At the same time, deregulation and the advent of foreign competition opened up what had been a relatively protected sector for LTCB. In October 1998, the government intervened, taking control of the bank. LTCB was eventually sold to foreign investors and reemerged as the Shinsei Bank.

An additional round of bank reforms was introduced in 1998 seeking to reduce the risk of a collapse of the Japanese banking system and provide institutional and financial mechanisms to accelerate the restructuring and consolidation of the sector. These measures entailed making funds of ¥60 trillion available to recapitalize "viable" banks, for failure resolution schemes including bridge banks and the nationalization of failed banks, and to be reserved for guaranteeing deposits at failed banks. Other measures included:

- The consolidation of existing agencies into an asset management corporation along the lines of the former U.S. Resolution Trust Corporation, to receive and dispose of bad assets.

- The creation of a new high-level body, the Financial Revitalization Commission (FRC), in the Office of the Prime Minister. The FRC's mandate is to help draft enabling legislation as well as to oversee the recapitalization of the banks and centralize all supervisory activities; the primary bank regulator, the Financial Supervisory Agency, was placed under the FRC's control.

The primary bank supervisory agency in Japan is the Financial Supervisory Agency (FSA). Prior to June 1998 that function had been fulfilled by the Ministry of Finance. The deep-rooted and systemic nature of Japan's banking crisis, as well as a number of scandals, discredited the Ministry of Finance and made the need for new institutions, with greater enforcement powers, pressing. Hence, the FSA was created. Although much of the FSA's staff came from the Ministry of Finance and initial expectations were mixed, the FSA demonstrated that it had clout by nationalizing the two biggest troubled institutions—Nippon Credit Bank and Long-Term Credit Bank. Considering the broad nature of bank reform in Japan and its commitment to clean up the banks' bad loans, the FSA is likely to have a substantial amount of work ahead.

As one of the major themes of this book is the rapid pace of change occurring in international banking, the case of Japan at the close of the 1990s and early 2000s demonstrates the process of globalization. Japanese banks must change to survive in the face of global competition and further deregulation. In a break with the past, Japanese banks are seeking to become more driven by financial intermediation while moving away from being the source of short-term capital. At the same time, considerable consolidation in the banking sector is occurring. A number of mergers were announced in 1999 and 2000, which included a three-way merger of Fuji Bank, Industrial Bank of Japan (IBJ), and Dai-Ichi Kangyo Bank (with assets of $1.3 trillion), Sanwa and Tokai Banks, and others. In addition, competition among Japanese banks is likely to increase; companies are likely to shift away from loans to capital markets, and the foreign presence in banking and finance will continue to expand.

Foreign banks operating in Japan theoretically are treated much the same as their Japanese counterparts. The reality has been different, as equal access to Japanese financial markets has been an ongoing source of tension between Japan and other G–7 countries. Foreign penetration of Japanese financial markets has been relatively slow and complicated by unofficial barriers and, in the past, a preference by Japanese financial consumers to stay with Japanese banks. The financial turmoil during the 1990s, however, has changed this situation somewhat, and foreign banks are making inroads into Japanese markets.

Japanese banks will continue to face substantial challenges over the next decade. Although they include some of the largest financial institutions in the world in terms of assets, Japanese banks still face pressure in terms of profitability and maintain relationships with sectors of the economy that will remain problematic, as in the cases of companies in agriculture, construction, and retail. Japanese banks must also move at a more rapid pace with those mergers already in motion. Competition has grown from both foreign institutions and nonbank Japanese institutions such as Softbank and Sony. This implies a greater need for technological innovation and unification of existing computer systems. Japanese banks confront the danger of wasting valuable time fighting over turf in announced mergers, while their counterparts increasingly expand into their traditional businesses. In addition, Japanese banks could well face macroeconomic problems if the country's public sector debt, calculated at around 120 percent of GDP at year-end 2000, is not brought under control. Expanding public sector debt could hurt the banks' bottom line if there were substantial problems with the Japanese Government Bond (JGB) market.

Euroland

Euroland is defined here as those countries in the European Union (Austria, Belgium, Denmark, Finland, France, Germany, Greece, Ireland, Italy, Luxembourg, Netherlands, Portugal, Spain, Sweden, and the United Kingdom). Although there are still national differences pertaining to certain specific practices, banking in Euroland countries is universal, and through legislation there are European Union–wide rules and regulations that each country has agreed to follow. The long tradition of international banking, the universal nature of business activities, the high level of economic development within the Union, and geographical location have guaranteed that some of the most significant institutions involved in international banking have their headquarters in London, Frankfurt, Madrid, Paris, and Amsterdam.

Major trends in Euroland are consolidation within national borders of banking systems, regional consolidation (as in the Nordic countries), and the search to find new revenue streams in a highly competitive environment. Following the emerging markets turbulence in 1997–98, it is also expected that the internationally oriented European banks will reduce their activities in those markets and instead focus more on lower-risk opportunities within Europe. One area of particular interest for European banks is the anticipated shift of money out of deposits and loans in banks and into equity markets. This expected development underscores another trend, the growth in continental Europe of shareholder power in the governance and direction of banks. While European banks are likely to enjoy new opportunities related to the creation of a single European currency, more active cross-border mergers are not expected to gain momentum. Factors such as different cultures and tax regimes, uneven economic development, and specific regulatory requirements are expected to be significant ongoing hurdles. As to the treatment of foreign banks, they fall under the jurisdiction of the relevant banking

STILL GROWING AFTER ALL THESE YEARS

John Plender

New York and Tokyo may be larger financial centers, but the City of London is unquestionably the front runner in international finance. It has achieved pre-eminence despite the relative decline of the British economy and the near-demise of sterling as a reserve currency.

No other financial centre in history has enjoyed such success while being semi-detached from the domestic economy. Yet surprisingly little research has been done to explain the nature of London's unique competitive advantage in international financial services....

Source: Financial Times, March 13, 1995.

authorities of each European Union member. That stated, each Union member has already implemented EU banking regulations that provide reciprocity in banking services. Foreign bank treatment is also a much easier issue because European banks are universal in operating.

United Kingdom   The banks operating in the United Kingdom make up one of the most important groups of banks within Euroland. There are some 200 banks in the United Kingdom, with a roughly similar number of representative offices of foreign banks.[9] The UK banking industry is broken down into four major groups: clearing banks, building societies, investment banks, and the foreign banking sector. It should also be added that London is by far the dominant financial center in the country as well as being a key international center. As in most major economies, UK banking is characterized by the rapid implementation of new technologies and consolidation. Consolidation has taken the form of the Royal Bank of Scotland's takeover of National Westminster Bank and rumors surrounding Barclay's attempt to take over Abbey National in 2000.

Clearing banks dominate the provision of financial services in the United Kingdom and play a significant role as international bankers. Products offered encompass documentary credits, bills, export finance, corporate finance, foreign exchange, and advisory services. Clearing banks have also moved into other non-deposit products following regulatory changes and today provide unit trusts, personal equity plans, and portfolio management services.

Clearing banks took their name from membership and control of various money-payments clearing houses. As membership of the clearing houses opened up to other institutions, they became known as retail or high street banks because of their nationwide branch networks. The dominant institutions within this sector are Barclays, National Westminster Bank, Lloyds Bank, the Royal Bank of Scotland Group, the Bank of Scotland, and Abbey National (formerly a building society). Two other institutions are significant, especially from the standpoint of their heavy involvement in international business: Standard Chartered PLC and Hong Kong Shanghai Bank (HSBC). (See Table 3.6.)

The UK's *building societies* still account for a significant share of the residential mortgage market, but they are in decline due to regulatory changes that allow them to convert into a bank. Until 1986, their primary focus was the provision of mortgage finance and the acceptance of deposits. Regulatory changes, however, allowed the building societies to diversify into life assurance, pensions, and investment products. The largest of these institutions converted into banks during the middle and late 1990s. Converts from building societies into banks include Abbey National and Halifax. Despite the shrinking numbers of this group, they do remain active as a force, with around seventy-five active societies as of 1998.

Investment banks (also called *merchant banks*) in the UK have traditionally provided services to the UK corporate sector. Institutions in this group include SBC Warburg, Schroders, Robert Fleming & Co., Ltd., Hambros, Singer & Friedlander Ltd., and N.M. Rothschild & Sons Ltd. Most of these banks can trace their history back to the eighteenth century, when they were heavily involved in bills of exchange. In the broad sense, investment banks are engaged in a wide range of businesses from lending and medium-term finance for exports to overseas project finance, investment management, and corporate finance. UK investment banks face tough competition from the investment bank operations of the clearing banks and foreign banks. Through the 1980s and 1990s, the numbers in the group declined. Institutions such as Barings and Morgan Grenfell were forced to seek foreign ownership to inject badly needed capital.

The foreign bank sector in the UK plays a significant role in making London a major international financial center. The British government has traditionally allowed easy access, pursuing an "open policy" designed to encourage London's

TABLE 3.6 Top Ten United Kingdom Banks by Assets, End–June 1999 (in US $ billions)	
Rank/Bank	*Assets (US$ billions)*
1. HSBC Holdings	$475.5
2. Barclays PLC	353.3
3. Nat West PLC	297.4
4. Abbey National PLC	273.5
5. Lloyds TSB Group	240.0
6. Halifax PLC	208.7
7. Royal Bank of Scotland	135.1
8. Bank of Scotland	95.8[1]
9. Nationwide Building Society	83.8
10. Standard Chartered PLC	79.6

Source: FitchIBCA.
[1] As of Feb. 1999.

key role in global finance alongside New York and Tokyo. As a *Standard & Poor's* report in 1996 noted: "Consequently, there are currently about 375 foreign-owned banking institutions active in the UK, over 200 representative offices and about 100 foreign securities houses. Virtually all the world's leading financial institutions have a physical presence in the London market."[10]

The primary bank regulatory institution in the UK is the Financial Services Authority (FSA), which replaced nine other regulatory bodies and became operational in 1998. Under the Financial Services and Markets Act of 2000, the FSA has four major objectives: maintaining market confidence; promoting public understanding of the financial system; the protection of consumers; and fighting financial crime. Before the emergence of the FSA, the primary bank regulatory institution was the Bank of England, the central bank, which was supplemented by a number of other regulatory bodies. The Bank of England continues to have roles that provide it some influence over banks. These functions include monetary policy, management of the country's stock register, and printer of bank notes. It also collects and publishes (via its Monetary and Financial Statistics Division) money and banking data in order to monitor developments in the financial system.

As a member of the European Union, the UK's banking law is also subject to EU statutes. The Bank of England's bank regulatory activities entail the licensing of new banks, supervision of their securities operations, and working with self-regulatory operations and recognized professional bodies. The Bank of England has traditionally followed an informal cooperative framework with its banks, supplemented by statistical returns, and on a regular basis, inspection-type visits. During the 1990s, regulation became more formalized due to market developments and new EU regulations.

France   France has one of the largest economies in the world, and its banks carry considerable weight within Euroland. Since the late 1980s, the French banking system has undergone considerable change, initially with a round of privatizations and most recently with a wave of consolidation as its major institutions are carefully sizing up merger candidates within France, while eyeing tough inter-European competition. As in other Euroland nations, French banks are universal in operation and are regarded as leaders in the area of *bancassurance*. The array of activities that falls under French universal banking includes:

- Accepting deposits
- Lending or providing other types of credit
- Cash management, transfer of funds, and payment services
- Foreign exchange operations
- Purchase and sale of gold and precious metals
- Purchase, sale, underwriting, and custody of securities
- Investment counseling and asset management
- Financial engineering
- Ownership and management of rental properties

- Ownership of nonbanks, including industrial enterprises
- Sale of insurance policies (through a subsidiary)

French banks were traditionally divided among savings institutions, retail banks, and specialized banks. This created a national banking system dominated by such institutions as Societe Generale, Banque Paribas, Banque Nationale de Paris, Credit Agricole and Credit Lyonnais. (See Table 3.7.) The distinctiveness of various credit institutions, however, was intentionally changed by the Banking Law of 1984, which was modified in July 1996. The banking law, especially after July 1996, sought to clarify and consolidate the banking system's regulatory structure and to eliminate perceived inequities. As *Standard & Poor's* noted: "It defines credit institutions broadly, thus eliminating restrictions on certain classes of organization that previously existed, and brings all credit institutions under the legal framework."[11]

The push to change the French banking system, which began in the 1980s, came from a number of fronts. The advent of the Socialist government under President François Mitterrand in 1981 resulted in the nationalization of the national banking sector. This gave way in the mid-1980s to deregulation, which encouraged the banks to significantly increase their lending capacity. The Socialists also recognized that nationalization of the banks was not the most brilliant of ideas and gradually reversed course. In 1987, some of the country's major banks, such as Societe Generale, Banque Indosuez, Banque Paribas, and Credit Commercial de France, were privatized. Unfortunately, the banks became heavily involved in lending to a speculative real estate industry. The bubble burst with the recession of

TABLE 3.7 Top Ten French Banks by Asset Size, December 1997

Rank/Bank	Total Assets (franc million)	Employees	Branches
1. Societe Generale	2,641,438	55,000	2,600
2. Credit Agricole	2,514,885	84,670	8,166
3. Banque Nationale de Paris	2,034,871	52,420	2,098
4. Credit Lyonnais	1,498,698	50,789	2,229
5. Campagnie Financiere de Paribas	1,468,211	20,000	N/A
6. Groupe Caisse d'Epargne	1,286,566	39,157	4,216
7. Groupes Banques Populaires	666,010	26,500	1,850
8. Credit Mutuel	648,951	23,700	N/A
9. CCF (Credit Commercial de France)	398,992	10,785	475
10. Natexis	299,300	3,313	N/A

Source: *The Banker,* January 1999, p. 38.

1992–93. This chain of events badly hurt a number of French banks, which were forced to contend with losses from bad commercial and property loans. The health of the banking system was also troubled by restrictive labor laws that resulted in overstaffing and the slowing of new labor-saving procedures. Consequently, the changes in French banking law enabled a more level playing field among credit institutions, pushing the weaker into mergers and, in some cases, forcing failures. At the same time, collective agreements with trade unions did allow some downsizing of employees through layoffs, relocations, or redeployment.

The primary bank regulator in France is the Commission Bancaire, which is attached to the Banque de France, the central bank. Two other bodies under the auspices of the Banque de France share bank supervisory authority—the Comite des Etablissements de Credit et des Entreprises d'Investissement or CECEI (the Credit Institutions and Investment Firms Committee) and the Comite de la Reglementation Bancaire et Financiere or CRBF (the Banking and Financial Regulatory Committee). The Banque de France coordinates the activities of the CECEI, CRBF, and Commission Bancaire and supplies staff. Moreover, the Banque de France's governor is chair of the CECEI and the Commission Bancaire. Consequently, the three bank supervisory bodies work in tandem, covering all aspects of banking in France:

- The CECEI is responsible for approving credit institutions and investment firms before they begin operations.

- The CRBF has responsibility for drawing up regulations concerning both credit institutions and investment firms in the areas of minimum capital requirements, publishing of financial information, and internal controls. In addition, it draws up regulations pertaining to depositor protection and the conditions under which credit institutions can carry out operations on their customers' accounts.

- The Commission Bancaire is the authority for supervising all credit institutions and monitoring their financial health; it interprets the regulations created by the CRBF and monitors their implementation; and it supervises regulations drawn up by the CRBF for investment firms. The Commission Bancaire conducts routine inspections, inspections motivated by problems in a specific bank, and systemwide examinations of a single area of activity.

The Banque de France's role in the banking system also includes functioning as the lender of last resort. To France's rubric of financial supervision should be added the Ministry of Finance, which appoints most members of the three banking committees within the Banque de France and of the Conseil des Marches Financiers (CMF), which was established by the 1996 Modernization Law and shares authority with the three institutions in regard to market activities.

The major trends in the French banking system are similar to those elsewhere in OECD countries, namely the push for consolidation, the implementation of new technology, and the quest for innovation. In terms of consolidation, the most significant development was the merger of Banque Nationale de Paris and Banque Paribas in 2000, which made it France's largest bank. At the same time, other European banks have become more active in France, as reflected by the sale of Banque Worms to a German bank in 2000.

Germany   As in the cases of the United Kingdom and France, Germany's banking system is universal. Based on the strongest Euroland economy (the third largest in the world), German banks constitute one of the most powerful groups in international banking. There are three major groups of universal banks in Germany: commercial banks (Kreditbanken); savings banks and their regional giro institutions (Sparkassen und Landesbanken); and cooperative banks and their regional giro institutions (Volks- and Raiffeisenbanken and the Zentralbanken). The giro is an electronic payment system widely used in Germany and other parts of Europe for consumer bill payments. Giros are credit transfers, in sharp contrast to the check system in the United States. In general, universal banks are involved in taking deposits, providing loans and mortgages, underwriting securities, and investing directly in securities including equities. Savings banks operate in three tiers—local savings banks, state savings banks, and the central savings bank. In contrast to the commercial banks, the savings banks are not profit-maximizing institutions, but are operated in the public interest. Cooperative banks have a similar three-tier structure, with depositors being shareholders. Other banking institutions in Germany include specialized banks (such as mortgage banks), building savings banks (Bausparkassen), and investment funds (Kapitalanlagesesellschaften). There are around 600 savings banks and 194 regional banks.

Germany's commercial banks are the most actively engaged in international banking. The Big Three—Deutsche Bank AG (with assets of $582 billion at year-end 1998), Dresdner Bank AG ($372.6 billion in assets), and Commerzbank AG ($288 billion)—together hold about 13 percent of the country's total banking assets (including their groups' mortgage subsidiaries) and exercise considerable influence on the rest of the economy through their shareholdings in major corporations, seats on advisory boards, and proxy votes. On the international side, all three have expanded their overseas operations, especially in investment banking. Deutsche Bank acquired Morgan Grenfell in 1989, and Dresdner Bank purchased Kleinwort Benson in 1995. Subsequently, Deutsche Bank acquired Bankers Trust in 1999. Outside of the Big Three, a number of the Landesbanks have expanded their range of activities to include international banking, as in the cases of Westdeutsche Landesbank Girozentrale and Bayerische Vereinsbank. (See Table 3.8.)

The primary supervisory authorities in Germany are the federal banking Supervisory Office (BAKred) and the German central bank, the Deutsche Bundesbank. *Standard & Poor's* describes this relationship: "Although BAKred is the primary bank regulatory and supervisory authority, it works closely with the Bundesbank, and the two are considered partners in the formulation of regulatory and supervisory policies."[12] In addition to BAKred and the Bundesbank, external auditors play a significant role, performing the examination function through various audits.

German banks are in the process of making substantial changes. The country's publicly owned banks are increasingly being forced to be more market driven and less dependent on the state for support as in the form of guarantees for the Landesbanks. These guarantees, referred to as Anstaltslast and Gewahrtragerhaftung, are believed to provide the Landesbanks top-notch credit ratings and allow them to borrow cheap money for expansion, with little regard to their underlying

TABLE 3.8 Top Ten German Banks by Assets, 1999

Rank/Bank	Total Assets (US$ billions)
1. Deutsche Bank AG	$844
2. Bayerische Hypo-und Vereinsbank (Proforma)	646
3. Dresdner Bank	399
4. Westdeutsche Landesbank Girozentrale West LB	391
5. Commerzbank	374
6. Landesbank Baden-Wuerttenberg	277
7. Bayerische Landesbank Gorozentrale	273
8. Deutsche Genossenschaftsbank	244
9. Bankgesellschaft Berlin AG	195
10. Norddeutsche Landesbank	172

Source: Merrill Lynch Fixed Income Research, BankScope, update 12 (April 2000).

financial strength.[13] Consequently, there is an increasing possibility that the Landesbanks may have weakened guarantees going forward or may face some type of restructuring to more accurately reflect who assumes risk. Another major trend in German banking is the shift away from cross-holdings between the banks and large companies. In July 2000, the German parliament passed a law that encourages this. Germany's four largest banks together hold $124.7 billion of equities, whose sale could generate tax-free profits (under the new law) of $80 billion.[14] This means that German banks will find the 2000s a decade of considerable change, demanding the development of new skills (as in mergers and acquisitions) and an ability to compete in international markets.

Emerging Market Banking Systems

The process of globalization has increasingly drawn attention to the various links between the banking systems of the developed countries and their counterparts in the developing group of nations. A number of banking systems crises throughout the 1980s and 1990s (such as in Argentina, Brazil, Mexico, and Venezuela) underscored the danger of poor supervision and regulation and the impact of bank failures on local, regional, and international economies. The Asian economic crisis in 1997–98 was, in part, a banking crisis. In Korea, Indonesia, and Thailand, local banks failed, were nationalized by reluctant governments, or limped along. The weak nature of Korean, Thai, and Indonesian banks in the aftermath of the crisis arguably lengthened the economic downturn due to a lack of credit necessary to restart businesses, facilitate trade finance, or meet payrolls.

Despite the periodic systemic banking crises in non-OECD countries, not all countries in Africa, Asia, Latin America, and Central and Eastern Europe have fallen victim to such downturns. In fact, the banking systems in much of Latin America (with a few exceptions like Venezuela) likely are on much firmer ground now than they were in the 1980s or early 1990s. Even Mexico's banking system, shell-shocked by the so-called tequila crisis of 1994–95, is completing the process of cleaning up problem assets, bolstering loan-loss provisions, and rebuilding weakened capitalization levels. And in the cases of Argentina and Chile, sound macroeconomic policies, prudent supervisory actions, and foreign investment have helped create relatively sound banking systems. Even in Asia, there has been an effort to upgrade local banks, so that they can compete in international, as well as local, markets, and depend less on high-interest margins from loans of dubious quality.[15]

Mexico

The Mexican banking system is universal in nature and is open to foreign banks. Since 1982, the banking sector has undergone nationalization, privatization, economic crisis, near collapse, and restructuring. In 1982, Mexico underwent a severe economic crisis that ultimately resulted in the rescheduling of its external debt. During that crisis, the outgoing Lopez Portillo administration nationalized the country's fifty-eight banks in an attempt to control the declining economic situation. This action also allowed the government a cheap source of funds, which resulted in a crowding out of private investment. As Mexico went through the process of restructuring its economy, it became important to reprivatize the banking sector. First, deregulation began in 1990, which allowed banks to switch to more credit activities. Next, from June 1991 to July 1992, the government sold the eighteen banks (the number left from the original fifty-eight institutions that were nationalized) at excessively high prices.

One of the problems that occurred in the postprivatization phase was that the banks rushed to provide credit, partly because many of the new bank owners had no previous experience in bank management. This meant that most banks had little ability to conduct adequate credit risk analysis related to their lending activities. Compounding the problem, the private sector was long starved for credit after having been crowded out by the public sector. However, as the public sector shifted from deficit financing to surpluses, the private sector suddenly found credit available. Consequently, the banks soon overextended themselves. One observer noted: "As a cumulative consequence of these factors, a 'bubble' economy emerged in Mexico whereby credit extended to the private sector mushroomed, often to the disregard of the risks inherent in such loans."[16] A major shock to the banking system came in the aftermath of the failed peso devaluation in December 1994, which precipitated a major economic crisis that has been dubbed the tequila crisis.

The 1994 peso crisis hit the Mexican banking sector hard. Many businesses suffered during the ensuing economic slump, which meant higher costs of capital (due to a rise in interest rates) and low demand for their products. Many of the loans from banks to the corporate sector had to be rescheduled. The dire straits in which Mexican banks found themselves were mirrored by the level of nonper-forming loans, which reached 30 percent of total loans established in 1995.

In response to the peso crisis and the substantial debt problem facing the bank-ing sector, the Mexican government created a number of institutions to help work out the debt. The government also intervened in a number of banks to prevent another collapse of the sector. Consequently, the Mexican government's approach to resolving the banking crisis was a combination of providing support for the banking sector through recapitalization, help in loan restructuring, and support for debtors. Additionally, efforts were made to improve bank supervision, and the banking sector was opened up to foreign investment after years of protection. These efforts, while significant, did not resolve the problem.

While the Mexican banking sector struggled to regain its strength following the 1994–95 crisis, it was rocked once again by the emerging markets turmoil in 1997–98. (See Table 3.9.) Already struggling under a burden of bad debt and ongo-ing deterioration in asset quality, a number of Mexico banks were in danger of fail-ure or once again had severe problems. Banco Serfin, one of the country's largest banks, was actually taken over by the government in July 1999. The government had already pumped $12.5 billion into Banco Serfin to keep it afloat after the December 1994 devaluation. One offshoot of this situation is that the banks have not been big providers of credit to the private sector, which has guaranteed a slower

TABLE 3.9 Top Ten Mexican Banks

Rank/Bank	Assets (US$ billions)	Per-cent change 97/98	Deposits	Per-cent change 97/98	Loans (US$ billions)	Per-cent change 97/98
1. Bancomer	$25.4	–6.2	$19.3	0.4	$17.99	–16.9
2. Banamex	25.3	–18.6	18.7	–13.2	16.3	–13.9
3. Banco Serfin	18.0	–7.3	11.6	–9.9	12.5	–3.6
4. Bital	10.3	12.8	5.7	–11.3	7.9	16.0
5. BBV Mexico	7.8	–0.1	5.3	–15.6	6.1	17.5
6. Banco Santander Mexicano	6.9	–13.2	4.99	–11.5	5.4	–5.9
7. Banco Mercantil del Norte (Banorte)	6.2	–2.1	4.37	10.0	4.66	–10.9
8. Inbursa	3.6	46.4	2.2	132.2	1.9	22.1
9. Banpais	2.86	3.6	2.7	52.9	1.98	–20.6
10. Citibank	2.78	44.0	1.7	26.7	2.09	56.8

Source: Latin Trade, September 1999, pp. 27-28.

pace of economic growth. This has forced the government to take further measures to restructure the banking sector.

A major move toward resolving Mexico's banking problems came in December 1998 when a compromise was reached in the Congress between the government party and a major opposition party. The debate over further financial reform was politically charged, especially considering that the cost of bailing out the banking sector, an estimated $100 billion, is equal to 20 percent of Mexico's GDP.

The future trends shaping Mexican banking are likely to be further consolidation, possibly greater foreign bank involvement, and a gradual recovery. The legislation adopted in December 1998 should set the stage for a stronger overall structure of banking more akin to that in other OECD economies and less like those in some of the more troubled emerging markets.

Mexico's central bank, the Banco de Mexico, plays an important role in regard to the nations financial system. While it is the key force in monetary policy and the issuer of bank notes, the Banco de Mexico operates as a reserve bank and lender of last resort for credit institutions. It also performs visitations at the intermediary facilities (banks) to verify and evaluate the information provided by banks and other institutions.

Indonesia

The Indonesian banking system collapsed in the late 1990s and is in the painful process of reconstruction. During the 1980s the combination of strong economic growth and financial liberalization allowed the banking system to enjoy a rapid expansion. The number of banks rose dramatically from 108 in 1988 to 232 in 1993, topping 250 in 1997. Following a universal model of banking with close ties to various conglomerates, the country rapidly became overbanked. Additionally, there was a lack of transparency and disclosure in financial transactions, creating an opaque system of business that thrived on secrecy. This condition was worsened by the weak nature of credit analysis in the banks, a situation promoted by the often political nature of lending.

Although the Bank of Indonesia, the central bank, recognized that there were too many banks and was inclined to encourage a consolidation of the sector, political influence precluded that policy from advancing in a meaningful fashion. The supervisory concern was that whenever the Indonesian economy hit a slowdown, many banks would find themselves overextended and hit by rising nonperforming loans. In 1997, Indonesia was hit by the Asian economic crisis. Exacerbated by the bungling of the International Monetary Fund (IMF) and the Suharto government, the banking system was plunged into a steep decline.[17] The fall of the government of President Suharto in May 1998 added a degree of political uncertainty to the situation, contributing to the systemic nature of the banking crisis.

Indonesia's banking sector will take several years to reconstruct. Since the end of 1997, the government has closed 57 banks, leaving it with 153 institutions.[18] The country's three largest banks—Bank Central Asia, Bank Danamon, and Bank Dagang Nasional Indonesia—were nationalized in 1998, and the process of nationalization and recapitalization was started in 1999 for nine more private banks,

SCRAMBLING FOR LIFEBOAT SEATS
Mark Landler

Jakarta, Indonesia—When Indonesia's economy began collapsing in August 1997, Rudy Ramli, president of Indonesia's fourth-largest private bank, gathered his top lieutenants for a pep talk. "If everybody is going to die," Mr. Ramli said, "we want to be the last ones to die."

Today, Mr. Ramli's bank, Bank Bali, is clinging to life, though he acknowledged that it is being strangled by bad loans and will need an infusion to stay afloat. What sounded alarmist in the summer of 1997 seems merely realistic in the autumn of 1998.

Bank Bali's woes illustrate just how thoroughly the Asian economic disaster has wrecked Indonesia's banking system. The vast majority of the country's 240 banks are insolvent—relics waiting to be taken over by the state or simply shut down. Even the few well-run banks, like Bali, have been infected by the disease, trapped by suffocating debts, a collapsed currency and social unrest that has led to panicky bank runs.

"Nobody trusts Indonesian banks," said Rizal Ramli, a prominent economist, who is not related to Rudy Ramli. "It is like we have no banks at all."

Source: New York Times, September 23, 1998.

---

including Lippo Bank and Bank International Indonesia. Reforms were made in 1999 to strengthen the central bank's supervisory role and to ensure its autonomy. The reforms clearly outlined the Bank of Indonesia's primary roles as being to protect the stability of the national currency (the rupiah); to ratify and implement monetary policy; to regulate and maintain a smooth payment system; and to regulate and supervise banks. Considerable attention was also given to making the bank of Indonesia more accountable and transparent in the implementation of its tasks.

In addition to the Central Bank of Indonesia's involvement in the process of reconstructing the banking sector, the government created the Indonesia Bank Restructuring Agency (IBRA). The process of bank reconstruction remains complicated by ongoing political connections between the government and certain bank owners, interbureaucratic squabbling between the central bank and the IBRA, and the difficult nature of the economy. These conditions prevailed in the late 1990s and continue to be factors in the early 2000s. Table 3.10 provides data reflecting the severe nature of the banking sector's situation.

India

The Indian banking system is universal in nature. Although reforms were enacted in the late 1980s and first half of the 1990s to modernize the Indian economy, reform of the banking sector has been slow. Simply stated, the financial sector is

TABLE 3.10 Indonesia: Banking System Balance Sheet (Rupiah 1,000bn)

	Dec. 1997	June 1998	Dec. 1998	Feb. 1999	Feb. 2000
Assets	528.9	1,013.9	762.4	704.2	800.6
Deposits	341.5	539.7	557.6	581.6	NA
Liabilities	482.2	959.6	861.0	902.2	NA
Equity	46.7	54.4	–98.5	–198	–19.3
Equity/assets	8.8%	5.4%	–12.9%	–28.1%	NA

Sources: RHB Securites as quoted by *Financial Times,* May 4, 1999 and the Bank of Indonesia web page.

dominated by the government, has been managed for political and social concerns, and has considerable problems that must be overcome before it is regarded as a more efficient, modern sector. In 1969, the government nationalized the fourteen largest commercial banks and subsequently took over six others; and it controls all banking through the Reserve Bank of India (the central bank).[19]

As of March 31, 1997, there were 299 commercial and regional banks in India, operating an estimated 63,500 branches.[20] The Indian banking system is dominated by publicly owned banks, the largest of which is the State Bank of India. The State Bank of India alone accounts for 26 percent of loans and 30 percent of deposits. Other significant state banks are the Industrial Development Bank of India, the Industrial Finance Corporation of India, the Industrial Credit and Investment Corporation of India (ICICI), and the Export-Import Bank of India. There are a total of twenty-seven public sector banks, which account for 80 percent of deposits and 90.8 percent of branches of all commercial banks.[21] The rest of the Indian banking system is accounted for by thirty-four domestic private sector banks (with around 9 percent of the deposits and 10 percent of all loans) and foreign banks (just under 8 percent of deposits and around the same amount of loans). (See Table 3.11.)

Retail banking has become an important segment of banking in India. In 1969 there were 8,200 branches; in 1996 there were 62,900 branches. The expansion of this business has been a positive force in mobilizing national savings. At the same time, India's banking sector faces substantial challenges. These include a weak credit culture in the banks, political interference, and a low level of technological innovation. In the past, lending was often politically inspired, not profit driven or constrained by credit concerns. This has led to a high level of nonperforming loans, which makes recapitalization difficult. India's ability to reform its banking sector is complicated by the inability of bank management in the public sector banks to lay off staff or close branches.

This situation is aggravated by strong employee unions that oppose many corrective actions, including automation; this has a negative impact on the quality of services and limits the range of products offered. Additionally, government interference continues. As a *Moody's Investor Service* report (November 1998) noted: "Banks are directed to water down commercial criteria with socially desirable goals e.g. lending to priority sectors such as agriculture and small industrial units that

TABLE 3.11 Top Ten Indian Banks by Assets

Rank/Bank	Assets (US$ billions)
1. State Bank of India	$52.5
2. Reserve Bank of India	35.2
3. Industrial Development Bank of India	16.3
4. Industrial Credit and Investment Corp. of India (ICICI)	13.8
5. Bank of India	12.7
6. Bank of Boroda	12.3
7. Canara Bank	11.3
8. Punjab National Bank	10.9
9. Central Bank of India	8.1
10. Union Bank of India	7.4

Source: Merrill Lynch Fixed Income, BankScope update 112 (November 1999) and the Bank of Indonesia web page.

have caused high problem loans in the past. Corporate governance issues arise from political appointments in key positions."[22]

India's primary bank regulator is the Reserve Bank of India. It provides supervision over the banks and is the lender of last resort. The Reserve Bank's support for the banking system was evident during financial year 1997–98, when the government spent Rupee 27 billion recapitalizing three nationalized banks. The recapitalization was made within the framework of the 8 percent minimum capital adequacy requirement, which the three banks were unable to reach. India, like many countries, has accepted the Bank for International Settlements (BIS) minimum capital adequacy standards, which require banks to put up 8 percent of their capital as a provision against potential risk.

Looking ahead, India's banking system will come under increasing pressure for change. This is already evident in the interest margin pressure, which is pushing banks to diversify into nontraditional lines of business and expand the range of banking products available to customers. Diversification has largely focused on the development of treasury and capital market activities, infrastructure lending, and retail banking (encompassing home lending and the provision of consumer finance). As with banks in other countries, the high reliance on fee income will augment revenue volatility, as income from trading and other fee-income activities can vary substantially from year to year.[23] The pressure to change will be particularly acute on public sector banks, due to their lower noninterest income revenue, high operating cost structure, and weak asset-quality position. Consequently, the future of banking in India is most likely to be marked by volatility, the introduction of new financial products, and eventually consolidation through mergers and acquisitions. Long protected from the pressures of the outside world, India's banks increasingly face the pressures of globalization, introduced in part by ongoing economic reforms. Along these lines, new measures were taken in 2000 to overhaul India's nineteen state banks by reducing government ownership from 51 percent to around 33 percent, which would allow them to recapitalize.[24] However, efforts to reform the banks have been started before, and this remains a major challenge for India in the twenty-first century.

China

China's banking system is transitory. The old model of dominant state banks channeling capital to particular sectors of the economy is gradually being dismantled. Four state banks dominated since the 1950s, but they functioned more as the state's cashiers rather than as banks. This was in tune with the statist orientation of the ruling Communist government. Commercial banks were not established until the late 1980s. Policy banks established to further rationalize the banking system between commercialized institutions and development banks were created only in 1994 and replaced by a more market-driven and competitive system. In the mid-1990s, a series of measures, seeking to improve regulatory supervisory, augment capital levels, and reduce problem loans, were introduced. Additionally measures were taken to commercialize the state banks (i.e., make them more market driven), allow the emergence of new commercial banks, and provide better guidelines for both banks and nonbank financial institutions in such areas as trade finance, investment banking, and negotiable instruments.

As of 1999, China's banking system consisted of 3 policy banks, 4 state commercial banks, 10 national joint-stock commercial banks around 88 city-based commercial banks, 3,240 urban credit cooperatives, and more than 41,500 rural credit cooperatives.[25] (See Table 3.12.) Despite the large number of institutions, the Big Four—the state-owned Bank of China, Agricultural Bank of China, China Construction Bank, and Industrial & Commerical Bank of China—control an estimated 80 percent of total banking assets.[26] All four are solely owned by the Ministry of Finance. Foreign bank participation is limited. As of 2000, there were more than 160 foreign banks that maintained branches or representative offices in China. Their operations, however, are highly restricted. At year-end 1999 only thirty-two foreign banks were active in providing domestic yuan businesses in Shanghai and Shenzhen.

Chinese banks have a low level of sophistication in terms of what products can be offered. Most banks provide rudimentary banking services such as deposit taking, lending, payment, and clearance. The small group of more sophisticated banks offer cash management, treasury, securities clearance, and other kinds of value-added services to corporate customers. Additionally, some of the larger retail-oriented institutions offer credit cards, mortgage loans, and other retail products. An even smaller group of banks provide Internet services, such as account access and transaction services.

Chinese banks confront difficult conditions, and reform of the sector is a priority of the government. While the banks face competition from nonbank financial institutions, they also must improve their performance with an eye to eventual entry of China into the World Trade Organization (WTO). One condition in WTO membership is the opening of domestic financial markets to greater outside competition. WTO membership also presents a challenge from another perspective: it is

TABLE 3.12 The Structure of China's Banking System (as of end 1998)

	Total Assets (RMB billion)	Market Share (%)	Total Loans (RMB billion)	Market Share (%)	Total Deposits (RMB billion)	Market Share (%)
State-owned commercial banks (4)	8,259	66%	6,231	69%	5,948	66%
Policy banks (3)[1]	569	5	552	6	1	0
National commerical banks (10)	1,148	9	584	6	835	9
City commercial banks (88)	457	4	220	2	364	4
Urban credit cooperatives (3,240)	561	5	401	4	608	7
Rural credit cooperatives (41,500)	1,143	9	881	10	1,216	13
Foreign banks (162)	283	2	223	2	40	0
Total (45,100)	12,420	100%	9,092	99%	9,012	99%

Source: China Financial Outlook 1999, PBOC Quarterly Statistical Bulletin.
[1]Policy banks' figures exclude Agricultural Development Bank of China.

feared that many of the more talented Chinese bankers will leave their current institutions to work for foreign banks that offer higher salaries.

At the same time, the state banks have a severe problem in the form of the country's 300,000 state-owned enterprises (SOEs). These companies account for only one-third of the country's industrial output, but they consume at least two-thirds of its credit resources.[27] This misallocation of credit is aggravated by the poor credit quality of most SOEs, as most are poorly managed, overstaffed, and awash in red ink. The challenge posed by SOEs and their relationship to the Big Four is further complicated by the fact that such enterprises still employ close to 50 percent of China's urban workers. Widespread closure of SOEs would obviously have political and social repercussions, despite the drag they have on China's public banking sector. In turn, the difficulty in bringing China's largest banks up to international capital adequacy standards leaves these institutions an ongoing concern to the rest of the banking sector as well as to the overall economy. Moreover, government ownership is likely to continue to undermine corporate governance, disturb lending behavior, and discourage performance incentives.[28] In 2000, the People's Bank of China, the central bank, released statistics on bank debt indicating that Chinese financial institutions need to write off an estimated 2.5 trillion yuan ($300 billion) in unrecoverable loans, a sum equal to 31 percent of annual GDP.

The problems of bad loans, poor credit analysis, and a lack of internal lending safeguards are not limited to the banks. Some of the country's nonbank financial institutions, namely the International Trust and Investment Corporations (ITICs) of provinces and cities, ran into problems in the late 1990s. The most spectacular failure was that of the Guangdong International Trust and Investment Corporation in October 1998, which included a default and rescheduling of foreign debt.

The bank regulatory authority is largely in the hands of the central bank, the People's Bank of China (PBOC). In the late 1990s, efforts were made to enhance PBOC's supervisory role and provide it with greater independence. In 1998, the PBOC's thirty-one provincial branches were reorganized into nine regional centers to augment regulatory authority and to counter interference from local governments (a major problem). The restructured central bank consists of a four-tier system with one head office (Beijing), nine regional offices, 326 city branches, and 1,827 county-level branches. The newfound independence of the central bank was evident in its forceful nature in closing down troubled local financial institutions. Although hardly omnipotent, the PBOC was able to overrule local governments and close the China Agribusiness Development Trust & Investment Corporation (1998), Hainan Development Bank, China Venturetech Company, GITIC, and twelve credit cooperatives in Guangxi Province and twenty in Guangdon Province.

Looking to the future, China's banking system faces substantial challenges. First and foremost is the pressing need to train more skilled bankers as well as regulators. With WTO looming on the horizon, local banks will find a smaller pool of talent. Second, stronger efforts will have to be made to clean up the portfolios of the publicly owned banks. This also implies an acceleration of reform of the SOEs. One step in the right direction was the creation in 1999 of the country's first asset management company—the Cinda Asset Management Corporation—with a mandate to assume control of a portion of the China Construction Bank's problem loans. However, the magnitude of the problem is huge, with estimates of nonperforming loans running from 30 percent to 65 percent of all assets. A third challenge will be adapting the right technology to help Chinese banks become more competitive. A fourth will be maintaining a role in disintermediation, especially as nonbank financial institutions continue to open their doors and challenge banks.

South Africa

Not all banking systems in the non-OECD set of nations are confronted by massive problems that threaten systemic collapse. Although the Republic of South Africa faces considerable challenges—high unemployment, the need to upgrade skills, and ethnic/racial tensions—it has one of the world's more sophisticated banking systems outside of the OECD. South Africa's banks benefit from the application of increasingly advanced technology and systems, sophisticated financial and risk management techniques, relatively stable competition due to the dominance of the major banks, low levels of problem lending, and solid bank supervision.

At end of 1998, there were forty-four registered banks in South Africa, four mutual banks, and a growing number of foreign banks. The six largest banks account for the bulk of the nation's banking business, though foreign banks have chipped away at that dominance. (See Table 3.13.) Nonetheless, the six largest South African banks (whose ranks include ABSA, First National, Nedcor, and Standard) account for almost 85 percent of total banking assets. Banks in South Africa follow the conglomerate, universal banking model, which allows them to offer a wide range of services. Among those financial services are commercial and investment banking, securities trading, derivatives trading, underwriting, fund management, and short-term insurance products. It is important to clarify that a bank is required to conduct business in equity securities and insurance through legally separate subsidiaries. Additionally, banking law prohibits the banks from making equity investments in corporate customers.

South African banking faced considerable changes in the 1990s. As the system of racial separation, apartheid, was dismantled, the country was welcomed back into the international economy. For the South African banking sector, this meant that foreign banks were now interested in accessing their home market. At the same time, the end of apartheid allowed South African banks to seriously consider banking opportunities in neighboring African countries—a business that had been officially denied them by many of the regional governments in protest of apartheid. The same factors allowed South African banks to expand their operations in large financial centers in North America, the United Kingdom, and Hong Kong, providing them with new income streams. Because of this expansion outside of the country, South African banks have also been forced to become sensitive to international market forces. This was reflected by the negative impact of the

---

TABLE 3.13 South Africa's Largest Banks, June 2000

Rank/Bank	Assets (US$ billions)
1. Absa Bank	$23
2. Standard Bank of South Africa	19.2
3. First Rand Bank	17.6
4. Nedcor	17.4
5. Investec Group	7.2
6. BOE	7.0
7. Development Bank of South Africa	2.4

Source: Merrill Lynch, November 2000.

Asian economic crisis in 1997–98, which contributed to a higher interest rate environment in 1998 due to the South African Reserve Bank's actions to protect the economy as well as to lower profitability in Asian markets.

Banking supervision is the responsibility of the Bank Supervision Department of the South African Reserve Bank under the control of the Registrar of Banks. It had a staff of sixty-eight as of year-end 1998. The South African Reserve Bank was established in 1921 and issues the country's bank notes. It is also the custodian of the country's gold and foreign exchange reserves, and it functions as a redemption bank, discount bank, and a supplier of credit to commercial banks and other financial institutions. Furthermore, the Reserve Bank formulates monetary and exchange rate policies and is the lender of last resort. It is believed that although the Reserve Bank has advocated a philosophy of market-based solutions to troubled situations, it would most likely intervene if any of the major four banks got into trouble. The country's Big Four are regarded as too big to fail, reflecting the belief that if one such institution were to fail, it would threaten the banking system's overall health.

Hungary

The Hungarian banking system has made a considerable transformation during its transition from Communism in the 1980s to a market economy in the 1990s. Under the old system, the state had considerable say in the allocation of credit, official interest rates were centrally set and reflected planners' growth priorities rather than availability of funds, and creditworthiness of the borrower was a foreign concept. Indeed, poor corporate performance was often rewarded with additional state subsidies. Although the political regime was to change in the late 1980s and early 1990s, old banking habits were hard to end. The legacy of the old banking regime was portfolios of bad loans, relations with clients that were not based on sound business planning, and a lack of credit skills necessary to develop a prudent lending culture within each bank. Consequently, the early 1990s were a period of upheaval for the Hungarian banking sector, witnessing a number of crises and state intervention in the sector to keep it afloat. Following the period of consolidation in the early 1990s, the Hungarian banking sector was reformed and became one of the stronger systems in Central Europe.

The Hungarian banking system is broken down between several large commercial banks (which are universal in nature) and a large number of smaller credit institutions. (See Table 3.14.) According to the National Bank of Hungary, the central bank, forty-three credit institutions were operating as incorporated companies (i.e., banks) on December 31, 1999.[29] The banks are divided into two groups, a handful of large and medium-sized banks that dominate the market and seventeen smaller banks that control only 7 percent of the market for loans. There were also 203 savings cooperatives and eight credit cooperatives.

Foreign bank involvement in the Hungarian banking sector is substantial. At year-end 1999, foreign banks owned 65.3 percent of the banking sector.[30] Large foreign banks, such as ABN AMRO, Citibank, Deutsche Bank, and Rabobank, are

TABLE 3.14 Top Hungarian Banks 2000 (Assets in US$ billions)

Rank/Bank	Assets (US$ billions)
1. OTP Bank	7.4
2. Magyar Kulkerekedmi Bank (MLB)	2.8
3. Kereskedelmi & Hitel Bank	2.2
4. ABN AMRO (Magyar)	2.0
5. Postabank & Savings Bank Co.	1.3
6. Budapest Credit & Development (Budapest Bank)	1.3

Source: Merrill Lynch Fixed Income Research, November 2000.

active in the Hungarian market. Although such a large foreign ownership always strikes a degree of nationalistic concern, the heavy involvement of large international banks has helped make the Hungarian banking sector more competitive and considerably more efficient. State ownership has shrunk considerably since the early 1990s, standing at 19.3 percent at the end of 1999. It is expected that the state ownership share will fall further as the decade proceeds.

The chief regulatory authority is the National Bank of Hungary, which operates through its Department of Banking Supervision. The central bank has sought to improve its supervisory role during the 1990s and now enjoys a reputation for prudent policies.

The major trends facing the Hungarian banking sector in the 2000s are consolidation, the implementation of new technology, and providing a credit flow to the country's major companies. Consolidation probably weighs the heaviest. There is considerable speculation that a country of 10 million does not necessarily need over forty banks. In 2000, consolidation began to take shape with the merger of K & H Bank, majority owned by KBC of Belgium, and the Dutch-owned ABN AMRO Hungary, a move that when finished will establish the second largest bank in the country.[31]

Russia

The Russian banking system has been marked by considerable volatility since the fall of the Soviet Union in 1992. The Soviet system was long dominated by the state monobank, Gosbank, which presided over the allocation of credit in the economy. As with other centrally planned economies, the Russian banking system functioned as a cashier for the government, channeling credit, and was open to political pressures. An understanding of credit and such concepts as profits and cash flow were largely unknown and not regarded as important. With the fall of Communism in the early 1990s, there was an explosion in the number of banks. Russia's shift to a market-oriented economy meant that there was a need for the services banks could provide. Consequently, from a handful of late Soviet institutions, Russian banks (as defined as operating credit organizations) reached 2,295 by January 1, 1996. (See Table 3.15.)

The dominant institutions are Sberbank and Vneshtorgbank. Both are state-owned banks. Sberbank is the state savings bank, and it is 58 percent owned by the central bank. It dominates retail deposit taking, controlling 80 percent of the market. Vneshtorgbank is 96 percent owned by the central bank, is the former bank for foreign trade, and holds a commanding force in the corporate sector. Combined, Sberbank and Vneshtorgbank account for more than 30 percent of the banking systems assets as of year-end 1999.

Russian banking remains in a state of transition. The shift to capitalism in the 1990s was not smooth, with banking prone to recurrent crises. While Russian banks were allowed to operate as universal banks, most managements lack the necessary expertise to be completely engaged in the full range of services offered. This became painfully evident in August 1998, when a large number of banks failed. According to one rating agency in January 2000: "In general, the Russian financial system operates under a peculiar and shifting logic, rooted in personality, politics, and brinksmanship, that has and will continue to frustrate creditors."[32] The rating agency also made note of "questionable banking and legal practices" in Russia as well as the "weak and arbitrary nature of its credit culture," as mirrored by:

- Confusion surrounding the settlement of forward contracts

TABLE 3.15 Operating Credit Institutions in Russia

Date	Number of Institutions
Dec. 31, 1995	1,476
Jan. 1, 1996	2,295
Jan. 1, 1997	2,029
Jan. 31,1998	1,686
Dec. 31, 1999	1,349
Dec. 31, 2000	1,311
Feb. 29, 2000	1,338
March 31, 2000	1,333
April 30, 2000	1,330
May 31, 2000	1,331
June 30, 2000	1,331
Sept. 30, 2000	1,322
Oct. 31, 2000	1,320
Nov. 30, 2000	1,316
Jan. 31, 2001	1,314

Source: Bank of Russia (Central Bank).

- Removal and reinstatement of banking licenses of bankrupt banks
- Russian accounting practices that have little basis in economic reality

Those shortcomings are compounded by a high level of arrears and lack of restructuring in the corporate sector; frequent bank collapses, which have led to a deep lack of trust in banks among the general population; collapse of financial services after the August 1998 crisis; poverty of most of the population; and lack of accessible banking services for much of the economy.[33] Moreover, Russian banks have been a target for organized crime. As one source commented: "Attracted by the early profits to be made in banking, organized crime clearly made determined efforts to penetrate the banking sector; the main evidence is the grisly trail of bank president's bodies left by contract killers over the years. It would be surprising indeed if capital originating from organized crime did not make up a substantial part of the Russian bank's capital."[34]

The Bank of Russia is Russia's central bank, and it has the primary responsibility for bank supervision and regulation. Under Article 4 of the Federal Law on the Central Bank, the Bank of Russia is the creditor of last resort for credit organizations and organizes the refinancing system; sets settlement rules for financial transactions; establishes and updates rules of conduct for bank operations and accounting and the reporting rules for the banking system; and conducts state registration for banks and revokes licenses of credit organizations and the organizations that audit them. The central bank also supervises the activities of banks and registers the issue of securities by banks in accordance with federal laws. Beyond the supervision and regulation of banks, the Bank of Russia conducts, on its own behalf or on the behalf of the government of the Russian Federation, all kinds of banking operations necessary for the central bank to implement its main policy objectives. This encompasses regulation of foreign exchange.

The Bank of Russia's track record as a bank supervisory agency has been difficult. It was founded in 1990, emerging from the Russian Republic Bank of the State Bank of the USSR. Starting with a small pool of bankers, the new institution was entrusted with the role of guidance for the commercialization of Russian banks in 1991–92, a highly politicized process. At the same time, it was under considerable pressure to maintain a steady flow of credit to enterprises to keep up productivity.

Although the flow of credit was eventually stanched and the bank reorganized to be more in line with a market-oriented economy, the Bank of Russia continues to have problems. A crisis in 1995 tested the central bank, especially in the aftermath in which new "bridge banks" were created to help restart the banking industry. The only problem with the bridge banks is that the assets of the previous insolvent entities have been transformed—while the liabilities have been left behind. This means bad debts continue to overshadow the banking system and public confidence is not forthcoming. Despite considerable strides in the right direction, Russia's bank supervision is still weak.[35]

The lack of sophistication in financial matters, the limited pool of talent, and the transitional nature of the economy combined to make the first years of Russian banking a painful experience. Looking ahead, Russian banking is likely to remain difficult. Russian banks must still deal with large numbers of depositors who lost money held on deposit during the 1998 crisis. They must also contend with foreign bank competition and the ongoing onslaught of new technologies. Additionally, Russia's regulators, legislators, and prosecutors have not kept up with all the change affecting the banking industry. The sad commentary about Russian banking at the beginning of the twenty-first century is that it lacks the confidence of the population, a critical lacuna. It will take considerable effort and time to gain popular trust in banking.

Islamic Banking

Any chapter examining banking systems around the world would be remiss without a mention of Islamic banking. Although most banks around the world adhere to a Western-based model that charges interest on loans, Islamic banks, which follow a different model that does not use interest, exist in a small number of countries, including Indonesia, Kuwait, Malaysia, Pakistan, Saudi Arabia, and Sudan. In 2000 there were an estimated 160 Islamic financial institutions, with total deposits of $100 billion.[36] The sector is growing as Islamic banking becomes better understood in both the West and lands where Muslims form a sizable market.

The Western banking model has long since sidestepped its religious problems with usury (i.e., the charging of interest on the use of money as a loan). In much of the Islamic world, however, usury remains an issue. Of particular concern is what is called *riba al-qarud,* the usury of loans, which involves a charge on a loan arising due to the passage of time, in other words, a loan at interest. The problem arises where a borrower of another's wealth enters into a contract to repay to that other person a preagreed amount in addition to the principal that was borrowed. In whatever fashion this increase occurs, if it is fixed in absolute terms at the outset of the transaction, the loan becomes a usurious one.

Under the Islamic banking code, interest is not paid, but share participations are paid at some date as earnings. For countries to create a just Islamic financial system, key measures that must be undertaken are to eliminate interest, minimize macroeconomic imbalances, and institute legal and institutional reforms.[37] It is important to emphasize that in contrast to Western banks, Islamic banks regard themselves as having a social responsibility, providing banking services to whoever needs them. The most prominent Islamic bank is the Islamic Development Bank, though many Western banks, such as Citibank and Hong Kong Shanghai Bank, have Islamic banking operations.

Islamic banking is still an evolving industry.[38] This is evident in that there is considerable discussion within the sector as to what is or is not an acceptable Islamic instrument. New products such as *ijara* (leasing) and *murabaha* (trade financing) have been added, but these remain open to debate. Acceptable accounting methodology is also a debated point. Indeed, as *Moody's Investor Service* noted: "Questions such as the validity of subordination of claims, or the liability of fund managers to make good initial investment values, are vital in assessing the creditworthiness of financial operations. Yet, issues such as these are often subject to divergent opinions and lack of precedent."[39] Despite being an industry in for-

TABLE 3.16 Supranational Lending Institutions as of June 30, 2000

Institution	Assets (US$ billions)
African Development Bank	$15.7
Asian Development Bank	49.9
Corporacion Andina de Fomento	6.2
Council of Europe Development Bank	17.7
European Bank for Reconstruction and Development	21.5
EUROFIMA	20.4
European Investment Bank	228.1
Inter-American Development Bank	88.3
World Bank	270.9
International Finance Corp.	40.5
Nordic Investment Bank	14.7

Source: Supranationals Maintain High Ratings, *Standard & Poor's,* Sept. 20, 2000.

mation, Islamic banking is expected to remain an active force in those countries where Islam has strong foundations.

Supranational Banks

In international banking there is one additional group of banks that exist—the supranationals. These are large multinational organizations, with memberships composed of countries, often along a regional line, such as with the African Development Bank, Caribbean Development Bank, European Bank for Reconstruction and Development, and Inter-American Development Bank. (See Table 3.16.) In general they have a specific mission, which is tied to economic development. Member countries usually provide capital in the form of subscriptions. These institutions also have the option to issue bonds, which are usually AAA rated.

The best known of these institutions is the World Bank, also known as the International Bank for Reconstruction and Development. The oldest of multilateral development banks, the World Bank commenced operations in 1946 and is owned by 181 countries. It provides medium- and long-term financing to developing countries at interest rates below those of private sector lenders. It also lends during periods of financial stress, when capital market access may not exist or commercial banks are not willing to make loans.

Since the Asian financial crisis there has been considerable debate about the usefulness of supranationals, including the World Bank. One argument is that World Bank policies made the economic crises worse in such countries as Indonesia. Some have called for the closing of the World Bank and other regional banks such as the Asian Development Bank. Despite such debates, these institutions provide badly needed capital to developing countries that would not be available elsewhere.

Citibank, N.A., in China

IVEY

Larry Li and Adrienne Young under the supervision of Professor David W. Conklin prepared this case solely to provide material for class discussion. The authors do not intend to illustrate either effective or ineffective handling of a managerial situation. The authors may have disguised certain names and other identifying information to protect confidentiality.

Ivey Management Services prohibits any form of reproduction, storage or transmittal without its written permission. This material is not covered under authorization from CanCopy or any other reproduction rights organization. To order copies or request permission to reproduce materials, contact Ivey Publishing, Ivey Management Services, c/o Richard lvey School of Business, The University of Western Ontario, London, Ontario, Canada, N6A 3K7; phone (519) 661–3208, fax (519) 661–3882, e-mail cases@ivey.uwo.ca.

> "We want to be totally global and totally local."
> —*John Reed, Chairman and CEO, Citicorp[1]*

Citibank at a Crossroads

In 1997, Citibank was still at an early stage in its China entry strategy. It was one of the strongest foreign banks operating in the People's Republic of China (PRC), but as a foreign bank it had only limited market access. It was licensed only to provide corporate banking services, and only to foreign-invested enterprises. It was licensed to operate branches in only three of the 24 Chinese cities open to foreign banks. In order to grow beyond these cities, and to expand from foreign corporate banking to the large and potentially lucrative domestic retail banking business, Citibank needed licenses from the central bank, And by preference, Citibank's China executives would have liked Citibank to be among the first foreign banks to get those licenses.

The bank's senior China staff knew that the People's Bank of China (China's central bank, or PBOC) would eventually open the China market to foreign banks, but they also knew the process would be slow. On the one hand, the PBOC was under pressure from the People's Congress, which hoped that commercializing and opening its banking sector would strengthen its bid for admission to the World Trade Organization. On the other hand, China's state banks were in appalling shape. Generally, they were run by bureaucrats, up to their knees in bad debts, still required to provide cheap funding to nearly bankrupt state enterprise, and unable to set their own deposit and interest rate levels. It might take them years to become properly competitive, and meantime it was up to the PBOC to see that strong foreign competitors like Citibank had no chance to bulldoze them out of the market. Mr. Chris Tibbs, the vice-president and head of corporate finance of

(continued)

Citibank's Chinese branch, was optimistic on this front. "The banking system in China is evolving faster than most other countries," he said in August 1997. "Generally speaking, the bureaucrats who are responsible for the financial market reforms are quite intelligent people. They know very much where they want to go. They are more efficient than most of the countries I have worked in (Japan, North and South America, and Hong Kong). I am optimistic that things will work out. PBOC operates in a very cautious but intelligent manner. The PBOC will not hold off our expansion. Actually, it is encouraging us to expand: it wants to use Citibank as a tool to force Chinese banks to become more competitive as soon as possible."

Though Citibank's senior China executives had worked hard to develop a good relationship with the PBOC, and were clearly positive about that relationship, they may also have had reason to be concerned. Citibank was one of the most powerful foreign banks in China, and given its deep pockets and obvious interest in emerging markets, the one that posed the most obvious competitive threat to China's struggling domestic banks. Should the PBOC feel that Citibank was too large, too ambitious or too successful in China, it might respond by braking Citibank's China expansion plans and give early licenses to smaller, less threatening foreign banks instead.

How could executives ensure that Citibank would maintain its first mover advantage in China? The Citicorp board wanted to see Citibank develop a major presence in retail banking. How could China executives ensure that Citibank would be among the first foreign banks to enter the domestic retail market? The most obvious option was a PBOC-sanctioned joint venture with a local bank, but Citicorp's chairman would almost certainly be opposed to the idea. Citibank didn't do joint ventures unless forced. Were there any viable alternatives? And if, despite Citibank's best efforts, PBOC opened China's retail market to other foreign banks before granting licenses to Citibank, how could Citibank establish its dominant position in a retail market?

Citibank Worldwide

Citibank, N.A. was the second-largest bank holding company in the U.S. in 1997 and was sole shareholder of Citibank, N.A. in China. The bank was significantly more international in scope than its international competitors: in 1997 it operated more than 3,400 locations in 98 countries, and, as recently as 1995, it derived 58 per cent of its net income from foreign operations. The bulk of that income came, furthermore, from its emerging market franchise.[2] The bank earned a net income of US$4.5 billion in 1996, with $294 billion in assets and $28.9 billion in capital.

Citibank had not always been a world-class success story, however. The bank suffered through a very difficult period in the late 1980s and early 1990s as a result of its decentralized decision-making structure and what *Euromoney* called a "near fatal brush with commercial real estate lending" in the U.S.[3] Thus, Chairman and CEO John Reed spent much of the early 1990s engineering the bank's recovery—a brutal but apparently successful process. One of his most well-known re-engineering efforts was the G–15.

(continued)

In 1993, at the height of the bank's real-estate lending crisis, he created a committee of the bank's top 15 business managers, who all reported directly to him. He required them all to fly to New York once a month for meetings that lasted an entire day and sometimes two, and were frequently highly confrontational, punishing all the managers involved, but analysts said it worked. By centralizing the decision making in New York and forcing his managers to fight him on every major strategic decision, he managed to repair the bank's balance sheet, rebuild its tier-one capital and restore its credit ratings by 1996.[4] Although the G–15 structure was modified later, decision making was still much more centralized in 1997 than it had been in the 1980s.

Another change Reed made was a re-orientation of the bank's strategic focus. Reed believed that Citibank's strategic advantage was in its international operations: global reach, local ties. The businesses where this advantage would be best leveraged, he hoped, were global relationship banking and global consumer finance. His focus after 1995 was, therefore, developing the bank's advantage as an international operation and, with it, developing those two lines of business. This focus would almost certainly drive all strategic decisions through the year 2000, including Citibank's decisions with regard to its China presence.

Citibank's Competitive Advantage: Its Global Network

> "When a multinational company wants to enter an
> emerging market it calls its lawyers, its
> accountants, the embassy and Citibank."
> —*Shaukat Aziz, head of Asia/Pacific global*
> *finance operations*[5]

Citibank executives, as well as most banking analysts, would probably agree that Citibank's only true and sustainable advantage in the 1990s was its sprawling global network which was important in serving its powerful list of corporate banking clients but crucial, too, in developing its consumer franchise in lucrative offshore markets.

This network, moreover, was extraordinarily strong in the emerging markets which were most attractive to Citibank's key corporate banking clients and to its own consumer finance division.

To provide an idea of the extent of Citibank's presence in and commitment to emerging markets at that time, Citicorp annual report statistics show that, while 58 per cent of total profits were provided by the bank's ex-U.S. operations in 1995, very little of this came from the developed world. In fact, slightly more than 47 per cent of total profits in 1995 came from the bank's 76-country emerging markets franchise. The Asia/Pacific region (where Citibank was particularly strong and which was considered a division of the emerging markets sector) brought in 23 per cent of the bank's net profit in that year.[6]

How had Citibank developed its emerging markets advantage?

(continued)

Time and Experience

Citibank had been in some of these markets for nearly 100 years. Where this had not been the case, Reed clearly believed in the value of first mover advantage, and had worked to ensure that Citibank was usually among the first foreign banks to get its foot in any emerging market door. The bank's relative experience in these volatile markets created a level of operational expertise that, in times of turbulence, other banks found difficult to match. This was a particularly valuable asset in attracting and keeping important multinational accounts.

Localization and Commitment

Citibank worked hard to develop close ties with the community and with the local central bank. Ninety-five per cent of Citibank's jobs held outside the U.S. in 1997 were held by locally hired staff. The bank had a well-established reputation for commitment, too, which made them popular with governments: unlike some other banks which moved into countries on the expectation of brisk profits and then moved out again when they were slow to materialize, Citibank moved in early with intent to stay. Executives (including John Reed) routinely emphasized the bank's ability and eagerness to help the local financial services industry grow. Employees were seconded to central banks. Technology was transferred. Locals were trained.

Citibank was not above currying political favor either: in Taiwan, for example, the bank "wowed Taipei" by bringing former U.S. President George Bush and former British Prime Minister Margaret Thatcher to visit in the 1990s. This seems to have worked particularly well. Rival bankers said, after that, Citibank got "just about anything they wanted from the central bank."[7] Someone, somewhere inside Citibank was almost certainly wondering how this model could be made to work for the bank in mainland China in 1997.

Technological Superiority

According to a Lehman analyst, Citibank was "ahead of the curve" with respect to technology and financial innovation[8] in the mid-1990s. Judging from the number of awards the bank won in 1996, this was not an uncommon view. Citibank was broadly perceived to be very strong in corporate banking services ranging from foreign exchange to cash management, debt capital markets to derivatives. And if this was the case in the U.S., it was even more obvious in emerging market nations where competition was less well developed, financial systems less evolved. It is also the reason Citibank won numerous awards as best bank overall: best emerging markets bank, best Asian bank, best foreign bank in China, best foreign bank in a number of other emerging markets.[9] In other words, Citibank could usually provide better corporate banking service than local banks in many of its markets, and competitive service in more markets than any of its "foreign bank" competitors.

(continued)

Human Resources Practices

According to Chris Tibbs, human resources development was one of the bank's most pressing issues in China. "The most challenging thing for us today is the human resource side of our business. Normally, a person needs to have about seven years of experience before he/she can be a capable manager. We only started branch banking activity in China three to four years ago, so we have trained local people to be successful managers for only three or four years." Despite this, the bank's human resources practices were broadly perceived as a powerful competitive advantage, in China and throughout Asia. Analysts in China said that Citibank people were frequently poached by other banks. Tibbs confirmed this, noting that the bank's counter-strategy (salary, environment and opportunity) was helpful in holding staff, and even in bringing them back. "As a matter of fact," said Tibbs, "our people who went to work for ABN-Amro want to return to Citibank. We are the college of banking and the best bank in the world."

Accounting Practices

The bank also had an advantage in Asia in its audit and accounting practice. This was particularly true in China, where Citibank was the bank the PBOC chose to work with to improve internal auditing within the domestic banking system. As of 1997, the PBOC was actually using Citibank's internal auditing standards as a guide for its own, and extending that standard to other Chinese banks. According to Chris Tibbs, in fact, the PBOC was so pleased with Citibank's recommended internal control system that they used it to audit the bank's new Beijing branch only six months after opening. "After our branch in Beijing had been open for about six months, we received a message from PBOC that it was going to audit us," said Tibbs. "It seemed strange that we had just been working for six months and it wanted to audit us. It turned out that it was because PBOC wanted to test its team of auditors, who were trained by us. This was the first time that Citibank was tested by its own students. After the team of auditors went through the auditing, Citibank suggested to them where they could possibly improve." Analysts wondered if, in China, this advantage was a sustainable one.

The Citibank Strategy

Focus on What We're Good At: Global Relationship Banking and Consumer Finance

Having identified those basic strengths, Reed defined a strategy in 1995: build on what the bank was already good at and on what was already profitable. And, as many analysts pointed out at the time, Reed's plan was much more about exclusion than most. As *Euromoney* put it in 1996, the strategy was "as much about what (Citibank) won't do as what it will do."[10] Thus Citibank was categorically uninterested in insurance or global investment banking. It wasn't interested in equities and it wasn't interested in lending on a large scale. If it was active in those areas in the past, it had generally

(continued)

been quick to get out of them, both domestically and internationally. And this would continue to be the case, according to the Reed plan, through the end of the century.

Global Relationship Banking (also known as GRB)

In focusing on the top 1,400 multinationals—most of them pursuing aggressive overseas growth strategies—Citibank was "serving global companies globally,"[11] an area where it had a distinct competitive advantage over both domestic and "foreign" banks in virtually all of the most attractive emerging markets.

In China, Citibank also had a strategy for targeting strong state-owned enterprises. "Our strategy," said Chris Tibbs, "is to identify 10 industries which would develop the fastest in a country, and target profitable companies within those industries. We are different from other banks in that we choose companies not only based on their numbers on the financial statements, but also the industrial sectors they are in, and the qualities of the management team."

In order to serve these customers seamlessly, each major Citibank GRB client had, by 1997, a "team" of its own. Bankers were encouraged to think of themselves as, for example, "on the Motorola team" instead of "in foreign exchange" or "from the HK office." And although, traditionally, large banks might focus on the higher-profile activities of lending and underwriting, Citibank focused primarily on profits to be made from lower-risk day-to-day transaction banking: fund transfer, custody, cash management, foreign exchange and securities trading. Other corporate banking services (trade services, lending and capital markets) were emphasized less heavily than in the past.

In the "Asian model" Citibank executives would apply in thinking about their China strategy, the GRB franchise usually represented an important platform, allowing Citibank to embed itself in new economies, hiring locally, developing a relationship with domestic regulators and (this was an emerging idea at Citibank) beginning to serve ambitious local companies as well as Western multinationals. With licenses and regulatory relationships in place, the consumer bankers could then move in,[12] offering whatever range of retail banking products was appropriate, marketing *Citibanking*® as the country's new premium banking product.

Global Consumer Finance

What Citibank aimed to provide worldwide was a one-stop shop for retail financial services. This would mean uniform service wherever consumers choose to bank, and with the convenience and reliability emerging markets clients probably associated more closely with their local McDonald's than with the kind of banking services they were receiving from their domestic banks. Citibank charged a premium price for these services but expected that, usually, the internationally-minded and newly wealthy business elite in these nations would be willing to pay more for first rate banking services.[13] Income

(continued)

statement figures suggest that they were. Consumer banking (which John Reed established at Citibank in the 1970s) was the largest and fastest-growing part of the bank by the mid-1990s,[14] supplying 48 per cent of its earnings in 1995.

What were the advantages fueling consumer banking growth in Citibank's emerging markets? Technology and first mover advantage, to begin with. But Citibank executives believed that one of their greatest assets in building consumer business was the Citibank brand.

Marketing the Experience: Citibanking®

In emerging market countries like China, Citibank had the capacity to develop what marketers like to call "strong brand equity." It had cachet as an overseas bank. It had or could develop a reputation as a bank that provides superior service to those with money. And those who had money (who were increasing in number in these countries, and who might already have had corporate banking relationships with the bank) were generally pleased to pay a premium for the level of reliable service and convenience—and the level of prestige—that they could only get from banking with Citibank. Citibank marketed its package of consumer banking services as an experience: "*Citibanking*®." This branding strategy was not yet an advantage in China as Citibank was not allowed to provide retail banking services there. That was, however, probably only a matter of time. Brand equity was perceived to be a great asset elsewhere in Asia, where Citibank's consumer banking business was growing at a very healthy clip. The importance of brand image to Citibank's consumer banking franchise should not be underrated, therefore, and would certainly be a factor in any discussion of joint ventures or strategic acquisitions.

Citibank's Joint Venture Strategy: A Few Final Comments

> "We are accelerating our plans to get fully engaged in our business directions … to fund the expansion of our franchise in the emerging market."
>
> —*John Reed*[15]

Citibank was strongly averse to joint venture relationships, entering into such agreements only when forced by central bank authorities.[16] Citibank operated in China, as in most countries, as branches of the parent, not subsidiaries. Chris Tibbs agreed with this negative attitude towards joint ventures (JVs). "We recognize that most JVs do not last very long," he said in August 1997. "JVs give an institution a short-term advantage, but not long-term benefit. A JV in China would be an expensive practice. We do not think that we need to do a JV in China. Up to three years ago, many institutions favored JVs. Now they realize that the environment in China is such that it is unnecessary for them to do JVs in order to get business. Today, foreign institutions are looking for majority shares of the partnership, or even 100-per-cent own-

(continued)

ership. The expansion of Citibank in China may be possibly through merger and acquisitions, instead of joint ventures." This made sense given the value Citibank placed on its own brand name, as well as the fact that, in the emerging nations where it was expanding most vigorously, the bank served its target clientele—top tier multinationals and later high-income retail clients—better than local banks were generally able to do.

The door was not, however, closed to the concept of growth through acquisition. John Reed suggested in 1996[17] that he was more comfortable with the concept of strategic acquisition than he had been in the past, as long as such an acquisition would build up one of the bank's key lines of business. The idea of an acquisition in China offered, at the very least, an opportunity to make another positive impression on China's central bank, the People's Bank of China. It might also impress Citibank executives as a way to reinforce their image as a committed foreign presence, deserving of access to the retail market. It would certainly, however, create branding issues. Thus, if Citibank's China staff were to propose an acquisition, they would do so with the expectation of significant concern from the Citicorp board.

For Chris Tibbs, the acquisition of an existing Chinese financial institution was not a likely scenario, or even a desirable one:

> "Acquiring a financial institution in China is not only not on our 'radar screen,' it is not something which I could see the government allowing anytime soon. Further, the time, resources, and market momentum lost in repairing someone else's wrecked bank (portfolio) is so significant that this is not one's rational dream of how to get ahead fast."

Citibank's Success in Asia

Earnings in the region grew in line with the economic boom of the 1980s and 1990s: net income from Asian operations grew about 30 per cent annually between 1983 and 1995[18] and Reed had been happy to invest resources there as a result, even when slashing in other parts of the world. Growth appeared to be leveling off by 1996, however,[19] in line with the slowdown in GDP growth in most Asian markets. Citibank may have become slightly less willing to invest in the region as a result, shifting attention, perhaps, to Latin America, where growth and profit potential were somewhat more boisterous.

Citibank in the PRC

Citibank had a long history in China, too, suggesting a deep institutional understanding of the nature of the market. The following is a brief timeline, indicating some of the bank's major China milestones:

1902: Citibank opened a branch in Shanghai, making it the first U.S. bank to establish operations in China.

1930s and 1940s: Citibank was one of the country's major foreign banks during this period, operating 14 branches in nine cities.

(continued)

WWII: Citibank's branches were all closed down or taken over by the communist government.

1984: Citibank opened its first office in Shenzhen and its first rep offices in Beijing and Shanghai. China had just allowed foreign banks to establish rep offices and, as usual, Citibank was one of the first banks in.

1991: People's Bank of China (PBOC) upgraded Citibank's Shanghai rep office to full branch status.

1993: Citibank moved its China headquarters from Hong Kong to Shanghai, one of only two banks to do so. Please note, however, that this appeared to have been a somewhat cosmetic move. Citibank's North Asia consumer-finance operations were based in Taipei, which Citibank viewed as a "launch pad" for the China market.[20] Corporate banking activity—syndicated lending, for example—was still based in Hong Kong.

1995: PBOC upgraded Citibank's Beijing rep office to full branch status.

December 1996: PBOC granted four foreign banks the right to conduct business in RMB (Renminbi, also known as "yuan," China's domestic currency). Citibank was among these banks. There were numerous restrictions, including the requirement that all affected banks move their Shanghai branches to Pudong, Shanghai's new financial district.

February 1997: Citibank moved its Shanghai branch to Pudong. The district was still under construction, and Citibank was the first foreign bank to make the move. The "old" branch in the Puxi district was downgraded to sub-branch status.

August 1997: Citibank now had the largest network among American banks in China, with branches in Beijing, Shanghai and Shenzhen, a sub-branch and national head office in Shanghai as well as rep offices in Xiamen and Guangzhou.[21]

Citibank's Position in the PRC in 1997

Profits are "okay but not spectacular."

> "(China is) a priority market for us and for many foreign direct investors. Now that we've put our network in place, we are ready to build the franchise. And we think we can help China as it goes ahead with economic development. At the same time, we want to help the country modernize its banking sector."
> —*John Reed, at the opening of the Beijing branch in 1995*[22]

(continued)

Hard Currencies: Moderately Profitable, Lots of Potential

As of June 1997, Citibank had branches in Shanghai (where it was one of about 50 foreign banks), Beijing (where it was one of about 10), and Shenzhen. Like other foreign banks in the PRC, Citibank was permitted to engage in:

1. hard-currency transactions (deposits, loans, etc.)
2. exchange of foreign currencies
3. buying and selling of stocks and securities

Statistics available for the market as a whole suggest that the China branches of foreign banks were performing, at the minimum, respectably. During the first four months of 1996, for example, the EIU reported that foreign financial institutions in China booked US$110 million in after-tax profit on total registered assets of US$24.6 billion. They had a large share of Shanghai's banking business, indicating their popularity with the local Foreign Invested Enterprise (FIE) community: holding 20 per cent of the city's forex balance they did 40 per cent of the loan business, 35 per cent of the foreign trade account business.[23] Lending was very impressive as well: US$16.6 billion— though this probably included syndicated loans to Chinese government borrowers (usually booked through Hong Kong) as well as loans granted to FIEs and booked through PRC branches.

Analysts said at the time that there was still considerable potential for growth in lending to the FIE community and, due to the extraordinary demand for infrastructure in China,[24] even more potential in lending to Chinese borrowers. To give an indication of the scale of business available to banks willing to develop relationships with Chinese borrowers, the State Planning Commission (which regulated offshore borrowing by Chinese corporate and state issuers) announced in early 1997 that foreign currency borrowing would total US$18 billion that year, up 63 per cent by comparison to 1996.[25] According to Chris Tibbs, however, this was not a particularly attractive market. The government exerted tight controls over total offshore borrowing and competition for business was reducing the lending margins. From February to August of 1997, for example, intense competition had tightened loan spreads by an average of 40 basis points. Tibbs felt that, in this environment, there wasn't enough money to be made in lending. And while some banks—the Japanese houses, for example—were having difficulty transforming their businesses, Citibank's response to the situation was to focus on providing fee-based transactional services: currency trading, advisory services, even underwriting and placement for corporations needing money.

Old-Fashioned Lending or Fee-Based Business?

Citibank's Tibbs believed that China's banking system would evolve more rapidly than most people expected or realized. And in this context he

(continued)

believed that Chinese state banks, because of their increasingly competitive attitudes and their enthusiasm for fee-based income, would become increasingly important competitive threats in the areas Citibank had targeted as most attractive.

> "We are facing threats from Chinese banks, which are fast in becoming very competitive," he said in August 1997. "We consider ICBC and China Bank of Communication the most competitive for us. ICBC, for example, is huge. It has not only an enormous number of branches, but also the most advanced MIS (Management Information System) in China. These give ICBC very clear competitive advantages over other Chinese banks. To give an example of the new competitive strength of Chinese banks, six months ago, it took about two weeks to transfer money from Beijing to Shanghai. Now it takes only two days. Yesterday we received a request from one of our clients, asking why we could not do it in one day. Considering it still takes two weeks for the similar money transfer in Italy or India, China's progress is very impressive. A few years ago, ATM machines were rare in China. Today they are everywhere."

As noted above, Citibank was also in 1997 one of only a few foreign banks permitted to deal in RMB. Was this strategically important? Was early access to a license a sustainable competitive advantage?

RMB Banking: Early Lead Gains No Sustainable Advantage, but the Market Had Potential

Unlike most of the 150 or so other banks in China, Citibank was allowed to engage in RMB transactions early in 1997. On December 23, 1996, the Shanghai branch of PBOC granted four foreign banks permission to do local-currency business in China. Citibank was one, and the others were HSBC, IBJ and BOT-Mitsubishi. This put Citibank in a somewhat privileged position because while this was something of a "test run" from China's point of view; by June 1997, only eight foreign banks (the other four are Standard Chartered, Sanwa, DKB, BOJ) had been approved to deal in RMB.

This looked, at first view, to have been a much more substantial competitive advantage than it really was. Independent analysts said at the time that none of the banks given RMB rights were likely to make "real inroads" into China's coveted RMB-banking market, primarily because the restrictive measures were "greater than most people expected."[26]

These restrictions, established to keep foreign banks from competing with domestic ones, were as follows:

1. Branches dealing in RMB must all be in the Pudong district of Shanghai (the city's new financial district).
2. They could accept RMB deposits from foreigners and foreign-invested enterprises (FIEs) but not from local companies or Chinese individuals.
3. They could make RMB loans and extend guarantees to FIEs and foreigners with offices in Shanghai, but not to the vast majority of local

(continued)

companies or individuals. They could, however, invest in RMB treasury and other bonds.

4. Total RMB deposits (liabilities) could not exceed 35 per cent of total foreign currency liabilities, excluding interbank deposits. Bankers considered this a very shallow deposit pool.[27] However, Citibank had a large foreign currency liability base, and so Tibbs felt that "this is in no way an impediment to our profitable growth."

5. Banks could also borrow RMB on the local interbank market and could "when necessary" borrow from the PBOC (though details were not clear, regulations were somewhat vague, according to EIU's FFO document, March 1997, and foreign bankers quoted in the Yatsko article). They must, however, lend at rates fixed by the PBOC, and as there was no interest rate swap market developed in China yet, this created the interesting question of how to hedge their interest rate risk on funds that were borrowed for purposes of on-lending.

As Tibbs explained:

> "The function of a bank's treasury is to manage the inherent risk involved in funding assets with terms longer than the underlying liabilities (deposits and inter-bank funding). Seeking to match funds or eliminate this 'exposure' would go a long way to reducing overall global bank profitability.... In any event, we are quite able in China to hedge foreign currency interest rate risk and provide these hedges to Chinese and foreign clients. (With local currency deposit rates at 3.0 per cent or less and PBOC-set lending rates at 9.18 per cent or more, depending on length of term, and with lending in local currency restricted by market convention—not regulation—to one year or less, there was very manageable risk in this situation.) Banks make money through arbitrage, not by avoiding it.... We help others to avoid it."

John Beeman, Citibank's country corporate officer for China, clearly agreed with analysts' assessment of near-term profit potential. He said in February 1997 that "on the scale (of Citibank's local currency business), our expectation for this year is that it will probably be relatively modest."[28]

In the long term, furthermore, the eight RMB-licensed banks would probably not be able to hold on to their advantage. The purpose of this exercise from Beijing's point of view was to be seen to be opening up the PRC's financial system so as to qualify for admission to the World Trade Organization. The reforms would, therefore, continue (albeit as slowly as possible) and more RMB licenses would inevitably be doled out. On the other hand, because China had given what the EIU calls an "open-ended commitment"[29] to allow more widespread foreign bank participation in RMB business, banks now approved to deal in RMB could eventually look forward to a much larger market. There would be fewer restrictions on the kind of business they could go after and fewer restrictions on the cities in which they could go after it. So medium-term profit potential for Citibank and its competitors was still unclear, but given the size of the country and the promising growth rate on

(continued)

the GRB side (among both FIE customers and new local corporate clients), it probably looked very enticing indeed.

And though the domestic retail market was still apparently closed to foreign banks, Citibank's retail banking franchise would be in an even stronger competitive position when the PBOC loosened its anti-competitive restrictions in that arena.

While other foreign banks and investment banks were competing strongly for corporate business, Citibank had a somewhat clearer field on the retail side: better technology and service capacity than most of the domestic banks; better network and local feel than the other foreign banks; and a brand name that, though new to most Chinese, already had some exposure among the elite and a certain amount of prestige. If one coupled that with the potential of the Chinese retail banking market, abounding in new wealth and already exhibiting interest in Citibank's high end product line, one could, perhaps, paint a picture enticing enough to make John Reed smile. Possibly quite broadly.

Credit Cards: Not Likely in the Near Term

While credit cards were an important and lucrative part of the Citibank consumer banking lineup elsewhere in Asia, Mr. Tibbs said that if the retail banking market were opened to foreign banks, Citibank was not optimistic about the credit card business in China in the near term. Why? The Chinese government and the PBOC had great sensitivity toward inflation. The government believed, analysts said, that along with corruption, one of the contributing factors to the 1989 Tiananmen problem was out-of-control inflation. Thus, from the point of view of the government, inflation constraint was a very important goal. The prevailing view in 1997, furthermore, was that if China was to maintain its exemplary rate of economic expansion, the national savings rate (40 per cent) would have to be maintained. Encouraging borrowing—via credit cards, for example—would increase inflation and discourage saving. Thus, analysts suggested, it would not be in the best long-term interest of either the country or its financial institutions to encourage hasty development of a retail credit card market. So, while Mr. Tibbs said Citibank did not see any risk of out-of-control inflation or of consequent currency devaluation in the last years of the millennium, Citibank was unlikely to push the expansion of credit cards in the PRC market.

Overall, then, analysts believed that Citibank's greatest competitive threat came from China's state banks: modernizing fast and possessed of vast branch networks. Nevertheless, most believed that if Citibank were allowed reasonably early access to China's retail markets, its success in China was probably assured, just as it had been elsewhere in Asia. As far as the board of directors was concerned, it was the job of Citibank's senior executives in China to ensure that these things happened. Those executives knew, too, that John Reed and the board were waiting for an outline of their plans.

---

[1]Bryan Batson, "Thinking Globally, Acting Locally," *China Business Review,* 20, no. 3. (May/June 1993): 23–25.

[2]Lehman Brothers Inc., Citicorp—Company Report, December 12, 1996.

(continued)

[3]Peter Lee, "Reed Reshuffles the Pack," *Euromoney*, April 1996: 34–39.

[4]Lee, "Reed Reshuffles the Pack."

[5]Lehman Brothers Inc., Citicorp—Company Report, December 12, 1996.

[6]Lehman Brothers Inc., Citicorp—Company Report, December 12, 1996.

[7]James Peng, "U.S. Giant Shakes Up Taiwan Banking, Eyes China," *BC Cycle,* 17 July 1996.

[8]Lehman Brothers, Inc., Citicorp—Company Report, December 12, 1996.

[9]Titles awarded by *Euromoney, Corporate Finance, Institutional Investor.*

[10]Lee, "Reed Reshuffles the Pack."

[11]Lehman Brothers Inc., Citicorp—Company Report, December 12, 1996.

[12]Kenneth Klee, "Brand Builders," *Institutional Investor,* March 1997, 89.

[13]Klee, "Brand Builders," 89.

[14]Lee, "Reed Reshuffles the Pack."

[15]Citicorp first quarter results from *Business Wire,* April 15, 1997.

[16]The only joint venture banking relationships Citibank had been involved in during recent times was a joint venture branch with the Bank of Hungary (Citibank re-acquired the last of the central bank's shares in 1995 and presently owned 100 per cent of the branch) and the Saudi American Bank, a joint venture bank with the Saudi central bank.

[17]At his December 1996 meeting with equity analysts, quoted in many analyst reports on Citicorp, including the Merrill Lynch report of January 24, 1997.

[18]Batson, "Thinking Globally, Acting Locally," 23–25; Lehman Brothers Inc., Citicorp —Company Report, December 12, 1996.

[19]Lehman Brothers Inc., Citicorp—Company Report, December 12, 1996.

[20]Peng, "U.S. Giant."

[21]"Citibank Gets RMB Business License," *BC Cycle,* 31 December 1996.

[22]"Citibank Willing to Wait for China Banking Reform, *Reuters,* October 30, 1995.

[23]Economist Intelligence Report, Financing Foreign Operations: China 1997, 32.

[24]The World Bank estimated in 1996 that Asia would need about US$1.5 trillion to fund its infrastructure needs for the next 10 years. A hefty chunk of that would go to China, and much of the money would, by necessity, be borrowed from foreign banks.

[25]FFO, 44.

[26]Pamela Yatsko, "Strings Attached: Foreigners Get Limited Entry into Renminbi Banking," *Far Eastern Economic Review,* January 16, 1997, 52.

[27]Ibid.

[28]"Citibank Opens Branch in Shanghai's Pudong: Reuters Asia-Pacific Business Report," *BC Cycle,* February 1997.

[29]Economist Intelligence Unit, China/Mongolia Report, First Quarter, 1997, 26.

Questions

1. Define universal banking, and provide examples of banking systems that follow this type of banking system. What do *Allfinanz* and *bancassurance* mean in this context?
2. What was the impact of the Glass-Steagall Act on the structure of U.S. banking? How did that piece of legislation make the U.S. banking system different from those of the United Kingdom, France, and Germany?
3. What were the major influences on the development of the Japanese banking system?
4. What were the causes for the crash of the Indonesian banking system in 1997–98?
5. What is Islamic banking? How does it differ from Western banking?
6. Mexico's banking system has had considerable problems since the 1994 tequila crisis. What measures did the Mexican government take to restructure the banking system?
7. What role do central banks play in bank regulation and supervision in the United States, Germany, France, and the United Kingdom? In each banking system, which government agencies share a supervisory role?

Notes

1. An example of the convergence in financial services is the Belgo-Dutch financial group, Fortis, which is now one of Europe's top ten financial institutions. See Neil Buckley, "Fortis Lifts Merger Benefit Estimates," *Financial Times,* November 22, 1999, p. 25.

2. E. H. White, "Before the Glass-Steagall Act: An Analysis of the Investment Banking Activities of National Banks," *Explorations in Economic History* (November 1986) 23, no. 22, pp. 33–55.

3. Anjali Kumar with Terry Chuppe and Paula Perttunen, *The Regulation of Non-bank Financial Institutions* (Washington, D.C.: World Bank, 1997), p. 7.

4. *Ibid.*, p. 20.

5. Miho Sunami and Koyo Ozeki, *"Japanese Banks Growing Threat to Credit Position of Regional Banks,"* Merrill Lynch Fixed Income Research (Tokyo), November 9, 2000, p. 2.

6. Tom Gove, *"Banking System Report: Japan,"* Thomson Financial, January 27, 2000, p. 6.

7. Norio Tamaki, *Japanese Banking: A History, 1859–1959* (New York: Cambridge University Press, 1995), p. xiv.

8. Kumar, *The Regulation of Non-Bank Financial Institutions,* p. 69.

9. Ian Linnell, "Bank Industry Risk Analysis, United Kingdom," *Standard & Poor's,* April 1996, pp. 3–4, put the number of banks at 224 institutions, 155 branch offices of banks incorporated outside the European Economic area, 146 organizations recognized as European authorized institutions, 208 representative offices of foreign banks, and 96 registered building societies, of which 82 were then active.

10. *Ibid.*, p. 8.

11. Elisabeth Grandin, "France, Bank System Report," *Standard & Poor's,* October 1997, p. 2.

12. Michael Zlotnik, "Germany, Bank System Report, *Standard & Poor's,* August 1997, p. 10.

13. Tony Major, "WestLB Split May Provide Model for German Banking" *Financial Times,* November 10, 2000, p. 20.

14. Kevin O'Brien, "Germany's Banking Bonanza", *Bloomberg Markets,* December 2000, p. 46.

15. "Asian Banks: Diminishing Returns," *The Economist,* April 29, 2000, pp. 73–74.

16. Christopher J. Mainlander, Reshaping North American Banking: The Transforming Effects of Regional Market and Policy Shifts, *CSIS Policy Papers on the America* (Washington, D.C.), July 1999, p. 18.

17. Steven Radelet, "From Boom to Bust: Indonesia's Implosion," *Harvard Asia Pacific Review,* Winter 1998–99, pp. 65–66.

18. Dan Murphy, "Banking: Paper Tiger," *Far Eastern Economic Review,* April 22, 1999, p. 68.

19. The Economist Intelligence Unit, *India/Nepal Country Profile 1997–98* (London: The Economist Intelligence Unit, 1997), p. 33.

20. Moody's Investor Service, *India: Banking Systems Outlook,* November 1998, p. 10.

21. *Ibid.*

22. *Ibid.*, p. 2.

23. Peter Sikora, "Bank Profit Pressure to Prevail in India in the New Millennium," *Standard & Poor's Credit Week,* May 3, 2000, p. 18.

24. Khozem Merchant and Angus Donald, "New Delhi to Cut Stake in State-Owned Banks," *Financial Times,* November 17, 2000, p. 8.

25. Charles X. Tan, "Banking System Outlook: China—The Start of a Long March," *Moody's Investor Service,* August 1999, p. 9.

26. James Kynge, "China's Banks Face a Cultural Revolution," *Financial Times,* April 27, 2000, p. 19.

27. *Ibid.*

28. *India: Banking Systems Outlook,* p. 13.

29. *National Bank of Hungary,* The Hungarian Banking Sector: Developments in 1999 (Budapest: National Bank of Hungary, 2000), p. 9.

30. *Ibid.*, p. 17.

31. Kester Eddy, "Banking Consolidation Takes Shape," *Financial Times,* Hungary Survey, November 22, 2000, p. III.

32. Richard Thomas, "Russia's Banks: A New Beginning or a Dead End?" *Standard & Poor's Credit Week,* January 19, 2000, p. 10.

33. *Ibid.*

34. Thane Gustafson, *Capitalism Russian-Style* (New York: Cambridge University Press, 1999), p. 82. Also see Rose Brady, Kapitalizm: Russia's Struggle to Free Its Economy (New Haven, Conn.: Yale University Press, 1999), pp. 114–115; and Stephen Handelman, *Comrade Criminal: Russia's New Mafiya* (New Haven, Conn.: Yale University Press, 1995).

35. As Andrew Jach noted: "Legal loopholes, outdated laws, and slow and contradictory decisions by those responsible for supervising and inspecting the sector have had little impact up till now." "Still Struggling to Inspire Confidence," *Financial Times, Russia Survey,* May 10, 2000, p. IV.

36. Farhan Bokhari, "Islamic Banking Survey," *Financial Times,* October 27, 2000, p. 1.

37. Nazim Ali, "Islamic Banking: Points of Law," *The Banker,* February 1999, p. 67.

38. See Andrew Cunningham and Elisabeth Jadison-Moore, Analysing the Creditworthiness of Islamic Financial Institutions, *Moody's Investor Service,* November 1999.

39. *Ibid.*, p. 5.

PART TWO

STRUCTURE AND FUNCTIONS OF THE INTERNATIONAL BANK

CHAPTER 4

INTERNATIONAL COMMERCIAL BANKING

As noted in the introduction, the world of international banking is in a constant state of flux, as bankers react to the myriad pressures produced by new competition, new technology, and enhanced globalization. Thus the bread-and-butter business of international commercial banking—accepting deposits and making loans—is increasingly being superseded by operations involving sophisticated financial instruments and an increased emphasis on nonlending activities. Even so, multinational corporations still look to their bankers to provide a wide variety of traditional and less-traditional services, in an ever-increasing number of venues around the world.

Multinational corporations expect a great deal from their bankers nowadays. Especially in the last two decades, as business has globalized at an accelerating pace, banks too have taken the plunge into overseas markets in unprecedented numbers. The decision to go abroad, from a banker's perspective, is often made in order to serve multinational clients who are demanding financial services in new markets, as the article about Rockwell illustrates. Moreover, banks hope to profit from a first-mover advantage—becoming the first big player in a new market—by opening up shop early and quickly in foreign countries. The rush by Western banks into Eastern and Central Europe in the 1990s illustrates the keen competition to gain this first-mover advantage. Citibank, of course, has virtually patented this strategy, becoming the biggest player in emerging markets around the world as a result. Citicorp boasts 2,000 branches, offices, or "money shops" in ninety countries; Barclay's has 2,000 branches, offices, or finance houses in seventy-five countries.

Structuring the Overseas Operation

Once a bank has made the decision to establish an overseas operation, the next decision is how to structure it. A variety of organizational units are possible. As we will see, the decision reflects a number of variables, ranging from tax considerations to the bank's internal resources.

ROCKWELL OPEN TO FOREIGN BANKS
WITH STRONG BIZ TIES

Rockwell may be looking for banks that can support its foreign business activities as international contracts are projected to contribute nearly half of the technology company's business within five years, according to CFO Michael Barnes. While the company maintains a 24-member bank group for its J.P. Morgan-led $1.5 billion revolver [revolving credit facility], only the Industrial Bank of Japan, Mitsubishi Bank, and Deutsche Bank have extensive ties in Asia, where Barnes said he expects the majority of Rockwell's growth to be centered. The company would consider expanding its bank group to include creditors that can help forge new business relationships from India to Australia, he said.

"With Rockwell's size and credit rating, borrowing is no problem," Barnes said. "We want a bank that can offer something well beyond that." That something, according to Barnes, is primarily a bank's ability to help the company develop business relationships in various countries, as well as provide project financing, cash management, and foreign exchange services. "We want a relationship in terms of something other than lending money," Barnes said. "I know it's not traditional, but that's my attitude," he added.

Source: Institutional Investor Inc. Bank Letter, June 17, 1996, p. 6.

Correspondent Banking

The lowest possible level of exposure to the foreign market may be achieved through a **correspondent banking** relationship. Correspondent banking involves using a bank native to the foreign market to provide services for the foreign bank. Correspondents provide a range of services to banks located in other countries that do not have local offices, or whose local offices are prohibited from engaging in certain types of activities. This relationship allows the foreign bank to provide trade-related and foreign exchange services for its multinational customers in the foreign market, without having to establish its own physical presence in the foreign market. For some large, money-center U.S. banks, providing correspondent banking services for non-U.S. banks is a major component of their business. Thus J.P. Morgan Chase, for example, may provide import/export facilities and foreign exchange services for smaller banks from Thailand or Peru, so that these banks do not have to incur the expense and exposure of setting up U.S. operations on their own.

Representative Office

While correspondent banks can be important sources of referrals for business, it is clear that banks sacrifice a great deal of potential income when they provide

US BANKS ADMIT TO SHORTFALL IN MONITORING CORRESPONDENT ACCOUNTS

Edward Alden

Top officials from the Bank of America and J.P. Morgan Chase admitted yesterday that the banks failed to monitor adequately their correspondent accounts for two Caribbean offshore banks that are said by congressional investigators to have laundered millions of dollars from proceeds from fraud, drugs, and internet gambling.

In testimony before the Senate governmental affairs committee, the banks said they should have been more alert to warning signs regarding the Swiss American Bank and the American International Bank. Both were licensed in Antigua to handle accounts for international customers, and both relied heavily on correspondent accounts in the US banks...

The hearings, which continue, are intended to throw a harsh spotlight on certain aspects of correspondent banking, in which US banks agree to provide a wide range of financial services for other foreign banks.

Several US banks have found themselves under intense scrutiny as a result of an investigation led by Senator Carl Levin, the ranking Democrat on the permanent subcommittee on investigations. Mr Levin said yesterday that correspondent banking has "become a gateway into the US financial system for criminals and money launderers..."

Source: The Financial Times, March 2, 2001.

---

international banking services through a correspondent rather than through their own operations. The next level of exposure is a **representative office** (also referred to as a rep office), in which the bank establishes a physical presence in the foreign market that has very limited functions. A rep office cannot provide traditional banking services. Its officers troll for business opportunities in the foreign market, but the office cannot accept deposits or lend funds on its own books. (Sometimes a rep office may generate some lending business as a result of its activities, but other offices must book this loan.) The rep office essentially serves as a liaison and marketing function for the parent bank, which is not legally present in the host country with regard to legal or tax liability. Rep offices are low budget and can be easily closed down, making them useful vehicles for exploring a new, high-risk market, like Lithuania or Albania in the mid–1990s. Rep offices may also be used in countries where the authorities do not permit foreign banks to set up full-service branches or subsidiaries.

Branch Office

Opening up a **branch** usually indicates a higher level of commitment to the foreign market than the rep office. A branch is an integral part of the parent bank, and it acts as a legal and functional arm of the head office, much as a branch of J.P. Morgan Chase in upstate New York is a part of the parent in New York City. In practice, though, major foreign bank branches are often quite independent, making most decisions locally. Citibank's country manager in Indonesia during the 1980s told a Harvard Business School class that, in accordance with Citibank's decentralized corporate philosophy, he had a very high level of autonomy. In my five years in Indonesia, he told the students, I *never* referred to New York on a loan decision. He further explained that as a senior credit officer of the bank, he (along with another senior credit officer) could extend loans up to the legal lending limit of the bank.[1]

Branches may perform all banking functions that are permitted by the host country, including accepting deposits and extending loans (unlike a rep office). (As Figure 4.1 demonstrates, branches are the most popular form of organizational structure for foreign banks in the United States.) Indeed, the predominant activity of foreign bank branches is extending credit, usually on a wholesale rather than retail basis. The branch is not a separate legal or financial entity from the parent, implying that the "full faith and credit" of the parent stands behind its branches everywhere in the world. Branches are usually not separately capitalized from the parent. This highlights the key disadvantage of a branch: The entire bank may be sued under local law for liabilities or other illegal acts committed by the branch and its staff, potentially putting all of the capital of the parent bank on the line.[2]

FIGURE 4.1 U.S. Banking and Representative Operations of International Banks as of December 31, 1999*

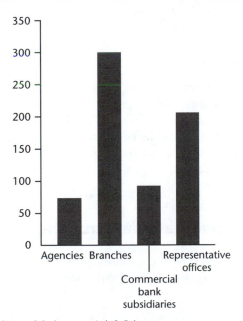

Agency

Like a branch, an **agency** is also an integral part of the parent bank. Agencies fall somewhere in between the branch and the rep office; they may perform more functions than a rep office, but they cannot perform all of the functions of a branch. In the United States, a foreign bank agency is not allowed to accept domestic demand deposits, but it may conduct full-scale lending operations similar to those of a branch. Agencies are used primarily for wholesale international commercial banking.

Subsidiary

The **subsidiary** eliminates the major disadvantage of the branch or agency—namely, potentially putting the entire capital of the parent bank on the line. A subsidiary is separate legally from the parent bank, organized under the laws and regulated by the authorities of the host country. It may engage in full banking activities as permitted by host country regulations. Banking subsidiaries may be established as a new organization, or through acquisition of an existing bank. The second advantage of a subsidiary over a branch is that it may offer a wider range of services. For example, U.S. banking regulations until late 1999 prohibited commercial banks from carrying on investment banking activities, such as securities underwriting or insurance activities. As a result, U.S. commercial banks set up merchant banking subsidiaries overseas to carry out these operations.

The primary disadvantage of a subsidiary is that it must be separately capitalized from the parent. This often requires a greater start-up investment than a branch, which relies on the parent's capital and borrowing power. There are also concerns that a subsidiary could end up competing with the parent if clear lines of communication are not maintained.

Consortium Banks

Banks may also join forces in entering new markets, in order to reduce the capital requirements and risks involved in new ventures. So-called **consortium banks,** which are nothing more than a group of banks forming a joint alliance to enter a new market, were popular in the 1970s but have since fallen into disfavor. The parent institutions found it difficult to share power and clients in the joint venture, and most of the consortiums have dissolved. The consortium bank remains a theoretical possibility, however.

Choosing an Organizational Structure

As we have seen, each type of organizational structure offers advantages and disadvantages. The bank's decision on which structure to choose will reflect several key factors:

- *The host country's banking laws.* The attitude of the host country as reflected in its laws, regulations, and policies toward financial institutions is probably the single most important factor in some countries, particularly emerging markets. Many countries prohibit or restrict the entry of full-service foreign banks, or limit their activities. Some governments do not allow foreign commercial bank branches; others prohibit fully owned foreign bank subsidiaries. While the United States and other major industrial countries place few restrictions on the entry of foreign banking institutions (see Table 4.1 for a list of the major foreign banks in the United States), other countries are more cautious. Under a World Trade Organization (WTO) pact accepted in December 1997, seventy member countries agreed to open their financial services sectors to foreign companies.[3] This is, however, just a first step toward truly free markets in banking services. Enabling legislation will be required in each individual country, often a lengthy and difficult process.

In the meantime, each country's attitude toward foreign banks will continue to heavily influence the banks' form of organization. In Argentina, Brazil, Chile, Mexico, and Peru, for example, liberalization in the 1990s has allowed a wave of foreign bank takeovers. Spanish banks, such as Banco Santander and Banco Bilbao Vizcaya (BBV), have been especially active in acquiring banks throughout Latin America. Similarly, a spokesperson from Chase Manhattan commented in 1998 that the bank hopes to profit from a recent decision by the Indian government to allow twelve new foreign bank branches per year instead of only eight.

- *The bank's resource constraints.* Banks are obviously limited by their own internal resource constraints, both financial and human, in considering how to enter foreign markets. The subsidiary, for example, generally requires more capital than a branch. The rep office requires the least amount of investment capital. Human resource constraints—the number of internationally

TABLE 4.1 U.S. Offices of Foreign Banks by Country of Origin

Bank	Total Assets (US$ millions)	Origin
Deutsche Bank AG	$112,892	Germany
HSBC Holdings Plc.	79,891	UK
ABN AMRO Bank	73,140	Netherlands
Bank of Tokyo-Mitsubishi	62,802	Japan
Societe Generale	58,377	France
UBS AG	50,166	Switzerland
Bank of Montreal	47,147	Canada
Banque National de Paris	43,408	France
Bank of Nova Scotia	32,217	Canada
Westdeutsche Landesbank Giroze	31,481	Germany
Bayerische Sparkassen-Und Giro	27,876	Germany
Sanwa Bank	25,145	Japan

Source: Federal Reserve Bank, March 2000.

experienced bank officers—are another concern. Rep offices need to be staffed with bankers who are strong in business development skills more than credit analysis; the opposite may be true of branches. Personnel constraints may become a serious issue for some banks, especially as their highly skilled and trained officers may be lured away by other financial institutions. Citibank is sometimes dubbed Citi-university, as Citibank-trained bankers are a highly prized commodity in many emerging market countries.

- *The bank's degree of commitment to a new market.* Some new foreign markets may have more obvious appeal than others, leading the bank to make a greater commitment at first, such as a branch or subsidiary. On the other hand, if a bank just wants to test the waters of a very young, very risky country, a rep office would be appropriate. Banks will often make their initial entry in a new market as a rep office, hoping to upgrade to a full-service branch once they are more comfortable. The *Nikkei Weekly* reported in December 1996, for instance, that Japanese banks with rep offices in Hanoi or Ho Chi Minh City, Vietnam, were anxious to upgrade their presence to full-fledged branches as their confidence in business prospects improved.[4] Another example of this wariness was the decision by ING, a large Dutch bank, to establish a rep office rather than a branch or subsidiary in North Korea in the late 1990s.

- *Tax considerations.* There can be important tax considerations as well. The earnings/losses of a foreign branch affect the parent's tax liability directly, since the branch is an integral part of the parent. Thus the parent may elect to set up the new unit as a branch in the early days, so that the parent can use its losses to offset tax liabilities at home. Once the branch begins to earn money, it can be converted into a stand-alone subsidiary, whose earnings are not taxed at home until they are remitted as dividends. One New York bank was reportedly dismayed when its new branch in Turkey, expected to generate losses for the first few years, surprised everyone by showing large profits from day one, upsetting the parent's elaborate tax planning strategy!

Empirical research by Jan Ter Wengel in the mid–1990s on banks' overseas organizational strategies revealed that banks find it easier to establish rep offices than branches abroad; that banks tend to send branches to richer countries and rep offices to the poorer markets; and that banks send low-cost rep offices rather than high-cost branches to larger countries with economies of scale in banking services. In other words, rep offices are commonly used in situations where the host country has strong banking institutions, regulations do not permit a higher form of representation, or profit opportunities are limited because of the country's low income level per capita. Subsidiaries may be employed as an investment alternative to branches in countries with liberal capital regulations and high income per capita.[5]

Scope of Foreign Banking Activities

Whatever the organizational form, foreign banking has exploded since the 1960s, as can be seen from Figures 4.2 and 4.3. Much international banking activity is still centered on London, where the financial know-how and technical skills

FIGURE 4.2 U.S. Offices of Foreign Banks: Total Assets (US$ billions)

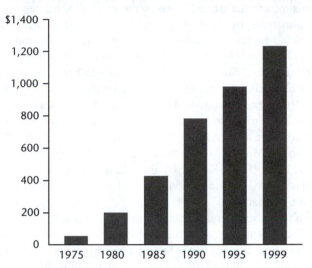

Source: "Selected Assets and Liabilities of U.S. Offices of Foreign Banks (year-end data)," Federal Reserve Board, March 2000.

FIGURE 4.3 Assets of Overseas Branches and Subsidiaries of U.S. Banks*

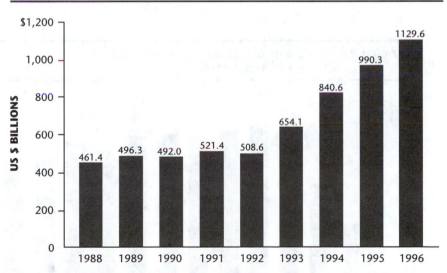

Source: Federal Reserve Board.
*Figures are as of December 31 for all years.

acquired through decades of experience have attracted more than 520 foreign banks (employing over 72,000 people). London remains the best city in the world for financial business, according to a recent survey, and is likely to retain this leadership position for the next decade.[6]

Foreign banks have also swarmed the U.S. market. At the beginning of the 1990s, there were around 280 foreign banks from more than sixty-five countries doing business in the United States, with over 1,000 offices nationwide. As Figure 4.4 illustrates, by 1999 foreign banks accounted for nearly one-fifth of total U.S. banking assets. U.S. authorities allow international banks to open up and compete on an equal footing with domestic banks. Most international banks operating in the United States focus on wholesale rather than retail business, and so they are relatively invisible to the average consumer. During the early 1990s the largest foreign presence in the United States, by far, was Japanese banks (Bank of Tokyo, Industrial Bank of Japan, Mitsubishi, Sanwa, Sumitomo, etc.); other big players were ABN AMRO Bank (Netherlands), National Westminster Bank (UK), Bank of Montreal (Canada), Credit Lyonnais (France), and Hongkong and Shanghai Bank (Hong Kong). By the end of the decade, the crisis in Japanese banking had provided more opportunities for non-Japanese overseas banks in the crowded U.S. market.

With regard to emerging market countries, Citibank still reigns supreme as the bank with a presence in more emerging markets than any other, although competition is mounting. Foreign banks have made the most progress in nations with stable and sophisticated banking systems, such as Chile and Singapore. In much of Asia, protectionist policies have prevented foreign banks from gaining much market share. Foreign banks are pouring into Central Europe (Poland, Hungary, the Czech Republic, and Slovakia) and, to a lesser extent, Eastern Europe (the Balkans and the former Soviet Union). Citibank has invested heavily in the region since the

FIGURE 4.4 U.S. Banking Operations of International Banks: Percentage of Total U.S. Banking Assets*

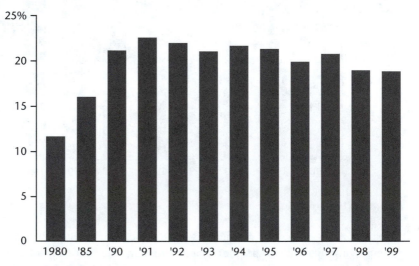

Source: Federal Reserve Board.

*Prior to 1993 data do not include assets booked at offshore offices of international banks.

fall of Communism and has gained a strong first-mover advantage, reflecting its excellent record in providing services to multinationals, blue-chip local companies, and high net worth individuals. In turn, this is sparking competition from the big Dutch banks, especially ABN AMRO, which are looking to Central and Eastern Europe as an engine of growth. Austrian and Italian banks are also drawn to the east.

Foreign banks (mostly Spanish, German, and Italian) are flooding into Latin America as well, especially as these economies have stabilized in the 1990s and many protectionist regulations have been eased or lifted entirely. In Mexico, where foreign banks were banned from taking part in the privatizations of several years ago, they are now welcome following the financial crisis of 1994–95. Foreign ownership of total bank assets in Mexico has soared from 2 percent to around 15 percent; in Hungary, the number has leaped from almost nothing to 40 percent. Foreign banks are increasingly welcome in emerging markets, reflecting a growing belief that they act to stabilize the local banking system, add liquidity, improve efficiency, and reduce costs.[7]

Functions of Global Commercial Banks

Credit Services

The primary function of a global commercial bank, of course, is to accept deposits and lend money. Indeed, lending is the cornerstone of global banking activity. Banks in overseas markets may lend money in local currency to local clients out of branches or subsidiaries in foreign countries, funded by local currency deposits or by local money-market borrowings. For example, Deutsche Bank's branch in Mexico City may lend pesos to a local car manufacturer, funded by peso deposits in its local branch. This is purely local business, in which the bank competes with domestic banks or with affiliates of other foreign financial institutions.

Alternatively, the bank may also engage in **cross-border lending,** in which a loan is made to a borrower in a country other than the lender's residence, and is denominated in a currency other than that of the borrower's currency. According to Federal Reserve Chairman Alan Greenspan in 1998, cross-border lending doubled in the previous decade. For example, Deutsche Bank's branch in London may loan U.S. dollars to the same car manufacturer in Mexico City. This loan is funded by dollars generated worldwide. (As Figure 4.5 illustrates, about half of all international bank lending is dollar-denominated.) Cross-border lending often takes the form of a **syndicated** facility, which will be discussed in the next section.

All lending activities, whether direct or syndicated, should generate revenue for the bank. The **spread** is akin to gross profit on the loan; it is the difference between the interest the bank earns on the loan and the interest it pays on its own borrowed funds. The spread should be sufficient to cover overhead, risk, and profits. Lending activities can also generate a variety of fees. One form of lending, for example, is the **revolving credit** facility (or "revolver"). This permits the customer to borrow, or draw down, up to a certain maximum amount over an agreed time period under an agreed interest formula. This formula is usually based on the **London Interbank Offered Rate,** or **LIBOR** (the interest rate paid between banks for

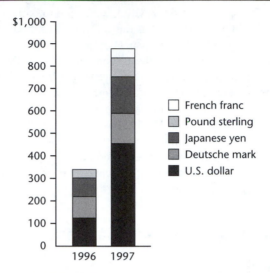

FIGURE 4.5 Currency Composition of International Bank Lending (US$ billions)

Source: BIS Consolidated Statistics, 1998, at www.bis.org.

dollars on deposit in London), plus a margin reflecting the borrower's creditworthiness. Thus General Motors, for example, might pay LIBOR plus $\frac{1}{4}$ percentage point, while Bolivia might pay LIBOR plus 3 percentage points. The bank, in turn, earns a commitment fee for standing ready to lend, whether or not the funds are actually disbursed. As we shall see, banks earn fees from a variety of lending-based services, such as syndicated loans and letters of credit.

Syndicated Loan Facilities

Syndicated loans are a central tool in international banking, widely used by banks to meet customers' needs for large-scale and/or high-risk loans. A syndicated loan is a credit extended by a group of banks to a single customer, usually on common terms. This permits the risk, which might be too large for one bank to accept on its own, to be shared out among a large group of banks. It also facilitates the extension of credits that would otherwise be too big for one bank to handle. Moreover, the syndication technique enables large and medium-sized regional banks to participate in international lending activities. Syndicated loans are accompanied by a weighty set of loan documentation and some standard legal agreements. For example, the agreement will usually specify the judgment currency and legal jurisdiction if the parties find it necessary to go to court; it will specify that all creditors are to be treated equally; and it will require the borrower, if a government, to waive its right to sovereign immunity (meaning that the banks can sue the government if necessary).

Syndication can be a handsome source of fee revenue for the lead bank or banks. In general, the borrower pays a commitment fee on the funds that are not disbursed, plus interest on the funds that are drawn down (usually, LIBOR plus a

OLIVETTI SECURES €22.5 BILLION LOAN FROM BANKS

Vincent Boland

Olivetti, the Italian telecommunications group, said yesterday it had secured a syndicated loan of €22.5 billion ($24.5 billion) from a consortium of banks to help finance its hostile €52.6 billion takeover bid for Telecom Italia.

Securing the financing—the biggest ever syndicated loan—is a boost to Olivetti's hopes of assembling the firepower it needs to pull off its takeover of the much larger Telecom Italia. The bid is also being financed by equity and bond issues....

Source: Financial Times, March 27, 1999, p. 19.

margin), as well as an agent fee. Typically, one or more large banks acts as lead or agent in the facility, gathering information for use in judging the creditworthiness of the borrower, organizing the loan, and selling it down to other participating banks. The lead institution must have the ability to market the credit to other financial institutions, and to perform the necessary tasks of structuring and pricing the credit. Chase Manhattan (now J.P. Morgan Chase) has long reigned as the top bank in syndicated lending worldwide, with around 25 percent market share, and it continues at the top of the ranks in the annual *Euromoney* survey. (See Table 4.2.)

The notion that syndicated loans reduce risk by sharing it out received a rude awakening in the 1980s, however. Credits to shaky Latin American borrowers, for example, were syndicated widely, often to unsophisticated regional institutions with little or no expertise in international lending. There is a tendency for participants in the syndication to rely heavily on the credit analysis of the larger, more sophisticated banks, and it is unclear to what extent the lead bank is responsible for the accuracy of the information presented on the borrower.

Thus it is not surprising that following a period of fast-paced growth in the 1970s, the syndicated loan market dried up after 1981 as a huge portion of bank resources were redirected into rescheduling problem loans to emerging market borrowers. Many bankers came to believe that the syndication process contributed to problems in unraveling the Third World debt crisis of the 1980s. Many small, regional banks were clearly in over their heads, and they became a weak link as the rescheduling process unfolded. (Why were local banks in Louisiana and Kentucky lending to Brazil in the first place?) By the mid–1980s, many banks had transferred or fired their syndication experts, and the banks closed down their syndication departments.

The process was accelerated by a tighter international bank regulatory regime, which emerged after the **Basel agreement** on capital adequacy was announced in 1988. This agreement required banks to maintain a certain ratio of capital to loans

TABLE 4.2 Syndicated Loans: Borrowers' Vote

1998 Rank	Bank
1	Chase Manhattan
2	Deutsche Bank
3	J.P. Morgan
4	Citicorp
5	Credit Suisse First Boston
6	Societe Generale
7	HSBC Markets
8	Barclays Capital
9	Merrill Lynch
10	ING Barings

Source: Euromoney, September 1998.

according to a complex and controversial formula, producing an era of retrenchment for many. For the next few years, international banks were forced to build up their capital bases and were drawn away from private sector lending toward sovereign lending (loans to governments and public sector entities), which require less allocations of risk capital. As a result, **"club" deals** became more popular in the late 1980s. Rather than a syndication of 100 or more banks, club deals were put together quietly by a handful of big banks.

As the 1980s gave way to the 1990s, however, the syndicated loan market began to rise from its ashes. With Third World debt issues resolved and capital adequacy levels healthy once more, banks began looking to rebuild their loan portfolios, while borrowers were eager to take advantage of the banks' willingness to lend once more. Syndicated loans can provide large amounts of funding very quickly and easily. They guarantee confidentiality to the borrower, which may be critical if the customer is raising funds for an acquisition or merger. Accordingly, by the middle to late 1990s, the revival in international syndicated lending had turned into a boom. (See Figures 4.6 and 4.7.)

The number of new syndicated loans hit a new record in 1996–97, amid increasingly fierce competition among banks to win the coveted (and lucrative) position of lead manager or agent. Spreads on loans to emerging market banks and subinvestment-grade European companies declined to unheard-of lows. Loans to Czech and South African banks, which would have been done at around 1.0 percentage point above LIBOR just 18 months earlier, were made at just 0.2 percentage points above LIBOR in 1997. Price differentiation between top-grade and second-tier borrowers, according to some observers, declined to dangerously low levels. Figure 4.8 illustrates, for example, that during 1997 the gap between spreads paid by developed country borrowers and developing country borrowers almost disappeared. Partly because banks were so keen to win mandates from emerging market borrowers in order to establish new relationships, major mispricing of credit

FIGURE 4.6 Announced Facilities in the International Syndicated Credit Market (US$ billions)

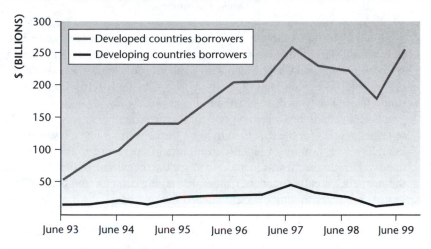

Source: Capital DATA; BIS, at www.bis.org.

FIGURE 4.7 New Syndicated Credits Worldwide (US$ billions)

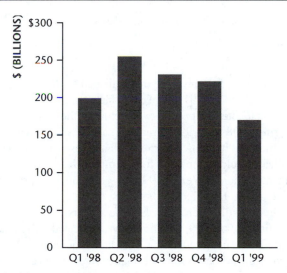

Source: BIS Consolidated Statistics, 1998, at www.bis.org.

risks undoubtedly occurred. Bankers insist, though, that they demanded more ancillary, fee-based business to accompany the low-cost loans.

Following the Asian financial crisis in 1997, the market for syndicated lending tightened up once more, and some of this mispricing has been corrected. In fact, the latest development is the use of *"market-flex"* clauses to protect bankers

TURNING THE TABLES
David Fairlamb

It looked at first as though 1998 would be a boom year for syndicated loans. In March, for example, an eight-strong group of banks including Barclays Capital and Chase Manhattan Bank was able to raise a massive €6 billion revolving credit facility for the U.K.'s General Electric Co, the first time a major loan was denominated in the new currency.

Indeed, conditions were so good that some Asian borrowers were able to tap the market for the first time in more than a year.... Just a few months later, however, liquidity suddenly evaporated in response to the financial upheaval in Russia. "It was incredible to see the magnitude of the change in the markets," recalls Jonathan Calder, managing director and head of the global secondary trading desk at Citicorp International...."All of a sudden the loan business was put on hold."

In that environment the terms on which banks were willing to lend tightened significantly. What's more, lenders increasingly insisted that their clients sign so-called market-flex contracts that specify provisional prices. That's a major shift away from traditional market practice, whereby banks give commitments to raise cash for their clients at a specified margin.

Source: Institutional Investor Inc. Bank Letter, January 1999, International Edition, p. 45.

against some of the risks involved in syndicated lending. These clauses, which were pioneered by Chase in 1997 and became increasingly popular in the next two years, allow lenders to alter the pricing or structure of the loan as market conditions fluctuate. During 1998 and 1999 spreads also rose sharply, especially on syndicated loans to emerging market countries such as those in Latin America. The strongly rated Chilean electric company, for example, was able to borrow at LIBOR plus 0.25 percentage points in early 1998; by year-end, the spread had widened to 2.25 percentage points. (As Figure 4.9 shows, though, the bulk of international syndicated credits are still taken up by U.S. borrowers.)

In the first half of 1999, volumes in the syndicated loan market soared once more, fueled by a boom in European mergers and acquisitions. Syndicated lending has reemerged as the primary source of finance for mergers and acquisitions, especially in the European market; nearly half of the new syndicated loans worldwide in the first half of 1999 were denominated in the euro, the new European currency introduced on January 1, 1999. Analysts expect the European syndicated loan market to continue expanding strongly, as long as merger and acquisition activity continues to expand.

Project Finance

Project finance is somewhat less susceptible to the boom-bust cyclicity of syndicated lending (see Table 4.3), but it too experienced a sharp resurgence in the early

FIGURE 4.8 Syndicated Credit Market: Weighted Average Spreads*

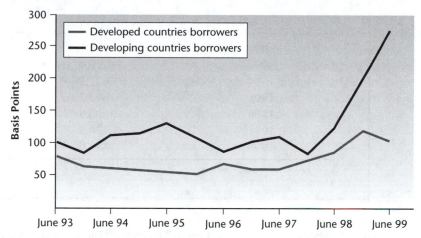

Source: Capital DATA; BIS, at www.bis.org.
*Spread over LIBOR on US dollar credits.

FIGURE 4.9 Announced International Syndicated Credit Facilities by Nationality of Borrower, 1997

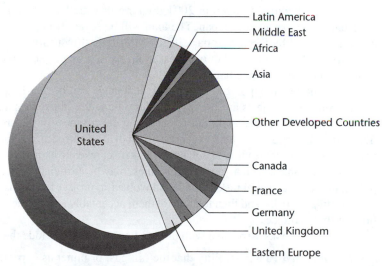

Source: BIS Consolidated Statistics, 1998, at www.bis.org.

to middle 1990s, followed by a dramatic reversal in 1997–98. Project finance refers to financing for large-scale capital projects, which are generally very large in scale, long in term, and high in risk. "Pure" project financing occurs when the debt is to be serviced only by cash flows attributable to the project itself, without recourse to the project's "sponsors" (those involved in an entrepreneurial and ownership

TABLE 4.3 Syndicated Loans: New Facilities Worldwide, 1992–1998

Year	Amount (US$ billions)
1992	$ 194.1
1993	279.4
1994	477.1
1995	697.7
1996	900.9
1997	1,136.3
1998	872.0[1]

Source: Bank for International Settlements.
[1]Estimate.

capacity). The borrower is the project itself. Thus project financing does not appear on the balance sheet of the sponsors, and it does not affect their financial structure or creditworthiness. For example, in 1996 a syndicate of banks provided project finance for the 12 billion peseta Elco Gas power station in central Spain, in which the sponsors were National Power of the UK, RWE of Germany, EDF of France, and ENE and Iberdrola of Spain. In November 1998, five big Japanese banks agreed on a ¥120 billion loan for Universal Studios Japan, the U.S. movie theme park that is scheduled to open in 2001, making this the largest project finance instrument ever executed in Japan. The loan will be repaid from the business revenues generated by the theme park itself. Multilateral institutions, such as the World Bank, frequently lend to or invest in infrastructure projects in developing countries alongside private bankers.

From the lender's point of view, project finance can be a risky proposition indeed. Since the projects are usually long term in nature, the debt maturities can stretch out even over several decades, increasing the riskiness of the credit. Moreover, infrastructure projects tend to generate cash in local currency, creating currency risk for banks that are lending in dollars. Even worse, revenue earned by local infrastructure companies, such as power companies, may be artificially manipulated by politicians. Thus a central task of bankers involved in project finance is to identify and quantify the risks, and then to allocate them acceptably among the various participants in the project.

A list of the risks associated with project finance would include the following:

- *Resource risk:* the possibility that the oil, gas, or minerals expected to be in the ground will not be present in sufficient quantities to service the debt.

- *Input risk:* the chance that the basic viability of the project will be threatened by the unavailability or high prices of key inputs such as energy or raw materials.

- *Completion risk:* the risk that the project will be delayed indefinitely, resulting in substantial cost overruns.

- *Market risk:* the risk that future demand for the product will decline.

- *Operating risk:* the risk that even after the project becomes operational, costs will change or critical elements such as labor or transportation will be disrupted.
- *Force majeure:* the possibility that so-called "acts of God" will occur to disrupt the project, ranging from warfare to weather.
- *Political risk:* the possibility that political conditions surrounding the project will become adverse.[8]
- *Regulatory risk:* the risk that is represented to the project's completion by changes in a government's rules and regulations pertaining to a certain industry. Such actions as tax hikes, prohibition of certain activities, and opening a market up to additional competition may negatively affect the outcome of the project as well as jeopardize its ability to repay the loan.

International project finance activity boomed during the first half of the 1990s, reflecting deregulation, privatization, and rapid economic growth in emerging market countries. The value of loans and bonds raised without official guarantees soared by 53 percent in 1995 alone, driven largely by activity in Asia, where rapid growth was putting severe pressure on the power and transportation infrastructure. As in the syndicated loan market, margins on bank lending in this sector narrowed sharply as competition intensified, and bankers showed more willingness to assume some of the aforementioned risks.[9] Also, as in the syndicated loan market, project finance activity slowed markedly following the financial crisis of 1997–98, especially in Asian and Latin American markets.

Trade Finance

Much less "sexy"—and much less risky—than syndications and project finance, trade finance is the bread-and-butter operation of international lending. Indeed, trade finance is the great-granddaddy of international banking. Prior to the 1960s, the international operations of U.S. banks were mostly limited to financing international trade. Even today, trade financing is an important revenue source for many international banks. The primary instrument of trade finance is the **letter of credit (L/C),** which allows the credit of the bank to be substituted for that of the customer. An L/C is a draft drawn by a company or individual on a bank, ordering it to pay a specified amount at a specified time accepted by the bank, to a named individual (or the bearer). In effect, the bank promises that payment will be made on the specified date. This facilitates international trade between a buyer and seller, who otherwise would not be willing to ship goods without some guarantee that payment will be made. Banks charge a fee for L/C business, and consider L/Cs contingent liabilities since most will never require the bank to make a payment.

There are other types of L/Cs as well. A **standby letter of credit** may be issued to reassure creditors that the bank will stand ready to make payment if the original borrower is unable. Companies routinely obtain standby L/Cs to back up their commercial paper offerings, for instance. A **performance letter of credit** obliges the bank to guarantee that its customer will perform some service as required; if the customer fails to provide the service, the bank will be forced to make restitution. All letters of credit provide fee income for the bank.

ASIA'S SOBERING WAKE-UP CALL
James Featherstone

Philip Crotty, head of Asian structured finance for Deutsche Bank, this year's biggest project-finance provider, reflects on the remnants of the business in south-east Asia: "It depends on the country to an extent, but I would say that most of the major projects—even ones that were under construction—have either been postponed or shelved indefinitely. And there are delays and renegotiations of contracts going on all over the place. Some sponsors have abandoned projects completely, others are trying to keep them warm and then resurrect them when conditions improve."

The market has been hit by devastating problems. Projects' ability to pay back dollar-denominated finance has been compromised where project revenues were in local currencies. In addition, as Asian economies have contracted, even local-currency revenues have slumped for most projects. Industry has reduced energy spending; fewer travelers are willing to pay to drive on toll roads; and weakness in commodity prices has hampered the revenue-raising abilities of oil, chemicals and mining projects....

Source: Euromoney, December 1998, p. 74.

Commercial Paper and Note Issuance Facilities

Commercial paper, or **CP,** is a standard financing technique for U.S. corporations. It refers to short-term promissory notes issued by strong corporate borrowers to sophisticated investors, usually other corporations, pension funds, mutual funds, and banks. Most commercial paper is issued for very short maturities, typically 90 days, and is rolled over at maturity. The issuing corporation is expected to provide a commercial bank loan backup facility to support its paper in the (unlikely) event of a market disturbance that might disrupt rollovers. While the commercial paper market has its origins in the United States, a lively Eurocommercial paper market has sprung up as well, primarily focused in London. Commercial paper is essentially a substitute for bank loans, although bankers do participate in the CP market both as underwriters and guarantors.

A **note issuance facility (NIF)** is a credit facility provided by a bank or group of banks under which the borrower may issue short-term Euro-notes (notes sold in the euromarket) over a given time period. The underwriting banks are committed to either purchase unsold notes or to provide guarantees that the notes will be repaid. Just as CP is an alternative to short-term bank lending, NIFs may be viewed as a substitute for syndicated lending. The major difference from the bank's viewpoint is that the syndicated loan uses bank capital, whereas the NIF provides fee-based income.

Credit Analysis in International Lending

Banks usually have a well-oiled mechanism for assessing the creditworthiness of their borrowers, both domestic and international. Credit analysis models vary from bank to bank, but most would include the following elements:

- *Collateral.* What is the quality of the collateral that the customer is offering? How easily can it be turned into cash? In other words, how liquid is it? Inventory of processed lumber, for instance, is higher-quality collateral than an inventory of unfinished refrigerators.

- *Cash flow projections.* How easily will the customer be able to service his or her debt? How reliable are his or her cash flow projections? How vulnerable are they to standard stress tests (e.g., higher interest rates, economic slowdown)?

- *Covenants.* Has the bank been able to insist on strict covenants? (These refer to conditions that the customer must fulfill in order to remain in good standing, such as requirements that the borrower maintain a certain level of cash, specified debt/equity ratios, current ratio, etc.) Will the bank be able to adequately assess the customer's adherence to these covenants in a timely fashion? What happens if the customer falls out of compliance with the covenants?

- *Character.* Many bankers believe that the *character,* or personal integrity of the borrower(s), is the single most important characteristic that they assess. Do we trust this person? Can we trust him or her with our depositors' money? Will he or she do everything humanly possible to ensure that the loan is serviced? This issue has become even more important since the 1980s, when many governments began to take a harder stance against money laundering. Know-your-customer programs, for example, exist in all U.S. banks, with banks being held responsible for knowing their customer—in a sense, moving past the traditional, less in-depth character review.

The process of credit analysis is well understood and well performed by major banks around the world. It becomes more complicated, however, when the banker is in New York and the loan is in Thailand rather than in Topeka, Kansas. International credit analysis is much more difficult than domestic credit analysis. First and foremost, differing accounting conventions make foreign financial statements difficult to read and understand. Latin American countries may make wide use of inflation accounting techniques, for instance, which are not used in the United States and Europe. Second, in many emerging market countries financial statements are not only different, but also suspect, as judged by analysts from the United States and other Western countries. Standards of transparency and accountability overseas may be much lower, creating unreliable and even misleading financial statements. This was indeed a major issue contributing to the financial crisis that hit Asia in 1997–98. Third, conventional tools such as credit reporting bureaus and credit histories may be nonexistent in foreign markets, making the banker's job much more difficult. Fourth, creditors must consider the absence of adequate bankruptcy laws and settlement procedures in many countries, which may offer little protection in the event of default. And finally, the process of

GITIC FAILURE HURTS OTHER BUSINESSES
James Harding

The fallout from a leading Chinese investment company's bankruptcy appeared yesterday to be spreading across China's financial industry after a leading provincial government-backed enterprise technically defaulted on a repayment due on a loan of $80 mln....

Fujian Enterprises told foreign creditors it would service the interest but be unable to meet the principal repayments on a syndicated loan falling due yesterday, a development likely to stoke bankers' concerns about lending to China. The technical default comes as other Chinese investment companies report difficulties honoring foreign debts in the face of a liquidity crisis caused by the retreat of international lenders from China risk following the closure of Guangdong International Trust and Investment Corporation (Gitic)....

Source: Financial Times, January 22, 1999, p. 3.

evaluating foreign credits is immeasurably complicated by the presence of ever-changing currency rates.

As the above article indicates, despite their best efforts bankers can still be caught unawares by a sharp deterioration in the creditworthiness of their borrowers. For example, in November 1997, Russia's "Gazprom signed one of the biggest syndicated loans ever for an emerging-markets borrower. Russia's gas company obtained $3 billion on respectable terms—paying 175 basis points over Libor for an eight-year maturity. And the deal was oversubscribed: 39 banks signed up for amounts ranging from $242 million apiece for arrangers Credit Lyonnais and Dresdner Bank Luxembourg, to $5 million each for ABN Amro and Mediocredito Lombaro."[10] As the world now knows, very shortly thereafter the Russian government defaulted on its domestic debt, and Russian credits became virtually untouchable.

Noncredit Services

Given the difficulty and risks inherent in overseas lending, it is hardly surprising that bankers have increasingly turned their attention to fee-based, noncredit services in overseas markets. These are activities that generate income, but do not require the bank to put its own capital at risk in the process. In mid–1998, for instance, Chase Manhattan announced that it planned to double its global asset management business from $167 billion in the next three years. Trust- and investment-related revenues were 15 percent of Chase's noninterest income in 1997.

Chase and other banks earn huge fees from global cash management, foreign exchange, custodial, and other noncredit services. Most banks consider this a key growth area, and they have focused a large chunk of their resources on improving technology and services in the arena of noncredit activities.

Global custody, the business of processing trades and keeping shares safe on behalf of fund managers, is one area of noncredit services that is acquiring a higher profile. The industry is dominated by U.S. players. (Bank of New York, Chase Manhattan, and State Street are the top three custody banks, together controlling about 40 percent of the international custody market.) The target market, however, is increasingly overseas as the market for private pension schemes in Europe explodes and the financial services industry mobilizes to handle the boom in pension investment. As financial assets worldwide soar and the pace of technological innovations accelerates, the international custody market is expected to grow by corresponding amounts over the next decade.[11]

Cash management is another high priority for international bankers looking to grow their noncredit services business. Cash management is the art of keeping corporate cash balances at the lowest level possible (ideally zero), since cash is a nonproductive asset, without jeopardizing short-term liquidity. To this end, bankers assist corporate cash managers in establishing **zero balance accounts,** which are emptied into interest-earning accounts at the end of every day; **controlled disbursement accounts,** which allow the company to estimate with a very high degree of accuracy the total volume of checks that will clear against its corporate checking account every day; and other, ever more sophisticated tools. The ultimate goal is to accelerate collections of receivables from customers, while delaying payables as much as possible—and to invest every penny, peso, and franc into interest-bearing overnight accounts. Idle cash is the ultimate disgrace. While corporate cash management within the United States and much of Western Europe has been quite sophisticated for many years now, these practices are spreading more slowly across the globe, and bankers are eager to capture the business of multinational customers as they export cash management practices around the world.

Last but not least, banks are active participants in various payments and clearing systems around the globe. A payments system may be defined as "the system of instruments and rules which permits agents to meet payments obligations and to receive payments owed to them." Banks act as clearing agents for their individual customers, and for their correspondent banks as well. The major payment systems include:

- SWIFT, the Society for Worldwide Interbank Financial Telecommunications, a cooperative company that transmits financial messages, payments orders, foreign exchange confirmations, and securities deliveries to nearly 7,000 financial institutions on the network, located in 190 countries. SWIFT's global network carried more than 1 billion messages in 1999, with an average daily value of over $5 trillion.[12]

- Fedwire and CHIPS, payment systems for high-value, U.S. dollar payments. Fedwire is operated by the Federal Reserve and is used for U.S. domestic funds transfers, while CHIPS (the Clearing House Interbank Payments System) is a private system used for the transmission and processing of international dollar payments.

- CHAPS, the London-based Clearing House Automated Payments System, which facilitates same-day sterling transfers.[13]

- Clearing houses, which include Euroclear, Cedel, and Clearstream, the dominant players in pan-European clearing and settlement of equities and bonds.

CHIPS AND THE GLOBAL ECONOMY

CHIPS is an on-line, real-time electronic payment system that transfers funds and settles transactions in U.S. dollars, the common currency of international business. It is the central clearing system in the United States for international transactions, handling over 95% of all dollar payments moving between countries around the world.

On a typical day in New York, well over $1.3 billion in business payments pass through CHIPS computers. This startling amount represents an equally startling volume of over 235,000 international transactions—foreign trade payments, foreign exchange, securities settlement, and Eurodollar transactions, as well as a growing number of domestic payments....

A private sector system, CHIPS is owned and operated by the Clearing House Interbank Payments Company L.L.C. The membership consists of 79 of the world's largest commercial banks....

Before CHIPS, bank transfers were made by hand, foot, and cable. A typical transfer:

A clothing importer in Barcelona, Spain asked her bank to send 1 million in U.S. dollars to a distributor in Milan, Italy, for a shipment of designer evening wear. Barcelona Bank A initiated a transfer of the $1 million from its account in its New York correspondent bank, Bank B, to pay the New York branch of Italian Bank C.

In New York, Bank B received the cabled instructions, translated the cable, and tested its authenticity. A typist prepared an official check and the required documentation for it. An account officer approved the check and signed it.

Bank B's messenger carried the check to the New York Clearing House for one of three daily exchanges, where the check and its backup documentation were passed to a Bank C messenger for delivery to the Italian bank office.

At Bank C, employees entered the check on the account ledger and typed the necessary records to account for the payment and notify their Milan customer of the funds received. Finally, they bundled the check together with

(continued)

the rest of the day's items for collection clearings and sent it back to the Clearing House for settlement at 10 a.m. the next business day.

As payments volume increased, these procedures and the accompanying paperwork and physical burden became overwhelming. An additional problem complicating the flow of funds was that books of account were closed at a fixed hour each afternoon, and banks could not be sure of some receipts until nearly closing time. Thus the banks made their credit decisions as late as possible before dispatching a check to the final payment clearing at the Clearing House. This delay crowded an inordinate number of payments into the final clearing and slowed the entire payment process.

With automation, the same transaction is now handled by CHIPS, transforming hours of manual labor into seconds of electronic transmission. To update the previous example:

Barcelona Bank A transmits instructions to its correspondent, New York Bank B, which verifies the transmission.

A terminal operator at Bank B enters the relevant information for the funds transfer into Bank B's CHIPS interface computer, with the identifying documentation.

The central CHIPS computer at the Clearing House, based on Bank B's information, edits and authenticates the message, stores the transaction, and causes a "store" acknowledgment message to be transmitted back to Bank B.

Subsequently, Bank B approves the stored transaction and releases it to CHIPS, which screens the payment against risk controls. CHIPS then sends a "receive" message to Bank C, automatically debits Bank B and credits Bank C.

Bank C notifies its Milan office by automated telecommunications message to pay the clothing exporter.

As the transactions occur, the Clearing House nets this transaction with all other transactions between the two banks and further nets the positions of each of these banks with all other transactions so that each participant on CHIPS has a single net position (which will be a debit or credit). At the end of the day, the Clearing House will send a summary report to each participant showing its net position.

Settlement of amounts due to and from the various banks is accomplished daily, using Fedwire, the public sector wire transfer system, to access reserve or clearing accounts on the books of the Federal Reserve. A CHIPS settlement account at the Federal Reserve Bank of New York is funded by the settling participants that are in a net debit position and drawn down by the Clearing House to pay those participants in a net credit position. The settlement account is brought to zero balance and closed daily. CHIPS payments executed throughout the day are irrevocable and made finally paid through settlement at the end of the day.

Source: www.chips.org.

CASE STUDY   Royal Bank of Canada in Thailand

IVEY

Bernice Scholten and Leslie Stephenson prepared this case under the supervision of Professor Paul Beamish solely to provide material for class discussion. The authors do not intend to illustrate either effective or ineffective handling of a managerial situation. The authors may have disguised certain names and other identifying information to protect confidentiality.

Ivey Management Services prohibits any form of reproduction, storage or transmittal without its written permission. This material is not covered under authorization from CanCopy or any reproduction rights organization. To order copies or request permission to reproduce materials, contact Ivey Publishing, Ivey Management Services, c/o Richard Ivey School of Business, The University of Western Ontario, London, Ontario, Canada, N6A 3K7; phone (519) 661–3208; fax (519) 661–3882; e-mail cases@ivey.uwo.ca.

Thailand, the country known as the "Land of Smiles," had little to feel good about after the brash headline appeared in *The Nation* on August 6, 1997: "IMF Takes Sledgehammer to Economy." Mark Bielarczyk, Country Manager for the Royal Bank of Canada's (RBC) office in Thailand, knew that the recent events would have a significant impact on the bank and found himself recounting the excitement leading up to the announcement.

RBC had re-entered Thailand on June 16, 1997, offering corporate and correspondent banking from its new office on Wireless Road. On July 2, following a sudden collapse in the financial and property sectors, and a lack of foreign reserves to defend the baht against speculation, the government reacted by floating the baht for the first time in thirteen years. This helped trigger the suspension of two-thirds of the country's finance companies, including Bank of Nova Scotia's minority interest in Poonpipat Finance and Securities Company Limited. By August 5, the International Monetary Fund (IMF) intervened and established a $16.7 billion bailout fund to help the country out of the financial crisis. This was the largest bailout fund since the Mexican peso crisis in 1992.

Thailand's 1997 financial crisis had created significant unrest. A recent American Express survey indicated Thailand had the greatest consumer pessimism in Asia and the economies of neighboring countries such as Indonesia and Malaysia were being negatively impacted by the instability. This had raised doubts with international investors about the sustainability of Southeast Asian economies. Bielarczyk had only hired one staff person and had inherited a handful of clients from the Singapore office. Perhaps the bank should cut its losses and focus its efforts elsewhere.

On the one hand, Bielarczyk knew based on experience that opening an office in an emerging market, such as Asia, required patience and persistence. These markets typically featured unique challenges including volatility in eco-

(continued)

nomic growth, poor information quality, political instability, and barriers to entry. Generally, the markets opened slowly and selectively. On the other hand, there was growing concern about whether the country could reform its system of political and economic management. Bielarczyk knew that corporately to fail in Thailand would affect RBC's ability to grow its commodity trade finance business, service multinationals, and produce solid returns from trading activities.

Bielarczyk would be meeting with Phil Brewster, Senior Vice-President and General Manager, Asia later that week and would be expected to provide an update on existing clients, new business contacts, and the potential in the region. Bielarczyk would need to present a strategy to Brewster about how the company should react to the crisis.

Background

In the early 1980s, RBC opened a representative office in Bangkok with limited operations. The office served as a marketing liaison only and could not solicit business in that jurisdiction. The bank's intention was to obtain a full branch licence. Unfortunately, the financial sector did not open as quickly as expected. With no demonstrated change in the regulatory environment, coupled with unexpected LDC (less developed countries) portfolio problems, the bank closed its office in 1986.

On May 23, 1997, the press release appeared in the *Bangkok Post* announcing that the office would be opening in June:

Thailand: Canadians Return to Financial Market

> RBC is making a comeback in the Thai financial market largely due to the many good opportunities identified. With our wide range of expertise, particularly in telecom, energy, mining and trade financing, our clients can expect top financial solutions to help them achieve their business goals.
>
> RBC has a strong commitment to Thailand and believes that the Kingdom has good potential to become a regional financial centre. Being a forward-thinking organization, we will work very hard to achieve our ultimate goal—a full branch licence to operate in Thailand.

The bank's intent was to commence with a staff of five people; the general manager would be an experienced banker from the network, with all other staff hired locally. Included in the local staff base would be individuals with account management, credit, and analysis skills, whose experience and familiarity with the marketplace would be important in developing the client base. Over the first two to three years, they would hire several Thai university graduates and train them in Canada before they returned to Bangkok to work. The capital equipment investment would reflect RBC's strong technological capabilities, from personal computers to communications.

Banking Industry
Canadian Banking System

The Canadian banking system was one of the most stable in the world. Since 1923, Canada had experienced only two bank failures (compared to some

(continued)

17,000 bank failures in the United States since 1921), and in both cases there were no losses experienced by either the deposit holders or bond holders. The Office of the Superintendent of Financial Institutions (OSFI) in Canada was responsible to the Minister of Finance of the Canadian federal government for the supervision of both banks and federally regulated non-bank financial institutions. The Canadian Bank Act required a bank to maintain adequate capital as well as adequate and appropriate forms of liquidity, and empowered the OSFI to direct a bank to increase its capital or to provide additional liquidity.

Revisions to Canada's Bank Act in 1987 and 1992 greatly reduced the barriers between the four pillars of Canada's financial services industry—commercial banking, investment banking, trust, and insurance. As a result, the major Canadian banks provided an extensive range of services within their marketplace, including insurance, money management, retail brokerage, and trust. In 1980, Canada had allowed foreign banks to enter its marketplace, and to date approximately 75 institutions had established operations in Canada.

Royal Bank of Canada

Founded in 1869, Royal Bank was Canada's largest financial institution, and North America's sixth largest bank, with assets of Cdn$245 billion in September 1997. Earnings in 1996 reached a record $1.2 billion and return on equity of 19.1 percent for the first half of 1997 was among the highest in the industry in Canada. Market capitalization in July 1997 was $20.4 billion. Royal Bank ranked first or second among Canadian financial institutions in earnings, market capitalization, and in virtually every financial service it delivered. The bank's 10 million personal, business, government, and financial institution clients were serviced through one of the world's largest delivery networks which included more than 1,600 branches and over 4,000 automated banking machines.

In an April 1996 survey, the Chief Executive Officers of the 1,000 leading Canadian companies selected the best-managed corporations in Canada. Royal Bank ranked number two, the highest of any financial institution in the country. Additionally, it was selected as number one among all companies regardless of industry in the categories of "Leader in Investment Value," "Leader in Responsibility" (measuring equality and charity), and "Leader in Financial Performance."

Internationally, Royal Bank operated in 35 countries through over 100 delivery units. The bank was strongly represented in the major international financial centers of the world, including New York, London, Frankfurt, Tokyo, Hong Kong, and Singapore. RBC's Chile office was opened in 1995, adding to its existing Latin American network of offices in Argentina, Brazil, Venezuela, and Uruguay. In addition to the above locations, the bank's European network included Spain, France, Switzerland, Netherlands, and Channel Islands. Business clients were offered a wide range of services including corporate banking, trade financing, treasury services, and investment banking.

Twenty-three percent of the bank's earning assets at October 31, 1995 were non-Canadian risk, producing 36 percent of its net income. RBC's international asset base increased 19 percent between October 1995 and

(continued)

April 1996 to US$30.4 billion. One of the bank's corporate goals was to increase the proportion of its business generated from non-Canadian sources.

RBC in Asia

The bank's Asia Pacific network of ten offices spanned seven jurisdictions, including Australia, Hong Kong, Japan, People's Republic of China, Singapore, South Korea, and Taiwan. Royal Bank had been operating in the region for more than four decades—in fact, in the early 1950s it was the first North American bank to begin doing business with China after the revolution. [Figure 1] outlines Royal Bank's history in Asia. The bank now had 400 employees based in Japan, Hong Kong, Singapore, Korea, China, Taiwan, Australia, and most recently, Thailand. The product offering focused on four major business lines—financial institutions and trade, multinational lending, treasury services, and global private banking. [Table 1] outlines the business assessment relative to trade services. The asset base as of April 30, 1996, was US$4.2 billion. This represented approximately 16 percent of RBC's total international earning assets.

Royal Bank had been marketing in Thailand for over 30 years. Initially, this was undertaken by representatives of the bank based in Hong Kong, as well as through RoyEast Investment and Orion Royal Pacific, joint venture partners. In the early 1980s, Royal Bank was granted authorized lending facilities for term loans to government entities, which included the Kingdom of Thailand, Electrical Generating Authority of Thailand, and Thai Airlines. The Royal had relationships with Thai banks, particularly Bangkok Bank, Thai Farmers Bank, and Siam Commercial Bank. In total, RBC provided facilities exceeding US$260 million for a number of locally incorporated groups. Recently, it had provided over US$100 million in facilities to more than 15 Thai corporations, both in Thailand and overseas.

While the bank's Asia strategy had been "status quo" in recent years while it had focused on consolidating its dominant position in Canada, there was now an aggressive plan in place for Asia. With a population of 2.8 billion people and unprecedented economic progress, Asia's need for financial services, by businesses and individuals, had grown exponentially. And although the financial environments in individual countries varied in degree of maturity, the potential of the region was evident.

BIBF Application

One of the primary challenges facing banks in Asia-Pacific was the ability to expand their delivery network to participate in the economic and social infrastructure development of the region. To successfully compete in and profit from this growth required an investment in the Southeast Asia network to increase presence, and to demonstrate commitment to both regional and multinational clients. For financial institutions that expected to reap long-term benefits in the country, the prescribed entry format (BIBF) had to be followed. New banks had been allowed to enter Thailand as Bangkok International Banking Facilities (BIBF) offices, as a representative office, as a branch with a banking licence, and as a Provincial International Banking Facility.

(continued)

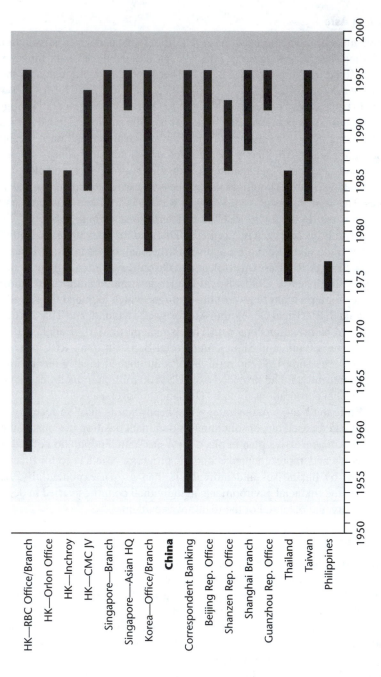

FIGURE 1 Royal Bank Asian Timelines

(continued)

TABLE 1 Business Assessment (June 1996)

Business Segment	*Trade Services*
Definition	• Delivery of trade products and services to Business Banking, Multinational, Correspondent Banking, and selected trade customers globally primarily on a short-term basis.
	• For RBC internal purposes. Financial Institutions & Trade (FI&T) includes all activities undertaken in Asia outside of Korea and Japan which would include general commercial lending which may or may not be trade-related.
Key Success Factors in This Business	• Centralized low-cost processing of documentation utilizing state of the art technology, electronic connection of processing centers with branches and client, and simple documentation to speed processing time.
	• Bank-to-bank trade (included in FI) is credit-driven: origination, structuring, and distribution critical.
	• Strong reputation in the marketplace.
	• Customer service; trained experienced staff.
	• Throughput: volume.
	• Large number of correspondent banking relationships.

Current RBFG Capabilities in Asia

Operations	• Trade conducted through branch offices in Shanghai, Hong Kong, Taiwan (2 offices), and Singapore under the direction of the VP Trade, Asia; other Southeast Asian countries are marketed out of Singapore.
	• Approximately 300 clients served, with a high concentration of business with one client in Hong Kong.
	• MTC (micro trade command) implemented in Singapore in 1995 at a cost of $1.8 MM which automates UC transaction processing for Singapore; to be implemented in Hong Kong (for HK, Tokyo, and Shanghai) and Taiwan over the next year and to interface with RIBS accounting system. It is the same

(continued)

TABLE 1 Business Assessment (June 1996) *(continued)*

Business Segment	*Trade Services*
	system used in Canada but customized for Singapore. This should result in full-time equivalent (FTE) savings (Canada eliminated 150 positions). Conversion costs are estimated at $150 M for each of HK and Taiwan and should result in saving 3–4 FTE positions at each location or $100 M/yr at each location.
Financial Results	• 1995 NIAT $8.9 billion forecasted to increase to $11.4 billion in 1996 (ROC of 18% and 17%, respectively). These results include loans to corporate clients (approx. 60% of gross revenue) and exclude bank-to-bank loans which are trade-related yet included in F1 results.
	• NIAT expects to grow 28% and 33% in 1996 and 1997, respectively.
	• ROC levels are strong and forecasted to grow further.
	• Global trade ROC for 1996 is 14%; Canada 12%, Europe 8%, US 28%. The Asian ROC could be overstated due to an under-allocation of capital; this issue is currently being examined.
Strengths	• Strong position with correspondent banks as a source of short-term trade finance business with more than 3000 correspondent banking relationships globally; 40% of foreign banks requiring Canadian services use RBC.
Weaknesses	• Lack of integrated marketing approach with other RBC products and units; lack of focused marketing strategy.
	• Account manager turnover and skill set not optimized due to lack of specialized training.
	• Lack of market coverage; no ground presence in Indonesia, Malaysia, Thailand, Vietnam; relatively few non-bank trade customers outside Canada.
	• Lack of management information systems (MIS) and cost/pricing methodology.
	• Low productivity due to lack of volumes and high fixed costs.

(continued)

TABLE 1 Business Assessment (June 1996) *(continued)*

Business Segment	Trade Services

Key Competitors
- Highly competitive, significant market activity due to ease of entry and large number of players threatens profitability.
- All global banks present including Citibank, Chase/Chemical, BNP, Societe Generale, HSBC, Standard Chartered, ABN-AMRO, and Deutsche.
- Citibank leading player with regard to centralization via imaging technology—all trade processing centralized in Penang (rent $.95 psf) and Hong Kong.
- CoreStates is active in trade processing and is used by BMO and many others.

Best Practices of Competitors
- Centralized, low-cost processing and use of technology.
- Large number of correspondent banking relationships.
- Focused approach to the market.

Opportunities for RBFG
- Adopt a more client-focused approach, segment and target market moving somewhat downmarket to large regional corporates to generate increased business.
- By 2000, total Asia exports, significantly intra-regional, will reach $2 trillion, up 65% which is the highest growth rate in the world (1993 intra-Asian trade flows were US $1,037 billion; 36% from Greater China [China, Hong Kong, Taiwan], 32% Japan and Korea, 24% Southeast Asia). Imports will total $1.5 trillion.
- Intra-Asian trade flows; or: Japan, Korea, China, and Taiwan are the origin of most flows; China and southeast Asia are the main destinations of the flows.
- Increasing Canada–Asia trade—by 2000, Canadian exports to Asia (excl. Japan) will total US $13 billion (up from $5.8 billion in 1994) and imports will be US $19.9 billion.

(continued)

TABLE 1 Business Assessment (June 1996) *(continued)*

Business Segment	*Trade Services*
	• Tap into increasing Latin America-Asia trade flows through our correspondent banking network.
	• Outsourcing our trade processing is an option (e.g., Citibank, CoreStates); even on a "white label" basis, however, this represents a degree of loss of control and RBC could install a similar system to that currently being put into Canada to retain control of documentation processing.
	• RBC can capitalize on its credit rating and strong reputation to generate business by linking customers globally (e.g., linking Asian with global commodities strategy).
	• Lending is the main basis of the Asian corporate banking relationship and the ability to secure trade finance business will likely go to those banks which maintain financing support.
Threats for RBFG	• Credit risks—lack of foreign exchange (FX); ability to repay (transfer risk); and illiquidity of local bank (F1 risk).
	• RBC loses clients who go into countries where we lack a ground presence as we are disadvantaged from providing a similar level of service to our competitors.
	• Lack of transparency in financials of customers impedes risk assessments.
	• Recent expansion in trade—the Bank has gone downmarket dealing with clients who essentially are independent business and trading companies with little capital and very high leverage.
Conclusion	• RBC is currently a high-cost producer lacking the necessary volumes to gain peak efficiencies; estimated processing efficiencies in Hong Kong and Taiwan vs Canada are 50%.
	• Trade is a core business in Asia and a core competency of RBC in Canada where volumes are relatively flat; to become a top

(continued)

TABLE 1 Business Assessment (June 1996) *(continued)*

Business Segment   *Trade Services*

20 global trade bank by 2000, Asian trade business must be further developed.

- There is a need to promote awareness of Asian trade capabilities in Canada.
- With the forecasted growth in Asian exports and intra-regional trade flows (e.g., Korea-Japan; China Triangle), the Asian market is very attractive for trade.
- Through enhanced market coverage and promotion of interbank referrals, attempt to increase the volume of export-related trade products.
- Prepare a business case to centralize processing of trade documents in Singapore which would require imaging technology (similar to current Canadian initiative) to reduce costs (offset by higher communication costs) and improve efficiencies. This could result in substantial FTE savings (perhaps as much as 50% of back office staff).
- Precisely define target market names; relationship-manage these targets with a view to enhancing revenue generation.
- Increase trade-specific training (as opposed to generic Visions and Values) to improve effectiveness of training dollars.
- Realign resources from back office/support/administrative staff to front-line revenue-generation staff (i.e., knowledgeable trade marketers) through downsizing, more effective training (our skill level requires upgrading), and introduction of technology. Add four trade marketers, reporting to VP Trade for Asia in Hong Kong, Tokyo, Singapore, and Seoul at a total estimated cost of $1.2 million (4 × $300 thousand) which will require $120 MM of new letter of credit (L/C) business to break-even (based on a 1% spread) which should be attainable based on expanding intra-Asian trade flows.

(continued)

TABLE 1 Business Assessment (June 1996) *(continued)*

Business Segment	*Trade Services*

- Lending as a stand-alone product should not be encouraged; however, as part of a trade finance relationship it should be encouraged.
- Involve VP Trade with country manager when setting country limits.
- More aggressive follow-up on advisements to Asian exporters.
- Upgrade Beijing to branch status to protect existing trade business done there as Beijing opens up.

A BIBF permitted entry into a strictly controlled marketplace, and served as the entry point to onshore lending in the future. These licences enabled the banks to extend loans within Thailand and abroad using money borrowed from overseas. Foreign banks were limited to just one office and were not permitted to deal in the local currency. Only certain transactions could be undertaken by a BIBF; these excluded certain types of trade business involving Thai goods or customers such as issuance of letters of credit or dealing in local currency. It did, however, provide the future possibility of upgrading to branch status, which permitted a larger range of business, including on-shore lending in the local currency. The BIBF represented an immediate investment to satisfy longer-term objectives. Local presence, combined with the ability to secure collateral, provided an opportunity to develop relationships with a much broader prospective client base than could be achieved from abroad. Also, physical presence permitted superior management of the political and economic risks prevailing in the marketplace.

Royal Bank opened a representative office in Bangkok in the early 1980s with a view to attaining full branch status. A representative office allowed it simply to develop relationships and refer and give advice. Unfortunately, the financial sector did not open as quickly as anticipated. Given no demonstrated change in the regulatory environment and Royal Bank's pressing LDC (less developed countries) portfolio problems, it decided to close the office in 1986. This action did not sit well with a country that believed foreigners should "weather the storm" and demonstrate their commitment to Thailand. Regulators have long memories and although there was some financial service liberalization in 1992 and some banks were "invited" to apply, Royal Bank was not one of them. In 1996, another round of foreign bank licensing occurred and Royal Bank was invited to apply. It was one of 21 applicants from around the world, and after six months of review and meetings with Thai regulators, it was one of seven successful applications and was granted a Bangkok International Banking Facility licence.

(continued)

As the bank expanded its BIBF presence, it expected significant benefits to accrue to Thailand:

- companies would receive funding at attractive prices
- sophisticated products would be offered, reflecting RBC's experience in specialized lending
- Thai personnel, both those working for RBC and those working with clients, would have their skills upgraded
- RBC's appetite for exposure, available to support trade in over 120 countries worldwide, would be available to support Thai exports
- technology expertise would be transferred to Thai employees and clients

A summary of expectations concerning the operation of the BIBF is outlined in [Table 2]. These estimates were considered conservative; business activities were expected to increase significantly as a result of participation in various growth industries in the country, including transportation, telecommunications, and energy.

The BIBF reported to the Senior Vice-President and General Manager, Asia based in Singapore. Expertise and familiarity with the marketplace were important in the development of a client base. [Table 3] outlines staff, premises, and capital costs for the initial five years.

The Thai Environment

[Table 4] provides an overview of the key factors relative to the markets in Southeast Asia. [Figure 2] summarizes the Royal Bank's presence in Asia.

Social   Thailand was situated on the Indo-Chinese peninsula and was bordered on the west by Myanmar and the Andaman Sea, on the east by Cambodia and

---

TABLE 2 Royal Bank of Canada Thailand BIBF Application June 1996

BIBF Feasibility Study Summary

	Year 1 (USD $)	Year 5 (USD $)
Assets	$225 million	$540 million
Revenue	$1,350,000	$3,100,000
Non-Interest	$720,000	$1,550,000
Pre-Tax Income	$595,000	$1,550,000
Capital Equipment Investment	$425,000	N/A
Staff Composition		
Experienced RBC staff	1	1
Locally hired team	4	9
Total	5	10

(continued)

TABLE 3 Royal Bank of Canada in Thailand

Staff Cost Estimates

Category	Number and Start Year	Detail	Year 1 USD	Year 2 USD	Year 3 USD	Year 4 USD	Year 5 USD
General Manager (Canadian Expatriate)	1, Year 1	Expatriate compensation package	$159,500	$175,500	$193,000	$212,300	$233,500
Senior Marketing Manager (5 years relevant experience)	1, Year 1	Salary, performance bonus, & other benefits	48,300	53,200	58,500	64,400	70,800
Operations Manager (5 years relevant experience)	1, Year 2	Salary, performance bonus, & other benefits		32,200	35,500	39,000	42,900
Marketing Manager (3 years relevant experience)	1, Year 3	Salary, performance bonus, & other benefits			35,500	39,000	42,900
	1, Year 5						42,900
Credit Analyst (Graduate with 2 years experience)	1, year 1	Salary, performance bonus, & other benefits	22,200	24,000	26,800	29,500	32,400
	1, Year 4					29,500	32,400
Secretary (2 years experience)	1, Year 1	Salary, performance bonus, & other benefits	9,700	10,600	11,700	12,900	14,200
Clerk (2 years experience)	1, Year 1	Salary, performance bonus, & other benefits	7,300	8,000	8,800	9,700	10,600
	1, Year 3				8,800	9,700	10,600
Driver allowance paid to managers (1 each for General Manager & Senior Marketing Manager)		Allowance	8,500	9,300	10,200	11,300	12,400
Total Staff Cost	10 staff		$255,500	$312,800	$388,800	$457,300	$545,600

(continued)

TABLE 3 Royal Bank of Canada in Thailand *(continued)*

Premises and Equipment Cost

Category	Number	Detail	Year 1 USD	Year 2 USD	Year 3 USD	Year 4 USD	Year 5 USD
Office Space	2,000 sq. ft.	@USD 2.01/sq. ft./mth in year 1	$ 48,200	$ 53,100	$ 87,600	$ 96,300	$106,000
	1,000 sq. ft.	@USD 2.44/sq. ft./mth in year 3					
General Manger's residence		Within 30 mins. driving distance of office	48,200	53,100	58,400	64,200	70,600
Depreciation—*Automobiles*		1 car for general manager	14,300	14,300	14,300	14,300	14,300
(5-year useful life)		1 car for senior marketing manager	6,800	6,800	6,800	6,800	6,800
Depreciation—*Office Equipment*		Computers and LAN server	7,300	7,300	10,900	10,900	10,900
(5-year useful life)		Data processing equipment	3,100	3,100	3,100	3,100	3,100
Depreciation—*Leasehold*		Improvements to office	26,200	26,200	39,300	39,300	39,300
Improvements (5-year useful life) space							
Utilities			8,100	8,900	9,800	10,700	11,800
Other miscellaneous			9,100	10,000	11,000	12,000	13,300
Total Premises and Equipment Costs			$171,300	$182,800	$241,200	$257,600	$276,100

(continued)

TABLE 3 Royal Bank of Canada in Thailand *(continued)*

Capital Costs

Category	Number	Detail	Year 1 USD	Year 2 USD	Year 3 USD	Year 4 USD	Year 5 USD
Club Membership	3	2 country clubs, 1 city club	$137,000				
Automobiles	2	1 Volvo	71,500				
		1 Toyota	34,300				
Leasehold Improvements		2000 sq. ft. @ THB 1625/sq. ft.	131,000				
		1000 sq. ft. @ THB 1625/sq. ft.			$65,500		
Personal Computers	5	Desktop PCs	18,100				
	5	Desktop PCs			18,100		
Data Processing Equipment	1	LAN server, cables, etc.	18,100				
		Computer, telecommunications hardware, fax, printers	15,600				
Total Capital Costs			$425,600	$0	$83,600	$0	$0

(continued)

TABLE 3 Royal Bank of Canada in Thailand *(continued)*

		Other Costs						
Category	*Number*	*Detail*	*Year 1 USD*	*Year 2 USD*	*Year 3 USD*	*Year 4 USD*	*Year 5 USD*
Club Membership	3	Annual fees	$ 2,000	$ 3,000	$ 3,000	$ 3,000	$ 4,000
Car Running Expenses	2	Petrol, maintenance, etc.	10,000	11,000	12,000	13,000	15,000
Insurance		Office and GM's residence	4,000	4,000	9,000	10,000	11,000
Banking License			20,000	22,000	24,000	27,000	29,000
Training			10,000	12,000	14,000	17,000	20,000
Travel			7,000	9,000	11,000	13,000	15,000
Audit			4,000	5,000	6,000	7,000	8,000
Entertainment			11,000	12,000	13,000	15,000	16,000
Legal and Professional			6,000	7,000	9,000	10,000	13,000
Postage and Courier			4,000	5,000	6,000	7,000	8,000
Telecommunications		Phone, fax, etc.	5,000	6,000	6,000	7,000	7,000
Data Processing Costs			42,000	47,000	51,000	56,000	62,000
Stationery			5,000	6,000	7,000	9,000	10,000
Total Other Costs			$130,000	$149,000	$171,000	$194,000	$218,000

(continued)

TABLE 4 Country Overview

	Canada (developed)	China (emerging) (2)	Hong Kong (developed)	Taiwan (developing)	Singapore (developed)	Malaysia (developing)
Ratings						
CRR	1	2–	2	2+	1	2
S&P	AA+	BBB	A	AA+	AAA	A+
Moody's	Aa2	A3	A3	AA3	Aa1	A1
Literacy rate	97%	80%	90%	92%	92%	60%
Secondary education	88%	48%	62%	44%	60%	58%
Higher education	42%	2%	10%	8%	8%	7%
Population	27 million	1.2 billion	6 million	21 million	3 million	20 million
Urban population as % of total	78%	29%	95%	56%	100%	46%
Income distribution (top 20% population/country earnings)	40%	42%	47%	41%	49%	54%
Foreign reserves—US$	12b	53b	52b	93b	60b	25b
Net debt (creditor) level—US$	430b	46b	(18b)	(54b)	(15B)	9b
GDP						
3-year avg—US$	493b	489b	111b	220b	69b	71a
Historical growth—5 year	1.6%	11%	5%	7%	8%	9%
Forecasted growth	2.90%	8%–10%	3.5%–5%	6.5%–5.5%	7%–6%	8%
GDP per capita—US$	18,015	408	18,652	10,516	23,980	3,622
GDP per capita at PPP—US$(1)	20,170	2,400	21,700	12,300	20,500	8,600
Trade—in US$						
Exports	132b	99b	135b	88b	96b	59b
Imports	122b	98b	141b	74b	96b	59b
Current account (1995)	(10b)	20b	(3b)	5b	15b	(7b)
RBC NIAT 1995		C$1.7m	C$0.8m	C$1.9m	C$0.8m	C$0.2m
Total revenues generated from country(4)						

(continued)

TABLE 4 Country Overview *(continued)*

	Indonesia (emerging)	Thailand (developing)	Vietnam (under-developed)	Philippines (emerging)	South Korea (developing)
Ratings					
CRR	2–	2	3	3+	2+
S&P	BBB	A	unrated	BB	AA–
Moody's	Baa3	A2	unrated	Ba2	A1
Literacy rate	84%	94%	89%	94%	97%
Secondary education	45%	33%	N/A	74%	87%
Higher education	20%	16%	N/A	28%	39%
Population	192 million	59 billion	72 million	67 million	45 million
Urban population as % of total	33%	35%	20%	45%	76%
Income distribution (top 20% population/country earnings)	42%	51%	49%	48%	42%
Foreign reserves—US$	16b	29b	.6b	6b	26b
Net debt (creditor) level—US$	88b	44b	18b	33b	44b
GDP					
3-year avg—US$	116b	143b	15(3)	63(3)	380b
Historical growth—5 year	7%	10%	8%	1.5%	7%
Forecasted growth	6.5%–7.5%	7%–9%	8.5%–9.5%	5%–6%	6%
GDP per capita—US$	909	2,411	215	941	8,539
GDP per capita at PPP—US$(1)	3,100	6,400	1,300	2,700	9,800
Trade—in US$					
Exports	40b	45b	4b	13b	96b
Imports	32b	49b	5b	21b	102b
Current account (1995)	(6b)	(12b)	(1b)	(4b)	(5b)
RBC NIAT 1995	—	—	—	—	—
Total revenues generated from country(4)	C$1.6m	C$1.4m	C$0.4m	N/A	C$0.8m

(continued)

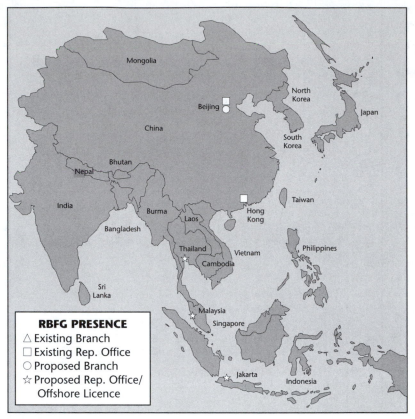

FIGURE 2 RBFG in Asia

the Gulf of Thailand, on the north by Laos, and on the south by Malaysia. The country covered a land area of 514,000 square km and consisted of 76 provinces which were divided into four regions: central, northern, north-eastern, and southern. Bangkok, the nation's capital, was situated in the central region and was home to approximately 10 percent of the total population. The official language was Thai, but English was often understood and used in commercial circles. Chinese, principally the Teo-chiew dialect, was also used in business.

According to the latest census, Thailand had a population of approximately 59 million, with an annual population growth rate of two percent. Most of the population was Thai; minority groups included Chinese, Indians, and Malays. Approximately 95 percent of the population was Buddhist, the remaining primarily Muslim, Christian, and Hindu. Freedom of religious belief was highly emphasized, with the king's royal patronage extended to all religions.

Political   Thailand was a constitutional monarchy and the king was head of state. The king appointed the prime minister on the recommendation of the Speaker of the House of Representatives. The prime minister was usually the

(continued)

leader of the core political party that formed the government. The latter was recommended to the prime minister by the political parties that formed the government and commanded the majority of votes in the House of Representatives. The appointment of the ministers in the cabinet was sanctioned by the king.

Thai politicians were seen as corrupt, incompetent, and responsible for the current economic crisis. General Chavalit Yongchaiyudh, Thailand's prime minister, took office in November 1996, but by August 7th, when he was sent to see the much-revered King Bhumibol, many expected his resignation to follow. Although his resignation did not occur, there were rumors of planned coups. The question remained whether Chavalit had any clout to form a strong team capable of steering the country out of the economic turbulence. Thailand's beleaguered finance minister had recently resigned, sending the currency and stock markets into a dive. He left after losing an intra-government battle over a plan to raise excise taxes for some consumer goods.

Economic   Thailand was an open economy with a significant volume of international trade. Its diverse private sector operated in the industries of agriculture, manufacturing, and services. The state favored the free enterprise system, but controlled certain industries to protect the public welfare or because the private sector showed no interest in developing them. Several industries were monopolized: utilities, tobacco, communications, arms and explosives, and air, rail, and motor transportation. Tourism was the country's most important foreign exchange source and was critical to the economy. With seven million people visiting a year, tourism represented 13 percent of the country's total export revenue.

In 1985, manufacturing outstripped agriculture in GDP share. Thailand was one of Asia's main agricultural exporters; it represented 11 percent of exports. Approximately 70 percent of the population was engaged in agriculture. Thailand was an important provider of rice, rubber, cassava, maize, and sugar to the world market but reliance on agriculture had been reduced due to the rapid growth in manufacturing and services. Manufactured products in Thailand accounted for 81 percent of exports. These included clothing, electronic parts and components, furniture, and jewelry. Thailand's principal trading partners were Japan, United States, European Union, Singapore, and Taiwan.

Between 1984 and 1990, Thailand's GDP growth rates averaged 11 percent per year, which made it the world's fastest-growing economy. From 1990 to 1995, annual growth rates averaged approximately eight percent. Inflation averaged five percent in recent years, which was impressive given Thailand's rapid growth. To keep pace with the country's growth, the government increased spending on infrastructure improvements such as road networks and telecommunications. Efforts were also underway to improve employee training and increase the number of workers with secondary and post-secondary education.

The currency was the Thai baht. It was fixed by the Exchange Equalization Fund of the central bank and was generally followed by the

(continued)

commercial banks. The Bank of Thailand, the central bank, was the Ministry of Finance's agent for public debt management, exchange control, and commercial bank supervision.

Thailand ranked in the top 25 of Canada's trading partners, with trade flows between Canada and Thailand increasing dramatically over the past three years. Major Canadian exports to Thailand increased 57 percent between 1993 and 1995 and included organic chemicals, wood pulp, paper, and building materials. Canada's imports from Thailand, such as electrical machinery, mechanical appliances, and fish, had grown almost 35 percent during the same period. This represented more than US$1.1 billion in trade business between the two countries.

Thailand was strategically located with respect to both Indochina and the Southern China region, and expected to continue as one of the fastest-growing economies in the world. It was anticipated that local companies would not only expand regionally, but that foreign companies would also want to service both the local and regional markets with new projects. The US$750 million announcement from General Motors in May 1996 was one such example. Royal Bank saw an important role in Thailand for the bank to assist such companies. [Table 5] outlines the top companies listed in Thailand. In addition, it was felt opportunities existed to lend to many more companies, with over 50 domestic companies having a turnover exceeding US$100 million. This growth was expected to increase by 10 to 15 percent per year as planned privatization was implemented.

TABLE 5 Top Companies Listed in Thailand (USD $ million)				
Rank[1]	Company	Sector	Sales	Total Assets
1	Airways International	Transportation	$2,203	$5,158
2	Ratchaburi Cement	Building	1,638	2,751
3	Saduak Petroleum	Energy	988	1,057
4	Damnoen Makro	Wholesale/ Retail	737	326
5	Rama Petroleum	Chemicals	609	2,359
6	Siphya Merchandising	Agribusiness	536	153
7	Sukhumvit Feedmill	Agribusiness	478	604
8	Mallee Development	Property	469	623
9	Ratchaburi City Cement	Building	422	1,109
10	Sala–Union	Textiles	406	541

Note: Opportunity exists to lend to many more companies, with over 50 domestic companies having a turnover exceeding USD $100 million. This is expected to grow by 10–15 per year as planned privatization is implemented.
[1]Ranked on sales; excludes banks and finance houses.

(continued)

Competitive Environment   The financial industry in Thailand comprised 15 domestic commercial banks, branches of 15 foreign banks, and approximately 100 finance companies. The five largest banks accounted for nearly 70 percent of the total banking assets and included Bangkok Bank, Krung Thai Bank, Thai Farmers Bank, Siam Commercial Bank, and Bank of Ayudhya. The foreign banks had only a seven percent market share. It was expected that the financial markets would be further liberalized, with plans in place to establish five new commercial banks, and to open branches of seven foreign banks currently operating under the offshore banking facility.

The Bank of Nova Scotia was the most active Canadian financial institution in Thailand. It established a representative office in Bangkok in 1980 and, in 1990, purchased a 25 percent interest in Poonpipat Finance and Securities Co. Limited. In 1993 it was granted a BIBF licence and was currently applying for a branch licence. In the mid–1980s, Canadian Imperial Bank of Commerce was active in Thailand, but subsequently closed its office.

Current Situation   After a decade of seven to eight percent annual growth, the Thai economy entered a dangerous and volatile phase. The country's exports were no longer booming; foreign investors were becoming concerned about the current-account deficit; and big loans to property developers had inflated a dangerous financial state. Bad debt continued to accumulate, causing more anguish in the financial system. The stock market plummeted to depths not seen in eight years. The currency fell prey to speculative attack.

Contributing factors to the Thai crisis were the typical litany of high debt, heavy borrowing, a large current account deficit, and a semi-fixed exchange rate system (the baht was tied to US$). Also, the banking industry had been deregulated without requiring adequate capitalization or proper lending controls—real estate was reckless. In June 1997, the central bank and the Ministry of Finance attempted to take control by ordering struggling finance companies to shore up their reserves against bad loans in response to a crisis of confidence that threatened the stability of the financial sector. The intervention came after the government had ordered the leading finance firm, Finance One, to merge with its long-time strategic rival, the country's 12th largest commercial bank, to avert Finance One's collapse.

The authorities' firm intervention contradicted the BOT's traditional preference for self-regulation and came after a year of mounting concern over the burden of non-performing loans carried by the finance sector. Loan defaults had been rising sharply because of tighter credit rules introduced by the central bank in late 1995 and high interest rates designed to bring inflation under control.

While the government had reassured the public that the baht would not be devalued, they could not withstand the pressure on the baht by speculators. The baht was, in effect, devalued 20 percent when the central bank could not halt its slide and had to unpeg it on July 2nd. Despite the country's good macroeconomic condition, Thailand had clearly lost sight of market discipline.

On August 5, 1997, the Thai government announced it had reached an agreement with the International Monetary Fund (IMF) on a tough program

(continued)

of economic and financial reforms to be introduced in return for a $16.7 billion package of loans. The reforms included the closing of another 16 finance firms, in addition to the 42 finance firms that were suspended earlier in the year. These firms were asked to merge with banks and other companies or submit other rehabilitation plans. The package also involved tax hikes, spending cuts, accelerated privatization, and potentially, the phasing out of public-utilities subsidies.

The program enabled Thailand to resume the rapid economic growth that it had enjoyed since the mid–1980s and allowed it to implement two of the three significant reforms that Thailand had long needed:

- the restoration of budgetary control
- the restructuring of the country's rickety and corrupt financial system

As a result of the bailout, the government were accountable to the IMF. They were required to report their reserves every two weeks and the central bank had to maintain foreign reserves above $24 billion, enough to pay for four months' imports. This figure would increase to $25 billion in 1998. The letter of intent also required the Thai government not to bail out troubled financial institutions by assisting their creditors. Implementing IMF conditions would be painful and unpopular, but without the credit package the reserves would be at risk of falling sharply since the private sector had to repay dollar-denominated loans at a time when foreign capital was flowing abroad.

Many Thais hoped the IMF rescue package would bail out the floundering economy and result in the reduction of the Value Added Tax (VAT) from its current level of 10 percent back to the previous seven percent. This, of course, would raise serious doubts about the commitment to the package. The government expected the VAT to increase revenue by 60–70 billion baht the following year on a broad range of consumer goods, services, and utilities. The government felt pressure to reduce consumption on non-essential goods and to cut public expenditures to achieve a balanced budget. Furthermore, the government hoped to:

- trim the current 950 billion baht budget for fiscal 1998 by 60–100 billion baht with cuts in all sectors apart from education and health
- cap inflation—less than five percent when the baht was floated in July— at 8.9 percent
- cut the current account deficit—8.2 percent of GDP at the end of 1996— to five percent in 1997 and three percent in 1998

Heading for a Recovery?

The Bank of Thailand's governor, Chaiyawat Wibulswasdi, was optimistic that Thailand's economy would turn around. He declared that the country was headed for recovery in three years, assisted by the country's new international credit line. Economic growth was expected to shrink to 2.5 to three

(continued)

percent this year, before improving to four percent in 1998 and five percent in 1999. The current account deficit would narrow to three percent of GDP.

The IMF might have helped to "plug the hole," but the country was clearly struggling to contain the effects of the currency devaluation and turn around an economy growing at its slowest pace since 1986. Without a doubt, the Thai crisis had triggered a reassessment of Southeast Asian and of individual economies. Problems around the region that investors had long ago discovered and discounted suddenly loomed larger and more sinister as markets began questioning the sustainability of Southeast Asia's economic miracle. International investors were growing more nervous about risk factors and local companies took a look at their practice of borrowing in dollars and looked for other ways to hedge.

Decision

The fallout from the Thai property market had been staggering. The financial sector, which once fed on relatively cheap offshore borrowing, was saddled with a staggering 547 billion baht ($17 billion) in property-related debt, much of which it would probably never recover. Growth had plunged and the government had been forced to accept a rescue line from the International Monetary Fund. Matters weren't helped by the government's muddled attempts to deal with the crisis, most of which came too late and brought confusion rather than clarity. The important question was when, and if, the country could reform its beleaguered, ill-fated system of political and economic management. The future looked uncertain at best.

Perhaps Royal Bank should cut its losses and focus its efforts elsewhere. Bielarczyk would be meeting with Brewster next week and needed to provide a status report and strategic direction for the country.

The Richard Ivey School of Business gratefully acknowledges the generous support of The Richard and Jean Ivey Fund in the development of this case as part of the Richard and Jean Ivey Fund Asian Case Series.

Questions

1. Why do you suppose that Citibank has been able to establish itself in so many countries around the world? How important is the first-mover advantage in international banking?
2. A large global bank is considering establishing operations in Lebanon. Should they establish a branch, a rep office, or some other type of operation in Lebanon? What factors does the bank need to evaluate?
3. Describe the ideal employee needed to staff each of the four main types of overseas banking operations. What background would you expect the chief officer of each operation to have?
4. What are the special features associated with syndicated lending?
5. Do you think that syndicated loans will become more or less common in the next decade? Why?

6. What is project finance? How does it differ from ordinary lending?

7. What are the risks associated with project finance? How can a lender mitigate these risks?

8. What is a letter of credit? Suppose that your customer, an importer located in Indonesia, asks you to provide a letter of credit to back his purchases from a supplier located in California. What risks and rewards are involved from the bank's point of view? Does your answer change if the importer is located in France? Russia?

9. What are the special challenges of international credit analysis, as opposed to domestic credit analysis? How can a bank meet these challenges?

10. Suppose that you work for a large global bank and that you are responsible for assessing the creditworthiness of a manufacturing client located in Brazil. What factors will you use to make your decision? How does this analysis differ from that used for a manufacturing client located in Louisiana? Belgium?

11. Why do bankers now place such a high priority on the development of noncredit services? Which noncredit services do you think offer real growth opportunities for international banks?

Websites

www.intlbanking.org	International Financial Services Association
www.123world.com.bank	Comprehensive list of official sites for banks, financial institutions, and central banks around the world
www.bankfacts.org.uk	British Banking Association
www.cib.org.uk	Chartered Institute of Bankers
www.iib.org	Institute of International Bankers
www.e-banking.org	Electronic Banking
www.obanet.org	Online Banking Association
www.aba.com	American Bankers Association
www.latinbanking.org	Latin American Federation of Banks
www.webbanker.com	Florida Bankers Association
www.aimhi.com/VC/tcfa	Chinese Finance Association
www.ibac.com	International Bankers Association of California
www.iboa.com	International Banking Operations Association
www.hkib.orh	Hong Kong Institute of Bankers
www.cba.ca	Canadian Bankers Association
www.swift.com	SWIFT
www.chips.org	CHIPS

Notes

1. Harvard Business School, *Citibank Indonesia,* Video: Interview with Mehli Mistri, Country Manager, Citibank Indonesia (Boston: Harvard Business School Publishing, 1988).

2. The landmark legal case in this regard arose from a dispute between Wells Fargo and Citibank. The dispute began when the Philippine government, on October 17, 1983, prohibited repayment of principal on eurodollar time deposits to foreign banks without central bank approval. Wells Fargo, which was scheduled to receive payment on $2 million in time deposits from Citibank's branch in Manila, sued Citibank in New York demanding that the parent make the payment out of its New York–based funds. The case went all the way to the Supreme Court, not once but twice, and took nearly

a decade to resolve. In the end, it was decided in Wells Fargo's favor, meaning that funds deposited in a foreign branch can be recovered from the U.S. bank's parent in New York under certain circumstances. For more information, see *Wells Fargo Asia Limited* v. *Citibank NA,* 936 F.2d 723 (2nd Circuit, 1991).

3. For details on this pact, go to www.wto.org.
4. "Japanese Banks Racing into Vietnam," *Nikkei Weekly,* December 9, 1996.
5. Jan Ter Wengel, "International Trade in Banking Services," *Journal of International Money and Finance,* 14, no. 1 (1995), p. 47.
6. James Mackintosh, "London Best for Business, Say Bank 'Outsiders,'" *Financial Times,* June 14, 2000, p. 10.
7. "Xenophile Urges: Love Affairs with Foreign Banks," *Euromoney,* April 12, 1997, p. 536.
8. Ingo Walter, "Project Finance: The Lender's Perspective," in David W. Pearce, Horse Siebert, and Ingo Walter, editors, *Risk and the Political Economy of Resource Development* (London: Macmillan Press, 1984).
9. "International Project Finance," *Financial Times Survey,* December 3, 1996, p. 51.
10. "Syndicated Lending: The Relationship Starts to Change," *Euromoney,* November 1998, p. 64.
11. "Global Custody," *Financial Times Survey,* July 14, 2000, p. 1.
12. The data and the preceding quote are from the SWIFT website, at www.swift.com.
13. Shelagh Heffernan, *Modern Banking in Theory and Practice* (New York: John Wiley & Sons, 1996), pp. 77–78.

CHAPTER 5

INTERNATIONAL
INVESTMENT BANKING

What Is Investment Banking?

According to one dictionary, an **investment bank** is "a bank whose function is provision of long-term equity and loan finance for industrial and other companies, particularly new securities."[1] This definition is accurate, but it hardly covers the full range of activities in which investment banks are involved. Indeed, we believe that investment banking is where a banker acts as a financial intermediary, providing long-term equity and loan finance for companies through underwriting of new securities, rather than when he or she loans money directly. Four functions form the core of investment banking activities:

1. Underwriting and selling of shares and bonds to investors.
2. Making markets in these securities for the investors who want to buy and sell them.
3. Advisory services: The selling of all manner of advice to large companies and governments (both local and central as well as foreign and domestic).
4. Supplementary business streams: These aforementioned business streams are supplemented by investment management, merchant banking, foreign currency trading, bridge financing, financial engineering (the packaging and sale of zero-coupon securities, mortgage-backed securities, other asset-backed securities, and derivatives), project financing, and leasing.

Considering the major business streams, we see that investment banking is different from traditional commercial banking. Indeed, investment banking is a higher-risk business: it depends on the ups and downs of stock markets, interest rates, and other intangible factors, reflecting the high degree of speculation involved.

To our definition of investment banking should be added the observation that not all investment banks are created equal. Like commercial banks, they come in all shapes and sizes. The largest firms are usually referred to as the **bulge bracket.** The term bulge bracket comes from the tendency of those firms' names to be printed larger and bolder on public offering announcements (known as **tombstones**) and on the front pages of prospectuses of new issues than the names of

J.P. MORGAN CUTS BACK SYNDICATED LOANS
Paul M. Sherer

J.P. Morgan & Co.'s loan business is shrinking—and the bank's executives couldn't be happier.

The U.S. investment bank has dropped to sixth this year from third in 1998 and second in 1997 in the ranking of the nation's lead banks in syndicated lending. It has led just 81 deals valued at $85 billion in the first three quarters of last year, according to Loan Pricing Corp.

But while loan volume is down, profitability is up. That's because a lot of the syndicated loans that J.P. Morgan made in the past were, in effect, loss leaders—cheap credit extended to borrowers in the hope that the borrowers would give more profitable business to the bank.

Credit Evolves Through Crisis

Now, J.P. Morgan is scrutinizing those longstanding relationships, first evaluating how much revenue the client generates from other business before extending loans. "There were a number of examples where the only thing we did with the clients was lend them money, and that was a losing proposition," explains J.P. Morgan credit chief William Demchak. "So either we got out of that lending relation" or began working the client on a range of products, he says.

J.P. Morgan's new approach to lending is part of a broader credit makeover that speaks volumes about the state of the global lending business. It shows how banks are evolving out of their traditional role of being holders of debt, and helps explain why companies' relative cost of borrowing has risen sharply over the past two years. In an effort to boost earnings, other banks are making more efficient use of capital, and even investment banks are trying to curtail their lending capital, too. Credit Suisse First Boston, for example, cut its equity capital devoted to lending from $3.2 billion at the start of 1997 to $800 million now.

Source: Asian Wall Street Journal, October 28, 1999, p. 21.

other firms making up the underwriting and distribution syndicate.[2] The bulge bracket firms during the early 2000s included Merrill Lynch, Salomon Smith Barney (now part of Citigroup, Inc.), Credit Suisse First Boston, Morgan Stanley Dean Witter, Nomura, Deutsche Bank, Lehman Brothers, Bear Stearns, and Chase Manhattan Securities. Those institutions not in the bulge bracket fall into the categories of **major bracket** (the second tier of investment banks), followed by **submajors** (the third tier of investment banks) and **regionals** (smaller institutions tied to geographical locations).

MORGAN STANLEY DEAN WITTER FACTSHEET

The Firm

Morgan Stanley Dean Witter is a global finance firm dedicated to the raising, trading and managing of capital to institutional and corporate entities around the world, with offices in New York, London, Hong Kong and other principal financial centers in 28 different countries. It has approximately 400 securities branch offices throughout the United States and more than 47,000 employees worldwide.

The Primary Businesses—Securities, Asset Management, Credit Services

Securities (Investment Banking/Sales & Trading/Individual Investor Services)

- Underwriting and private placement of debt and equity in U.S. and global capital markets.
- Financial advisory services for mergers and acquisitions, privatizations, and restructurings.
- Sales, trading and market making for U.S. and foreign equities and equity-related securities.
- Distribution and trading of fixed income products, including corporate, government and asset-backed securities.
- Full-service brokerage and global economic, industry and portfolio research.
- Trading of spot, forward and futures in foreign exchange and commodities as well as trading of derivatives.
- Securities lending and financing in connection with investment banking services.

Asset Management (Investment Advisory, Global Custody, Principal Investing)

- Dean Witter Inter-Capital and VanKampen American Capital provide investment advisory services to proprietary open- and closed-end funds; Morgan Stanley Asset Management and Miller Anderson & Sherrerd provide global portfolio management services for institutions.
- Morgan Stanley Services provides global custody and correspondent clearing services.

(continued)

- Principal investing in mergers & acquisitions, restructurings, and leveraged buy-outs; venture capital.
- Other asset management services include NOVUS Financial, investment consulting and insurance agency activities and commodities pool and real estate management.

Credit and Transaction Services (Credit Cards, Outsourcing and Direct Brokerage)

- NOVUS Services offers general purpose credit cards for use on NOVUS network, including Discover Card, Private Issue Card and various co-branded and affinity cards in the U.S.
- SPS Transaction Services provides technology-based outsourcing services.
- Discover Brokerage Direct offers financial services through its Internet site and automated telephone system.

Source: Supplied by Morgan Stanley Dean Witter.

Characteristics of Investment Banks

The organizational structure of investment banks varies considerably. There are the large, global multifunctional investment banks such as Morgan Stanley (see box above) and smaller boutiques. As Marshall and Ellis observed: "There is not any one 'typical' organization, and what works for one firm may not work for another. Much of the organizational structure is often related to the internal politics and alliances within the firm."[3] In a broad sense, there are three organizational structures in investment banking—the partnership, the conglomerate unit, and the public firm. The partnership held sway in the early days of investment banking, but it has declined considerably in numbers, with Goldman Sachs being one of the last major firms to have had this structure. The conglomerate unit places the investment bank as part of a group of companies held by a particular institution, and it is answerable to the parent company. The public firm operates on the premise that it functions at the behest of the shareholders. The ownership of the firm has been sold to the public through a share sale, hence providing the shareholders the right to elect the board of directors. That board is responsible for the general strategy and policy of the company.

Investment banks range from being full-service shops, offering everything, to boutiques, which specialize in a few select services. It is important to underscore that while boutiques have had a certain mystique attached to them, they operate in a highly competitive environment and the most successful usually

TOP 10 INVESTMENT BANKS
DOUBLE GLOBAL BUSINESS

Edward Luce

The world's leading 10 investment banks have almost doubled their share of fee-based and advisory business in the global capital markets since 1990, according to the Stern business school in New York. They now have 77 percent of the market.

The growing concentration of market share in the hands of the top banks has coincided with an explosion in the global capital markets during the 1990s, from total volume of less than $1,500bn at the start of the decade to almost $4,000bn last year, the Stern study showed.

The findings, which are based on statistics from Securities Data, the US information group, showed that the top 20 investment banks increased their share of global capital markets business from 80 percent in 1990 to 97 percent last year.

The top 10 banks are Goldman Sachs, Morgan Stanley Dean Witter, Merrill Lynch, Salomon Smith Barney, Credit Suisse First Boston, Warburg Dillon Read, Deutsche Bank, J.P. Morgan, Chase Manhattan and Lehman Brothers.

Source: Financial Times, March 1, 1999, p. 20.

maintain a relationship with at least one of the larger firms to be effective. The potential awkwardness of this situation is eased by the reality that many of those working at boutiques had previously worked at a larger firm, reflecting the ongoing importance of relationships in the investment banking world.

One well-known boutique was Wasserstein Perella & Co., which was established when the two individuals of those names opted to leave First Boston and carry on their mergers and acquisitions business on their own. At First Boston the team of investment bankers under Bruce Wasserstein and Joseph Perella had been enormously successful. In 1987, they left the larger firm due to differences over resource allocation. In February 1988, Wasserstein and Perella opened their doors with the objective of providing custom-tailored strategic advice and services to corporations and investors worldwide. The firm developed three lines of business: (1) advising a global base of clients on matters of corporate strategy, mergers and acquisitions, divestitures, restructurings, and corporate finance; (2) engaging in specialized research, underwriting, sales, and trading of debt and equity securities; and (3) managing investment funds and products that seek superior risk-adjusted returns to investors. With a client base of Fortune 500 companies, Wasserstein Perella & Co. became an attractive asset to larger investment banks, especially to European institutions looking to expand into the U.S. market. In 2000, Wasserstein Perella & Co. entered into negotiations with Dresdner Bank, which was seeking to complement its investment bank operations. By early 2001, it appeared that the merger was going to happen.

Another point of consideration is that while the distinction was made in the United States and Japan between commercial and investment banking activities (up until the 1999 repeal of the Glass-Steagall Act in the United States), universal banks around the rest of the planet, particularly in Europe, never had to deal with these concerns. Universal banks almost by definition are involved in investment banking. At the same time, New York City, often referred to as Wall Street, is the primary hub for this industry, with London and Tokyo also playing significant roles. This means that U.S. banks work alongside their many foreign counterparts in New York, placing universal banks involved in investment banking activities alongside U.S. commercial banks with securities subsidiaries.

Examples of non-U.S. investment banks include the German Dresdner Bank, which operates its investment bank operations through its Kleinwort Benson wing, Spain's Banck Santander Central Hispano, and Deutsche Bank, one of the world's largest banks. Deutsche Bank is Europe's largest bank group, with assets of over $800 billion. It is also one of the most active non-U.S. investment banks, especially after taking over Bankers Trust. As a key player in London, Tokyo, and New York, Deutsche Bank is active in a wide range of securities and investment products. Deutsche Bank's prominent role was noted by *Moody's Investor Service:* "It is one of perhaps 10 to 15 institutions globally that is poised to be a possible survivor of the battle for a leadership role in investment banking."[4]

One last defining point is that in securities underwriting the funding is provided by the investing public, in sharp contrast to a loan syndication, through which funding is provided by the particular bank or group of banks. At the same time, the differences between commercial and investment banking are narrowing, with an ongoing number of commercial banks willing to try their hand at investment banking. The incentive is profitability, especially in the area of underwriting.

Functions of Investment Banks

Now that we have provided the big picture of companies spanning the globe, helping to lubricate the wheels of international capitalism, how exactly do investment bankers ply their trade? In a broad sense, the functions of an investment bank can be broken down into two major categories—revenue-generating activities and support activities. In the former category fall primary market making, secondary market making, trading, corporate restructuring, financial engineering, and other revenue-generating activities, such as advisory services, investment management, venture capital, and consulting. Under support activities come clearing, internal finance (also referred to as funding), and information services.

What Is Underwriting?

Underwriting is defined as the providing of long-term equity and debt finance for corporations and governments, largely through the issuance of new securities. It should be clarified that governments do not issue equity, which implies ownership. **Equity,** defined as shares of ownership generally with voting rights, is one option for companies to raise capital. Governments issue debt (bonds) and do not issue equity. A **bond** is a financial instrument issued by companies or governments as a method of long-term financing. Bonds are usually at least several years in duration, are repayable on maturity, bear a fixed or floating rate of interest, and may be convertible into common or preferred stock. Bonds can be very long-term in maturity; the Walt Disney Compnay has actually issued ninety-nine-year bonds, popularly referred to as "sleeping beauties"!

Underwriting is big business and underwent a massive expansion during the 1980s and early 1990s. As one source noted: "From 1983 to 1993, the volume of new commercial loans increased from $404 billion to $443 billion, an annual compound rate of increase of less than 1 percent. Over the same decade, new **commercial paper (CP)** issues grew from $184 billion to $554 billion, an increase of almost 12 percent per year. In addition, corporate bond issues rose over the same 10-year period from $643 billion to $2.27 trillion, a 13 percent annual increase."[5] (Commercial paper is a short-term IOU, or an unsecured money market obligation, issued by prime-rated commercial firms and financial companies, with maturities from 2 days up to 270 days.[6] CP is often a critical element of corporate financing.) The sheer weight of these underwriting numbers had an impact in the late twentieth century, forcing a number of commercial banks to change track. Among the most prominent in making a shift into more traditional investment banking activities were J.P. Morgan, Bank of America, Chase Manhattan, and Barclays. Not all such attempts were successful, but the temptation continues, considering the large volume of underwriting.

Who are the customers of investment banks in the underwriting side of the business? In other words, who issues these securities? Issuers include industrial firms, public utilities, and high-tech companies as well as banks, insurance companies, and governments and subnational entities (municipalities, states, provinces, and publicly owned utilities). For example, both the Republic of Italy and the City of Naples have issued dollar-denominated debt in the U.S. market. Government-issued debt is referred to as **sovereign debt,** reflecting the understanding that such debt is backed by the full faith and credit of that particular country's sovereign government and is thus regarded as the best credit from that country, above corporate debt. In terms of the bond market, the largest issuers of bonds are from the United States and other industrialized countries, though countries and corporations from Asia, Latin America, Central and Eastern Europe, and Africa have also issued debt. (See Table 5.1.)

Winning the Mandate

The job of the investment bank is to handle the underwriting process; issuers choose an investment bank based on its prowess in this area. Table 5.2 presents the leading bookrunners (the main bank involved in the transaction—i.e., the "keeper of the book") for international bond issues. The underwriting process has a number of stages. Before investment bankers reach the stage of the actual underwriting and

TABLE 5.1 International Bond Issues: Breakdown by Country of Borrower (US$ billions)

	1983	1989	1991	1993	1995	1997	1998
Industrial Countries	**$60.3**	**$240.4**	**$282.9**	**$408.0**	**$330.5**	**$639.8**	**$909.7**
United States	7.3	15.8	21.1	24.8	68.5	182.8	320.1
Japan	14.0	97.5	72.1	61.0	33.2	37.9	53.3
Developing Area	**2.5**	**2.6**	**9.4**	**45.6**	**22.1**	**59.7**	**56.1**
Latin America	—	—	5.0	23.7	11.1	38.3	41.7
Asia	2.2	1.9	4.1	13.0	9.7	15.6	10.5
Middle East	0.2	0.7	0.3	8.9	1.3	5.8	3.9
Eastern Europe	**0.1**	**2.4**	**2.0**	**7.0**	**1.6**	**2.1**	**19.0**
International Organizations	**13.4**	**10.3**	**14.4**	**20.4**	**15.2**	**26.9**	**106.4**
Total	**$76.3**	**$255.7**	**$308.7**	**$481.0**	**$369.4**	**$728.5**	**$1091.2**

Sources: Data adapted from *Financial Statistics,* OECD, various issues; Bank for International Settlements.

TABLE 5.2 All International Bonds (All Currencies) Bookrunners, 1/1/99–5/15/99

Rank	Managing Bank or Group	No. of Issues	Total (US$ millions)	Share (%)
1	Merrill Lynch	226	$58,891.87	9.44%
2	Salomon SB	139	58,785.50	9.42
3	Deutsche Bank	202	47,684.19	7.64
4	Morgan Stanley DW	183	46,967.60	7.53
5	CSFB	134	35,585.51	5.70
6	Goldman Sachs	83	33,760.00	5.41
7	Warburg D.R.	124	33,403.52	5.35
8	J.P. Morgan	100	31,576.06	5.06
9	ABN Amro	112	30,259.11	4.85
10	Lehman Brothers	95	28,904.56	4.63
11	Dresdner KB	88	25,581.32	4.10
12	Paribas	73	21,463.07	3.44
13	Commerzbank	77	17,364.97	2.78
14	Barclays Capital	53	17,334.95	2.78
15	Bear Sterns	43	13,817.49	2.21

Source: International Financial Review, May 15, 1999, p. 11.

forming syndicates, the process of winning a mandate from a customer to bring a new security to the market is an essential step. A potential issuer with financing needs does not go to the phone book and randomly look up investment banks! Reputations, track records, and relationships are critical to investment banking.

Investment banks devote a considerable amount of time and care to developing relationships in the underwriting process. If the relationship is well developed, the investment banker can win the mandate to manage the issuance of equity or debt (bonds). This process is highly competitive and often entails making numerous presentations as to what makes Investment Bank A better than Investment Bank B, not to mention the traditional wining and dining and invitations to corporate skyboxes for sporting events and other modes of entertainment. To win a mandate an investment banker must demonstrate an understanding of the client's strategic and operational plans, be ready to assist with credit rating issues, and contemplate the *aftermarket* (i.e., will the issue need to be supported in the secondary market following issuance, and what type of research will be used to monitor the issuer going forward?). If the mandate is won, the winning investment bank becomes the lead manager of the deal and has the option to form a syndicate to help it issue the new security in the primary market.

Underwriting is also called **primary market making.** This is because the primary market is the first market in which a security trades as opposed to the secondary market, where *aged* or *seasoned* securities are allowed to trade. Aged or seasoned refers to the period of time between issuance and when the bonds or stocks are permitted to trade in the secondary market.

Preparing the Issue

Potential issuers have a menu of options to select from in choosing the right instruments, ranging from equity to debt (with fixed or floating interest rates). In the bond area, they can also choose to issue a global bond (or eurobond), which is issued in New York, London, and Tokyo simultaneously and usually in dollars, a Yankee bond (only issued in the United States and in U.S. dollars), a Samurai bond (issued in Japan and in yen), and so on. The global bond is usually used in the event of a large multibillion-dollar issue and seeks to tap investors in the world's three largest markets (the United States, Europe, and Japan).

Also taken into consideration is the need to register the upcoming issue with the proper authorities, as is the case in the United States with the establishment of a *shelf.* Under Rule 415 of the U.S. Securities Code a corporation is allowed to file a registration for a securities issuance and then take up to two years to sell the securities in the U.S. market. The shelf is this two-year window of opportunity. Registration is done to ensure supervision of the underwriting process and to prevent financial fraud, especially as companies must by law provide a certain level of disclosure about their financial position. Corporate issuers also have the option to sell an entire issue to one or more institutional buyers, such as insurance companies, without registering the issue for public sale. Such an issue is known as a *private placement.* Finally, eurobond issues that are taken to the euromarket need not be registered with any national authority.

Being the lead manager of a deal is the most profitable position in the business. At the same time, the lead manager of a new issue must balance advocacy for the client and objective evaluation. He or she must conduct a thorough investigation of the issuing corporation, examining financial, marketing, and production matters involved in the transaction. This thorough investigation process is referred to as **due diligence.**

In the underwriting process, the investment banker purchases securities from the issuer, as principal, and assumes the risk of distribution to ultimate investors.[7] The distribution syndicate that is formed in the underwriting process helps diversify the risk associated with taking a new issue to market. The number of firms involved depends on the size of the issue. Instead of one institution risking its reputation in the market, that risk is spread among a number of investment banks. There are several distinct groups within the syndicate: the *managers* (who play the major role in leading the issue through the sale), the **bulge bracket** (the largest investment banks in the country and the deal), the *major bracket* (the second tier of investment banks), the **mezzanine bracket,** and the *submajor bracket* (the third tier of investment banks). The *mezzanine bracket* refers to small firms that have special relationships with either the issuer or the lead manager. Considering that a bad execution of a new issue will decidedly be remembered by most investors and make subsequent deals with that issuer much more difficult, great care is taken to achieve good execution.

Commitment or Best Efforts?

A typical underwriting transaction entails either a commitment by an investment bank to purchase a whole issue (called a *firm commitment*) or the investment bank's decision to take the entire deal on a *best efforts* basis, which is selling as much as the market will absorb, but with no guarantees. Almost all underwriting deals are the former, firm commitments by which the underwriters guarantee that they will sell a specified minimum quantity of the issue at the offering price.[8] If the underwriters are unable to sell the guaranteed amount, they must take it on their own books. The critical idea in this process is that the security is already largely sold by the date of issuance, greatly reducing the risk of assuming a large portion of an unwanted issue on the investment bank's books. It should also be noted that the firm commitment is an insurance policy for the issuer and is factored into the terms of compensation.

In contrast to a firm commitment, a best efforts underwriting does not provide any guarantee. Simply stated, the investment bank agrees to do its best to distribute the securities, with the understanding that any unsold securities will be returned to the issuer. A third alternative is the *standby underwriting,* which is used when the issuer offers the securities to existing shareholders through a rights offering and uses the underwriters only as a backup for any securities not taken through the rights offering.[9] A *rights offering* occurs when a company needs additional capital. It has the option to offer new securities to the public (beyond what it has already issued) by first granting what are called subscription rights to existing shareholders in direct proportion to the number of shares they currently own.

The IPO

A company raising capital by selling common stock to the public for the first time is known as an *IPO* (*initial public offering*). The actual process of launching a new issue includes the following:

- A due diligence meeting between the issuers (i.e., the company) and investment bankers in the *cooling-off* period prior to moving to the actual sale. The due diligence meeting is used to review the company and address any last-minute issues. (The cooling-off period is the time before the actual sale of the security. During this time there are certain prohibitions as to what type of information can be given to potential buyers, while investment bankers make the final decision to pursue the sale of the issue based on their due diligence findings as well as indications of investor interest.)

- The pricing of the new issue, based on stock market conditions and estimates of the value of the company.

- Deciding the effective date, which is the first date on which the securities can be sold to the public.

- Delivery of a *final prospectus* (the printed results of the due diligence investigation), required with each sale of a newly issued security.

- Sale of the securities: after the final due diligence meeting, the syndicate sells the securities to the public.

- Dealing with a *sticky issue:* this is when there is considerably less demand than supply and the underwriter has the option of stabilizing the security by bidding for shares in the open market.

- *Customer settlement:* buyers of public offering securities are expected to pay for the securities on the transaction settlement date, which is normally the fifth business day from the public offering date.

- Disbursing proceeds: when the offering is completed, the underwriting manger allocates underwriting profits and commissions. Syndicate members derive their revenues from the underwriting or gross spread, which is the difference between the offering price to the public and the proceeds to the issuer. There are three components of the gross spread: the management fee, the underwriting fee, and the selling concession. The first goes to the managers for their role in preparing the offering. The second is the portion of the gross spread that is intended to cover the many miscellaneous costs associated with the underwriting (excluding those costs that the issuer must bear directly). The last is paid to the firms in the syndicate based on the number of shares they are responsible for selling.

Some of the most active firms in underwriting are Merrill Lynch, Salomon Smith Barney, Nomura, Deutsche Bank, Credit Suisse First Boston, and Morgan Stanley. Although investment banks are the dominant group, commercial banks in the United States are also active, such as J.P. Morgan and Chase Manhattan Bank. (See Table 5.3.)

TABLE 5.3 Leading Issuers of West European Corporate Bonds, as of June 30, 1999

Rank/Bank	Amounts (US$ millions)	No. of Issues
1. Deutsche Bank	8,542	28
2. Morgan Stanley	8,257	37
3. Goldman Sachs	7,229	17
4. Dresdner Kleinwort Benson	6,721	19
5. Lehman Brothers	6,664	11
6. Merrill Lynch	6,460	24
7. Warburg Dillon Read	8,542	29
8. SG	5,158	9
9. J.P. Morgan	5,051	17
10. Credit Suisse First Boston	4,294	20
11. Chase Manhattan	4,160	8
12. Banque Nationale de Paris	4,135	12
13. Barclays Capital	4,004	14
14. Paribas	3,819	16
15. ABN Amro	3,763	14
16. Mediobanca	3,042	5
17. Donaldson, Lukfin & Jenrette	2,694	3
18. Salomon Smith Barney	2,661	12
19. Banco Blibao Vizcaya	2,142	6
20. Commerzbank	1,826	5
Others	14,232	NA
Total	113,396	

Source: Capital Data Bondware as quoted in *Euromoney,* September 1999, p. 105.

Secondary Market Trading

Secondary market making covers dealer activity and brokerage activities, with trading (speculation and arbitrage) playing a significant role. **Arbitrage** is the buying and selling of assets between two or more markets in order to profit from any differences in the prices quoted in these markets. By simultaneously buying in a lower-priced market and selling in a higher-priced market, an arbitrageur can make a profit from any disparity in prices between them.

Secondary market trading (as in the case of the primary market making) requires traders, salespeople, and support from research. There is an ongoing quest to find relative value—that is, the weighing of the value of one asset versus another, usually in the same asset class. If, for example, one bond is cheaper and is equal in creditworthiness than another more expensively priced bond, then good relative value has been discovered.

On the bond side, research identifies the relative value, traders take a position, and the sales force finds buyers. At the end of the day, a sale is made and the investment bank's secondary market desk (hopefully!) makes a reasonable profit from the trade. Internal finance for the traders is also essential, as it provides the necessary funding to put on a trade and hold a position—sometimes at a loss for a period of time before prices rise and profits can be realized.

In secondary market trading in the bond market, the desk is required **to mark its book to market** prices at the close of business each day. This is also called daily settlement, which is done to accurately reflect the value of what the trading desk holds and is part of the process of self-regulation. With mark to market, the traders realize their paper gains and losses in cash on the results of each day's trading. The trader may withdraw the day's gains and must pay the day's losses. Failure to accurately mark to market can result in large losses, especially if market prices move strongly against the desk's position.

Emerging Markets Trading

One of the major areas that has developed is a secondary market for trading the debt of developing countries. Referred to as emerging markets, this arena for trading Argentine, Brazilian, Mexican, and other developing country debt began in the early 1980s following the defaults of a number of Latin American countries and slowly expanded through the 1990s into a multitrillion-dollar market. The trading volume in emerging markets debt rose from around $2 trillion in 1993 to a little under $6 trillion in 1997, before falling to a little under $2 trillion in 1999.[10]

It is important to clarify that what was traded was commercial bank debt at a deep discount. In time, much of this debt was converted into bonds, known as Brady bonds, named after former U.S. Treasury Secretary Nicolas Brady, who was responsible for the creation of these instruments. Countries with Brady bonds are limited to Argentina, Brazil, Bulgaria, Ecuador, Mexico, Nigeria, Panama, Peru, the Philippines, Poland, and Venezuela. As instruments of rescheduled debt, they are an asset class that is limited and will over time disappear. However, the explosion of trading in Brady bonds has opened traders' eyes to the possibilities inherent in financial instruments of emerging market countries—and this will not disappear.

As the emerging markets business has expanded, paralleling a recovery in Latin America and the opening up of Central and Eastern Europe, investment banks have dedicated entire departments to deal with emerging markets, from trading and sales to research and relationship banking to help gain new issue business. While there are tremendous profits to be made in this area, the 1994–95 Mexican tequila crisis, the Asian contagion of 1997–98, and the Russian debt default of 1998 also indicate that there can be large losses as well. One negative development in emerging markets was the partial default of Ecuador on its Brady bond obligations in 1999. This was the first case of a default on Brady bonds and could set the stage for other such defaults.

It is also important to underscore the connections between emerging markets and U.S. markets. Although the political and economic development of countries as diverse as Argentina and Brazil on one hand and Côte d'Ivoire and Indonesia on the other affect emerging markets, the most significant factor is the direction of U.S. markets, in particular, the high-yield market. Taking this one step further, the direction of interest rates set by the U.S. Federal Reserve and the ups and downs of the New York Stock Exchange and the NASDAQ are usually reflected in the price for Argentine, Brazilian, and Russian debt and equities. In this sense, emerging markets are wholly locked into the globalized financial system. All the same, banks must be aware of domestic developments affecting nations in Asia, Eastern and Central Europe, and Latin America.

Advisory Services

Investment banks offer a wide range of advisory services to their customers. These advisory services, according to one source, "include any activity in which an investment bank provides advice, recommendations, or opinions in exchange for a fee."[11] Consequently, investment banks offer a wide range of advice, with regard to the restructuring of a clients' balance sheet for asset/liability management purposes; taking public companies private and taking private companies public; or assisting in bankruptcy workouts. The bottom line on advisory services: Advice that used to be given away freely or attached to a particular underwriting deal is now unbundled as a separate revenue activity.

Within the realm of advisory services *corporate restructuring* is a relationship-based activity pursued by investment banks and, if successful, can be highly lucrative. The investment bank is used to help expand or shrink the corporation depending on industry conditions. Expansion comes with mergers, consolidations, acquisitions, and most activities related to the enlargement of a firm or redefinition of the scope of its operations. Investment bankers work with firms to help them with *horizontal mergers,* between two firms in similar businesses; *vertical mergers,* between two firms involved in different stages of production for the same product; and *conglomerate mergers,* between two firms in largely unrelated business streams.

Takeovers and Leveraged Buyouts

One of the best-known areas of corporate restructuring, especially after a wave of such activity in the 1980s, is that of *takeovers*. There are different kinds of takeovers. The *friendly takeover* is a process by which the acquiring company will make a financial proposal to the target enterprise's management and board of directors, which entails a merger or consolidation of activities as well as allowing the management of the target firm to retain their positions after the deal is done.

A *hostile takeover* occurs when the target firm has clearly indicated that it does not want to be acquired and the acquiring firm decides to proceed despite this opposition. The target firm, also armed with its own set of investment bank advisors, might opt to create a *poison pill defense* to deter the raider. The basic idea in a poison pill defense is to make the hostile takeover so costly to the enemy corporate raider that any victory would be beyond the value of the company. The role of the investment banker in this process is to provide advice on either how to launch a hostile takeover or how to create a poison pill. Frequently, investment banks are found on both sides of such a struggle. One calculated risk for an investment bank is that if the hostile takeover fails, it most likely will never do business with either the acquiring firm or the target again.

One of the areas of corporate restructuring that has gained considerable attention is that of the leveraged buyout (LBO). Simply stated, an LBO is an investment technique in which the assets of the company are hocked in order to buy it, much like real estate deals in which second and third mortgages are used. As one observer noted: "The LBO firms would buy companies in partnership with their management. By being made equity partners, those managers were given incentives to trim costs and augment efficiencies."[12] In the 1980s there was a massive wave of mergers, acquisitions, spin-offs, proxy battles, and buyouts that helped reshape U.S. industry and, after considerable upheaval, made it more competitive in global markets. Investment banks, like Drexel Burnham Lambert, were active in developing the initial techniques for LBOs and have continued to play a role in such activities. (Not Drexel, though; it collapsed in the late 1980s. This story highlights the risks inherent in investment banking.)

While corporate restructuring through the use of LBOs is a lucrative area of business for investment banks that possess the expertise to make use of junk bonds, bridge financing, and venture capital, it has become a political issue as well. The displacement of large numbers of workers caused by the breaking up of companies, seemingly at the whim of Wall Street fat cats lacking any moral compass, provides many politicians an easy target.

Financial Engineering and Derivatives

Investment banks offer other services beyond underwriting, secondary market trading, and advisory services. These activities are supplemented by foreign currency trading, **bridge financing** (lending for a short duration to cover a financial gap until other means of financing are available, such as a bond issue), *financial engineering,* project financing, leasing, investment management, and merchant banking. Financial engineering is among the best known of these activities and will be explained here. (Foreign currency trading and project financing are explained in Chapters 4 and 8.) We define financial engineering as the application of **derivatives** to manage risk, which entails the packaging and sale of zero-coupon securities, mortgage-backed securities, other asset-backed securities and derivatives. Also in this category are collateralized mortgage obligations (CMOs), collateralized bond obligations (CBOs), and collateralized loan obligations (CLOs). CMOs, CBOs, and CLOs all are securities backed by other securities. For example, a CBO is a debt security backed by a pool of investment-grade or high-yield bonds, and a CMO is a bond secured by a portfolio of mortgages and offering a fixed redemption date.

While there has been considerable hype over financial engineering, derivatives in particular, the simple truth is that these instruments offer high reward, but often with high risk. What exactly is a derivative instrument? According to Robert W. Kolb, a derivative "is a financial instrument based upon another more elementary financial instrument. The value of the financial derivative depends upon, or derives from, the more basic instrument. Usually, the base instrument is a cash market financial instrument, such as a bond or a share of stock."[13] In a number of investment banks, derivative instrument groups make markets in such things as interest rate swaps and interest rate caps and floors.

The derivatives industry clearly is big business. As one source noted: "Derivatives have become the largest market in the world. The size of the derivatives market, estimated at $55 trillion in 1996, is double the value of all U.S. stocks and more than ten times the entire U.S. national debt."[14] (See Table 5.4.)

Derivatives are not for the financially unsophisticated. In theory, they allow users to buy or sell credit risk. Two views exist about the value of derivatives. One view is that they contribute to the concentration of risk, as the main clients will be institutional investors, insurance companies, and big banks. A second view is that derivatives will eventually diversify risk, which has traditionally been concentrated, because retail banks that mainly lend to their neighborhood will have an opportunity to hedge that risk through new instruments. Whatever one's view, derivatives remain high risk for those unequipped to handle such instruments. Certainly the case of Orange County, California, in 1994 exemplifies a situation in which the wrong person bought the wrong product, resulting in the bankruptcy of the Orange County municipal government as well as a plethora of lawsuits against the investment banks involved.

While Orange County represents one case of problems with derivatives, other cases exist. These include Bankers Trust transactions with Gibson Greetings and Procter and Gamble, and Barings Brothers. The last case was the most dramatic, as it resulted in the demise of a venerable investment bank due to the trading activities

TABLE 5.4 Markets for Selected Derivative Financial Instruments: Notional Principal Amounts Outstanding[1] (US$ billions)

	North America	Europe	Asia-Pacific	Other	Total
1986	518.1	13.1	87.0	0.0	$618.2
1990	1,268.5	461.2	560.5	0.2	$2,290.4
1991	2,151.7	710.1	657.0	0.5	$3,519.3
1992	2,694.7	1,114.3	823.5	1.8	$4,634.3
1993	4,358.6	1,777.9	1,606.0	28.7	$7,771.2
1994	4,819.5	1,831.7	2,171.8	39.5	$8,862.5
1995	4,849.6	2,241.6	1,990.1	106.8	$9,188.1
1996	4,839.7	2,831.7	2,154.0	59.3	$9,884.7

Source: IMF, International Capital Markets, November 1997.

[1]Selected derivative instruments include interest rate futures, both short-term and long-term instruments; interest rate options; currency futures; currency options; stock market index futures; and stock market index options.

ORANGE COUNTY'S DERIVATIVES PROBLEM
Paul Stiles

On the surface Orange County looks like this: the Orange County Investment Pool (OCIP) was a $7.4 billion fund in which 187 different municipal bodies—school systems, cities, public agencies, pension funds— invested. The fund was run by the county treasurer, Robert L. Citron, a man highly regarded by his superiors for his consistently high returns; his average of 9.4 percent was a full percentage point higher than the California State fund. Citron's investment strategy included two important elements: leverage (using borrowed money to boost returns) and interest rate risk. Citron leveraged his fund primarily through the use of reverse repurchase agreements, known as "reverse repo." This entailed lending securities from OCIP as collateral for loans, using the loans to buy more securities, and then lending out these securities as well. By repeating this process Citron leveraged his fund to approximately $20 billion, almost three times its size—an extraordinary amount for a municipal fund—greatly enhancing both his potential returns and his downside risk. Citron also bet heavily on interest rates— specifically, that they would stay flat or decrease—always a risky strategy. He did so using a complex derivative called an inverse floater, which responds inversely to changing rates: when rates go up, the instrument pays less. Both of these strategies, involving billions of dollars in securities, were mainly pursued through a single broker, Merrill Lynch.

Citron's troubles began in February [1995], when the Fed began hiking rates, reducing revenues from his inverse floater positions. By the summer OCIP was down 7 percent and in need of cash. To raise money Orange County issued a $600 million taxable note through Merrill. Citron used this money to continue the fund's investment strategy and buy more securities, primarily from Merrill. As rates continued to rise, the fund continued to get hammered. In October, available cash reserves dropped by half, sounding a loud warning chime. It wasn't until December, however, that Orange County was able to price the complex portfolio, revealing a massive $1.5 billion loss (the final tally was $1.7 billion, 23 percent of the fund). Shortly thereafter the county defaulted on its first loans.

Source: Riding the Bull: My Year in the Madness at Merrill Lynch (New York: Random House, 1998), pp. 246–247.

of one trader, Nicholas Lesson, based in Singapore. Simply stated, Lesson made the wrong bet in a trade and lost his firm around $1 billion, which wiped out the net worth of Barings Brothers, forcing the bank to declare bankruptcy. It was ultimately bought by ING, the Dutch investment bank, for one dollar.[15]

Despite the issue of risk, the derivative market is not expected to disappear any time soon. Derivatives have increasingly become a low-margin, high-volume business as the various instruments have become familiar to market participants. In a sense, the well-publicized problems related to Orange County, Procter and Gamble, and Barings have alerted potential investors that derivatives offer risk, though that risk can be properly managed. Moreover, the derivative product has become more standardized, a little more plain vanilla than it was before Orange County and Barings. Another important factor in the maturing of the derivative market is its globalization. There has been a steady increase in derivatives in the United States as well as in Europe and Asia through the 1990s, a trend expected to continue in the 2000s. Moreover, the major U.S. derivative exchanges, the Chicago Mercantile Exchange and the Chicago Board of Trade, have established links with foreign exchanges, such as the Marche à Terme International de France (MATIF), London International Financial Futures Exchange (LIFFE), and Deutsche Terminborse (DTB).[16]

Other Investment Banking Services

Investment management is the investment of other people's funds. In this, investment bankers function as managers for a wide variety of investment vehicles, including real estate partnerships, venture capital pools, money market funds, and mutual funds. For example, with asset fund managers, the fundamental objective is to provide superior returns by utilizing the best relative value global credit strategies in an interest rate neutral framework. Investment banks also structure and manage many specialty investment vehicles issued through trusts. Since the mid-1980s, the funds management business has exploded due to the large-scale shifts in households' saving behavior and deregulation of financial industries. Simply stated, households have made a shift from maintaining their savings in the bank (at low interest rates) to investing in the stock market or in other investment-oriented instruments that beat the savings interest rates. The deregulation of financial markets has opened the door to a universe of new products, which have proved exceedingly attractive. In 1985, the ten largest institutional investors in the United States managed assets worth $969 billion; in 1995, that number had risen to $2.4 trillion.[17] Consequently, investment management has become a highly competitive business, with companies such as Fidelity Investments going head-to-head with banks such as Barclays for market share.

It is often difficult for an investment bank to become involved in investment management, and not all such institutions participate in this line of business. In particular, it is expensive to establish an investment management business due to the costs associated with acquiring the right personnel, and there is a distinct danger of losing money. Losses in investment management do not project the correct image of an investment bank that is capable of making money, which can damage the more traditional role of raising capital. Consequently, considerable care is given to having a disciplined relative value trading approach, with diversification among credit names, industry sectors, geography, and asset classes. There is also attention given to having tight controls on concentration, leverage, and credit ratings (especially in the bond business).

Merchant banking is the direct investment of the bank's own money in a particular asset not directly related to the investment bank's traditional business. This can mean that the investment bank provides what is called **venture capital** for a start-up company (or a venture) it believes will be highly successful, but is in need of capital and has little or no track record. High-tech companies, especially those involved in the Internet during the late 1990s, represented a major area of such activity. The company, in turn, provides equity shares, which over time will be either sold back to the company or sold on the market, both at a profit for the investment bank. Merchant banking expanded as an activity during the 1980s and continued through the 1990s as a lucrative, though risky, area of business. An added incentive for investment banks' involvement in merchant banking is that the provision of venture capital at a critical juncture in a company's life can help cement a relationship that will ultimately lead to additional demand for more traditional investment banking services. It should also be clarified that merchant banking activities are not limited to providing venture capital for start-up companies, but can also include addressing capital needs that may arise during a corporate restructuring.

Support Systems

While revenue-generating activities are the raison d'être of investment banks, these activities do not exist in a void. One last point needs to be mentioned in providing a proper definition of investment banking: the role of supporting industries. Behind the façade of a few financial hot shots making the big deals is a substantial infrastructure of human capital. For the types of multimillion-dollar bond and equities issues (as well as the increased volume) that came in the 1990s, investment bankers needed a lot of help from strong supporting casts. As Samuel L. Hayes III and Philip M. Hubbard noted: "But behind the news clips and the mega deals is an army of accountants, lawyers, filing clerks, stock custodians, specialized printers, and record-keeping and computer experts without which there would be no story and no deal."[18]

Although investment banks have not always relished having to hire and depend on supporting industries, there is a grudging recognition that a failure to have an adequate human skills infrastructure can limit business development. Hayes and Hubbard point to the massive upsurge in business that occurred on Wall Street in the 1960s: "Stock trading was so fast and furious that the back offices of leading securities firms were literally buried in paperwork. The NYSE, in desperation, closed each Wednesday in an effort to unclog the logjam of record-keeping, broken trades and handling of certificates."[19] Closure of the market, of course, meant that an entire day's worth of buying and selling was lost. As the investment banking business became more globalized and the volume of new issues rose dramatically in the 1990s, success for those banks involved was often defined by the quality of supporting services.

The Players

The major players in international investment banking are from the United States, Europe, and Japan and are led by large integrated global financial institutions that emerged during the 1990s—Citigroup, Inc., Merrill Lynch, Morgan Stanley Dean

BAYERISCHE LANDESBANK PRODUCT OVERVIEW

Investment Banking

- Money investment in securities, leaseholds and participations under risk spreading aspects, as well as supervisory activities as trustees.
- Purchase of investment fund certificates.

Portfolio Management

- Portfolio management
- Asset management

Securities Business

- Securities trading
- Issuing business
- Research and investment advisory service
- Safe Custody service
- Interest rate and currency derivatives
- Securities derivatives

Money Market and Foreign Exchange Trading

- MM lending/borrowings
- Spot trading
- Forward dealings

Source: www.blb.de/english/investmentbanking/309.htm, 2000.

Witter, Goldman Sachs, Deutsche Bank, Union Bank of Switzerland (UBS), Credit Suisse, and a few others. As Erik Banks noted: "These institutions had the ability to offer specialist corporate finance services (including M&A and advisory), issue debt, equity and hybrid securities, produce research in support of new issues, trade securities on a secondary basis and structure complex financial risk management solutions via derivatives. This broad range of services fueled incremental advisory and new issue mandates, which repeated itself."[20] In other words, each of these investment banks had achieved a critical mass that provided them with a vast range of products (traditional as well as new), a depth of talent and experience, and a global reach, all of which are difficult to replicate under one roof by many other banks. British merchant banks as a group were unable to compete with this type of global competitor and, with a few exceptions, one by one have been purchased by larger U.S. or other European banks.

What helped elevate a small group of firms into the "super global" elite of investment banks was the ability to effectively establish operations in U.S.

financial markets in the 1980s and 1990s. The size and scope of U.S. markets meant that foreign institutions lacking a meaningful presence in the United States were effectively unable to provide their clients with the full range of products and services demanded. As Banks noted: "By the 1990s the capitalization of the U.S. equity markets was greater than the combined capitalization of Japanese, German and British markets, while the U.S. corporate bond market accounted for two thirds of total global corporate bonds outstanding."[21]

To deal with the wide range of international investment banking business, firms such as Goldman Sachs, Lehman Brothers, and Credit Suisse First Boston have established global networks of salespeople, traders, research analysts, bankers, and back-office people necessary to run sophisticated computer systems. This has also meant that to seriously play in the game of international investment banking, firms must set up offices in such locations as New York, London, Paris, Tokyo, Hong Kong, and Singapore, and possibly Mexico City, Buenos Aires, São Paolo, or Mumbai (Bombay). (See Table 5.5.)

While investment banks constitute one group of players, another key player is the investor. Investors come in all shapes and sizes, but the real money comes with the large institutional investors, such as insurance companies, a large array of European and U.S. mutual funds, and corporations with excess cash. Although some investors are willing to assume risk (as in high-yield markets and emerging markets), most institutional and individual investors are risk adverse and prefer securities with solid investment-grade ratings.

While much of this chapter has centered on Wall Street, we emphasize that, like commercial banking, investment banking is a twenty-four-hour-a-day business and is conducted around the world. Investment banking operations actively hub out of Tokyo, Hong Kong, Singapore, Mumbai, São Paolo, Milan, Paris, Frankfurt, Amsterdam, London, and New York. U.S. firms are clearly major players, but hardly the only players. Investment banking has certainly become more international in recent years, in large part because of the liberalization of capital markets, first in Europe and lately in Asia. The United Kingdom's "Big Bang," which was launched by the Financial Securities Act of 1986, created an institutional framework for securities market regulation and brought substantial changes to the London stock market. As Roy C. Smith and Ingo Walter noted: "In consequence, trading volume in the United Kingdom more than doubled; many of the British brokers and dealers merged into other, stronger groups; competition increased greatly; and large integrated securities firms, such as S.G. Warburg, Merrill Lynch, and Goldman Sachs, increased their market share."[22]

London's Big Bang was followed by similar moves throughout Europe, in particular, in France, Germany, Italy, and Switzerland. The push to a single European market in 1992 and the creation of a single European currency in 1999 added greater pressure for European stock markets to upgrade their technology, improve the interconnections among their markets, and streamline their operating procedures. All of this helped stimulate higher levels of capital market activities, which benefited the business operations of investment banks. Outside of Europe, capital market liberalization measures have been introduced in Australia, Canada, New Zealand, and, in the late 1990s and early 2000s, in Japan and Korea.

TABLE 5.5 Largest Securities Houses in the United States

Rank/Firm	January 1, 1998 Capital (US$ thousands)
1. Merrill Lynch & Co.	$51,419,000
2. Morgan Stanley Dean Witter & Co.	39,747,000
3. Salomon Smith Barney Holdings Inc.	27,592,000
4. Lehman Brothers Holdings Inc.	24,784,000
5. Goldman Sachs Group L.P.	21,774,000
6. Bear Sterns Companies Inc.	14,789,047
7. Paine Webber Group Inc.	5,911,342
8. Donaldson, Lufkin & Jenrette	4,513,347
9. Credit Suisse First Boston	3,736,126
10. BT Alex. Brown Inc.	2,360,000
11. UBS Securities LLC	2,161,700
12. NationsBanc Montgomery Securities LLC	1,838,530
13. Chase Securities Inc.	1,778,868
14. Prudential Securities Inc.	1,660,098
15. Charles Schwab Corp.	1,506,166
16. J.P. Morgan Securities	1,453,942
17. A.G. Edwards Inc.	1,414,148
18. SBC Warburg Dillon Read Inc.	1,412,211
19. D.E. Shaw & Co.	1,384,779
20. Deutsche Bank Securities Inc.	1,370,709
21. CIBC Oppenheimer Corp.	1,331,873
22. Nomura Securities International Inc.	1,094,881
23. Bank of Tokyo-Mitsubishi Trust Co.	1,067,533
24. Daiwa Securities America Inc.	945,522
25. Societe Generale Securities Corp.	888,278

Source: The Wall Street Journal Almanac 1999, (New York: Ballantine Books, 1999), p. 162.

Major Trends in Investment Banking

The major trends in investment banking at the end of the twentieth century are the ongoing globalization of the financial marketplace; a larger amount of money going into international markets, partly from the growth of pension funds in the United States, Canada, Europe, and Japan; the reemergence of commercial banks in investment banking; and an increasing emphasis on financial innovation pushed by technology. These trends also point toward greater consolidation in the industry, a process well advanced as reflected by the formation of Citigroup, which was formed from Citibank, Travelers Insurance, and Salomon Smith Barney. It is also seen in acquisitions by European banks of U.S. institutions in the late 1990s and early 2000s, as in

DRESDNER, WASSERSTEIN TALK

Germany's Dresdner Bank is in talks to acquire New York investment bank Wasserstein Perella & Co., sources close to the situation told CNNfn.com Tuesday.

Negotiations between the two firms are advanced and a deal could be announced by the end of the week, the sources said. However, the acquisition could still fall apart.

Wasserstein Perella & Co. declined to comment. Dresdner also declined to comment.

Dresdner is interested in the New York–based Wasserstein's merger and acquisition, high yield and equity practice, a source said. The bank's purchase of Wasserstein could cost between $1.2 billion and $1.5 billion, the *Wall Street Journal* reported Tuesday.

A Dresdner-Wasserstein merger comes on the heels of Credit Suisse First Boston's agreement to buy Donaldson, Lufkin & Jenrette for $11.5 billion on Aug. 30. Swiss Bank UBS also agreed on July 12 to purchase securities firm Paine Webber for about $12 billion.

Speculation that J.P. Morgan is also up for sale has caused the firm's shares to soar. J.P. Morgan shares rose $2.56 to $171.88 in afternoon trading Tuesday.

An M&A Boutique

The privately held Wasserstein was founded by Bruce Wasserstein and Joseph Perella in 1988. Perella quit the firm in 1993 to head Morgan Stanley Dean Witter's global investment banking business. Wasserstein currently has about 600 employees with offices including London, Paris, and Frankfurt, Germany.

Wasserstein is strong in investment banking and ranks fifth in the U.S. as an adviser on mergers and acquisitions. Wasserstein advised Axa Financial in the $11.5 billion sale of Donaldson, Lufkin & Jenrette to Credit Suisse First Boston. Wasserstein also helped Philip Morris in its $14.9 billion acquisition of Nabisco Holdings Corp. and advised Time Warner in its $128 billion merger with America Online. Time Warner is parent of CNN.fn.com.

The acquisition would strengthen the standing of Dresdner's investment banking unit, Dresdner Kleinwort Benson, a practice that now ranks 14th in the M&A area in the United States and seventh in Europe.

Dresdner Kleinwort Benson has about 8,000 people worldwide in its bond, stock and corporate finance businesses, with about 1,000 based in the United States. While Dresdner Kleinwort is a top M&A adviser in the United Kingdom, the investment bank has failed to make a dent in the competitive U.S. market.

European-based investment banks have had a tough time making inroads in the coveted mergers and acquisitions market, said analyst Evagelos Kavouriadis, of Sanford Bernstein. Morgan Stanley Dean Witter, Goldman Sachs, Salomon Smith Barney, UBS and Credit Suisse First Boston

(continued)

comprise the top five investment banks in the global M&A market. Dresdner is ranked seventh, Kavouriadis said.

"The deal will help Dresdner immensely in the U.S. because Wasserstein is strong in the U.S. and Dresdner is not," said Kavouriadis.

Dresdner is expected to pay about $1.2 billion to $1.5 billion for Wasserstein, which is too high Kavouriadis said.

Dresdner may also have problems retaining top executives if the deal does go through.

"Dresdner would have to let Wasserstein run the group from the U.S. if they wanted to make it grow," Kavouriadis said.

However, Dresdner does not have the best luck with acquisitions, failing in April to purchase Deutsche Bank. In May, Dresdner Bank chairman Bernd Fahrholz said the firm would be looking to expand in key sectors globally, especially in the United States and Japan. Dresdner is also looking to expand its local presence in the European target markets of France, Italy, Spain and Scandinavia.

"They are now trying to recoup," Kavouriadis said. "Dresdner is trying to regain momentum."

CNN Financial, September 12, 2000, at http://cnnfn.cnn.com/2000/09/12/deals/dresdner.

---

the cases of Credit Suisse First Boston buying Donaldson, Lufkin & Jenrette, UBS's purchase of Paine Webber, and Dresdner Bank's buying of Wasserstein Perella & Co.

At the same time, investment banking faces some difficult challenges. Investment banks once made considerable profits as intermediaries, matching buyers with sellers and charging a fee for that service. With the advent of computers and global information networks, the intermediary role has declined and is likely to decrease further. Large investors are actively seeking to improve their information networks and bypass, where possible, investment bank commissions. A growing number of exchanges, such as the Arizona Stock Exchange and the United Kingdom's Tradepoint, actually allow fund managers the option of trading securities directly with each other. All of this has meant that investors, such as fund managers, are demanding more from investment banks for less money. In turn, these trends have put profit margins under pressure. An additional factor vis-à-vis shrinking profit margins is that many commercial banks have been willing to try their hands at investment banking. From the standpoint of commercial banks, the top-tier borrowers are a declining pool and investment banking allows a profitable use of capital. The waves of new competition from commercial banks have caused greater personnel costs for investment banks, in particular for good traders and research analysts.

Investment banks have been forced into making difficult decisions about resource allocation. In some cases, the more-profitable side of the business has helped subsidize some of the less-profitable business streams. This is done to maintain the full range of investment bank services that customers may demand, especially as customer needs change over time.

Another trend in investment banking is the development of the European securities markets due to the shift to a single European currency, the euro. The eleven countries that have adopted the euro represent a new horizon for business development in a number of areas. First and foremost, the euro is likely to allow a deepening of the financial markets, helped along by the convergence of tax and regulatory controls. Hand in hand with this has come deregulation of pension, investment, and savings restrictions. All of this provides fertile opportunities for European and other investment banks willing and capable of offering asset management. The aging population within Europe is also growing, providing asset management new outlets from the standpoint of pension funds. Additionally, the single currency unit and corporate reforms in a number of countries are pushing the development of a European high-yield market.

Investment banks confront difficult decisions in the early 2000s. As they have subsidized unprofitable businesses with the profits of healthier ones to maintain their wide range of services, tough decisions will have to be made in trimming these areas to contain costs and in offering specialized services. One way investment banks have responded to shrinking profit margins has been to take greater risks. While this has resulted in bigger profits, it is a course of action fraught with risks. There have several well-publicized disasters. Barings lost $1.40 billion and its survival as an institution in bad derivatives trading in 1995, Daiwa lost $1.1 billion in bond trading in the same year, and Chase Manhattan lost $0.16 billion in bond trading in 1997. Consequently, investment banks face substantial trade-offs between achieving profitability, achieving the correct level of risk, and staving off competition from commercial banks. Consolidation will provide a group of bigger players with deeper pockets, but they will still find the environment highly competitive and constantly changing.

Questions

1. What are the three core functions of investment banking? How does investment banking differ from commercial banking?
2. What is underwriting? Describe the underwriting process. Who assumes the risk?
3. What is a private placement?
4. What role does a syndicate play in the underwriting process?
5. What is primary market activity? What does secondary market activity entail?
6. Investment fund management has become big business in the 1990s. What trends are driving the expansion of this business?
7. What are the major trends in investment banking in the early 2000s? What are some of the major challenges facing investment banking?
8. What are the three organizational structures for investment banking?
9. What attributes does an investment bank need in order to be successful? Who do you think will dominate the industry in the next decade?
10. What do you predict will be the future of mergers between investment banks and commercial banks? Will the two blend easily?

Notes

1. C. Pass, B. Lowes, L. Davies, and S. J. Kronish, *The Harper Collins Dictionary of Economics* (New York: Harper Perennial, 1991), p. 273.
2. John E. Marshall and M. E. Ellis, *Investment Banking and Brokerage: The New Rules of the Game* (New York: McGraw Hill, 1993), p. 6.
3. *Ibid.*, p. 27.
4. Linda J. Montag, Tobias Grun, and Samuel S. Theodore, *Deutsche Bank AG, Moody's Investors Service Report,* December 1999, p. 3.
5. Hazel J. Johnson, *The Banker's Guide to Investment Banking: Securities and Underwriting Activities in Commercial Banking* (Chicago: Irwin Publishers, 1996), p. 2.
6. Thomas Fitch, *Dictionary of Banking Terms* (New York: Barron's Educational Series, 1997), p. 98.
7. Hazel J. Johnson, *The Banker's Guide to Investment Banking,* p. 2.
8. John E. Marshall and M. E. Ellis, *Investment Banking and Brokerage,* p. 67.
9. *Ibid.*
10. Jonathan Fuerbringer, "The Wounds Haven't Healed in Emerging Markets Debt," *New York Times,* November 28, 1999, p. A7.
11. John E. Marshall and M. E. Ellis, *Investment Banking and Brokerage,* p. 267.
12. Connie Bruck, *The Predators' Ball: The Insider Story of Drexel Burnham and the Rise of the Junk Bond Raiders* (New York: Penguin Books, 1989), p. 99.
13. Robert W. Kolb, *Financial Derivatives* (Malden, Mass.: Blackwell Publishers, 1997), p. 1.
14. Frank Partnoy, *F.I.A.S.C.O.: Blood in the Water on Wall Street* (New York: W. W. Norton & Company, 1997), p. 15.
15. As Kolb noted of the Barings affair: "Nicolas Leeson, a trader for Barings Bank stationed in Singapore, was supposed to be conducting index arbitrage between Japanese stocks and future contracts on the Japanese index. Such trading involves taking equal and offsetting positions in stocks and futures, which were traded in both Japan and Singapore. Although the details remain somewhat unclear, it seems apparent that Leeson did exactly the opposite in late 1994 and early 1995. Through the futures markets, Leeson made very large one-sided bets that Japanese stocks would rise. The Kobe earthquake, however, rocked the entire Japanese economy and led to a dramatic drop in the Japanese stock market. The highly leveraged bets on a rising Japanese stock market turned out to be giant losers. In a short period, Leeson's trades lost about $1 billion. These losses completely exhausted the net worth of Barings, which declared bankruptcy and was acquired by a Dutch investment bank." Robert W. Kolb, *Financial Derivatives,* p. 246.
16. International Monetary Fund, *International Capital Markets: Developments, Prospects, and Key Policy Issues* (Washington, D.C.: International Monetary Fund, November 1997), p. 123.
17. *Ibid.*, p. 120.
18. Samuel L. Hayes III and Philip M. Hubbard, *Investment Banking: A Tale of Three Cities* (Boston: Harvard Business School Press, 1990), p. 324.
19. *Ibid.*
20. Erik Banks, *The Rise and Fall of the Merchant Banks* (London: Kogan Page Ltd., 1999), p. 477.
21. *Ibid.*, p. 470.
22. Roy C. Smith and Ingo Walter, *Global Banking* (New York: Oxford University Press, 1997), p. 303.

CHAPTER 6

INTERNATIONAL RETAIL AND PRIVATE BANKING

Serving the banking needs of individuals, wealthy or poor, has traditionally not been one of the "sexier" areas of international banking. Aspiring bankers in training programs seldom clamor to go into branch banking rather than the high-gloss fields of mergers and acquisitions or foreign exchange trading. Senior bankers, nonetheless, have become increasingly interested in retail and private banking services over the past decade. These areas offer the allure of a stable client base, less volatility in earnings, and lower capital requirements than other areas such as investment banking. They satisfy two needs: the urge to increase fee-based income rather than lending-based income, and the need to offset the competitive decline in traditional corporate lending services. (Since the Basel agreement of 1988, banks have been under pressure to maintain higher levels of capital to support their lending operations. These capital adequacy requirements have increased the attractiveness of nonlending business.) Accordingly, many banks have made the strategic decision to focus their international expansion efforts on two areas offering stable, fee-based income: private banking and retail banking.

International Retail Banking

While international private banking has evolved from the stodgy stereotype of wealth conservation into one of the most exciting areas of modern banking, the retail side of the business in some ways remains the neglected stepchild. Retail banking, or the provision of banking services to individual customers, has never had the glamour and allure of corporate or investment banking. Moreover, barriers to internationalization have made this area in some ways a backwater as other banking services have expanded and globalized.

What exactly is retail banking? A subset of commercial banking, retail banking refers to the provision of banking services for individuals. This includes deposit taking; consumer lending for home, car, and other purchases; credit card services; transaction services; and even insurance and investment management services for individual clients. It is a high-volume business, long valued for its ability to gather cheap deposits and generate high-margin loans. However, branch banking has been one of the last areas within banking to globalize. In the 1990s, though, some banks developed international ambitions for their retail banking business. Especially within

BUILDING CONSUMER BANKING INTERNATIONALLY

C onsumer banking is the least developed direction in the international expansion of most banks. The main reason for this lies in the high barriers to entry into this business. Economies of scale present key organizational and technological barriers. In consumer banking, acceptable economies come from having tens of thousands (and millions in mass retail), rather than hundreds of clients. It is expensive to accumulate these numbers and build proper distribution networks to serve them. An acquisition may seem to provide a shortcut, but it often comes with a price tag brought on by the costs of integration, including the costs of adjusting brand image and performance. In addition, there are soft barriers to entry. A "foreign" image does not automatically translate into a high quality image in fresh markets.

Moreover, foreign banks, more than domestic ones, are under suspicion of being "here today, gone tomorrow" operations. Finally, the environment for consumer banking is often largely unknown outside the domestic banking system and, partially as a result of this, is considered high-risk in credit terms....

Source: Peter L. Bernstein "The New Religion of Risk Management" *Harvard Business Review* (March/April 1996), p. 47.

Latin America, banks are beginning to regionalize their retail banking operations. Mexican and Chilean banks have bought some Argentine rivals, while others are moving in on their own. Banco Itau, a technologically sophisticated Brazilian bank, is moving into the Argentine market as well. Infisa, a Chilean-based financial services group, plans a $750 million investment project to set up Latin America's first regional retail bank. Retail banking remains tremendously important for most international banks because of its ability to generate relatively cheap funds through retail deposits. This has motivated many European mergers and acquisitions over the past decade.

Nonetheless, the globalization of retail banking may prove a difficult process. While banks have aggressively globalized their wholesale operations, banking for individual customers has stubbornly remained a largely local business. The barriers to internationalization are substantial. One problem is product differentiation: Unlike in corporate and investment banking, retail banking products, customs, and regulations differ greatly from country to country. New entrants often face an uphill battle against established local players with large branch networks. Thus there are still no powerful regional players in the European Union, despite the flourishing single market in goods and services. Local branding remains critical in retail banking, while local habits and product preferences are sizable barriers to globalization. Local regulations, too, inhibit multinational providers of financial services from aggressively entering new markets. The process of obtaining a mortgage, for example, differs widely across the European Union, creating vastly different sets of customer needs and preferences in this key area.

Testifying to the difficulty of international expansion in retail banking, several banks have tried and failed in this process since the 1980s. The major exception to this trend is Citigroup, which has succeeded in creating a global brand name in consumer banking. The strategy of building global recognition of its "Citi" brand name has made it the first truly global consumer bank. In South Korea, for instance (where most foreign banks focus on the wholesale sector), Citibank has a strong presence in retail banking with more than 200,000 individual clients. Citigroup's income data reflect the importance of global consumer banking to its bottom line. (As Table 6.1 indicates, in 1997 global consumer banking accounted for just about half of Citibank's total revenue.) Even Citigroup, though, faces some hurdles. Its appeal overseas is largely limited to sophisticated customers with an international

TABLE 6.1 Citibank: Business and Geographic Distribution of Revenue

Total Revenue ($ millions)[1]

	1997	1996[2]	1995[2]
Business Distribution			
Global Consumer			
Citibanking	$6,030	$5,796	$5,441
Cards	5,190	5,274	5,066
Private Bank	1,130	1,043	929
Global Corporate Banking			
Emerging Markets	3,888	3,444	2,895
Global Relationship Banking	4,384	3,744	3,627
Corporate Items	994	895	720
Total	**$21,616**	**$20,196**	**18,678**
Geographic Distribution			
United States	9,802	9,344	8,843
Western Europe	3,323	3,365	3,352
Other[3]	719	586	564
Total Developed Markets	13,844	13,295	12,759
Latin America [4]	3,314	2,743	2,493
Asia-Pacific	3,475	3,286	2,738
Other[5]	983	872	688
Total Emerging Markets	7,772	6,901	5,919
Total	**$21,616**	**$20,196**	**$18,678**

Source: Citibank Financial Report 1997.
[1] Indicates net interest revenue and fees, commissions, and other revenue.
[2] Reclassified to conform to the 1997 presentation.
[3] Includes Japan and Canada.
[4] Includes Mexico, the Caribbean, and Central and South America.
[5] Includes Central and Eastern Europe, Middle East, and Africa.

perspective, and its penetration is significant only in countries where local bank service is relatively poor. In industrialized countries such as the United Kingdom, even Citi has had little success competing head-on with domestic financial institutions, and it has largely limited its ambitions to export finance.[1] (See Figures 6.1 and 6.2 for Citibank locations worldwide.)

International Branchless Banking?

In this environment, the hopes of bankers interested in expanding their retail operations internationally are pinned on a few specific areas. One is the proliferation of online, or "direct," banks. Currently, bankers lose money on eight out of ten retail customers; 10 percent of retail customers generate 60 to 70 percent of the profits in this area. Internet banking may help to solve these problems, by offering economies of scale and low transaction costs, as well as access to a well-heeled target market. In fact, the cost of an average transaction with a bank teller is just over $1.00, compared with three or four cents for an Internet transaction. Moreover, Internet-savvy customers tend to be high-balance types, the customers that bankers most want to attract.[2]

Thus the proliferation of "direct" (online) banks and brokerages across Europe is not surprising. Internet-only banks are springing up, while traditional banks, too, are sensing the advantages and launching themselves into cyberspace. Branch networks are increasingly expensive white elephants, while direct banks can be housed in cheap real estate well away from the financial centers and staffed by cheaper

FIGURE 6.1 Location of Citibank Branches Around the World*

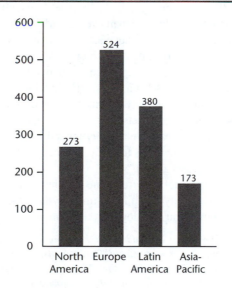

*Number of offices.
Source: www.citigroup.com.

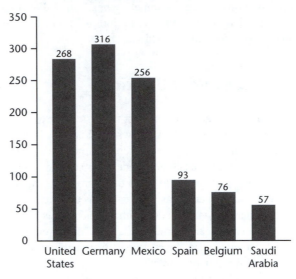

FIGURE 6.2 Number of Citibank Branches per Country

Source: www.citigroup.com.

personnel. Thrifty German customers, for example, are a rich target. German retail banking has long been plagued by inconvenient hours and poor customer service at traditional banks, opening a window of opportunity for Internet banks to jump through. In addition to lower costs and better customer service, Internet banks offer the appeal of attractive demographics. Internet households tend to be younger, more affluent, and better educated than average. Most important, they tend to maintain higher bank balances and produce a higher demand for financial products and services, making them more amenable to cross-selling of other bank services.[3]

While Internet banking has expanded dramatically in the past few years in line with Internet growth, it has been slower to develop than online stockbroking. Nonetheless, most analysts expect an explosion in online banking. Some markets hold out especially strong prospects for growth, such as online mortgages and retail loans. Deutsche Bank forecast in early 1999 that the online mortgage market would grow from $4.2 billion in 1998 to $250 billion by 2003 (business in this area expanded tenfold in 1998 alone).

Internet banking is not risk-free. One problem is the ease of Internet banking scams, which have already taken in an unlucky few. (As the saying goes, on the Internet no one knows you're a dog.) As the *Financial Times* reports:

> *Illegal banks have always existed but thanks to the Internet they can now reach a wider market and operate more easily. They can also disappear as quickly as they arrive by simply pulling the plug on their Web server and relocating to another offshore regime with lax regulation. In 1997, the government of Antigua, a Caribbean island, had to warn Internet users about a virtual bank operating from the island*

TWILIGHT OF THE TELLER?

David Woodruff

E ighteen months ago, Paul McNamara closed out his account at the Bank of Ireland and moved to First Direct, a novelty on the European scene: a bank that has no traditional branches. Like First Direct's 850,000 other customers, the 31-year-old McKinsey & Co. management consultant simply picks up the telephone or sits down at a computer terminal to pay bills or handle other transactions. "Bank opening hours tend to be at crunch working hours, when I don't have time," says McNamara, who lives in London.

Busy young clients like McNamara are fueling growth of these new "direct" banks and brokerages around Europe. First Direct, a unit of HSBC Group's Midland Bank PLC subsidiary, adds 12,500 new customers a month. Bank 24, a three-year-old Deutsche Bank offshoot that offers banking and brokerage services, will nearly double its German customer base this year, to 450,000. Traditional banks are edging into cyberspace, with their own telephone and computer banking services. So by 2001, figures Boston Consulting Group Inc., 51 million Europeans, or about one in six, will be banking that way....

Source: Business Week International Edition, July 20, 1998, p. 16.

---

under the genuine-sounding name of the European Union Bank. It offered interest rates that were too good to be true—an astonishing 21 percent—and the Antiguan government suspected that the Russian mafia was behind the bank. The directors disappeared, taking with them some of the customers' deposits.[4]

U.S. authorities are concerned about the proliferation of businesses posing as banks on the Internet. These companies are not banks, as they are not legally chartered by state or federal governments, and their deposits are not insured, but consumers are not always aware of these subtleties. Thus these operations may be easily confused with legitimate banks doing business on the Internet, posing a threat to consumers and legitimate banks alike.

Moreover, the technological requirements of Internet banking require large up-front investments, which may not pay off immediately. As a result of high start-up costs and intense competition, only a few direct banks are profitable so far. At the same time, competition from Internet upstarts is threatening traditional banks. ABN Amro announced in early 2000 that it would close one in six of its Dutch branches, in a restructuring that bank officials attributed to the arrival of Internet-based competitors. A senior bank official commented, "The Internet and e-commerce are creating a more severe competitive world."[5] The advent of the common European currency, the euro, is expected to make direct banking across borders much easier in the future, though. Over time, Internet banking should provide customers with better convenience and lower fees, while providing bankers with lower costs and better access to retail customers across borders.

International Credit Card Issuance

One area in which U.S. banks have made substantial inroads overseas is in the marketing of consumer credit via credit cards. The European credit card market is vastly underdeveloped by U.S. standards. Conventional wisdom holds that Europeans shun credit cards, preferring to use cards that directly debit their bank accounts. These direct-debit cards, which are widely used throughout Europe, are unattractive from the bank's viewpoint, offering only a small transaction fee rather than the 18 to 22 percent on outstanding balances available from credit cards. U.S. invaders, however, have proved that Europeans do not have a cultural aversion to credit cards.

The first stop for U.S. financial institutions in their move into the European credit card business was the UK. Big British banks like Barclays still dominate the market (Europe's largest credit card market), but in recent years U.S. issuers have

---

CHARGE!

Charles P. Wallace

Americans don't know jack about soccer, right? It was bad enough when the Germans crushed the U.S. team in the opening round of the World Cup in Paris without raising a sweat, but when the Yanks got thrashed by the Iranians too, well, case closed. So, who would have guessed the origin of those plump envelopes dropping through British mailboxes earlier this year? The envelopes contained a really fantastic chance to attend the World Cup final match and get a low 6.9% interest rate on a MasterCard until April 1999. And—surprise!—they were coming not from Britain's Barclay Bank or even the French bank Credit Lyonnais. No, the offers arrived from a bank with headquarters all the way across the Atlantic—Capital One in Glen Allen, Va.

The mailing was just the latest skirmish in a full-scale U.S. invasion of Europe's credit card business—an invasion that has already seen the intruders gather a huge chunk of territory. While Americans may have a lot to learn about soccer, U.S. banks are teaching their European cousins some painful lessons in the marketing of consumer credit. And for the American institutions, the push comes none too soon. With credit card growth leveling off in the U.S. and American consumers surfing among low-ball teaser rates, U.S. lenders see Europe as a way to jump-start growth....

Source: Fortune, September 28, 1998, p. 189.

carved out a substantial position. They now control around 7 percent of the British market and are heading into continental Europe with the aid of marketing tools undreamed of by their European competitors. Household Finance (HFC), for example, roared into the British market in 1994 with a Visa card jointly issued with General Motors, which gave holders savings of up to $4,000 on new GM cars; more than 500,000 people signed up. HFC then established a joint venture with British Gas to issue a credit card dubbed Goldfish, which offered a rebate on utility bills. Backed by an expert marketing campaign, the Goldfish card won 700,000 new customers by the end of 1997, accounting for fully 18 percent of all new credit card accounts in the UK.[6] While barriers to internationalization still exist (including a more stringent regulatory climate in Europe than in the United States), the growth prospects for marketing-savvy U.S. banks in international credit card operations are impressive.

International Private Banking

As the article observes, private banking—the provision of wealth management services to high net worth individuals—is an ever more attractive market for banks. ("High net worth" individuals have traditionally been defined as people fortunate enough to possess a net worth of $1 million or more. As we shall see, this definition is undergoing some revision, though.) Private banking is hardly a new business,

CALM AMONG THE STORM
Stephen Timewell

A s the world's financial markets are tossed about by continuous storms, private banking is standing firm.

In an ocean of financial turmoil private banking appears to be a sea of tranquillity and bankers are striving ever harder to find their way there. The prospect of high quality fee income has always been attractive but at times of volatile earnings in many areas, especially in investment banking, the stability and growth potential of private banking revenue streams have even more appeal.

With the private banking market estimated to approach $25 trillion by 2000 and growing at an average 8% a year bankers are competing intensely for a slice of the expanding pie and recent financial crises have not dimmed their enthusiasm. "In terms of market there is a colossal opportunity that will expand in the future," says Ian Woodhouse, private banking specialist at PricewaterhouseCoopers....

Source: The Banker, January 1999, pp. 47–48.

although its nature has changed dramatically in the past two decades. Private bankers have evolved from golf-playing buddies (who, according to fabled reports, once upon a time delivered food delicacies to imprisoned clients) to sophisticated financial engineers.

What exactly do private bankers do? They provide both traditional and not-so-traditional banking services for high net worth (rich) individuals. These services include:

- *Deposit-related activities* (establishing money market accounts, savings accounts, certificates of deposits, commercial paper, bankers acceptances, Treasury bills, money market funds, etc.)
- *Credit extension and personal lending*
- *Corporate lending*
- *Investment management* (including custodial services, real estate services, handling investments in precious metals, currencies, commodities, and artwork), and the provision of financial and tax advice

As we will discuss later, the services demanded of private bankers are changing quickly and dramatically as the client base evolves. Traditional products, such as offshore accounts, mutual funds, and international tax advice, are quickly being supplemented by newer and sexier products tailored for newer and sexier clients. For example, private banking clients are increasingly likely to be dotcom millionaires rather than old-money types. These newer millionaires may be serial entrepreneurs, who require substantial lending facilities to fund their newest venture. (They may also require some fancy financial engineering to turn their paper assets into real cash.) These clients are likely to demand more sophisticated investment management products, including alternative investment vehicles such as hedge funds and derivatives. Even on the traditional asset management side, private bankers now are often expected to offer clients the investment funds of different managers as well as their own funds. In serving the needs of newly minted millionaires, private bankers are even known to provide psychologists to help Silicon Valley parents deal with "affluenza"—the scourge that turns newly rich kids into spoiled brats![7]

Serving the Private Banking Client

Whether they are old money or dotcom, private banking clients are seeking to satisfy a number of (occasionally conflicting) goals. First and foremost is secrecy. Traditionally, wealthy individuals have sought out international private banking services for the purpose of moving their funds offshore to evade the scrutiny of domestic regulatory and tax authorities. As financial barriers have tumbled worldwide, this has become somewhat less important. It has also become much more difficult to guarantee. The U.S. government, for example, has become much more aggressive in demanding that overseas banks turn over information that may be related to criminal activities. At the same time, even the famously tight-lipped Swiss bankers have become more willing to cooperate with government authorities in relation to criminal investigations.

Discretion may be of declining importance to the private banking relationship, but it is still a critical element. In mid–1999, Swiss officials moved aggressively to defend themselves against pressure from the European Union (EU) to relax their bank secrecy laws further. Switzerland's economics minister noted, "We absolutely agree that bank secrecy must not be used to protect criminal elements and money laundering." He added, though, that Switzerland had already changed its laws to accommodate this belief, and that further amendments were unnecessary. Underlying his stance, of course, is Switzerland's strong position in the private offshore banking market (it controls around one-third of the total market), and the belief that secrecy is an advantage in this market. Concluded the Swiss minister: "There is a tradition of discretion in this country and bank secrecy is part of the culture of individual treatment of bank customers."[8]

Many international private banking clients are also seeking safety for their funds. One experienced private banker testified about her field in the 1994 trial of two private bankers from American Express International who were accused of money laundering. She noted that private banking clients "usually come from countries that are in turmoil of some sort," and are seeking to shelter their funds in a safe haven overseas.[9]

While private banking clients are certainly concerned with safety and secrecy, the data do not entirely support the assertion that they come from countries "in turmoil." In fact, as Figure 6.3 illustrates, Europe and North America account for 59 percent of the high net worth individual market, with an additional 18 percent from Asia. In Europe alone, an estimated $6 trillion is held by people with more than $1 million in investable assets. This misstatement, in fact, probably reflects lingering misperceptions that are common in the fast-changing world of private banking.

FIGURE 6.3 Where the World's Wealthy Live (millions of high net worth individuals)

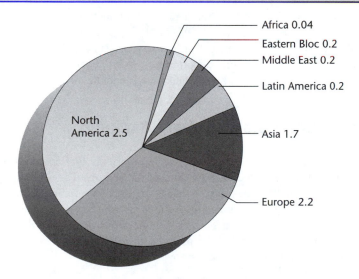

Source: Gemini Consulting and Merrill Lynch World Wealth Report 2000. *The Financial Times* (July 7, 2000).

In addition to safety and confidentiality, then, wealthy individuals in need of private banking services are motivated by the quest for yield and performance. The "typical" private banking client has evolved over the years, from the scion of a wealthy family primarily concerned with conserving his wealth, to the new-money entrepreneur who is more interested in achieving high yields on her newfound riches. Thus there is, at times, a built-in contradiction between the desire for yield and the desire for security. A top private banker at Merrill Lynch explains, "Most clients will come in and say they want to preserve their capital and get 20%. Sadly, those two goals are not compatible." The private banker's job is to determine what kind of performance the client really wants, that is, what combination of risk and return the client can stomach.[10]

The final expectation, on which all private banking clients agree, is top-flight service. Private banking remains a relationship-driven business, revolving around the personal ties between bankers and their clients. Personal relationships in this area are so important that private bankers are known as "relationship managers." (Other bankers derisively call them "meeters and greeters," "butlers to the rich," or "poodle-walkers."[11]) In the aforementioned testimony, a senior bank official explained that private bankers assiduously cultivate close ties with their clients. They remember birthdays, get to know families, and visit their clients at home a dozen or so times a year.[12]

Bankers who can fulfill these needs—secrecy, security, yield, and service—for their private banking clients are operating in a high-stakes market. The size of the market for wealth management services for high net worth individuals is usually estimated at around $25 trillion in 2000. According to reputable reports in the *Financial Times,* in 1999 alone another 1 million people became "high net worth individuals," and the market is forecast to grow at 12 percent per annum over the next five years.[13] Moreover, this market offers the prospect of relatively stable, high-quality profits. In 1997 global banks earned around $100 billion from managing $17.4 trillion in wealth.[14] The relationship-driven nature of the market suggests that once a client forges close ties to a private banker, he or she will remain for the long term. (See Figures 6.4 and 6.5.) This market is even more attractive in the wake of the Asian financial turmoil of 1997–98, offering good growth prospects and minimal risk to offset volatile earnings from other areas, such as securities trading. It even offers valuable cross-selling opportunities, since private banking clients will often invest in products created by the bank's investment banking division.

Competition in Global Private Banking

Considering these attributes, it is hardly surprising that competition for international private banking clients has intensified sharply. The Swiss banks, traditionally dominant in the private banking market, are facing fierce competition, especially from U.S. financial institutions. Private banking remains critical to the health of the big Swiss banks. Union Bank of Switzerland (UBS) derived around two-thirds of its first half 1998 pretax profit from private banking activities; the comparable figure at Credit Suisse was 33 percent.

FIGURE 6.4 Citibanking Accounts (In Millions)

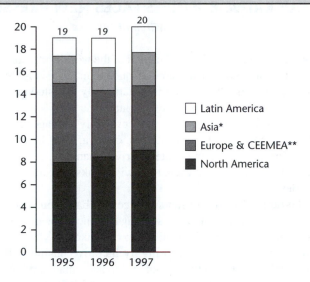

*Including Japan.
**Central/Eastern Europe, Middle East, and Africa.
Source: "Global Consumer: Citibanking," Citibank Financial Report, 1997.

FIGURE 6.5 Citibank–Private Bank: Managed Client Business Volumes ($Billions)

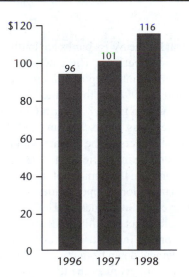

Source: "Global Consumer: Private Bank," Citibank Financial Report, 1997, 1998.

LUCRATIVE BUSINESS FACES NEW PRESSURES
William Hall

S witzerland is the undisputed capital of the world's offshore private banking industry. Swiss banks are reckoned to manage close to SFr 4 trillion
of assets. Around a third of all internationally invested private assets are
believed to be managed out of Switzerland.

London, the nearest competitor, probably manages less than half as
much as the combined totals of Zurich, Geneva, and Lugano, Switzerland's
three main private banking centers. Private banking, unlike global investment banking, is one area where the Swiss banks have always been the market leaders.

The recipe for Switzerland's success is based on several well-tested
ingredients: political neutrality, a strong currency, low inflation, respect for
client privacy, and a multilingual group of bankers.

Swiss private banking is a highly lucrative business. In the first six
months of 1999 UBS's private banking division made pre-tax profits of Sfr
1.4 billion on assets under management of Sfr 659 billion. Credit Suisse
earned Sfr 1.1 billion on assets under management of Sfr 440 billion.

The importance of private banking for UBS can be seen in the fact that the
division employs less than a fifth of the group's 48,000-strong workforce and
uses only 5 percent of group capital, yet is generating half UBS's profits....

Source: Private Banking Survey, *Financial Times,* October 27, 1999, p. SIII.

With so much at stake, the Swiss banks are battling to maintain their position
in the face of growing competition. The emergence of the new UBS from the
merger of UBS and Swiss Bank Corporation created the largest private banking
institution in the world in 1998. In the United States, however, the merger of
Citibank and Travelers Group in 1998 to form Citigroup created another private
banking giant to rival the Swiss. Deutsche Bank and HSBC in particular are determined to become global leaders in the private banking business; Merrill Lynch,
too, is aggressively expanding in this field. In 1998, for instance, it launched a new
brokerage house in Japan from the remains of the failed Japanese house Yamaichi,
in a bid to capitalize on unexplored opportunities in providing banking services for
the thrifty Japanese savers.[15] Subsequently, HSBC set up a $16 billion joint ven-
ture with Merrill Lynch to target 50 million affluent customers expected to be seeking investment advice on the Internet. This reflects a growing interest in serving
the needs of the next segment down from traditional private banking clients—affluent individuals who may not yet meet the threshold of $1 million in liquid finan-
cial assets, but who are well on their way. Competition to penetrate this market is
expected to be especially fierce in the next decade.

TABLE 6.2 Leading Private Banks Worldwide

Company	Assets Under Management (US$ billions)	Staff (no.)
UBS	422	7400
Credit Suisse	288	8400
Deutsche Bank	180	5400
Chase Manhattan	150	2500
Citibank	140[1]	4000
Merrill Lynch	137[2]	9500
ABN Amro	133	N/A
HSBC	121	3000
BNP Paribas	100	2400
J.P. Morgan	80	1387
Pictet & Cie	80	1500
Julius Baer	78	2000

Source: FT research, *The Financial Times,* Private Banking Survey, July 7, 2000.
[1]Includes loans and deposits.
[2]International private clients only.

The international private banking business is still dominated by a few heavy-weights—UBS, Citigroup, Merrill Lynch, and Credit Suisse. (See Table 6.2.) Overall, however, it is still a fragmented industry in which no single player has more than a 10 percent market share. Some medium-sized, niche players, such as Geneva-based Pictet & Cie with its focus on client relationships, are extremely successful. (See Figure 6.6.) Indeed, during 1999 UBS lost market share to smaller and more aggressive Swiss competitors such as Julius Baer, which enjoyed a 35 percent increase in funds under management. Among other problems, UBS reportedly failed to address rising demands among its wealthy clients for online banking services.[16] As the *Financial Times* observed in its 2000 survey of private banking, "Switzerland is still the capital of the world's offshore private banking industry, with a market share of around one-third. But the day when the Swiss banks could sit back and wait for wealthy private clients to approach them has disappeared. 'The biggest are the Swiss but the best are the Americans,' says Michael Lagopolous, head of private banking at Royal Bank of Canada."[17]

A Dangerous World?

The attractions of the private banking business should not blind bankers to its risks. Any business that is founded, at least in part, on the need for secret financial transactions may drift into unpleasant byways of international finance.

The BankBoston case illustrates some of the pitfalls of international private banking. There should have been plenty of red flags along the way. Carrasco was making a large number of loans out of a small office in New York, and private bankers were

FIGURE 6.6 *Financial Times* Advertisement: "Geneva's Private Bankers"

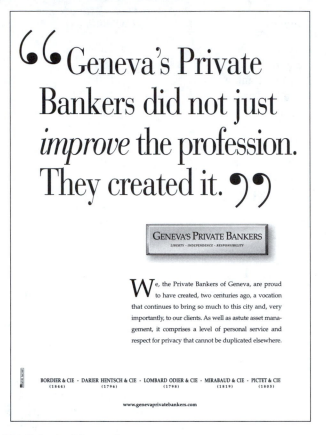

Source: Geneva Private Bankers Association. www.gbpg.com.

handling some sizable corporate loans. (In fact, private bankers do often handle corporate finance transactions for their clients, making these irregularities difficult to detect.) BankBoston officials say that there are two reasons they did not detect the problems. First, most of Carrasco's irregular loans were around $1 million, an amount that he could approve on his own. Second, Carrasco failed to disclose that the firms to which he was lending were all connected to one Argentine businessman.[18]

The bottom line for BankBoston was around $70 million in loan losses and a great deal of very public embarrassment. The incident sent shock waves throughout many global banks, as bankers wondered whether it was an isolated case of a rogue employee—or an indicator of systemic problems in the world of international private banking. The case illustrates the dangers of the financial secrecy that lies at the very heart of private banking. According to one banking regulator, officials are concerned that "regulatory compliance in the private banking area may not be as effective as it is in other areas of the banking business."[19] Even more worrisome, clients who earned their money illegally, such as drug traffickers and international arms dealers, may open private banking accounts and use them to launder their profits into "clean" overseas

PRIVATE BANKING: A DANGEROUS WORLD

Peter G. Gosselin and Steve Fainaru

Change was bearing down on BankBoston's international private bank even before its senior vice president, Ricardo S. Carrasco, vanished in the poof of bad loans last winter.

The bank's traditional role as a safe haven for wealthy foreigners was shrinking as countries around the world dismantled the financial barriers the bank once made its living helping clients to circumvent. Competitors were tripped up by scandals that seemed to reveal private banking's dirty little secrets: that some banks want their clients' business almost no matter what it is, and that some bankers want their customers' extravagant lifestyles, even if they can't afford them.

Before Carrasco's disappearance, BankBoston executives confidently predicted they would sail past any trouble that change brought. Since then, they have sought to portray the problem as one of a lone rogue, and nothing more.

But banking industry leaders and government officials say that the case is about considerably more than an individual banker gone bad. They say that it offers a rare glimpse into one of the most hidden recesses of banking: its elaborate courtship of the international super-wealthy and the $100 billion a year to be made tending their estimated $17.4 trillion in fortunes....

Source: Boston Globe, June 10, 1998, p. 1.

accounts. Corrupt foreign officials are another concern. (In 1998, responding to criticism, Citibank adopted a new policy against seeking out public figures as private bank clients—even though such public officials only account for around 350 of the private bank's 40,000 customers.) To avoid breaking the U.S. federal law that prohibits banks from knowingly accepting illicit funds, private bankers are supposed to check out their clients carefully under "know your customer" guidelines.[20] In practice, however, these guidelines may be uncomfortable or impossible to follow. The need to provide safe, confidential financial services for international customers thus leads some private bankers into the morass of money laundering and financial fraud (see Chapter 12 for a more in-depth discussion on money laundering).

Trends: New Money and the Emerging Affluent

The fast-changing nature of private banking clients and services in the 1990s provides a new set of challenges and opportunities. As noted earlier, private banking clients are evolving in nature. Until fairly recently, most international private banking clients were mainly concerned with avoiding taxes in their home countries. Once the private banker helped them move their funds into safe havens abroad, they were mostly content just to park the money and conserve it for future generations.

CITIBANK ADMITS LAPSES IN OVERSIGHT HELPED FOREIGNERS LAUNDER MILLIONS

Nick Anderson

Citibank, confronted by a stinging new Senate investigation of money laundering, on Tuesday acknowledged lapses in oversight of its "private banking" operations during the 1990s—operations that helped foreign leaders and their relatives move millions of dollars overseas in questionable transactions.

A report by the Senate permanent investigations subcommittee charged that the foreigners, with Citibank's help, used deliberately opaque networks of shell corporations, offshore trusts and other instruments to shield their identities as they secretly transferred money out of their own countries.

Among the most glaring incidents cited by the subcommittee were those involving the brother of former Mexican President Carlos Salinas de Gortari; the president of Gabon, an oil-producing nation in west Africa; the sons of a former Nigerian military strongman; and the husband of a former prime minister of Pakistan....

Source: Los Angeles Times, November 10, 1999, p. C3.

Nowadays, however, both industrialized and emerging market countries have largely removed the financial barriers that private bankers were paid to help avoid.

Moreover, the private banking client nowadays is increasingly likely to be a new-money type, who demands better investment performance and more sophisticated financial services than the old-money families. The 1980s and 1990s witnessed a surge in first- and second-generation riches created out of newly successful businesses around the globe. This new breed of private banking clients earned rather than inherited their wealth, and they usually demand a more active approach to their wealth management as well. New-money active investors now account for around 28 percent of private banking clients, and this proportion is expected to continue rising sharply. In turn, this shift in emphasis is creating pressure for change within banking institutions. The new-money investors, for example, increasingly derive their funds from their own growing businesses—so they demand a capability in corporate finance from their private bankers. A 1998 survey found that a whopping 82 percent of private bankers questioned intended to make significant operational changes in order to cope with intense competition; some 14 percent planned fundamental strategic shifts.[21] Reflecting the need to provide more sophisticated financial services for their clients, bank executives are actively working to strengthen the skills of their private bankers in these areas. No longer is it sufficient to know the best places for lunch and golf, and to provide a high level of discretion and service.

In fact, nowadays an increasing number of private bankers are drawn from the investment banking side of the institution.

In addition, private bankers are starting to cast their net over a potentially much larger market segment than in the past. They are targeting the emerging affluent population, especially in Europe—the growing group of high-income professionals who may not yet be high net worth according to the traditional definitions, but are underserved by banking institutions.[22] As this group matures and enters a wealth accumulation stage of life, it is expected that they will add significantly to the growth potential of private banking services.

Questions

1. What are the barriers to globalization in retail banking?
2. In what ways has Citibank managed to overcome the barriers in Question 1? Suggest strategies for other banks interested in globalizing their retail operations.
3. Is Internet-based banking a threat or an opportunity to banking institutions worldwide?
4. What are the barriers to entry in Internet banking? Risks?
5. How did U.S. banks enter the international credit card market? Do you foresee any pitfalls for U.S. banks in this market?
6. What impact do you expect the euro to have on the development of retail banking markets in Europe? How can banks position themselves for this?
7. Why have banks focused more attention on private banking operations in the 1990s? What is the attraction of private banking?
8. In what way is the market for private banking services changing? Do these changes represent threats to or opportunities for international bankers?
9. What are high net worth individuals seeking in their private bankers? What are the competitive strengths of Swiss banks in this area? U.S. banks?
10. To what extent do you believe that private bankers should protect their clients?
11. How does private banking intersect with money laundering? How can bankers safeguard their institutions to avoid becoming involved in shady financial transactions through their private banking operations?
12. Do you believe that private banking should be more tightly regulated? If so, how and by whom? If not, why not?

Websites

www.e-banking.org	Electronic banking
www.obanet.org	Online Banking Association
www.jpbg.ml.com	Private banking, money laundering
www.mastercard.com	Mastercard/ACCESS
www.visa.com	Visa
www.link.co.uk	ATM Network
www.banking.com	Banking Services

Notes

1. George Graham, "The Difficulty of Banking on the World," *Financial Times,* October 29, 1997, p. 18.
2. Scott Wooley, "Virtual Banker," *Forbes,* June 15, 1998, pp. 127–128.
3. David Woodruff, "Twilight of the Teller?" *Business Week International Edition,* July 20, 1998, p. 16.
4. Geoffrey Nairn, "Increase in Crimes Is the Darker Side of e-Business: Fraud," *Financial Times,* July 7, 1999, p. 3.
5. Gordon Cramb, "ABN Amro to Cut Branches and Shed Jobs," *Financial Times,* January 19, 2000, p. 30.
6. Charles P. Wallace, "Charge!" *Fortune,* September 28, 1998, p. 189.
7. *Financial Times Private Banking Survey,* July 7, 2000, p. 1.
8. William Hall, "Swiss Set to Defend Bank Secrecy Law," *Financial Times,* April 20, 1999, p. 2.
9. Anthony De Palma and Peter Truell, "A Mexican Mover and Shaker and How His Millions Moved," *New York Times,* June 5, 1996, p. A1.
10. George Graham, "Stronghold in Times of Trouble," *Financial Times Private Banking Survey,* November 9, 1998, p. S1.
11. Peter G. Gosselin and Steve Fainaru, "Private Banking: A Dangerous World," *Boston Globe,* June 10, 1998, p. 1.
12. Anthony De Palma and Peter Truell, "A Mexican Mover and Shaker and How His Millions Moved," p. A1.
13. *Financial Times Private Banking Survey,* July 7, 2000, p. S1.
14. Peter G. Gosselin and Steve Fainaru, "Private Banking: A Dangerous World," p. 1.
15. Stephen Timewell, "Calm Among the Storm," *The Banker,* January 1999, pp. 47–48.
16. William Hall, "Swiss Banks in Market Share Rise," *Financial Times,* February 3, 2000, p. 28.
17. William Hall, "'World's Wealthy Press for Service," *Financial Times,* July 7, 2000, p. 1.
18. Steve Fainaru and Peter Gosselin, "Bank Boston Sues Argentine for $62 Mln," *Boston Globe,* April 23, 1998.
19. *Ibid.*
20. Anthony De Palma and Peter Truell, "A Mexican Mover and Shaker and How His Millions Moved."
21. George Graham, "Private Banks Respond to Fierce Rivalry," *Financial Times,* February 15, 1999, p. 2.
22. George Graham, "Stronghold in Times of Trouble," p. S1.

CHAPTER 7

OFFSHORE FINANCIAL CENTERS

Offshore financial centers usually have a certain sense of mystery around them. More than one James Bond movie has taken place in the Bahamas, Switzerland, or Hong Kong, revolving around the use of offshore bank accounts by diabolical archvillains scheming to take over the planet. Indeed, offshore financial centers are founded on the concepts of bank secrecy, confidentiality, and no or low taxes—all of which reflect an opaque nature of conducting business. Offshore financial centers provide a venue for money matters beyond the prying eyes of business competitors, tax authorities, and vengeful spouses involved in divorce proceedings. At the same time, offshore financial centers certainly are not just for crooks. Indeed, they have their own set of rules and regulations as well as international treaties, all of which provide a legal foundation for business that is oriented to obtaining and maintaining legitimate financial intercourse. Consequently, for companies and individuals in politically unstable countries, doing business in an offshore financial center, with an established bank having international credentials, often makes more sense than putting money and other securities into old mattresses, hidden stashes in the wall, and in the backyard. Although bank secrecy remains controversial, there has been an erosion of the once airtight nature of a banker's confidentiality due to growing pressure from international law enforcement concerned with money laundering and other types of financial fraud.

Offshore financial centers differ from "onshore" banking in that the financial services offered are usually not available to the local population. In other words, an offshore financial center exists for the benefit of foreign customers, a distinction often strictly upheld by local laws. Indeed, the *Oxford Dictionary of Finance and Banking* defines offshore banking as, "The practice of offering financial services in locations that have attractive tax advantages to non-residents."[1] Moreover, not all the services offered by an offshore financial center—fund management, brokering, insurance, holding company registration, fiduciary services, and Internet gaming—may be permitted those banks operating onshore.

While there are differences among venues, all offshore financial centers share a number of key elements. These include the following:

1. Low or no taxes.
2. Services are provided mainly, but not exclusively, for nonresident clients.
3. There are no or few foreign exchange controls.

FINANCIAL TIMES SURVEY: GUERNSEY

The traditional image of a tax haven as a sun-kissed island of palm trees and cocktails on the beach can take a serious battering during an autumn week in Guernsey. The island, alas, is subject to the vagaries of northern European weather.

The people who regulate the island's financial sector would claim, in any case, that part of their job is to shatter prejudices about offshore financial centres. Guernsey—like its competitor centres in Jersey and the Isle of Man—is fighting hard to dispel the notion that it is primarily a safe deposit box for suitcases of cash being spirited out of the taxman's reach.

But there are more than rain clouds hanging over Guernsey and other offshore centres. The UK government, the European Union, the Organisation of Economic Co-operation and Development, and the Financial Stability Forum (a grouping of finance ministers, central banks and regulators) are all turning the spotlight on the centres' activities as the clamour grows for an end to the myriad distortions that persuade those who can afford it to invest "offshore."

Guernsey, having built up its financial services industry steadily in the past 20 years, is extremely sensitive to these investigations and the wider attacks on "tax havens." The phrase sends a chill through officials there, who insist it is no such thing.

Source: Financial Times, October 21, 1999, p. 11.

4. Geographical proximity to a major economy (like Luxembourg and Switzerland to Germany, or Bermuda and the Bahamas to the United States) and good communications (as well as good hotels).

5. A legal regime that upholds bank secrecy.

6. A high degree of political stability is also important—no one wants to put their money into a country that cannot guarantee personal safety or the ability to extract one's funds.

Additionally, international banks generally play a dominant role in the offshore financial center, for they have the necessary structure for providing the varied services required by a global clientele that ranges from major multinational corporations to wealthy individuals.

Another factor is that offshore finance can offer a helpful economic activity to countries with few natural resources. It is not a coincidence that a great number of offshore centers are either small countries, such as Luxembourg and Liechtenstein in continental Europe, or islands such as Vanuatu and Nauru in the South Pacific. (See Table 7.1.) Generally speaking, offshore financial centers are limited in population size and natural resources, which forced them to adopt development

TABLE 7.1 Offshore Financial Centers

The Americas	Europe and the Middle East	Asia-Pacific
Anguilla	Bahrain	Cook Islands
Aruba	Cyprus	Hong Kong
The Commonwealth of the Bahamas	Gibraltar	Lubuan Island (Malaysia)
Barbados	Guernsey	Palau
Bermuda	Ireland (Dublin)	Nieu
British Virgin Islands	Isle of Man	Singapore
Cayman Islands	Jersey	Vanuato
Grenada	Liechtenstein	
Montserrat	Luxembourg	
Netherlands Antilles	Monaco	
Panama	Switzerland	
Turks and Caicos Islands		
Uruguay		

strategies—such as offshore finance—that use the country's comparative advantage in location and human capital. Another economic sector that is often found in offshore financial centers is tourism, as the two tap some of the same competitive advantages. This is very much in evidence in Caribbean offshore financial centers, such as Anguilla, Aruba, and the Cayman Islands, that combine "sun and sand" with international banking.

Points of Origin

Offshore financial centers emerged with the creation of the nation-state, which became particularly pronounced after the Treaty of Westphalia in 1648. Although the movement of funds and other types of securities from the scrutiny of the authorities in one country to another with looser government controls was not referred to as offshore banking, cross-border flows of capital in the seventeenth through the twentieth centuries were often arranged to find a home for "hot money." As Ingo Walter noted: "With the advent of the sovereign states, and the ability to transfer financial resources between them, came the possibility of secrecy seekers to solicit protection offshore. The principle of sovereignty of states insures that foreigners will have limited insight, strictly controlled by domestic law and policy; anything more is politically unacceptable."[2]

For banks involved in offshore finance, there are clear-cut rules and regulations governing operations, both from the country in which the institution has its license and in the offshore center. The level of supervisory regulation varies from location to location, ranging from tight supervision from local authorities on the alert for possible criminal penetration of the center to intentionally lax supervisory practices aimed at receiving the maximum amount of business. The latter types of centers operate with the view that "money has no smell."

While there are advantages to using offshore financial centers, there are also disadvantages. Those who favor offshore banking centers argue that law-abiding citizens and companies have the right to their financial privacy. Moreover, unnecessary and excessive financial disclosure requirements may hurt the companies' ability to compete, as business secrets could be divulged. This latter case might, for example, cause an investment fund to incorporate in an offshore financial center, such as the Bahamas.

The argument against offshore financial centers is that they provide the means by which individuals and companies can willfully evade the payment of taxes, which is an obligation to the state. Loss of tax revenues for the government means a reduced ability to pay for public services, ranging from national security to adequate funding for primary education and basic health care. (On the other hand, of course, tax minimization—as opposed to tax evasion—is a legitimate and necessary element in corporate financial engineering.) Additionally, the very nature of bank secrecy and confidentiality is likely to attract unsavory business elements involved in international criminal activities. These concerns were evident in the comment in a U.S. government report on possible money laundering operations in Antigua and Barbuda: "Antigua has an active offshore financial services industry which continues to be largely unregulated. This loosely-regulated environment has led, in recent years, to a substantial increase in the number of offshore banks registered in Antigua. Several of these banks have links to Russia and many to offshore entities in other jurisdictions, generating concern about investors and depositors of questionable origin."[3] Offshore financial centers (attractive because of zero taxation) encourage capital flight from countries with high tax regimes.

Whatever the arguments for and against offshore financial centers, they are not likely to disappear anytime soon. The end of the Cold War opened the door to new offshore financial centers eager to acquire business and be more lax in their supervision. Banks in Latvia and Slovakia have actively advertised on the Internet. As one bank in Latvia offered: "At Paritate Bank confidentiality can be enhanced through private investment accounts and the use of several other jurisdictions. Again, this does not always shield the investor from income reporting for tax purposes, but does protect investment privacy."[4] The Latvian bank is hardly the only institution around the world offering the same set of services.

Unease about the use of offshore financial centers to evade taxes and to launder the ill-gotten gains of criminal activities has given these centers a dubious reputation. It is important to recall that, while in some cases this reputation is amply justified, offshore financial centers also provide a variety of legitimate business services. In a broad sense, international offshore financial centers provide the option to establish a wide range of accounts and corporations. Most centers offer licenses for offshore banks and various kinds of holding companies. Additionally, banks and other financial institutions operating in such centers must be able to provide services to deal with such things as grantor trusts, annuities, asset protection

INTERNET ADVERTISEMENT FOR PARITATE BANK IN LATVIA

If overseas banking and investing fits your financial needs, you will want to consider Paritate Bank. Located in Riga, Latvia, Paritate offers both conventional banking and full range of investing services. If you are doing business in Eastern Europe and the former Soviet Union Paritate offers an intimate understanding of those markets, as well as invaluable contacts. But Paritate's advantages are not limited to its geographic location. Latvian banking and tax laws and Paritate's expertise make it competitive with any other bank in the world. The ease with which a Paritate account can be established is unmatched. Paritate's unique PC banking software allows you to manage your account from anywhere.

In a world characterized by political uncertainty, financial and market volatility and rapidly changing values, consistency and continuity are virtues. Throughout its history, Paritate Bank has been built on working partnerships with the clients. It is in this spirit of partnership, hard work, and personal service that the Bank has developed and it is in the same spirit that the Bank moves forward. Distinctive style of service and strong commitment to clients around the world truly set it apart.

Source: Taken from Paritate Bank's website, December 20, 1998, at www.paritate.lv. aboutparitate.htm.

trusts, discretionary trusts, and family limited partnerships. An asset protection trust is a special form of irrevocable trust, usually established for preserving and protecting part of one's wealth offshore against creditors. A grantor trust is established by a person who creates a trust or transfers real property to another entity. A discretionary trust is a grantor trust in which the trustee has complete discretion as to who among the class of beneficiaries receives income and/or principal distributions. Family limited partnerships are created for family estate planning and some asset protection. These arrangements, offered in many offshore financial centers, are meant to provide flexibility as well as the utmost privacy.

While there are a number of offshore financial centers to look at, we have selected Switzerland, Luxembourg, the Bahamas, Singapore, and Hong Kong. These are some of the best-known and well-managed offshore financial centers.

Switzerland

One of the persistent stereotypes of Switzerland is that of young Heidi, high up the mountainside, happily tending her goats. And how can one forget those quaint Swiss dressed up in lederhosen and green Alpine hats, merrily yodeling to their neighbors. While Switzerland often comes across as the land of creamy milk chocolate and cuckoo clocks, that is a façade with the economic foundations based on international trade and, for the purposes of this book, global finance. Switzerland remains one of the world's major offshore financial centers, providing a highly sophisticated range of services for its select clientele.

Switzerland as an offshore financial center evolved because of a convergence of historical and geographical reasons. Throughout most of Switzerland's existence as an independent nation, economic development was rudimentary. Lacking adequate land for extensive cultivation and landlocked, Switzerland also had to wrestle with isolated valleys, high mountain passes, decentralized administration, and regional differences. Until the nineteenth century, mercenaries were the country's major export. Despite these challenges, the Swiss began a long steady march to becoming an important offshore financial center and tourist center. In 1850, the federal government began issuing its first national currency, named the franc. This was key to establishing Switzerland as an offshore financial center—the Swiss franc was relatively stable and was to become attractive as a refuge currency in times of international crisis and tourism. This made other Europeans aware of the existence of this small landlocked country in the midst of Western Europe. Political stability only increased the country's attractiveness.

Another factor that helped the advancement of Switzerland as an offshore banking center was the development of a sophisticated banking sector. Credit Suisse, the country's first universal bank, was founded in 1856. Swiss Bank Corporation was created in 1872 as a result of a merger of six small banks. Union Bank of Switzerland (UBS) was established in 1912 by the merger of the Bank of Winterthur and the Toggenburger Bank. All three institutions were highly involved in international finance and became significant players in international capital markets, all of which helped elevate Switzerland's role as a financial center. It was no mistake that, in a 1999 survey of the most globalized banks conducted by *The Banker,* Credit Suisse Group and the merging Union Bank of Switzerland and Swiss Banking Corporation conducted over 67 percent of their business outside of Switzerland, which put these institutions in the top five most globalized banks.[5]

Political turmoil in Europe during the 1914–1945 period reinforced Switzerland's claim of being a safe harbor. Switzerland's neutrality was upheld in both the First and Second World Wars, which helped it attract funds from a wide range of individuals and companies. Following the Second World War, Switzerland emerged as one of the truly dominant offshore financial centers, well known for its airtight secrecy and numbered accounts. Numbered accounts worked in such a way that some banks agreed to replace an account name with a special code number. The number (or a series of letters and digits) was the only way a bank clerk could identify the account. To ensure secrecy, the actual owner's name was known only to the bank manager and recorded in a special ledger located in the manager's private safe. With a central European location and with a strong tourist sector, Switzerland's tough bank secrecy attracted considerable overseas money. At the end of 1977, identified foreign deposits on hand in Switzerland were about $50 billion, and in 1980 there were 4,887 banks (including branches serving 3,000 towns), trusts, and other financial institutions.[6] Although other nations fumed about tax cheats running off to Switzerland to store their wealth, there was little to be done about Swiss bank secrecy and the services provided. Moreover, the Swiss clearly regarded their nation's banking facilities as a part of an offshore center, not as a tax haven.

Switzerland's traditions of bank secrecy and being an offshore financial center have not always provided an easy mechanism to maintain a competitive edge in the global economy. Swiss bankers have had problems in the late 1990s with hard questions over their holding of Jewish money during the Second World War and well beyond that time as well as charges of money laundering. While the issue of Jewish money has become an emotive and complicated political issue with reparations gradually forthcoming, the Swiss have taken more comprehensive action on money laundering. Although the Swiss have not introduced any restrictions on international capital movements and continue to place an emphasis on bank secrecy, they did criminalize money laundering in 1990 and put anti–money laundering legislation in place in 1994. In 1997, a new Swiss Money Laundering Law was passed in Parliament, extending the scope of existing money laundering regulations to nonbank financial institutions and establishing an obligation to report suspicious transactions.[7] Moreover, in the same year, the country's high court ordered the transfer of assets belonging to the late Philippine President Ferdinand Marcos to that country, stating that it was against Swiss national interests "to serve as a safe haven" for flight capital or criminal proceeds.

The Swiss are also active in the supervisory activities of the Bank for International Settlements (BIS), based in Basel, Switzerland, are part of the Council of Europe Convention on Money Laundering, and are in the Financial Action Task Force (FAFT), initially organized by the industrialized nations to counter money laundering activities. It has also cooperated with the U.S. authorities. As the 1997 *International Narcotics Control Enforcement Report* stated: "Switzerland cooperates with the United States on money laundering issues and there have been several successful operations in which the Swiss have seized bank accounts and shared assets with the United States."[8]

Although airtight bank secrecy is eroding, Switzerland remains one of the most respected offshore financial centers. The issue of reparations for wartime Jewish money and money laundering have brought tough questions to the Swiss authorities and bankers, but efforts have been made to preserve the offshore banking function for a well-heeled clientele that includes wealthy individuals (with legitimate sources of income) and corporations. As banking and related services play a significant role in the Swiss economy, both in terms of wealth generation and in employment, efforts are being made to maintain Switzerland's leading role as one of the world's best-run offshore financial centers.

The Grand Duchy of Luxembourg

Another leading offshore financial center is the Grand Duchy of Luxembourg, strategically located between Germany, France, and Belgium. Smaller than Switzerland, with only 2,586 square kilometers and a population of 425,000, this landlocked country turned to offshore finance in the mid-twentieth century.

Luxembourg's economic development was initially dominated by the steel industry, in particular, the Arbed Group. In the 1960s and 1970s, however, intense international competition in the steel industry made it critical to diversify. Consequently, during the late 1970s growth in the financial sector picked up considerably. By 1980, the number of banks in the country had risen from 37 in 1970 to 111, employing 4.6 percent of the total workforce.[9] In this process, the government pursued a hands-on policy to enhance the attractiveness of Luxembourg as a location for financial activity.

The reasons for considering Luxembourg for offshore banking, as advanced by the Luxembourg Bankers' Association, are a politically stable and sound national environment, a very broad range of services offered, a multicurrency environment, professional multilingual staff, discretion and confidentiality, experienced banking control, competitive fiscal framework, and top-ranking banking institutions.[10] Much of this was echoed in a 1999 Organization for Economic Cooperation and Development study: "The absence of monetary reserve requirements for banks, tax advantages over neighbouring countries, a liberal regulatory environment, and the rapid implementation of EU directives in Luxembourg law, combined with a favourable geographical location at the heart of Europe and a qualified and multilingual labour force have been central in creating competitive advantages in financial services."[11] Consequently, at the close of the 1990s more than 200 banks have been established in the Grand Duchy, accounting for 17 percent of GDP, 20 percent of the central government revenues, and 9 percent of employment.[12]

The activities of international banks have been supplemented by the development of other financial opportunities in the Grand Duchy. Luxembourg is the home to a growing number of investment funds, holding companies, insurance and reinsurance companies, financial intermediaries, and Cedel, a clearing house for transactions in marketable securities. According to the Luxembourg Bankers' Association, 82 insurance companies and 229 reinsurance companies have selected Luxembourg as their base.

Luxembourg's bank secrecy, upheld by Clause 16 of the 1981 Banking Act, has long been a point of attraction as well as a keystone of the Grand Duchy's reputation as a tax haven. This combination helped create the myth of Belgian dentists taking the train to Luxembourg to deposit their earnings in an effort to keep them out of the hands of Belgian tax authorities. Indeed, secrecy applies to applications from foreign banks, which are approved by the Luxembourg Banking Authority, while a high level of confidentiality applies to bankers in Luxembourg handling the business of establishing holding companies, selling eurobonds, and exporting and importing capital. An important component of Luxembourg's secrecy is extended to the creation of holding companies. The guiding law for this is the Holding Company Act of July 1929 (as revised in 1983 to allow mutual funds also to benefit from its terms), which exempts these corporations from paying tax on income, interest on bonds issued, royalties, capital gains, and sales of securities.[13] At the close of the 1990s, Luxembourg had more than 6,000 holding companies, functioning as vehicles for joint ventures, mergers, takeovers, and managing the investments of wealthy individuals. Additionally, under the Law of August 10, 1915, SOPARFIs (Sociétiés de participation financiere) can be established. In contrast to holding companies whose core business is to acquire, manage, and exploit participations in domestic or foreign companies, the SOPARFIs' activities are not limited solely to securities investments.

The Grand Duchy of Luxembourg's sustained push into the big league of offshore finance has forced it to deal with charges of money laundering occurring in its jurisdiction. In 1989, anti–money laundering legislation was passed. The law pertains only to narcotics-related money laundering, though it calls for suspicious transaction reporting in the financial and insurance sectors. Further tightening of anti–money laundering measures followed the international closure of Bank of Credit and Commerce International (BCCI) in 1991, and efforts were made in 1997 and 1998 to widen the penal code's definition of illegal money laundering. Luxembourg is a member of the Financial Action Task Force and is a party to the 1988 United Nations Drug Convention.

Luxembourg is likely to continue to be one of the world's leading offshore financial centers. At the same time, it faces a number of tough challenges, as its membership in the European Union may lead to changes in bank secrecy and tax policy. Considering the significance of offshore finance and banking to the country, the government will do all that it can to maintain the Grand Duchy's competitive position.

The Commonwealth of the Bahamas

Whereas Switzerland and Luxembourg are well-established offshore banking sectors in the heart of postindustrial Europe, the Bahamas provides an example of a non-OECD country that has opted for a similar path of economic development. Located fifty miles off the coast of the United States and forming the northern border of the Caribbean Sea, the Bahamian economy shares with other offshore financial centers a pronounced emphasis on offshore finance to co-lead its development (behind tourism). One of the top ten offshore financial centers in the world, the Bahamas has a tradition of confidentiality, privacy, anonymity, and no direct taxation, which has been complemented by considerable political stability (uninterrupted parliamentary government), excellent communications, and a talented local workforce characterized by a high level of literacy. Additionally, its geographic location and modern communications mean that the Bahamas is easily accessible, and the time zone in which it falls allows operations in the island-state to trade in the New York, Toronto, and London markets at various times of the day.[14] Easy access to the United States and a thriving tourist sector have also helped develop the Bahamas as a offshore financial center.

Long a British colony, the Bahamas achieved its independence in 1973 through a peaceful shift of power from London to locally elected authorities. Tourism was already a well-established industry, and financial services were an attractive second sector. Though the first offshore operation was established in the Bahamas in 1936 as the Bahamas General Trust Company, it was not until the 1960s that the offshore sector began its rapid expansion. Today, according to the Central Bank of the Bahamas, banking accounts for 15 percent of GDP, employs 3,608 people, and contributes $240 million in direct expenditure to the economy. Moreover, offshore banking in the Bahamas is said to manage assets valued at around $200 billion. At the beginning of 1997 there were 425 institutions licensed to conduct banking and/or trust business with the public, 20 of which were designated by the Exchange Control to deal in Bahamian or foreign currency and gold.

The offshore financial sector provides services that entail the creation of holding companies, the establishment of foreign banks in the offshore sector, private banking and trust business, discretionary fund management, and mutual fund back-office administration. In 1997, there were 60,000 international business corporations. Portfolio management and international investment have emerged as important components of offshore financial activities. Under Bahamian law, an account can be opened with proper identification and a bank reference.

Key legal foundations for the Bahamas offshore financial center are the Banks and Trust Companies Regulation Act of 1965, as amended in 1980, and the Companies Act of 1966, as amended. These laws provide the bedrock for the main types of financial activity of domestic commercial banking, international commercial banking, and international trust banking. Section 10 of the Banks and Trust Companies Regulation Act of 1965 provides the basis for bank secrecy, which at inception was sweeping in nature.

The Bahamas' preservation of secrecy is strongly upheld by the government, attorneys, and bankers as an essential element to the continued success and expansion of the Commonwealth as a major offshore financial center. This stance puts the Bahamas at times at loggerheads with the United States, as in the case of litigation between the United States and the Bank of Nova Scotia (discussed below). The situation in the 1980s was complicated by the use of the Bahamas as a drug trafficking conduit from Colombia to the United States and allegations of high-ranking corruption in the governments of Prime Minister Lynden O. Pindling.

In 1983, the United States clashed with both the Bahamas and Canada over an incident involving the Bank of Nova Scotia, a Canadian bank operating in the United States and the Bahamas. U.S. authorities had long contended that bank secrecy was being used by U.S. tax evaders and drug smugglers to launder millions of dollars through Caribbean tax havens like the Bahamas. In the case of Nova Scotia, the bank refused to compromise the confidentiality of a customer. In August 1983, the Canadian bank was forced to give a Florida grand jury bank records belonging to a client of its Nassau office after being threatened with a $50,000-a-day fine imposed on the bank's Florida branch. The Bahamas government condemned this action as an infringement on Bahamian sovereignty and contrary to international law. Shortly thereafter, in 1984, there was an internal inquiry into Prime Minister Pindling. Although Pindling was acquitted, his name resurfaced later in the case of Colombian drug trafficker Carlos Ledher, who confessed to paying the Bahamian government $3 to $5 million in 1980–81, with part of the pay-off allegedly going to the head of state.

Following these events, the reputation of the Bahamas as an offshore financial center fell under a cloud in the 1980s. As business dropped off, the government was forced to become more proactive. Failure to clean up the Bahamas' image in international financial circles would have threatened a key foundation in the economy, with long-term repercussions for the nation's well-being. A change of government in the early 1990s further helped the Bahamas present a cleaner image, seeking to gain the right clients and not those involved in laundering criminal proceeds.

During December 1996, the Central Bank of the Bahamas issued guidance notes to financial institutions on money laundering that explained how to apply the Commonwealth's now comprehensive anti–money laundering law. Furthermore, the Central Bank has created an internal unit to monitor compliance of financial reporting requirements. Working with the Ministry of Finance, efforts have been made to tighten regulations, better screen potential customers, and share information. At the same time, the government passed comprehensive anti–money laundering legislation and the implementing regulations in 1996. The passage and implementation of these laws allowed the Bahamian Drug Enforcement Unit (DEU) to conduct several money laundering investigations in 1997 and 1998. The Bahamas is also a member of the Caribbean Financial Action Task Force, a spin-off of the Financial Action Task Force, founded to improve regional responses to money laundering.

Hong Kong and Singapore

The two major offshore financial centers in Asia are Hong Kong and Singapore. Both are former British colonies and have enjoyed geostrategic locations that have helped stimulate their development as trading and financial hubs. Among the similarities shared by Hong Kong and Singapore are strong economies with extensive international links, relative political stability, state of the art communications, excellent air and sea transportation links, English-speaking labor pools, well-developed service infrastructures in the legal, accounting, and insurance sectors, and a British-influenced efficient civil service.[15] The last point is important, because it underscores that both Hong Kong and Singapore uphold the rule of law in the financial sector. Despite the number of similarities, Hong Kong and Singapore's early development as offshore financial centers had a number of noteworthy differences.

Singapore sits in a time zone that allows it to enjoy overlapping business hours with the major Asia-Pacific financial centers (Hong Kong, Tokyo, and Sydney) as well as with London, Paris, and Switzerland. Because of this, Singapore has been able to develop a more active international money market, in particular, the Asian dollar market, than Hong Kong. According to the Monetary Authority of Singapore (MAS), the island-state's central bank, Singapore is only behind London, New York, and Tokyo in foreign exchange trading, with an average daily trading volume of $167 billion in 1997.

Singapore also benefits from its attractiveness to multinational corporations looking for a regional headquarters in Southeast Asia. With a reputation for law and order, cleanliness, and efficiency, Singapore attracts many multinational corporations. The emergence of a competent offshore financial center was a bonus for many of these companies. At the same time, the concentration of multinational corporations, a favorable tax regime, and location also attracted a growing number of banks.

Singapore, according to the MAS, is the fourth largest foreign exchange trading center in the world, the fifth largest trader in derivatives, and the ninth largest offshore lending center. There are more than 700 financial institutions, local and foreign, operating in Singapore, participating in a wide range of financial services, including trade financing, foreign exchange trading, derivatives trading, financial advisory services, syndication, underwriting, mergers and acquisitions, and specialized insurance products. According to the MAS, as of March 1998, there were 154 banks, 80 merchant banks, 19 finance companies, 163 insurance companies, 90 stockbroking companies, and 156 investment advisors.

With the increasingly global nature of competition in offshore banking, Singapore embarked on a review of its policies in regulating and developing its financial center in 1997. The review was followed in 1998 by a number of reforms, including better transparency and disclosure. In particular, attention was given to improving disclosure of loan-loss provisions, off–balance sheet items, and significant exposures. These actions sought to enhance Singapore's reputation for maintaining a competitive and prudently run offshore financial center, an important signal to an international banking market rattled by the Asian financial crisis of 1997–98.

Hong Kong's location near Korea, Japan, Taiwan, and mainland China, which contain a number of capital-hungry governments and corporations, helped it develop a regional capital market. This development was reinforced by the attractiveness of Hong Kong as a headquarters and regional office location for many multinational corporations and financial institutions. Consequently, while Singapore emerged as a key offshore center for currency dealings and a link to the eurodollar market, Hong Kong evolved as a major hub for the arrangement, syndication, and management of eurocredits to borrowers from the Asia-Pacific area. Today, Hong Kong is the world's sixth largest international banking center in terms of external transactions and has the representation of 79 of the top 100 banks. According to the Hong Kong Monetary Authority, the central bank, at end-November 1998, there were 174 licensed banks, 62 restricted banks, and 105 deposit-taking companies in Hong Kong.

Bank secrecy plays a key role in attracting and maintaining business in Hong Kong's and Singapore's offshore banking sectors. The key legislation for Singapore's bank secrecy is the Banking Act of 1970, under which tough bank secrecy laws are enshrined. The banking law also provided for the legality of numbered accounts, which could only be penetrated by an order of a Judge of the Supreme Court for the purposes of civil or criminal proceedings. Hong Kong's bank secrecy laws are upheld by its Banking Ordinance. The criminal penalties for violating Hong Kong's bank secrecy laws can be both monetary and imprisonment.

Like other major offshore financial centers, Hong Kong and Singapore have been forced to take measures to deal with money laundering. In November 1997, the Hong Kong Monetary Authority issued a revised Guideline on the Prevention of Money Laundering under Section 73 of the Banking Ordinance. Similar guidelines were promulgated in July 1997 by Hong Kong's Securities and Futures Commission to cover equities transactions and related institutions.

Hong Kong reverted back to Chinese sovereignty on June 30, 1997. Under the agreement with the United Kingdom and the People's Republic of China, Hong Kong became a Special Administrative Region (SAR). This allowed Hong Kong to become a part of China again, but it maintained its own set of laws and way of government. Although concerns have been raised that China would not uphold Hong Kong's rules and regulations, hence eroding confidence in Hong Kong as an offshore financial center, this has not occurred. Hong Kong, in fact, weathered its transfer to China as well as Asia's 1997–98 financial crisis and maintains its role as a major offshore financial center.

In the late 1990s, concerns about maintaining confidence, the need to bolster the financial system, and the necessity of sustaining Singapore's competitiveness as a regional financial center moved the authorities to implement a reform package. The key elements of that package include raising the amount of public funds placed with private asset managers, permitting public funds to invest in approved trusts, lifting controls on brokerage rates, encouraging bank mergers, and increasing bank disclosure toward the U.S. level.[16] Although not all these measures pertain to offshore financial activities, most do.

International Banking Facilities

The emergence of well-known financial centers and their active development in the 1960s and 1970s eventually resulted in the creation in the United States of international banking facilities (IBFs). These institutions were vehicles that permitted a bank to accept time deposits from non-U.S. residents free of reserve requirements and of interest rate ceilings, as well as to lend to nonresidents exempt from most local (but not federal) income taxes. Beginning in December 1981, banks in the United States were allowed to open IBFs. By 1983, more than 400 banking institutions had established them, with total assets of around $200 billion.[17] The globalization of banking and capital markets liberalization in the late 1980s and 1990s gradually made IBFs less attractive to investors.

Looking Ahead

Looking ahead, one of the most significant challenges for offshore financial centers will be to reinvent themselves. The offshore banking industry has become highly competitive, almost cutthroat. This has left some of the more astute centers and their bankers looking for salvation in telecommunications and e-commerce to bolster their competitive edge. In 2000, a number of offshore centers, such as Bermuda, Singapore, the Isle of Man, and Jersey, introduced legislation for doing business on the Internet.[18]

The business of providing offshore financial services is a multibillion-dollar activity, and countries such as the Bahamas, Singapore, Luxembourg, and Switzerland are on the cutting edge. They are well known, have extensive legislation, and have taken measures to reduce criminally related activities through enhanced enforcement and, in certain cases, information sharing with other nations. While offshore banking activities in centers such as Cayman Islands, the British Virgin Islands, and Luxembourg have come under greater official scrutiny, there remain a number of other locations where the screening process is much more lax and criminal penetration much more profound. The process of globalization, however, is pushing all offshore financial centers into greater competition, which creates difficulties in maintaining adequate supervisory measures. As the twenty-first century begins, there is likely to be a more pronounced split between those offshore centers that want blue-chip customers and those willing to accept cash with no questions asked. Consequently, the debate about offshore financial centers and their role in international banking will continue.

Questions

1. What are the key elements that all offshore financial centers share?
2. What are the advantages and disadvantages of going to an offshore financial center?
3. What factors contributed to the emergence of Switzerland and Luxembourg as important offshore financial centers?
4. Hong Kong and Singapore are major offshore financial centers in Asia. Compare and contrast the development of each city as an important offshore financial center.
5. What is an International Banking Facility?

Suggested Reading

Diamond, Walter. *Tax Havens of the World,* Vol. 1. New York: Matthew Bender, 1974–1983.
Higgins, J. Kevin. *The Bahamian Economy: An Analysis.* Nassau, The Bahamas: The Counsellors Ltd., 1994.
Jones, Michael Arthur. *Swiss Bank Accounts: A Personal Guide to Ownership Benefits and Use.* New York: Liberty Press Books, 1990.
Permanent Subcommittee on Investigations of the Committee on Governmental Affairs, U.S. Senate. *Crime and Secrecy: The Use of Offshore Banks and Companies.* Washington, D.C.: U.S. Government Printing Office, 1985.
Walter, Ingo. *The Secret Money Market: Inside the Dark World of Tax Evasion, Financial Fraud, Insider Trading, Money Laundering and Capital Flight.* New York: Harper Collins, 1990.

Notes

1. Brian Butler, David Butler, and Alan Isaacs, editors, *Oxford Dictionary of Finance and Banking: From International to Personal Finance* (Oxford: Oxford University Press, 1997), p. 249.

2. Ingo Walter, *The Secret Money Market: Inside the Dark World of Tax Evasion, Financial Fraud, Insider Trading, Money Laundering and Capital Flight* (New York: Harper Collins, 1990), p. 185.

3. U.S. Department of State, Bureau of Narcotics Affairs, *International Narcotics Control Enforcement Report 1997* (Washington, D.C.: U.S. Department of State, 1997), p. 112.

4. Taken from Paritate Bank's website, at www.paritate.lv.aboutparitate.htm.

5. Stephen Timewell, "Going Global," *The Banker*, February 1999, p. 40.

6. Report made by the Permanent Subcommittee on Investigations of the Committee on Governmental Affairs, U.S. Senate, *Crime and Secrecy: The Use of Offshore Banks and Companies* (Washington, D.C.: U.S. Government Printing Office, 1985), p. 125.

7. U.S. Department of State, *International Narcotics Control Enforcement Report 1997*, p. 112.

8. *Ibid.*, p. 113.

9. *Luxembourg* (Luxembourg: Editions Binsfeld, 1980), p. 21. The number of banks was data provided by the Luxembourg Bankers' Association.

10. The Luxembourg Bankers' Association, "Banking in Luxembourg: Facts and Figures, June 1998."

11. Organization for Economic Cooperation and Development, *OCED Economic Survey Belgium/Luxembourg 1999* (Paris: Organization for Economic Cooperation and Development, 1999), p. 133.

12. *Ibid.*

13. Walter Diamond, *Tax Havens of the World, Vol. 1* (New York: Matthew Bender, 1974–1983), p. 15.

14. J. Kevin Higgins, *The Bahamian Economy: An Analysis* (Nassau, The Bahamas: The Counsellors Ltd., 1994), p. 68.

15. Yoon S. Park and Jack Zwick, *International Banking in Theory and Practice* (Reading, Mass.: Addison-Wesley Publishing Company, 1985), p. 151.

16. Organization for Economic Development and Cooperation, *OECD Economic Outlook 1998* (Paris: Organization for Economic Cooperation and Development, 1998), p. 146.

17. Yoon S. Park and Jack Zwick, *International Banking in Theory and Practice*, p. 151.

18. Ed Crooks, "Islands Look to E-commerce Boost," *Financial Times*, July 27, 2000, p. 10.

CHAPTER 8

BANKING ON THE FOREIGN EXCHANGE MARKET

The foreign exchange (FX) market is the largest unregulated financial market in the world. As Figure 8.1 indicates, around $1.5 trillion changes hands every *day* on the foreign exchange markets, and global banks are major players in this market. Banks trade foreign exchange in part to provide a service for their customers, both retail and wholesale. (According to its annual report, in 1998 the volume of global FX transactions handled by Citibank exceeded the gross domestic product of the United States—$8.5 trillion.) Retail customers need foreign currency when they travel abroad; corporate customers need foreign currency when they do business overseas. It would be misleading, though, to view foreign exchange operations at international banks as purely a service for their customers. Banks also participate actively in FX markets to *take a position,* or speculate, on the direction of foreign currency movements, and to earn trading profits for their own bottom lines. The move to business activities such as FX trading reflects part of the ongoing shift of banks away from traditional deposit-taking activities to more fee-income and speculative activities.

FIGURE 8.1 Summary of Global Activity in Foreign Exchange Markets (average daily turnover in US$ billions)

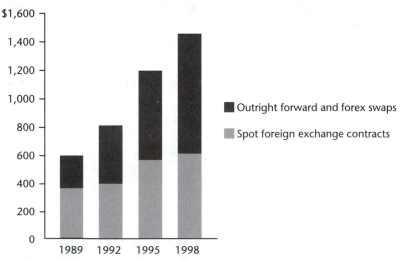

Source: The BIS Consolidated International Banking Statistics, 1998, at www.bis.org.

TURBULENCE IN CURRENCIES LIFTS US BANKS
Simon Kuper

The foreign exchange industry continued its strong recovery in the third quarter of 1997, as several large US banks reported currencies revenues more than doubling compared with the same period last year.

Bankers said the growth was due mainly to the return of volatility to the currency markets. Exchange rate moves were sharp, although many were swiftly reversed. For example, the dollar rose to DM 1.89 against the D-mark and then dropped about 15 pfennigs during the quarter, while sterling at one point fell almost 30 pfennigs from DM 3.08....

Klaus Said, head of foreign exchange at J.P. Morgan, said: "Volatility is always a positive double whammy. Unless you get your positions completely screwed up, it will benefit earnings." He said volatility rather than any change in strategy was almost the sole cause of growth at Morgan.

Last year, stability in the currency markets led some bankers to argue that the industry had embarked on a long downturn. Many traders were sacked and trading floors closed, but the resulting fall in capacity has helped several banks increase their profits this year.

Citibank, the market leader in foreign exchange, reported a 97% rise in foreign exchange trading revenues for the third quarter of this year to $435 million compared with the same period in 1996....

Source: Financial Times, October 28, 1997, p. 38.

This is a demanding business. It involves high risks and high returns. Speculating on foreign currency movements is not quite as risky as gambling in Las Vegas, if you possess specialized knowledge of key markets, market variables, and government policy trends that may give you an edge over other speculators. At times, however, the similarities are uncomfortable. The currency is the bottom line of a country. Everything eventually washes out in the foreign exchange markets, so that the currency rate will come to reflect political factors, economics, financial issues, personalities, weather, culture, and dumb luck. This makes FX trading both a serious challenge and an opportunity for market participants, including banks.

FX Market: Who, What, Where, When, Why, and How?

The foreign exchange market is an oddity, unlike any other market in the world. There is no physical location for FX trading, like the New York Stock Exchange. Rather, the foreign exchange market consists of thousands of traders throughout the world, linked together by computers, telephones, and even telexes. Most trading takes place among dealers in New York, London, and Tokyo. London remains

GLOBAL FX MARKETS

In its triennial survey of FX trading, released in late 1998, the Bank for International Settlements (BIS) estimates the total size of the "traditional" FX market in 1998 at $1.5 trillion per day. (To put this in perspective, this compares with around $50 billion in stock trades on an extraordinarily heavy trading day for the New York Stock Exchange.) The BIS found that dollar trading still dominates the market. Indeed, a whopping 87 percent of all currency trades still involve the U.S. dollar. (See Table 8.1.) The Deutsche mark was the second most commonly traded currency, followed by the Japanese yen, UK pound, French franc, Swiss franc, and Canadian dollar. However, trading in emerging market currencies such as the Czech koruna, the South African rand, and East Asian currencies is increasing rapidly.

Also, the dollar's dominance may well be challenged by the emergence of the euro, which came into being on January 1, 1999, and is eventually expected to replace eleven West European currencies. The euro, which represents a bloc of countries that is slightly larger than the U.S. in terms of world trade and gross national product, may well prove a serious competitor to the dollar. Governments may choose to hold their foreign exchange reserves in euros rather than dollars, and multinational corporations, too, may choose to invoice their foreign sales in euros. This would produce a gradual increase in euro trading on FX markets, and a corresponding decrease in dollar trades.

TABLE 8.1 Currency Distribution of Global Traditional Foreign Exchange Market Activity[1] (% shares of average daily turnover)

Currency	April 1989	April 1992	April 1995	April 1998
U.S. dollar	90%	82%	83%	87%
Deutsche mark[2]	27	40	37	30
Japanese yen	27	23	24	21
Pound sterling	15	14	10	11
French franc	2		8	5
Swiss franc	10	9	7	7
Canadian dollar	1	3	3	4
Australian dollar	2	2	3	3
ECU and other EMS currencies	4	12	15	17
Other currencies	22	11	10	15
All curencies	**200**	**196**	**200**	**200**

Source: BIS Consolidated Statistics. 1998. www.bis.org.

[1] Whenever reported on one side of transactions. The figures relate to reported "net-net" turnover; i.e., they are adjusted for both local and cross-border double-counting, except for 1989 data, which are available only on a "gross-gross" basis.

[2] Data for April 1989 exclude domestic trading involving the Deutsche mark in Germany.

the number one FX market, followed by New York in the second position and Tokyo at number three. (The London market benefits immeasurably from having a time zone that allows it to overlap with the end-of-day activities in Asia and the morning business hours in North America.) These three centers together account for nearly 60 percent of all FX business.

In theory, all convertible foreign currencies (i.e., currencies that may be freely traded without government involvement) may be traded by any foreign exchange dealer anywhere in the world. In reality, though, some currencies are relatively scarce on FX markets and require a specialized trader to perform a large, well-priced deal. For example, the most efficient trades in Scandinavian currencies are still done by Scandinavian banks in their home markets. By the same token, a trader in Rio de Janeiro might have a difficult time giving a timely, well-priced quote on the South African rand.

The FX market is often described as a twenty-four-hour market. It is certainly true that FX trading does not open and close at set times, like the New York Stock Exchange. A trader with access to a computer terminal or telephone can execute FX deals at any hour. (In fact, senior traders in New York often do crawl out of bed in the middle of the night to check their positions and do a few deals with Tokyo.) The market essentially moves around the globe in line with international time zones, from the Far East to the Middle East to Europe to New York to Chicago to the West Coast and back to the Far East again.

The liveliest time in the markets, however, is during the New York morning, when traders in both London and New York are actively trading. This is when the markets are the deepest and the most liquid; thus it is by far the best time to execute large trades. The bulk of FX trading takes place during this window of time. Woe betides the hapless customer who tries to execute a big or difficult trade with a New York bank on a Friday afternoon! The markets may be too sleepy for the New York trader to resell the foreign currency at a reasonable price (the trader's counterparts in Europe are already out celebrating the week's profits), and so he or she will make the customer pay dearly for making the bank hold the position over the weekend.

Banks and their multinational customers form the backbone of the FX market. (See Table 8.2.) Multinational corporations (MNCs) trade foreign exchange for business purposes, such as trade and investment overseas. Corporate treasurers use FX markets to hedge against adverse swings in currency rates, in order to protect their investments and earnings streams. Also, some MNCs speculate on FX movements just as banks do. These companies go way beyond hedging to protect their positions, by building up large positions to take bets on future FX rates. Allied-Lyons of the United Kingdom, for example, took heavy positions on its expectations of dollar weakness (e.g., selling the dollar short), and they lost nearly $300 million on these FX dealings in 1991 when the dollar unexpectedly shot up against the pound.

Central banks are also key participants in FX markets, although these days the central banks of industrialized countries are much less apt to intervene in currency markets to try to influence the direction of currency movements than they were in the 1970s and 1980s. The ill-fated interventions of the central banks of Thailand and Korea in 1997 only reinforce the concept that such interventions do

TABLE 8.2 *Euromoney* Foreign Exchange Poll, 1998–99

FX Trading Rank by Market Share

1999	1998	Bank	Estimated Share (%)
1	1	Citibank/Salomon Smith Barney	7.75%
2	2	Deutsche Bank	7.12
3	3	Chase Manhattan Bank	7.09
4	—[1]	Warburg Dillon Read	6.44
5	4	Goldman Sachs	4.86
6	—[2]	BankAmerica	4.39
7	6	J.P. Morgan	4.00
8	5	HSBC	3.75
9	11	ABN Amro	3.37
10	8	Merrill Lynch	3.27

Source: Euromoney, May 1999. www.euromoney.com
[1]SBC Warburg Dillon Read ranked 7, UBS 19.
[2]BankAmerica ranked 12, NationsBank 73.

not necessarily work. (However, intervention is far from dead; witness the European Central Bank's efforts in 2000 to prop up the wilting euro.) In addition, large investment funds have become increasingly important players on FX markets in the past decade. Of these, perhaps the most notorious are the giant hedge funds such as Long-Term Capital Management (LTCM) of Greenwich, Connecticut. Hedge funds are private investment pools that borrow huge amounts of money to trade securities and currencies. According to Federal Reserve Board Chairman Alan Greenspan, a hedge fund "is structured to avoid regulation by limiting its clientele to a small number of highly sophisticated, very wealthy individuals…. it seeks high rates of return by investing and trading in a variety of financial instruments."[1] Hedge funds are often managed very aggressively, and they may take massive positions in expectation of foreign currency swings.

The investment funds, obviously, participate in FX markets in the hopes of earning a trading profit. Similarly, banks profit in various ways from their participation in FX trading. First, they make money from the **spread** between the bid and ask price on foreign currency. (The bid price is the price to buy dollars; the ask price is the price to sell dollars.) Obviously, if a bank buys low and sells high, it will profit from the spread between these two rates.

Spreads in FX trading have been driven down to razor-thin levels over the past decade, however. In this environment, it is fortunate that banks can also profit from their **proprietary trading** activities in FX markets, in which the banks' traders take a position on the direction of the foreign currency and place their bets accordingly. If the bank's senior yen trader believes that the yen will increase in value, for example, he or she will buy up yen and hold them for the expected increase in value. Since currency values fluctuate constantly, and trades are usually in huge denominations

HOW FX RATES ARE DETERMINED

It is well established that, over the long run, currencies adjust to reflect the relative economic fundamentals of the countries they represent. If the U.S. economy is fundamentally stronger than Canada's, over time the U.S. dollar should strengthen against the Canadian dollar. The trouble is that over the long term, as the great economist John Maynard Keynes observed, we're all dead. In the meantime, figuring out what makes currencies fluctuate can be a challenging task indeed.

The bedrock of traditional currency forecasting is the **purchasing power parity (PPP)** theory, which postulates that under perfect conditions, exchange rates adjust for relative inflation. If U.S. inflation is 5 percent and Mexican inflation is 30 percent, the Mexican peso should fall by roughly 25 percent against the dollar. Conditions are very rarely perfect though, and in real life PPP has proved a very flawed indicator of currency trends. Thus economists look at other economic fundamentals as well for clues to currency directions. Currencies should be influenced by the country's balance of payments, for instance, and by its record of economic growth. Countries that attract sizable inflows of foreign capital should see their currencies strengthen. A country with sensible macroeconomic policies should have a stronger currency than one with high inflation, high government borrowing, and poor productivity levels.

A host of other factors influence FX traders as well. Some governments still intervene in FX markets by buying and selling their own currencies, to try to push foreign exchange rates to a desired level. In addition, market psychology and expectations are critical. FX markets tend to be wary of socialist governments, for example, and will often bid down the value of a currency when a leftist government is elected. Traders are also painfully aware of each other. This creates a kind of "Keynesian beauty contest" situation, in which judges vote for the contestant that they think the other judges will select, not the one that they prefer. If traders believe that their counterparts will sell the Russian ruble, they will too, regardless of whether they believe the ruble really deserves to be sold short.

Finally, FX traders keep a close eye on world events. They tend to rush into safe haven currencies like the U.S. dollar or Swiss franc at times of global uncertainty (like the death of a Russian or Chinese leader, for example). If oil prices rise, traders will buy up U.S. and Canadian dollars, UK pounds, and Norwegian kronor (the currencies of strong oil producers), while selling off the currencies of countries such as France, Italy, and Japan that are more dependent on oil imports.

Putting together all these factors to form a consistent and reliable method of exchange rate forecasting is a Herculean task. Some forecasters rely on increasingly sophisticated econometric models, which draw on economic and

(continued)

financial data to produce a forecast for the currency based on historical relationships. Others use technical models, which produce short-term trading
guidelines based on recent patterns of market behavior. Others still create a
kitchen-sink approach, which throws in some econometrics, some technical
modeling, and a large dollop of experience and judgment to produce the final
forecast. The results of these forecasts are mixed at best. A famous paper by
Richard Meese and Kenneth Rogoff demonstrates that the random walk
model, which forecasts that tomorrow's exchange rate will be the same as
today's, outperforms all other models in terms of mean forecasting error.[1]

[1]Richard A. Meese and Kenneth Rogoff, "Empirical Exchange Rate Models of the Seventies,"
Journal of International Economics, 14 (February 1983), pp. 3–24.

(the normal interbank minimum is $5 million per trade), it only takes a very small
increase in the yen to net the bank a tidy profit. In fact, most bank traders only hold
positions for a matter of minutes before they cash out. As the article at the beginning
of the chapter notes, FX traders make their money from currency volatility.

Forecasting currency movements has long been more of an art than a science,
although computer-based models have always been a popular tool. At the turn of
the decade, however, changes in the fundamentals of currency flows have contributed to some adjustments in the prevailing wisdom on currency analysis. First,
the volume of cross-border capital flows has mushroomed; the gross inflow of funds
to the United States ballooned from $142 billion in 1990 to $715 billion in 1999.
Second, the composition of these funds has shifted, largely due to a huge increase
in the volume of equity-related flows. Thus currency analysts must pay more attention to issues that affect long-term, bricks and mortar type investment flows.

These factors are increasingly of interest to currency analysts and traders, in part
because of the perplexing and persistent weakness of the euro since its birth in January 1999—in defiance of all the economic fundamentals. The euro has been expected
to gain ground essentially since the day it arrived. Despite these expectations, though,
during its first eighteen months the euro stubbornly refused to respond to an acceleration of economic growth in the eurozone, a continued current account surplus, and
declining interest rate differentials between the eurozone and the United States. In
fact, the hapless euro tumbled by 23 percent in its first eighteen months of life.

This has prompted currency experts to turn to new methods of analysis. For
one thing, the role of volatile and fickle short-term capital flows is now given much
more emphasis in currency forecasting models. Similarly, FX analysts are turning
more attention to the overall investment environment of a country, in order to determine the likely direction and volume of foreign direct investment. As the following article demonstrates, though, the art of currency analysis continues to confound
and frustrate even the most experienced of practitioners.

MYSTIFYING MOVES TEST ECONOMISTS
Christopher Swann

The foreign exchange market is a capricious beast at the best of times. But the movements of the world's largest currencies have been particularly mystifying over the past year.

Seldom has the divergence between economic fundamentals and the performance of currencies been so stark.

Traditional currency analysis, based on economic growth, interest rates and current account balances would, for example, have dictated a rising euro and a falling yen. In fact, the reverse has happened.

The refusal of currencies to obey textbook economics has helped bring new analytical tools to the fore—most notably the study of capital flows and market positioning....

Source: Financial Times, June 2, 2000, p. 4.

Emerging Trends in FX Trading

Bank consolidation, corporate mergers, the single European currency for the majority of European Union members, the Asian financial crisis of 1997–98, and the growing role of technology all contribute to new realities in the business of foreign exchange, creating new opportunities and threats in the process. Profits have been decidedly volatile for banks in the FX business. Profits growth slowed dramatically in the early 1990s, leading some to issue doom-and-gloom scenarios for the future of foreign exchange profitability. Banks slimmed down their trading capabilities, and some began to focus on alternative revenue sources. In 1997, however, the FX markets came roaring back. Currency volatility made this a banner year for the FX trading business at most banks. The big players and some niche players seemed to benefit the most; Standard Chartered, for example, made nearly $200 million on FX trading in 1997, one-half of this directly related to the upheaval in Asian currency markets. (See Figure 8.2.) Similarly, some banks made huge profits on the Brazilian devaluation of early 1999. Chase Manhattan reportedly earned $150 million from the devaluation, more than twice its net income in Brazil for all of 1998.[2]

Even so, it is evident that banks are under pressure on FX profits. Increased competition and the proliferation of new technologies have combined to drive down the spreads between bid and offer prices. In particular, the introduction of electronic broking systems and the Reuters FX trading system in the mid-1990s have made dealing prices more transparent, thus bringing down spreads. Now, banks make only a tiny profit on most trades.[3] (Internet trading is the next frontier, but so far most players still prefer the personal contact of a telephone deal for large trades.) Cheaper

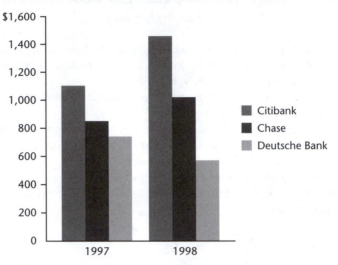

FIGURE 8.2 Revenue from Foreign Exchange Trading Operations (US$ millions)

Sources: Citibank, Chase Manhattan Bank, and Deutsche Bank Annual Reports, 1998. [Note: Deutsche Bank report originally in DM. Exchange rate (DM/$): 1.7905 (12/31/97); 1.6767 (12/31/98). Source of exchange rate: Bloomberg.]

technology also allows information to be shared more widely. If every trader has the same information at the same time, profit opportunities decline precipitously.

A second dampening factor is the newfound trend toward European currency stability. On January 1, 1999, eleven major European countries joined the euro-zone, linking their national currencies to a new currency, the euro, at fixed rates and intending to move exclusively to the euro over the next few years. Obviously, this removes eleven currencies from FX trading at one fell swoop. Most European currencies had been relatively stable for the past few years as well, in the run-up to the euro. Currency stability removes profit opportunities from the markets. Even worse, within Europe it has meant that governments have finally accepted market realities, removing sitting targets represented by fundamentally weak currencies propped up by a combination of official intervention and high interest rates. Currency speculators know that eventually such currencies will fall, and place their bets accordingly. In 1992, for example, George Soros bet against the British pound and won approximately $1 billion! In the good old days, betting against central banks was a windfall profit opportunity. *Forbes* magazine reported in 1992: "The month of wild trading and sheer excitement that wrecked the European Exchange Rate Mechanism was ... good times for leading U.S. banks with big foreign exchange operations, especially Citicorp, J.P. Morgan, Chemical Bank, Bankers Trust, Chase Manhattan, First Chicago, and BankAmerica. Together, in the third quarter, they netted before taxes $800 million more than what they normally earn in a quarter from trading currencies."[4]

As the turn of the century approached, however, central banks smartened up. Traders can no longer exploit the policy errors of central banks by betting against their currencies. Most central banks (except for some emerging market countries)

HOW? THE MECHANICS OF FX TRADING

Foreign exchange traders adhere religiously to a set of conventions that can make their dealings seem strange and mysterious to the uninitiated. FX rates are quoted in two ways: American or European terms. These rates are reciprocals of each other.

American	European
$.667 = SF 1.0	SF 1.5 = $1.0
$.0080 = Yen 1.0	Yen 125 = $1.0
$1.55 = Pound 1.0	Pound .645 = $1.0

In practice, European terms are used for all currencies except for the pound sterling. (Inexplicably, the euro, too, is quoted in American terms.) Currency rates are also quoted in terms of a bid/ask price. If the quote is $1.5434–36 per UK pound, this means that $1.5434 is the bid rate, or the price at which the bank will *buy* sterling. The ask (or offer) price is $1.5436, the rate at which the bank will *sell* sterling. The difference between the bid and ask prices is the spread, or the bank's gross profit on the deal. This spread should be large enough to cover overhead, risk, and profits.

There are three primary types of transactions in the FX market. A **spot** deal is a trade for current value at current prices. In reality, though, spot deals have an actual value date of two business days (next business day in the North American market). A **forward** trade is when the two sides agree today to buy/sell the foreign exchange at some future date at a price that is agreed on today. Forward currencies trade at a **premium** or **discount** relative to their spot rate; the premium or discount reflects interest rate differentials. Finally, a **swap** involves both a spot and forward contract, or two forwards. This is the simultaneous purchase and sale of foreign exchange for two different value dates, with the same counterparty.

have stopped defending unrealistic currency rates. This means that the days of easy FX profits for banks are over.

As a result, banks must offer more and improved services to win foreign exchange business from their multinational clients. Part and parcel of this is a tendency to downplay plain vanilla spot transactions, and to pay increasing attention to increasingly sophisticated foreign exchange transactions, such as **derivatives**. Derivatives are financial instruments that derive their value from an underlying instrument, in this case foreign exchange. Thus FX derivatives include options, futures, forwards, and swaps. While futures and forwards have long been part of the FX business, the creation of new and sophisticated instruments based on these

INTEREST RATE PARITY, FORWARDS, AND SWAPS

In a forward deal, the two parties agree to trade currency at some future date at a preagreed rate. (Note: The forward market is *not* equal to the futures market!) Rates in the forward market are quoted in terms of premium and discount. For example:

Spot	1.5370 SF/$	1.5350 $/pound
1 Month Forward	1.5320 SF/$	1.5270 $/pound

In these examples, the Swiss franc (SF) is trading at a forward premium against the dollar (it is worth more on the one month forward than it is worth on the spot market), and the pound is at a forward discount against the dollar. (Remember that the SF is quoted in European terms and the pound in American terms.)

The forward premium/discount is usually quoted in terms of points added to or subtracted from the spot rate, both bid and offered. The points are sometimes called a **swap rate.** For example,

Spot	1.4273/90 SF/$		
1 Month	.0030/.0020	*or*	30/20

How do you know whether to subtract or add? The convention is that if the points are quoted with the larger number first, you *subtract.* If the smaller number is first, you *add.* In this case, you subtract because the larger number is first. This gives us outright forward rates of 1.4243/70. Thus the Swiss franc is at a forward premium against the dollar.

The premium/discount is often evaluated in terms of percent per annum, calculated as follows:

Spot	1.8200 $/euro
6 Month Forward	1.8450 $/euro

Step 1: Find the premium/swap rate. In this case,
        $1.8450 - 1.8200 = .0250.$

Step 2: Multiply by twelve months and divide by six months to annualize.

Step 3: Divide by the spot rate.

Step 4: Multiply by 100.

So,

$$.0250 \times 12/6 = .05,$$

and

$$(.05/1.8200) \times 100 = 2.75 \text{ percent per annum}$$

What determines the premium/discount? According to the interest rate parity theory, certain forces will work toward making investment yields and

(continued)

borrowing costs equal in different countries and currencies. Thus there should be no advantage to borrowing or investing in any particular money market; there should be equality between the rate of return on domestic assets and on hedged foreign assets. This means that the premium/discount should be equivalent to the interest rate differential between the two currencies, in order to offset differences in borrowing costs. In the above example, the euro is trading at a 2.75 percent per annum forward premium against the dollar. This tells us that interest rates in the eleven eurozone countries (on a weighted average basis) should be 2.75 percent lower than U.S. interest rates.

derivatives is a competitive and complex operation. As the 1999 *Financial Times* survey on FX observes, bankers are turning more and more to "the rapidly growing market in exotic FX derivatives."[5] According to the BIS, spot FX transactions increased by only around 15 percent from 1995 to 1998 to total $600 billion per day, while over-the-counter FX options doubled in the same period to a gross outstanding daily value of $141 billion.

The foreign exchange markets have changed dramatically over the past decade, and further transformations are under way. The most obvious development in FX markets is explosive growth. Global foreign exchange trading has expanded rapidly with the liberalization of cross-border financial flows and with the proliferation and increased sophistication of the technology that has helped to reduce transactions costs (and profits).

COVERED INTEREST ARBITRAGE

The mechanism necessary to maintain the spot and forward exchange markets in the state of equilibrium described by interest rate parity is known as **covered interest arbitrage.** When the market is not in equilibrium, the conditions for riskless or arbitrage profits exist. The arbitrageur, usually a FX trader at a major bank, will move to take advantage of these conditions by executing a covered interest arbitrage transaction. He or she invests in whichever currency brings the higher return on a covered basis, as described in Figure 8.3. This process of covered interest arbitrage drives the market toward the equilibrium described by interest rate parity. Slight deviations from equilibrium provide the opportunity for small riskless profits; however, should the trader hesitate for even a few minutes, the opportunity will disappear.

(continued)

FIGURE 8.3 Covered Interest Arbitrage

Morning. William Wong, an arbitraguer for Hong Kong & Shanghai Banking Corporation, Hong Kong, arrives at work Tuesday morning to be faced with the currency quotations shown in the "Morning Quotation Box" below. He has access to several major Euro-currencies for arbitrage trading. On the basis of the quotations below he decides to execute the following CIA transaction:

Step 1: Convert $1,000,000 at the spot rate of ¥106.00/$ to ¥106,000,000 (see "Start").
Step 2: Invest the proceeds, ¥106,000,000, in a Euroyen account for six months, earning 4.00% per annum, or 2% for 180 days.
Step 3: Simultaneously sell the proceeds (¥108,120,000) forward for dollars at the 180 day forward rate of ¥103.50/$. This action "locks in" gross dollar revenues of $1,044,638 (see "End").
Step 4: Calculate the cost (opportunity cost) of funds used at the Eurodollar rate of 8.00% per annum, or 4% for 180 days, with principal interest then totaling $1,040,000. Profit on CIA at the "End" is

$$\$1,044,638 \text{ (proceeds)} - \$1,040,000 \text{ (cost)} = \$4,638$$

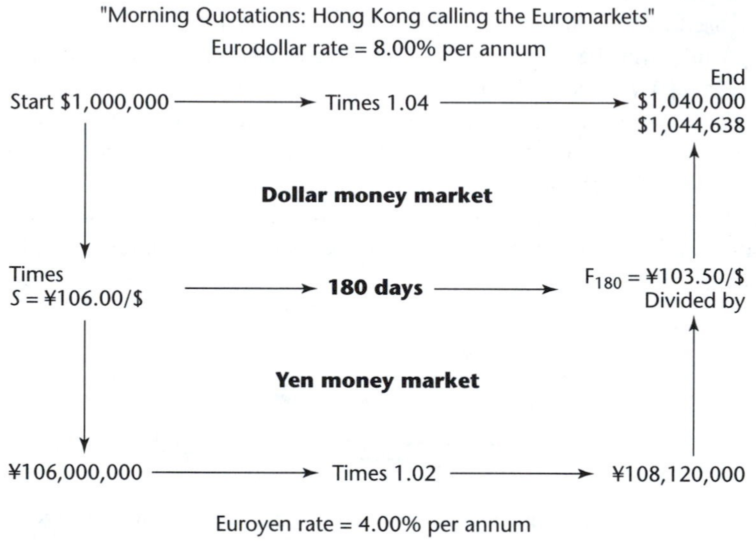

"Morning Quotations: Hong Kong calling the Euromarkets"
Eurodollar rate = 8.00% per annum

Source: Adapted from David K. Eiteman, Arthur I. Stonehill, and Michael H. Moffett, *Multinational Business Finance*, 8th edition (Reading, Mass. Addison-Wesley Publishing Company, 1998), pp. 123–125.

Part and parcel of this growth is the entrance of new players, bringing new muscle and mind-set into the world of currency trading. For years, the large international banks, securities houses, corporate treasurers, and central banks dominated FX trading. For the most part, these are conservative institutions, heavily regulated and closely observed by stock analysts and shareholders. Now, they are joined in the FX markets by institutional investors with huge portfolios of assets and capital: hedge funds, pension funds, and insurance companies are a

CURRENCY SWAPS

A **currency swap** is a foreign exchange agreement between two parties to exchange a given amount of one currency for another and, after a period of time, to give back the original amounts swapped. Currency swaps may be negotiated for maturities up to ten years and beyond. The swap bank or dealer acts as intermediary in this transaction.

A typical currency swap first requires two firms to borrow funds in the markets and currencies in which they are best known. For example, a Japanese firm would typically borrow yen on a regular basis in its home market. If the Japanese firm were exporting to the United States and earning U.S. dollars, however, it might wish to construct a natural hedge that would allow it to use the U.S. dollars earned to make regular debt service payments on U.S. dollar debt. If the Japanese firm is not well known in the U.S. financial markets, though, it may have no ready access to U.S. dollar debt. Thus it could participate in a currency swap, as shown in Figure 8.4. The Japanese firm could swap its yen-denominated debt service payments with another firm that has U.S. dollar debt service payments. The Japanese firm would then have dollar debt service without actually borrowing U.S. dollars.

The swap markets are dominated by the major money-center banks worldwide. After being introduced on a global scale in the early 1980s, currency swaps have grown to be one of the largest financial derivative markets in the world, a major source of both risk and opportunity for bankers.

FIGURE 8.4 Creation of a Currency Swap Through a Swap Dealer

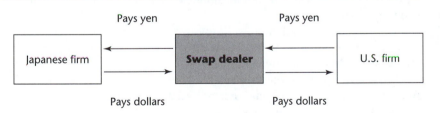

A Japanese firm can swap its U.S. dollar-denominated debt payments for the Japanese yen-denominated debt payments of a U.S. firm through a swap dealer. The swap dealer searches out matching currency exposures and plays the role of a middleman, providing a valuable currency management service for both firms.

Source: David K. Eiteman, Arthur I. Stonehill, and Michael H. Moffett, *Multinational Business Finance,* 8th edition (Reading, Mass.: Addison-Wesley Publishing Company, 1998), p. 256..

---

few examples. Overall, the flows generated by these investment groups are far greater than those of banks, which are subject to official regulations and must limit their risk accordingly. (Hedge funds were made famous overnight by George Soros's Quantum Fund, which "mugged" the Bank of England in 1992 as described above; they became infamous in 1998 with the debacle of Long-Term Capital Management.) They are largely unregulated, and operate primarily by taking highly leveraged, speculative positions. There are around 3,000 hedge funds operating around the world today, with an estimated $400 billion of money from investors.

The ultimate role of these new players in the FX markets is a matter of intense debate. Critics argue that they are immensely destabilizing, with the power to make or break currencies with a few computer keystrokes. Some politicians, especially in emerging market countries, warn that the hedge funds are big and bold enough to force a devaluation, and reap the profits afterward. There is no doubt that hedge funds are indeed powerful enough to move currency markets. In October 1998, for example, yen purchases by a handful of huge hedge funds, apparently to repay yen loans, reportedly pushed the yen up quite dramatically and unexpectedly against the U.S. dollar.

On the other hand, supporters argue that hedge funds in fact play a stabilizing role in world financial markets, by acting as "enforcers" who ensure that countries enact sensible economic and financial policies. Soros might argue, for example, that he was only making the Bank of England pay the price for its own ill-consid-

MYSTERIOUS SPECULATORS CREATE RISKY NEW WORLD

Junichi Miura

When the dollar plunged by more than 11 yen on October 7, [1998,] rumors flew fast and furious among traders at New York's foreign exchange market.

One said hedge funds were selling off huge amounts of dollars. No, another said, the funds were holding their dollars and were just waiting to unload the currency at the right moment.

Whichever was true, when the smoke cleared, one fact was clear: hedge funds were at the heart of the most dramatic selling of the U.S. currency since it was put on the floating exchange rate system in 1973....

An economist at the New York branch of Sanwa Bank estimated that hedge funds dislodged more than $20 billion on October 7.

Given that any central bank can only intervene with, at most, several billions of dollars a day, the amount is staggering.

Many economists believe that it is now practically impossible for monetary authorities to compete against hedge funds to control the direction of a market....

Source: Daily Yomiuri (Tokyo), October 23, 1998, p. 1.

ered policies in the early 1990s—and, perhaps, acting as a deterrent to other countries that might be tempted into similar policy mistakes. Another hedge fund manager, David Shaw of DE Shaw, says that hedge funds are a "positive force." By making money from market inefficiencies, he explains, they perform a crucial job "from a social welfare point of view."[6]

Whatever the outcome of this debate, the bottom line is that new, more aggressive companies are embarking on huge speculative transactions in FX markets. Also, building an FX business is a tougher challenge today. Setting up a trading system and hiring staff is extremely expensive, thus increasing the challenge—and profit opportunities—of FX trading accordingly. One by-product is a much greater

A FRENZIED MARKET

It is impossible for mere words and pictures to fully express the frenzied pace and activity of the FX markets. To give the reader some sense of a typical day in the markets, this is excerpted from one of the thousands of websites devoted to FX market activity. It describes activity on one, relatively quiet day in late 2000.

September 15, 2000

As expected, SWF [Swiss franc] backed up into 1.7700s before turning around for a speedy dip to our long anticipated downside target of 1.7500, courtesy of ECB's (European Central Bank) verbal threat of intervention. As planned, we made an SWF buy (long) entry at 1.7700 which was in a nice position to catch the whole distance of +200 points. But, as it is often the case, the market rose against us just high enough to trigger our 1.7750 cut loss order before nosing down below 1.7500. Perhaps this is (as some viewers insist) the doing of market's big boys who are reading our trade plans against us, or perhaps this is the showing of market's poetic justice to carve back a bit of our early boastful profit. In our opinion, the latter is more likely. Now that SWF dipped down to complete the touchdown at 1.7500, the dollar bulls have one less concern to be worried about as they turn to focus once again on the benchmark 1.8000. We will back up our SWF's buy (long) orders a bit to let the market make this move. Our next main battle line will be drawn at SWF 1.8000. We will do a hit-and-run buy (long) trade at SWF's previous high of 1.7920. Both EUR [euro] and GBP [British pound] are near their crucial lows which would turn out to be major technical buying levels if given the right credible intervention scares. We move down their buy (long) entries to 0.8480 and 1.3900. JPY [Japanese yen] seems to flirt with 108.00 level again, so we will stay off its buying plan for now....

Source: ForexATS, at www.FOREX-ats.com/dailyshow/html.

concentration of FX business. Increasingly, FX trading is concentrated in London, and among a decreasing number of global banks. Only the very biggest banks have the financial muscle to sustain the liquidity and credit risk involved in the very large scale, high-stakes FX trading that dominates the markets today. The head of FX and commodities trading at J.P. Morgan says, "Single spot trades of $500 million or $1 billion are quite frequent now. These can be risky, with potentially good returns for the banks, but it will only be the largest FX firms more comfortable with risk which can execute these deals." For the most part, the U.S. regional banks have exited the business of FX trading (aside from deals to service their customers), and several Japanese banks have been weakened so badly by their financial crisis of the late 1990s that they have withdrawn as well.[7]

Finally, the advent of the euro places a big question mark over the future of FX trading activity in European currencies. The euro is all about eliminating financial inefficiencies in the market; thus it will eliminate opportunities for traders who profit from inefficiencies. While many questions remain, there are two impacts that seem certain. First, euro versus dollar trading will take off (although euro/dollar dealing was off to a slow and cautious start during 1999 and 2000). Second (and perhaps more ominously), banks will show increasing interest in trading emerging market currencies to replace the lost profits of intra-European trading. Dealing in emerging market currencies suffers from decreased liquidity, increased volatility, and increased uncertainty compared with trading in well-established West European currencies. As a result, this trend may well increase the riskiness of FX trading by banks in general.

Managing Risk in FX Trading

FX trading inevitably involves taking on risk. Essentially, there are two forms of risk involved in FX markets from the bank's viewpoint: settlement risk and trading risk. *Trading risk* consists of the possibility that the currency you purchase will decline in value before you can resell it. To take a simple example, suppose that Citibank purchases 5 million yen from a corporate customer who has received the yen in payment for a sale to its Japanese customer. At the time that Citi purchases the yen, the yen/dollar exchange rate is 250 yen/dollar, so the 5 million yen are worth $20,000. If the yen declines to 260/$, the 5 million yen are only worth $19,230; if the yen goes up to 240/$, the 5 million yen have now increased in value to $20,833.

When Citi purchases the yen, it essentially has two choices. First, Citi's trader can immediately resell the yen to another bank. This will earn the bank a small profit from the spread between its bid price and its offer price (the price at which it resells). Alternatively, the trader can decide to take a position on the yen. If the trader believes that the yen should rise in value, perhaps because he or she is expecting an announcement of favorable economic news from Japan later that day, the yen can be held in anticipation of this price rise with plans to resell it later in the day (or even tomorrow) at a higher price.

This kind of activity, speculation, is where the big profits (or big losses!) are in the FX market. Bank managers must choose their preferred position along the

FIGURE 8.5 Yen Historical Price (yen/$)

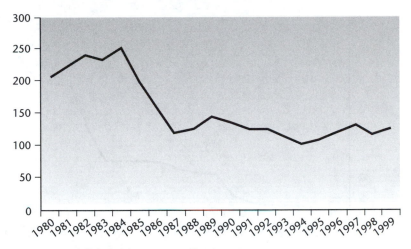

Source: Bloomberg, Historical Price Traded Currency, at www.bloomberg.com.

FIGURE 8.6 British Pound Historical Price ($/GBP)

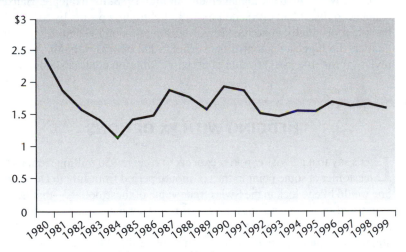

Source: Bloomberg, Historical Price Traded Currency, at www.bloomberg.com.

risk/return trade-off curve, and plan accordingly. Managers monitor traders' positions on a real-time basis, and they set strict trading limits for each trader. It is especially important to separate the functions of the trader from those of back-office personnel who are responsible for recording and monitoring the trades. The importance of these controls has been graphically demonstrated by several incidents in which traders managed to evade controls and build up huge currency

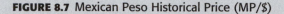

FIGURE 8.7 Mexican Peso Historical Price (MP/$)

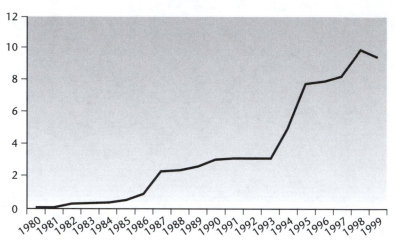

Source: Bloomberg, Historical Price Traded Currency, at www.bloomberg.com.

positions, only to take correspondingly huge losses eventually when the positions were uncovered by bank management. In mid-1988, for example, Bankers Trust announced that it had overstated its 1987 FX trading profits by $80 million. The bank had originally announced FX trading gains of $338 million in the fourth quarter, the biggest such profits ever recorded by a U.S. bank. A management review of the true market value of certain FX option contracts, however, led it to

HEDGING WITH FX OPTIONS

L et's say that a Swiss exporter expects to receive $50 million from a U.S. customer at some point in the six-month period from July to December. She would like to lock in the Swiss franc value of these dollars—that is, execute a **hedge.** Since she does not know the exact date of the payment, she prefers to hedge with an **option,** which gives her the right, but not the obligation, to complete the trade, rather than a forward or future contract.

Her banker offers to sell her a **call option** on Swiss francs (SF), which gives her the right to buy SF at an agreed-on price, called the **strike price,** at any time in the next six months. (This type of option is called an **American option,** since the exporter has the right to exercise the option at any point in the six-month period. By contrast, a **European option** may only be exercised on its maturity date.) In exchange for this right, she pays the banker a **premium** up front:

Strike price on SF call: SF 1.30/$
Premium: SF 0.04/$

(continued)

Thus the **floor value** of this option, or the worst price she can possibly get for her dollars, is equal to the exercise price minus the premium:

$$\text{Floor Value} = \text{exercise price} - \text{premium}$$
$$= 1.30 \text{ SF/\$} - 0.04 \text{ SF/\$}$$
$$= 1.26 \text{ SF/\$}$$

This means that the exporter is now assured of getting at least 1.26 SF for every dollar that she receives, regardless of what happens to the SF/$ exchange rate on the FX market. Whether or not she decides to exercise the option, however, depends on what the SF/$ spot exchange rate does.

Case I: SF Declines to 1.45 SF/$

In this case, the exporter decides not to exercise the option. She is better off selling the dollars in the spot market for 1.45 SF/$ than exercising the option. Her net value is 1.45 SF/$ minus the premium that she paid for the option, or 1.45 SF/$ − 0.04 SF/$. (Note that this calculation ignores the opportunity cost of borrowing the SF 0.04/$ premium, since this was an up-front cost. If the opportunity cost was 5 percent per annum, then the total value of the premium was really 0.04 SF/$ × 1.025 for a six-month period.)

Case II: SF Rises to 1.15 SF/$

In this case, the exporter does exercise the option. She is better off selling the dollars through the option contract at the strike price of 1.30 SF/$ than she would be in the spot market at 1.15 SF/$.

What about the banker who sold the option? His maximum gain on this contract is limited to the premium that he received up front. His downside risk, on the other hand, is potentially unlimited and depends on how far the SF rises. In Case II, for example, the banker would have to buy the dollars from the exporter at 1.30 SF/$, and then resell them in the spot market at only 1.15 SF/$, a substantial loss on $50 million. Bankers try to protect themselves against such losses by constructing elaborate hedging strategies related to options sales. The complexity, volatility, and poor liquidity of many FX derivatives such as options contracts makes it very difficult to value and monitor banks' positions in these markets, however. This is an ongoing concern for bank managers and regulators.

reduce its profits estimate to $258 million.[8] Since then, banks have developed increasingly sophisticated risk management models for FX trading, in order to calculate the sensitivity of their profits to literally millions of what-if scenarios. (However, as the article below illustrates, this has not eliminated the potential for big FX miscalculations.) Ultimately, FX trading success rests on a combination of discipline, courage, capital, technical skills, experience, luck, and effective internal control procedures.[9]

The second kind of FX trading risk is called **settlement risk,** or sometimes **Herstatt risk.** Because of differences between time zones and the operating hours of national payments systems, banks often pay out their side of a foreign exchange deal before they actually receive any payment in return. This means that a bank may be exposed to heavy losses if its counterparty collapses before making payment. In 1974, the collapse of Germany's Bankhaus Herstatt with $620 million of uncompleted trades sent shivers through the international financial world. (When Herstatt failed, German regulators closed the bank down at 3:30 P.M. in Frankfurt—after it had been paid the foreign exchange it was owed in Europe, but before it made its dollar payments to banks in the United States. Eventually, U.S. banks lost up to $200 million.) Since then FX trading volume has ballooned, and a collapse today could be far more damaging. These fears escalated after the failure in 1990 of the U.S. investment bank Drexel Burnham Lambert; the closure of the Bank of Credit and Commerce International (BCCI) in 1991; and the collapse of Barings Brothers in 1995.

The central banks of many Western countries have been expressing increased concern about settlement risk, and urging private banks to come to grips with this risk. Bankers tend to consider Herstatt risk as very low, however, contending that the market can handle such incidents. The BIS, in turn, criticizes this complacency. A consortium of international banks, CLS Services, is working on the ultimate solution: creating a bank, the Continuous Linked Settlement (CLS) Bank, to carry out the continuous linked settlement of FX transactions. This will not be operational until 2001 though, and even then it will not eliminate all of the risk involved in FX transactions.

For most large global banks, the risks of FX are well worth taking. Their multinational clients are converting more and more money into other currencies as businesses globalize; pension and other huge funds are increasingly investing abroad, requiring FX services; and world trade is growing at a faster clip than the world economy. Thus big banks with the best technology and access to the biggest multinational customers are poised to benefit from increasing concentration in this industry.

CHASE FIRES SENIOR TRADER AS MISSTATED PROFITS COST £36M

Gary Silverman

Chase Manhattan has fired a senior trader over misstated profits and will reduce its trading revenues in the fourth quarter by $60m (£36m).

The third largest US bank yesterday said it had uncovered errors in the accounts of its proprietary trading department, which trades the bank's own money. No customer accounts were affected, it added.

(continued)

The case is not believed to involve a rogue trader such as Nick Leeson, the man who brought down the UK's Barings Bank. It is thought to focus on incorrect reporting of complex trading positions....

The trader was dealing in foreign exchange forward contracts and interest-rate swaps, a source said. Some of the contracts involved were cutomised and illiquid. In such cases pricing is rarely automatic and traders often have discretion in calculating the returns on their trades.

The case illustrates the difficulties large financial institutions have in calculating the value of some trades....

Source: Financial Times, November 2, 1999 p. 1.

CASE STUDY   Conflict on a Trading Floor (A)

Research Assistant Jerry Useem prepared this case under the supervision of Professor Joseph Badaracco as the basis for class discussion rather than to illustrate either effective or ineffective handling of an administrative situation. This case is based on a paper written by a recent MBA graduate of the Harvard Business School, and has been partially disguised.

> And before a blind person you shall not put a stumbling block.
> —*Leviticus, 19*

Background

From March of 1986 through May of 1988, I worked on The FirstAmerica Bank's main trading floor in New York. I began as an assistant and eventually became a salesperson on the non-dollar derivative products desk where futures, options, and other items whose values are based on another security are traded in foreign currencies. I specialized in cross-currency interest rate swaps.

As an assistant, I had worked with three vice presidents, and particularly closely with a top salesperson named Linda. In fact, Linda had been instrumental in recruiting me to the bank in 1986. She had a reputation on the floor for her extremely volatile and hot-tempered nature, but was highly respected for her ability to close deals. She was very aggressive, both in pursuing new business and in ensuring that she received full credit for any profitable transactions.

After about six months on the job, in September 1986, I began to work with Linda on a new transaction for one of her largest accounts, Poseidon Cruise Lines. I had assisted her with a number of clients by that point and had become familiar with her working habits and idiosyncrasies. During the year and a half that Poseidon had been a client of FirstAmerica, Linda had developed a close relationship with the treasurer and the chief financial officer of the cruise lines. Poseidon had transacted many small, simple deals through FirstAmerica—mostly short-term financing transactions that involved borrowing $20 million or $30 million from a credit line. The new Poseidon deal, however, was the largest transaction I had seen at the bank and it had a fairly complex structure. Essentially, Poseidon wanted to finance the construction of a new cruise ship to be built by a French shipyard. The ship would be one of the largest and most luxurious in their fleet. Construction was to be completed over a five-year period at a total cost of approximately $700 million.

(continued)

Poseidon faced several challenges in this undertaking. First, the French shipyard had provided a schedule of the payment dates and amounts that comprised its bid for the project. Poseidon was obligated to make these payments in francs. As a U.S. corporation with most of its cashflow in dollars, these payments exposed Poseidon to significant currency risks. Second, the French government had agreed to subsidize the transaction by allowing Poseidon to borrow the francs it needed at a below market rate. The government did this with many major construction contracts. While Poseidon's executives felt that the ability to borrow francs cheaply definitely helped offset their risk, they were uncertain how to value this benefit. Third, while the treasurer and CFO of Poseidon were fairly active in the currency markets, neither of them had executed transactions of this size or complexity. They were uncertain about the French currency markets and about the possibility of hedging exchanges several years in the future. They were also unfamiliar with complex financial structures.

The Transaction

Over a period of approximately three months, Linda worked with the CFO to devise a structure that would result in the lowest possible all-in cost in dollars. They agreed that Poseidon should be completely hedged from all currency exposure. The structure Linda developed had three main components. First, Poseidon was obligated to make a 10% downpayment to the shipyard at the time the contract was signed. FirstAmerica, with the largest currency trading operation in the world at the time, would work to obtain the best possible spot price for this purchase of approximately $70 million of francs. Second, over the first three years of the transaction Poseidon was obligated to make a series of equal monthly interest payments to the shipyard on the outstanding balance of the purchase. FirstAmerica and Poseidon would enter into a "cross-currency interest rate swap," in which FirstAmerica would pay to Poseidon, on each payment date, the francs it needed to make its payments. In return, Poseidon would pay FirstAmerica an even stream of U.S. dollars on the same dates, in predetermined amounts. This would effectively convert Poseidon's franc obligation into a dollar one. The third part of the structure involved the actual principal payments which were to be made at the end of the years three, four, and five. These were large individual payments which Linda proposed to hedge by having Poseidon purchase the francs from FirstAmerica in three "forward" contracts, effectively locking in the future exchange rates.

Although they had looked at a number of hedging alternatives, including buying foreign currency options, buying French government bonds or exclusively using forwards, Linda tried to convince the CFO that this combination made the most sense. She told him that by hedging through large, long-term contracts, Poseidon would save on transaction costs because there would be fewer transactions to make. Linda also argued that Poseidon could save significantly by giving FirstAmerica sole responsibility for the financing. There was very little liquidity in the forward franc markets further than one year out,

(continued)

she explained, and the Poseidon deal was so large it could dramatically move the entire franc market. She argued that if Poseidon "shopped" the deal, market participants would certainly try to profit from the knowledge and, by positioning themselves in front of the deal, they would dramatically increase Poseidon's costs. Impressed with her arguments, the CFO agreed to Linda's plan. From an objective standpoint, the plan was probably as least as good as the other hedge options. However, the crucial matter of how much Poseidon would pay for these transactions was still under discussion.

The Questions

As I assisted Linda throughout this process, I became aware of several issues that led me to question the way she conducted business. First, by dramatically exaggerating the need for secrecy in the transaction, she managed to convince Poseidon not to speak with other investment banks. This meant that Poseidon, because it lacked the sophistication and the market contacts to effectively price the structure itself, had to trust Linda on the fairness and accuracy of the pricing. While any salesperson would love to have a customer in this position, I wondered about the way Linda had achieved it. There was some truth to her argument that shopping the deal would disturb the market, but I learned from the franc traders that the cost of such "slippage" would probably not exceed 10 basis points (1/10 of 1%) on the transaction. Since Linda planned to use her exclusive relationship to charge Poseidon significantly more than that, I questioned the propriety of her argument.

The second issue that troubled me was the actual price that Linda quoted. Since forward points and swap rates are both determined by the interest rates in the relevant countries, the prices Linda quoted for the transaction can best be expressed in terms of interest rates. She told Poseidon that she could effect their transactions at a three-year franc rate of approximately 12.80% and a five-year rate of approximately 13.40%. While these rates represented significant premiums above current French government bond rates, Linda explained that the differential existed because of the credit risk of dealing with a corporate counterpart and because of market illiquidity. While there was a kernel of truth to these arguments, I knew that the rates Linda quoted were on average 80 basis points higher than the rates the traders needed for FirstAmerica to profitably hedge its positions. This profit margin, on the average size of the exchanges over their average lives, meant that Linda was charging Poseidon a fee of roughly $12.5 million to hedge their risk. The most profitable transaction I had ever heard of at the bank until that point had earned fees of $2.3 million, and there was no clear reason why the Poseidon deal should be worth that much more. Most disconcerting of all, however, was the fact that Linda explained to the CFO that FirstAmerica would net profits on the deal of approximately $1.2 million.

The Dilemma

As we prepared to execute the trades, we were in almost constant contact with the treasurer and CFO. I performed and sent numerous analyses illus-

(continued)

trating the benefits of the transaction under a wide variety of possible economic scenarios. Ultimately, though, the two executives still had doubts about the structure and the fairness of the pricing. They told me they would not execute the trade unless they could see for themselves that three- to five-year French borrowing rates for a corporation with Poseidon's credit rating were actually hovering in the 12.50% to 13.50% range.

When I told Linda about this condition, she was visibly shaken. She told me to stay at my desk and watch the phones. Then she went to speak with one of the forward franc traders for about half an hour. When she returned, she still looked extremely nervous and agitated, but she seemed to have recovered some of her infectious confidence. She told me to pull up a particular Telerate page, print it out, and fax it to Poseidon. Telerate was a widely used computer information service that listed up-to-the-moment trading prices and interest rates from around the world. Linda said I should also call the CFO to let him know the information he wanted was on the way. When I commented that, with the transaction hanging in the balance, it might look better if she called herself, she became quite angry. She told me to just do it and stop asking questions.

I called up the page, which was in a part of the information system I had not used before. I noticed that the section was for non-dollar bonds with trading restrictions. The French bonds in question, it appeared, were subject to a 10% government withholding tax if held by foreign investors. Although it was not mentioned on the page, the rates incorporated the return of the withholding tax, effectively increasing the yields by 100 to 120 basis points. This withholding tax would not apply to an off-balance-sheet transaction like a swap or a forward. I picked up the printout and returned to my desk. After thinking for a few seconds, I leaned over to Linda's desk and asked if she was aware of any withholding tax on the bonds. She told me to stop interrupting and send the fax immediately.

I opened my Rolodex to get the CFO's fax and phone numbers and then picked up the phone. As I started to place the call, I wondered if I could actually send the fax.

I was truly torn at that moment. My immediate reaction was to follow the instructions I had been given—for four reasons. First, Linda was my direct superior at the bank and her instructions had been very clear. I strongly believe that it is important to respect the wishes and requests of people in positions of authority. (My background in team sports, my family, and my religious upbringing each reinforced this commitment.) Second, despite the fact that I disliked many of Linda's habits and attitudes, I felt indebted to her for helping me get my job. She was the first FirstAmerica employee to interview me as a college senior and, ignoring my lack of experience or training, she recommended me for a position that is normally held by someone with an MBA. I felt that since she had been willing to "bend the rules" to help me, I certainly owed her enough to return the favor.

Third, as an employee of the bank, I had a responsibility to help my desk make as much money as possible. A transaction like the Poseidon one would noticeably increase all of our bonuses; this deal alone could add $500,000

(continued)

to $1 million to Linda's bonus, and I stood to make an extra $30,000 to $40,000, or as much as 70% of my base salary. The transaction would also help the bank show positive earnings at an extremely difficult time (the North American real estate market was deteriorating rapidly) and might even improve the bank's share price. In this sense, by helping to ensure that the transaction was completed, I would provide clear benefits to the employees, managers, and shareholders of the bank.

Finally, and perhaps the most pressing of all, I had just begun my new job and felt that I had a great deal of potential. It was extremely important for me to be seen as a dedicated professional who could be completely trusted. To challenge my boss directly and to risk losing an extremely large and profitable transaction would almost certainly end my career at FirstAmerica. In addition, if I could not help execute a large and profitable transaction because of nagging doubts, I had to wonder if I could ever hope to be successful in the industry.

On the other hand, there were four good reasons why I felt I could not send the fax or call the CFO. First, I firmly believe that all people have an obligation to be honest. I am an observant Jew, as well as (I'd like to think) a generally decent human being. I feel that basic honesty in human interactions is a crucial building block for an enjoyable and happy world. Although I did not consciously formalize the dilemma into a religious question at the time, the religious beliefs that my family instilled in me did affect the way I looked at the problem. Having grown up in a small but tightly-knit Jewish community, I was raised in the modern orthodox tradition, which holds that people should obey the laws of the Torah while interacting with the modern world as much as possible. The experience that most strengthened my commitment to Jewish belief was the year I took off from college to go to Israel in order to work and study in a small settlement south of Jerusalem. There, I spent 10–12 hours a day at a Yeshiva, or Jewish seminary, studying Jewish law and tradition. I recalled from my studies that there are several specific commandments in the Jewish tradition that prohibit lying or intentionally misleading others. The one that seemed most directly applicable is "And before a blind person you shall not put a stumbling block" (Leviticus, 19). While Linda was not asking me to lie directly, the information I was asked to convey was certainly misleading enough to make me uncomfortable.

The second reason I felt I should not send the fax was my professional responsibility to the client. I felt that when I, as a person in a service industry, accepted a new job, I was committing myself to acting in that client's best interest. In banking, there is always a tremendous tension because every dollar the banker earns ultimately comes out of the pockets of his clients. I knew that I would have to live with this conflict in every transaction I pursued, but the harm being done to Poseidon Cruise Lines seemed too large to ignore.

(continued)

Third, while I knew that the transaction could have significant benefits for the bank's employees and shareholders in the short term, it was quite possible that gouging a major client could have a tremendous negative impact in the long run. In addition, if the amount of profit Linda had built into the trade ever became public knowledge, many of our other clients would almost certainly turn away. Linda evidently felt that the risk of a negative outcome was great enough that she did not want to call the CFO herself. Last of all, it was possible that there might be professional benefits from staying completely honest and guarding the client's interest. Perhaps a senior person at FirstAmerica would be outraged by Linda's behavior and would reward me for not getting involved.

I reflected for a moment on the various senior people I might talk to. I had already spoken with the person most closely involved with the details of the transaction, the floor trader, Roger. Roger was a very bellicose individual who did not take kindly to interference from junior salespeople. Nonetheless, overcoming my reluctance to approach him, I asked him what he thought about the prices Linda was quoting. "Hey, whatever she wants to do, it's her deal," was his response. Roger was aware of Linda's tactics, and was surprised that she would take such a risk, but his attitude was that if she could get away with it, she should do it. Her methods worried him somewhat, but only from the standpoint that Poseidon might discover the profits we were making and back out of the deal.

Next up in the company hierarchy was the sales manager for derivatives, Peter. Unfortunately, Peter was a totally ineffective manager. He had been an undistinguished salesperson for 25 years, and had been promoted to sales manager simply by virtue of the fact that he was the oldest person on the trading floor. Having built his career by executing the same simple transactions over and over again, Peter did not have a good feel for the more complicated derivative products that had appeared on the market in recent years, especially anything not based in U.S. dollars. As a result, he exercised very little control over salespeople like Linda. If he had wanted to investigate Linda's deal, he would have had to ask a trader to examine the numbers for him. Essentially, he would have been over his head, and I knew from his risk-averse disposition that he would not want to put himself in such a controversial situation. Thus, although it was Peter's job to prevent the people under him from committing improprieties, I felt that alerting him to Linda's intentions would not be an effective course of action.

Finally, if I had wanted to take the issue still higher up the management ladder, I could have gone to the senior vice president who managed FirstAmerica's entire 550-member trading floor team. I had seen this man only once, at a breakfast for new hires where he delivered a brief talk to 50 of us. For me, a junior salesperson, to approach him with the intention of "blowing the whistle" on my boss would have been incredibly intimidating. In fact, I could hardly contemplate it at the time.

Questions

1. Who are the key participants in FX markets?
2. Why do multinational corporations need to trade foreign currencies?
3. Why do commercial banks enter FX markets? How do they profit from FX market transactions?
4. What role do central banks play in FX markets? How has this role evolved in recent years?
5. How did FX speculators like George Soros profit from the activities of central banks?
6. How does FX trading differ from other trading activities? How does FX trading differ from the other activities in which banks engage?
7. As the stockholder of a major international bank, would you want the bank to participate actively in the FX market? Why or why not?
8. Why have spreads in FX trading been reduced in the past decade? What trend do you predict for the future?
9. What regulations and restrictions exist on the FX market? Should the FX market be more heavily regulated? If so, why and how? If not, why not?
10. Explain how and why banks speculate in FX markets. How is this different from gambling in Las Vegas or Monte Carlo?
11. What are the key risks associated with FX trading from a bank's point of view?
12. How can banks protect themselves against the risks associated with FX trading?
13. What is the euro? How will it influence FX market activity in coming years?

Problems

1. Suppose that U.S. interest rates are 8 percent per annum and UK rates are 12 percent per annum. If the spot $/pound exchange rate is 1.50, what should the twelve-month forward rate be? Should the pound be at a forward premium or discount against the dollar?
2. Look at today's newspaper to find spot and forward exchange rates for the pound, euro, Japanese yen, Swiss franc, and Mexican peso against the dollar. Which of these currencies are at a forward premium against the dollar, and which are at a discount? What does this tell you about interest rates in the UK, Euroland, Japan, Switzerland, and Mexico vis-à-vis those in the United States?
3. You are a U.S. exporter expecting to receive a euro 10 million payment from your French customer in exactly six months. You wish to lock in the dollar value of this payment. Using forward rates from today's newspaper, explain how you can hedge this payment. What are the costs? Opportunity costs?
4. In the previous problem, now assume that you do not know the exact date of the payment from your French customer. Your banker offers you an option with the strike price set at today's spot rate. The premium is 3 percent of the face value of the contract. Under what circumstances do you prefer the option to the forward contract? Using different exchange rate scenarios, demonstrate when you would exercise the option and what your net costs are.
5. From the banker's point of view, does the forward contract suggested in Problem 3 or the options contract suggested in Problem 4 present more risk? How can the banker deal with these risks?
6. Today's spot SF/$ rate is 1.2487 SF/$. The $/euro rate is 1.1132 $/euro. What is the SF/euro cross-rate?

7. Yesterday's spot Can\$/US\$ rate was 1.4100. What factors could have caused the movement to today's 1.3850 Can\$/US\$ rate?

8. Given the following spot and forward rates, in each case calculate the percentage forward premium/discounts on the Japanese yen.

	Spot JY/$	Forward JY/$	# Days Forward
a.	170	175	30
b.	170	175	90
c.	148	160	180
d.	165	145	360

9. If the one-year Mexican interest rate is 9 percent, the one-year U.S. interest rate is 3 percent, and the spot exchange rate is 6.50 MP/\$, what should the one-year MP/\$ forward rate be if no arbitrage opportunities are present?

10. You agree to purchase pounds through a two-year forward contract at a rate of 1.75 \$/pound. The contract amount is \$5 million. If the spot exchange rate on the pound two years from now is 2.00 \$/pound, what is your dollar gain or loss on the contract?

Suggested Readings

"Central Bank Survey of Foreign Exchange and Derivatives Market Activity in April 1998: Preliminary Global Data." Basel, Switzerland: Bank for International Settlements, 1998. This is the definitive source of data on foreign exchange trading throughout the world, published every three years.

Gonnelli, Adam. *The Basics of Foreign Trade and Exchange.* New York: Federal Reserve Bank of New York, Public Information Department, 1993. This is a free guide available to anyone who requests it from the Fed.

Krieger, Andrew, with Edward Claflin. *The Money Bazaar: Inside the Trillion Dollar World of Currency Trading.* New York: Times Books, 1992. It is virtually impossible to give readers a taste of the pace and activity in foreign exchange markets, but this book provides an accessible and fascinating account of the FX trading business from one of its most colorful players, Andrew Krieger.

Shirreff, David. "FX: Plotting the Death of Settlement Risk." *Euromoney,* May 1998, pp. 70–72. A good guide to settlement risk issues.

Websites

N.B.: There are many fee-based websites offering foreign exchange trading services and advice; we have limited our list to free websites.

www.wiso.gwdg.de/ifgb/currency/htm	Links to FX sources
www.bloomberg.com	FX rates, history, news
www.pacific.commerce.ubs.ca/xr	Historical FX rates, analysis, and projections
www.cme.com/market/currency/index/html	Chicago Mercantile Exchange

www.newsbrokers.com   News and analysis on major
                                    financial markets

www.FOREX-ats.com   FX trends analysis, strategies,
                                    trading results

www.bis.org   BIS data on FX trading

Notes

1. Testimony of Federal Reserve Chairman Alan Greenspan, "Private-Sector Refinancing of the Large Hedge Fund, Long-Term Capital Management," before the Committee on Banking and Financial Services, U.S. House of Representatives, October 1, 1998, p. 1.

2. Simon Romero, "As Brazil Devalued, Some Got Rich," *New York Times*, March 26, 1999, p. C4.

3. There are several excellent sources of information on this topic. First and foremost is the annual survey of foreign exchange markets in the *Financial Times*. This chapter draws on data in the June 5, 1998, and June 25, 1999, surveys. In addition, see Anthony Currie, "FX: A Tough Race Gets Tougher," *Euromoney*, May 1998, pp. 53–64. *Euromoney* magazine publishes an annual survey of foreign exchange traders and banks, which is widely respected and quoted throughout the industry. Information here is from the May 1999 survey.

4. Thomas Jaffe and Dyan Machan, "How the Market Overwhelmed the Central Banks," *Forbes*, November 9, 1992, pp. 40–42.

5. "Foreign Exchange Survey," *Financial Times*, June 25, 1999, p. S1.

6. William Lewis and Andrew Hill, "The Return of the Hedge Funds," *Financial Times*, September 24, 1999, p. 23.

7. Anthony Currie, "FX: A Tough Race Gets Tougher," *Euromoney*, May 1998, pp. 53–64.

8. Anatole Kaletsky, "Bankers Trust Overstated Its 1987 Foreign Exchange Profits," *Financial Times*, July 21, 1988, p. 28.

9. Julian Walmsley, *The Foreign Exchange and Money Markets Guide* (New York: John Wiley & Sons, 1992), pp. 407–410.

PART 3

RISK MANAGEMENT

CHAPTER 9

BANK CRASHES

The importance of understanding bank failures or crashes is likely to grow as financial markets become more globalized, because the linkages between banking systems increasingly function as channels for the spread of crises, much like a contagious disease spreads by contact or close association. Indeed, much has been written about the problem of **contagion** in regard to the 1997–98 Asian financial crisis. One lasting impression from the experiences of such countries as Indonesia, Thailand, and Korea is that failures spread throughout the banking system as sick institutions infect the healthy and drag them down into insolvency. No doubt the future will be marked by new financial crashes, some involving banks, both local and international. Understandably there is a deep apprehension of systemic risk in the financial sector and in particular banking, which is magnified by the public's relative lack of understanding of financial matters.

There is nothing new about bank failures. The past is littered with failed institutions, distraught people who lost their deposits, and a disturbing number of suicides. The early Italian banks were forced to deal with defaults by European monarchs, some of which resulted in failures. Down the path of history, the Dutch, English, Scots, French, Austrians, Germans, Japanese, and Americans have all faced the same problems. Some of the best-known modern cases are those of Bankhaus Herstatt, Franklin National Bank, Banco Ambrosiano, Continental Illinois and Penn Square, Johnson Matthey Bankers, U.S. Thrifts, Bank of New England, Barings, and Bank of Credit and Commerce International.

The seriousness of banking failures is underscored by the fact that they have occurred in most OECD countries and many developing economies. The list of banking crises in OECD countries includes Spain (1977–85), where estimated losses reached almost 17 percent of GDP; Finland (1991–93), with estimated losses equal to 8 percent of GDP; Sweden (1991), 6 percent of GDP; and Norway (1987–90), around 4 percent of GDP.[1] The U.S. savings and loan crisis (1984–91) cost about 3 percent of GDP. The cost of Japan's protracted banking crisis, beginning in 1990 and continuing into the first decade of the twenty-first century, has yet to be tallied, but it has already run into the hundreds of billions of dollars. The developing world has not been immune from large-scale banking failures. In the last two decades of the twentieth century, there were banking crashes with heavy costs in Venezuela (losses equal to 14 percent of GDP), Bulgaria (14 percent of GDP), Mexico (12–15 percent of GDP), and Hungary (10 percent of GDP).

THE BANKING PANIC OF 1893
(IN THE UNITED STATES)

Elmus Wicker

[Preceding this passage, the stock market had crashed in May 1893.]

D *uring the first week of June there were city-wide runs in Milwaukee, Spokane, and Chicago. Unrest spread during the second week to Omaha and Detroit. Los Angeles and San Diego bore the brunt of bank suspensions in the third week. The Plankinton Bank of Milwaukee closed on June 1 with deposits of $2 million; it had survived a "hard run" on May 13, the proximate cause of which had been the failure of a large furniture manufacturer who had amassed a debt of over $200,000 to the bank. Since that time there had been continuous withdrawals by large depositors. The bank's closing triggered a run on other banks in the city as well as the state.*

There were three weeks of relative calm in Chicago after the suspensions of Chemical National and Columbia National banks in early May. On June 3, there was a renewal of banking unrest. Herman Schaffner and Company, the largest commercial paper house in Chicago, was forced to close with deposits of $850,000. The private bank had allegedly used funds to invest heavily in street railway bonds. As a result of the stock market collapse in May, the bottom had dropped out of the market for such bonds. The head of the firm committed suicide by renting a boat and rowing out into Lake Michigan, never to return. Alarm spread immediately among small depositors in the Jewish community. There followed runs on every savings bank in Chicago. Long lines of frightened depositors appeared at all of the savings banks. June 5 was described as the most exciting day in Chicago's financial affairs in a decade. The savings banks continued to pay depositors with one notable exception: the Dime Savings Bank, which only paid a percentage of deposits and then invoked the thirty-day notice rule. There were no savings banks suspensions in Chicago. They were all financially sound as evidenced by their ability to meet depositors' demands. An editorial in the *Chicago Tribune* on June 7 contained the estimate that 4,000 depositors withdrew $1 million in two days!

Source: Elmus Wicker, *Banking Panics of the Gilded Age* (New York: Cambridge University Press, 2000), p. 64.

Argentina, Chile, and Côte d'Ivoire have also had their fair share of banking problems, while weak banking systems in key Asian countries were a key contributor to the Asian financial crisis of 1997–98.

SALE OF JAPANESE BANK LIKELY TO PRIVATE U.S. EQUITY FUND

Stephanie Strom

The Japanese government is close to selling the Long-Term Credit Bank of Japan to an American-led investor group, a transaction that would put a financial icon of the country's postwar reconstruction in foreign hands.

The anticipated sale of Long-Term Credit to a group led by Ripplewood Holdings, a New York-based private equity fund, would for the first time give foreigners control of a Japanese bank.

Long-Term Credit was nationalized last October as part of an effort to overhaul the nation's financial system, laden with hundreds of billions of dollars worth of bad debts as a legacy of the speculative lending boom of the late 1980's....

Source: New York Times, September 24, 1999, p. C2.

Defining the Terms

What is a **bank crash**? Simply stated, a bank crash is a failure of a financial institution (usually a deposit-taking institution) caused by a number of factors. If enough banks crash (or seem in danger of crashing), the banking system may reach such a condition that it is unable to provide payments or allocate credit, its traditional role. In a broader sense in which banks also play an important role in securities markets, a bank crisis can also result in a lack of liquidity for the buying and selling of bonds, stocks, and other financial instruments. Along these lines, economist Charles Kindleberger noted that "a crash is a collapse of the price of an asset, or perhaps the failure of an important firm or bank. A panic, 'a sudden fright without cause,' from the god Pan, may occur in asset markets or involve a rush from less to more liquid assets. Financial crisis may involve one or both, or in any order."[2]

A banking crisis occurs when fear that payments will not be available at any price precipitates a desperate action on the part of the public to obtain cash. Mobs of depositors appear at the bank and its branches, demanding their money in what is called a **run.** The liquid reserves in the banking system are quickly drained. This in turn results in an effort to restore reserves, in which the banks may call loans, refuse to extend new credit, or sell assets. This leaves the authorities (central bank, or lender of last resort) in the difficult position of either having to close the bank that has experienced the run, or providing the bank with a line of credit as well as visible support for the institution in an effort to restore public confidence.

Although we have already mentioned contagion, a further definition is worthwhile. Contagion is a systemic risk that cumulative losses will occur from an event that puts in motion a series of successive losses along a chain of institutions or markets that constitute a system. Contagion is also used in regard to conglomerates, reflecting the likelihood that the losses of one activity may shrink the capital available to support the activities of other parts of the organization.

What Causes Crashes?

Banks are regarded as being more vulnerable to failures than other companies. In a sense, they are often perceived as being more fragile than many other firms and more open to contagion. Three reasons support this view:

1. Low capital-to-assets ratios (high leverage), which provides little room for losses

2. Low cash-to-assets ratios, which may require the sale of earning assets to meet deposit obligations

3. High demand debt and short-term debt to total debt (deposits) ratios (high potential for a run), which may require hurried asset sales of opaque and nonliquid earnings assets with potentially large fire-sale losses to pay off running depositors[3]

Yet what actually sparks a crash? Crashes take place for a number of reasons. Crashes occur after a long period of calm conditions marked by fierce competition between financial institutions; long credit cycles in which banks have been able to continue lending for a long period to increasingly more indebted borrowers; and after a period of financial innovation. Bank failures can also be caused by financial fraud. The actual catalyst for a banking crash is often a panic, which is initiated by an abrupt shift in the perceived riskiness of a bank or a financial market. The problem is that failure at one bank causes people to become apprehensive about the safety of their funds at other banks.

As already noted, panics can lead to runs, which occur when individual depositors suddenly demand currency because of concern about the safety of their deposit. The most vivid impression of a run on a bank is that of crowds of people rushing to the bank and demanding back their money. There were many cases of bank runs in the 1990s in Indonesia, Russia, and Brazil and in 2000 in Ecuador. There can also be silent runs, which happen when large financial institutions, foreign banks, or corporations sell their negotiable CDs or commercial paper of banks that demonstrate signs of financial weakness. As confidence evaporates, the selling of commercial paper accelerates, eventually resulting in severe funding problems for the bank. This occurred in 1984 with Continental Illinois, then the seventeenth largest bank in the United States. Although Continental Illinois was saved by a federal loan, other banks in similar circumstances were not as fortunate and have been forced to close their doors.

Goldstein and Turner, in a comprehensive study on banking crises in developing economies, identified eight catalysts for an actual crash. These include both external and domestic causes:[4]

1. Macroeconomic volatility, both external and domestic
2. Lending booms, asset price collapses, and surges in capital inflows (as in Chile in the early 1980s)
3. Increasing bank liabilities with large maturity or currency mismatches
4. Inadequate preparation for financial liberalization, which allows banks to take excessive risks in areas where they have little or no experience (as in the Nordic countries in the late 1980s and early 1990s)
5. Heavy government involvement and weak controls on connected lending (Indonesia and Korea in the late 1990s)
6. Weakness in accounting, disclosure, and legal framework (as in Asia in 1997–98)
7. Distorted incentives for owners, managers, depositors, and supervisors (much of Central and Eastern Europe in the 1990s)
8. Exchange rate regimes that are open to considerable volatility

An additional factor on the list should be **regulatory forbearance,** defined as the putting off of tough actions on the part of regulators in the hope that a bank will recover on its own. As a World Bank report notes: "The reluctance of ever-hopeful regulators to control risk-taking or to preemptively close banks with deteriorating loan portfolios has made many banking crises worse."[5] There have been cases where regulators have waited too long to act, with the crisis eventually slipping out of control and becoming difficult to remedy. The issue of regulatory forbearance also carries with it a political dimension: The role of the state must be carefully balanced between being too heavy-handed and allowing market forces to run riot. Somewhere in the middle of these two poles is probably the most attractive stance for regulators, but political viewpoints cannot be ignored.

It is worth discussing the international dimensions further. Goldstein and Turner emphasize that one cause of a banking crash can be large swings in the terms of trade. What this refers to is when there is a major and unexpected disruption in either imports or exports, which leaves a company with outstanding obligations that it cannot service. If prices for Company A's products suddenly fell in international markets, the expected level of income would suddenly be much lower. Consequently, when a bank's customers suddenly discover that the terms of trade have turned sharply against them, their ability to service existing loans is likely to be impaired. A second external factor for bank failures is volatility in international interest rates and their effect on private capital flows. As Goldstein and Turner note: "Not only do fluctuations in international interest rates affect (either directly or indirectly) the cost of borrowing (at the margin), they diminish the relative attractiveness of investing in emerging markets."[6] This can mean volatility in capital flows, which can create distortions in local markets, hence problems for banks.

A third external factor identified by Goldstein and Turner is real (i.e., inflation-adjusted) exchange rate volatility. Real exchange rate volatility can cause difficulties for banks either directly or indirectly: directly when there is a currency or maturity mismatch between bank liabilities and assets, or indirectly when exchange rate volatility creates large losses for bank borrowers. A fourth factor is volatility in international securities markets. A bad trade can result in the loss of millions, sometimes billions of dollars. This situation can be compounded by efforts to conceal losses, as was the case of Barings in 1995 when a rogue trader made a bad bet on Japanese securities and then exacerbated the problem by attempting to conceal the trade. Ultimately, Barings incurred a $1.4 billion loss that forced one of England's oldest and most reputable banks into bankruptcy.

Barings is hardly alone in suffering from fraud. In 1995, it was revealed that the New York branch of Daiwa Bank was hit by a loss of $1 billion caused by a senior trader. Upon closer scrutiny it became evident that the money had been lost over a ten-year period but was covered up through the sale of securities stolen from customer accounts, which were replaced by forged securities. Other well-known cases of fraud involve the French bank, Credit Lyonnais and its involvement with Giancarlo Parretti and MGM, and Banco Ambrosiano. The last-mentioned was notable for the death of its chairman Roberto Calvi, who was found dangling from an orange rope beneath Blackfriar's Bridge in London. Consequently, fraud can be added to the list of factors contributing to a bank failure.[7]

Once a banking (or financial market) crash is in motion, runs, panics, and asset devaluations often occur. Liquidity in securities markets evaporates. Credit becomes a scarce commodity. The government is then forced to intervene in an effort (not always successful) to prevent contagion and stave off a recession. As a crash progresses, there is usually more than one failure. This relates to one of the biggest concerns about bank (as well as securities market) crashes, systemic risk. As globalization has proceeded hand in hand with financial liberalization, banking systems are highly connected and the problem facing one system is often a problem confronting others. As economist George Kaufman noted:

> [B]ecause banks are closely intertwined financially with each other through lending to and borrowing from each other, holding deposit balances with each other, and the payments clearing system, a failure at one bank is believed to be more likely to spill over to other banks and to do so more quickly. Thus, the banking system is seen as more susceptible to systemic risk.... I define systemic risk as the probability that cumulative losses will occur from an event that ignites a series of successive losses along a chain of institutions or markets comprising a system.[8]

Dealing with Crashes

As panics and runs hit a banking system, governments can play a critical role in containing the crisis. They can also, as happened all too often in the past, inadvertently make matters worse. An example of this was in the United States when the stock market crashed in 1929. Instead of providing liquidity to the banking system when panicked depositors made runs on banks and the banks frantically called in loans (many of them to people who borrowed to buy stocks now worth far less then their purchase price), the Federal Reserve raised interest rates, which dried up any liquidity. Without credit, the crisis only worsened.

When confronted by a banking failure, the primary objective of the government is to contain the damage, restore confidence to the public, and avoid or contain contagion. Bank regulators often have a choice in how to intervene and for how long. They often make use of a bank holiday (usually around a weekend) during which to intervene in a bank, briefly closing the doors. This time is used to assess the damage and either suspend or revoke the bank's charter. As the regulators come to terms with the scope and nature of the problems, they can assess what to do: either close the bank and liquidate the assets or make the intervention temporary, inject capital, and put into place new management intending to eventually reprivatize the bank.

If the goal is to return the bank to private hands, the state may also create a *bad bank* in which to put most of the troubled or nonperforming assets (usually loans). Simply stated, a bad bank is an asset management company set up to manage nonperforming assets of problem banks. This allows the newly restored bank, under new management, to restart with a clean slate. The bad bank, with a management selected by the government, will then proceed to sell the bad assets at a discount to investors. Another option is restructuring, which allows the bank's management and regulators to come up with a plan to reorganize the bank and return it to financial health. The decision about whether to return the bank to private ownership is called resolution and involves a determination of how much it will cost to restore the bank.

Regulators and their respective governments must also consider what is called the **"too big to fail" doctrine.** This emerged most noticeably in the United States in 1984, when the Office of the Comptroller of the Currency stated that the eleven largest banking firms were "too big to fail," implying that they would receive de facto 100

JAKARTA SHUTS THREE COMMERCIAL BANKS

Sander Thoenen

I ndonesia yesterday closed three commercial banks, nationalised one, merged four state banks and offered matching funds to banks that boost their capital.

As part of the government's first comprehensive banking reforms, Bambang Subianto, the finance minister, announced the closure of Bank Dagang Nasional Indonesia, one of the country's 10 largest banks, as well as Bank Umum Nasional and Modern Bank.

He formalised the nationalisation of Bank Danamon, which boasts an extensive branch network, but delayed a decision on the largest bank, Bank Central Asia, as well as on Bank PDFCI and Bank Tiara Asia.

The government's plan for these seven banks, among 55 taken over by the government, was widely regarded as a test of its will to take and inflict pain to save the banking sector.

"We can only revive the economy if we tackle the banking sector," said Ginandjar Kartasasmita, coordinating minister for economy, finance and industry....

Source: Financial Times, August 23, 1998, p. 7.

percent deposit insurance. In other words, even though a bank may have substantial problems that may threaten its solvency, the bank may also be one of the largest banks in the financial system and its failure could have considerable repercussions on the rest of the economy. These repercussions could include a drastic reduction in the money supply of the national economy, with significant negative effects on economic activity. Additionally, a massive bank failure could raise the cost of credit intermediation and reduce demand, thereby cooling economic growth. The ultimate fear is that the failure of a large bank could cause a financial black hole, capable of sucking in other banks and businesses that have credit and debt relations with the bank. In this case, widespread bankruptcies would be one consequence, which would result in a lack of confidence in the health of the stock market (where most major banks are listed and partially depend on share prices for their capitalization).

One other major consideration in the "too big to fail" doctrine of bank supervision and regulation is that banks play a critical role in the payments and settlement systems for the payment of goods and services, securities transfers, foreign exchange, and other aspects of international capital flows. With a major failure in one country, complications could be quickly transmitted to other countries via contagion.

Any type of regulatory intervention must take into consideration **moral hazard,** in which banks are apt to avoid the proper due diligence in the belief that governments will cover or pay for their mistakes. The *Oxford Dictionary of Finance and Banking* applies an even stronger definition: "The incentive to cheat in the absence of penalties for cheating."[9] The moral hazard issue was evident in Asia's 1997–98 financial crisis, especially in Indonesia, Korea, and Thailand. It was also an issue in the U.S. Federal Reserve's orchestration of a rescue for the U.S. hedge fund Long-Term Capital Management in 1998, due to concerns over the impact on major banks, both in the United States and in Europe. In a sense, there must be a concern that bankers will take advantage of a regulatory authority that is too willing to bail them out for assuming too much risk or making imprudent lending decisions that ultimately jeopardize the bank's solvency.

In the United States, the "too big to fail" issue also included a discussion of the role of deposit insurance, especially after the 1980s. It was argued that under this policy large banks enjoyed 100 percent deposit insurance that completely protects all uninsured depositors and general creditors. Along this line, the de facto insurance coverage for all depositors and creditors of large financial institutions raises serious questions about competitive equity, market efficiency, financial sector structure, and overall economic stability.[10] Periodic suggestions for reducing the taxpayer's exposure to bank failures have included more market discipline by reducing the insurance coverage and ongoing deregulation, which occurred throughout the 1990s.

Bad Banking, Bad Policies, and Bad Luck: Bank Failures in the Nordic Countries

In the late 1980s and early 1990s, the banking systems in the Nordic countries of Finland, Norway, Sweden, and, to a lesser extent, Denmark ran into substantial problems. Of the Nordic countries, only Iceland avoided crises that threatened to become systemic. Later, one of the former governors of the Norwegian central bank commented that the bank crisis that swept through the region was a combination of "bad banking, bad policies, and bad luck." Although a systemic collapse was avoided in each country, the risk that a majority of key banks could go under was something very much on the minds of governments. In the case of Norway alone, the state intervened in twenty-two banks in the 1988–91 period. In each country the authorities were able to effect a prudent exit strategy from the crisis that left the banking system functioning, while troubled individual banks were dealt with by a combination of state intervention, asset sales, government-guided mergers, the use of bad banks, and, in a few cases, closures. Considering the high level of economic development in the Nordic countries, this regional banking crisis teaches two valuable lessons: (1) no economy is immune from a banking crisis, and (2) prudent policies from both the public and private sector can reduce the downside impact of negative macroeconomic conditions.

What were the root causes of bank crashes in the Nordic countries? The causes were hardly singular in any country, but multiple and interrelated. In the late 1980s, there was a move to liberalize the banking systems in the Nordic countries. Competitive pressure was growing from continental Europe, the United Kingdom, and the United States. Denmark was the first to open up local banking systems, but the others soon followed. Key measures included the withdrawal of a number of restrictive foreign exchange limitations, incentives to develop money market borrowing mechanisms, and an easing of lending guidelines. With the exception of Denmark, all of the Nordic countries had heavily regulated capital flows during most of the postwar period. It is important to underscore that access to international capital markets was a major factor in providing foreign funding when local bank lending picked up. Indeed, it has been asserted that without this access to foreign funding the rapid growth in lending by Norwegian, Swedish, and Finnish banks would have been impossible.[11]

As access to foreign funding opened up, banks in all four Nordic countries moved to rapidly increase bank lending. Norway led the way, and the other three followed. In part, this reflected stronger economic growth combined with deregulation. Added to this was the reaction of regulatory authorities. As one observer noted: "The details of the deregulatory processes differed, but in each country the authorities felt that banks needed to adjust to an unregulated equilibrium; and that this equilibrium entailed a substantially higher level of bank lending. Initially rapid growth in lending could be rationalized as normal adjustments to a new regime."[12]

By the late 1980s and early 1990s macroeconomic factors conspired against the Nordic banks. Deregulation was launched during a period of strong economic growth. Even as lending soared to new highs, however, economic conditions gradually began to deteriorate. (See Table 9.1.) When asset bubbles burst, a number of banks were overextended, lacked proper internal controls, and were inadequately reserved for what was to be a sharp spike in nonperforming loans. The property and construction sectors were particularly problematic in terms of asset deterioration. In Sweden, the situation was aggravated by recurrent budget deficits and low efficiency in industrial production.[13]

TABLE 9.1 Real GDP Growth Rates in the Nordic Countries: Boom & Bust (%)

	1986	1987	1988	1989	1990	1991
Denmark	3.6%	0.3%	1.2%	0.2%	1.0%	1.1%
Finland	2.4	4.1	4.9	5.1	0.0	−6.3
Norway	3.6	2.0	−0.1	0.9	2.0	3.1
Sweden	2.4	3.0	1.7	2.7	1.6	−1.1

Source: OECD, *OECD Economic Outlook*, June 2000, p. 245.

The economic deterioration was worst in Finland. The end of the Soviet Union and the collapse of that country's economy was a major blow, considering that it was Finland's major trade partner. Norway's banks were also hard hit by problem loans, mainly in the shipping sector (hit by a fall in international demand) as well as in shipyards, petroleum, and fishing. Asset-quality problems in the mortgage business and export finance also produced big losses.

How did the Nordic countries resolve their respective bank crises? Throughout the region, it was recognized at an early stage that the crisis was systemic and that prompt measures were required. A major objective of the Nordic governments was to contain the negative impact on other sectors of the economy. This was rooted in the need to protect the payments system and avoid a domestic credit crunch as well as retain the confidence of foreign banks in the national banking sectors.

Well before the crisis, Denmark, Finland, and Norway had founded bank insurance funds, which helped reduce the impact of the crisis. Yet the insurance funds were not adequate for the full scope of the problem, and government intervention had to be more pronounced. In Finland and Sweden, governments were directly engaged at an early stage, unlike in Denmark where the authorities were able to let the insurance fund and the private sector banks resolve the problems. Government funds for troubled banks were created in 1991 in Norway, in 1992 in Finland, and in 1993 in Sweden. The authorities also opted to close some banks. This was done in only three cases—one in Denmark and two in Norway. In each case the banks were small, with limited customer bases.

The Swedish government also decided to nationalize some troubled banks as in the case of Nordenbanken, the country's second largest bank. Already 80 percent government owned in 1991, Nordenbanken was forced to make substantial provisions for loan losses incurred in a slowing economic environment. Confronted with a lack of public confidence in one of Sweden's most prominent banking institutions, the government repurchased the 20 percent of the private sector stock and injected capital in 1992. It then split Nordenbanken into a good bank and a bad bank, which was named Securum AB. It was entirely owned by the Swedish government and assumed over 60 billion krona of bad loans from Nordenbanken. Some $800 million of government funds was injected into the good bank Nordenbanken in order to guarantee a $609 million loan to save Sweden's largest savings bank, which was in trouble from overlending. Ultimately, the recapitalization of Nordenbanken was equal to 6.4 percent of Sweden's GDP.

The Nordic countries were able to surmount their difficulties and eventually restore their banking sectors to health. In the 2000s the Danish, Finnish, Norwegian, and Swedish banking sectors are regarded as healthy. Moreover, the tough measures taken in the 1990s helped set the stage for more competitive banking systems, which have been able to deal with rival institutions from the rest of Europe. In addition, the Nordic banks have engaged in considerable consolidation, forcing bank regulators to act in greater concert and with better transparency and disclosure, all aimed at avoiding another major banking crash.

Bank Crashes in Central and Eastern Europe

The countries of Central and Eastern Europe have witnessed a considerable transformation of their banking systems since the fall of Communism and the shift to market-based economies. Throughout the region, from the more advanced cases of Hungary and the Czech Republic to the more problematic cases of Russia, Ukraine, and Kazakhstan, bank failures were part of a dramatic upheaval of polit-

ROMANIANS RUN SCARED OF THEIR FAILING BANKS
Phelim McAleer

Nicolae Cinteza, director of supervision at Romania's central bank, points to five bottles of pills on his desk as he gulps coffee and chain smokes. The difficulties and stresses involved in regulating the Romanian banking sector are taking their toll....

According to Radu Gheta, vice-president of Alpha Bank and the head of the Romanian Banking Association, 1999 was the industry's most difficult since deregulation. During the year, the Romanian Bank for Foreign Trade (Bancorex) and Bank Agricola, two of the country's large state-owned banks, experienced difficulties, which led to Bancorex merging almost overnight with the Romanian Development Bank. Bad debts of $1.7 bn from both institutions were taken over by the new State Resolution Agency (Avab). Avab has recovered less than $100 m.

According to Mr. Cinteza, the problems in the sector reflect the banks' continued failure to adapt. "It is a problem of mentality after 50 years of communism. Before 1989 lending was the most important part of banking. The management of some Romanian banks has not changed their mentality. When you put all your money in one business, in lending, when the economy deteriorates as it has in Romania, the banks suffer," he said....

Source: Financial Times, July 6, 2000, p. 16.

ical and economic systems in the past decade. While most of the region's banking systems are now relatively healthy, the 1990s were a period of considerable transition. The radical nature of this transition was captured by Michael Borish and Fernando Montes-Negret: "The collapse of central planning in Central and Eastern Europe and the former Soviet Union and the opening of their formerly socialist economies to the West presented enterprises and banks in these countries with an inescapable imperative: the need to undergo radical restructuring by means of privatization, divestiture, liquidation, and/or reorganization."[14]

In the beginning, commercial banks emerged from monobanks, which had been the mainstay of centrally planned economies. The passage from one bank to many was not smooth, and it was filled with a number of problematic legacies. First and foremost, most of the new banks inherited the loan portfolio and deposit base as well as the clients of the old institution. This meant that they assumed relationships with state-owned enterprises (SOEs), the vast majority of which were also struggling to survive, retool, and become more competitive. This situation was not helped by the considerable debt problems of many SOEs, something rooted in the old Communist system in which profits did not matter. Under Communist rule, access to credit was an issue of political connections rather than creditworthiness. Despite the demise of Communist rule, the new banks were often under political pressure to continue operating as before. The SOE problem was compounded for the banks by loan portfolios that were often excessively concentrated either in individual industries or in geographical regions. There was also a lack of a credit culture in the banks; generally the concept of creditworthiness was hazy at best. According to one study, banks in Central and Eastern Europe, "having functioned for many years as mere instruments of bureaucratic control, lacked the most elementary skills in evaluating creditworthiness in a market economy; even the system of accounting did not correspond to the basic standards used in the capitalist system."[15]

The combination of struggling companies, weak corporate governance laws, a lack of skilled people, and new competition put Central and Eastern European banks and their borrowers under considerable strain. As markets took hold, there was a large and expanding stock of nonperforming loans, which created solvency problems for many banks. Consequently, most banking systems went from having one or two banks to a large number in the early transition stage, and then to a sharp reduction in numbers due to spikes in nonperforming and troubled loans. In Kazakhstan, there was a shift from one bank to some 5 specialized banks and 72 commercial banks shortly after independence in 1992. At year-end 1993, there were 184 financial institutions, of which 177 were private banks; by 1997, the number of banks had fallen to 83.[16] The bumpy path of reform and SOE problems helped trim the numbers.

In the 1990s governments in Central and Eastern Europe were forced to deal with bank fragility, including failures. Poland followed a decentralized approach to resolution of bad debt burdens. Polish banks were put in charge of loan recovery from their clients, while providing assistance to those institutions that appeared capable of working out their problems. Nonperforming loans fell from 60 percent of total bank loans in 1991–92 to 8 percent by 1995.[17] In Hungary, recapitalization schemes for the banks began in 1992, with a large-scale swap of bad loans (which were consolidated into a specially formed new fund) for government securities. This measure, however, failed to stem the crisis in the banking sector. By 1994, bank crashes led to the government holding around 90 percent of the banking sector, with a cost equal to 6 percent of GDP. The Hungarian government then went through the difficult process of restructuring the banking sector, selling off assets to foreign banks, and tightening bank supervision. By the end of the decade, these tough measures paid off, with the Hungarian banking sector performing in a relatively healthy fashion and with a considerably shrunken government-owned sector (under 30 percent), though with a high level of foreign ownership.

In the Czech Republic (which was Czechoslovakia until 1992), the transition from a monobank system to commercial banks began in 1989 with enacting legislation. In January 1990, Komercni Banka and Vseobecna Uverova Banka were established to assume commercial banking activities in the country. Other private banks were to follow, while foreign banks were granted licenses to operate in the country. As the Czech National Bank would later note about the transition: "This was a highly complicated and risky manoeuvre involving the reconstruction of the institutional and legislative framework."[18] While bank activities rapidly expanded, with the banks playing a role in the privatization of the corporate sector, business conditions were difficult due to new competition and heavy demands made on the banks' small core of expertise. Furthermore, the business environment was complicated by the "velvet divorce" between the Czech Republic and the Slovak Republic in 1992. The troubled nature of the Czech banking system began to make itself felt in 1992, but turned acute in 1993 with the problems of Kreditni a Prumyslova Banka, which suffered from shortcomings of liquidity and capital and was finally taken over by the government.

In responding to the growing problem in the banking sector, the Czech government followed a centralized approach to resolving the problems of failing banks, nonperforming loans, and troubled SOEs by creating what was referred to as a "loan hospital," the Konsolidachni Banka, to work out the nonperforming loans. Under this system, the banks swapped their nonperforming loans for government bonds at a discount. It was then left to the bad bank (the loan hospital) to arrange a workout with the troubled companies. Although the Czech Republic was eventually able to stabilize its banking system, this approach was complicated by interlocking directorates and structural weaknesses at the firm and bank levels, which undermined overall competitiveness and raised serious questions about governance, management, and the depth of initial reforms. Bank failures and license revocations occurred throughout the 1994–96 period. Although the number of banks peaked in 1994 at fifty-five, of which thirty-two were Czech and fifteen dominated by foreign capital, the attrition rate was high. By 1997, the total number of Czech banks had fallen to forty-five.

Dismayed by the inability of the loan hospital approach to deal with the ongoing problems in the banking sector, the government was forced to use other measures. These included direct intervention through government takeover of banks with the intention to reprivatize them or to merge them with stronger institutions, closure, or government assistance in dealing with bad loans. At the same time, there was a marked improvement in bank supervision. Throughout the 1990s, new measures were introduced to close banks, introduce conservatorships, sell banks, and improve relations with other national bank supervisors. Moreover, the Czech Republic moved to harmonize its banking legislation and prudential rules with European Union standards as part of the preparatory process for European Union accession. By the beginning of the 2000s, the Czech banking system had gradually improved, foreign ownership was up and forcing positive competitive changes, and the remaining banks under government control were set to be sold in a competitive auction.

It should be noted that Hungary and Poland took more resolute action earlier and were willing to allow foreigners a larger role in their banking systems than was the case in the Czech Republic, where the process of bank reform was hindered by politics and painful economic decisions as well as a recession in 1998–99. A common point for all three Central European countries is that they resolved their banking crises through a combination of government intervention (through closures, temporary takeovers, creation of bad banks, etc.) and allowing foreign banks to take a larger role. Additionally, all three countries made concerted efforts to improve bank supervision, with an eye to joining the European Union sometime in the second half of the 2000s.

Korea's Banking Crisis

During the 1997–98 Asian financial crisis, the Korean banking system imploded under the weight of substantial bad loans, accumulated through bad practices over the course of several decades. Although it can be argued that the actual crisis was sparked by international banks actively providing capital to local companies (to which there is some truth), the Korean banking system was ready for a major meltdown in the late 1990s. The liberalization of foreign credit restrictions revealed a lack of adequate monitoring systems, which in turn reflected the weakness of the underpinning banking system. Large-scale overseas borrowing on the part of Korean corporations and easy access to credit at home ultimately set the stage for a major banking crisis. As in the cases of Central and Eastern European countries, the nature of the Korean banking system was a major force in the crisis.

Throughout much of the post–Korean War (1950–53) period, Korean banks were essentially extensions of government policy. During the lengthy dictatorship of Park Chung Hee (1961–1979) in particular, the banking sector came under the control of the government, which used the sector as a means of allocating credit to those sectors deemed important to national economic development. Moreover, access to credit was used as a political tool to either reward loyalists in the large industrial conglomerates, called *chaebols,* or to punish by withholding credit those seeking too much autonomy from the government. In addition, the government up until the 1980s appointed the top management of the banks. Bank presidents were appointed by the Ministry of Finance, to which they were beholden. Although minor changes were made in the 1980s to provide more autonomy to the banking sector, bankers generally continued to follow the government lead on where loans were made. This system also meant that little emphasis was placed on credit analysis, as political connections proved more important than creditworthiness. In those cases where companies got into trouble, banks would provide additional funds in the expectation that the government would help bail them out if they got into trouble. Moral hazard was indeed a major issue in Korean banking. The state-guided banking approach also fostered a lack of credit culture, leaving one analyst to comment on the low skills of banking executives, "who had done little more than process government orders."[19]

Another complicating factor for Korean banks was their overconcentration in lending. The Korean economy was dominated by the *chaebols,* who were heavily concentrated into the top five of Daewoo, Hyundai, SK, Lucky Goldstar, and Samsung, a group that also made up a sizable amount of the country's GDP and exports. The view that "size matters" gave the *chaebols* an image of "too big to fail." As one analyst commented: "This dulled the commercial judgment of those making lending and investment decisions, worsening the *chaebols'* debt burden on the very eve of the financial collapse. Banks lent widely to the *chaebols,* ignoring group or single-borrower limits. Firms neither kept nor disclosed consolidated accounts, despite the existence of widespread cross-guarantees, making it effectively impossible to assess firms' cash flows and debt-carrying capacity."[20]

When the financial crisis struck Korea in November 1997, the country's financial structure was more precarious than initially thought. The banks were exceedingly fragile and would prove to be hard hit by the crisis. At year-end 1997 Korea had 33 banks and 2,069 nonbank financial institutions. By end-April 2000, the number of banks stood at 10 and nonbank financial institutions numbered 440.[21] As the Korean government moved to deal with the crisis, it was forced to reschedule some of its foreign debt, begin a restructuring of the corporate sector, and gain assistance from the IMF. As to the banks, the government ultimately closed five banks and merged a number of others, and created the Korean Asset Management Company (KAMCO). KAMCO was part of the government program under which banks sought to purge their balance sheets of nonperforming loans through sales to that institution, which functioned as a bad bank.

While progress was made in restructuring the banking sector, Korea's banks continue to face tough challenges. The corporate sector has continued to represent problems, in part due to the slow pace of reform in that sector as well as the troubles of Daewoo, which tumbled into bankruptcy in 1999 and 2000, and Hyundai, which has substantial debt problems but proved to be too big to fail. Faced with these issues, the government sought to regain momentum in 2000 by introducing new measures, some of which seek to improve bank supervision. At the same time, the slow reform of the corporate sector has hurt the government banking reform, with its emphasis on reprivatization and supervision as the keys to a sounder financial system and a government commitment to a more hands-off approach. Despite the end of the crisis, Korea's banking system remains fragile, and the possibility of a new round of crashes cannot be ruled out.

The Rescue of Long-Term Capital Management

One of the most dramatic rescues in which "too big to fail" was used occurred in 1998, with a hedge fund named Long-Term Capital Management (LTCM). The term

UK BANK LOSSES OF $12 BN BLAMED ON WORLD TURMOIL

Richard Adams

The near collapse of Long-Term Capital Management, the US hedge fund, and the Russian government's debt default last year contributed to UK-based banks suffering trading losses of … $12.2 bn, official figures revealed yesterday.

The losses were the result of trading conditions in the second half of last year, according to Britain's Office for National Statistics….

Source: Financial Times, March 23, 1999, p. 6.

hedge comes from the expression "to hedge one's bets." A hedge fund is a limited partnership, which by definition exists for the benefit of a small group of investors, either wealthy individuals or institutions. Unlike mutual funds, which are open to the broader public and are allowed to advertise, hedge funds are prohibited from advertising.[22] Hedge funds in small numbers have operated since the 1920s and for a long time were largely unregulated. Since the 1920s hedge funds have grown in number, hitting 215 in 1968 and reaching around 3,000 in the late 1990s.

Considering the nature of exclusiveness as well as legal and proprietary reasons, hedge fund managers have traditionally been very reluctant to disclose specifics about their operations. In 1977 *Institutional Investor* noted of the relationship between hedge funds and the rest of the securities industry: "Today, they [hedge funds] are still targets for an uncanny number of unsavory market rumors, the victims of smear campaigns accusing them of just about everything short of pilfering the napery from the New York Stock Exchange dining room…. hedge funds are so often branded as villains by other sectors of the investment community."[23] Considering the secretive manner in which LTCM operated and the threat that it came to pose to a number of U.S. and European banks, many of those suspicions were revisited in 1998.

LTCM was founded in 1994 by former Salomon Brothers derivatives trader John W. Meriwether, who brought with him a team of Ph.D. economists and a firm belief in the ability of highly complicated models to accurately forecast the direction of markets. LTCM was to concentrate on relative value trades in bond markets around the world. Traders placed multimillion-dollar bets on the direction of bonds in Italy, Japan, the UK, and the United States. Eventually, they diversified into equity markets and emerging markets, such as Russia and Brazil. To make such large trades, LTCM borrowed huge amounts of money from Wall Street banks and investment houses as well as from a number of major European institutions. With little capital of its own, LTCM was able to leverage its initial capital twenty to thirty times. This allowed a small firm in Greenwich, Connecticut, and London to amass very large trades, which initially reaped huge profits.

What made LTCM a problem to banks was the lending they provided the hedge fund. When market conditions were good, LTCM's secretive ways and arrogance were tolerated and credit freely flowed to the firm. However, when market conditions deteriorated (across the board) and many of the huge bets failed, LTCM was suddenly vulnerable and so were its creditors. The much-vaunted models were left wanting as LTCM faced what has been referred to as the financial world's equivalent of a "perfect storm"—everything went wrong at the same time. As *Business Week* noted: "Interest rates moved the wrong way, stock and bond prices supposed to converge diverged, and liquidity dried up in some crucial markets."[24] In addition, LTCM traders came to rely too heavily on their models. They sought to rule out what has been called "animal spirits." As Roger Lowenstein noted: "The professors overlooked the fact that people, traders included, are not always reasonable. No matter what the models say, traders are not machines guided by silicon chips; they are impressionable and imitative; they run in flocks and retreat in hordes."[25]

By September 1998 LTCM had amassed $100 billion in assets, most of them borrowed and falling daily in valuation. In addition, the hedge fund had entered into thousands of derivative contracts, amassing more than $1 trillion worth of exposure. LTCM simply did not have the ability to meet its obligations. For its creditors, LTCM suddenly loomed as a major potential loss, coming during a period of high market volatility. Among those at risk were Bankers Trust, Chase Manhattan, Merrill Lynch, Goldman Sachs, UBS, and J.P. Morgan. Consequently, the U.S. Federal Reserve decided to step in and lead a private sector rescue of LTCM. The rescue was justified because a sudden and disorderly retreat from LTCM's positions would have posed unacceptable risks to the U.S. economy and, by extension, the international economy, already fragile after the Asian financial crisis and the Russian ruble default in August 1998. The Fed also stressed that it was really a government-guided rescue in that no public funds were involved.

The Fed-led rescue raised criticisms of crony capitalism and bailing out a wealthy few. Along these lines, it was pointed out that complacent Westerners blamed Asia's financial crisis in 1997–98 on the closed, secretive, and incestuous elite systems in which the state came to the rescue when the time came to balance the books. The United States, IMF, and World Bank told Asian governments to put their houses in order, make their systems more transparent, and be subject to the laws of the market. As one Western observer noted: "Above all, they [governments] must stop propping up failing banks or enterprises on the pretext of some connection with a crony or his hangers-on."[26] Consequently, when the Fed moved to corral banks into rescuing a highly secretive hedge fund and the benefactors of such a rescue were an elite few, an outcry arose.

Although there was considerable resistance to bailing out LTCM, the Fed was able to pull together a rescue package for the hedge fund. The main thrust of the package was an infusion of $3.5 billion by LTCM's major creditors in return for a 90 percent share in the fund and a promise that a supervisory board would be established in which the banks dominated. The crisis was averted, and the international financial system continued along.

THE SAGA OF LTCM

The source of the trouble seemed so small, so laughably remote, as to be insignificant. But isn't it always that way? A load of tea is dumped into a harbor, an archduke is shot, and suddenly a tinderbox is lit, a crisis erupts, and the world is different. In this case, the shot was Long-Term Capital Management, a private investment partnership with its headquarters in Greenwich, Connecticut, a posh suburb some forty miles from Wall Street. LTCM managed money for only one hundred investors; it employed not quite two hundred people, and surely not one American in a hundred had ever heard of it. Indeed, five years earlier, LTCM had not even existed.

But on the Wednesday afternoon of September 23, 1998, Long-Term did not seem small. On account of a crisis at LTCM, McDonough had summoned—"invited", in the Fed's restrained idiom—the heads of every major Wall Street bank. For the first time, the chiefs of Bankers Trust, Bear Stearns, Chase Manhattan, Goldman Sachs, J.P. Morgan, Lehman Brothers, Merrill Lynch, Morgan Stanley Dean Witter, and Salomon Smith Barney gathered under the oil portraits in the Fed's tenth-floor boardroom—not to bail out a Latin American nation but to consider a rescue of one of their own. The chairman of the New York Stock Exchange joined them, as did representatives from major European banks. Unaccustomed to hosting such a large gathering, the Fed did not have enough leather-backed chairs to go around, so the chief executives had to squeeze into folding metal seats.

Although McDonough was a public official, the meeting was secret. As far as the public knew, America was in the salad days of one of history's great bull markets, although recently, as in many previous autumns, it had seen some backsliding. Since mid-August, when Russia had defaulted on its ruble debt, the global bond markets in particular had been highly unsettled. But that wasn't why McDonough had called the bankers.

Long-Term, a bond-trading firm, was on the brink of failing. The fund was run by John W. Meriwether, formerly a well-known trader at Salomon Brothers. Meriwether, a congenial though cautious mid-westerner, had been popular among the bankers. It was because of him, mainly, that the bankers had agreed to give financing to Long-Term—and had agreed on highly generous terms. But Meriwether was only the public face of Long-Term. The heart of the firm was a group of brainy, Ph.D.-certified arbitrageurs. Many of them had been professors. Two had won the Nobel Prize. All of them were very smart. And they knew they were very smart.

For four years, Long-Term had been the envy of Wall Street. The fund had racked up returns of more than 40 percent a year, with no losing stretches, no volatility, seemingly no risk at all. Its intellectual supermen had apparently been able to reduce an uncertain world to rigorous, cold-blooded odds—on form, they were the very best that modern finance had to offer.

(continued)

This one obscure arbitrage fund had amassed an amazing $100 billion in assets, virtually all of it borrowed—borrowed, that is, from the bankers at McDonough's table. As monstrous as this indebtedness was, it was by no means the worst of Long-Term's problems. The fund had entered into thousands of derivative contracts, which had endlessly intertwined it with every bank on Wall Street. These contracts, essentially side bets on market prices, covered an astronomical sum—more than $1 trillion worth of exposure.

If Long-Term defaulted, all of the banks in the room would be left holding one side of a contract for which the other side no longer existed. In other words, they would be exposed to tremendous—and untenable—risks. Undoubtedly, there would be a frenzy as every bank rushed to escape its now one-sided obligations and tried to sell its collateral from Long-Term.

Panics are as old as markets, but derivatives were relatively new. Regulators had worried about the potential risks of these new securities, which linked the country's financial institutions in a complex chain of reciprocal obligations. Officials had wondered what would happen if one big link in the chain should fail. McDonough feared that the markets would stop working; that trading would cease; that the system itself would come crashing down.

Source: Roger Lowenstein, *When Genius Failed: The Rise and Fall of Long-Term Capital Management* (New York: Random House, 2000), pp. 5–6.

The Roles of the IMF and the World Bank

There is considerable debate about the roles of the IMF and the World Bank in dealing with international banking crises. The World Bank's mandate is to provide technical assistance in economic development for a wide range of countries, as well as long-term loans earmarked for sectorial development. In this capacity, the World Bank has played a role in supporting bank reforms and during times of crisis has been a supporting institution. The mandate of the IMF differs in that its primary task is to promote international monetary cooperation by providing itself as the machinery for consultation and collaboration on international monetary problems. Crucially, the IMF is to provide "confidence to members by making general resources of the Fund temporarily available to them under adequate safeguards, thus providing them with opportunity to correct maladjustments in their balance of payments without resorting to measures destructive to national or international prosperity."[27] This means that during a crisis of confidence, as in a banking crisis, the IMF can provide short-term loans to help restore confidence. Such loans are often made in tandem with the World Bank and other multilateral institutions.

The IMF also has an annual look at each member country's economy under what is called an Article IV consultation. This examination involves a close and ongoing dialogue with monetary and finance officials at both the technical and policymaking levels. Since the Asian financial crisis of 1997–98, the IMF has taken a

BANKING SCANDALS RATTLE ASIANS AND WORRY LENDING AGENCIES

Wayne Arnold

Banking scandals have rippled across Indonesia and Thailand this month, and bankers and securities analysts predict that they are likely to worsen, intensifying pressure on the two countries' governments and providing a growing source of consternation to lenders at the World Bank and the International Monetary Fund....

In Indonesia, officials prepared to expand an investigation of questionable payments by Bank Bali to include that country's central bank, after an IMF request that they do so. The Bank Bali scandal has involved Indonesia's President and his brother and provoked calls for the resignation of the nation's top financial officials.

IMF and World Bank officials have sounded stern warnings that Indonesia needs to clear up the Bank Bali mess expeditiously. On Tuesday, the World Bank's country director, Mark Baird, said it would be difficult to continue providing funds if Indonesia did not resolve the case to its satisfaction. The IMF's Asia-Pacific director, Hubert Neiss, said in Jakarta today that a lingering scandal could be "a disaster scenario." He declined to speculate further or in any detail at this stage....

Source: New York Times, August 26, 1999, p. A10.

closer look at banking and financial supervisory policies, which gives it greater understanding of the issues facing a particular country. Moreover, it is recognized that a blowup in the banking sector can put an IMF restructuring program at risk. As Karin Lissakers notes: "A fiscal blowout of the banking system can blow a huge hole in the government budget, as demonstrated by both industrial and developing country banking crises, that leaves both the banking system and the Fund's stabilization plan in a shambles. However, Fund conditionality through a well-designed adjustment program that also addresses banking problems can be an effective means of permanently improving the performance of member countries' financial sectors."[28] This also means that the IMF (and the World Bank) must work with other international organizations, such as the Bank for International Settlements and regional development banks, in dealing with both the prevention and resolution of bank crashes that threaten to become systemic crises and spread through contagion.

The IMF has been active in dealing with banking system crises in Asia, Latin America, and Eastern Europe. In November 2000, it launched an effort to help Turkey through a crisis of confidence caused by problems in the banking sector, which stemmed from ten banks under state administration in Turkey. A criminal investigation into corruption around the banks prompted foreign investors to sell Turkish treasury bills and stocks. This sell-off triggered a solvency crisis among a handful of

IMF BEGINS TURKISH BANKING CRISIS

Leyla Boulton

Officials from the International Monetary Fund last night began consulta-
tions with the Turkish authorities on urgent measures to stem a crisis in
the banking sector and safeguard a wider economic reform programme.

The experts' arrival in Ankara coincided with a statement by Horst
Kohler, the IMF managing director, who said the talks would focus on banking reform. He also hoped the discussions would be concluded "expeditiously" so that the IMF could approve an emergency loan sought by Turkey
at a December 21 board meeting.

"This suggests that once they are convinced the Turks are prepared to
close down all banks which are currently not viable, then the IMF is likely
to provide additional financing," said Jurgen Odenius, Commerzbank's
emerging market strategist, who used to work for the IMF.

Source: Financial Times, December 4, 2000, p. 24.

banks, which had made themselves vulnerable by borrowing heavily to finance traditionally lucrative treasury bill holdings. Apprehensive of the liquidity squeeze and
bank failures, the central bank exceeded funding limits worked out with the IMF in
an earlier economic restructuring agreement. What brought the IMF into the crisis
was that the Turkish problem was threatening to spread into other emerging markets
and German bank stocks (those institutions with heavy Turkish exposure).[29] Ironically, the Central Bank of Turkey's governor, Gazi Ercel, had stated in October 2000,
"we all agree that the highest priority should be given to crisis prevention measures
described as the adoption of consistent macroeconomic and exchange rate policies,
sound debt management, and prudential supervision of financial system."[30]

The Turkish banking crisis and other such crises underscore the role of the IMF
as an international lender of last resort—or something very close to it. Although this
role is highly controversial, as it raises issues of moral hazard, the IMF remains the
only game in town to handle this type of role. The Bank for International Settlements has a different role, more akin to an international bank supervisor and in a
limited sense at that. The track record of such BIS actions is exceedingly limited,
whereas that of the IMF is extensive. In fact, the missions of the IMF make its role
as a lender of last resort almost a logical extension of its other activities.

Conclusion

Bank crashes are part and parcel of international banking. They have a long history and will be part of the future. As reflected by the cases demonstrated in this
chapter, there are a number of similarities worth noting. These include the neces-

sity of prudent regulation on the part of the authorities in preventing bank crashes, the need for prompt action once a banking crisis occurs, and the importance of transparency and disclosure in financial transactions. International cooperation is also highly important from the standpoint of ongoing globalization of financial markets and the threat posed by contagion. In addition, the path out of a bank crisis—that is, the restructuring process—is difficult and takes considerable political will, as many tough decisions must be made that may not be popular with the public.

Questions

1. Drawing on specific examples cited in the chapter, what are the leading indicators of a banking crisis?
2. Are developing countries or developed countries more susceptible to banking crises? Why?
3. What steps can be taken to prevent future banking crises? Who should be responsible for taking these steps?
4. What is the IMF's role in preventing and managing banking crises?
5. In your opinion, what are the lessons of the LTCM saga for bankers? For regulators?
6. Explain the role of moral hazard in banking crashes.
7. What steps may be taken by government and regulators to help contain a banking crisis? What is the role of "bad banks"?
8. Do you believe that Central and Eastern European countries are more susceptible to banking crashes than other countries? Explain your answer.

Notes

1. Morris Goldstein and Philip Turner, *Banking Crises in Emerging Economies: Origins and Policy Options* (Basel, Switzerland: Bank for International Settlements, 1996), p. 5. Also see Benton E. Gup, *Bank Failures in the Major Trading Countries of the World: Causes and Remedies* (Westport, Conn.: Quorum Books, 1998).
2. Charles Kindleberger, *Manias, Panics and Crashes: A History of Financial Crises* (New York: John Wiley & Sons, 1996), p. 97.
3. These views are well stated by economist George G. Kaufman, "Bank Fragility: Perception and Historical Evidence," Chicago University Working Paper No. 96–6 (1996).
4. Morris Goldstein and Philip Turner, *Banking Crises in Emerging Economies*, pp. 4–8.
5. World Bank, *Entering the Twenty-First Century: World Development Report 1999/2000* (New York: Oxford University Press, 2000), p. 77.
6. Morris Goldman and Philip Turner, *Banking Crises in Emerging Economies*, p. 10.
7. Benton E. Gup, in *Bank Failures in the Major Trading Countries of the World*, pp. 46–67, argues that nonperforming real estate loans, even more than fraud, are the primary causes for bank failures.
8. George G. Kaufman, "Banking Failures, Systemic Risk, and Bank Regulation," *Cato Journal*, 16, No. 1 (Spring/Summer 1996), p. 3 of the Internet version http://www.cato. org/pubs/journal/cj16n1-2.html.

9. Brian Butler, David Butler, and Alan Isaacs, editors, *Oxford Dictionary of Finance and Banking: From International to Personal Finance* (New York: Oxford University Press, 1997), p. 227.

10. For more on this argument, see Dennis Jacobe, "It's Time to End the Too-Large-to-Fail Doctrine," *Savings Institutions*, 111, No. 2 (1990), pp. 23–25.

11. Sigbjorn Atle Berg, "Bank Failures in Scandinavia," in Gerard Carpio Jr., William C. Hunter, George Kaufman, and Danny M. Leipziger, editors, *Preventing Bank Crises: Lessons from Recent Global Bank Failures* (Washington, D.C.: The World Bank, 1998), p. 198.

12. Ibid.

13. See Assar Lindbeck, Per Molander, Torsten Persson, Olof Petersson, Agnar Sandmo, Birgitta Swedenborg, and Niels Thygesen, *Turning Sweden Around* (Cambridge, Mass.: The MIT Press, 1994).

14. Michael Borish and Fernando Montes-Negret, "Restructuring Distressed Banks in Transition Economies: Lessons from Central Europe and Ukraine," in Gerlad Caprio Jr., William C. Hunter, George G. Kaufman, and Danny M. Leipziger, editors, *Preventing Bank Crises: Lessons from Recent Global Bank Failures* (Washington, D.C.: The World Bank, 1998), p. 69.

15. Roman Frydman, Andrzej Rapaczynski, and Joel Turkewitz, "Transition to a Private Property Regime in the Czech Republic and Hungary," in Wing Thye Woo, Stephen Parker, Jeffrey Sachs, editors, *Economies in Transition: Comparing Asia and Europe* (Cambridge, Mass.: The MIT Press, 1997), p. 75.

16. United Nations, *World Economic and Social Survey 1999: Trends and Policies in the World Economy* (New York: United Nations, 1999), pp. 146–147.

17. *Ibid.*, p. 148.

18. Czech National Bank, *Report on Banking Supervision in the Czech Republic* (Prague: Czech National Bank, December 1999), pp. 6–7.

19. Mark L. Clifford, *Troubled Tiger: Businessmen, Bureaucrats and Generals in South Korea* (Armonk, N.Y.: M. E. Sharpe, 1997), p. 207.

20. Donald Hanna, Suktae Oh, and Cliff Tan, *Korean Financial Restructuring: Where to from Here?* Salomon Smith Barney Economics, November 23, 2000, p. 6.

21. *Ibid.*, p. 8.

22. For more on hedge funds, see Jess Lederman and Robert A. Klein, editors, *Hedge Funds: Investment and Portfolio Strategies for the Institutional Investor* (New York: McGraw-Hill, 1995).

23. John Thackray, "Whatever Happened to the Hedge Funds?" *Institutional Investor*, May 1977, pp. 71–74.

24. Peter Coy and Suzanne Woolley, with Leah Nathans Spiro and William Clasgall, "Failed Wizards of Wall Street," December 1, 1998, atBusinessweek.com/1998/38/b3596001.htm.

25. Roger Lowenstein, *When Genius Failed: The Rise and Fall of Long-Term Capital Management* (New York: Random House, 2000), pp. 234–235.

26. Ibrahim Warde, "Crony Capitalism: LTCM, a Hedge Fund Above Suspicion," *Le Monde Diplomatique*, November 1998, at www.monde-diplomatique.fr/en/1998/11/04warde2.

27. Articles of the International Monetary Fund, Article I, at www.imf.org/external/pubs/ft/aa/aa01.htm.

28. Karin Lissakers, "The Role of the International Monetary Fund," in Caprio et al., *Preventing Bank Crises: Lessons from Recent Global Bank Failures*, p. 30.

29. Leyla Boulton, "Turkey Seeks Further Loan from IMF," *Financial Times*, November 30, 2000, p. 3. Also see Leyla Boulton and Martin Wolf, "Turkey's Economic Tremors," *Financial Times*, December 5, 2000, p. 19.

30. Gazi Ercel, Governor of the Central Bank of the Republic of Turkey, "The Role of the Private Sector in Crisis Prevention and Crisis Resolution," Conference of the Global Capital Market Reinvesting Bretton Woods Committee, Montreal, October 23, 2000. Available through the Turkish Central Bank's website, at tcmb.gov.tr/yeni/evds/konusma/ing/2000/Reinventing.html.

CHAPTER 10

SUPERVISION AND REGULATION

The supervision and regulation of banks involved in international activities is an important element of a functioning global economy. Without proper bank supervision, problems can arise that undermine the ability of banks to act as the main facilitators of credit and managers of national payment systems. Problems that have cross-border implications for other banking systems may include:

- Self-lending through conglomerates and holding company structures
- Contagion from other financial markets
- Poor credit policy guidelines
- Bad management

Each of these elements was evident during the Asian economic crisis in 1997–98, which was in part caused by a lack of prudent bank supervision. This created an environment in which transparency and disclosure were lacking, credit controls were weak or nonexistent, and patronage inhibited needed remedial action. The so-called Asian contagion, which rolled into Russia and Brazil in 1998 and 1999, amply reflected the ability of problems in one financial market to spread to others with devastating repercussions. Consequently, proper banking supervision and regulation are needed to ensure a sound and efficient environment for international banking as well as the workings of the global economy. Although there is no single international bank regulator, the Basel Accord has established important guidelines for home country bank supervision and international cooperation on cross-border banking issues. A central component of international supervision, the Basel Accord will be discussed in this chapter.

What do supervision and regulation mean? The former usually refers to the enforcement of regulation, with the latter meaning laws or guidelines, often passed by national legislative bodies. A more comprehensive definition of supervision was provided by a World Bank Discussion Paper:

It includes: (a) authorization of institutions in the regulated business, (b) licensing and approval in the field of regulated business, (c) issuing rules stipulated in law and drafting guidelines for the conduct of regulated business, and (d) performing the actual task of supervision on an ongoing basis. These tasks are by no means separate nor independent of each other; to the contrary, together they form an integrated set of duties to be performed in a consistent, logical and efficient manner preferably by one competent authority per sector of the financial system.[1]

BASEL BUST-UP

In June, when a central-bankers' committee proposed revisions to the famous Basel Accord, which determines how much capital internationally active banks must set aside against their loans, their plans were broadly welcomed. The original accord was so flawed that some felt it was operating perversely. Since it did not always require more capital for riskier borrowers—indeed, often the reverse—it was encouraging banks to take more risks, not fewer. Yet the June revisions are now under such heavy attack that the whole idea of a new accord is in danger.

The aim of the revision, everyone has agreed, was admirable enough: to tie banks' capital more closely to the riskiness of their portfolios. The riskier these are, the more capital banks ought to hold. The problem was, as ever, how to assess the risk. One idea was to follow the risk-management models used by the banks themselves. But the committee found that these were, for the time being, insufficiently developed. One banker dismisses them as a "philosopher's stone."

Another notion was to use ratings from credit-rating agencies, such as Standard & Poor's or Moody's. Although the committee was not all that keen on this idea, it could find nobody else to do the job. There were oddities, such as that unrated borrowers would get more favourable treatment than lowly rated ones. But the biggest problem, it now transpires, is that there is little support for the use of rating agencies—and, not least, that the agencies themselves are unhappy with the idea. For their part, banks think they know their borrowers better in any case. "A lot of banks don't have any confidence in the agencies, because they have better relationships and information," says Harald Benink of Maastricht University.

Although external ratings will probably appear in some form, many banks would prefer a third option: to use their internal ratings as a way of setting capital. "They are one way of solving the dilemma," says one member. Unfortunately, this idea was inserted in the June proposals only at the last minute, because some countries had been opposed to using such ratings at all. Details of how they might be used, indeed any details at all about them, were notable in June for their absence.

Committee members now say that the technical details are being thrashed out; a progress report is due later this year. The two biggest questions are over how to make different banks' ratings comparable and how to link capital to them. The subcommittee responsible thinks that comparability could be achieved by using such techniques as "expected-default frequency," which measure the likelihood of default. But capital needs to be set aside more for unexpected losses than expected ones.

Source: The Economist, October 16, 1999, p. 77.

While it is generally recognized that prudent bank supervision and regulation are important components in making the international financial system work, there is no single global bank regulator. Bank supervision remains a function of the particular nation-state, with the location of the bank license being called the home country. Control over national banking systems is still a realm of sovereignty that most governments are reluctant to surrender. Even within the European Union, which has created common banking laws and a central bank, bank supervision remains under the control of each member government. Thus, there is no single regulator with the scope and authority to oversee major multinational financial institutions, such as Deutsche Bank or Goldman Sachs. Despite the absence of one overarching international bank regulator, efforts have been made to construct a framework of common practices, such as internationally recognized capital adequacy standards and more uniform regulatory mechanisms to deal with money laundering. Nonetheless, the lack of a global banking supervisor—in a world of increasingly global banks—has created a patchwork of regulators that leaves many holes in the safety net.

CRISIS IN THE MAKING

John Plender

Since the launch of European economic and monetary union on January 1, [1999,] the pace of consolidation among the larger banks of the eurozone has been breathtaking.

In Italy two giants, San Paolo-IMI and UniCredito Italiano, are proposing to merge with Banca di Roma and Banca Commerciale Italiana respectively. In Spain the big link-up is between Banco Santander and BCH, while in France Banque Nationale de Paris is stalking Societe Generale and Paribas, both of which would prefer a merger of their own.

So far the merger wave has been contained, for the most part, within national borders. But it is clear that some of the deals are intended to be intermediate stages on the way to the development of supra-national champions. This raises big questions for banking supervision. The most indelicate is: what happens when one of the new euro-behemoths runs into trouble?

There is no clear answer. For the European Central Bank has no decisive legal mandate to act as a lender of the last resort in a banking crisis. So, despite Emu [the European monetary unit], banking supervision is still handled at the national level.

If banking history has one consistent message, it is that large-scale changes in the structure and regulation of this highly leveraged industry are almost always followed by failures of banking supervision and financial crises. In particular, liberalization has an unremitting capacity for exposing flaws in the system.

Source: Financial Times, April 12, 1999.

The Legal Regime

At the beginning of the twenty-first century, most countries have well-established public policies for the regulation and supervision of banks. Since banks function as the depositors of the public savings, facilitators of capital in the economy, and managers of the nation's payment systems, there is a pressing need for prudent regulation and supervision at the national level. Good bank supervision and well-administered banks are obviously in the public interest. Although there is no supranational bank regulatory authority, each nation delegates regulatory and supervisory powers to either a central bank (or monetary authority) or to a number of parties. Despite the differences in national bank regulatory systems, there is a common concern that the regulatory and supervisory regime support the lender of last resort, deposit insurance, and/or investor of last resort functions that governments may have to perform to maintain confidence in the financial system.[2] In the aftermath of the Asian financial crisis, there has also been greater consensus about the need for greater transparency for government involvement and ownership in the banking system, limits to connected lending, better public disclosure of banks' financial condition, and safeguards against regulatory forbearance (i.e., the government's willingness to allow certain practices despite potential risks). This also means that a legal regime must be in place that upholds the rule of law and provides a legal foundation for the existence and working of a banking system.

Another element key to the legal regime supporting proper banking supervision is that bank regulatory agencies must be provided with broad rule-making authority. Financial markets evolve, and as they do, regulatory agencies need a degree of flexibility to adapt their methodology and retrain their staff. While this is true of mature financial markets, as in the United States and Japan, it is even more accurate of emerging financial markets in Asia, Latin America, and the Middle East. In the latter cases, the regulatory bodies often play a role in the development and regulation of the financial markets and related institutions.[3]

Key elements of a legal regime supportive of banking supervision include basic laws pertaining to the licensing of banks, mechanisms for proper supervision and governmental and legislative support, and flexibility to enact, when required, new laws and regulations. The legal regime should support the supervisory agency in imposing the following safeguards for the protection of the public: banks and their related entities must maintain accurate books and records (i.e., adequate transparency and disclosure), efficient systems for the processing, transfer, and safekeeping of financial instruments; there need to be independent auditors; and banks must provide disclosure of meaningful accounts in an accurate and timely fashion. And, while it is essential to have the right laws on the books, implementation of the law is equally significant. More than one bank crisis has occurred because of poor supervision stemming from a lack of political will on the part of the authorities to carry out the law. Indeed, in some cases, political interference from the government has been the root cause of more systemic failures, as exemplified by Indonesia in 1997–98.

There are three areas of commonality among bank regulators around the planet: an emphasis is placed on corporate authorizations, risk assessment, and sanctions. The first area pertains to the licensing of new charters, geographical and product expansion, mergers and acquisitions, and bank failures. Any time a bank enters a new line of business, it must seek supervisory approval. Risk assessment concerns the risks in individual bank operations as well as what risks are posed to the entire banking system. Risk assessment is done by both on-site and off-site examinations. On-site examinations are conducted by trained bank examiners, who actually spend time at the particular institution they are reviewing. The last area, sanctions, pertains to the enforcement and compliance process, which can encompass formal agreements, cease and desist orders, removal of management, and civil and criminal penalties.

The globalization of banking has clearly made bank supervisors aware of such risks as contagion, poor capital adequacy, and financial fraud (see Chapter 12 on money laundering). It has also raised questions as to how to properly supervise such entities as conglomerates that have multiple lines of business, sometimes not financial in nature. Consequently, bank regulators must be alert to the threat of contagion and the need to maintain close monitoring of the relationships between the regulated entities and the rest of the companies making up the conglomerate. The collapse of BCCI (Bank of Credit and Commerce International) in 1991 was a painful reminder of this pitfall. BCCI evaded serious scrutiny for years by operating between Luxembourg, the United Kingdom, and the Cayman Islands in such a way that the Luxembourg authorities were unaware of most of its activities and the Bank of England had very limited authority. The BCCI debacle was an illustration of the failures of cross-border banking supervision in the modern global economy.

Transparency

Another issue arising from the financial crises and scandals during the 1980s and 1990s is **transparency.** While there has been considerable discussion linking the lack of transparency and corruption in Asia, the actual definition must be broader. As already observed, the Nordic banking crises had little to do with corruption, but were largely due to adverse macroeconomic events and poor bank supervision. Consequently, we define transparency as (1) the need to make visible financial transactions underpinning the disclosure of the level of nonperforming loans (as well as clear definitions of such terms). This also includes the level of working capital and its relationship to what is theoretically available to the bank (hidden assets, real estate, and other assets). Moreover, transparency includes (2) how accurate bank statements are pertaining to risks and strategies.[4] Critical to improving transparency is the need to have adequate resources and human capital.

Complicating the achievement of greater transparency are the increasingly complex and dynamic activities of banks over the last couple of decades. As one report notes: "Many banks now have large-scale international operations and significant participation in securities and/or insurance businesses in addition to traditional banking activities. Their product lines change rapidly and include highly sophisticated transactions, and they have complex legal and managerial structures."[5] Consequently, the task of providing timely, accurate, relevant, and sufficient disclosures of qualitative and quantitative information that enables users to make a proper assessment of risk has become far more challenging. In the aftermath of the Asian financial crises of the late 1990s, this complex challenge also carried with it a greater need for international coordination.

Any improvements made in transparency and disclosure will be a huge help in averting future bank/financial crises. Clearly, awareness of problems makes responding an easier process. (Table 10.1 lists the official bank regulatory/supervisory

TABLE 10.1 Bank Regulatory/Supervisory Agencies in Selected Countries	
Canada	Office of the Superintendent of Financial Institutions (OSFI)
Germany	Federal Banking Supervisory Office
Greece	General Inspectorate of Banks (part of the Bank of Greece)
Hong Kong	Hong Kong Monetary Authority (HKMA)
Italy	Bank of Italy (central bank)
Jamaica	Central Bank of Jamaica
Japan	Financial Supervisory Authority
Mexico	Banco de Mexico (central bank)
Russia	The Bank of Russia (central bank)
Singapore	Monetary Authority of Singapore (MAS)
South Africa	Bank Supervision Department of the South African Reserve Bank under the control of the Registrar of Banks (also, Financial Service Board for securities business)
Sweden	Financial Supervisory Authority
United Kingdom	Financial Services Authority, with indirect support from the Bank of England
United States	Office of the Comptroller of the Currency (OCC) (national banks)
	Federal Reserve Board (bank holding companies)
	Federal Deposit Insurance Corporation (FDIC)
	State banking authorities
Venezuela	Superintendency of Banking

agencies in selected countries.) However, transparency and disclosure alone will not avert all crises, especially those stemming from macroeconomic factors.

A Private Sector Element

The prudent governance of a banking system also has a private sector component. As one former U.S. bank regulator noted: "It is first and foremost the responsibility of bank management and directors to establish the policies, practices, and procedures for the banks under their fiduciary stewardship."[6] Without a system in which the regulatory authorities and banks work well together, banking can be a highly risky business for the bankers as well as the public who depend on the banks to function prudently.

The globalization of financial services and the need for prudent supervision has become increasingly important around the world. In the past decade, the asymmetry between national regulation of banks and the increasingly international nature of the banking industry has become glaringly apparent. In the late 1990s efforts were stepped up to improve cross-border supervision and to widen the international dialogue. Such efforts included the Group of Ten (countries), the Bank for International Settlements, and new regional central bank and supervisory group forums that have been established in the Americas and Asia. At the G–7 summit in Denver in July 1997, the leaders of the United States, Japan, Germany, France, Italy, the UK, and Canada announced several new measures to help reinforce international bank supervision:

- Steps toward the establishment of a multilateral network of supervision appropriate to today's global markets and global institutions
- Progress toward a framework of strong supervisory principles for the major globally active financial institutions
- New steps to improve transparency
- Steps to reduce risk in payment and settlement systems
- Endorsement of a concerted international strategy to help emerging economies to strengthen their financial systems, including a new, universally applicable set of core principles for effective banking supervision[7]

The articulation of such initiatives was apt, considering the financial crisis that was already beginning to strike Asia. Certainly, the July 1997 G–7 summit declaration to reinforce international bank supervision was timely as it recognized the risks of cross-border contagion and the role that open, yet weakly supervised, banking systems could play in this. A central player in strengthening international banking supervision, as envisioned by the G–7, is the Bank for International Settlements.

The Bank for International Settlements (BIS)

As international banking evolved and became a significant area of economic activity, governments were increasingly faced with the difficult issue of how to provide prudent supervision and regulation of those institutions with activities in jurisdictions beyond their authority. While it is difficult to monitor a British bank's activities in Argentina, the risks posed by such business to the health of the British banking system could not be easily overlooked. Consequently, in the late nineteenth century a modicum of cooperation existed between the Bank of England and the Banque de France, which helped to contain contagion when certain banks got into trouble, as during the Barings Crisis of 1890. Such cross-border cooperation, however, was limited due to the relatively small number of international banks, which were largely concentrated in a handful of European countries, namely England, France, Germany, and Austria. In Japan, the activities of the country's fledgling banks were domestic in orientation, and cross-border issues were not of major significance. Although the United States had a sizable number of banks, most were not international in their business orientation. Moreover, international bank regulatory supervision involving the United States was decidedly limited by the absence of a central bank until 1912–13. Regulators also depended on the help of private bankers, as when the British in 1890 turned to the Rothschilds for help and the Americans to J. P. Morgan during the financial panic of 1907.

The move to greater international regulatory cooperation began during the Great Depression. The collapse of the U.S. stock market in 1929 and subsequent devastation of the U.S. banking sector, along with the frail health of the major European economies, caused a serious reassessment of the need for better cross-border cooperation. One offshoot of this was the creation of the Bank for International Settlements (BIS), which was based in Geneva, Switzerland. The initial impetus for the BIS came from the Young Plan, implemented to help the German government make its reparation payments as agreed by the Treaty of Versailles, which ended World War I. The BIS was prevented from serving as a significant venue of international monetary cooperation, in part because the U.S. Congress refused to allow the Federal Reserve Board to join. Nonetheless, the BIS was to outlive the Young Plan and evolve into what some have described as a "central bank for central bankers."

The BIS, which opened its doors in 1930, is the world's oldest international financial organization. The primary mission of the BIS, according to Article 5 of its Original Statutes, is "to promote the co-operation of central banks and to provide additional facilities for international financial operations."[8] Consequently, the BIS has three key roles. First, it is "an important forum for international monetary and financial cooperation between central bankers and, increasingly, other regulators and supervisors." This role helped provide the impetus for the standardization and implementation of BIS capital adequacy ratios for banks. A second role for the BIS is that of a bank, "but one whose depositors are limited to central banks and international financial institutions." This has meant that a significant portion of the world's foreign exchange reserves are held on deposit with the BIS. The BIS's third role is to function as an agent or trustee in connection with various international financial agreements.

The BIS seeks to reflect changes in global finance by providing technical expertise and information-sharing forums to a growing membership. Throughout most of the BIS's existence, its membership and leadership were limited to the small group of industrialized nations (including the United States, which eventually joined). This changed in the 1990s as an effort was made to reflect the rise of a number of Asian economies as well as to take into consideration the importance of several sizable developing countries (such as Brazil, China, and India). Consequently, in 1996 and 1997 nine central banks from Asia, Latin America, the Middle East, and Europe were admitted, reducing the earlier heavy concentration of BIS shareholding central banks in the OECD countries. As of March 31, 1998, forty-five central banks had rights of representation and voting at general meetings of the BIS, including institutions from Brazil, China, India, Korea, Russia, Saudi Arabia, Singapore, and South Africa.

The Basel Committee and Capital Adequacy

Efforts have been made on the part of national governments to cooperate, share information, and provide prudent international banking guidelines. In the last area, the Basel Committee on Banking Supervision was established by the leading OECD countries in December 1974 to improve collaboration among bank supervisors. The impetus to create such a committee came from the progressive globalization of financial markets as well as the ongoing process of financial innovation. A forerunner to the Basel Committee was the Standing Committee to the Group of Ten Central Banks, which was established in 1971 due to growing regulatory concerns related to the emergence of the eurocurrency markets. In particular, the problems related to the 1974 collapse of Bankhaus Herstatt in Germany and that of the Franklin National Bank in New York in 1971 convinced bank supervisors of the need for better coordination. Both bank failures briefly threatened the financial health of banks in other countries, raising apprehension about cross-border contagion risk. Simply stated, the problems of a bank failure in one country could rapidly become a problem for banks in other countries due to the proliferation of interbank financial transactions. Even if regulatory authorities were competent and proactive in their own jurisdictions, contagion from another country was beyond their control.

The Basel Committee is one of the most significant organizations dealing with international bank supervisory issues. Its secretariat is provided by the BIS, and each member government sends representatives. The Basel Committee's work covers three major areas:

1. It is a forum for discussion on the handling of specific supervisory problems.
2. It coordinates the sharing of supervisory responsibilities among national authorities in respect of banks' foreign establishments. The goal of this is to ensure effective supervision of banks' activities worldwide. The committee responsible for this area of work produced the Basel Concordat in 1983, which was strengthened in 1992 when members agreed on minimum standards for the supervision of international banking groups and their cross-border establishments.
3. The Basel Committee seeks to enhance standards of supervision among its members.

The third area of work for the Basel Committee covers considerable scope and is important to the health of the global financial system as it seeks to improve standards of supervision, especially vis-à-vis solvency, so as to help strengthen the safety and soundness of international banking. In 1988, this committee produced a highly

THE FAILURE OF BANKHAUS HERSTATT

The failure of Bankhaus Herstatt in 1974 sent shock waves through the international banking system, giving bank regulators in a number of countries considerable food for thought about the dangers of contagion. The significance of the affair was that the actions of one bank in one country as well as those of its regulator could have an impact well beyond national borders.

Bankhaus Herstatt was a small bank in Cologne, Germany, active in the foreign exchange market. In 1974, the bank was hit by substantial losses in the foreign exchange market, threatening its solvency. German banking authorities, upon learning the situation, acted on June 26, withdrawing the bank's license and ordering it into liquidation during the banking day, but after the close of interbank payments systems in Germany. Prior to the announcement, several of the bank's counterparties had via their branches or correspondents irrevocably paid Deutsche marks to Bankhaus Herstatt on that day through the German payments systems against anticipated receipts of U.S. dollars later the same day in New York in respect of maturing spot and forward transactions. Complicating matters, Bankhaus Herstatt's New York correspondent bank, upon the termination of the German bank's business at 10:30 A.M. in New York (3:30 P.M. in Germany), suspended outgoing U.S. dollar payments from Bankhaus Herstatt's account. This action left Bankhaus Herstatt's counterparty banks exposed for the full value of Deutsche mark deliveries made. Additionally, banks that had entered into forward trades with the German bank not yet due for settlement lost money in replacing the contracts in the market. Still other banks had deposits with Bankhaus Herstatt that were imperiled by the bank's collapse.

Although the damage threatened by the failure of Bankhaus Herstatt was contained and contagion was averted, the affair clarified the danger of cross-border contagion risk and helped influence thinking in official policy circles about the need to improve international supervisory relations.

important agreement to develop a common framework for capital measurement that would enable the capital adequacy of all banks to be judged on a roughly comparable basis and to use the framework to set minimum capital guidelines. The Basel Accord required a ratio of capital to risk assets of at least 8 percent. "Capital" was defined as paid-in capital, retained earnings, tax-loss carry-forwards, preferred stock, subordinated debts, hidden assets, and loan-loss reserves that had been set aside for future possible losses (as opposed to specific loans that had already gone bad). Risk assets meant those assets potentially in danger of complications that would create problems for repayment. The Basel Accord pertained to the banks of all member countries that had agreed to adhere to the capital adequacy ratios. It should also be stated that although all banks involved in international business were expected to adhere to the capital adequacy ratios, there were no hard and fast penalties to be exacted on the part of the BIS.

Under these capital adequacy standards, capital was divided into Tier 1 and Tier 2 capital to cover different types of exposure. (See Table 10.2 for Tier 1 and Tier 2 capital adequacy ratios for selected Asian banks at the end of 1998.) The more important of the two is Tier 1 capital, which is primary capital defined as common equity, qualifying noncumulative perpetual preferred stock, and minority interests less goodwill. Tier 2 is secondary capital defined as nonallocated loan-loss reserves, subordinated debt, and all preferred stock that does not count as Tier 1 capital. (The capital positions of selected European banks are shown in Table 10.3.)

The 1988 capital adequacy agreement required banks to hold a capital cushion equivalent to 8 percent of total assets, with half of this cushion in the form of Tier 1 capital. Assets are weighted according to risk, with 100 percent weighting for most loans but only 50 percent for residential mortgages, 20 percent for short-term interbank credits, and zero for most government credits. Internationally active banks were expected to maintain the reserves of 8 percent of total assets. If the bank fell below that level, it was supposed to be subject to unspecified penalties to be implemented by local regulatory authorities.

Although the implementation of capital adequacy standards was initially undertaken by OECD countries, its acceptance has gained ground throughout the world, especially in the 1990s. Today most countries have internationally recognized capital adequacy standards that were initially inspired by the Basel Committee. Critics, however, charge that these simplistic weightings have created distortions in international capital markets. By the end of the 1990s, there was a serious effort to reform and update the capital adequacy standards.

TABLE 10.2 Capital Adequacy Ratios for Selected Asian Banks, Year-End 1998						
	Hanvit Bank (Korea)	*Chohung Bank (Korea)*	*Philippines Saving Bank*	*Krung Thai Bank (Thailand)*	*Maybank (Malaysia)*	*Hang Seng (Hong Kong)*
Tier 1 capital ratio (%)	6.0%	0.2%	23.7%	9.0%	9.4%	17.5%
Tier 2 capital ratio (%)	6.0	0.2	0.0	0.0	1.8	NA
Total capital ratio (%)	12.0	0.4	23.7	9.0	11.2	21.3
Source: Flemings Banking Research, August 1999.						

TABLE 10.3 Capital Position for Selected European Banks, Year-End 1998

	Tier 1 Capital (US$ millions)	Total Capital (US$ millions)	Weighted Risks (US$ millions)	Tier 1 ratio (%)	Total capital ratio (%)
Abby National	$4,878	$568,402	$57,977	9.3%	10.2%
Allied Irish	2,938	352,369	39,113	7.5	11.1
Bank of Ireland	3,706	275,301	31,109	8.8	11.3
Barclays	8,112	1,025,991	109,781	7.4	10.7
BBV	6,588	605,184	73,227	9.0	12.1
BNP	8,112	1,055,587	109,781	6.4	10.4
Commerzebank	10,337	1,224,446	164,076	12.0	17.8
Credit Suisse	24,198	1,135,270	202,078	12.0	17.8
Deutsche Bank	15,944	2,025,257	232,905	6.8	11.5
Lloyds TSB	7,280	737,168	83,300	8.7	11.3
NatWest	8,048	730,303	96,400	8.3	13.2
Royal Bank of Scotland	3,240	438,304	49,090	6.6	11.2
Standard Chartered	2,668	255,890	32,498	8.2	12.7
Unicredito	9,900	1,412,088	128,500	7.2	9.1

Source: Flemings Bank Research, August 1999 p. 22.

Debating the Basel Accord

Debate about the usefulness of the Basel Accord was heightened by the 1997–98 Asian financial crisis. In response to that crisis, the Basel Committee on Banking Supervision released twenty-five core principles for effective banking supervision that cover licensing and structure, prudential regulations and requirements, methods of ongoing banking supervision, information requirements, formal power of supervisors, and cross-border banking.[9] Supervisory authorities from around the planet endorsed the core principles at the annual meetings of the IMF and the World Bank in October 1997. The principles are designed to function as a basic reference for minimum requirements for effective banking supervision and are to be applied to the supervision of banks in each nation's jurisdiction.

While there was widespread agreement on the twenty-five core principles for effective banking supervision, there was less consensus about the role of the capital adequacy guidelines in creating the 1997–98 crisis. Those favoring the Basel Accord and the capital adequacy guidelines argue that they have strengthened the environment in which international banking is conducted. This is because the amount of capital maintained in banking systems has risen, pricing discipline has improved, and systemic risk has declined. (See Table 10.4.) Although the last point appears odd in light of the problems that occurred in Asia and Russia, banking systems in the developed world were able to weather the crisis partly due to their larger capital bases.

Critics of the Basel Accord argue that the capital adequacy rations have been widely used by the equity and credit markets to measure the riskiness of banks—that is, the lower a bank's capital adequacy ratios, the greater the risk for problems. Consequently, just meeting the regulatory minimums was often no longer suffi-

---

TABLE 10.4 Incentives for Adequate Risk Assessment in Banking Systems

Country	Capital Adequacy Ratio (Basel definition) Minimum Actual Ratio, 1995	Ratio, 1996	Maximum Lending to a Single Borrower (% of capital)	Sub-standard Loans (1996) Months of Arrears	Provision-ing %	Non-perform-ing Loans, as % Age of All Loans (1996)
Korea	8	9.1	15%	6+	20–75%[1]	0.8
Mexico	8	13.1	10–30	3+	Variable	12.2
Hong Kong	8	17.5	25	None	None	2.7
Indonesia	8	11.9	10–20	3–6	10	8.8
Malaysia	8	11.3	30	6–12	Variable	3.9
Thailand	8	9.3	25	6+	7 1/2–15[1]	7.7
Taiwan	8	12.2	3–5	6+	Variable	3.8
Argentina	12	18.5	15	3–6	1–25[1]	9.4
Brazil	8	12.9	30	3–6	20–100[1]	5.8
Chile	8	10.7	5	1–2	20[1]	1.0
Russia	8	13.5	50–100	N/A	Variable	15.1
United States	8	12.8	15	3+	Variable[2]	1.1
Japan	8	9.1	20	6+	None	3.4
Germany	8	10.2	25	None	None	N/A

Source: Organisation for Economic Cooperation and Development, June 1999 p. 180.

[1]Conditions depend on types of collateral and guarantees.

[2]An allowance for impaired loans should be based on the present value of the expected future cash flows of the loan, or at the loan's observable market price or at the fair value of the collateral if the loan is collateral dependent.

cient, as markets exacted a higher standard, reflected in the valuation of equity shares or bonds. Furthermore, a number of banks conscious of the capital adequacy issue vis-à-vis assuming greater risks made a decision to shy away from credit risk—for which they are required to set aside capital—to interest-free risk, which requires little or no capital. One other factor is that a number of banks, mostly in the United States, adopted risk-shifting techniques, such as securitization and credit derivatives (financial instruments created to hedge credit risk; see Chapter 5 for a fuller explanation), to avoid having to set aside capital for some of the loans they originated or to deliver the high capital ratio that markets demanded. One last argument was noted by Flemings Research:

> *Despite the creation of a common framework, many [bankers] claimed "regulatory arbitrage" allowed banks from weakly regulated countries to unfairly leverage their narrow capital bases. That is to say, these banks would set up foreign subsidiaries or branches in developed countries that were, in and of themselves, adequately capitalised. However, their parent organisation was, due to gaps in regulation in their home country, inadequately capitalised. Therefore, adequate capitalisation was an illusion but one that developed country regulators—limited to their home markets— were unable to address.[10]*

Proposals have been made to reform the Basel Accord. In 1999, the BIS suggested a "three pillars" approach, which centered on quantitative capital requirements; supervisory review; and market discipline through enhanced transparency. It was envisioned that the new accord would be based on an internal ratings-based approach to credit risk. This internal ratings method would be applicable to those institutions that have in place strong internal ratings systems accompanied by robust internal controls. Along these lines, it was suggested that greater emphasis should be placed on credit ratings and mathematical risk models, such as Value-at-Risk (VAR) models, which would include pricing. The latter would indicate a shift to a more market-based model for the Basel Accord, which many banks obviously favor. They argue that a market-based system would be more in tune with the reality that bankers face in their day-to-day operations. As Flemings Bank Research commented: "Bank managers would like to be able to allocate capital on the basis of these models partly to prevent distortions, but also to simplify their own lives by allowing themselves to use one model for the regulatory and internal purposes." The entire discussion revolves around two questions: how to make different banks' internal ratings comparable, and how to link them to capital. Added to this, of course, is a third question—how much capital should be set aside? Should the minimum 8 percent ratio be scrapped?

There are no simple answers to the questions thrown up by the new debate concerning the Basel Accord and capital adequacy ratios. Indeed, the devil is in the details, with substantial challenges remaining in the harmonization of definitions, interpretations, and policies. Whatever the outcome, the banks in the OECD countries are in a relatively strong position to handle most prudential set-asides. Banks in a number of emerging market countries are in a less-desirable situation and will be forced to scramble if the new guidelines are more stringent.

Other Supervisory Efforts

The continuing challenges posed by the globalization of banking and related financial services as well as ongoing financial innovation have forced governments to establish regional supervisory groups. Most of these organizations work with the BIS, the IMF, and the World Bank. The following are some of the major regional groups:

- Latin America: CEMLA (Centro de Estudios Monetarios Latinamericanos)
- Asia-Pacific: EMEAP (Executive Meeting of East Asian and Pacific Central Banks), SEANZA (Central Banks of Southeast Asian, New Zealand, and Australia), and SAARC (South Asian Association for Regional Cooperation)
- Middle East: GCC (Gulf Cooperation Council)
- Africa: SADC (South African Development Community)

In addition to these bodies, other organizations involved in supporting more prudent banking are the OECD, the World Bank, the IMF, and the regional development banks—the European Bank for Reconstruction and Development, the Inter-American Development Bank, the Caribbean Development Bank, the Asian Development Bank, and the African Development bank.

The IMF

One of the most important institutions providing support for international cooperation in better banking is the IMF. The IMF maintains various training programs, sends teams of experts to help governments formulate and implement improved regulatory and supervisory systems, and provides support for multilateral and bilateral supervision. IMF technical assistance seeks to strengthen the financial infrastructure of member countries through advice on upgrading their monetary and fiscal management, foreign exchange and capital market development, the design of payment systems and deposit insurance arrangements, and the development of the legal framework for banking. In addition, the IMF works with member countries to establish prudential regulations and supervisory capabilities, especially in the area of entry and exit of banks and strategies for bank systemic restructuring (in those cases where there has been a collapse of the banking system).

In the aftermath of the Asian financial crisis of 1997–98, in which unsound banking practices played a significant part in the economic collapse, the IMF compiled a list of sources of banking system problems. These are as follows:

- Weak internal governance of banks leaves the system vulnerable to macroeconomic shocks.
- Financial deregulation, competition, and innovation outstrip the capacity of banks to manage risks prudently.
- Financial deregulation takes place before adequate prudential regulation and supervision are in place.

- Weak and insolvent financial institutions are allowed to continue operations, thus weakening the entire system.

- Capital account liberalization occurs before the soundness of the domestic financial system and macroeconomic policy is assured.

- Declining business profits, together with excessive corporate indebtedness, lead to a deterioration in asset quality.

- Overexpansionary monetary and fiscal policies spur lending booms, excessive debt accumulation, and overinvestment in real assets, which drive up equity and real estate prices to unsustainable levels.

To counter this roster of banking system problems, the IMF also compiled a list of best practices. It supported the development by the Basel Committee of its Core Principles for Effective Banking Supervision, a set of twenty-five principles flexible enough to be applied to banking systems in developing economies. In early 1999, the IMF Executive Board presented its Framework for Sound Banking, which entails the following:

- Strengthening internal governance by bank owners, boards of directors, and managers

- Increasing transparency and the role of market forces

- Limiting distortions imposed by public sector policies

- Controlling risk through regulatory and supervisory oversight

- Strengthening the broader structural framework

- Fostering national and international supervisory coordination

The Asian economic crisis of 1997–98 provoked considerable debate about the need to create a new international architecture, which obviously raises tough questions about the condition of global banking and securities supervision. The IMF, the leadership of the G–7 countries, central bankers, and academics are all pondering the question of how to limit the damage of sharp and unexpected market reversals. Possible measures may include getting the private sector to take more of the strain of financial crises, tougher supervision of banking systems in developing nations, and greater transparency nationally and internationally with regard to financial data. One response to this was by the UK's last governor to Hong Kong, Christopher Patten: "None of this should do any harm, and some of it may even do a bit of good. But it is not going to prevent further financial breakdowns. Technology has added immeasurably to the speed and scale with which disaster can strike, and the foolishness that has characterized every business crash since the tulip mania of the seventeenth century cannot be legislated out of existence by well-intentioned global concordats."[11]

One other offshoot of the debate arising from the Asian financial crisis is the debate about the IMF's role as a lender of last resort. Although the IMF has not been officially proclaimed as the international lender of last resort, it continues to be the only institution capable of fulfilling that role. During the Asian financial crisis the IMF made loans to Korea, Russia, and Brazil, subject to policy conditionality. In

2000, when Argentina was hard hit by a lack of confidence, the IMF was again active in holding support. It did the same for Turkey in late 2000, when a banking crisis resulted in a major investor stampede from the country, reducing its foreign exchange reserves.

The idea of the IMF riding to the rescue of every crisis that hits developing economies has also struck resistance from those worried about moral hazard. It is reasoned that if the IMF is there to bail out every government that makes a mistake, investors will be more at ease in buying such securities as sovereign bonds or making loans. Indeed, investors will come to expect an IMF rescue and take little care to accurately measure risk. Consequently, steps have been made to reduce the moral hazard problem by "bailing in" investors as in the case of Ecuador with its partial default on Brady bonds in 1999. In addition, member countries are expected to support the IMF's role as a lender of last resort through improvement of standards for corporate governance, transparency, and the provision of relevant information. As the IMF's chief economist Stanley Fisher commented: "I will argue that the International Monetary Fund, although it is not an international central bank, has undertaken certain important lender of last resort functions in the current system, generally acting in concert with other official agencies—and that role can be made more effective in a reformed international financial system."[12]

BancZero New Product Development

*Charles M. Williams Fellow Alberto Moel and Professor Marco Iansiti prepared this
case as the basis for class discussion rather than to illustrate either effective or
ineffective handling of an administrative situation.*

> "Porqué no podemos compjretar la transaccion del
> swap? Ya estamos a Diciembre, y empezamos a
> trabajar en esto en Junio. Que está pasando?"[1]

That was the complaint made by Fernando Manzanilla, head of derivative
products sales in BancZero's Mexico City office, to Ricardo Elizondo, Technology and Operations new products manager. For more than six months, T&O
had been working on a currency swap product requested by the Developing
Markets Sales and Trading front office in Mexico City. Local clients were asking for a flexible currency hedging alternative to existing products; in response,
the front office had created a financial product that met those needs, and
aggressively marketed it. At the same time, it requested that T&O begin developing the technology and operations infrastructure to handle the offering. Yet,
with clients eager to close the transaction, T&O was still not yet ready.

Manzanilla and Elizondo were arguing about the status of the project as
they prepared for a project review meeting with Susan MacLaughlin, worldwide head of Risk Management, and a member of the board of directors.
Manzanilla had been pressuring Elizondo to finish the project, but Elizondo
remained concerned about a number of unresolved operational issues.

The Financial Services Industry

Financial intermediation was as old as money itself—Sumerian documents dat-
ing from around 3000 BC showed the granting of loans for agriculture, for example, while Hammurabi's code, written around 1800 BC, contained sections on
the regulation and granting of credit.[2] Beginning in the 12th century AD in the
Italian city-states of Genoa, Florence, and Venice the first formal banking institutions appeared, taking deposits and making loans to merchants, governments,
and royalty. Even derivatives were not new; organized exchanges for trading
financial futures and other early derivative instruments were set up in Amsterdam as early as the 17th century. How the activities of borrowing, lending, and
investing were carried out, however, altered dramatically, so that by the late 20th
century the following broad institutional forms could be distinguished:

> *Commercial Banks* granted credit to individuals and companies, and
> took demand and interest bearing deposits.

(continued)

Investment Banks made loans and granted credit to large corporations, institutions, and governments; loans were funded by issuing liabilities, which were bought by other large institutions. Investment banks also underwrote new securities on behalf of corporations and governments, structured transactions such as mergers and acquisitions, and gave financial advice.

Traders and Market Makers engaged in the buying and selling of securities, both in organized exchanges and markets, such as the New York Stock Exchange (NYSE), and in over-the-counter (OTC) transactions. These institutions bought and sold for their own account and for their clients.

Investment Management firms collected funds from individuals and institutions, pooled the funds, and invested them in other securities in search of a financial return.

A single bank or financial services company might have units dedicated to different functions. For example, most large banks had investment banking, trading, and investment management divisions, thereby offering a broad range of financial services.

Innovation in Financial Services[3]

Always a hallmark of the financial services industry, innovation accelerated swiftly with the advent of electronic computing in the late 1940s and early 1950s, which led to increasingly lower transactions costs. By the mid 1990s, the decision to implement a financial innovation was generally based on a simple cost-benefit tradeoff. When transactions costs were reduced, the incentive to introduce an innovation previously considered unprofitable was greater. As the costs to change were reduced, it became profitable not only to introduce new products and services and develop new markets, but to modify existing institutional arrangements (including geographical presence) more elastically. Much smaller shifts in customer preferences or smaller reductions in operating costs were sufficient to trigger changes previously deemed not cost-effective.[4]

Merton[5] postulated that the financial system's evolution could be viewed as an innovation spiral, in which organized markets and intermediaries competed with each other statically and complemented each other dynamically. Indeed, the history of innovative financial products suggested a pattern whereby products first offered by intermediaries would ultimately migrate to markets. For example:

Junk bonds. Junk bonds arose from the untapped borrowing needs of small companies, and from the realization that these firms' default risks did not justify the high interest rates charged. Junk bonds linked investors in search of higher yields with borrowers willing to pay them. With the establishment of junk bond markets, mutual funds, pension funds, and individual investors were able to purchase these bonds directly, allowing this new class of investors to fund corporate issuers that had previously depended on banks as their source of financing.

(continued)

Mortgage bonds. Similarly, the rise of national mortgage markets allowed mutual funds and pension funds to purchase mortgages from thrift institutions, and to compete with these same institutions as funding sources for residential mortgages.

Interest rate and currency swaps. The exchange of fixed income assets and liabilities across asset and liability classes and currencies lowered companies' borrowing costs. For example, company A, able to borrow favorably in yen at floating rates, might want fixed rate dollar financing, while company B could borrow at low fixed dollar rates, but wanted floating rate yen liabilities. A swap, arranged through a financial intermediary, lowered the borrowing costs of both companies. Swaps began in 1982 as specialized over-the-counter transactions but quickly became commoditized and widely traded.

When products had standardized terms and were widely available, and when enough information about them existed to determine a fair price, financial markets tended to be more efficient than intermediaries, which were better suited for low-volume custom products. As new products, such as options and swaps, entered the market, their terms became standardized, and their transaction volume increased; they therefore moved from intermediaries to markets. The proliferation of new trading markets in these products, moreover, made the creation of new custom-designed financial products more feasible. The new market boundaries could extend geographically (e.g., derivatives in Mexico) or along new segments of existing markets (e.g., swaps of different terms). The increase in transaction volume in these new markets reduced transactions costs. This led intermediaries to develop more new products and trading strategies, which in turn led to still more volume, repeating the cycle.

Growth in the markets was propelled both by intermediaries, who created the new products, which formed the basis of new markets, and by increasing transaction volume in existing markets. On the other hand, intermediaries used markets as the building blocks for constructing new customized products. Hence, even though markets and intermediaries competed, they also complemented each other in the innovation spiral.

The financial innovation cycle was characterized as follows:

Low capital investments. New product development did not require large capital investments, only human capital.

Low cycle times. Development of new financial products was rapid, and new products were sold to clients based on meeting customer needs at lower costs. Sometimes new products filled an otherwise latent need.

Low barriers to entry. Financial products were not patentable and could not be copyrighted, and were therefore quickly copied by competitors, reducing first-mover advantage.

Fast testing cycle. Financial products could be quickly tested in the marketplace, determining their success or failure rapidly and leading to a fast(er) innovation cycle.

(continued)

BancZero

BancZero, headquartered in New York City, was the holding company for a number of subsidiaries that provided a wide range of financial services around the world. One of the largest banks in the United States, BancZero had achieved great success in the securities business. Important to its ability to make large inroads in well-established markets and gain market share were its credit rating and large, stable capital base.

Because BancZero carried out a strict credit screening process, the amount of its bad debts was substantially smaller than that of other banks its size. Although some claimed that BancZero was too conservative and lacked creativity in its lending policies, from the bank's standpoint, most of loans it denied did not offer sufficient returns given the risks involved. Additionally, BancZero was rather cautious when increasing transactions with a particular customer. It increased the size of its exposure only if the additional risk provided a more than adequate return.

BancZero aimed to attract and retain clients with a broad range of financial service needs, for example, market-making in foreign exchange, derivatives, fund raising from various markets, advisory, and mergers and acquisitions services. Large conglomerates needed such services, and BancZero focused on increasing its transactions with these corporations rather than expanding the size of its client list.

Overseas divisions were important sources of profit. BancZero had established an unrivaled position in Europe and in parts of Latin America, far ahead of other commercial and investment banks. It had recently turned its attention to the emerging markets of Asia and Latin America. Investors from advanced countries were eager to enter emerging markets, and clients in the developing countries were beginning to need the bank's skills.

BancZero's internal organization consisted of Corporate Finance, providing comprehensive services for institutional clients; Markets, serving market clients; and Asset Management, offering investment management services to clients. The Legal, Technology and Operations (T&O), Financial, and Audit divisions supported the other three divisions, as shown in [Figure 1]. The basic rule in BancZero's structure was to create an organization that benefited clients. Its practical formulation was an established procedure by which employees of various divisions formed a "relationship team" for each client and cooperatively provided comprehensive services.

In all of its businesses, BancZero and its subsidiaries operated in an highly competitive environment, especially with respect to services and pricing. In the US, it faced competition from other money center bank holding companies: investment banks, many regional and foreign banks, and a wide range of non-bank financial institutions. Globally, the firm faced competition from investment banks, commercial banks, and universal banks in the money centers of Europe, Asia, and Latin America.

(continued)

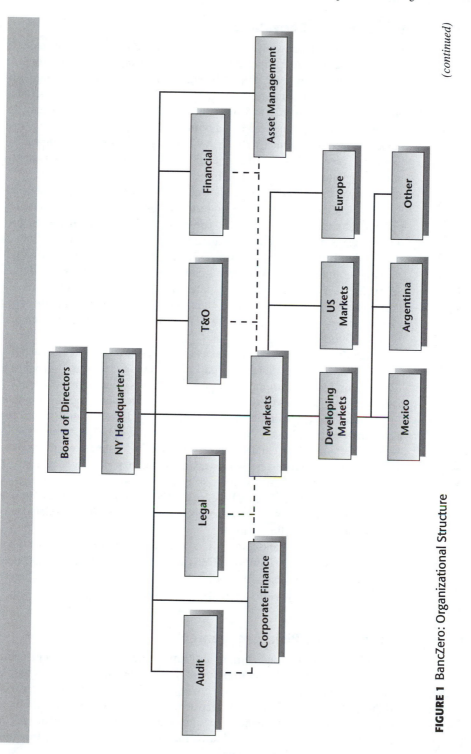

(continued)

FIGURE 1 BancZero: Organizational Structure

BancZero and Derivatives

A financial instrument whose value was *derived* from an underlying asset or index, derivatives were structured as contracts or agreements wherein the underlying asset was interest rates, foreign currencies, securities, commodities, or financial or commodity indices. Examples of derivatives included options, futures, forwards, and swap contracts. With a strong presence in the derivatives market, BancZero had a number of competitive advantages that made it a desirable counterparty for a wide range of clients: a strong capital base, high credit rating, expertise developed over many years, global distribution capabilities, and long-standing client relationships.

Derivative contracts were either negotiated with specific counterparties (over-the-counter) or were standardized contracts executed and traded on an exchange. Negotiated over-the-counter derivatives included forwards, swaps, and specialized options contracts. Standardized exchange-traded derivatives included futures and options contracts. Although over-the-counter derivatives were generally not traded like securities in an exchange, they might be terminated or assigned to another counterparty. The terms of the agreement, the timing of cash flows, and other special considerations were generally determined by a contract written and signed by both parties.

BancZero utilized derivatives extensively in its trading and asset and liability management operations. As part of its trading activities, it acted as a dealer in derivative instruments to meet clients' risk management needs by structuring transactions that allowed clients to hedge their exposure to prices of securities and commodities, financial indices, and interest rates. BancZero also took positions based on its assessment of market expectations and to benefit from price differentials between different instruments and across markets. And it used derivatives extensively as hedges to transactions carried out with clients as part of the client's risk management activities. Members of the local sales organization and the local office senior management, unlike most other bank employees, were compensated in part with a negotiated percentage of the transaction amount.

As an end user, BancZero utilized derivative instruments in the management of its asset and liabilities. Derivatives were used to hedge exposures to interest rate or currency fluctuations, and to modify interest rate characteristics of balance sheet instruments, such as loans, short-term borrowings, or long-term debt.

BancZero and Risk Management

With the increasing flow of trade and capital, derivatives proved efficient tools for managing risk and implementing basic business strategies across national borders; they essentially were innovations responding to new needs in the global marketplace. As a derivatives dealer, BancZero was oriented towards helping clients manage risk, not trading for its own account. The average credit quality of its derivatives exposure was well above the high quality of its traditional loan portfolio.

(continued)

BancZero was extremely careful in minimizing the risks inherent in its derivative operations. These included market, liquidity, credit, legal, and operational risks (described below). Comprehensive risk management processes had been developed to facilitate, control, and monitor risk-taking, and control mechanisms were in place at different organizational levels. Especially important was the Risk Management group, in New York, headed by Susan MacLaughlin, a member of BancZero's board. MacLaughlin had a bachelor's degree in mathematics and a Harvard MBA. Her 20-year career at BancZero had spanned a variety of functional assignments, including credit analysis, capital budgeting, and large loan approvals. Previous to her current assignment, MacLaughlin had been the world wide head of Technology and Operations and was instrumental in spearheading BancZero's push into emerging markets. She was known both for her sense of humor and uncanny ability to mediate between the salespeople and the operations staff.

Risk Management included an independent group that oversaw the overall risk profile at BancZero, as well as specialized units within Audit, Legal, Financial, and Technology and Operations. All these groups were involved in monitoring risks from a variety of perspectives and ensuring that businesses were operating within established corporate policies and limits. New businesses and changes to existing ones were subjected to new product reviews to convince this group that all significant risks were identified and adequate control procedures in place.

Market Risk

Market risk represented the uncertainty that future cash flows were exposed to due to changes in the value of portfolios of derivative instruments. This risk was a consequence of BancZero's derivative exposures in the market-making, position-taking, and asset and liability management activities in the interest rate, foreign exchange, equity, and commodity markets.

Estimating potential losses arising from changes in market conditions was a fundamental element of managing market risk. BancZero employed a value-at-risk methodology to estimate such potential losses, whose main measure was "Value at Risk" (VaR). This measure took into account numerous variables that could cause a change in the value of the portfolio of derivative contracts, including interest rates, foreign exchange rates, securities and commodities prices, and their volatilities, as well as correlations between these variables.

With VaR, BancZero estimated potential market risk related to using derivatives in trading, position-taking, and asset and liability management activities. Management set global daily VaR limits for each of these business activities. The level of risk a business should assume was based on overall objectives, the business manager's experience, client requirements, market liquidity, and volatility. Within these global limits, business managers set regional, local, product, and trader limits as appropriate.

On a daily basis, BancZero estimated VaR for each derivative instrument and for all derivative instruments combined. Similar daily estimates were made for asset and liability management activities. Risk Management

(continued)

reviewed a daily report of profit and loss, total positions, and BancZero's global market risk profiles.

Credit Risk

Credit risk arose from the possibility that counterparties might default on their obligations to BancZero. When a derivatives counterparty had an outstanding obligation to the bank, this represented an implicit asset to the firm whose probability of payment was linked to the counterparty's credit quality. BancZero was also exposed to credit risk in the payment and securities settlement transactions for its own account as well as for clients.

Managing credit risk had both qualitative and quantitative aspects. The qualitative aspect involved determining the creditworthiness of the counterparties. Credit officers evaluated the credit quality of the firm's liabilities and counterparties and assigned internal credit ratings based upon this evaluation. These officers, along with the business managers, were responsible for credit screening and monitoring. Credit officers with direct knowledge of the client's creditworthiness set credit limits for individual clients and counterparties. Risk Management regularly reviewed established limits and actual levels of exposures.

The quantitative aspect of credit risk consisted of measuring credit exposure to the counterparties. BancZero's senior management, located predominantly in New York, was responsible for establishing the framework of policies and practices required to measure such risk. BancZero measured credit exposure in terms of both current and potential credit exposure given the counterparty's current and expected credit quality.

Liquidity Risk

Liquidity risk arose in the general operation of BancZero's derivative transaction activities and in the management of derivatives positions. The major liquidity risk in derivative transactions was that of being unable to liquidate a position in a timely manner at a reasonable price.

Legal Risk

Legal risk came about from the uncertainty of the enforceability, through legal or judicial processes, of the obligations of BancZero's derivative counterparties. BancZero tried to remove or minimize such uncertainty through constant consultation with internal and external legal counsel in all countries where it had offices or clients. It took extreme care in drafting contracts that were enforceable and valid in all countries where the firm conducted business.

Operational Risk

Operational risk represented the potential for loss caused by a breakdown in information, communication, transaction processing, or settlement systems. BancZero attempted to eliminate or reduce operational risk by maintaining a thorough system of internal controls, which included maintaining key backup facilities and undertaking regular error-recovery planning. Internal

(continued)

controls also involved the establishment of systems and procedures to monitor transactions and positions, and extensive documentation of all derivatives transactions.

BancZero and New Product Development

At BancZero, new product ideas could originate from the client, who suggested the new product to the bank, from traders and salespeople, who saw a market need, or from business managers, who realized that the bank had to offer a given product as part of its business strategy. The process was driven by a search for new forms of revenue. A new product assumed various forms.

- **New business.** Any new activity that exposed the firm to operational, financial, or other risks not previously encountered and which required that a new support infrastructure be introduced (e.g., establishing a securities lending desk).

- **New financial product.** Any introduction of a new service within an existing business that required a significant change in operating or support procedures (e.g., a new kind of derivative contract). As in a new business, a new product might also expose the firm to certain risks.

- **New instrument.** The trading of a new security within an existing product line. New instruments represented products that were currently traded but differed in terms of the issuer or the country of the instrument. For example, currency swaps, widely available in the US, would be a new instrument in Mexico.

- **New market.** Any business initiative that resulted in developing a new market for either an existing or new product.

- **New location.** Any new business initiative that involved either locating professional staff in a new office or required significant change in the legal or capital structure of an existing location.

In the past, whenever a new product was proposed, either through internal idea generation, or in response to competitive pressures, an *ad hoc* team would form, led by the person most interested in the product's success. The team leader would converse with different functional groups and discuss the new product's requirements. Each functional unit would then work on developing the product according to its own priorities and schedules. The process was not formalized, but there was enough implicit knowledge and experience among the people involved that it moved along reasonably well.

However, changes in the marketplace and the increased unease that the growth of derivatives was causing for market players had led to a recent change. The increasing rate of product innovation and the firm's increased emphasis on risk management were straining the informal new product development policy. The lack of accountability, unclear reporting relationships, and lack of formal authority were causing confusion among the people entrusted with developing and implementing new products, leading

(continued)

senior management to formulate a new product approval process. The motivation behind this move was to introduce a structured process by which the new product's risks and requirements would be clearly documented and dealt with.

The New Product Approval Process

The objectives of BancZero's new product approval process were to ensure that:

- The risks associated with new products were defined, analyzed, and understood, and procedures to manage then were in place prior to product launch.

- The needed support infrastructure would be put in place in a timely manner to permit smooth and well-controlled operation.

- Any conflicts or overlaps with existing businesses were identified and resolved, important inter-entity linkages were defined and control procedures in place before proceeding.

- The pace of the product's expansion was consistent with the bank's capacity to manage the risks associated with the new product.

Given the dynamic nature of financial innovation and a firm's strategy to compete in servicing the constantly changing needs of sophisticated clients, it was difficult to provide an all-purpose definition of "new product." As a result, business judgment was required to determine what constituted a new product and for which special risk management review. As a general guideline, a new product was any new or modified financial instrument, trading activity, or business venture that resulted in risks that deviated from those already taken in existing products or which entailed significant incremental risks.

The standard operating procedure at BancZero for a new product was the following (see [Figure 2]):

1. A proposal was written for the new product. Proposals for a product were usually initiated by a sales and trading or corporate finance professional. The new product proposal usually included the following:

•*Description:* Product overview, features, benefits, target market, expected volumes, revenues, risk profiles of targeted client base, transaction steps, and typical work flow.

•*Risks:* Description of types (types of market risks, types of credit risks, etc.), measurement and reporting methods, potential controls.

•*Financial information:* Projected impact, start up costs, price schedules, accounting, tax implications, funding.

•*Implementation plan:* Responsibilities of key support groups, timing and availability of personnel and systems.

(continued)

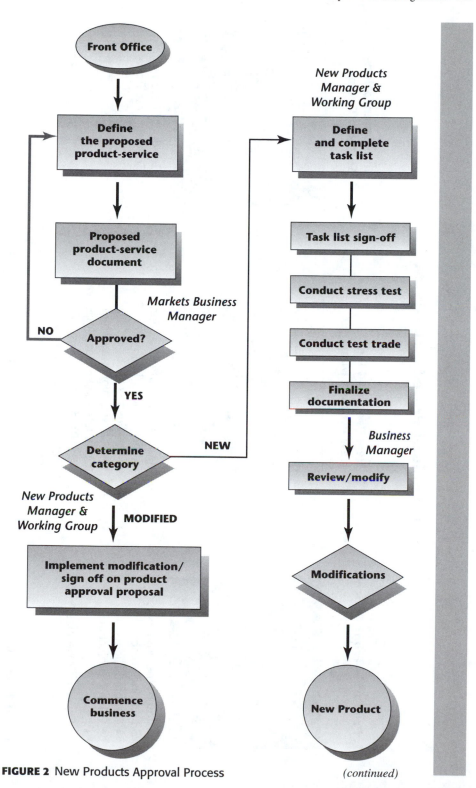

FIGURE 2 New Products Approval Process

(continued)

New Products Procedure Overview

1. Proposal—Front Office

Document the business or products including:
- Targeted clients
- Volume projections
- Risks
- Expected revenues

2. New Product Plan— New Product Manager

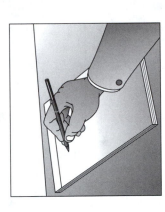

A. Agree on the categorization of the product (i.e., new or modified)
B. Identify the Working Group
C. Complete the Product Approval New Products Checklist
D. Obtain approval for New Products Implementation

3. Implementation— Support Group

A. Conduct Stress Test
B. Conduct Test Trade

(continued)

FIGURE 2 (continued)

2. Once the business manager approved the product proposal, a new products manager from the operations area became responsible for coordinating the product introduction and ensuring that deadlines were met. The new products manager's role in product introduction had several components (see [Figure 3]):

- Gain consensus on product categorization. This step was critical to the entire process because the conclusions reached would determine the degree of effort required to implement the product. The new products manager completed a product approval proposal [Figure 4] with information gathered from the product sponsor, which was then distributed to the various support disciplines. Based on their response, the new products manager could either submit the product to a detailed new product approval process, or obtain sign-off from the support groups, indicating that the new product could be handled, and then advise the front office that the new product was ready.

- Identify the working group. The new products manager had to identify a working group to sign off on the product. The working group included (but was not limited to) representation from the business group (e.g., Sales and Trading, Corporate Finance), Operations, Legal, Financial, Audit, and Risk Management. Clearly, judgment was needed to determine the applicability and relative importance of the items for each product under review, and the need to involve various functions in the review.

- Complete a "new product task list" if a full new product approval process was required. A new product task list [Table 1] ensured that key issues had been addressed prior to sign-off. Each support group completed the relevant section of the task list, which became part of the final document. Each discipline was expected to document its findings and opinions. Every new product had to be signed off by the business managers and support groups involved before it was introduced.

- Manage the implementation of all tasks required to commence business in the product. Implementation included completing all steps in the workplan described in the new product task list, and a test trade to verify and clarify procedures. Also, the new products manager generally produced interim status reports and a final post-implementation report on the product introduction, ensured that sign-offs had been obtained, and maintained documentation.

The role of the new products manager was central to the successful introduction of new products. That individual had to understand the product completely, and then assign tasks to each group to get things done; he or she had to understand the concerns of each functional group and know when to apply pressure to get things done.

The new product cycle depended strongly on the product's complexity, novelty, and urgency and could range from one-and-a half to three months. Simple products required shorter documentation cycles, a shorter new product task list, and usually went through fewer development cycle iterations.

(continued)

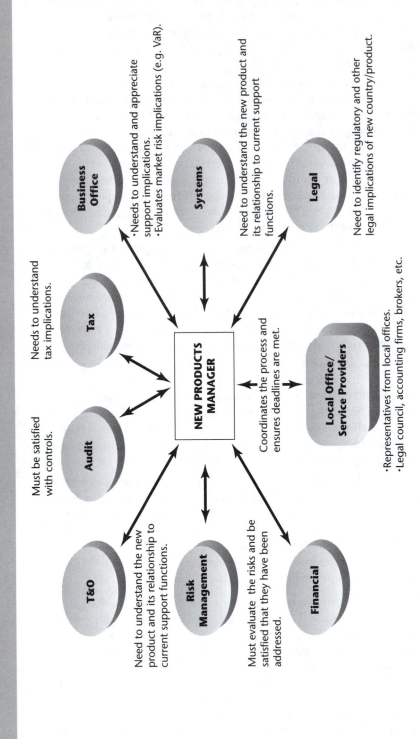

(continued)

FIGURE 3 Role of New Products Manager

This form is to be utilized by the T&O New Products Manager to efficiently determine the ability of the various groups to support the new product while submitting it to a detatiled new product approval process. This form will be used for any products which in any form deviate from something previously done, i.e., different currency, country, etc.

In the description/transaction flow section, the product specialist will include a short description of the product/transaction, with accompanying processing flows. The description will include volume projections, targeted clients, and expected revenues. The description will also illustrate the differences between this and other similar products/ transactions. The completed form will then be furnished to representatives of the groups listed below for signoff. In the event that three (3) or more groups determine that the product/ transaction represents a significant increase in risk, operational procedures, or in resources needed to adequately support this transaction, a detailed new product approval process will be initiated. Additionally, there may be instances where a single group has an issue of such magnitude that the product/transaction may be unable to be implemented (i.e., the Legal department deems the activity to be illegal). This short form process is designed to efficiently and expediently bring light to such instances, as well as hasten the introduction of products/transactions in a controlled environment.

Description of Product/Transactional Flow

Expected Profitability (include revenue and estimated costs): $
Expected Volumes (one-off or expected to be repeated—how frequently):

Area	Name	Significant Change Yes/No	Date
Financial	_____	_____	_____
Legal	_____	_____	_____
T&O	_____	_____	_____
Tax	_____	_____	_____
Other	_____	_____	_____
New Products Manager	_____		_____
Marketer/ Sponsor	_____		_____
Business Manager (last)	_____		_____

FIGURE 4 Product Approval Proposal   *(continued)*

TABLE 1 Detailed New Product Approval Task List

Task to Be Completed During Analysis	Primary Accountability	Other Area(s) involved
Business Strategy		
Sponsor new strategy.	Business Manager	Risk Management
Understand and document the economics of the new activity.	Business Manager	Legal + Finance
Define the capital requirements for the new product.	Business Manager	Risk Management
Regulatory and Legal Risks		
Identify applicable regulatory restrictions for product or business.	Legal	
Verify client/counter party power and authority to enter into activity under its local laws and regulations.	Legal	
Determine if the applicable entity is legally authorized to do the business.	Legal	
Determine what legal documentation is required.	Legal	Business Manager
Develop and implement monitoring and review procedures to ensure compliance.	Business Manager	Legal + Audit
Designate the supervisor responsible to ensure that the product is sold only to clients/counterparties for which it is suitable.	Business Manager	Legal + Audit
Determine if sufficient resources are available to support regulatory and legal requirements.	Business Manager	Legal
For Securities Activity Only		
Check if there are any insider trading concerns.	Legal	Audit
Ensure the traders are properly registered and/or all salespeople qualify for regulatory purposes.	Legal	Trading/Sales Mgrs. + Audit

(continued)

TABLE 1 Detailed New Product Approval Task List *(continued)*

Task to Be Completed During Analysis	Primary Accountability	Other Area(s) involved
Credit Risks		
Identify and analyze the risks of product.	Business Manager	Audit
Define procedure for monitoring exposures.	Business Manager	Audit
Market Risks		
Identify and analyze market risk.	Business Manager	Risk Management
Specify management's intention. (Hold positions, actively trade, or both?)	Business Manager	Risk Management
Approve pricing methodology.	Business Manager	Risk Management
Define procedures to independently test traders' valuation.	Business Manager	Financial + Audit
Determine hedging approach.	Business Manager	Financial
Establish separate VaR or other trading limits.	Business Manager	Risk Management
Define how to independently monitor those limits.	Business Manager	Risk Management
Establish and monitor special interim limits to control the new product expansion in a measured gradual manner.	Business Manager	Risk Management
Operational and Control Risks		
Verify if all departments involved in trading/processing this new product are able to handle the expected volumes.	Business Manager	T&O + Audit
Determine if the staff's and management's level of expertise is adequate.	Business Manager	T&O + Audit
Develop and document control procedures to enable contingency processing.	Business Manager	T&O + Audit

(continued)

TABLE 1 Detailed New Product Approval Task List *(continued)*

Task to Be Completed During Analysis	Primary Accountability	Other Area(s) involved
Operational and Control Risks (continued)		
Define and, if necessary, develop credit and market risk monitoring systems.	Business Manager	T&O + Audit + Legal
Specify adequate controls for physical settlements and fails.	T&O Manager	Financial + Audit
Develop capability to report daily credit usage.	Business Manager	T&O + Financial
Define management reporting requirements in conjunction with front office.	Business Manager	T&O + Audit
Provide accurate position data to front office on timely basis.	T&O	Business Manager + Audit
Ensure that P&L is compared and positions are reconciled on a daily basis to the back office.	Business Manager	T&O + Audit + Financial
Ensure that the transaction will be recorded daily on the general ledger.	Business Manager	T&O + Financial + Audit
Ensure that the new activity is being coordinated with other relevant offices.	Business Manager	T&O + Financial + Audit
Verify that the necessary new accounts/securities/books are being/have been opened.	Business Manager	T&O + Financial + Audit
Ensure that all deal/transaction documentation is maintained in a secure location, and is in compliance with all regulatory requirements.	Business Manager	T&O + Audit + Legal
Document and provide systems requirements to Systems Support.	Operations Manager	Audit

(continued)

Complex products could involve many more people's effort and attention. Also, an urgent need for the new product could sometimes cause the product description document and other documentation to be written at the end of the product development cycle, instead of at the beginning.

The most important new product development phases were the stress test and the test trade. The stress test calculated the product's impact on the bank's balance sheet and income statement to extreme changes in market variables. Extreme currency and interest rate volatility was simulated, and the value of the profit and loss position calculated for a large range of extreme values. The test's purpose was to predict, with as much certainty as possible, the effect of a new product on the bank's bottom line. A potentially highly profitable product might not be allowed to proceed to the test trade stage if the risks involved in transacting the product were too high.

The stress test was usually designed and executed by a quantitative support person in the front office. It involved developing extensive software, typically a couple of weeks' worth of intense programming. The work would be based on existing software models developed by the New York office. Although the stress test was run in a standalone system, not linked to any real market transactions, real market data was used to analyze the potential market risks associated with the new product. Running a full stress test, therefore, required market information and a clear description of the product's functionality.

In a test trade, a simulated transaction involving the new product was performed using actual systems and procedures. The objective was to validate the product's operational side. The test trade was used to reconcile all remaining technical and operations loose ends in the product development cycle, and to prepare the system for an actual client transaction. The number and extent of unresolved issues at the time of the test trade varied with the product, with more complex and novel products requiring more cleanup work after the test trade.

Running a test trade typically meant simultaneously coordinating the activities of several dozen people scattered in New York, London, and other offices, since the bulk of the systems development group was in New York, yet bookkeeping operations (i.e., the tracking of the transaction through its life) were in London given its convenient time zone. A successful test trade might take two to three hours, with the group in constant contact to verify that the software executing the transaction was actually working as specified in all locations. During this time, considerable effort was usually spent debugging software and information flow problems. A test trade might be repeated a few times over the course of a few days until the system worked as required.

BancZero's Mexico City Office

The Mexico City office had been opened to take advantage of new business opportunities in emerging Mexican markets. The office's management [see Figure 5] was all transferred from other BancZero offices, mainly from Buenos Aires and New York. Fluent in Spanish and English, staff members

(continued)

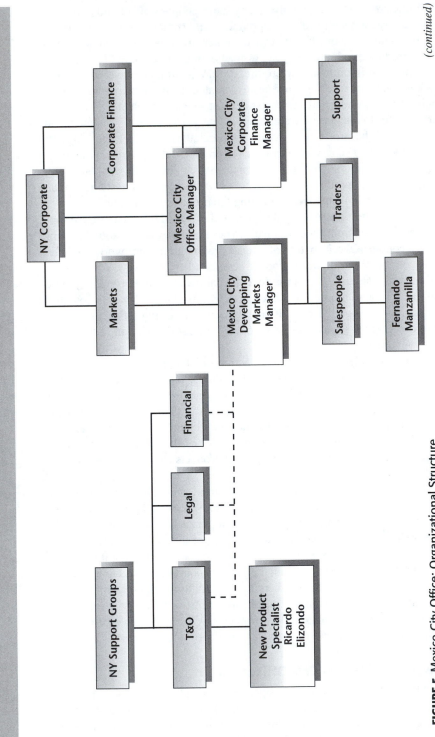

FIGURE 5 Mexico City Office: Organizational Structure

(continued)

were experienced local hires from other investment banks and brokerage houses. In addition to opening the office, hiring local staff, transferring systems and management, and establishing client relationships, the office had to cope with volatile economic conditions. The startup phase was chaotic.

The head of derivative product sales, Fernando Manzanilla, was hired from a competing investment bank, where he had been head of sales and trading—and one of the most successful salespeople in the bank's history. The T&O new products manager, Ricardo Elizondo, was hired from a large local bank, where he had been assistant comptroller. Elizondo had asked for a sales position but was told that the biggest need was in T&O management.

Elizondo's job was to make sure that a host of financial products were ready for transacting, while at the same time putting out fires in other areas where he had previous expertise. Initially, the bank offered basic financial services, such as currency exchange and government bond trading. Even these relatively simple products required a major effort, however, since legal approval and permits had to be obtained, systems purchased, and operational procedures developed, all of which occupied the time and effort of Elizondo and the office's other support groups.

The salespeople were making a strong effort to obtain new business from local companies, selling BancZero as a full-service operation willing to provide unusual financial expertise, for example in derivatives and complex financial transactions, that was unavailable elsewhere. The clients, eager to enter into such transactions, would work with the salespeople in creating transactions tailored to their needs. The salespeople, in turn, would request that the support groups develop a certain transaction capability or a new product.

Currency Swaps in Mexico

One such new product was currency swaps. A swap contract obligated two parties to exchange two defined cash flow streams at specified intervals, for a specified period of time. Suppose, for example, that Mexican Company A, a real estate concern, had borrowed abroad US$10 million for 5 years at a fixed rate of 10% a year to purchase and develop land for houses. Company A would build and sell these houses to Mexican clients, who would finance their purchase by taking a mortgage in Mexican pesos (at Mexican interest rates fixed, say, at 20% per year). Thus, Company A would have Mexican peso assets and US dollar liabilities. To service its US dollar borrowings, Company A would have to take in the Mexican peso payments from the home buyers and convert them into US dollars at prevailing spot rates in order to make the US dollar interest payments, thereby exposing Company A to foreign exchange risk. To avoid this, Company A could enter into *currency swap* with BancZero: BancZero would make Company A's US dollar interest payments and in exchange, Company A would forward the home buyers' Mexican peso payments to BancZero.

But now BancZero would be exposed to *exchange rate* risk. For example, if the currency depreciated from 7.50 pesos/dollar to 15 pesos/dollar, the incoming cash flow from the Mexican company would be the same, but

(continued)

twice as many pesos would be required to make the US dollar interest payment. The swap would also expose BancZero to *interest rate* risk. If interest rates in the US dropped from 10% to 8%, BancZero would be paying 10% to the US counterparty when the market demanded only 8%. Thus, the liability that BancZero took on by agreeing to pay the US dollar cash flow would be larger when revalued at the 8% cost of capital. This would impact BancZero's balance sheet and thus reduce its ability to make new loans. Similarly, if interest rates in Mexico increased from 20% to 30%, the asset that BancZero held from Company A would be worth less, since BancZero was receiving 20% for the loan, when the market was willing to pay 30%.

Also, by entering into the swap, BancZero became exposed to *credit risk,* both from the home buyers and from Company A. If a home buyer defaulted on the mortgage, Company A would still be obligated to pay BancZero the fixed amount. However, since Company A's cash flow was now reduced, its ability to service its debt to BancZero would be also reduced. This would imply that BancZero would want to charge Company A a higher interest rate for the loan. However, the contract specified a fixed 20% interest rate, and thus BancZero would effectively be lending money to Company A at rates below those demanded by the market.

BancZero, as a large diversified bank, however, had the ability to hedge some of these risks. It could hedge exchange rate risk by buying dollars forward to cover the US dollar interest payments, i.e., agreeing to purchase US dollars in the future at a pre-agreed price. This way, if the currency depreciated, BancZero would be insulated from currency fluctuation. But in the Company A case, BancZero would not be able to hedge all its risks, since some of the hedging instruments necessary to fully insulate BancZero from all risks with Company A either were not available in Mexico, or the fees charged by the counterparties to take on the risk were too high.

In exchange for providing the swap, therefore, BancZero would charge an intermediation fee plus a spread on the cash flows exchanged, in order to cover some of its risk exposure. The salespeople had presented this product to clients, who were more than willing to enter into transactions with BancZero under BancZero's terms.

The Swap Project

Manzanilla first proposed currency swaps to BancZero's business management group in Mexico City in May, six months after the office opened. A number of clients had requested peso/dollar currency swaps, and Manzanilla realized the new product had great potential as a revenue source. The office manager gave verbal approval to proceed with new product development, which was entrusted to Elizondo. The office manager and Elizondo agreed that the project was of sufficient size and complexity to require significant changes in operational and support procedures. Thus, the new product had to be subjected to a full new product approval process review [Table 1].

The complexity of currency swaps was far above anything the office had developed to date. The number of unanswered questions was staggering, and their resolution involved dozens of people in Mexico, New York,

(continued)

and London, where all offshore swap transactions were eventually logged. The existing software systems would require extensive modification to handle the new product. Regulatory approval had to be obtained. The product's impact on the income statement and the VaR limits for the office had to be calculated from the ground up.

As a first step, Elizondo went through the new product task list, assigning each task to the relevant group, and estimating the completion time. In late June, in a teleconference with all the support groups (shown in [Figure 3]), Elizondo outlined the tasks to be completed, the corresponding deadlines, and the estimated product introduction date. The group agreed that a late September test trade would not be unreasonable. The salespeople proceeded to talk to potential clients, indicating that actual trades with BancZero as a counterparty would be available in early October. The clients, although slightly disappointed with the time lag, agreed to wait for BancZero to prepare the systems for the trade. Meanwhile, rumor had it that the competition was working on similar products, but clients were willing to wait for BancZero on the strength of its relationships, reputation, and credit quality, and the knowledge that the bank would not introduce a new product before it was ready.

Previous time commitments on the part of Elizondo, the salespeople, and the working group made progress slow. The legal aspects of the transaction occupied the internal and external counsels' time, who had to negotiate with the regulatory authorities for permission. Software development had to be transferred to New York, since Mexico City had neither the resources nor the time to modify the systems to handle the new transaction. The financial group had difficulty determining credit lines and credit standards for the proposed counterparties, since no precedent existed for the transaction.

General product meetings were held every two weeks. The status of the currency swap project and of other projects was discussed, and revised schedules proposed. The product design was modified several times in response to regulatory constraints on the kinds of booking allowed by the Mexican regulatory authorities. Each modification involved small changes in the task list, sometimes resulting in backtracking and repeating work previously completed.

By mid-September, it was clear that the late September test trade would be delayed. Particularly troublesome was the pricing and valuation model. An existing US–G7 pricing model, used to price currency swaps between the US dollar and European currencies and the Japanese yen, was modified to support the Mexican peso. However, the peso was a particularly volatile and unstable currency, and the model's assumptions regarding currency stability had to be reexamined. Meanwhile, the authorities had not responded to the request for executing currency swaps, so it was agreed to proceed with the test trade without the regulatory approval once all the systems worked. The assumption was that if the systems worked, regulatory approval would be a formality. Based on a late September review of the progress to date, the group agreed to a late October test trade, with actual client trades as soon as regulatory approval was obtained.

Work proceeded in ironing out the issues with the pricing and valuation model, and with the booking system. E-mail and phone communications

(continued)

between New York, London, and Mexico City were constant. Since the swaps' booking system was in London, the time difference made communicating with the systems staff difficult; people had to be tracked down for multiple conference calls, where progress was discussed and new deadlines set. The salespeople scoped out the marketplace for potential competitive pressures. It was not clear whether competing products were ready, or competitors were just "fishing" for business.

In mid-October, it was clear there were too many systems issues to be completed for the test trade to run at the end of the month. Against salespeople's objections, the test trade was again delayed, until the end of November, to give the support group time to wrap up loose ends. Fortunately, regulatory approval was obtained in late October, making system completion the priority. The Mexico City office manager put on pressure for the work to be finished, giving the currency swap product the highest priority in the office.

However, in late November, just before the test trade, the product failed the stress test, which was carried out by members of Manzanilla's staff in Mexico City. The preset VaR limits were easily broken under the extreme volatility of exchange rates and interest rates. The office manager ordered an analysis of Mexican interest rates and currency volatility to determine the historical probability of such volatility. A similar study for the G7 currencies had indicated that such a stress test failure would be extremely unlikely. However, the Mexican markets were unstable enough that the likelihood of a large loss was much higher.

The test indicated that the probability of a slight loss was less than 5% (a "slight" loss could amount to as much as 2% of the principal of the transaction—principals were typically tens of millions of dollars). The probability of a large loss (more than 10% of principal) was as high as 1%. On the other hand, testing estimated that the expected return for BancZero was above 10% of principal.[6]

A group of senior risk managers from New York flew to Mexico City to determine the level of risk that the bank would be willing to bear in order to roll out the product. Raising the VaR limits or reducing the dollar amount of the swaps was discussed. Manzanilla compiled a future forecast of interest rate volatility which showed that extreme future swings were unlikely, but senior management was not convinced.

The Test Trade

By December, the situation had come to a head. The competition was rumored to be ready to roll out a similar product. The systems people were ready to carry out a test trade, regulatory approval had been obtained, and support work almost completed. But senior management in New York was wary of allowing a test trade without a satisfactory resolution of the stress test. They felt that risk exposure should be further analyzed before the product was authorized.

However, performing a significant amount of analysis and modifying the product to meet the current stress test standards could take three or four weeks,

(continued)

or longer if changes had regulatory, legal, or operational implications. Alternatively, raising the VaR limits or changing other stress test specifications was discussed, but no precedent existed for such changes. Manzanilla pushed for either approval of the product or a waiver of the checklist sign-off. He felt strongly that his clients were about to defect to competing banks for similar products.

Ultimately, the decision lay with Susan MacLaughlin, the opinionated head of the risk management group in New York.

---

[1] *"Why can't we close this swap deal? It is now December, and we started work on this back in June. What's going on?"*

[2] Homer, S. (1977), *A History of Interest Rates*, 2nd Ed., New Brunswick, NJ, Rutgers University Press.

[3] This section is based on the work of Merton and Hayes, cited below.

[4] See, for example, Hayes, S. L. III (1993), *Financial Services: Perspectives and Challenges*, S. L. Hayes III, ed., Boston: Harvard Business School Press.

[5] See for example, Merton, R. C. (1993), "Operation and Regulation in Financial Intermediation: A Functional Perspective" in *Operation and Regulation of Financial Markets*, P. Englund, ed., Stockholm: The Economic Council.

[6] For comparison, in a typical G7 trade, the probability of a slight loss was less than 1%, the probability of a large loss was less than 0.1%, but the expected returns to BancZero were on the order of 1%.

Conclusion

It is likely that there will always be international banking crises that will be followed by a clamor for better regulation. At the same time, governments are likely to continue to be reluctant to surrender this element of sovereignty over their banks. This combination leads to ongoing convergence of banking practices and better cooperation between regulatory agencies, yet leaves the door open to the occasional unexpected hiccup caused by ongoing financial innovation and globalization.

Questions

1. What is the Bank for International Settlements?
2. What is the Basel Accord? How did it evolve, and what were the forces behind it?
3. One of the key measures proposed by the Basel Accord is capital adequacy. What is capital adequacy, why is it regarded as important, and how does it relate to international banking supervision?
4. What is the significance of Bankhaus Herstatt to international banking supervision?
5. What are the three core areas of responsibility for the Basel Committee on Banking Supervision?
6. What role does the International Monetary Fund play in international banking supervision? Should the IMF's role as a lender of last resort in international crises be expanded?

Notes

1. Anjali Kumar with Terry Chuppe and Paula Perttunen, *The Regulation of Non-bank Financial Institutions: The United States, the European Union and Other Countries* (Washington, D.C.: The World Bank, 1997), p. 70.

2. Robert Bench, "The Role of Regulation and Supervision in the Global Banking System," in William H. Baughn, Thomas I. Storrs, and Charles E. Walker, editors, *The Bankers Handbook* (Homewood, Ill.: Dow Jones Irwin, 1988), p. 1187.

3. Anjali Kumar, *The Regulation of Non-bank Financial Institutions,* p. 14.

4. Eric Rosengren, "Will Greater Disclosure and Transparency Prevent the Next Banking Crisis?" paper presented at a conference jointly sponsored by the Federal Reserve Bank of Chicago and the International Monetary Fund, 1998.

5. Basel Committee on Banking Supervision, *Enhancing Bank Transparency,* September 1, 1999 (Basel, Switzerland: Basel Committee on Banking Supervision), p. 3.

6. Robert Bench, "The Role of Regulation and Supervision in the Global Banking System," p. 1190.

7. Karin Lissakers, "The Role of the International Monetary Fund," in Gerald Caprio Jr., William C. Hunter, George G. Kaufman, and Danny M. Leipziger, editors, *Preventing Bank Crises: Lessons from Recent Global Bank Failures* (Washington, D.C.: The World Bank, 1998), p. 28.

8. From the Bank for International Settlements website, at www.bis.org/about/profgh.htm, 1998.

9. The World Bank, *Global Development Finance: Analysis and Summary Tables* (Washington, D.C.: The World Bank, 1998), p. 45.

10. Flemings Research, "Global Banking, Changes in Banks' Capital Requirements," August 1999, p. 7.

11. Christopher Patten, *East and West: China, Power and the Future of Asia* (New York: Times Books, 1998), p. 114.

12. Stanley Fischer, On the Need for an International Lender of Last Resort," a paper prepared for delivery at the joint luncheon of the American Economic Association and the American Finance Association, New York, January 3, 1999, at www.imf.org/external/np/speeches/1999/010399.HTM.

CHAPTER 11

RISK MANAGEMENT

As the Chase official notes, a banker's job is to manage risk, not avoid it. After all, if bankers never took on any risk, they would never make any loans! They could spend worry-free days on the golf course and in the sun. Of course, they would never make any money either. Thus risk management is a central function of all banks, whether domestic or international. Bankers classify risk into six basic categories:

1. **Credit risk:** the risk due to default or failure by a borrower or counterparty to fulfill its contractual obligation. ABN Amro states in its annual report, "Credit risk encompasses all forms of counterparty exposure in relation to lending, trading, hedging, settlement and other financial activities."[1]

2. **Market risk:** the bank's exposure to adverse changes in the value of financial instruments caused by a change in market prices or rates, including interest rates, exchange rates, securities prices, and commodity prices.

3. **Liquidity risk:** the risk that sufficient cash flows will not be available to meet the bank's financial commitments at some point in time. The importance of liquidity transcends the individual bank, since a liquidity shortfall at a single institution can have systemwide repercussions.

4. **Interest rate risk:** the risk that earnings and returns will fluctuate in line with changes in interest rates.

5. **Operational risk:** potential losses due to a breakdown in information, communication, transaction processing, settlement systems and procedures, fraud by employees or outsiders, or unauthorized transactions by employees.

6. **Cross-border risk:** potential losses arising from the bank's operations in overseas markets. This can stem from loans outstanding or other investments made in a particular location beyond national borders. (Cross-border risks are so central to the operations of a multinational bank that we have devoted an entire chapter, Chapter 14, to this topic.)

Two other types of risks could be added for those banks heavily involved in international securities markets: **call risk** and **legislative risk.** The former is the risk that a bond might be called before maturity and an investor will be unable to reinvest his principal at a comparable rate of return. Legislative risk comes into play as most national legislative bodies (congress, parliament, etc.) have the authority to change laws affecting securities. The risk is that such a change in law might

TAKING THE DANGER OUT OF RISK
Timothy O'Brien

What's the difference between being rich and being poor? asks a joke currently making the rounds on Wall Street. Answer: About 30 seconds.

These days, huge sums of money are made and lost on Wall Street at unforgiving speeds. Lately, mostly lost. Indeed, many of the financial service industry's biggest players, battered by global economic turmoil and rapid-fire market shifts, have reported dismal earnings for 1998.

But not Chase Manhattan. Amid the wreckage of a volatile year that included the near-collapse of one of the country's most esteemed hedge funds, the ouster or replacement of several well-regarded banking executives and a broad retreat from speculative markets, Chase still raked in gobs of money....

Chase's performance is all the more remarkable for having occurred in a year that tripped up other financial Goliaths, including Citigroup, Merrill Lynch and Goldman, Sachs. It has proved to be a bank adept at corralling—at least for the time being—the bogeyman haunting all of Wall Street: risk.

"We're in the business of risk management, not risk avoidance," said Marc J. Shapiro, Chase's vice chairman for finance and risk management. "We have to take risks to make money."

But, he added, "people in this organization have been through some pretty tough times over the last 10 or 15 years, and nobody wants to go back there." ...

Source: New York Times, January 20, 1999, p. C1.

adversely affect a security. Alternatively, legal risks might arise when a counterparty lacks the legal or regulatory authority to engage in a transaction.

This chapter will focus primarily on credit and market risk, with some additional commentary on operational risk and interest rate risk issues. (International bank supervision and regulation is covered separately, in Chapter 10.) While these are not the only important risks to affect international bankers, they do take on a different and more challenging aspect in the international environment.

Credit Risk Management

Credit risk is the risk that borrowers may not be willing or able to service the loan. For example, in 1998 the Russian government decided to impose a ninety-day moratorium on its domestic debt payments, causing an estimated $6 billion in losses to banks and securities dealers. The art of estimating the future recovery rate on a loan includes a number of factors:

- The relative bargaining position of lenders and borrowers
- The underlying bankruptcy code and its enforceability
- The bank's access to collateral in the event of default
- The seniority of the loan or bond, and whether or not it is secured
- The availability of secured collateral and its value at a time of financial distress
- The role of multiple creditors[2]

A glance at these factors with the Russian case in mind is instructive. Which player is more powerful at a time of geopolitical uncertainty, bankers or the Russian government? How likely are Russian courts to enforce bankruptcy proceedings against their own government? What collateral could the bank collect? (Nuclear weapons, perhaps? Or maybe the bank could seize the Russian embassy in Washington?) With the benefit of hindsight, it becomes apparent that these credits could easily become impaired, and that the banks could have little real recourse in such an event.

Credit risk management techniques are probably among the best-developed tools in a banker's briefcase. Bankers have long experience in assessing and managing credit risk, although the development of new products, such as exotic derivatives, is placing new demands on these tools (see Chapter 13). Explaining credit risk management in *Financial Markets and Institutions,* Frederic Mishkin and Stanley Eakins point out:

> The concepts of adverse selection and moral hazard ... provide a framework for understanding the principles that financial institution managers must follow to minimize credit risk and make successful loans.
>
> Adverse selection is problematic in loan markets. This is because bad credit risks (borrowers most likely to default) are the ones who usually line up for loans—in other words, those who are most likely to produce an *adverse* outcome are the most likely to be *selected*. Borrowers with very risky investment projects in mind have much to gain if their projects are successful, and so they are the most eager to obtain loans. Clearly, however, they are the least desirable borrowers because of the greater possibility that they will be unable to pay back their loans.
>
> Moral hazard is a problem in loan markets because borrowers may have incentives to engage in activities that are undesirable from the lender's point of view. In such situations, it is more likely that the lender will be exposed to the *hazard* of default. Once borrowers have obtained a loan, they are more likely to invest in high-risk investment projects—projects that pay high returns to the borrowers if successful. The high risk, however, makes it less likely that the loan will be paid back.
>
> To be profitable, financial institutions must overcome the adverse selection and moral hazard problems that make loan defaults more likely. The attempts of financial institutions to solve these problems help explain a number of principles for managing credit risk: screening and monitoring, establishment of long-term customer relationships, loan commitments, collateral, compensating balance requirements, and credit rationing.[3]

Despite these safeguards, the system is by no means infallible. The chairman of the New York Federal Reserve Bank, William McDonough, complained in 1999:

> Let me be a bit more specific about some of the weaknesses found in credit risk management techniques. For example, some institutions routinely performed

TECHNIQUES OF CREDIT RISK MANAGEMENT

- *Screening* refers to the collection and effective review of reliable information on prospective borrowers by the financial institution. When a bank makes a personal loan to you, it asks for a great deal of personal information—salary, marital status, and so on—which it uses in evaluating your creditworthiness. The same process applies to a business loan, in which case the banker might look at data on the company's profits and losses, assets and liabilities, and prospects for future success. "The bottom line is that, be it for personal or business loans, financial institutions need to be nosy."

- *Monitoring.* To reduce the risk that borrowers will engage in risky activities after the loan is obtained (moral hazard), bankers write provisions into loan agreements that place boundaries on the borrowers' activities. For example, bankers may require that during the loan period companies maintain certain financial ratios or refrain from paying out dividends.

- *Long-term customer relationships,* another key principle of credit risk management, offer bankers a way of minimizing the costs of information collection and making it easier to screen out bad credit risks. Also, long-term relationships give the borrower a more pressing incentive to avoid risky activities that would endanger its relationship with the financial institution, thus helping bankers deal with even unanticipated moral hazard contingencies.

- *Loan commitments.* A loan commitment commits the bank, for a specified period of time, to provide the borrower with loans up to a given amount at an agreed-on interest rate. This promotes the long-term relationship with the customer, in turn facilitating the collection of information.

- *Collateral,* or property promised to the lender as compensation if the borrower defaults, reduces the banker's losses in the case of a loan default. Collateral requirements offer important protection to banks, and they are extremely popular in both personal and business loans.

- *Compensating balances* are a particular form of collateral that may be required when a bank makes commercial loans. This occurs when a bank requires the borrower to maintain a certain minimum amount of funds in a checking account at the bank. For example, a business getting a $10 million loan may be required to keep compensating balances of at least $1 million in its checking account at the bank. If the borrower defaults, this $1 million in compensating balances can be taken by the bank. Compensating balances thus serve not only as collateral, but they also decrease the likelihood of default, by helping the bank monitor the borrower and minimizing moral hazard.

(continued)

- *Credit rationing* occurs when lenders refuse to make loans, or restrict the size of the loan, even though borrowers are willing to pay the stated interest rate or even a higher one.

Adapted from Frederic S. Mishkin and Stanley G. Eakins, *Financial Markets and Institutions,* 3rd edition (Reading, Mass.: Addison Wesley Longman, 2000), pp. 620–624.

credit assessments using sparse, often unaudited financial information from valued customers, some of which had recorded substantial profits in previous years. Moreover, institutions that received intermittent financial statements and had infrequent contacts with the counterparties were left to make periodic assessments using stale information in a rapidly changing market. This insufficient information impeded the setting of prudent credit limits and terms, including collateral requirements and contract covenants.

Many risk managers also failed to account fully for the risks involved in new financial products. Non-traditional products such as equity repos and credit derivatives challenged existing credit analysis systems and methodologies. In addition, relatively few financial institutions attempted to stress test credit exposures and even fewer anticipated a market environment as adverse as what we experienced in the third quarter [of 1998].[4]

Most bankers readily acknowledge that the system is flawed. In particular, as McDonough notes, the emergence of new and exotic **derivatives** products (financial instruments whose value is derived from an underlying asset) presents new challenges to traditional credit risk management systems (see Chapter 13 for a fuller discussion of derivatives and risk management). However, it is also true that credit losses are a part of doing business for a bank; the trick is to find an acceptable level of credit losses that still permits aggressive business development efforts.[5]

Market Risk Management

By virtue of their participation in various and diverse markets around the globe, banks are constantly exposed to price fluctuations in these markets that can affect the value of their trading portfolios. This is the meaning of market risk. Bankers have developed increasingly sophisticated and quantitative methods to assess market risk, partly thanks to the proliferation of increasingly sophisticated computer capabilities. The two primary methods of modeling market risk involve an assessment of **Value at Risk (VaR),** which essentially measures market risk in everyday, normal market conditions, and **stress testing,** which looks at market risk in abnormal market conditions.

Value at Risk

VaR methodology allows banks to measure statistically probable losses that their trading portfolios could incur over a certain period of time. From a given set of

FAILURES OF RISK MANAGEMENT: BARINGS

On February 26, 1995, the Queen of Great Britain woke up to the news that Barings PLC, a venerable 233-year-old bank, had gone bankrupt. Apparently, the downfall of the bank was due to a single trader, 28-year-old Nicholas Leeson, who lost $1.3 billion from derivatives trading. This loss wiped out the firm's entire equity capital.

The loss was caused by a large exposure to the Japanese stock market, which was achieved through the futures market. Leeson, the chief trader for Barings Futures in Singapore, had been accumulating positions in stock index futures on the Nikkei 225, a portfolio of Japanese stocks. Barings's notional positions on the Singapore and Osaka exchanges added up to a staggering $7 billion. As the market fell more than 15 percent in the first two months of 1995, Barings Futures suffered huge losses. These losses were made worse by the sale of options, which implied a bet on a stable market. As losses mounted, Leeson increased the size of the position, in a stubborn belief he was right. Then, unable to make the cash payments required by the exchanges, he simply walked away on February 23. Later, he sent a fax to his superiors, offering "sincere apologies for the predicament that I have left you in."

Because Barings was viewed as a conservative bank, the bankruptcy served as a wake-up call for financial institutions all over the world. The disaster has revealed an amazing lack of controls at Barings: Leeson had control over both the trading desk and the "back office." The function of the back office is to confirm trades and check that all trading activity is within guidelines. In any serious bank, traders have a limited amount of capital they can deal with and are subject to closely supervised "position limits." To avoid conflicts of interest, the trading and back-office functions are clearly delineated. In addition, most banks have a separate risk-management unit that provides another check on traders.

Source: Philippe Jorion, *Value at Risk* (New York: McGraw Hill, 1997), pp. 29–30.

inputs (historical prices), the bank calculates the maximum loss, or VaR, that it might experience to a given level of probability. For example, using historical market data, the bank may estimate its VaR, or the most it would be expected to lose in 99 out of 100 trading periods. With tongue only partially in cheek, practitioner Barry Schachter offers three definitions of VaR:

1. A forecast of a given percentile, usually in the lower tail, of the distribution of returns on a portfolio over some period; similar in principle to an estimate of the expected return on a portfolio, which is a forecast of the 50th percentile.

2. An estimate of the level of loss on a portfolio which is expected to be equaled or exceeded with a given, small probability.

FAILURES OF RISK MANAGEMENT: DAIWA

Daiwa's case provides a striking counterpart to the Barings disaster. On September 26, 1995, the bank announced that a 44-year-old trader in New York, Toshihide Igushi, had allegedly accumulated losses estimated at $1.1 billion. The losses were of a similar magnitude as those that befell Barings, but Daiwa, the 12th-largest bank in Japan, managed to withstand the blow. The loss absorbed "only" one-seventh of the firm's capital.

Apparently, Igushi had concealed more than 30,000 trades over 11 years, starting in 1984, in U.S. Treasury bonds. As the losses grew, the bank said, the trader exceeded his position limits to make up for the losses. He eventually started selling, in the name of Daiwa, securities deposited by clients at the New York branch. The bank claims that none of these trades were reported to Daiwa and that Igushi falsified listings of securities held at the bank's custodian, Bankers Trust. Apparently, the bank failed to cross-check daily trades with monthly portfolio summaries.

As in the case of Barings, the problem arose because at some point Igushi had control of both the front and back offices. Unlike other Japanese workers who were rotated regularly, he had been hired locally. In their home market, Japanese banks rely on a group spirit that acts as an internal safety mechanism; in overseas operations, such an approach can be fatal.

Source: Philippe Jorion, *Value at Risk* (New York: McGraw-Hill, 1997), pp. 33–34.

3. A number invented by purveyors of panaceas for pecuniary peril intended to mislead senior management and regulators into false confidence that market risk is adequately understood and controlled.[6]

More precisely, VaR measures the worst possible loss that a bank could expect to suffer over a given time interval, under normal market conditions, at a given confidence level. For example, a bank might calculate that the daily VaR of its trading portfolio is $35 million at a 99 percent confidence level. In plain English, this means that there is only 1 chance in 100 that a loss greater than $35 million would occur under normal market conditions on any given day.[7] It should be clear, though, that this is not a *maximum* loss; for example, if a bank regularly measures VaR at the 99 percent confidence level, the actual losses should exceed its estimate 1 percent of the time, or 1 day out of 100.

Partly because it is easy to understand, VaR has become widely accepted and used in the past decade. Another practitioner comments that the evolution of financial risk management over the past five years "can be summarized as a quest to describe risk concisely through a single number, Value-at-Risk." He points to two events in particular that have led to widespread adoption of VaR in the financial sector. First was the BIS meeting at Basel in 1995, at which major central banks

ING GROUP: VaR

Important control instruments employed are Value-at-Risk (VaR) position estimates, stress-testing scenarios and daily profit and loss statements. VaR models are based on estimated volatilities by means of historical data. The VaR calculations are based on market movements in the previous twelve months within a 99% one-sided statistical confidence level. On this basis, an assessment is made of the potential loss that could accrue in the event of adverse market movements if the trading positions remained unchanged for a time interval of one trading day. In December 1997, ING introduced an integrated system for calculating trading risks that provides consolidated VaR on a daily basis. The system meanwhile covers 90% of all trading activities. In accordance with the Basel Capital Accord ING has raised the confidence level for its VaR calculations in 1998 from 97.5% to 99%. The following table shows the overnight VaR based on this new system at year end 1997 and 1998 on the trading positions as well as the highest, lowest and average overnight VaR for each risk category in 1998.

Source: ING Group Annual Report, 1998.

Value-at-Risk by Category (millions of guilders)

	Year-end 1997[1]	Year-end 1998	Maximum 1998	Minimum 1998	Average 1998
Foreign Exchange	11.9	4.1	24.1	2.8	11.3
Equities	26.1	14.1	42.2	12.3	28.1
Emerging Markets	17.5	28.4	41.5	18.0	28.7
Interest	12.0	31.0	49.0	5.4	24.0
Subtotal	67.5	77.6			
Diversification Effect	(22.6)	(26.9)			
Total	44.9	50.7			

Source: Annual Report 1998 of ING Group.
[1]Figures adjusted from confidence level of 97.5% to 99%.

proposed new rules amending the 1988 Basel Accord requiring financial institutions to hold certain levels of capital against their exposure to market risk. The 1995 proposal, which was adopted a year later, created an incentive for banks to develop sophisticated internal risk measurement systems to calculate VaR and thus

CITICORP: VaR

The price risk of trading activities is primarily measured using the Value-at-Risk method, which estimates, at a 99% confidence level, the potential pretax loss in market value that could occur over a one-day holding period. The Value-at-Risk method incorporates the market factors to which the market value of the trading position is exposed (interest rates, foreign exchange rates, equity and commodity prices, and their implied volatilities), the sensitivity of the position to changes in those market factors, and the volatilities and correlation of those factors. The Value-at-Risk measurement includes the foreign exchange risks that arise in traditional banking businesses as well as in explicit trading positions. The volatility and correlation assumptions used in the Value-at-Risk computations are based on historical experience. The Value-at-Risk method is not a predictor of future results or worst-case scenarios, but rather a statistical estimate of potential risk....

The following table summarizes Citigroup's Value-at-Risk in its trading portfolio as of December 31, 1998 and 1997 along with the 1998 average.

Source: Citigroup Annual Report, 1998, pp. 41–45.

Citigroup's Value-at-Risk in Its Trading Portfolio (US$ millions)						
	Citicorp			*Salomon Smith Barney*		
	12/31-1998	*1998 Average*	*12/31-1997*	*12/31-1998*	*1998 Average*	*12/31-1997[1]*
Interest Rate	$13	$16	$23	$75	$67	$57
Foreign Exchange	7	8	8	3	17	12
Equity	5	7	8	15	9	11
All Other (primarily Commodity)	1	1	—	11	11	11
Covariance Adjustment	(11)	(14)	(14)	(33)	(34)	(30)
Total	15	18	25	71	70	61

Source: Citigroup Annual Report, 1998 pp. 41-45.

[1]In 1998, Salomon Smith Barney adopted the use of a 99% confidence level rather than the previously used 95% confidence level, primarily for consistency with capital guidelines issued by the Federal Reserve Board and other U.S. banking regulators. The amounts in the table provide the restated VaR at the 99% confidence level.

J.P. MORGAN: RISKMETRICS

Safety in Numbers

Every afternoon at 4:15 (Eastern time), Dennis Weatherstone, chairman of J.P. Morgan, an American bank, is handed a sheet of paper. Written on it are estimates of how much money the bank would lose should prices in the markets in which it has open positions move by a certain amount. Condensing so-called market risk in this way is no mean achievement: the bank's 120 risk-taking units churn out 20,000 transactions a day. It is also a feat beyond all but the most sophisticated financial intermediaries. Few companies, banks or fund managers can even work out the riskiness of their positions, let alone boil down the information as J.P. Morgan can. Most would like to be able to.

Now they are being given a helping hand. On October 11th J.P. Morgan bared all. First, the bank published the methodology (dubbed Risk-Metrics) that it uses to calculate its overall market risk. It is a two-step process. The first step works out the volatility of each individual position. The more volatile a market, the more the bank stands to lose. But for a portfolio of instruments that information may well overstate its risks. To work out its overall risk, the bank also looks at the correlations between those markets: how much (or little) they move together. The smaller the correlation between the markets in which it has positions, the less risky its overall positions.

Morgan has gone further by also publishing daily the information needed to implement its methodology—namely the volatilities of, and correlations between, more than 300 different financial instruments....

Source: *The Economist,* October 15, 1994, p. 102.

avoid more regulatory requirements. Second was the decision by J.P. Morgan in 1994 to make its RiskMetrics system available free of charge over the Internet, which provided financial data and methodology to calculate a portfolio's VaR.[8]

The exact computation of VaR will depend on assumptions about:

- The distribution of price changes, normal or otherwise
- The extent to which today's change in the price of an asset may be correlated to past price changes
- The extent to which the characteristics of mean and standard deviation (volatility) are stable over time
- The relationship between two or more different price moves
- The data series to which these assumptions apply

For the most part, financial managers use historical market data on various financial assets to create their VaR model. In developing its RiskMetrics model, for example, J.P. Morgan refines the model to account for different types of market risk: trading market risk and investment portfolio market risk. Trading market risk is short-term, whereas investment portfolio managers take a much longer time horizon.

J.P. Morgan's general definition for VaR is the maximum estimated losses in the market value of a given position that may be incurred before the position is neutralized or reassessed. Thus,

$$\text{VaR}_x = V_x \times dV/dP \times \Delta P_i$$

V_x: the market value of position x

dV/dP: the sensitivity to price move per \$ market value

ΔP_i: adverse price movement over time i; for example, if the time horizon is a day, then VaR becomes daily earnings at risk:

$$\text{DEAR} = V_x \times dV/dP \times \Delta P_{\text{day}}$$

(See Figure 11.1 for an example of VaR.)

J.P. Morgan specifies the following assumptions in its measure of VaR:

- Prices of financial instruments are assumed to follow a stable random walk. Thus, price changes are normally distributed.

- Price changes are serially uncorrelated; there is no correlation between the change today and changes in the past.

- The standard deviation (volatility) of the price or rate changes is stable over time; that is, past movements may be used to characterize future movements.

- The interrelationships between two different price movements follow a joint normal distribution.

The assumptions of a normal distribution and no serial correlation are controversial, because of evidence that financial markets do not follow a random walk and the presence of autocorrelation. However, J.P. Morgan justifies the assumptions by pointing out that other distributions are unsuitable; for example, if another type of distribution was assumed, it might not be possible to measure risk in terms of standard deviation.[9]

While VaR is undoubtedly a valuable tool in risk management, it suffers from some drawbacks as well. Most of these drawbacks are related to the differences between market realities and the assumptions that are necessary to make the VaR computation possible:

- *Markets are not normal.* A central assumption of VaR calculations is that market returns are described by the statistical notion of a normal distribution, or the standard bell-shaped curve. However, in reality this assumption is often violated.

- *Portfolios are nonlinear.* Many VaR calculations assume that portfolio value moves in strict proportion to changes in market prices. However, the relationship between the value of the portfolio and the market value of the stock cannot be described by a straight line when the portfolios include derivatives, as they usually do in modern international banks.

- *Volatility is not a constant.* Unfortunately, risk managers cannot rely on historical averages of volatility to indicate future trends. Volatility is the key determinant of option values, and so the difficulty of measuring volatility is

FIGURE 11.1 J.P. Morgan: RiskMetrics

Example 1: A single position Value at Risk example

Definitions	Value at Risk = the forecasted amount that may be lost given an adverse market move = Amount of Position * Volatility of Instrument
	Volatility = % of value which may be lost with a certain probability, e.g., 95%
Position	A U.S. investor is long 140 million Deutsche marks
Market/Risk Information	DEM/USD FX Volatility: 0.932% FX Rate: 1.40 DM/USD
Value at Risk	VaR_{USD} = DEM 140 million * 0.932% / 1.40 DEM/USD = USD 932,000

Example 2: Two-position Value at Risk example

Definitions

$$VaR = \sqrt{VaR_1^2 + VaR_2^2 + 2p_{12}VaR_1VaR_2}$$

VaR_1 = Value at Risk for Instrument 1

VaR_2 = Value at Risk for Instrument 2

p_{12} = Correlation between the price movements of Instrument 1 and 2

Position   A U.S. investor is long DEM140 million ten-year German bunds (the U.S. investor is therefore also long Deutsche marks)

Market/Risk Information

Bund volatility:	0.999%
DEM/USD FX Volatility:	0.932%
Correlation:	-0.27

Interest rate risk	DEM 140 million * 0.999% / 1.40 = USD999,000
FX risk	DEM 140 million * 0.932% / 1.40 = USD932,000

Value at Risk

$$VaR_{USD} = \sqrt{(999,000)^2 + (932,000)^2 + 2 * (-0.27) * 999,000 * 932,000}$$

= USD 1.17 million

The undiversified risk, assuming a perfect correlation between instruments, is simply the sum of the individual risks. For example, with a + 1.0 correlation this would be USD999,000 + USD932,000 = USD1.93 million. We look at the undiversified risk with respect to the diversified risk (our typical *VaR* calculation). The difference between the two is the diversification benefit to the investor due to correlation ($1.93 million − $1.7 million = $760,000).

Source: J.P. Morgan, "Introduction to Risk Metrics" (1995), at www.RiskMetrics.com, p. 15.

especially harmful in calculating VaR for portfolios containing options—another standard element in the portfolios of international bankers.

- *Markets move together, but nobody knows how.* Many of the greatest financial risks in today's world arise from co-movements among market risk factors. VaR models do include statistical correlations, but these tend to be very imperfect descriptions of the way markets move together when they make big moves (for example, the spread of Asian contagion in 1997–98).[10]

Stress Testing

As noted in the previous section, VaR captures the essence of a bank's risk in the normal market environment. What if market conditions turn abnormal, though? An endless variety of scenarios can be invented for abnormal market conditions, ranging from a bomb blast on Wall Street to an assassination in Moscow. To measure the bank's exposure to losses in disordered markets, risk managers turn to stress testing. This is a technique that relies on computer modeling of different scenarios, and computation of the results of those scenarios on a bank's portfolio.

For example, risk managers may devise a scenario in which the Mexican peso is suddenly devalued by 30 percent. All assets in the bank's portfolio are then revalued using the new environment, creating a new estimate for the return on the portfolio. Many such scenarios lead to many such exercises, so that a range of values for return on the portfolio is derived. By specifying the probability for each scenario, managers can then generate a distribution of portfolio returns, from which VaR can be measured. The advantage of this method is that it allows risk managers to evaluate possible scenarios that may be completely absent from historical data. As Chase Manhattan explains in its 1998 Annual Report:

> Portfolio stress testing is integral to the market risk management process—co-equal with, and complementary to, VaR as a risk measurement and control tool. Chase's corporate stress tests are built around changes in market rates and prices that result from pre-specified economic scenarios, including both actual historical and hypothetical market events....
>
> Stress test scenarios are chosen so they test "conventional wisdom" and focus on risks relevant to the positions taken in Chase's portfolios. A key to the success of stress testing at Chase is continuous review and updating of stress scenarios. This is a dynamic process that is responsive to changes in positions and economic events, and looks to prior stress tests to identify areas where scenario refinements can be made. Corporate stress tests are performed approximately monthly on randomly selected dates. As of December 31, 1998, Chase's corporate stress tests consisted of seven historical and hypothetical scenarios. These historical scenarios included the 1994 bond market sell-off, the 1997 Mexican Peso crisis and the 1997 Asian markets crisis....[11]

Indeed, Chase apparently had good reason to laud its risk management system. It began stress testing its entire trading and loan portfolio in late 1997 to analyze how it would perform in a wide variety of unforeseen market downturns—essentially devising numerous plots that could lead to disaster, and analyzing their impact on the bank. Based on the results of this analysis, Chase management devised an incentive package that reduced compensation if risk

BIS STUDY ON STRESS TESTING

In April 2000, the Bank for International Settlements (BIS) published the findings of its Working Group on Macro Stress Testing established by the Committee on the Global Financial System. The group interviewed risk managers at more than twenty large, internationally active financial institutions to learn about the current state of the art in stress testing.

The BIS learned that most of the interviewed firms do indeed use stress tests to supplement VaR, reflecting the limited usefulness of VaR in measuring firms' exposure to extreme market events. The financial institutions relied mostly on four different techniques in stress testing, described below:

Stress Testing Techniques

Technique	What Is the "Stress Test Result"?
Simple sensitivity test	Change in portfolio value for one or more shocks to a single risk factor
Scenario analysis	Change in portfolio value if the scenario were to occur (hypothetical or historical)
Maximum loss	Sum of individual trading units' worst-case scenarios
Extreme value theory	Probability distribution of extreme losses

Stress tests provide information summarizing the firm's exposure to extreme, but possible, circumstances. The risk managers interviewed by the Working Group included the following when discussing some of the specific ways stress tests are used to influence decision making:

- Manage funding risk
- Quantify tail risk
- Provide a check on modeling assumptions
- Set limits for traders
- Determine capital charges on trading desks' positions

The Working Group also interviewed risk managers on the limitations of stress tests. One well-understood limitation is that there are no probabilities attached to the outcomes. The lack of probability exacerbates the issue of transparency and the seeming arbitrariness of stress test design, a point readily acknowledged by the risk managers. Also, system incompatibilities

(continued)

across business units make frequent stress testing costly for some firms. Thus risk managers noted that the heavy computational burden imposed by full revaluation of complex options limits the frequency of their stress tests. Finally, the Working Group noted that none of the interviewed firms systematically integrates market and credit risk in stress testing.

Source: Committee on the Global Financial System, "Stress Testing by Large Financial Institutions: Current Practice and Aggregation Issues" (Basel, Switzerland: Bank for International Settlements, April 2000), available at www.bis.org.

taking did not lead to appropriate rewards, helping it create a more conservative risk profile overall.[12]

Certainly, VaR is subject to "event risk" and thus must be augmented by stress testing. However, stress testing, too, is subject to some serious flaws. First, the method of predicting scenarios is by its very nature completely subjective; bad or implausible scenarios lead to bad measures of VaR. People tend to do a poor job

MERRILL LYNCH INVESTIGATES "ILLEGAL TRANSFER" OF $40M

David Ibison

Merrill Lynch, the US investment bank, is investigating an alleged fraud involving the illegal transfer of $40m of one of its client's funds into a Swiss bank account.

The funds belonged to one of the bank's largest clients in the Middle East—Arab International Bank—and were sent to a UBS account in Geneva in six tranches between 1996 and 1998.

Internal documents obtained by the *Financial Times* pinpoint problems with Merrill Lynch's internal supervision and management controls which contributed to the alleged fraud.

The documents reveal five of the six fund transfers were ordered by an Arab International employee who died three months before the transactions were conducted. The other was ordered by a person unauthorized to conduct fund transfers....

Merrill Lynch said, "We have full confidence in our controls—unfortunately in this case there was a clear abuse of trust by an employee who went to great lengths to conceal his activities."

Source: Financial Times, January 7, 2000, p. 17.

of brainstorming scenarios that have never occurred before. Second, the choice of scenarios may be affected by a bank's portfolio position itself, that is, where the portfolio is invested. Finally, stress testing techniques handle correlations poorly. Typically, stress testing examines the effect of a large movement on one financial variable at a time, so it is not well suited to large, complex portfolios such as those held by international banks. Accordingly, this method should be viewed as a complement to, not a replacement, for VaR. Its greatest value is in helping managers evaluate the worst-case effect of a large movement in key variables—providing that they have created the proper scenario to spur this movement.[13]

Operational Risks

Of all the risk categories, operational risks are probably the most difficult to quantify and, therefore, model. Operational risks range from "rogue trader" losses to the risk of a computer or telephone outage disrupting operations systems in critical areas. The best safeguard against most operational risks is the old-fashioned standby, internal control. However, even the best-managed banks cannot always protect themselves from fraud, theft, or operational disasters.[14]

LLOYD'S INSURES ROGUE TRADE RISK

Jim Kelly

A syndicate at the Lloyd's of London insurance market said yesterday it had sold its first insurance policy covering banks for the risk of "rogue trading." SVB Syndicates, a managing agency, launched the policy last October. It said the buyer was a "large New York based financial institution with global operations." The risks associated with traders under pressure were graphically illustrated by the collapse of the Barings merchant bank in 1995 following the losses run up by the Singapore-based trader Nick Leeson. Barings suffered losses of £800m ($1,336 m). In many cases, such losses are not covered by fidelity policies because the trader has not been involved in fraud for personal gain. SVB's policy provides cover for a trading loss which has been concealed by a trader or falsely recorded. The cover of up to $300m extends to commitments in excess of permitted limits, trading in unauthorized instruments and trading with unapproved counterparties. To qualify, banks will have to show they have the necessary internal controls in place.

Source: Financial Times, February 3, 1998.

Interest Rate Risk

Banks are by their very nature constantly exposed to interest rate risk, the riskiness of earnings and returns related to changes in interest rates. The first step in assessing interest rate risk is to determine which assets and liabilities are rate-sensitive, that is, which have interest rates that will be reset (repriced) within the year. If a bank has more rate-sensitive liabilities than assets, then a rise in interest rates will reduce the net interest margin and income, and a decline in interest rates will raise the net interest margin and income.

The sensitivity of bank income to changes in interest rates can be measured more directly using gap analysis (also called income gap analysis), in which the amount of rate-sensitive liabilities is subtracted from the amount of rate-sensitive assets. This calculation, known as GAP, can be written as

$$GAP = RSA - RSL$$

where   RSA = rate-sensitive assets
                 RSL = rate-sensitive liabilities.

Then, multiplying the GAP times the change in the interest rate immediately reveals the effect on bank income:

$$[\text{change in}] \, I = GAP \cdot [\text{change in}] \, i$$

where   [change in] I = change in bank income
           [change in] i = change in interest rates.

This analysis is known as basic gap analysis, and it focuses only on the effect of interest rate changes on income. An alternative method for measuring interest rate risk, called **duration gap analysis,** examines the sensitivity of the market value of the financial institution's net worth to changes in interest rates. This is based on the concept of duration, which measures the average lifetime of a security's stream of payments. The bank manager can figure out the effect that interest rate changes will have on the market value of net worth by calculating the average duration for assets and for liabilities, and then using those figures to estimate the effects of interest rate changes.[15]

Limits to Modern Risk Management Techniques

Despite the increasingly complex computer-based techniques such as VaR and stress testing at their disposal, and even insurance policies to cover some operational risks, bankers still cannot rest easily. Even the most modern and sophisticated methods of assessing risk are not foolproof, reflecting their assumptions of key factors such as volatility or their dependence on historical relationships to forecast the future. Following some well-publicized risk management failures in 1998 (see Chapter 9 for a discussion of financial crashes), one prominent rating agency warned that financial institutions needed to take "corrective action" to mend their risk

THE NEW RELIGION OF RISK MANAGEMENT

Peter L. Bernstein

The science of risk management is capable of creating new risks even as it brings old risks under control. Our faith in risk management encourages us to take risks we otherwise would not take. On most counts, that is beneficial. But we should be wary of increasing the total amount of risk in the system. Research shows that the security of seat belts encourages drivers to behave more aggressively, with the result that the number of accidents rises even as the seriousness of injury in any one accident may diminish.... I have concerns about a similar process at work today among conservative institutional investors who use broad diversification to justify their large exposure in untested areas. Diversification is not a guarantee against loss, only against losing everything at once.

Yet nothing is more soothing and authoritative than the screen of the computer, with its imposing arrays of numbers, luminous color schemes, and artfully composed charts. That is not the worst of it. As we sit and stare at the data and the graphs, we are so absorbed in what we are doing that we tend to forget we are operating a gadget whose mind is at rest. Computers exist to answer questions, not to ask them....

Source: Harvard Business Review, (March/April 1996) pp. 47.

management practices. Observers fretted about the degree of confidence that bankers place in computer-driven risk models, and especially on the basic assumptions that underlie these models (with regard to correlations between different financial markets, for example, or the availability of market liquidity in times of stress). Taking a similar tone, the Institute of International Finance (IIF) found in a recent report that while most large banks were satisfied with their systems for assessing market and credit risk, those systems were in fact working in isolation from each other and dealt inadequately with linkages between various categories of risk. Also, the IIF warns that banks do not make sufficient allowance for liquidity risk, or the chance that markets might dry up in times of stress—making it impossible to sell out of positions without incurring huge losses.[16] This underlines the old joke: Emerging markets are markets from which you cannot emerge in an emergency.

Questions

1. Why is moral hazard a problem in making loan decisions? What can bankers do to counteract this risk?

2. A senior Fed official is quoted as commenting that credit risk management is still not infallible. Why do you suppose this is? Can you suggest remedies to improve the traditional techniques of credit risk management?

3. What is VaR? How is it calculated? Why is it used?

4. What are the strengths of using VaR techniques for assessing market risk? Weaknesses?

5. What are the strengths and weaknesses of using stress testing techniques for assessing market risk?

6. Suppose you work for the risk manager of a major international bank, and she asks you to devise ten scenarios to use in stress testing the bank's portfolio. What scenarios would you use? What probabilities would you attach to each scenario?

7. What kinds of risks do the Barings and Daiwa case studies underscore? Suggest management techniques for avoiding the fate that befell Barings and Daiwa.

8. What is operational risk? How can banks measure and assess this type of risk?

9. What is interest rate risk? How can banks measure and assess it?

Websites

www.RiskMetrics.com	RiskMetrics
www.rims.org	Risk and Insurance Management Society
www.GloriaMundi.org	Value at Risk resources
www.isda.org	International Swaps & Derivatives Association
www.riskworld.com	News and views on risk management

Notes

1. ABN AMRO Annual Report, 1998.

2. Suresh Sundaresan, "Mastering Risk: Lenders and Borrowers Demand a Creditable System," *Financial Times Survey*, May 16, 2000, p. 2.

3. Frederic S. Mishkin and Stanley G. Eakins, *Financial Markets and Institutions*, 3rd edition (Reading, Mass.: Addison Wesley Longman, 2000), pp. 619–623.

4. William J. McDonough, Remarks Before the Bond Market Association in New York, January 1, 1999, available at www.federalreserve.gov.

5. A full discussion of credit risk management in financial institutions may be found in R. Boffey and G. N. Robson, "Bank Credit Risk Management," *Managerial Finance*, 21, No. 1 (1995), pp. 66–768.

6. Barry Schachter, "An Irreverent Guide to Value at Risk," at www.GloriaMundi.org/var.

7. Philippe Jorion, *Value at Risk* (New York: McGraw-Hill, 1997), p. xiii.

8. Paul Glasserman, "Mastering Risk: The Quest for Precision Through VaR," *Financial Times Survey*, May 16, 2000, p. 6.

9. This discussion of J.P. Morgan's RiskMetrics model is adapted from Shelagh Heffernan, *Modern Banking in Theory and Practice* (New York: John Wiley

& Sons, 1996), pp. 194–195. A full discussion of VaR must begin with an understanding of probability theory and other statistical methods, which are beyond the scope of this textbook. For the student interested in more detail, please refer to Heffernan or Philippe Jorion, *Value at Risk*.

10. Paul Glasserman, "Mastering Risk: The Quest for Precision Through VaR," p. 6.

11. Chase Manhattan Annual Report, 1998.

12. Timothy O'Brien, "Taking the Danger Out of Risk," *New York Times*, January 20, 1999, p. C1.

13. Philippe Jorion, *Value at Risk*, pp. 196–199.

14. For an excellent report on operational risks in financial institutions, see Mark Parsley, "Risk Management's Final Frontier," *Euromoney*, September 1996, pp. 74–78.

15. This discussion is adapted from Frederic S. Mishkin and Stanley G. Eakins, *Financial Markets and Institutions*, pp. 624–626. Since interest rate risk is generally covered in money and banking textbooks, and does not raise any additional issues in the international context, we have devoted very little attention to it here. If the student has no background in the management of financial institutions and would like more information, please refer to the Mishkin/Eakins text, pp. 620–624, or Shelagh Heffernan, *Modern Banking in Theory and Practice*, pp. 184–193, for a fuller discussion.

16. George Graham, "Banks Urged to Improve Risk Management Procedures," *Financial Times*, March 22, 1999, p. 4.

CHAPTER 12

MONEY LAUNDERING

Money laundering usually conjures up images of exotic locations, silk-suited financial intermediaries, and Rolex-wearing drug lords. The environment in which "hot money" or drug profits are transformed into "clean" legal tender or assets is perceived as glitzy and fast-paced. What is often missing in this picture is the tedious filling out of Currency Transaction Reports (CTRs) by bank clerks in the United States, long hours of negotiations between teams of experts to create multilateral anti–money laundering agreements, and the methodical work of building cases against suspected money launderers that cut across international frontiers.

With vast profits (estimates range between $300 to $500 billion), secret trade routes, and the power to buy influence, the criminal consortia involved in this commerce have become an international force of which banks must be fully aware.[1] For any bank involved in international business, the issue of money laundering cannot be easily sidestepped. Banks in many countries are legally required to have anti–money laundering measures in place that alert the bank's own management as well as the authorities to what they regard as suspicious transactions. Failure on the part of a bank to have implemented the proper measures can result in criminal and civil actions against the particular institution. The burden of recognizing a "suspicious transaction," however, falls heavily on bankers who are untrained in law enforcement.

Defining Our Terms

What exactly is **money laundering**? Money laundering is the act of transforming profits earned from a criminal activity into legal profits. While drug trafficking usually earns the headlines for generating such profits, other activities that fall within this rubric include arms smuggling; trafficking in stolen art, body parts, nuclear secrets, and weapons; money used by terrorist groups; kidnapping for ransom; pariah states undertaking financial transactions to evade international sanctions, in order to acquire technologies and components for weapons of mass destruction; and individuals seeking to avoid paying their taxes (not a criminal act in every country, but certainly not something that local authorities smile upon). There are three phases of money laundering:

1. Placement: Phase one is the placement of currency into a financial services institution. This can be a bank, a brokerage house, or so forth.

2. Layering: Phase two is the movement of funds from institution to institution to conceal the original source and ownership of the funds.

CLEARING MUDDY WATERS

Nancy Birdsall and Devesh Kapur

The international financial community must be more transparent if laundering of ill-gotten gains from emerging markets is to be stopped. The perennial problems of money laundering and corruption in emerging markets have been highlighted again by Russia. The Bank of New York is alleged to have helped shift more than $10bn in ill-gotten gains out of Russia into private bank accounts in the west, at the same time as the number of Russians below the official poverty line has risen from 33m to 55m in the past year. How should the international community respond?

The favoured solution on Wall Street, at the International Monetary Fund and in the US Treasury to this and other financial and economic problems of emerging markets is more transparency in the financial accounts of emerging-market governments. But, as evident from the sheer size of capital flight from Russia, the demands for more transparency on the part of those countries are oddly self-serving. What about greater transparency on the part of private parties in the market themselves?

Source: Financial Times, September 13, 1999.

---

3. Integration: Phase three is the time when the funds, having been "washed," are reinvested into a legitimate business.

In providing an accurate definition of money laundering, we must understand another term: **flight capital.** According to one financial dictionary, flight capital is, "The rapid withdrawal of capital (flight capital) from a country as result of loss of confidence in its government."[2] This, however, only provides part of the picture. Flight capital is also referred to as "hot money," which moves from one point to another, driven by possible gains or concerns about government policies. In many regards, it is difficult to make a distinction between legitimate and illegal flight capital. The legal component of flight capital is usually after-tax money flows from one country to another; it is usually properly documented, remains on the books of the entity from which it was transferred, and is generally believed to be beneficial in terms of promoting economic growth. Moreover, the legal component of flight capital flees to safety. The illegal component of flight capital seeks out secrecy, motivated by a desire to be accumulated in a concealed fashion. As one expert noted: "The illegal component is almost always tax evasion. It is improperly documented, or it is dependent on a preceding or a following transaction that is properly documented. It disappears from any record in the country from which it is transferred."[3]

Another term in money laundering, directly related to the three phases, is **smurfing.** Named after small blue cartoon characters, smurfs are individuals who help move the funds from one institution to another or from one country to another.

A smurfing operation will involve a major coordinator (a "Papa Smurf"), who will direct his smurfs to make deposits of drug profits at a large number of banks, usually at numbers just below local reporting requirements, like drug-smuggling airplanes that fly below radar screens.

Money laundering operations are attracted to locations that are defined by extensive bank secrecy laws, weak financial regulatory regimes, lax enforcement, and corruption. At the same time, extensive money laundering occurs in many countries, including the United States and the United Kingdom, which have some of the toughest anti–money laundering measures in place.

One key motivation to launder illicit profits is that cash itself is a problem. As one observer noted: "It [cash] is heavy and unwieldy. In $100 denominations, cash is three times the weight of drugs that generate it; 450 paper bills weigh one pound. In the more common street-level denominations of $10 and $20 bills, it is at least 15 to 30 times the weight of its equivalent value. To move cash around the world in quantities and with the speed demanded by the operations of the major cartels is difficult, if not impossible."[4]

Since the United States is the biggest drug market in the world, it generates billions of dollars in profits, a significant amount of which seeks to exit U.S. borders and find its way back into the hands of those who earned it. Considering the scope of international money laundering, the activity clearly represents a threat to the integrity of a nation's financial institutions. Consequently, since the late 1980s the United States, the European Union countries, and others have sought to take extensive countermeasures to deal with the problem. As the U.S. government stated, in its 1997 annual report on international money laundering:

> Due to the high integration of capital markets, money laundering can also negatively affect national and global interest rates as launderers reinvest funds where their schemes are less likely to be detected rather than where rates of return are higher because of sound economic principles. Organized financial crime is assuming an increasingly significant role that threatens the safety and security of peoples, states and democratic institutions. Moreover, our ability to conduct foreign policy and to promote economic security and prosperity is hindered by these threats to our democratic and free-market partners.[5]

Serious efforts have been made to prevent money laundering in most OECD countries. The result of these efforts has been to reduce the amount of money laundering occurring in the banks, but to increase the flow of illicit cash through nonbank financial institutions. Even in the United States, money laundering operations continue, targeting both the banks and, more often, the over 200,000 nonbank financial institutions in the country.

Money Laundering: A Long History

There is nothing new about money laundering. Although it is difficult to pinpoint exactly when money laundering began, it can be traced to the 1930s in the United States. Stimulated by Prohibition in the United States, criminal groups needed a subterranean financial system that was impervious to the effects of fiscal and monetary policy and was indifferent to tax collectors.

SWISS, RUSSIANS SEEK TO CUT FLOW
OF DIRTY MONEY

S wiss and Russian ministers sought ways yesterday to stem billions of
dollars in Russian underworld money that is reported to be flowing into
Swiss bank accounts. The Swiss justice minister, Arnold Koller, and the
Russian interior minister, Sergei Stepashin, held talks aimed at boosting
cooperation in the battle against organized crime, money laundering, and
drug trafficking, the Justice Ministry said.

The talks were a further sign of a commitment in both countries to fight
against activities that posed "a great challenge to the rule of law," the ministry said. Swiss prosecutors say Russian crime organizations have laundered
$40 billion through banks in Switzerland since communism collapsed in
1991. Swiss federal police said in January that they suspected more than 90
Swiss-based companies were fronts for Russian organized crime.

The Justice Ministry said that next month, Russia will ratify two Council of Europe conventions on extradition and legal assistance in criminal
investigations. But analysts say it is unclear when the Russian parliament
will adopt them. Passage of the conventions would lay the legal groundwork
for effective legal cooperation, said the ministry.

Switzerland's banking secrecy laws have earned it a reputation as a haven
for dirty money, prompting authorities to impose tight rules against money
laundering. A law last year led to a boom in tipoffs to the authorities and the
freezing of $190 million in dubious wealth, an official said in December.

Source: Boston Globe, March 3, 1999, p. A11.

The pioneer often credited with creating the first major criminal drug-related
money laundering ring in the United States is Meyer Lansky, who came into his
own in the 1930s and figured prominently into the 1950s.[6] Lansky was upset by
Al Capone's arrest and conviction on charges of tax evasion in 1931. He was
allied with Salvatore "Lucky" Luciano, who led a coup against the old mafia
dons who were opposed to trafficking in heroin. Heroin trafficking soon brought
a huge inflow of cash, and some mechanism was needed to help wash the money
and keep it out of the hands of U.S. tax collectors. Hence, in 1932 Lansky
allegedly made his first foray into Swiss banking, opening a new cash route.
Under Lansky's guidance, the hot money was collected in New York and sent
through Canada to Switzerland. This was in operation through the 1940s, but in
the 1950s and 1960s the route changed. Mob-run banks in Miami would directly
transfer funds to Switzerland, or the funds would be smuggled to the Bahamas
(where they entered the legal banking system) and then transferred to bank

accounts in Switzerland. Another route until 1959 was through Cuba via the many mafia-owned casinos.

Meyer Lansky was not the only individual involved in international money laundering. Other hot money mandarins included Tibor Rosenbaum, founder of the Banque de Credit Internationale and implicated in helping run guns from Czechoslovakia to the Stern Gang in Palestine as the paymaster to Israel's secret service, the Mossad; and Allen J. Lefferdink, who moved his operations to Bermuda, dealt with U.S. heroin dealers in Vietnam, and handled capital flight in Latin America. One of the more interesting characters to surface in this murky world was Frank Peroof in the 1960s, who ran a small fleet of planes to carry currency illegally out of Argentina, Chile, and Peru. He was also involved in smuggling emeralds out of Colombia, which no doubt showed some of the local talent new horizons for business.

The range of these activities, along with the establishment of secret trade routes and havens for hot money in Europe and the Caribbean, clearly set the stage for the expansion of the Colombian drug cartels in the 1970s. As criminal groups from Medellín and Cali gradually climbed up the success ladder of drug trafficking, displacing the Cubans in Florida and eventually carving up the North American market in the early 1980s, the need to launder large amounts of money became urgent. By the mid–1980s, money laundering routes were opened throughout the Caribbean and were spreading to Europe. The opening up of Central and Eastern Europe and the creation of new countries out of the former Soviet Union and the former Yugoslavia, combined with the liberalization of financial markets around the planet, guaranteed the ongoing endeavors of money laundering operations. By the end of the 1990s, money laundering operations were being conducted by criminal organizations around the world, while law enforcement agencies and bank regulators sought to prevent these actions, in part by creating an international anti–money laundering regime.

It would be erroneous to portray all money laundering operations as either North or South American and European or to indicate that the 1930s was the jumping-off point for the beginning of money laundering in its broadest sense. There are what is referred to as underground or parallel banking systems, which enable the avoidance of any conventional paper record of financial transactions. The best known of these underground systems are the hawalah and chop systems.

The Indian **hawalah system** has existed for a considerable period of time and rarely involves "the physical movement of cash, or for that matter anything other than tokens which are regarded within the special structure of the system as the equivalent in value to the relevant cash sums."[7] The system depends on considerable trust and simplicity—the money launderer places an amount with the underground bank, with the identifying receipt for a transaction being something as innocuous as a playing card or postcard torn in half.[8] Half is held by the customer, and half is forwarded to the overseas hawalah banker. The launderer then presents her receipt in the target country to obtain her money, thus exporting cash out of the country and limiting the risk of detection. The key point of this compensation system that makes it attractive to money launderers in much of South Asia is that it is a paperless and practically recordless banking system, which can transfer substantial amounts of wealth.

Related to the hawalah system is the **chop system,** which is used throughout the overseas Chinese communities in Southeast Asia, Canada, and the United States. The chop system is also a largely paperless remittance system, operating on the basis of a chop or a mark that identifies the carrier as someone who can be trusted. A carrier of a chop can travel from Hong Kong, where he has asked for credit, to Los Angeles, where upon demonstration of the chop he receives the money.

The Burden on Bankers

In a globalized economic system, there is no escape from the problem of money laundering. Indeed, intentional failure to apply the law is called **willful negligence** and is regarded by most law enforcement authorities as a criminal act with severe penalties. In most countries, banks are now required to report **suspicious transactions** and to establish internal controls to shield the bank or its branches and subsidiaries from any money laundering operations, including employees who may have turned to work with criminal organizations. Suspicious transactions include such things as a deposit made just below the $10,000 currency transaction reporting limit (in the United States), an excessive cash flow from a business in an area that is economically depressed, or someone showing up at the teller's window with a suitcase of cash. Simply stated, it is anything that raises any questions out of the ordinary about the origin of the money. Realistically, though, it is not always easy for a banker to identify suspicious transactions. Criminal groups go to extreme lengths to conceal their laundering operations, using dummy corporations, wire transfers, and smurfs. Nevertheless, the banker is also required to cooperate with law enforcement, especially during criminal investigations.

An extremely important element of any money laundering prevention program for banks is the implementation of a "Know Your Customer" program, which seeks to verify the background of the clients of the bank. This extends to all aspects of bank business, including private banking and letters of credit. It is expected that banks make it an explicit policy that business transactions will not be conducted with customers who do not provide evidence of their identity. A good Know Your Customer program will also monitor accounts and take appropriate action if there are unusual patterns in account activity.

Equally important as knowing their customers, banks are also required to have adequate record-keeping systems of transactions. In a number of countries, records of currency purchases of monetary instruments over a certain value are required. Customer identification is required for the records, helping to provide law enforcement with a paper trial when conducting investigations. Such records are also useful to a bank's internal compliance to flush out smurfing operations.

To briefly summarize, international banks are urged to comply with laws, cooperate with law enforcement authorities (when the need arises), and make reasonable efforts to determine the true identities of all customers requesting the institution's services. Failure to do so will have negative consequences.

Anti–Money Laundering Laws in the United States

The United States probably has the most comprehensive and some would argue the most burdensome set of anti–money laundering laws to which bankers must adhere. One of the most important laws pertaining to bankers and money laundering prevention is the Bank Secrecy Act (BSA) of 1970 and its enabling regulations. The purpose of the BSA is create a paper trail for criminal, tax, or regulatory investigations by requiring record keeping for transactions of $10,000 or more in value. Later amendments to this law allow the government the authority to lower the $10,000 benchmark in the course of an investigation.

Other significant money laundering laws in the United States include the Comprehensive Crime Control Act of 1984, the Money Laundering Control Act of 1986, the Anti–Drug Abuse Act of 1988, and the Annunzio-Wylie Anti–Money Laundering Act of 1992. The Money Laundering Control Act subjects individuals to criminal liability for knowing participation in any laundering of money and authorizes the seizure and forfeiture of cash or property related to such cash.

The Annunzio-Wylie Act allows the regulators to revoke the charter of a federally chartered bank, federal branch, federal agency, savings association, or credit union after a conviction for money laundering. Before revoking a license, a regulator must consider:

1. The extent to which directors or senior executive officers were involved
2. Whether the institution had policies and procedures in place designed to prevent money laundering
3. The degree to which the institution cooperated with law enforcement officials
4. Whether the institution now has in place procedures to prevent the recurrence of the offense
5. The effect of the forfeiture of the franchise on the local community's interest in adequate credit and depository services

Failure to adhere to the various rules and regulations pertaining to money laundering in the United States can carry both civil and criminal penalties for bankers. On the civil side, bankers are subject to civil penalties of up to $100,000 for willful violations of the reporting or record-keeping requirements of the BSA. Moreover, a separate violation occurs each day the violation continues and at each branch, office, or place of business where a violation occurs or continues. As for criminal penalties, violators are subject to up to $250,000 in fines, up to five years of imprisonment, or both.

One of the earliest and best-known cases pertaining to a bank being penalized for failure to adhere to the various rules and regulations pertaining to money laundering in the United States was that of the Bank of Boston. The Bank of Boston had two problems. Although U.S. authorities had indicated a more stringent adherence to the filing of Currency Transactions Reports in 1980, the bank continued to conduct currency transactions with foreign banks, including its own subsidiaries, without filing CTRs. It did this until 1984.

The second problem was probably more serious and compounded the lack of compliance in the first. As Robert Powis noted: "Another problem encountered by Bank of Boston was that one of its branches had been doing business with a notorious crime figure for years. The individual owned a realty business, and the branch exempted the business from the currency reporting requirements even though it did not qualify for an exemption under Treasury regulations. For years, the mobster and his brothers would bring shopping bags full of cash into the bank and make deposits or buy cashier's checks."[9] By 1985, Bank of Boston's compliance problems, ranging from the failure of its Know Your Customer program to the failure to file CTRs, resulted in considerable negative publicity as well as criminal charges being leveled against the bank. Ultimately, Bank of Boston pled guilty and was fined $500,000.

Laws Around the World

In the UK, bankers operate under similar pressures in regard to money laundering as in the United States. In December 1990, the UK issued a set of guidelines to assist and compel banks in detecting and stopping money laundering, such as reporting suspicious transactions. The set of guidelines for banks was prepared by the banking industry with the participation of the National Drug Intelligence Unit, Customs and Excise, the police, and the Bank of England. The guidelines concentrate on the banks' statutory duty to alert the enforcement agencies to suspected criminal activity. As in the United States, the consequence of not abiding by the statutes and guidelines is potential criminal liability; the benefits of compliance are exoneration from potential criminal and civil liability rising from breaching of client confidentiality.[10]

The UK guidelines require banks to identify all customers personally, if possible through a face-to-face meeting, mirroring the implementation of the Know Your Customer approach. The guidelines also define reliable forms of identification: the passport is preferred, but other acceptable forms of identification include an armed forces identity card, an employer identity card, and a driving license. Moreover, banks must keep records for up to six years to facilitate investigations.

As in the United States, UK bankers are expected to report suspicious transactions. The UK guidelines indicate that the staff of the institutions subject to the guidelines must be encouraged to cooperate completely with law enforcement agencies and to provide prompt notice of suspicious transactions. While banks are subject to the guidelines, they also pertain to building societies, insurance companies, and investment firms.

Other key pieces of legislation in the UK's anti–money laundering regime include the 1986 Drug Trafficking Offences Act, the 1987 Prevention of Terrorism Act, the Criminal Justice (International Cooperation) Act of 1990, and the Criminal Justice Act of 1993. The first-mentioned provides the police with the authority to investigate suspected drug-derived assets, to freeze them, and, upon conviction, to confiscate them.[11] The same law makes it a criminal offense to assist a drug trafficker in retaining or making use of his drug-related assets. Under the 1987 Prevention of Terrorism Act, an offense is committed by anyone who facilitates retention or control of terrorist funds. The Criminal Justice Act of 1990 made it possible to prosecute anyone who conceals, disguises, converts, transfers, or removes property from the jurisdiction of the courts, or helps someone do just that, when he or she knows or suspects that the property represents the proceeds of drug trafficking.[12] The Criminal Justice Act of 1993 extended the power of the court to prosecute money laundering as a crime in itself.

The United States and the UK are hardly alone in creating anti–money laundering legal and regulatory regimes to protect their banking systems. The European Union's banking regulations and supervisory practices guidelines require bankers to know their customers so that money launderers will find it harder to operate; to comply actively with existing legislation and law enforcement agencies in the fight against money laundering; to improve record-keeping systems so that suspicious activities can be detected early; and to train staff so that they can recognize and will report money laundering activities.[13]

Australia operates with a currency transaction reporting system similar to that in the United States. Any cash transaction of US$10,000 and over must be reported. The data are then electronically sent by the banks and financial institutions to the Cash Transactions Reports Agency. In Japan, banks are required to report all domestic cash transactions in excess of 30 million yen and all foreign cash transactions in excess of 5 million yen.[14] Additionally, in those cases where drugs are involved, prosecutors can put banks and financial institutions in the dock on money laundering charges.

Adventures in Money Laundering

To put international money laundering and the problem it poses for banks into perspective, let us examine the cases of the Bank of Credit and Commerce International (BCCI), the ongoing problems confronting Antigua and Barbuda's offshore banking center, and Russia's emergence as a potential money laundering catastrophe.

The Bank of Credit and Commerce International

One of the most notorious cases of financial fraud was that of the Bank of Credit and Commerce International, sometimes referred to as the Bank of Crooks and Criminals International or Bank of Cocaine and Criminals International. Before BCCI was brought to heel by international law enforcement authorities in 1991, it operated in seventy-three countries and was a major force in such financial centers as New York, London, Geneva, Paris, and Hong Kong. As Peter Truell and Larry Gurwin noted:

> BCCI had outwardly seemed like a normal financial institution, with attractively designed branch offices, its own travelers' check business, and a reputation for financing international trade. But behind this convincing façade, BCCI was a criminal enterprise that catered to some of the most notorious villains of the late twentieth century, including Saddam Hussein, the blood-thirsty ruler of Iraq; leaders of the

Medellín drug cartel, which controls the bulk of the world's cocaine trade; Khun Sa, the warlord who dominates heroin trafficking in Asia's Golden Triangle; Abu Nidal, the head of one of the world's leading terrorist organizations; and Manuel Noriega, the drug-dealing former dictator of Panama.[15]

BCCI was established in 1972 in Luxembourg by a Pakistani banker by the name of Aga Hassan Abedi. Supported by the financial muscle of wealthy individuals in the Persian Gulf, in particular, Sheik Zayed bin Sultan Al-Nahayan, the ruler of Abu Dhabi, BCCI eventually grew to be a bank with assets of around $20 billion in the early 1990s. By 1987, BCCI was conducting banking operations through offices and branches (capable of taking deposits and making loans) in the UK and through offices in the United States, with its U.S. headquarters in New York City.

BCCI's rapid expansion into the world of international banking had not gone unnoticed. It had developed a reputation for offering highly professional services and special treatment for wealthy customers, in particular for those coming from the developing world. Using bank secrecy in such locations as Luxembourg, the Bahamas, and other offshore financial centers, BCCI was able to attract both legitimate business and less savory types of individuals—those involved in the world of transnational crime. In 1986 rumors began to circulate that something was amiss at BCCI. As Robert Powis noted: "Rumors started to circulate in 1986 that the solvency of BCCI was in doubt. Other rumors suggested the bank had its hands in shady transactions involving money laundering, arms shipments, and bribery."[16]

The negative rumors about BCCI gained momentum in 1988 when the bank was indicted in Florida for money laundering. By 1989, BCCI was announcing that it had large losses from bank loans amounting to $500 million. Growing questions about BCCI's reputation and solvency ultimately caused runs on the bank in the UK in 1991. By July 1991 regulators in seven nations seized control of BCCI operations in their countries, citing huge losses and widespread fraud. The embarrassment of the BCCI scandal hit far and wide, especially as a number of central banks, such as that of Jamaica, held some of their deposits with the rogue bank. BCCI demonstrated that international anti–money laundering efforts, created by a number of agreements in the late 1980s, were not so well established as many financial regulators and their counterparts in enforcement had hoped. In the aftermath of the BCCI scandal, international efforts to improve anti–money laundering operations were put into place through North America, Europe, and parts of Asia. BCCI, if nothing else, heightened the awareness of banking regulators and bankers that there was a pressing need to better know one's customers as well as one's bank.

Islands in the Sun: Antigua and Barbuda

Much of the Caribbean is ideal for money laundering. The many island-states of the region are close to major drug producing countries, are on major drug trafficking routes, have relatively small governments (which also means limited law enforcement and supervisory capabilities), and have tourist-based economies that are largely cash-intensive. Added to this mixture are offshore banking facilities and good communications. In addition, many Caribbean countries indeed are attractive places to visit, spend money on casinos, and set up offshore banks to help bring into circulation drug profits. Although many Caribbean countries have taken measures to reduce the problems with money laundering, Antigua and Barbuda have troubled records. As a U.S. Government report noted in 1997: "Antigua, with an active offshore financial services industry, stringent bank secrecy and limited regulatory capabilities, continues to be one of the most attractive financial centers in the Caribbean for money launderers. As such, Antigua has a growing international reputation as a haven for dirty money."[17]

This situation, which carried on through the end of the decade, resulted in a dark cloud hanging over the Caribbean nation's offshore banking operations (with some forty-seven offshore banks and thousands of international business corporations), and strained relations with the United States, the UK, and other Caribbean nations. In March 1999, the U.S. Treasury warned banks and other financial institutions to treat transactions with Antigua with extra caution because of concerns that it was softening its laws against money laundering. Accordingly, the U.S. Treasury noted that recent amendments by Antigua to its legislation "further erode supervision, stiffen bank secrecy and weaken international law enforcement and judicial co-operation."[18]

UK BANKS WARNED OVER DEALINGS WITH ANTIGUA

George Graham and Canute James

The British government last night warned UK banks to be on their guard when dealing with financial institutions from Antigua. The Caribbean island had on Friday announced an overhaul of its banking supervision board and promised to improve its money laundering legislation.

Although the UK Treasury welcomed Antigua's promised overhaul of its financial services rules, its announcement implies that international suspicion about the island financial centre continues unabated. The US Treasury had already issued a warning to US banks on dealings with Antigua, which joins the Seychelles and Austria as the only two countries singled out for criticism by the international community because of their money laundering rules. The US State Department identified Antigua in a recent report as a money-laundering centre and a key transit point for South American cocaine bound for the US and Europe.

In London yesterday Patricia Hewitt, economic secretary to the Treasury, said: "The UK is determined to take a global approach to combat money laundering. As part of the G7 initiative on financial crime, we have signalled our willingness to identify jurisdictions which fail to meet minimum standards."

UK banks are to be encouraged to report any suspicious transactions involving Antiguan institutions to the National Criminal Intelligence Service, especially large or unusual movements for which there is no obvious economic purpose.

However, there is no obligation to report all transactions involving Antigua, or to avoid dealings with Antiguan citizens. The Antiguan government

(continued)

last week named a new board of overseers for offshore banks, replacing members when the US had accused it of being tied to the institutions they were supposed to regulate.

Lester Bird, the prime minister, also promised changes to the island's money laundering legislation, responding to US and UK complaints that it had recently weakened measures intended to stop criminal activity.

He confirmed that Antigua was receiving help from a British Foreign Office consultant.

Antigua has launched several successive efforts to clean up its offshore financial businesses. It closed down several Russian-owned offshore banks which government officials said had laundered money for the Russian mafia.

But last year it amended its laws again to strengthen bank secrecy and restrict co-operation with overseas law enforcement authorities.

The British government said last night this seriously eroded the ability of Antigua to counter the threat from money launderers. Antigua also drew the attention of British regulators as the home of the European Union Bank, the subject of a Bank of England warning two years ago after it advertised for deposits on the Internet, though it was not authorized in the UK. The bank has since collapsed.

Source: *Financial Times,* April 19, 1999, p. 7.

Antigua's reputation in regard to money laundering and like-minded activities was initially tarnished in the mid–1990s when it was revealed that weapons purchased for the Antiguan military made their way to the farm of Gonzalo Rodriguez Gacha, one of the top members of Colombia's Medellín cartel. As one observer commented: "The regionwide and complex relationship among drug trafficking, arms trading, and government corruption was evident from the murky involvement of an Israeli 'special envoy' appointed by the government of Antigua and of an Israeli specialist in guerrilla warfare who had previously been sought in Colombia for training narcoterrorists; from the possible Panamanian links to the affair; and from reports that a training camp was to be financed by the Medellín cartel for Colombian and Sri Lankan Tamil terrorists."[19]

Concerns about Antigua's involvement in money laundering operations were reinforced by the 1996 findings of British authorities who had been invited by the Caribbean government to examine its offshore incorporating statute. Deficiencies discovered included no notification provisions for a change in beneficial ownership of an offshore entity, no provision to revoke an entity's license, and no independent vetting of applications for bank licenses.

The findings of the British authorities and growing international pressure on the Antiguan government led to the December 1996 enactment of a comprehensive money laundering prevention act that criminalized the laundering of the proceeds of specified serious crimes, such as blackmail, counterfeiting, drugs, extortion, false accounting, forgery, fraud, illegal deposit taking, robbery, terrorism, and theft. The law also required record keeping by banks and nonbank financial institutions, mandated the reporting of suspicious transactions, and provided for the establishment of a Supervisory Authority to receive and analyze suspicious transaction reports. Furthermore, it included statutes for asset forfeiture and a mechanism for international legal assistance.

Even though Antigua's government has passed a substantial anti–money laundering law, its implementation is lacking. The government was slow to staff the Supervisory Authority and the Ministry of Finance was glacial in providing guidance to implement the mandated suspicious transaction reporting requirements. Furthermore, efforts were made to weaken some of the new regulations in 1999, which raised concerns that the government did not take matters too seriously.

An additional factor in Antigua's less-than-stellar reputation in dealing with money laundering is its lack of cooperation with the authorities of other countries in dealing with a number of investigations, including the collapse in 1997 of an Internet bank, the European Union Bank (EUB) of Antigua Limited, and the Caribbean American Bank. EUB failed in August 1997, when the two Russian founders of the bank absconded with $10 million of depositors' funds. After the two left Antigua and the bank ceased operations, the government revoked its license. Cooperation with a U.S. investigation, however, led to only limited access to bank records due to Antigua's strict bank secrecy laws. In the case of the Caribbean American Bank, a director of that Antiguan-registered institution was convicted in the United States of laundering $3.4 million in advanced fee fraud proceeds in 1997. Antiguan authorities were slow to provide records of the bank. One of the most glaring examples of Antigua's difficulty with money laundering was noted in a U.S. government report:

> *Since April 1994, US Department of Justice attorneys have attempted to work with the GOAB [Government of Antigua and Barbuda] to enforce a May 1994 criminal forfeiture order for USD 7.5 million entered by the United States District Court in Boston against John E. Fitzgerald, a convicted racketeer and drug money launderer. Instead of enforcing the forfeiture order, the GOAB appears to have obtained the funds from Swiss American Bank where the funds were on deposit. A larger portion of funds were then transferred directly into the national treasury. Repeated requests by the US to Antigua for explanations and documents have gone unanswered, except for representations that the relevant bank records had disappeared in a hurricane.*[20]

In 1999, following the U.S. Treasury warning about Antigua, the government of Prime Minister Lester Bird pledged to cooperate with the United States to ease concerns about money laundering in the Caribbean country's offshore banks. Moreover, promises were made to amend Antigua's legislation and strengthen the supervision of the offshore financial sector. Efforts by the Antiguan government finally bore fruit by 2000, when the Caribbean country was not placed on an international blacklist of noncooperative countries that lacked adequate transparency and disclosure. A report from the Financial Action Task Force (FATF), an international anti–money laundering organization discussed later in this chapter, stated: "The authorities of Antigua and Barbuda have achieved impressive results, especially since 1999, in revising the anti–money laundering framework, in accordance with the FATF 40 recommendations."[21]

Russian Tales

In the second half of the 1990s Russia emerged as a problem country for money laundering, clearly posing a risk for international banks. The breakup of the Soviet Union, the upheaval of a new capitalist order, the emergence of a powerful criminal class, and ongoing political uncertainty in the 1990s provided the necessary conditions to encourage large-scale money laundering operations. As Stephen Handelman, author of *Comrade Criminal,* noted in 1995: "Criminal cartels, believed by the police to control as much as 40 percent of Russia's wealth, infiltrate stock exchanges and the real estate market. Gangsters not only open bank accounts; they open banks."[22] This sentiment was reflected by *The Economist* in 1999, which when commenting on the Russian laundering of IMF funds stated: "[T]he scandal has confirmed Russia's status as the world's leading kleptocracy."[23]

Since 1992 the IMF has lent over $20 billion to Russia to assist in the Yeltsin government's reform of the economy and help stave off financial collapse. Throughout the 1990s, the Russian economy was largely in disequilibrium and lurched from crisis to crisis. With an external debt burden of around $150 billion, debt default continued to threaten. Consequently, Western governments, the IMF, and international banks were willing to lend money to Russia to avoid an economic crash and any concomitant threat of a slide into political chaos that could pave the way for a return of the Communists.

Although the Russian economy is largely privatized, considerable problems have continued to prevent a shift to self-sustaining economic growth. These include poorly defined business regulations, a lack of transparency and disclosure in financial transactions, ongoing interference by government officials, and the strength of criminal organizations that have come to permeate widespread sectors of the Russian economy. The opaque nature of conducting business in Russia even existed within the government. This was made evident in 1999 when it was revealed that Russia's central bank had apparently moved IMF funds out of Russia to Fimaco, a firm it controlled in the Channel Islands, without informing the international organization. In February 1999, Sergei Dubinin, the former head of the Russian central bank, acknowledged that Russia transferred part of its hard currency reserves to Fimaco between 1993 and 1997 to try to shield them from foreign creditors. Russia's prosecutor general alleged that up to $50 billion of central bank reserves may have been transferred offshore over the past five years.

Many of the problems associated with Russia and money laundering stem from the treatment of that country as a special case by the IMF and international banks. Simply stated, no one in the West wanted Russia's experiment with democracy and capitalism to fail. Consequently, lending to Russia had political undertones. This also meant that lending criteria for Russia were lax. The overall nature of the problem was compounded by the encouragement given international banks to establish operations in Russia by Western governments. Additionally, international banking in Russia was lucrative for those who understood the environment and were able to stomach a high degree of volatility in terms of the economic and political situations. At the same time, setting up shop in Russia carried substantial risks, the least of which was knowing your customer.

As *The Economist* noted: "[I]t is virtually impossible to tell whether the money is earned legitimately. That is because crime is not at the margin of society: it is at its very centre.... half of Russia's banks are thought to be controlled by crime syndicates."[24] All of this was brought home by the Bank of New York scandal, which erupted in 1998–99.

The Bank of New York, like many international banks, is active in moving money around the globe. In 1993, Benex International was founded by a Russian émigré, Peter Berlin. Initially involved in arranging shipments of stereos and other electronic products to Russia from the United States, according to reports Berlin eventually turned to something much more lucrative, the movement of funds out of Russia. Estimates of capital flight from Russia vary from 1992 to 1997 cumulatively to be within the $60 billion to $150 billion range. In 1996 Benex International opened an account with the Bank of New York. That bank was hardly a random choice: Berlin's wife, Lucy Edwards, was an executive at the Bank of New York and had been recently promoted to a prestigious position at the bank in London drumming up commercial clients in Russia.

Although the exact date that Benex International became involved with moving money is not known, it is evident that by 1996 it had become one of the most heavily used pipelines for sending out cash. As a U.S. Congressional Research Service report noted:

> *Between October 1998 and March 1999, around $4.2 billion was processed at the Bank of New York through accounts under the control of a company that reportedly was used by Russian businessmen to "launder" illegally obtained funds from Russia. The account was kept open to allow investigators to follow the trail of funds, and an estimated total of at least $10 billion (with some estimates going as high as $15 billion) is believed to have been processed through the account.[25]*

In 1998, however, investigations in the United States, the UK, Russia, and Italy raised a number of questions about the origin of the money flow, strongly suggesting that it came from Russian gangs operating out of northern Italy, a laundering and stock manipulation case involving another Russian émigré, and a kidnapping case in Russia. By August 1999, Berlin and Edwards were indicted on charges of operating a money transferring business without licenses in the United States, and their bank accounts were frozen. The investigation is ongoing.

The Bank of New York scandal forced many banks to reassess their involvement in Russia. The Bank of New York was not the only institution that may have been used by Benex International. Moreover, the 1998 economic crash in Russia and the external default at the same time only added incentives for banks to exit the country. Clearly these were some of the reasons behind the decision by Barclays Bank to end its twenty-five-year presence in Moscow by closing its office. The ongoing problem of money laundering in Russia resulted in the Financial Action Task Force putting the Eurasian country on an international blacklist for bankers and regulators. The FATF took this action because Russia lacked comprehensive customer identification requirements, a reliable transaction reporting system, a fully operational financial investigative unit, and effective and timely procedures for providing evidence to assist in foreign money laundering prosecutions.[26]

International Regulatory Efforts

Considering the threat that international money laundering and other forms of financial fraud pose to the security of national banking systems and, through them, national economies, efforts are being made to counter the problem through a number of international and regional efforts that share the ultimate goal of establishing an international anti–money laundering regime.[27] One of the initial forces in this regard was the Basel Committee on Banking Regulations and Supervisory Practices Statement of Principles in 1988. Working through the Bank for International Settlements, the Basel Committee encouraged banks to undertake to know their customers, spot suspicious transactions, and cooperate completely with law enforcement agencies. Many of these concerns were taken up in the broader-gauged 1988 United Nations Convention Against Illicit Traffic in Narcotic Drugs and Psychotropic Substances (also referred to as the Vienna Convention). The UN convention commits signatory countries under Article 3 to take measures to enable its competent authorities to prevent and suppress the acquisition, possession, transfer, or laundering of proceeds derived from or used in illicit drug trafficking.

Probably the most significant group that emerged within the anti–money laundering regime is the Financial Action Task Force (FATF). The FATF was established at the G–7 Economic Summit in Paris in 1989. It is an intergovernmental body whose purpose is to develop and promote policies to combat money laundering. The underlying idea behind the organization is that money laundering is a complex economic crime that cannot be effectively controlled by conventional law enforcement methods. Consequently, it is important to pool the resources of law enforcement agencies with those of regulatory agencies, central banks, and finance ministries. This provides a comprehensive approach to a complex problem. The FATF has twenty-six national members (mainly OECD countries) and two international organizations—the European Commission and the Gulf Cooperation Council.

The initial work of the FATF was to help member countries to adopt anti–money laundering legislation, ultimately creating an international anti–money laundering legal regime. Along these lines, it released in April 1990 forty recommendations seeking to establish a global consensus on legislation and banking actions to curb the flow of drug proceeds through banking and nonbanking financial institutions. While much of the FATF-suggested legislation was adopted, the organization also conducted mutual evaluations of its members. This was done to measure how each country had done in implementing its new laws. Another FATF function is to provide technical assistance to groups outside of its ranks. Along these lines, the FATF has worked with the Caribbean Financial Action Task Force, the Council of Europe, the Offshore Group of Banking Supervisors, the Asia Pacific Group on Money Laundering (APG), and the Organization of American States. In 1997, the FATF created a regional ad hoc group on Central and Eastern Europe to support, coordinate, and exchange information between it and the nations that were formerly in the Eastern bloc and that are in the process of transition from centrally planned economies to market-based ones.

Has the FATF worked? Although it cannot be argued that the FATF has halted all money laundering operations in international financial flows, it has a positive impact in creating a more uniform set of anti–money laundering international rules and regulations. Through two rounds of mutual country evaluations, it has forced countries to not only implement laws, but to practice them as well. Equally important, the FATF has provided an international forum of cooperation against international money laundering that has stimulated greater cross-border law enforcement actions, as in the case of U.S. and Colombian investigations against the Cali cartel's money laundering operations in the early 1990s. Furthermore, the FATF has sought to work with the international banking community and provides useful information for banks, such as its annual money laundering typologies report.

The FATF was also successful in compiling a highly controversial blacklist of countries and territories that have lacked in cooperation and in dealing with the problem of money laundering. The purpose of the blacklist was to "name and shame" countries seen as money laundering havens. A total of fifteen countries were placed on the list, including the Bahamas, Cayman Islands, Dominica, Panama, Israel, Lebanon, Liechtenstein, Russia, the Philippines, Cook Islands, Marshall Islands, St. Kitts-Nevis, Nauru, and Niue. Despite protests from the targeted countries, most governments responded to the blacklisting by trying to bring their laws into line with the FATF guidelines on transparency, international cooperation, and reporting of suspicious transactions.[28] At the same time, a number of banks cut off correspondent relations with banks in targeted countries, giving the blacklist a sting.

The task of establishing a functioning international anti–money laundering regime is difficult. Yet money laundering and international crime are not likely to disappear, and they are factors with which bankers will be forced to contend. Consequently, banks will have to continue to know their customers, maintain internal compliance programs, and be on the lookout for suspicious transactions.

Citibank Mexico Team: The Salinas Accounts

Ivey

*David T. A. Wesley prepared this case under the supervision of Professor Henry W. Lane
solely to provide material for class discussion. The authors do not intend to illustrate
either effective or ineffective handling of a managerial situation. The authors may have
disguised certain names and other identifying information to protect confidentiality.*

*Ivey Management Services prohibits any form of reproduction, storage or
transmittal without its written permission. This material is not covered under
authorization from CanCopy or any reproduction rights organization. To order copies
or request permission to reproduce materials, contact Ivey Publishing, Ivey
Management Services, c/o Richard Ivey School of Business, The University of Western
Ontario, London, Ontario, Canada, N6A 3K7; phone (519) 661-3208; fax (519) 661-
3882; e-mail cases@ivey.uwo.ca.*

> Mexico was … a country of smoke and mirrors,
> where yesterday's heroes are today's villains and
> today's champions of justice may be tomorrow's
> crooks.
>
> *Andres Oppenheimer—Senior
> Correspondent,* Miami Herald[2]

O n July 4, 1995, Amy Elliott, head of Citibank's Mexico Team, had just
returned from Switzerland, where Swiss narcotics agents were encouraging her to lay a trap for the wife of one of her clients,[3] Raul Salinas, who
had been arrested in Mexico a few months earlier on charges of murder, illegal enrichment and laundering money for the Mexican drug cartel.

The fate of one of her former employees, who had recently been sentenced
to 10 years imprisonment for managing the account of a convicted money launderer, provided food for thought. If she co-operated with narcotics agents, perhaps she could avoid the same fate. On the other hand, she had to consider her
obligation to her client, who, as the brother of Mexico's most popular president in recent history, was believed by some to have been falsely accused by
his political enemies. Another consideration was whether, by co-operating with
authorities, Citibank could be liable for violating Swiss bank secrecy laws.[4]

Company Profile

Citibank was established in 1812, and by the end of the 19th century had
grown to become the largest bank in the United States, and the first to establish a foreign trading department. In 1914 the bank established its first overseas office in Buenos Aires, Argentina, and shortly thereafter began to
aggressively expand across South America and Asia. In 1929, Citibank
became the largest bank in the world.

(continued)

By the early 1990s, Citibank had grown to more than 3,400 branches in 100 countries, and was considered the world's most global bank. Of the company's 90,000 employees, more than 50,000 resided outside the United States.

In Mexico, Citibank had more than 65 years of history, and was the only foreign bank permitted to operate in that country following the nationalization of Mexico's banks in 1982. In the 1990s, more than 20 per cent of the bank's revenues came from Latin America.

The Mexico Team

Amelia Grovas Elliott, a Cuban American, began working for Citibank in 1967. In 1983 she became head of the bank's Mexico Team, consisting of 10 private bankers, at Citibank's New York office. The Mexico Team specifically sought out clients with a net worth of at least $5 million and at least $1 million of available liquid assets to invest with the bank. In the early 1990s, the Team managed accounts for about 250 Mexican clients.

Private banking services included deposit taking, mutual fund investing, personal trust, estate administration, funds transfers and establishing offshore accounts and trusts. Service was very personal. Bankers typically knew their clients well and understood their specific needs. Elliott explained:

> We visit our clients 10 to 12 times a year in their country. They come back three or four times to New York. We see our clients a lot. It's obviously a growing kind of thing and not just in knowing your customer, but making sure you know what's going on. Because the relationship can grow deeper the more you know the person, we go to their homes, visit their family, go to their business, and remember birthdays. It just increases the depth.[5]

Raul Salinas

On May 11, 1992, Elliott received a phone call from the Mexican Minister of Agriculture, Carlos Hank Rhon, one of the wealthiest men in Mexico and a long-standing client of Citibank. He wished to arrange a meeting between Elliott and Raul Salinas, brother of Mexican President and Harvard educated economist, Carlos Salinas. Salinas was in need of private banking services, and the agriculture minister had recommended Citibank.

John Reed, CEO of Citibank, was a personal friend of President Carlos Salinas, and Citibank had been working for some time to further its Mexican operations.[6] Securing the account of the president's brother could only serve to advance the Mexico Team's profile and possibly Elliott's career.

Later in the week, Salinas flew to New York to discuss his financial needs. There, Salinas stated that he had recently sold a construction company and needed a bank to provide confidential investment of the proceeds. Salinas explained:

> I do not want anyone in Mexico to know that I am moving large amounts of money out of the country. If the public finds out that I am not reinvesting the money in Mexico, it could harm my brother's political career.[7]

(continued)

As such, confidentiality was a prime consideration. Rhon told Salinas that he believed Citibank could provide the type of confidentiality that Salinas was seeking. Apparently, Salinas was assured that indeed it could.

Normally when new accounts were opened, the bank followed strict procedures that made the process somewhat bureaucratic. Elliott explained:

> The relationship manager would be discussing the prospective client with his or her supervisor throughout the entire process. It's a complex kind of sale, so it has a fairly long lead-time, especially if you're not physically located in Mexico.[8]

In order to smooth the way as much as possible for Salinas, bank references and background checks were waived. Citibank policy allowed for such exceptions. In Salinas' case the waiver was allowed on grounds that he was a "known client and referred by a very valuable client of long standing." In most cases bank references did not provide useful information anyway and were viewed as a mere formality. Furthermore, this was the president's brother. Elliott noted:

> You can trust some Mexican officials, some not. If you get to know them, it's fairly obvious if they can be trusted. Public figures in Mexico are talked about a great deal. Generally speaking, it's a fairly small and tight upper crust.[9]

On May 26, 1992, Salinas was approved as a Citibank client. A chequing account was opened at the New York office under the name of his accountant, Juan Guillermo Gomez Gutierrez.

The Salinas Accounts

An "investment optimization" strategy had to be devised that would both conceal the identity of the account holder and produce a superior return on investment. In order to avoid a potential information leak, nobody at Citibank Mexico would be advised about the accounts.

Deposits made in Mexico would be done in the name of Salinas' fiancée, Patricia Rios Castañon. Rios delivered cheques, denominated in pesos, of between US$3 million and $5 million. The teller delivered the cheques, which were made payable to Citibank, to a manager at the branch, who then wired the money to New York.

Five corporations were opened in the Cayman Islands on behalf of Salinas. The main corporation was Trocca Private Investment Company, and the others were created to act as shareholders and directors of Trocca (see [Figure 1]). The principal shareholder, Tyler Ltd., received the transferred funds in a concentration account in New York where they were converted from Mexican pesos to U.S. dollars. The concentration account was designed as a transfer point of funds wired from Mexico to offshore corporations, and allowed the holder to mix both personal and business deposits in one account. The only record that showed Salinas as the owner of the company was held in Cayman where bank secrecy laws could protect his identity.

(continued)

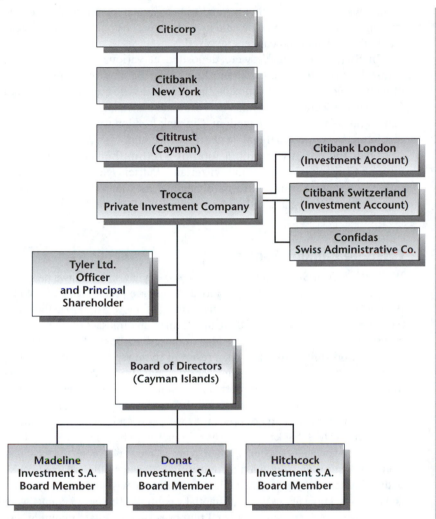

FIGURE 12.1 Trocca and Related Companies

Source: U.S. General Accounting Office.

From Trocca, funds were transferred to Citibank Switzerland. Salinas was assured that, while the scheme was complicated, it provided the best protection of his identity. She explained:

> By using a corporation in Cayman as the account holder, the source of ownership will be concealed from people who have no reason to know.
>
> The reason for the account in Switzerland is their very strict secrecy laws. A Swiss banker can be put in jail if they divulge the confidentiality of the name of an account.[10]

Salinas understood the value of the Swiss accounts. He had visited Switzerland on many occasions to take part in equestrian competitions in Lucerne, and to visit his two nephews who were attending school there.

(continued)

Salinas was well aware of Switzerland's international reputation for secrecy, and since his identity would be held in confidence, he could have direct contact with the banks and bankers involved.

In Switzerland, funds were deposited at various banks, including Citibank Zurich, Banque Pictet and Julius Baer Bank. Trocca, not Salinas, officially held the funds at Citibank Zurich. Funds were transferred back and forth between Zurich and London in order to take advantage of higher money market rates in the United Kingdom. Citibank London was not made aware that Salinas was the beneficial owner of the account.

Over the next two years, a total of $100 million was transferred through Citibank to accounts in Switzerland. Patricia Rios Castañon, who, in 1993, became Salinas' third wife, handled most of the transactions. A large portion was transferred on November 30, 1994, the last day of Carlos Salinas' presidency.

Offshore Banking Secrecy

While the United States had its own bank secrecy laws, these laws provided less protection than most offshore jurisdictions (see [Table 1]). Federal law required that banks report all financial transactions above $10,000 to the Internal Revenue Service (IRS). If the bank deemed any transaction to be suspicious in nature, the bank was also required to contact the Criminal Investigation Unit of the IRS. As a result of these reporting requirements, banks operating in the United States were exempted from liability to their customers for reporting account information, even without customer consent.[11]

Investors have used the services of offshore banking in jurisdictions that provided greater protection of privacy, as well as tax advantages and limited legal liability. U.S. banks used offshore branches to hold information about the beneficial owner of accounts, where bank secrecy laws protected the client from disclosure. This provided a competitive advantage that allowed banks with offshore branches to attract clients who did not wish banking regulators and others to know about their substantial wealth. While such accounts were usually used for legitimate and legal purposes such as estate planning, tax shelters and reduced legal liability, they have also attracted those engaged in illegal activity, such as money laundering, investment fraud and tax evasion.

The main instrument for concealing wealth was the Private Investment Company (PIC). These were shell companies registered by banks in the offshore jurisdictions and used solely to hold the funds of clients. PICs, since they were not in the client's name, could be used to transfer funds in any country of the world without drawing the attention of regulators or others to the beneficial owner. Information about the beneficial owner was held secretly and safely in the offshore branch.

While many offshore jurisdictions provided the aforementioned benefits, the U.S. General Accounting Office[12] identified nine where U.S. bank subsidiaries and branches held substantial accounts (in excess of $1 billion). These were the Bahamas, Bahrain, the Cayman Islands, the Channel Islands, Hong Kong, Luxembourg, Panama, Singapore and Switzerland.

(continued)

TABLE 1 Relevant Bank Secrecy Laws: United States[1]

The Right to Financial Privacy Act of 1978

... as amended, the Privacy Act provides that it shall not preclude any financial institution, or any officer, employee, or agent of a financial institution from notifying a government authority that such institution, or officer, or employee, or agent has information that may be relevant to a possible violation of any statute or regulation. Such information may include only the name or other identifying information concerning any individual or account and the nature of any suspected illegal activity.

The Bank Secrecy Act and the Currency and Foreign Transactions Reporting Act, 1970

... all domestic and foreign currency transactions of more than US$10,000 must be reported within 15 days.

... Financial institutions must file a Currency Transaction Report (CTR) for each deposit, withdrawal, exchange of currency, or other payment of transfer, by, through, or to such financial institution which involves a transaction of currency of more than $10,000.

...the Report of International Transportation of Currency or Monetary Instruments (CMIR). Every person or entity must file a CMIR who physically transports, mails, or ships, or causes to be physically transported, mailed, or shipped, currency or other monetary instruments in an aggregate amount exceeding $10,000 on any one occasion.

... financial institutions are required to maintain for a five-year period, a variety of records, such as copies of signature cards, bank statements, and checks drawn for more than US$100.

Violation of the Bank Secrecy Act provides for jail terms up to 10 years and fines from US$1,000 to US$500,000.

---

[1] Campbell, D., *International Bank Secrecy*, Sweet and Maxwell, London, 1992.

(continued)

All of these locations, with the exception of Bahrain, had regulations that required the reporting of suspicious transactions to local authorities. And, in most jurisdictions, U.S. law enforcement could gain access to individual accounts to investigate certain criminal acts. Only Bahrain, Luxembourg and Singapore did not allow access for these purposes. On the other side, without a legal mandate to provide information, bankers could face fines or imprisonment for violating secrecy laws in several jurisdictions, including the Cayman Islands and Switzerland (see [Tables 2 and 3]). Furthermore, Switzerland allowed for third parties to take civil action against banks, and as a result, many bank officials expressed concern over the liability to their banks of breaching confidentiality in these jurisdictions.[13]

A Swiss judge had the power to overturn secrecy obligations for the purpose of criminal investigations conducted in Switzerland. Under most conditions, the same was true for crimes committed outside of Switzerland, provided that international law enforcement officials formally requested assistance, and the crime was also considered illegal in Switzerland (i.e. drug trafficking). A 1977 treaty signed between Switzerland and the United States allowed for co-operation between these countries, even when the crime was not considered illegal in Switzerland.[14]

U.S. banking regulators relied heavily on self-monitoring by banks to prevent offshore accounts from being used for illegal purposes. A "know your customer" (KYC) policy was considered the most effective of the self-monitoring measures implemented by the banks. Most banks stipulated under KYC policy that clients had to submit bank references and other information related to the origin of their wealth. Banks also monitored accounts for unusual or large transactions that could be a sign of illegal activity. However, a study by the Federal Reserve Bank of New York concluded that "in general ... client profiles contained little or no documentation on the client's background, source of wealth, expected account activity, and client contacts and visits by bank representatives,"[15] even though such information was believed to be critical in preventing the illegal use of offshore accounts.

The Hobbs Act

The Hobbs Act was a federal law enacted in the United States in 1951 to allow prosecution of corrupt American government officials. Specific unlawful activities under the Hobbs Act included extortion, fraud against a foreign bank, kidnapping, narcotics and robbery. The law could be used against foreign nationals and institutions if any aspect of illegal activity occurred in the United States. Therefore, if the proceeds of drug trafficking were either held in the United States or transferred through the United States, the law's jurisdiction would become extra-territorial.[16]

In 1994 Antonio Giraldi, a former banker in Elliott's Mexico Team, was arrested and tried for violations of the Hobbs Act. At the time, Giraldi was employed by American Express Bank International. In 1989, Giraldi secured

(continued)

a client who deposited $21 million over a very short period and was later discovered by U.S. federal agents to be laundering money for the Mexican drug cartel. Elliott was asked to testify against her former employee.

Elliott explained to the federal court that it was a banker's responsibility to know the client, and that an experienced banker should be able to spot irregularities in an account. Citibank had specific guidelines used to protect the bank from becoming an instrument for drug money laundering:

> "Know your client," at least in our bank, is part of the culture. It's part of the way you do things. It's part of the way you conduct yourself. If you come in with a prospect or the name of a prospect, you will be sure to be asked, "Who is this person, what do they do, who introduced them to you," by at least three or four people higher than you. It's just the way it is … It's too risky to not do the due diligence, not to know who you are dealing with.[17]

No direct evidence was provided that proved Giraldi knew of the illicit origins of the money. Nevertheless, the court convicted Giraldi and sentenced him to 10 years imprisonment on the grounds that he had been negligent in not determining the source of his client's wealth. In Giraldi's case, "willful blindness" was deemed the same as having knowledge.[18] A female colleague who helped Giraldi with the accounts was also sentenced to three years in prison.[19]

The Murder Investigation

On February 13, 1995, the lead story in the Mexican news briefs that were delivered daily to Elliott's office by e-mail reported that Raul Salinas was under investigation for the murder of his brother-in-law, Jose Ruiz Massieu. As Salinas was one of Elliott's most important clients, she called him. Salinas claimed:

> Those allegations are absolutely false. They are lies made up by my brother's enemies. He made some unpopular decisions in order to modernize Mexico and this attack against me and my family is a result of that.[20]

Although it seemed unlikely that the former president's brother could be formally charged, she decided to prepare a profile which, under bank policy, should have been completed when Salinas first became a client. Filling out the form, it became apparent that she had very little information about Salinas and the sale of his construction company. She had never visited the company, and did not even know its name.

On February 27, Salinas was arrested and formally charged with murder by Mexican authorities. A few days later, Mario Ruiz Massieu, the victim's brother and former chief investigator in the case, was arrested by U.S. Customs agents at the Newark Airport, also in connection with the murder. Ruiz Massieu, a professional civil servant, had somehow amassed millions of dollars, which had recently been deposited in a Texas bank. Within days allegations began to surface that both men had developed close ties with the Mexican drug cartel.[21]

(continued)

TABLE 2 Relevant Bank Secrecy Laws: Cayman Islands[1]

Banks and Trusts Companies Law, 1989

… provides for the preservation of secrecy on the part of the Inspector of Banks and Trust Companies and any person authorized to assist him in his functions.

It prohibits the disclosure of any information, by the Inspector or his staff, of the affairs of a licensee or any customer of a licensee and provides a penalty of a fine not exceeding CI $10,000, or a term of imprisonment not exceeding one year, or both for contravention of this law.

Confidential Relationships Law, 1976

… as amended, provides that, if any person in possession of confidential information, however obtained, divulges it or attempts, offers, or threatens to divulge it to any person not entitled to possession, or who willfully obtains or attempts to obtain confidential information is guilty of an offense and is liable on summary conviction to a fine not exceeding CI $5,000, or for imprisonment of a term not exceeding two years, or both.

In addition, where such person solicits such information for himself or another for reward or being a professional person entrusted with such information, the above mentioned penalties are doubled.

Section 3(2)(b) of the Law provides a number of cases in which the law has no application. These are as follows:

1. Any professional person acting in the normal course of business or with consent, express or implied, of the relevant principal;
2. A constable of the rank of Inspector or above investigating an offense committed or alleged to have been committed within the jurisdiction;
3. A constable of the rank of Inspector or above, specifically authorized by the Governor in that regard, investigating an offense committed or alleged to have been committed outside the Islands which offense, if committed in the Islands, would be an offense against its laws; or

(continued)

TABLE 2 *(continued)*

4. The Financial Secretary, the Inspector, or in relation to particular information specified by the Governor, such other person as the Governor may authorize;

5. A bank in any proceedings, cause, or matter when and to the extent to which it is reasonably necessary for the protection of the bank's interest, either as against its customers or against third parties in respect of transactions of the bank for, or with, its customer, and

6. The relevant professional person with the approval of the Financial Secretary when necessary for the protection of himself or any other person against crime.

… as amended, provides in section 3A that, where it applies, the following provisions shall apply:

Whenever a person intends or is required to give in evidence in, or in connection with, any proceeding been tried, inquired into, or determined by any court, tribunal, or other authority, any confidential information within the meaning of the Law, he shall, before doing so, apply for directions … Upon hearing an application under subsection (2), a judge shall direct:

1. That evidence be given; or

2. That evidence shall not be given, or

3. That the evidence be given subject to conditions which he may specify whereby the confidentiality of the information is safeguarded …

… a bank should disclose information … Where disclosure is under compulsion by … the Mutual Legal Assistance Treaty (signed by the United Kingdom, United States, and Cayman Islands), or the Misuse of Drugs Law (of the Cayman Islands).

---

[1] Campbell, D., *International Bank Secrecy*, Sweet and Maxwell, London, 1992.

(continued)

TABLE 3 Relevant Swiss Bank Secrecy Laws and Regulations[1]

... the right to privacy refers to a person's right to protection of his or her person in the sense referred to by article 28(1) of the Swiss Civil Code ... Violation of the right to privacy is also tantamount to a tort under articles 41 et seq. of the Code of Obligations. Thus a bank can not only be held liable on contractual grounds but also toward third parties.

Article 47 of the Federal Law on Banks and Savings Banks of November 8, 1934
As amended,

1. Whoever divulges a secret entrusted to him or of which he has become aware in his capacity as officer, employee, mandatory, liquidator, or commissioner of a bank, as representative of the banking commission, officer, or employee of a recognized auditing company and whoever tries to induce others to violate professional secrecy, shall be punished by imprisonment for not more than 6 months or by a fine of not more than 50,000 Swiss francs.

2. If the act was committed by negligence, the penalty shall be a fine not exceeding 30,000 Swiss francs.

3. The violation of secrecy remains punishable even after termination of the official or employment relationship or the exercise of the profession.

4. Remaining reserved are federal and cantonal provisions concerning the duty to testify in court to give information to a government authority.

(continued)

TABLE 3 (continued)

Swiss Penal Code, Article 305 bis

1. Whosoever undertakes actions which lend themselves to defeat the ascertainment of origin, the discovery or collection of assets which, as he knows or must assume, emanate from crime, will be subject to punishment by imprisonment or a fine.

2. In severe cases punishment is penal servitude up to five years or imprisonment. Added to this penalty of detention is a fine of up to 1 million francs. A severe case is if the perpetrator:
   a) acts as a member of a criminal organization;
   b) acts as a member of a criminal organization whose purpose is the continued practice of money laundering;
   c) realizes a large turnover or considerable profit from professional money laundering activities.

3. The perpetrator will also be subject to sentencing if he commits the principal act of violation abroad and such act is also punishable in the place of perpetration.

Lack of Due Diligence in Financial Transactions

Whosoever professionally accepts, keeps in safe custody, assists in the investment or transfer of assets which are the property of others and fails to apply the relative due diligence called for in establishing the identity of the economic beneficiary, is subject to punishment by imprisonment of up to one year or a fine.

---

[1] Campbell, D., *International Bank Secrecy*, Sweet and Maxwell, London, 1992.

(continued)

In early March, Citibank's vice-president of legal affairs was contacted by a senior official at the bank and asked to investigate the Salinas accounts. Elliott was instructed to immediately report any activity on Salinas' accounts to the vice-president of legal affairs.

During the summer, the Swiss federal prosecutor and agents of the Swiss Central Narcotics Division contacted the executive vice-president of Citibank's office in Switzerland. They reported that at one of Salinas' residences in Mexico City, Mexican authorities had discovered phony identification which linked Salinas to a safety deposit box at Citibank Switzerland. The safety deposit box was believed to contain documentation valuable to the investigation that was being conducted by Mexican authorities.

Citibank Switzerland referred the matter to Elliott, who met with Swiss narcotics agents shortly thereafter. A senior agent asked Elliott to make arrangements with Patricia Rios de Salinas to remove any documents that were being held in the safety deposit box. She was to use the pretext that they were no longer secure due to an internal investigation by the bank. Since the agents, under Swiss law, were not permitted to enter the bank in order to seize the contents of the box, they planned to arrest Rios, documents in hand, while she was leaving the bank. The Swiss federal prosecutor asked Elliot to not discuss the matter with Citibank's vice-president of legal affairs, among others.

An article in the June 24 *New York Times*, "Score One for Salinas,"[22] revived doubts about Salinas' guilt. "We will get Mario!" began the fifth paragraph, which quoted a Mexican government official. The article continued:

> The [June 22] ruling of the U.S. magistrate in Newark, Ronald J. Hedges, also revived broader questions about the case against Raul Salinas.... Most of the witnesses whose credibility Hedges challenged in New Jersey when they implicated Mario Ruiz Massieu are lined up in Mexico to testify against Raul Salinas.... Hedges sharpened the public focus on doubts that have long existed about changes, gaps and contradictions in the testimony.... The most important witness left against Salinas is a congressional aide ... [who] was probably the first person Hedges had in mind when he complained of being handed testimony from witnesses who changed their stories, contradicted themselves and said they had been tortured into confessing.

The U.S. magistrate further criticized Mexican prosecutors for having "picked and chosen" from testimony given against Salinas, and for having "glossed over" testimony that called into question the credibility of the witnesses.

Perhaps Salinas had been telling the truth. Perhaps this was a ploy by his family's enemies to undo the reforms begun by Raul's brother. Furthermore, neither Mexican nor Swiss authorities could offer any evidence linking Raul, or anyone in his family, to drug trafficking.

However, any feelings of vindication had to be balanced with knowledge of the fate of Giraldi and Elliott's testimony against him. The court, when passing sentence, had declared:

(continued)

A rational jury could have found it incredible that carelessness and honest mistakes could account for the complexity required to give the transactions the appearance of legitimacy.

The court's opinion was largely based on Elliott's testimony about Citibank's meticulous "Know Your Customer" policy, a policy that she herself may have violated.

[1]*This case has been written on the basis of published sources only. Consequently, the interpretation and perspectives presented in this case are not necessarily those of Citibank or any of its employees. Many of the events documented in this case were adapted from "Private Banking: Raul Salinas, Citibank, and Alleged Money Laundering,"* United States General Accounting Office, *October 1998.*

[2]*Oppenheimer, A., Bordering on Chaos, Little Brown & Co., New York, 1996.*

[3]*Raul Salinas' Testimony, "Murder, Money, and Mexico: The rise and fall of the Salinas Brothers,"* The Corporation for Public Broadcasting, *1998. Also see "How a Mover and Shaker Manoeuvred His Millions,"* The New York Times News Service, *June 2, 1996.*

[4]*Under article 28(1) of the Swiss Civil Code, a bank could be held liable, both on contractual grounds and by third parties, for violating a client's right to privacy.*

[5]*Amelia Elliott quotations throughout this case were adapted from official testimony given by Amelia Elliott in United States vs. Antonio Giraldi, May 12, 1994, cited in "Murder, Money, and Mexico: The rise and fall of the Salinas Brothers,"* The Corporation for Public Broadcasting, *1998.*

[6]*"How a Mover and Shaker Manoeuvred His Millions,"* The New York Times News Service, *June 2, 1996.*

[7]*Raul Salinas quotations throughout this case were adapted from official testimony given by Raul Salinas to Swiss prosecutors on December 6, 1995, cited in "Murder, Money, and Mexico: The rise and fall of the Salinas Brothers,"* The Corporation for Public Broadcasting, *1998.*

[8]*United States vs Antonio Giraldi, May 12, 1994, cited in "Murder, Money, and Mexico: The rise and fall of the Salinas Brothers,"* The Corporation for Public Broadcasting, *1998.*

[9]Ibid.

[10]*Ibid.*

[11]*Campbell, D.,* International Bank Secrecy, *Sweet and Maxwell, London, 1992.*

[12]*The General Accounting Office is the investigative arm of the U.S. House of Representatives.*

[13]*"Money Laundering: Regulatory Oversight of Offshore Private Banking Activities,"* United States General Accounting Office, *June 1998.*

[14]*EWJ Newsletters, Grendelmeier, Jenny, and Partners, Switzerland, 1998.*

[15]*"Money Laundering: Regulatory Oversight of Offshore Private Banking Activities,"* United States General Accounting Office, *June 1998.*

[16]*"U.S. Laundering Law Applies in Salinas, other Corruption Case,"* Money Laundering Alert, *January 1996.*

[17]*United States vs Antonio Giraldi, May 12, 1994, cited in "Murder, Money and Mexico: The rise and fall of the Salinas Brothers,"* The Corporation for Public Broadcasting, *1998.*

[18]*"Business crime: Appeals court thumps money-launderer,"* International Commercial Litigation, *London, November 1996.*

[19]*"Legal Guide to White Collar Crime,"* International Financial Law Review, *London, July 1995.*

[20]*Official testimony given by Raul Salinas to Swiss prosecutors on December 6, 1995, cited in "Murder, Money and Mexico: The rise and fall of the Salinas Brothers,"* The Corporation for Public Broadcasting, *1998.*

[21]*Real-life soap opera,* Time, *March 20, 1995.*

[22]*"Score One For Salinas,"* The New York Times News Service, *June 24, 1995.*

Questions

1. What is money laundering, and why are bankers concerned about it? What are the three phases involved in laundering ill-gotten gains?
2. Considering the threat money laundering poses for international finance, what are bankers required to do to prevent this criminal act?
3. What is a suspicious transaction?
4. Suppose that you are a banker and a new customer comes in with an $8,000 cash deposit. Is this a "suspicious transaction"? Should you report it to the authorities? What risks do you run?
5. What is the significance of the Bank of Credit and Commerce International to money laundering? What are the lessons of the BCCI affair?
6. What are the consequences to a bank for failure of compliance with money laundering laws? Are there any notable cases of compliance failure?
7. What is the Financial Action Task Force? Why was it established, and what role does it play in combating money laundering?
8. What are the consequences of Russian criminal activity with regard to money laundering?

Notes

1. Bureau of International Narcotics and Law Enforcement Affairs, U.S. Department of State, *International Narcotics Control Strategy Report, 1997* (Washington, D.C.: U.S. Department of State, March 1998), p. 1.

2. Brian Butler, David Butler, and Alan Isaacs, editors, *Oxford Dictionary of Finance and Banking: From International to Personal Finance* (Oxford: Oxford University Press, 1997), p. 51.

3. Comments from Raymond Baker; see "Event Transcript: Criminal Money Laundering and Illegal Capital Flight," A Brookings Press Release, September 29, 1999, p. 2.

4. David Andelman, "The Drug Money Maze," *Foreign Affairs*, July/August 1994, p. 94.

5. Bureau of International Narcotics and Law Enforcement Affairs, *International Narcotics Control Strategy Report, 1997*, p. 2.

6. R. T. Naylor, *Hot Money and the Politics of Debt* (London: Unwin Paperbacks, 1987), pp. 21–22.

7. Barry A. K. Rider, *Fei Ch'ien Launderies—the Pursuit of Flying Money* (New York: Oceana Publications, August 1994), p. 17.

8. "Understanding Money Laundering," *The Hindu*, October 17, 2000, p. 14.

9. Robert E. Powis, *The Money Launderers: Lessons from the Drug War—How Billions of Illegal Dollars Are Washed Through Banks and Businesses* (Chicago: Probus Publishing Company, 1992), p. 290.

10. Bruce Zagaris, "Money Laundering: An International Control Problem," in Scott B. MacDonald and Bruce Zagaris, editors, *International Handbook on Drug Control* (Westport, Conn.: Greenwood Press, 1992), p. 29.

11. Jeffery Robinson, *The Laundrymen: Inside the World's Third Largest Business* (London: Pocket Books, 1998), p. 34.

12. *Ibid.*, p. 35.

13. *Ibid.*, p. 36.

14. Ibid.

15. Peter Truell and Larry Gurwin, *False Profits: The Inside Story of BCCI, the World's Most Corrupt Financial Empire* (New York: Houghton Mifflin, 1992), p. xvii.

16. Robert E. Powis, *The Money Launderers*, p. 169.

17. Bureau of International Narcotics and Law Enforcement Affairs, *International Narcotics Control Strategy Report*, 1997, p. 39.

18. Anthony P. Maingot, "The Offshore Caribbean," in Anthony Payne and Paul Sutton, editors, *Modern Caribbean Politics* (Baltimore: The Johns Hopkins University Press, 1993), p. 263. Also see Canute James, "Antigua to Act on Money Laundering," *Financial Times*, April 13, 1999, p. 8.

19. Anthony P. Maingot, "The Offshore Caribbean," p. 263.

20. Bureau of International Narcotics and Law Enforcement Affairs, *International Narcotics Control Strategy Report*, 1997, p. 39.

21. Financial Action Task Force, *Financial Action Task Force on Money Laundering: Review to Identify Non-cooperation Countries or Territories: Increasing the Worldwide Effectiveness of Anti–Money Laundering Measures* (Paris: Financial Action Task Force), June 22, 2000, p. 2.

22. Stephen Handelman, *Comrade Criminal: Russia's New Mafiya* (New Haven, Conn.: Yale University Press, 1995).

23. "Russian Organized Crime: Crime Without Punishment," *The Economist*, August 28, 1999, p. 7.

24. *Ibid.*, p. 5.

25. William H. Cooper, "Russian Capital Flight and the Banking Scandals: An Examination of Definitions and Data," Congressional Research Service Report for Congress, September 23, 1999, p. 5. Also see Timothy O'Brien and Lowell Bergman, "Tracking How Pair West from Russia to Riches," *New York Times*, October 19, 1999, p. A12.

26. Financial Action Task Force, *Financial Action Task Force on Money Laundering*, p. 9.

27. Scott B. MacDonald, "Frontiers for International Money Regulation After BCCI: International Cooperation or Fragmentation?" in *The American Society of International Law Proceedings of the Eighty-Sixth Annual Meeting, Washington, D.C., April 1–4, 1992*, pp. 191–196.

28. Edward Alden, "Blacklist Leaves A Mark on Money Laundering," *Financial Times*, December 5, 2000, p. 4.

CHAPTER 13

DERIVATIVES

The complexity and size of the derivatives market poses a unique challenge to risk managers at financial institutions. As the article explains, a derivative is a financial agreement whose value is linked to, or derived from, changes in the value of some underlying asset, such as stocks, currencies, or commodities. (In the foreign exchange market, the forwards, futures, options, and swaps described in Chapter 8 are all types of derivatives.) Companies use derivatives to help manage their exposure to imponderables such as changing interest rates and raw material prices. For example, a wheat trading company may purchase an option to buy wheat in ninety days at a price that is agreed on today, thus relieving managers of the need to worry about wheat prices over the next three months. In effect, the manager is purchasing an insurance policy for protection against the risk of higher wheat prices.

Derivatives may be used to control the risks associated with fluctuations in prices for foreign exchange, commodities, and interest rates. This is called **hedging,** a strategy used to reduce risk. For example, think of a Canadian construction company that is bidding on a project in France. Payment will be in euros over the next ten years; however, there is substantial uncertainty associated with these payments. First, the company's managers do not know whether they will win the bid and hence the contract. Second, even assuming that the company does win the bid, the timing of the payments is uncertain, since they will be linked to certain milestones in the construction process. Third, since the value of the euro fluctuates against the Canadian dollar, the company cannot know for certain how much it will earn in C$.

In this situation, an option would be ideal. The company purchases a **call option** on Canadian dollars, giving it the right but not the obligation to exchange euros for C$ in the future at a certain prespecified rate called the **strike price** or **exercise price.** Thus if the construction company fails to win the bid, or if the euro rises against the C$ to a rate higher than the strike price, the company can just throw the option in the wastebasket. It was essentially a form of insurance. On the other hand, if the company does go forward with the project and the euro/C$ rate falls below the strike price, then the company exercises the option to purchase C$ at the strike price. This enables managers to hedge against all of the risks described above, thanks to the foreign exchange options market.

The risk profiles of the option writer and purchaser are, however, fundamentally asymmetrical. The option purchaser's downside risk is limited to the premium, or price he paid for the option, while his upside potential is unlimited. If the price of the underlying asset moves against the purchaser, he simply exercises the option;

DERIVATIVES: A MIXED BAG FOR U.S. BANKS
Matt Murray

The good news for banks: Derivatives are booming. The bad news: Derivatives are back in the hot seat.

The big banks' aggressive marketing and use of derivatives is again under scrutiny, following the near-collapse of Long-Term Capital Management. Executives at several major banks have privately acknowledged that they traded with Long-Term Capital without a full overview of its risky strategies. In their eagerness to do business with the high-flying hedge fund, many banks also were willing to cut corners on fees and margin calls....

Companies such as J.P. Morgan & Co. and Chase Manhattan Corp. have been aggressively selling products designed to hedge risk throughout the long bull market. In the search for new clients, they have spread the use of derivatives from major international corporations to smaller companies, some of lower investment grade, not to mention such risky but profitable customers as hedge funds.

Derivatives, which are investments whose value is derived from underlying securities or some other asset, have become "a very important driver of earnings, an area of growth that's out of its infancy stage," says Judah Kraushaar, a bank analyst at Merrill Lynch & Co....

The total face amount of all derivatives sold by commercial banks jumped 21% to a record in the second quarter from a year earlier: to $28.2 trillion, according to the Office of the Comptroller of the Currency. That is four times the size of the market at the end of 1991. The figures for the second quarter, the most recent for which data are available, don't include Wall Street investment banks, which needn't report their sales....

Source: Wall Street Journal, September 29, 1998, p. C1.

---

his cost is equal to the premium. If the price of the underlying asset moves in his favor, he discards the option and sells the asset in the spot market, reaping the gains. His net gain is equal to his profit on the spot market asset sale, minus the premium he paid on the discarded option. From the writer's point of view, however, the opposite is true. The writer's gain is limited to the premium she received. If the purchaser does not exercise the option, then the writer has a profit equal to the premium. If the purchaser does exercise, however, then the writer has a loss equal to the difference between the current spot price of the underlying asset and the exercise price of the option (minus the premium received). Depending on the size of movements in the underlying asset market, the option writer could face a substantial loss indeed. Since most over-the-counter (OTC) options are written by financial institutions, managing the risk involved is a critical endeavor for banks worldwide.

However, derivatives may also be used for **speculation,** or taking on risk in anticipation of gains. The unique characteristic of derivatives is their ability to create exposure to a market very cheaply via high levels of leverage, either to assume risk or to reduce it. This dual nature of derivatives is what makes them so difficult to control, since it can be well nigh impossible to determine when a derivatives trade is for hedging purposes or when it is speculative.

Derivatives may be traded on regulated exchanges, as many options and futures are, or on the unregulated over-the-counter (OTC) market arranged privately between banks, corporations, hedge funds, and other big players. OTC derivatives are tailored for specific parties, and remain off the banks' balance sheet; they are also more difficult to manage, measure, and understand. Not surprisingly, it is the OTC derivatives market that has come under attack in the past decade. Certainly it has grown to spectacular proportions. (See Figure 13.1.) According to the Bank for International Settlements (BIS), the global OTC derivatives market as of June 1999 stood at a whopping $81.5 trillion (notional amount outstanding).[1] (See Table 13.1.)

Plain Vanilla Derivatives

Most derivatives are in fact of the plain vanilla variety, despite the proliferation of exotic instruments that have given the industry something of a bad name. Indeed, the plain vanilla interest rate and currency swaps that help to mitigate market risk have now become standard tools of treasury management for mainstream corporations. Once viewed as glamorous and perilous, they have now achieved wide-

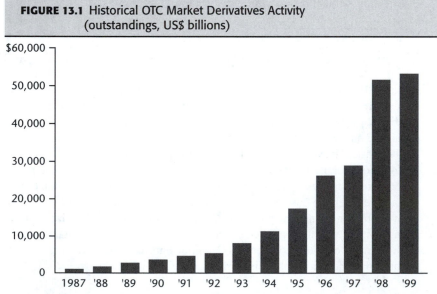

FIGURE 13.1 Historical OTC Market Derivatives Activity (outstandings, US$ billions)

Source: International Swaps & Derivatives Association, at www.isda.org.

TABLE 13.1 The Global Over-the-Counter (OTC) Derivatives Markets[1]
Amounts Outstanding (US$ billions)

	Notional Amounts		
	End-June 1998	*End-Dec. 1998*	*End-June 1999*
A. Foreign Exchange Contracts	$18,719	$18,011	$14,900
Outright forwards and forex swaps	12,149	12,063	9,541
Currency swaps	1,947	2,253	2,350
Options	4,623	3,695	3,009
B. Interest Rate Contracts[2]	$42,368	$50,015	$54,071
FRAs	5,147	5,756	7,137
Swaps	29,363	36,262	38,372
Options	7,858	7,997	8,562
C. Equity-Linked Contracts	$ 1,274	$ 1,488	$1,511
Forwards and swaps	154	146	198
Options	1,120	1,342	1,313
D. Commodity Contracts[3]	$ 452	$ 416	$441
Gold	193	182	189
Other	259	234	252
Forwards and Swaps	153	137	127
Options	106	97	125
E. Other[4]	$ 9,331	$10,388	$10,536
Grand Total	$72,144	$80,318	$81,459
Memorandum Item:			
Exchange-Traded Contracts[5]	$14,256	$13,549	$15,501

Source: BIS Quarterly Review, February 2000. www.bis.org

[1] All figures are adjusted for double-counting. Notional amounts outstanding have been adjusted by halving positions vis-à-vis other reporting dealers.

[2] Single-currency contracts only.

[3] Adjustments for double-counting estimated.

[4] For end-June 1998: positions reported by institutions participating in the triennial *Central Bank Survey of Foreign Exchange and Derivatives Market Activity* but not in the semiannual surveys; for subsequent periods: estimated positions of these reporting institutions.

[5] Sources: FOW TRADEdata; Futures Industry Association; various futures and options exchanges.

spread acceptance. Many of the complex financial instruments under the umbrella of derivatives can be broken down into four main categories:

1. **Swaps.** The two parties to a swap agree that for a certain period they will exchange regular payments. In an interest rate swap, for example, one institution pays the other a fixed rate of interest (say, 8 percent), while the counterparty pays a floating rate of interest (say, LIBOR plus $\frac{1}{2}$). This enables the company with floating-rate liabilities to turn them into fixed-rate ones, and vice versa.

OPTION VALUATION

At this point, the canny reader must be wondering what our Canadian manager had to pay for the privilege of hedging his foreign exchange risk. In fact, the purchaser of an option pays an up-front fee, or **premium,** to the writer of the option. Option premiums fluctuate so rapidly as a result of price movements in the underlying assets (in our example, the euro and the Canadian dollar) that computerized models are necessary to value them properly. To understand how options are valued, we must introduce some parameters.

Like the option purchased by our Canadian friend, most options traded in the world are **American options,** meaning that they can be exercised at any time before expiration. (**European options** are much less flexible; they may only be exercised on their expiration date.) This suggests that premiums must at least be equal to the profit an investor could obtain if he immediately exercised the option. **Intrinsic value** is the value of an option that is immediately exercised. An option buyer would never exercise an option when the underlying asset price is below the exercise price, because she would lose money. (Such an option is said to be *out of the money,* and the intrinsic value of this option is zero.) When the asset price is above the exercise price, the option is *in the money,* and its intrinsic value is the difference between the asset price and the exercise price.

An option will generally sell above its intrinsic value. For example, let's say that a call option on gold with a strike price of $400 is worth $10 when the spot price of gold, the underlying asset, is $402. The difference between the option premium and its intrinsic value is the **time value** of the option. Here, the intrinsic value is $2 ($402 − 400) and the time value is $8 ($10 − 2).

Studies indicate that option values depend on just four variables. The influence of each of these variables on a call, or buy, option can be described as follows:

1. *Exercise price.* The value of an option depends critically on the relationship between its strike price and its current asset price. The higher the exercise price, the lower the premium for call options on the same asset with an identical expiration date.

2. *Interest rate.* The value of a call option is an increasing function of the interest rate. Options reduce the opportunity or financing cost for claiming an asset. Thus as interest rates rise, this feature of options becomes more valuable, raising the price of the option.

3. *Volatility.* The value of an option increases with the volatility of the underlying asset, because options are perfectly protected against downside risk. The buyer's loss is limited to the premium paid, but his or her potential gain is unlimited.

(continued)

4. *Time to expiration.* The value of an option is an increasing function of the time to expiration, because the levering advantage mentioned earlier increases with time, and because the opportunity for the underlying asset price to far exceed the exercise price increases over time.

Three out of the four variables for determining option premiums can be measured precisely. Unfortunately, underlying asset volatility is represented by the standard deviation of returns and must be estimated. The most famous option valuation model was developed by Black and Scholes in 1973 and remains the basis for option valuation worldwide.[1] These formulas are a useful approximation, but several of their key assumptions are not valid in the real world. The limits to option pricing formulas present risks of their own.

Adapted from Bruno Solnik, *International Investments,* (Reading, Mass.: Addison Wesley, 2000), pp. 520–524.

[1]F. Black and M. Scholes, "The Pricing of Options and Corporate Liabilities," *Journal of Political Economy*, June 1973.

2. Options. An option gives the holder the right, but not the obligation, to buy/sell something in the future at a price that is determined today. For instance, a Japanese exporter wanting to protect the yen value of his dollar receivables might buy **put options** giving him the right to sell dollars in the future at a certain yen/dollar exchange rate. This would guarantee him a certain yen value in the future, while still giving him the opportunity to benefit if the dollar rises on foreign exchange markets.

3. Futures. Largely traded on regulated exchanges, these contracts are less worrisome to regulators. The buyer or seller of a futures contract puts up a margin at the outset, which acts as a buffer against subsequent price changes. The margin is then adjusted regularly, depending on whether the contract has gone down in value.

4. Forwards. Like futures, forward contracts are agreements to buy or sell at some date in the future, at a price that is agreed on today. Forwards, however, are privately arranged between counterparties and are not traded on regulated exchanges. Forward contracts do not usually involve margin calls; rather, they are founded on the general creditworthiness of the counterparties.

In fact, most common derivatives may be classified as one or a combination of these four basic types. These linear contracts (forwards, swaps, futures, and options) are essentially building blocks for more complex products, such as the exotic options described below. Any asset with derivative features may be priced as the sum of its various components. A convertible bond (a bond that is convertible into equity), for example, is equivalent to a position in a straight bond plus an option to purchase stock. Similarly, the convertible's value-at-risk (VAR) can be reconstructed from the VAR of its components.

It is important to underscore that while complex and increasingly exotic derivatives products tend to grab the attention, the bulk of banks' activities in this area is concentrated in the plain vanilla derivatives products. Interest rate swaps account for most of banks' swap activities, and fixed versus floating rate swaps are the most common form of interest rate swap. (See Figures 13.2 and 13.3 for an indication of currency and interest rate swaps volume.)

FIGURE 13.2 Interest Rate Swaps (outstandings, US$ billions)

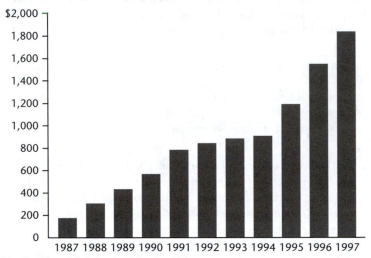

Source: International Swaps & Derivatives Association, at www.isda.org.

FIGURE 13.3 Currency Swaps (outstandings, US$ billions)

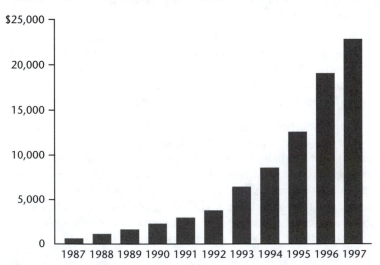

Source: International Swaps & Derivatives Association, at www.isda.org.

INTEREST RATE SWAPS

In a basic (or plain vanilla) interest rate swap, one counterparty has an initial position in a floating-rate obligation, while the other has an initial position in a fixed-rate obligation. The first counterparty can reduce its exposure to interest rate risk by swapping with the second counterparty. The second counterparty is exposed to more interest rate risk after the swap occurs and bears the risk in anticipation of a return.

Let's consider an example, in which the swap covers a five-year period and incorporates annual payments on a principal amount of $10 million. This principal is called a notional principal, because it is an amount used as a base for calculations but is not an amount actually transferred between the counterparties. Bigco agrees to pay a fixed interest rate of 10% to Bankco. Bankco in return agrees to pay to Bigco a floating rate equal to 3% above LIBOR. Figure 13.4 summarizes the payments in the swap transaction.

If LIBOR is 8% when the first payment is made, Bigco must pay $1 million (10% × $10 million) to Bankco; Bankco owes $1.1 million [(8 + 3)% × $10 million] to Bigco. Netting the two payments, Bankco pays $100,000 to Bigco. Generally, only the net payment is exchanged.

Why might firms and financial institutions participate in interest rate swaps? One motivation is to transfer interest rate risk to parties that are more willing to bear it. Second, one party may have better access to long-term fixed-rate capital markets than another. For example, in an early U.S. swap transaction in 1982, the Student Loan Marketing Association (Sallie Mae) and ITT Financial were counterparties. Sallie Mae had a portfolio consisting mostly of floating-rate assets, while ITT Financial had a portfolio consisting mostly of fixed-rate assets. Before the swap, Sallie Mae used its status to borrow in an intermediate-term fixed-rate debt market, while ITT Financial borrowed using commercial paper. After the swap, Sallie Mae paid ITT Financial's floating rate, while ITT Financial paid Sallie Mae's fixed rate. The swap gave both counterparties a better match with their assets.

Source: R. Glenn Hubbard, *Money, the Financial System, and the Economy* (Reading, Mass.: Addison Wesley, 2000) pp. 234–235.

FIGURE 13.4 Payments in a Swap Transaction

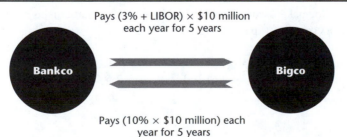

Pays (3% + LIBOR) × $10 million
each year for 5 years

Bankco   Bigco

Pays (10% × $10 million) each
year for 5 years

Source: R. Glenn Hubbard, *Money, the Financial System, and the Economy*, 3rd ed. (Reading, Mass.: Addison Wesley, 2000), p. 235.

CURRENCY SWAPS

In interest rate swaps, counterparties exchange payments on fixed-rate and floating-rate debt. In currency swaps, counterparties exchange principal amounts denominated in different currencies. For example, Le Taste Company might have French francs and want to swap the francs (or equivalent in euros) for U.S. dollars. Big Steel Company might have U.S. dollars and be willing to exchange those dollars for francs.

A basic (plain vanilla) currency swap has three steps. First, the two parties exchange the principal amount in the two currencies. (Note the difference from the interest rate swap, in which the counterparties deal in the same currency and can pay only the net interest amount.) Second, the parties exchange periodic interest payments over the life of the agreement. Third, the parties exchange the principal amount again at the conclusion of the swap.

Suppose, for example, that the current spot exchange rate between French francs and U.S. dollars is 5 francs per dollar, or FF 1 = $0.20. Le Taste has FF 50 million and would like to exchange the amount for dollars. In return, Big Steel would pay $10 million to Le Taste at the beginning of the swap. Let's assume that the swap is for a five-year period and that the parties make annual interest payments. The U.S. interest rate is 8 percent, and the French interest rate is 10 percent. Hence Big Steel will pay 10 percent interest on the FF 50 million it received, for an annual payment of FF 5 million. Le Taste will pay 8 percent interest on the $10 million it received, for an annual payment of $800,000. (In practice, the two firms will make net payments.) At the end of five years, Le Taste and Big Steel again exchange principal amounts. Le Taste pays $10 million, and Big Steel pays FF 50 million, ending the swap.

Why might firms and financial institutions participate in currency swaps? One reason is that firms may have a comparative advantage in borrowing in their domestic currencies. They can then swap the proceeds with a foreign counterparty to obtain foreign currency for, say, investment projects. In this way, both parties may be able to borrow more cheaply than if they had borrowed directly in the currency they needed.

Over the past decade, interest rate swaps and currency swaps have become more complex. On the one hand, this complexity serves the commercial and financial interests of the transacting parties. On the other hand, many policymakers worry that defaults by some key participants could precipitate a crisis in swap markets.

Source: Reprinted with permission from R. Glenn Hubbard, *Money, the Financial System, and the Economy* (Reading, Mass.: Addison Wesley, 2000), pp. 235–236.

Derivative War Stories

Despite the sophistication of managers and computers handling these deals, the size and complexity of derivatives markets has become increasingly worrisome in the past decade. During the 1990s, an ugly series of well-publicized losses and unseemly arguments among participants in derivatives markets underlined the risks inherent in these markets. A brief timeline is presented in the box on page 363.

The Bankers Trust/P&G debacle, in particular, highlights some of the pitfalls of these markets. The argument erupted over some leveraged interest rate swap instruments purchased by P&G, which were allegedly promoted as a form of protection against sharp interest rate fluctuations but apparently were highly speculative. Bankers Trust (BT) eventually agreed to swallow a large portion of the losses, in a painful reminder that OTC derivatives largely fall outside of the scope of regulatory authorities.[2] In its legal case against BT, P&G charged that BT officials deliberately misled and deceived P&G about key aspects of the derivatives being peddled. Unfortunately for BT, a recording system routinely taped conversations involving some of these transactions. For example, a BT employee is heard saying, "They would never know. They would never be able to know how much money was taken out of that," referring to BT's huge profits on the deal. Responds his colleague, "Never, no way, no way."[3]

Financial Hydrogen Bombs?

These misadventures have led some government officials to warn that since derivatives activity is concentrated in a few big financial institutions, there is a growing possibility of a market crisis leading to a taxpayer-financed bailout. While this is a controversial viewpoint, there are some grounds for concern:

- *Inadequate information.* Disclosure practice has lagged behind market developments, making it extremely difficult for unbiased observers to assess how much risk is involved in derivatives positions. Since the value of derivatives positions changes minute by minute in the markets, and their value in any case incorporates big assumptions about the future, published financial statements cannot possibly convey a full picture of the risks being taken.

- *Concentration.* The giant derivatives market rests on about twelve global financial institutions, which account for more than half of all derivatives business worldwide. This is a good news/bad news story. Since the highly specialized derivatives business requires a fair amount of capital and expertise, there has been a shakeout among banks as the better-capitalized, stronger commercial banks have pushed into territory once dominated by investment banks. The shakeout process is painful, but it should winnow out the weaker players and leave the industry in the hands of the strongest. On the negative side, the

BNDES TO LAUNCH NEW DERIVATIVE IN ELETROBRAS

The equity arm of the Brazilian Development Bank (BNDESpar) will hold an unprecedented auction of nearly R$ 90 million shares and options in federal power company Eletrobras. BNDESpar director Sargio Weguelin explained that the auction represents the launch of a new product on the Brazilian capital market. The product allows investors to buy a share, a put option and two call options.

The new product is a special type of derivative and is new even for the international market. "Our intention is to increase liquidity in Eletrobras shares on the market and make it more interesting for international investors," said Weguelin.

Source: Gazeta Mercantil Online, August 22, 2000.

IBJ INTRODUCES "RAIN" DERIVATIVE CONTRACTS
Gillian Tett

As the rainy season gets under way in Japan, the Industrial Bank of Japan is trying to make a new financial splash.

The bank has become the first Japanese group to launch so-called "rain" derivatives, which offer Japanese companies compensation if their business suffers as a result of unusually wet or dry weather.

The scheme differs from a traditional insurance policy since it uses a mathematical formula based on rainfall levels to determine payouts—rather than an insurance company's assessment of actual "damage."

And IBJ is targeting the scheme at the leisure, retail and tourism sectors in Japan, whose profits can be dampened by unpredictable bouts of rain. "It rains a lot in Japan so we think there will be demand," explained Hiroshi Matsui of IBJ....

Source: Financial Times, June 19, 2000, p. 24.

increasing concentration of the industry suggests higher risk. Banks, brokerage firms, or derivatives dealers could be brought down by just one market mishap, big bet gone bad, or rogue trader. The collapse of just one big player would have devastating ripple effects on the rest of the market.[4]

- *Difficulty of valuation.* Related to the first issue is the impossibility of devising an impartial and accurate valuation of a firm's derivatives position. Options especially are difficult to value from the seller's point of view, since they may or may not be exercised. Standard accounting practice such as marking to market (updating the value of a position according to current market rates) is impractical when there is no real market, as often occurs with OTC derivatives. Instead, financial institutions use complex computer-based models that calculate value based on assumptions about probability, volatility, and future costs. (Recall the certainty among the BT officials that P&G would never be able to figure out how much profit BT made on the deal.) However, these models are only as good as the assumptions on which they are founded.

- *Liquidity.* Moreover, market prices may not fully reflect the illiquidity of the more complex derivatives, in which a few institutions make a market and liquidity can evaporate in difficult circumstances. Most computer models simply assume adequate market liquidity.

- *Supervisory challenges.* As the article on Sumitomo notes, the temptation for traders to fail to report their true positions is certainly not unique to derivatives markets, but it is especially difficult to detect when the valuation process is so complex and senior management may not fully understand the instruments and markets in which their traders are dealing. Complex derivatives require special monitoring because in illiquid situations, which often occur, management must rely on traders' assessment of values.

Reliance on increasingly complex computer models to value derivatives and manage their risk brings its own set of rewards and challenges. As derivatives expert Philippe Jorion explains, linear VAR models adequately describe the risks of linear derivatives, such as forwards and swaps. However, these models perform poorly in representing the risks of options, because of the nonlinear nature of these derivatives. Jorion warns that the technology behind the creation of ever more complex derivatives instruments seems to have advanced faster than our ability to control it. Also, he worries that agents in trading activities often have incentives to engage in risk-taking activities that may not be in the best interests of their company.[5]

Nonetheless, many observers believe that increased regulation is not the answer. Many derivatives market players point out that the market is already highly regulated. Its biggest participants include commercial banks, investment banks, and highly rated corporations, which already rank among the world's most heavily regulated entities. Moreover, for the past fifteen years the derivatives market has in fact performed very nicely, avoiding any market-specific disasters. Problems have been institution-specific, such as those related to LTCM and Orange County, or event-specific, as in Russia's 1998 default. Each problem was also associated with fraud, incompetence, or force majeure; thus they do not reflect any failings on the part of the market. Finally, derivatives market growth is slowing to more sustainable levels as the market matures. According to International Swaps & Derivatives Association (ISDA) data, outstanding swaps contracts rose by 12 percent in 1999, compared with a 75 percent increase during 1998.[6] And as Jorion points out, the market risks of derivatives involve changes in contract market values, not notional or outstanding amounts—so the figures on outstanding contracts far surpass the actual risks involved.[7]

The trouble is that the nature of derivatives makes it easy for traders to take massive positions with relatively small amounts of capital, and then to lie about it. It is dismayingly easy to disguise and deceive in the derivatives market, as many financial institutions have learned. Thus one bank analyst warns, "Risk management across the system has generally improved, but derivatives have always been a major exception."[8] Or as veteran Wall Streeter Felix Rohatyn says, "Twenty-six year olds with computers are creating financial hydrogen bombs."[9]

CAPS, COLLARS, AND FLOORS

While most financial derivatives are of the plain vanilla variety, the variations on these basic structures can be remarkably sophisticated and complex. Many of the most interesting and innovative derivative products are based on options. OTC interest rate options, for example, often take the form of *caps* and *floors*. An interest rate cap option is based on an agreement between buyer and seller stating that if the chosen index, say the three-month London interbank offer rate (LIBOR), is above the agreed-on exercise price at prespecified dates in the future, the seller will reimburse the buyer for the additional interest cost until the next specified date. A floor option is the opposite. A five-year cap on the three-month LIBOR can be broken down into a series of nineteen European options with quarterly strike dates. The option premium may be paid in the form of a single front-end payment (e.g., 2 percent of the face value) or a yearly cost paid regularly (e.g., 0.5 percent per year).

As an illustration, consider a five-year 10 percent cap on the three-month LIBOR for $1 million. The current LIBOR is 8 percent, and the yearly cap premium is 0.5 percent. If the LIBOR stays below 10 percent over the next five years, the cap option will be useless. Conversely, if the LIBOR rises above 10 percent at some of the specified exercise dates, the seller will pay the difference in interest costs. For example, if the LIBOR rises to 12 percent, the cap buyer receives a payment equal to the difference between the market LIBOR (12 percent) and the exercise price (10 percent). In this case, the quarterly payment is

$$\$1 \text{ million} \cdot \frac{(12\% - 10\%)}{4} = \$5000$$

Contracts like this are usually purchased by companies as insurance against a rise in interest costs on their floating-rate borrowings. They are usually written by banks, which may hedge their option writing by borrowing funds at a variable rate with an interest cap. For example, the bank may engage in the following operations:

- Lend money to company A at LIBOR + $\frac{7}{8}$ percent
- Borrow money from investors at LIBOR + $\frac{3}{8}$ percent with a cap at 10 percent
- Sell a cap option at 10 percent to company B for $\frac{1}{2}$ percent per year

(continued)

This enables the bank to hedge its cap writing and end up with a margin of 1 percent.

Collars, which offer both a floor and a cap on interest rates, are another attractive instrument for management of long-term interest rate risk. These complex packages are quite common in international finance. Their use requires expertise on the part of bankers, and a solid understanding of the pricing of these multiple options.

Source: Adapted from Bruno Solnik, *International Investments* (Reading, Mass.: Addison Wesley, 2000), pp. 516–517.

SOME PAINFUL LESSONS

April 1994

Kidder Peabody dismisses Joseph Jett and accuses him of recording phantom profits of $350 million on trades involving derivatives created by stripping the interest and principal from bonds and selling them separately.

Sept.–Oct. 1994

Bankers Trust is sued by Gibson Greetings and Proctor & Gamble over derivatives losses, which amounted to $21 million for Gibson and a $200 million settlement for P&G.

December 1994

Orange County, California, reports a $1.5 billion loss, largely because of investments in derivatives, leading to the resignation of the county's treasurer, Robert L. Citron, and lawsuits against Merrill Lynch, among others.

February 1995

Barings, Britain's oldest investment bank, announces a loss, which ultimately climbs to $1.38 billion, related to derivatives trading in Singapore by Nicholas W. Leeson.

September 1998

Long-Term Capital, a hedge fund led by John W. Meriwether, is rescued by a group of financial institutions after its big derivatives positions turn sour.

Source: David Barboza and Jeff Gerth, "On Regulating Derivatives," *New York Times*, December 15, 1998, p. C1.

YAKULT IS HIT BY A £ 483M LOSS ON DERIVATIVES TRADING

Bethan Hutton

Yakult Honsha, the Japanese company best known for its fermented milk drink, said early today it had been hit by losses of ¥ 105bn (£ 483m) stemming from derivatives and other financial dealings.

The chairman, Jun Kuwahara, and a vice-president are to resign over the losses, although the president, Sumiya Hori, seems likely to stay for the moment....

Yakult is not the first Japanese company to suffer from heavy losses on trading in derivatives or other financial instruments. Earlier this year the Industrial Bank of Japan said it had lost $120m from derivatives trading; Bank of Tokyo-Mitsubishi last year incurred a loss of $83m on its swaps book; and Daiwa Bank lost more than £ 670m because of trading in US Treasury bonds by an employee in its New York office....

Source: Financial Times, March 20, 1998, p. 1.

RISK AND REWARD: LOSS FOCUSES ATTENTION ON DETECTING UNAUTHORISED TRADES

Tracy Corrigan

The $2–3m loss suffered by Sumitomo Finance International on its interest rate options book last autumn, after a desk manager concealed his real trading position from senior management, has highlighted once again the importance of tight management controls in the derivatives markets....

Although failure to report true positions to management is not a risk peculiar to the derivatives market, it may be less likely to be detected, because the valuation of positions is so much more complex, and senior management, or in some cases the traders themselves, may not fully understand the instruments they are dealing with. In the case of over-the-counter options, as in this instance, the lack of liquidity and ready price information is a further element....

In the Sumitomo Finance case, it appears that tighter controls might have forestalled the problem.

The manager of the interest rate options desk had to record the value of his positions in management reports submitted to his chief executive, but he gave falsely inflated values in order to hide his true position. He then persuaded an employee with another firm, which he knew was used by Sumitomo's accounts department to check those valuations, to quote inflated prices that corresponded with those in his own internal management reports.

(continued)

"In my experience there are a lot of banks where a trader believed to be of exceptional quality reports direct to the top," said Mr. Derek Ross, a Touche Ross partner who advises banks and securities firms in this area. "It's easy to develop a culture which allows the trading room to develop without controls."...

Source: Financial Times, May 24, 1993, p. 20.

MYTH NUMBER 3: THE ENORMOUS SIZE OF THE FINANCIAL DERIVATIVES MARKET DWARFS BANK CAPITAL, THEREBY MAKING DERIVATIVES TRADING AN UNSAFE AND UNSOUND BANKING PRACTICE

The financial derivatives market's worth is regularly reported as more than $20 trillion. That estimate dwarfs not only bank capital but also the nation's $7 trillion gross domestic product. These often-quoted figures are notional amounts. For derivatives, notional amount is the amount on which interest and other payments are based. Notional principal typically does not change hands; it is simply a quantity used to calculate payments.

While notional principal is the most commonly used volume measure in derivatives markets, it is not an accurate measure of credit exposure. A useful proxy for the actual exposure of derivative instruments is replacement-cost credit exposure. That exposure is the cost of replacing the contract at current market values should the counterparty default before the settlement date.

For the 10 largest derivatives players among U.S. holding companies, derivative credit exposure averages 15 percent of total assets. The average exposure is 49 percent of assets for those banks' loan portfolios. In other words, if those 10 banks lost 100 percent on their loans, the loss would be more than three times greater than it would be if they had to replace all of their derivative contracts.

Derivatives also help to improve market efficiencies because risks can be isolated and sold to those who are willing to accept them at the least cost. Using derivatives breaks risk into pieces that can be managed independently. Corporations can keep the risks they are most comfortable managing and transfer those they do not want to other companies that are more willing to accept them. From a market-oriented perspective, derivatives offer the free trading of financial risks.

The viability of financial derivatives rests on the principle of comparative advantage—that is, the relative cost of holding specific risks. Whenever comparative advantages exist, trade can benefit all parties involved. And financial derivatives allow for the free trading of individual risk components.

Source: Thomas F. Siems, "10 Myths About Financial Derivatives," Case Policy Analysis No. 283, September 11, 1997, available at www.cato.org/pubs.

Questions

1. What are derivatives? What is the difference between derivatives and other financial instruments?
2. Under what circumstances are derivatives used for hedging purposes, and under what circumstances are they speculative? Give examples of each type of transaction.
3. What is the difference between the risk profile for the purchaser and the writer of an option?
4. Why have derivatives markets experienced such rapid growth in recent years? Do you think that this growth will continue in the next decade?
5. What is an interest rate swap? What risks are involved from the bank's point of view?
6. What is a currency swap? What risks are involved from the bank's point of view?
7. Why do you think that derivatives were involved in so many scandals and financial crises in the early to middle 1990s?
8. What can be done to prevent further meltdowns arising from derivatives trades in the future?
9. Is it true that derivatives are "financial hydrogen bombs"?

Suggested Reading

Hull, John C. *Options, Futures, and Other Derivatives,* 3rd edition. New York: McGraw Hill, 1997. This is a good textbook for graduate and advanced undergraduates. It assumes that the reader has some prior knowledge of finance, probability, and statistics, but no previous coursework on swaps or other derivatives.

Partnoy, Frank. *F.I.A.S.C.O.: Blood in the Water of Wall Street.* New York: W. W. Norton & Company, 1997. This is a highly readable and fascinating account of the adventures of one Wall street derivatives trader.

Smithson, Charles W., Clifford W. Smith Jr., and Wilford D. Sykes. *Managing Financial Risk: A Guide to Derivative Products, Financial Engineering and Value Maximization.* New York: McGraw Hill, 1995. This book is aimed at corporate finance professionals, and it provides in-depth explanations of forwards, futures, swaps, options, and exotic derivatives.

Websites

www.fiafii.org	Futures Industry Association
www.isda.org	International Swaps & Derivatives Association
www.futuresguide.com	A guide to the futures market
www.optionstrategist.com	A guide to the options market
www.numa.com	Financial derivatives
www.margrabe.com/dictionary/html	Derivatives dictionary
www.appliederivatives.com	Online magazine about derivatives trading

Notes

1. *BIS Quarterly Review*, February 2000, at www.bis.org.

2. Richard Waters, "Putting Back the Trust into BT," *Financial Times*, May 13, 1996, p. 19.

3. Kelley Holland, Linda Himelstein, and Zachary Schiller, "The Bankers Trust Tapes," *Business Week*, October 16, 1995, p. 106.

4. David Barboza and Jeff Gerth, "On Regulating Derivatives," *New York Times*, December 15, 1998, p. C1; and *Financial Times*, Survey: Derivatives, June 28, 2000, p. 1.

5. Philippe Jorion, *Value at Risk* (New York: McGraw Hill, 1997), pp. 315–316.

6. *Financial Times*, Survey: Derivatives, June 28, 2000, p. 1.

7. Philippe Jorion, *Value at Risk*, p. 23.

8. Matt Murray, "Derivatives: A Mixed Bag for U.S. Banks," *Wall Street Journal*, September 29, 1998, p. C1.

9. Philippe Jorion, *Value at Risk*, p. 23.

CHAPTER 14

COUNTRY RISK AND GLOBAL DEBT CRISES

The shift from domestic to cross-border lending adds a new layer of risk, and therefore risk management, to the banker's portfolio. In addition to the everyday issues of credit analysis that shadow every financial transaction, new and more challenging concerns arise with regard to the provision of overseas finance, such as foreign exchange risks, legal risks, and country risk. One large North American bank characterizes the additional credit risks involved in international lending as follows:

- *Quality of management*
- *Quality of information,* relating to worries about different accounting systems, "fudging" of data, and timeliness of data
- *Liquidity/refinancing risks* (there are very few lenders in some markets, and global capital flows can be erratic and unpredictable)
- *Foreign exchange risk*
- *Legal risks* relating to the enforceability of contracts
- *Corruption*
- *Personal safety*

The bottom line: All cross-border loans by international commercial or investment banks involve country risk—the possibility that these loans will be impaired by economic or political events in the foreign country. Bankers involved in cross-border lending are exposed to a variety of factors that could make the borrower unable (or unwilling) to service its loan. Most important, the individual borrower's ability to meet its external debt obligations is influenced not only by its own circumstances, but also by the ability of the country as a whole to meet external obligations. Thus, when a bank participates in international lending or securities underwriting, it must assess country risk as well as the creditworthiness of the individual borrower. The bank needs to set limits on its exposure to each country, usually in the form of overall country limits as well as sublimits for different maturities, individual borrowers, industries, and regions. This is the process that we call country risk analysis.

Special Issues in Cross-Border Lending

In assessing cross-border risk and setting limits on exposure, the banker is also aware of the special issues that affect cross-border lending. One enduring ques-

THE LION'S SHARE: AS ONE BANK SHOWS, BANKRUPTCY IN RUSSIA IS A REAL CAT FIGHT

Andrew Higgins

In a conference hall on the Moscow River last fall, Russia's sluggish march toward the free market was all set to take a bold stride. For the first time, a big Russian bank was officially going bankrupt.

For a country where insolvent businesses often stagger on no matter how infirm they are, the harsh discipline of the marketplace would provide a bracing tonic. It was a step the International Monetary Fund had been urging for years, and 300 or so creditors were on hand, including dozens of American and European bankers hoping to recover millions of dollars owed them.

Almost half a year later, a few still hope, but many have given up. Instead of an orderly liquidation, the test case has become a brawl in which some of the West's premier financial institutions have been muscled aside by a cluster of Russian companies linked to a 32-year-old Moscow metals trader. The battle has featured bogus credit claims, murky offshore companies and menacing phone calls. One thing it hasn't had much of is money....

Source: Wall Street Journal, April 5, 1999, p. 1.

tion revolves around how to assess different classes of borrowers in international markets. Walter Wriston, the former chairman of Citibank, is known for (among other things) his famous pronouncement that countries do not go bankrupt. The idea is that countries have control over their own supply of money (they can always print more), and so they cannot go bust. While theoretically true, this sentiment can lead us into dangerous territory when it underpins the standard assumption that governments are better credit risks than private sector companies.

One way of examining this is to realize that the present value of a country's future national income—the best definition of its wealth—must be greater than its external liabilities.[1] Hence countries do not go bust. Governments do, however. Moreover, countries may reinvent themselves—witness the disappearing nations of Central and Eastern Europe such as Czechoslovakia and the Soviet Union in the 1990s. Thus it appears that in some cases private sector companies may be longer-lived and more creditworthy than sovereign borrowers. (Would the rational banker prefer lending to the government of Albania or to Microsoft?) Dealing with any political entity is fraught with risk. As the Bible warns us, put not thy trust in princes.

Lending overseas, whether to private or sovereign borrowers, is further complicated by the issue of legal recourse and discipline. Among the unusual legal characteristics of international lending is the sad reality that legal recourse against a defaulting government offers little protection to the lender. For obvious reasons, creditors are reluctant, and often unable, to seize the assets of deadbeat governments. (Imagine a world in which Deutsche Bank hires mercenaries to seize oil tankers on the high seas in repayment of the oil exporting country's debt!) Thus disciplinary action rests largely on the threat of no new loans. This, however, may be an empty threat if the bankrupt country has powerful geopolitical protectors, or if the fate of the banks is inextricably tied up with that of the debtor. The old saw is instructive: If I owe you a million dollars, I'm in a lot of trouble. If I owe you a billion dollars, you're in a lot of trouble.

Definitions of Risk

What, then, do we mean by country risk? Conceptually, this refers to the possibility that a borrower will be *unwilling or unable* to service its debt in a timely fashion—the risk from cross-border lending that arises from events to some degree under the control of the government of the borrowing country. More precisely, a definition of country risk should encompass the following factors:

- **Political risk:** the risk that political factors might impair a borrower's ability to repay. Political risk encompasses a vast array of possible events, ranging from nationalization or expropriation to damage from civil strife, political turmoil, and corruption. It refers to the possibility that political decisions or events in a country will affect the business climate in such a way that investors will lose money, or not make as much money as they originally expected. Political risk forecasting involves an attempt to project "harm" to the investor resulting from political decisions. For example, the departure of a (relatively) reformist president in Venezuela in 1993 was followed by the accession of the elderly populist Rafael Caldera, who immediately imposed a punishing regime of price and foreign exchange controls. The fall of Suharto in Indonesia in 1998, which led to a major debt rescheduling, is another potent example. Compared with most types of economic or business forecasting, political risk forecasting remains a very underdeveloped art. The opening of Eastern and Central Europe in the 1990s, for instance, was foreseen by virtually no one.

- **Transfer risk:** the risk that a commercial borrower might be unable to service its debt because the government restricts access to foreign exchange. In other words, the commercial borrower has earned sufficient revenue to service the debt, but is not permitted to convert local currency into foreign currency for the purposes of debt service.

- **Sovereign risk:** the risk that the government as a borrower may prove to be uncreditworthy. This refers to the risk that the sovereign borrower (or a private borrower with a public guarantee) will be unwilling or unable to make payments on its foreign obligations. One of the most recent of sovereign defaults, of course, was the case of Russia in 1998, followed in 1999 by Ecuador.

From the banker's point of view, country risk refers to the potential for loss of assets that the bank has loaned across borders in a foreign currency. Thus, whereas sovereign risk relates to the credit risk of the government as borrower, country risk involves the credit risk of all borrowers in the country taken as a whole. It is important to recognize that our definition should *not* exclude private sector borrowers. After all, when a country is unable (or unwilling) to meet its external debt service obligations, the ability of the private sector to gain access to foreign currency to pay off its debts is severely compromised.

Methodologies of Country Risk Analysis

The assessment of country risk, then, involves both qualitative and quantitative analysis of political, social, economic, and natural conditions in the country in which the borrower operates; additionally, it requires a judgment of the degree to which these factors will affect the borrower's ability to service its loans. In practice, country risk assessment is dauntingly complex, incorporating a vast array of social, political, psychological, historical, political, and social factors. One prominent sovereign risk analyst in New York describes himself as a historian, relative value strategist, detective, and storyteller.

The task is immeasurably complicated by the tricky psychology and herd instinct of financial markets. As another analyst observes, "Markets are like wild hurricanes, subject to random events that no one can predict."[2] It is indeed difficult to predict the madness of crowds, as the aptly named Asian contagion of 1997–98 demonstrates.

Accordingly, despite numerous attempts at quantification and modeling, most practitioners confess that country risk analysis remains more art than science. The multivariate sources of country risk force a multidisciplinary approach. As Table 14.2 illustrates, a systematic method of country risk analysis typically results in some sort of index, including a variety of weighted variables that add up to a sum for each country.

Banks became more analytical in their approach to country risk beginning in the 1970s. Aside from anything else, advances in the computer industry suddenly facilitated the use of more quantitative, sophisticated methodologies than the technology allowed just a few years earlier. But even more important were shocks in the international environment, ranging from revolutions in Iran and Nicaragua to civil war in Lebanon. Bankers were abruptly—and painfully—reminded of the pressing need for political risk analysis as a key element in country risk analysis.

As these events unfolded, bankers gradually increased their emphasis on systematic country risk analysis. While the use of quantitative models increased, for the most part banks to this day rely on structured qualitative analysis of country risk, coupled with a weighted checklist to score all countries on a common scale of risk in order to facilitate comparability. Many banks, rating agencies, and consulting services have developed proprietary country risk rating models, but all models contain several basic elements:

1. *Political analysis.* An important facet to the political country risk analysis challenge is an attempt to predict the *willingness* of sovereign governments to continue servicing foreign debt. The variables used to assess this may include any or all of the following:

      Depth and experience of government bureaucrats

      Political intrusiveness on economic management

Political links with foreign partners
Past behavior under stress
Regime legitimacy and stability
Ethnic tensions
Corruption
Political turmoil

2. *Economic analysis.* Next, the analyst assesses the probable future economic performance of the country, as an essential step to determining the country's likely future *ability* to service its foreign debt. This analysis should include, at a bare minimum:

Monetary and fiscal policy
Global economic environment
Natural resources
Export diversification
Stability of the banking industry
GDP growth and inflation rates

3. *Financial analysis.* Finally, analysts examine various indicators of a country's international liquidity position, to provide further clues as to its future capacity to service foreign debt. The indicators include:

Foreign indebtedness, both in absolute terms and relative to GDP
Debt service payments relative to exports
Current account
Capital inflows/outflows
Exchange rate stability
Foreign exchange reserves[3]

In Table 14.3, for example, at first glance it appears that Brazil is the highest-risk country, with a total foreign debt burden of $235 billion. Brazil's debt service level, the percentage of its export revenues that are used to service foreign debt, is also the highest at nearly 56 percent. However, measured against GDP the foreign debt looks less worrisome. By contrast, Chile's foreign debt/GDP and current account/GDP ratios both suggest that in 1998 the country was carrying a heavy debt burden and running a large deficit on its goods and services trade with the rest of the world, relative to its GDP. All of these data pale by comparison to a country like Nicaragua, though, which in 1998 was running a current account shortfall equivalent to nearly one-quarter of its GDP, and carrying a foreign debt burden equivalent to over 300 percent of its GDP!

Limits to Country Risk Analysis

As the foregoing discussion indicates, most attempts at country risk analysis incorporate roughly the same universe of variables in an effort to contrast and rate risks across countries. All models create a list of risk factors and attempt to evaluate these factors for each country. Then, the analyst consolidates his or her analysis of risk factors into some quantifiable index, using weightings, so countries

TABLE 14.1 Selected Country Exposure—Chase Manhattan Bank (US$ billions)

	December 31, 1998	*December 31, 1997*
	Total Cross-Border Exposure	*Total Cross-Border Exposure*
Latin America		
Brazil	$ 3.2	$ 4.8
Argentina	2.8	3.2
Mexico	2.2	2.9
Chile	0.9	1.5
Colombia	0.8	0.8
Venezuela	0.4	1.0
All Other Latin America[1]	1.0	0.8
Total Latin America	11.3	$15.0
Asia		
Korea	$ 2.4	$ 5.3
Indonesia	1.2	2.2
Thailand	0.9	1.4
Subtotal	4.5	8.9
Hong Kong	$ 0.8	$ 1.1
Singapore	0.8	1.6
Philippines	0.6	0.9
Malaysia	0.6	0.9
China	0.6	0.7
All Other Asia	0.5	0.6
Total Asia, excluding Japan, Australia and New Zealand	$ 8.4	$14.7
Japan	$ 6.9	$ 8.8
Australia	1.9	2.8
New Zealand	0.6	0.3
Total Japan, Australia, and New Zealand	$ 9.4	$11.9

Source: Financial Reports, 1998, The Chase Manhattan Corporation. www.chase.com.
[1]Excludes Bermuda and Cayman Islands.

may be compared. The multidisciplinary nature of country risk requires an integrated approach to analysis combining both quantitative and qualitative factors, as well as the insights and wisdom of experienced practitioners. The integrated approach will always factor in basic indicators such as domestic instability, foreign conflicts, and the economic and political climate of a country. In addition, most studies reveal that an overvalued exchange rate, a big current account deficit

TABLE 14.2 Institutional Investor Country Credit Ratings,[1] March 1999		
Rank	*Country*	*II Credit Ranking*
1	Switzerland	92.7
2	Germany	92.5
3	United States	92.2
4	Netherlands	91.7
5	France	90.8
6	United Kingdom	90.2
7	Luxembourg	89.9
8	Austria	88.7
9	Norway	86.8
10	Japan	86.5
11	Denmark	84.7
12	Belgium	83.5
13	Canada	83.0
14	Finland	82.2
15	Ireland	81.8
16	Singapore	81.3
17	Spain	80.3
18	Sweden	79.7
19	Italy	79.1
20	Portugal	76.1
21	Taiwan	75.5
22	Australia	74.3
23	New Zealand	73.1
24	Iceland	67.0
25	UAE	62.5
26	Hong Kong	61.8
27	Chile	61.8
28	Malta	61.7
29	Czech Republic	59.7
30	Slovenia	58.4
31	Cyprus	57.3
32	China	57.2
33	Poland	56.7
34	Kuwait	56.5
35	Greece	56.1
36	Hungary	55.9
37	Saudi Arabia	54.4
38	Israel	54.3
39	Mauritius	53.7
40	Botswana	53.5

(continued)

TABLE 14.2 Institutional Investor Country Credit Ratings,[1] *(continued)*

Rank	Country	II Credit Ranking
41	Oman	53.3
42	South Korea	52.7
43	Qatar	51.7
44	Malaysia	51.0
45	Bahrain	50.7
46	Tunisia	50.3
47	Thailand	46.9
48	Uruguay	46.5
49	Mexico	46.0
50	South Africa	45.8
51	Colombia	44.5
52	India	44.5
53	Egypt	44.4
54	Barbados	43.5
55	Philippines	43.3
56	Trinidad and Tobago	43.3
57	Morocco	43.2
58	Estonia	42.8
59	Argentina	42.7
60	Slovakia	41.3
61	Panama	39.9
62	Croatia	39.0
63	Costa Rica	38.4
64	Latvia	38.0
65	Brazil	37.4
66	Namibia	37.3
67	Jordan	37.3
68	Turkey	36.9
69	Lithuania	36.1
70	Peru	35.0
71	Venezuela	34.4
72	Sri Lanka	33.3
73	Lebanon	31.9
74	Paraguay	31.3
75	El Salvador	31.2
76	Romania	31.2
77	Papua New Guinea	30.4
78	Ghana	29.5
79	Seychelles	29.1
80	Bulgaria	28.6

(continued)

TABLE 14.2 Institutional Investor Country Credit Ratings,[1] *(continued)*

Rank	Country	II Credit Ranking
81	Swaziland	28.5
82	Libya	28.1
83	Dominican Republic	28.1
84	Bolivia	28.0
85	Jamaica	28.0
86	Indonesia	27.9
87	Kazakhstan	27.9
88	Vietnam	27.8
89	Iran	27.7
90	Guatemala	27.2
91	Zimbabwe	26.5
92	Ecuador	25.5
93	Algeria	25.2
94	Bangladesh	25.0
95	Nepal	24.4
96	Cote D'Ivoire	24.3
97	Kenya	24.1
98	Gabon	23.2
99	Syria	23.0
100	Senegal	21.7
101	Pakistan	20.4
102	Malawi	20.4
103	Uganda	20.3
104	Russia	20.0
105	Honduras	19.8
106	Burkina Faso	18.8
107	Myanmar	18.7
108	Uzbekistan	18.3
109	Tanzania	18.3
110	Cameroon	18.1
111	Mozambique	17.9
112	Ukraine	17.2
113	Nigeria	16.8
114	Togo	16.6
115	Benin	16.3
116	Ethiopia	16.2
117	Zambia	16.1
118	Guinea	15.4
119	Mali	15.4
120	Grenada	14.7

(continued)

TABLE 14.2 Institutional Investor Country Credit Ratings,[1] *(continued)*

Rank	Country	II Credit Ranking
121	Cuba	12.4
122	Belarus	11.9
123	Nicaragua	11.6
124	Angola	11.5
125	Haiti	11.2
126	Georgia	10.9
127	Albania	10.7
128	Congo Republic	9.7
129	Yugoslavia	8.9
130	North Korea	7.8
131	Liberia	7.6
132	Sudan	7.6
133	Iraq	7.1
134	Sierra Leone	6.3
135	Afghanistan	6.2
136	Congo	6.1
	Global Average Rating	40.9

Source: Institutional Investor, March 1999. www.iimagazine.com/research/99/countrycredit/

[1]This exclusive, semiannual survey ranks the creditworthiness of countries on a scale of 0 to 100, with 100 signifying the least chance of default..

TABLE 14.3 Major Latin American Debtor Countries, 1998

Country	Current Account (US$ billions)	Current Account/ GDP (%)	Foreign Debt (US$ billions)	Foreign Debt/GDP (%)	Debt Service (%)
Argentina	−$15.00	−4.3	87.99	25.3%	47.1%
Brazil	−35.60	−4.6	235.08	30.3	55.9
Chile	−5.18	−6.3	30.83	37.5	28.0
Colombia	−6.70	−6.7	33.60	33.6	21.0
Mexico	−16.65	−3.7	157.95	35.1	32.7
Venezuela	−1.30	−1.4	35.15	37.0	22.0

Source: Political Risk Services, *Country Forecasts,* 1999.

(relative to GDP), a decline in exports, and weak economic activity are almost always present before a major crisis. Thus the key points of any analysis will include economic structure and growth, inflation and interest rate structure, budget and public sector debt, key foreign debt ratios (foreign debt to GDP, foreign

THE ECONOMIST: "COUNTRIES IN TROUBLE: WHO'S ON THE SKIDS," 1986

In December 1986, *The Economist* presented a "non computer-modeled" technique for looking at countries to determine who will get into trouble for the remainder of the decade. The magazine noted, "The lives of countries, even very small ones, are so long, complicated and mysterious that it often seems hopeless to try to understand what is going on in them now, let alone what they might be like in a few years." Nonetheless, the authors continued, sharp reverses in the fortunes of a country do not come entirely out of the blue, either. Thus the article presents sixteen variables, with individual weightings, aimed at determining how much risk that country will present over the next few years. The variables are:

Falling GDP per person (8 points)

High inflation (5 points)

Capital flight (4 points)

High and rising foreign debt as a proportion of GDP (6 points)

Decline in food production per person (4 points)

Raw materials as a high percentage of exports (6 points)

Being near a superpower or trouble spot (3 points)

Democratic, totalitarian, authoritarian (7 points)

Longevity of regime (5 points)

Legitimacy of regime (9 points)

Generals in power (6 points)

Armed insurrection or war (20 points)

Urbanization (3 points)

Islamic fundamentalism (4 points)

Corruption (6 points)

Ethnic, religious, and racial tension (4 points)

The Economist's variables are, of course, related to general business conditions in a country rather than the specific risks of cross-border lending. Moreover, some of the analysis appears dated today. To some extent, this reflects the bias in the 1980s toward focusing on large-scale disruptions such as the fall of the shah in Iran, rather than the kind of politically motivated shifts in business climate that became more common in the 1990s. *The Economist*'s model does not take account of connections between markets, as reflected by the Asian contagion in the late 1990s. Also, most analysts in the late 1990s would place a much heavier weight-

(continued)

ing on corruption, displacing the relatively benign view of "crony capitalism" that prevailed in an earlier decade.

Nonetheless, *The Economist*'s analysis is still intelligent and relevant. It represents a "deeply unscientific"—and, thus, credible—attempt to combine economic, political, and social indicators into a meaningful assessment of risk in an arena in which scientific methods seem pointless. Especially welcome is the article's recognition that the serious risk of a country's becoming unstable depends on an odd mixture of

a. Things going objectively wrong (like a sagging economy) in ways that a large number of people can understand and be hurt by, and

b. The ability of these people to display their anger in ways that the state cannot control.

Source: Based on "Who's on the Skids?" *The Economist,* December 19, 1986, pp. 69–72.

---

debt to exports, and debt service), current account trends, foreign exchange reserves, and politics.

But one reality should never be lost here: Let the banker beware! Most country risk assessment models represent an effort to *quantify* information in some way, to put risks within a country into a broader context to facilitate informed comparisons. The ultimate goal is to rate and compare countries in terms of these risks, and to determine how political risks may be measured against other more conventional types of hazard such as fire, theft, and natural disaster.

However, the unfortunate reality is that country risks do not behave like other types of risk. Thus, the models that we use to assess these risks are seriously limited. One problem is related to the use of inaccurate and inconsistent data in producing models. Even macroeconomic data are not always timely and reliable; major countries regularly revise their data in ways that can make a big difference. In January 1990, for example, the Chinese government announced that China enjoyed a $5 billion balance of payments surplus in 1989, even though the Bureau of Customs reported a deficit due to "accounting differences." Changes in reporting method also matter; thanks to a different method of calculating GDP, Italy forged ahead of the United Kingdom in reported economic size for the first time in 1993 (to the consternation of the British government!). Inaccurate or missing data can also be critical, as in funds flows related to drug transactions or money laundering. Finally, it can be very difficult to obtain critical data in a timely manner. Whether due to design or sheer inefficiency, governments often do not release data on foreign exchange reserves quickly enough to enable analysts to spot sharp reverses.

Even with regard to quantifiable factors, then, the numbers used in creating country risk models may be suspect. Remember the cardinal rule of economic modeling: GIGO! (Garbage in, garbage out.) Risk by its very nature arises from events in the *future,* so country risk analysis must be forward-looking. However, the statistical data used in the quantitative models are historical data, by their nature backward-looking. Moreover, the further forward the analyst looks, the greater the likely margin for error becomes. In a discipline as dynamic as country risk assessment, the pitfalls of projecting the past into the future should be obvious. Even worse, much of what affects country risk—the degree of social cohesion, a tradition of peaceful problem resolution—is simply unquantifiable.

In sum, anything meant to *simplify* this very complex topic should be suspect. Most commercial risk analysis services produce "quantitative" measures of country risk to meet market demand, but these numbers are softer than ripe peaches. Anything that tries to quantify the unquantifiable should be treated with the utmost caution.

Modern Debt Crises

Latin America in the 1980s

Nowhere are the limits to country risk analysis more evident than in the litany of debt crises that have erupted in the past two decades. The modern era of debt crises

---

THE WORLD'S A DANGEROUS PLACE: CAUTIOUS FINANCIAL INSTITUTIONS TAKE GLOBAL CREDITWORTHINESS DOWN A NOTCH

Harvey D. Shapiro

A dozen of the biggest banks in the U.S. and Europe have formed a committee to reassess their global lending practices. Money managers everywhere are reassessing overseas stock and bond investment. Financial institutions have suddenly taken a stronger interest in analysis of currency fluctuations. All in all, in the wake of the financial debacles in Asia, Russia and Brazil, these institutions have become decidedly more wary about international investing, especially when it comes to emerging markets. As the International Monetary Fund observed in its most recent World Economic Outlook report, internationally active financial institutions and other asset managers appear to have engaged in a wholesale reassessment and repricing of financial risk.

That skepticism has led to a sharp downturn in the perceived safety of overseas investment. And, not surprisingly, for the first time in more than five years, *Institutional Investor*'s exclusive survey of international financial managers registered a decline in global creditworthiness…. Predictably, the country that saw the sharpest decline in its risk rating was Russia, whose government restructured and in effect defaulted on a huge load of foreign debt after the autumn devaluation of its currency….

Source: Institutional Investor Inc. Bank Letter, March 1999.

began in the 1980s in Latin America. Without a doubt, Latin America was bad news for the global banking system in those years. The Mexican debt moratorium in 1982, and its prolonged and painful aftermath, brought commercial banks in major countries to the brink of collapse. It precipitated a frenzied, multilateral quest on the part of governments, multilateral institutions, and banks for some resolution that would keep the banks solvent and not punish borrowing countries unduly. Whether these goals were ultimately met is still a matter of debate.

Bankers generally date the onset of 1980s debt crisis as the infamous "Mexican weekend" of August 1982 when Mexico informed its creditors that it was unable to service its external debt obligations. Brazil soon followed suit, and for the next few years voluntary lending by banks to developing countries essentially ceased. At first, the notion of writing off a substantial portion of the $200 billion plus that banks held in Latin American debt was unthinkable—a disaster for the banks, and a **moral hazard** for the borrowers. (If failure to repay debts was rewarded by banks writing off those debts, who would ever bother to repay?)

Soon, however, Mexico's liquidity problems mushroomed into a regional nightmare, as sovereign insolvency became epidemic. From 1980 to 1994, no fewer than sixty-eight governments engaged in multilateral restructuring of their official or commercial bank debts. Some 380 individual restructuring operations took place. Eleven countries restructured their debt ten or more times, in negotiations often repeated year after year. Mexico alone went through twelve separate restructurings between 1983 and 1990.[4] These operations were a weary burden for both bankers and debtors, engaging a disproportionate share of management time and attention from both sides.

In part, the debt crisis defied solution for so long because of everyone's inability to comprehend the extent of the disaster. At first, the banks treated the problem as a crisis of liquidity rather than solvency, essentially temporary in nature and solved with recourse to the usual techniques of temporary emergency finance. Thus principal was rescheduled and new loans were extended, largely in order to protect the banks from the dire consequences of having to formally declare that the loans were nonperforming (as, of course, they were in any real sense).

Gradually, as the arrears mounted and economic reforms in debtor countries lagged, there was a dawning recognition that this was a severe crisis of solvency rather than liquidity. The turning point came in 1987, when Citibank broke ranks with its peers and created a $3 billion provision against its $14.8 billion sovereign debt exposure, in effect acknowledging that a substantial portion of this debt might never be repaid. Other banks in the United States, Canada, and the UK rapidly followed suit. By the end of 1987, the nine biggest U.S. money center banks had established $12.9 billion in reserves against their loans to developing countries. The banks continued to argue for public consumption that the debt was still 100 percent recoverable, but their actions spoke otherwise and the emergence of a secondary market (in which the debt traded at well below face value) further undercut these claims.[5]

The fact was that at the time of the Mexican weekend in 1982, the banks were monumentally ill-prepared for this shock. Major banks faced a grave problem, thanks to their high degree of exposure to developing countries, and in particular to their heavy concentration in a few large Latin American debtor nations. In fact, Latin American exposure was equivalent to twice the capital base for major U.S.

banks. The region accounted for 7–10 percent of the assets of Chase Manhattan, Chemical, Citibank, and Manufacturers Hanover, and it was responsible for an even greater proportion of profits. Thus banks were deeply vulnerable to a crisis in this region. They reacted quickly, by redlining Latin America (no new voluntary lending), and by reducing their vulnerability to its troubles by aggressively increasing capital and reserves. Eventually, banks became adept at selling, swapping, and writing off/down their loans to risky countries.

These actions set the stage for resolution of the crisis by the late 1980s. In effect, the debt crisis was over for the banks well before it ended for the borrowing countries. Big U.S. banks returned to profitability by 1988, signaling the end of the debt crisis from the bankers' perspective. Facing other credit problems and efforts by regulators to force them to increase their ratio of capital to assets (capital adequacy), banks increased their capital and slowed asset growth during the second half of the 1980s, strengthening their financial position. However, the borrowing countries were still staggering under the weight of foreign debt that, in many cases, exceeded the level of the country's GDP. Efforts to continue servicing debt and to implement economic austerity, compounded by the banks' unwillingness to lend new funds, resulted in a "lost decade" for Latin America in which growth disappeared and social conditions deteriorated dramatically.

Nonetheless, the seeds for a return to progress were being sown. The next turning point was the promulgation of the Brady Plan in 1989 (named for U.S. Treasury Secretary Nicholas Brady). The Brady Plan introduced nothing that was radically new—essentially, it embraced much that was already happening, namely, provisions for debt reduction based on economic restructuring. However, its most important contribution was the tacit recognition of all parties that the debt would never be fully repaid. Also, the Brady Plan laid the groundwork for substantial funds to be made available to facilitate the debt reduction process. In addition, the increased emphasis placed on economic reforms provided new impetus to countries such as Mexico and Argentina, which moved ahead aggressively to privatize their economies and introduce market-oriented policies.

The results were gratifying. The debt crisis ended with a whimper rather than a bang, as the 1994 restructuring agreement between Brazil and its creditors finally allowed everyone to agree that this unpleasant episode in the history of international bank lending was indeed over. About 80 percent of the money that had been lent by commercial banks to developing countries had been restructured, and the four largest debtors (Brazil, Mexico, Argentina, and Poland) had all revamped their debt. At this point, the remaining problem countries (mostly in Africa) were much too small to pose a threat to the stability of the international financial system.

As the crisis petered out in the early 1990s, though, much attention turned to the burning question of where to affix the blame. After all, a crisis that threatened the stability of the world's largest banks and resulted in a decade of lost growth and opportunity for vast swathes of the developing world should be blamed on someone! In the mutual recriminations that flew freely, there was no shortage of potential villains.

From south of the equator, the prevailing view was that greedy and shortsighted bankers brought the crisis on themselves. Clearly, this was not the bankers' finest hour. They were blinded by their belief that countries do not default, as well as by the urgent pressure on them to increase margins. By the late 1970s, competitive pressures had forced margins on lending to creditworthy borrowers, such as OECD governments, down to a level where banks were unable to earn a profit on those loans. As a result, bankers turned their attention to the developing world, where margins were much richer, conveniently overlooking the fundamental risk/return trade-offs that underpin these margins. Bankers rushed to developing countries with checkbook in hand and competition intensified, driving down margins in these markets as well. As the inherent conflict between banker-as-salesperson and banker-as-credit-analyst sharpened, the quality of risk management declined.

The oil boom after 1974 also contributed to the debt crisis. Simply stated, the massive influx of money into the OPEC nations created a need to recycle those dollars. As Saudi, Kuwaiti, and Iranian petrodollars flowed into Western banks, the local authorities, concerned about inflation, encouraged the recycling of petrodollars out of the United States, the UK, and France and into the developing world. Banks were a primary force in this process of recycling.

In hindsight, the competitive factors that led bankers to overlend so grossly in the 1970s and early 1980s seem obvious. The profitability of lending in developing countries rather than OECD countries was a powerful lure. Citicorp, for example, earned 32 percent of its overall net income in Latin America and the Caribbean from 1977 to 1982, on only 16 percent of its assets. Much of this derived from one country, Brazil, which provided 17 percent of Citicorp's net income on just 4 percent of total assets! Several years earlier, Indonesia was the prime engine of profitability, to the point where senior bank officials were reportedly fond of saying, "Around here, it's Jakarta that pays the check."

In addition to profitability pressures, banks were also under pressure from their domestic customers to make loans to overseas affiliates. One banker from a large money-center institution cites the example of Caterpillar, a potential client with which the bank had been pursuing a relationship for years. According to the banker, Caterpillar management told the bank that it would have to "go the extra mile" and lend to Caterpillar's customers in Africa and Latin America if it wanted to become a house bank. The bank did, and made many loans to developing countries that it later came to rue.[6]

At the same time, structural factors as well were contributing to the bankers' missteps. With the benefit of hindsight, it is clear that the big banks' policy of frequent personnel shifts and reorganizations contributed to a severe lack of accountability. By the time that a credit went sour, the banker responsible for the credit was often on the other side of the world. Moreover, the custom of syndicating credits to developing countries created a false sense of security. Bankers believed that by spreading the risk of this lending around via syndications, they were reducing the risk. John Maynard Keynes, many years ago, lamented bankers' herd instinct when it comes to risk: "A sound banker, alas, is not one who foresees danger and avoids it, but who, when he is ruined is ruined in a conventional way along with his fellows so that no one can blame him."[7] This rather aptly describes the syndication process, which, rather than reducing risk, added immensely to the problems of restructuring the loan once it went bad. As countries entered the restructuring process, the terms of syndication generally required that all participating banks agree unanimously on any changes to the loan agreement. However, the different needs and viewpoints of, literally, hundreds of banks from around the world needlessly complicated this process, and gave a disproportionate share of the power to smaller banks.

While it is clear that banks were, in some cases, lending without due regard to risk/return issues, it is also true that no one was forcing the developing countries to borrow! Thus debtor countries must shoulder their share of the blame as well. Mismanagement and corruption in many countries contributed immeasurably to the problem. According to some estimates, around 10–20 percent of the money lent to Latin America before 1982 simply disappeared. Mismanagement by companies and governments accustomed to operating in small, highly protected domestic markets resulted in further losses. As a result, in many cases foreign borrowing failed to create a base of export-oriented, productive investments that could be used to repay the debt.

Finally, the role of the multilateral institutions in contributing to, and eventually resolving, the debt crisis remains one of great controversy. The IMF and the World Bank played a key role in facilitating both debt restructuring and economic restructuring in developing countries. Most of the time, commercial banks refused to sign on to a restructuring package until the borrowing country had obtained an IMF seal of approval for its economic policies. Backers of the IMF point to the market-oriented, liberal economic policies that were thus spawned in developing countries around the globe. On the other hand, naysayers are disturbed by the IMF's dogmatic insistence on one-size-fits-all austerity policies, and charge that the Fund is insensitive to different cultural environments as well as social and economic nuances.

At any rate, these debates were not resolved by the ensuing events of the 1990s. For no sooner was the debt crisis of the 1980s formally declared to be over, than Mexico tumbled off another cliff.

Mexican Tesobono Crisis, 1994–95

In December 1994, the Mexican government found itself unable to service its *tesobonos,* a series of short-term government bonds, a situation that escalated with remarkable speed into a full-fledged financial crisis for the country. The roots of the Mexican tesobono or tequila crisis, as it came to be called, were well established and not at all difficult to detect. First, the government's policy of maintaining a strong exchange rate via high real interest rates and a budget surplus made the process of economic restructuring more difficult and costly than expected. Highlighted by gaping trade and current account deficits, the data presented a worrisome picture of a country struggling to adjust to free trade with its powerful neighbor. Second, political turmoil (in the form of a rebellion in the impoverished southern state of Chiapas and a number of high-level assassinations, including the ruling party's presidential candidate) erupted at a delicate moment in the economic restructuring process, when the country was heavily dependent on foreign capital inflows to finance its external payments deficit.

Mexico's problems quickly expanded into a crisis for the entire region. The "tequila effect" (referring to the hangover that drinkers get the day after a tequila binge) brought uncertainty to all of Latin America, as other governments frantically sought to decouple their countries from Mexico's troubles. Notwithstanding these efforts, a broadly based sell-off of Latin American equities and currencies ensued, as countries with large current account deficits and low foreign exchange reserves were seen as vulnerable. The tequila or spillover effect was strongest in Argentina and, to some extent, Brazil, but the entire region was affected in some way.

By the standards of the 1980s debt crisis (and the later Asian contagion as well), however, the 1994–95 crisis was remarkably short and shallow. Recovery from Mexico's 1994 troubles proved to be, in retrospect, painless and smooth compared with the Mexican weekend of 1982! The IMF and the United States responded rapidly to Mexico's liquidity difficulties, pulling together a massive rescue package that left no doubt as to the support Washington's southern neighbor was to receive. Moreover, the Mexican authorities also responded quickly, putting together a credible stabilization program, which helped to restore credibility in a short period of time. As a result, the crisis never really spread outside Mexico, never threatened any international banks or the global financial system, and had very limited repercussions on the Mexican political system, compared with 1982. By 1996, Latin America was growing strongly again, and private capital flows to the region were running at record levels.

Asian Contagion, 1997–98

Perhaps the ease of recovery from Mexico's tesobono crisis contributed to a sense of complacency among bankers and investors with regard to the risks of what were, by the mid–1990s, called emerging markets rather than developing countries. At any rate, international lending to emerging markets by the mid–1990s was booming.

The party came to an abrupt end in mid–1997, when a crisis was, improbably, ignited by the July 1997 devaluation of the Thai baht. While the baht is not exactly a premier currency on world markets, this devaluation set off a chain of events culminating in Russian devaluation and default almost exactly a year later. By the dawn of 1999, the repercussions of the Asian virus were threatening to engulf Latin America as well as the muscular U.S. economy itself. As 1999 came to a close, the major Latin American countries seemed to be out of danger for the moment, but tiny Ecuador had been forced into default, setting a new and worrisome precedent in the annals of international lending.

The rapid spread of the crisis reflected a number of unfortunate convergences. First of all, a sharp decline in world commodity prices, exacerbated by the decline in growth and demand in much of Asia, was a serious blow to many emerging market countries still dependent on exports of price-sensitive commodities. Second, political instability or paralysis in several pivotal countries, including Japan and Russia, fueled the crisis. Third, doubts about the IMF—underfunded and under fire—and its ability to play a key role in resolving this latest crisis added to the uncertainty. Fourth, the severity of the crisis reflected in part the overleveraged nature of companies in many of the borrowing countries, compounded by the fact that huge chunks of their debt were denominated in foreign currencies. In a sense, this was a leverage crisis that was parlayed into a foreign debt crisis due to the currency of denomination of the debt. Finally, and most important, the deeply intertwined nature of global financial markets spread financial panic around the globe at unheard-of speeds.

The last-mentioned point underscores the differences between the origins of the 1997–98 financial crisis and the 1980s debt debacle. At the same time, there are many similar elements as well. Indeed, newspaper reports indicate that at least a year before the Thai devaluation, warnings at Citibank that Asia looked like precrisis Mexico had precipitated some steps to reduce the bank's exposure. According to reports, the bank managed to weed out its weakest Asian customers and cut its exposure to shaky business sectors, avoiding the worst when the crisis hit. At Citibank, many members of its Asian staff were veterans of the Latin American debt crisis and 1994 Mexico. These experienced bankers noted some warning signs in Asia:

1. Bankers falling all over themselves to lend money

2. Exchange rates artificially fixed to the dollar

3. Current account deficits

4. Very weak and poorly supervised financial systems

5. Real estate speculation

STUDY SHOWS HOW WORLD BANKS PANICKED OVER ASIAN TROUBLES

Edmund L. Andrews

After viewing Asia for years as a promised land for lending and investing, despite growing signs of trouble, Western and Japanese financial institutions panicked last fall and shut down the flow of new capital to troubled countries, according to a study prepared for the world's major banks made public today.

The study documents how within the span of a few months, foreign banks and investment companies did a U-turn from greed to fear, slashing new loans and investments to the five most troubled Asian countries by $100 billion. That amount equals two-thirds of the new money funneled to Asia the year before....

The data provide the first concrete evidence of how the powerful and mercurial flow of international money both propped up and then helped unravel the countries now in crisis. It does not suggest that foreign banks caused the crisis, which most economists believe had its origins in irresponsible borrowing by Asian countries themselves....

But the study does provide a graphic picture of how foreign banks fell over themselves to lend more money year after year and how surprised they seem to have been when currencies and stock markets from Indonesia to Thailand collapsed....

Source: New York Times, January 30, 1998, p. D1.

According to some sources, Citibank cut its exposure to Thailand and Indonesia by half beginning in 1996. One newspaper noted, "It wasn't just Citibank's Latin American expertise that helped it prepare for trouble in Asia; it was also terror of repeating the pain of that era."[8] Moreover, experienced bankers have learned that one reliable early warning sign of trouble to come is when high net worth individuals start moving their money out of their country and into dollars. Thus institutions with large private banking units, such as Citibank, may have observed such a trend beginning in 1996 and adjusted their positions accordingly. At any rate, its past experience certainly helped Citibank and other major institutions reduce their risk tolerance, perhaps permanently. These moves did not completely insulate Citibank as recession loomed in a region that supplied 23 percent of its earnings in 1996, but they undoubtedly helped to cushion the blow.

Even so, it is fair to say that no one really foresaw the depth of the downturn that began with the Thai devaluation. The fast pace of expansion and competition among foreign banks entering Asian markets in the early 1990s underlines the role of these lenders in facilitating and contributing to the crisis. As in pre–debt crisis Latin America, there is no doubt that global banks lent overgenerously to Thailand, Indonesia, and other Asian countries, perhaps on the assumption that if they got into serious trouble the IMF would bail them out (an example of moral hazard). At any rate, it is self-evident that international banks were not innocent bystanders to this crisis. They placed huge amounts of their capital at risk in Asia, continuing to pour funds into problem countries until mid–1997. According to the Bank for International Settlements (BIS), Japanese bank exposure to troubled Asian debtors at year-end 1997 was a whopping $114.8 billion, by far the largest exposure, followed at a distance by German banks at $48.6 billion, French banks at $42.8 billion, and British banks at $32.2 billion.[9] As the World Bank noted, the lax regulations and dubious financial practices in Asian countries were aggravated by "undisciplined foreign lending"—a classic case of too much money chasing too few good investments.

The World Bank in fact reserves some of its sharpest comments for the role of financial institutions from the most advanced economies in the Asian crisis. The Bank notes, "Loans came from countries with seemingly well-regulated and transparent financial institutions operated by sophisticated managers without government intervention. Yet foreign lenders and investors were not restrained by inadequate financial statements, high short-term debt, or the unhedged foreign exchange exposure present in the financing structure of most Asian banks and firms." The subtext: fools and their money are soon parted.[10]

The issue of transparency is a central theme of the Asian crisis. The term **transparency** is not in fact well defined, but basically it refers to the provision of clear, credible information about the economy and all important actors and transactions in the economy. (The concept of transparency is discussed in more detail in Chapter 10.) In the aftermath of the Asian meltdown, it soon became clear that the lack of transparency contributed immeasurably to the severity of the crisis. Janet Yellen, chair of the Council of Economic Advisers, comments:

> [T]he crisis countries favored centralized and behind-the-scenes mechanisms for the allocation of capital. The particular institutions varied from the captive banks of the

Korean chaebols to the finance companies of Thailand to government-linked banks in Indonesia, but in general a large part of capital allocations were not made by a decentralized open capital market via arms-length transactions; instead, decisions were made out of the public eye and often were based on personal and business relationships or governmental influence more than on reliable accounting or other information about the borrowers or their investment projects.... One thing we may have learned from the East Asian experience is that in the long run, reliance on such behind-the-scenes relationships for capital allocation may lead to increasingly poor investment decisions.[11]

Then, just as troubles erupted, the banks turned off the spigot. As Table 14.4 illustrates, international banks abruptly began pulling their money out of Asia in the second half of 1997. South Korea and Thailand were the hardest hit, but every country in the region suffered as the bankers executed a dramatic U-turn and headed for the exits. According to a study by the Institute for International Finance (IIF), after years of unrestrained lending to Asia despite mounting signs of trouble, Western and Japanese bankers panicked in fall 1997 and shut down the flow of new capital to the troubled countries. (See figure 14.1.) The IIF study stops short of suggesting that the foreign banks caused the crisis, but it highlights the combination of irresponsible borrowing and shortsighted, greedy bankers caught by surprise by the collapse of currencies and stock markets.[12]

Why, exactly, were bankers caught by surprise? Apparently country risk analysis before the Asian crisis was woefully inadequate for the task of predicting future developments in these countries. Analysts were blindsided by the crisis, lulled into complacency by generally positive credit trends, strong macroeconomic growth, the tendency toward more countries getting ratings and more countries issuing debt, and the political pressure to play down political risks. In this environment, analysts fell into some classic traps:

1. Political risks were understated in some key countries, such as Indonesia and India. In part, this was due to the role of sovereign governments as clients and users of financial services—and governments tend to be thin-skinned about bankers' assessment of domestic policies.

2. Financial markets and institutions tolerated the lack of transparency and disclosure in Asia as long as market trends remained positive.

3. Analysts placed a heavy emphasis on positive track records and the Asian miracle story. This is the classic tendency to project the past into the future, allowing negative factors to be obscured by the Asian success story.

4. Too much trust was placed in ratings. Market participants believed that rating agencies were impartial referees, when in fact they, too, were competing for position in a crowded market.

5. The emergence of new factors (i.e., ballooning levels of private sector dollar-denominated debt) was not given enough attention.

6. The globalization of financial markets was vastly underestimated.

7. The herd instinct of financial markets—the "madness of crowds"—was vastly underestimated.

Thus it seems clear that bankers fell into some of the very same traps that plagued them in 1980s Latin America. At the same time, however, bankers side-

TABLE 14.4 Net Capital Flows to Twenty-Nine Major Emerging Market Economies (US$ billions): How the Banks Helped Create the Emerging Market Crisis

	1993	1994	1995	1996	1997	1998
Total	$197.7	$196.2	$269.6	$331.8	$297.9	$195.6
Public	22.5	26.2	40.9	3.6	36.9	52.5
Private, of Which	175.2	170.0	228.7	328.2	261.0	143.1
Banks	25.2	43.4	99.5	120.4	30.9	−29.1
Other Creditors	66.2	30.0	23.4	78.8	88.7	49.4
Direct Investment	40.6	67.2	81.4	93.3	116.2	120.4
Portfolio Equity	43.2	29.4	24.4	35.7	25.2	2.4

Source: Institute for International Finance, as quoted in the *Financial Times,* April 21, 1999.

FIGURE 14.1 Cross-Border Loans to Developing Countries (US$ billions)

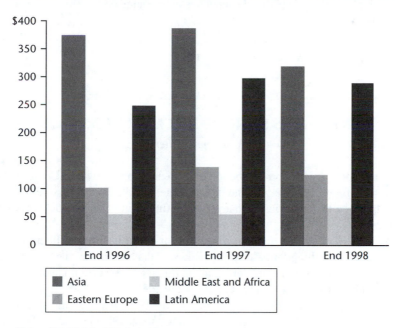

Source: BIS Consolidated Statistics, 1998, at www.bis.org.

stepped some of the worst snares. The threat to the world financial system posed by Asia and Russia together in 1997–98 paled in comparison with that of Latin America in the 1980s. Most important, the risk to banks from the 1997–98 financial turmoil was to their earnings potential, not their stability. It was a pocketbook issue, not a basic solvency one.

This is not to say that the Asian contagion did not clobber banks. Indeed, there was a long list of prestigious international financial institutions reporting heavy

IMF ATTACKS CREDIT RATING AGENCIES
Edward Luce

C redit rating agencies should devote more resources to the rating of emerging market countries if they are not to repeat the mistakes they made prior to the Asian crisis of 1997, according to the International Monetary Fund.

In its annual report on international capital markets, the IMF said the signals sent by credit rating agencies had become an increasingly important determinant of how markets behave.

In some cases, the decisions made by the agencies, including the rapid downturn of the sovereign ratings of South Korea and Thailand, had accelerated the dramatic outflow of capital from these countries. This had made a bad situation worse.

"Rather than being an important independent stabilizing force, the major credit rating agencies did not behave very differently from the vast majority of participants," it said. "While the ratings assigned prior to the crisis were too high, it is arguable that the agencies overreacted and in some cases went to the other extreme."

Source: Financial Times, September 9, 1999, p. 4.

ILLNESS LESS SERIOUS BUT MORE CONTAGIOUS
Stephen Fidler

I nvestors may be worried about Russia generating a new phase of a worldwide financial crisis, but the threat to the world's financial system is not yet seen to be as serious as that posed by the Latin American debt crisis of the 1980s.

Mr. Charles Dallara, managing director of the Institute of International Finance, a Washington-based think tank, said the current Russian crisis, with the turmoil in Asia, did not yet equal the threat to the world financial system posed by Latin America's debt crisis of the 1980s.

Many analysts now conclude that if the debt owed by Latin American governments to US, European, and to some Japanese banks in the 1980s had been recognized at its market value, many of the world's main banking institutions would have been bankrupted by that crisis....

The current crisis offers nowhere near the same kind of risks to the world's banking system, because banks hold nowhere near the same volumes of debt, in general, and because they are mostly better capitalized....

Source: Financial Times, August 28, 1998, p. 2.

losses from the Russian and Asian crises. Citicorp cut its third quarter 1998 earnings by $200 million because of losses related to Russia; Bankers Trust took a $350 million pretax trading loss related to holdings of Russian securities. The losses were not just confined to New York banks either; Barclays Bank took a charge of 250 million pounds in 1998 to cover potential losses on Russian lending and securities business, while big Swiss and Japanese banks also reported large losses. These losses surely suggest that banks failed to properly assess the risks associated with doing business in emerging markets such as Russia, repeating the missteps of the 1970s and 1980s.

On the whole, however, the big Western banks by the late 1990s were well capitalized and could absorb these losses with relative ease. The extent of U.S. banks' exposure to Russia was minimal compared with that to Latin America in the 1980s. Moreover, this time around the banks took quick action to write down possible losses by up to 85 percent, limiting the damage. According to estimates, U.S. money-center banks had $58.5 billion outstanding in loans to Latin America in 1984, compared with total capital of $26.7 billion and reserves of $4.1 billion. By contrast, the same banks had total exposure to Russia of just $6.4 billion in 1998, set against total capital of $92 billion and reserves of $15.9 billion.[13] Even Russia plus Asia did not pose a real threat to the global financial system. Although banks' exposure to troubled Asian countries was large in absolute terms, it was much smaller in proportion to the banks' capital bases. The largest cross-border exposure to Korea was in Japan, where banks had $22.5 billion outstanding as of June 1997 according to the BIS. Even this figure, however, was dwarfed by the mountain of problem loans held by Japanese banks in domestic markets.

Since the banks were better capitalized and the volume of debt held by banks was much lower, the 1997–98 crisis offered much less systemic risk. Also, the nature of the banks' exposure had changed dramatically since the early 1980s. The aggregate exposure data cover a variety of different risks. In particular, trade finance—letters of credit secured by goods in transit—makes up a large proportion of credits to Asia. This type of lending is generally considered high quality, boasting a much better repayment record than other types of credit. The nature of the banks' exposure had changed in other ways as well. In 1982 banks lending to Latin America were involved largely for their own account. After the debt crisis exploded, the banks learned to minimize their exposure to worrisome countries, emphasizing instead their role as underwriters and wholesalers. As a result, much of their activity in emerging markets by the mid–1990s was off–balance sheet, noncredit services rather than straightforward lending exposure.

Of course, by the mid–1990s the banks had forgotten some of the pain of Latin America, and they were aggressively lending to some emerging markets. Even so, as noted above, the magnitudes were much smaller and more manageable than in the 1970s and 1980s. Moreover, even in straight lending the rules had changed. In the early days of lending to Latin America, syndicates of big U.S. banks were the lenders, and the borrowers were Latin American governments. Asia in the 1990s looked very different; most of the loans were from Japanese and European banks, with U.S. banks in a distant third place, and most of the loans were not to governments but to private sector borrowers. At first glance, this appears to be more

CURRENCY CONTROLS ARE GETTING A HEARING AMID ASIAN CRISIS

David Wessel and Bob Davis

For better than a year, the Treasury and the International Monetary Fund have lectured shaken governments that the only prudent response to their financial crisis is to move more rapidly toward unfettered markets, for everything from cars to currency. And until recently, these governments paid heed.

But it hasn't worked—at least not nearly as well as the advocates hoped.

Now, some of the afflicted countries are moving in the opposite direction, erecting new barriers to the free flow of money across borders. More appear likely to follow. The result is the most serious challenge to the free-market orthodoxy that the globe has embraced since the end of the Cold War.

Declaring that "the free market has failed disastrously," Malaysian Prime Minister Mahathir Mohamed this week said his country will no longer allow its currency to trade outside its borders. Russia has unilaterally refused to pay some of its foreign debts. Some Latin American governments are flirting with new controls on the flow of money across borders....

All this hasn't been lost on Wall Street. As Goldman, Sachs & Co. economists note in their newsletter this week, "So far, countries whose currencies have not been freely convertible have done best. This raises the risk that at some point, other countries will decide to impose capital controls. The exact consequences for the U.S. outlook are not clear, but they would certainly be negative." The Goldman economists see a threat to the profits of U.S. multinational corporations, particularly financial institutions, that have benefited from an increased openness to foreign direct investment....

Source: Wall Street Journal, September 4, 1998.

---

promising. In the 1980s, sagging Latin American economies were incapable of generating enough foreign exchange to repay the lenders. Hence, debt reduction and Brady bonds eventually emerged to help resolve the dilemma. However, the more powerful and internationally competitive Asian economies, especially South Korea, should prove capable of generating more income, enough for full repayment as long as the debt is spread out over a long enough period of time.[14]

In other ways, however, the different nature of banks' exposure to emerging markets in the 1990s appears less benign. In contrast to the earlier era, in the 1990s international banks were heavily involved in trading securities of emerging markets—generating huge losses when these markets tanked. Chase Manhattan, for example, took a huge loss ($150–200 million pretax in one week alone) in emerging markets securities trading in late 1997. This bank, like many others, was caught holding vast quantities of emerging market bonds that it no longer wanted, and trying to unwind complex derivatives positions in an illiquid market. Thus the shift from straightforward lending to noncredit operations such as securities trading and foreign exchange trading in emerging markets carries its own set of risks. The nature of the exposure is different, but the risk is still substantial. This underscores the ultimate finding: In contrast to the 1980s, the 1990s Asian crisis was not a bank solvency issue, but rather a threat to banks' earnings power.

The Asian crisis, however, has had a profound impact on conventional wisdom toward free markets and capital controls. For at least the past decade, the IMF and other purveyors of financial wisdom have told emerging market governments that the true path to free market prosperity begins with the lifting of all controls on capital flows. Until the 1997–98 free fall, most of their clients were pleased with this advice, as hundreds of billions of dollars in foreign investment inflows fueled an unprecedented increase in living standards. However, the events of 1997–98 illustrated the dangers of this approach as well. Countries as far-flung as Brazil and Malaysia were hard hit as foreign capital fled for the exits, while those that had refused to lift capital controls—China, India, and to some extent Chile—were largely insulated from the crisis. The lessons that may be drawn are obvious, and they have led to calls around the world for reimposition of capital controls.[15] In turn, the prospect of renewed capital controls raises lending risks around the world (borrowers may not be allowed to service foreign currency denominated debt), and it may even result in controls on capital inflows as Chile used to impose.

Bankers and Hedge Funds

Speculators—and the huge **hedge funds** that they manage—have been widely and popularly blamed for the spectacular collapse of emerging markets currencies and equities in the 1990s. The truth is much more complex, of course, and includes

---

EDITORIAL: LESSONS FROM A HEDGE FUND CRISIS

A worried group of leading US bankers goes into a secret, smoke-filled meeting on Wall Street and emerges with a plan to stop contagion spreading through US markets. September 1998? No, October 24, 1929, at the start of the crash, when J.P. Morgan and its allies famously stepped into the market in an attempt—briefly successful—to restore confidence.

One should perhaps not draw parallels between that event and Wednesday night's rescue of Long-Term Capital Management, the US hedge fund, other than to note that Wall Street has a history of working together in times of financial peril.

But the bailout of Long-Term Capital demonstrates the extent to which the global financial crisis is now touching the US. It must also raise fresh concern about the prudence international banks have shown in their lending to hedge funds....

Source: Financial Times, September 25, 1998, p. 23.

bankers who were not necessarily trying to create market turmoil but undoubtedly made a substantial contribution nonetheless as they raced in and out of fragile markets at warp speeds. One of the more intriguing chapters of the Asian contagion saga, however, is the role of hedge funds—and the bankers who bankrolled them.

Hedge funds are in fact absurdly misnamed investment funds for the very rich, which operate essentially beyond the reach of disclosure or regulatory requirements. They are deliberately structured in ways that allow them to avoid the disclosure requirements that apply to brokerage firms, banks, and other financial institutions. Hedge funds operate with low levels of capital and extraordinarily high levels of leverage, usually supplied by bankers and brokerage houses. Hedge funds, one would hope, are effectively supervised by the banks that lend to them, which are in turn supervised by the government.

This comfortable belief, however, was challenged by the spectacular near-collapse of the (also) misnamed Long-Term Capital Management (LTCM) hedge fund in late 1998. Using sophisticated quantitative models, LTCM was betting on all kinds of securities in many markets, but when emerging markets turmoil sent securities plunging in tandem in midyear, the fund's highly leveraged positions were decimated. (LTCM was apparently using Value-at-Risk [VAR] models to measure their risk, at least at the beginning of their difficulties. This should highlight the dangers of excessive reliance on the VAR models discussed in Chapter 11.) According to reports, LTCM had over $120 billion in positions on just $5 billion of capital. Apparently, almost every major Wall Street securities firm and many large commercial banks extended generous credit lines to this secretive and highly leveraged fund.

LTCM's huge losses focused attention on the risk posed to the global financial system by these hedge funds. The Federal Reserve Bank of New York made the extraordinary decision to broker a rescue, helping to put together a consortium of fourteen financial institutions that injected $3.6 billion into the failing hedge fund in order to stave off bankruptcy. Needless to say, the Fed came under intense criticism for this action, but officials insisted that their concern was to stabilize financial markets rather than to protect LTCM's rich and well-connected owners and creditors. Fear of the unknown played a major role—the complex and secretive nature of LTCM's business meant that no one could really predict the impact of its collapse. While this was a serious concern, critics also worry about the moral hazard aspects of the LTCM bailout. If high-flying financial speculators are persuaded that they will be rescued in the event of a disaster, this obviously reduces their incentive to manage risks prudently.

Observers also marvel at the extent to which the best and brightest bankers on Wall Street and around the world underwrote LTCM. UBS—the world's second largest bank and a bastion of Switzerland's renowned banking establishment—took a $682 million charge on its loans to LTCM; Sumitomo Bank of Japan had invested $100 million with LTCM, and even the Italian central bank had invested a small portion of the country's foreign exchange reserves with LTCM for management!

In the wake of the LTCM debacle, of course, many bankers wonder whether the proliferation of huge investment funds outside the regulatory net may pose a threat to global banking systems. In this context, there are many calls for expanded regulation of these firms. No doubt, it was naive of bankers to act as counterparties to LTCM's bets and as financiers of its activities. However, the banks were enticed by the opportunity of lucrative business with LTCM. They could earn fat commissions on business with a company that traded as frequently and in such large volumes as LTCM.

In the end, responsibility for reining in hedge funds rests with the bankers. The Chairman of the Federal Reserve, Alan Greenspan, argues convincingly that regulating the hedge funds would just drive them overseas to unregulated environments. Rather, he believes that the best way to control their proclivity for risk taking is for their lenders to assess their risks and to deny them credit when necessary. Thus banking supervisors can be the second line of defense by pushing bankers to ensure that their risk assessments are adequate. In the end, the responsibility belongs to the banks.

The Future of Country Risk

The 1997–98 financial turmoil highlights the weakness of the international financial system, and possibly the need to strengthen or restructure it. Global markets were once again near crisis, reeling under the weight of aggressive lending by foreign banks to shaky countries such as Thailand and Indonesia; heavy borrowing by speculative hedge funds to invest in volatile emerging markets; and substantial, unhedged foreign borrowing by private sector companies in Asian countries. The common denominator, of course, is undisciplined foreign lending based on inadequate risk assessment of emerging market countries.

The consequences of poor country risk analysis are still unfolding. Emerging market countries are still teetering, but the banks were punished as well. ING, the Dutch financial group, announced plans in late 1998 to cut 1,200 jobs at ING Barings, its corporate and investment banking arm, because of the downturn in emerging markets. This is undoubtedly the tip of the iceberg. Many leading banks saw profit declines linked to emerging markets debt and/or LTCM. In particular, many banks endured a plunge in trading and commission income following the sharp decline in equity markets worldwide. In sum, all investment and commercial banks were hammered to varying degrees because of weak markets and global economic turmoil. The crisis of 1997–98 may have subsided, but its legacy is a reminder of the boombust cyclicity and inherent riskiness of lending in these markets around the world.

The financial crisis of 1997–98 poses some fresh challenges to the country risk analysts who failed to predict it. The old methodologies of country risk assessment must now be revamped to fit the new environment; methodology must catch up with globalization of financial markets. A wish list for future risk analysts would include the following:

1. More awareness of potential linkages for contagion (e.g., geographical links, similar economies)
2. More awareness of the identity and likely behavior of short-term creditors
3. Better transparency and disclosure
4. Improved regulatory environments

5. A better understanding of domestic banking systems, especially in emerging markets

6. Greater emphasis on certain risk factors, such as short-term capital flows, currency risks, regulatory risks, and legal/contract enforcement risk

7. With respect to political analysis, new emphasis on type of political system, autonomy of various branches (such as the central bank), the rule of law, the role of the military, and the power of the ruling elite

The prime lesson of Asia's meltdown may prove to be that globalization has forever changed the world, creating more volatility and risk than anyone thought possible a decade ago. Moreover, transparency and disclosure are critical. In the go-go lending atmosphere of the early 1990s, there was some tendency to shrug at poor disclosure and sloppy financial statements because of the rush to enter hot emerging markets. Perfectly sane bankers lent on the basis of Indonesian balance sheets that would have been torn apart in Kansas. Finally, what goes up must come down, and bankers must be prepared for the down as well as the up. Experience matters; junior traders who never saw a bear market before panicked, creating an unheard-of herd mentality—the madness of crowds.

There is much talk, of course, of crisis prevention systems to avert another meltdown. In most of the suggestions being put forth, the IMF plays a leading role as an arbiter and early warning system. The Bank for International Settlements (BIS) has suggested a more refined classification of risk than was previously used in supervision and capital requirements, highlighting the dynamic interplay between financial market developments and supervisory responses. There is one unavoidable reality, however; no crisis prevention system will reduce the need for good country risk analysis—or make the job any easier!

TABLE 14.5 A guide to market euphemisms	
Asia	Adventure playground for western bankers. Home of world-beating companies with the wrong form of corporate governance. Missionaries from the International Monetary Fund (qv) are busy imposing Anglo-American gospel to promote mergers, acquisitions, downsizing, etc., distracting firms from making globally competitive products. Long-awaited Asian century will thus be delayed.
Banking Crises	What crises? Alan Greenspan, the chairman of the US Federal Reserve, has abolished them.
Black-Scholes	(Rhymes with black holes). Exotic mantra that absolves option traders from applying critical intelligence to their work. Otherwise, an option pricing model that facilitates lucrative volumes of turn-over for Wall Street and London. See also dynamic hedging and Nobel Prize winners.

(continued)

TABLE 14.5 A guide to market euphemisms *(continued)*

Bubble	Killjoy term for the current bull market in equities which, as every investment banker will tell you, are risk free. It is anyway the patriotic duty of Americans to keep buying, otherwise the US economy will grind to a halt. "Only coconuts go down as well as up"—Goldman Sachs, 1998.
Contagion	What happens when a dozen or so traders talk on the phone or the golf course about the next country to sell short. Global financial village provides ideal breeding conditions for this epidemic phenomenon. As profitable for financiers as a plague for physicians. Makes nonsense of theory of portfolio diversification (qv).
Convergence	Notion that most financial instruments in any hedge fund or bank portfolio will observe a rule of inexorable mutual attraction, so providing convergence player with a free lunch. No empirical evidence to support this rule. Some claim that belief in convergence is closely correlated with bankruptcy and bail-outs.
Crony Capitalism	Degenerate form of relationship banking, more politely known as "Asian values." Paradoxically prevalent on Wall Street (see LTCM) and in 10 Downing Street, although bribery is less explicit. Can inflict crushing losses on investors outside the loop and reputational damage on naïve politicians.
Dollar	The greatest brand name in global finance. Threatened with depreciation as a result of current account deficit heading for 4 percent of US gross domestic product; also by arrival of the new European currency, the euro (qv). Or not, as the case may be, since this is a currency forecast and worth about as much as any other currency forecast.
Dynamic Hedging	Wall Street's answer to the philosophers' stone, whereby each and every change in security prices requires fund managers to trade ferociously in the derivatives markets for the benefit of investment bankers.
Emerging Market Economies	Fair game for hedge funds and proprietary traders. Contain real people, who live with savagely deflationary consequences of swings in capital flows that range up to 15 percent of GDP. But it's all their fault because of crony capitalism (qv).

(continued)

TABLE 14.5 A guide to market euphemisms *(continued)*

Euro	A virtual currency that comes into being in January without any notes or coins. To be administered by a central bank as secretive and unaccountable as a hedge fund. Big business wild about it.
George Soros	Not to be confused with Stanley Druckenmiller, who runs the Soros hedge fund. The real George Soros is a great philanthropist, who recently made headlines with his call for Mr. Druckenmiller to be restrained before he sinks another emerging market economy.
Globalization	Ghastly cliché. Avert gaze and move on.
Hedge Funds	Engine of contagion; honey-pot for investment bankers, who derive profits from brokering, money lending, stock lending, clearing fees and handy inside knowledge from these secretive institutions. Prone to charge outrageous fees for providing leveraged access to rising markets. Meaning and derivation of name a total mystery. Redeeming feature: they get up the nose of Mahathir Mohamad (qv).
IMF	Unfailing commitment to deflationist policy provides rare fixed point in a fast-moving financial world. Convenient butt for profligate governments and megaphone economists. Legitimate target for all others.
Investment Banks	Hedge funds in disguise, which front for real hedge funds. They sport huge balance sheets perched on a slender wedge of capital and produce volumes of research showing hedge funds are the safest investments known to man (apart from investment banks). Focus of intense battle in which employees grab more and more profit at the expense of managers and shareholders.
Irrational Exuberance	Wall Street in sober mood.
Japan	Alas…
Long Term	For fuddy-duddies, next Wednesday. For all others this afternoon.
Long-Term Capital Management	Respected specialist in leveraged levitation which manages the official reserves of the Bank of Italy. Also manages the personal savings of the heads of Merrill Lynch, Paine Webber and other securities firms. Presumed defunct in September but rose

(continued)

TABLE 14.5 A guide to market euphemisms *(continued)*

	from the dead on the third day with a little help from the Fed. Now trading furiously as ever under the supervision of crony creditors.
Mahathir Mohamad	Malaysian prime minister who, like George Soros, believes untrammelled capitalism is dangerous. Nonetheless wants to lock up the great philanthropist. Has locked up deputy prime minister Anwar Ibrahim instead.
Moral Hazard	Economists' jargon for great deals where banks grab the profits while taxpayers pay for losses.
Nobel Prize Winners	Subtle marketing device deployed by hedge funds, notably LTCM whose board was adorned by Myron Scholes (Black-Scholes, qv) and Robert Merton. Modern version of the yea-saying aristocratic directors of yore known as guinea pigs after the guineas they raked in.
Oskar LaFontaine	Germany's answer to Mahathir Mohamad.
Portfolio Diversification	Theory which claims that investing abroad will either deliver a higher reward at the same degree of risk, or the same reward at a lower degree of risk. Has cost US investors a fortune. Fund manager overheard at pension fund trustee meeting: "You will be delighted to hear that our grotesque underperformance has been achieved at a much lower degree of risk than otherwise."
Proprietary Trading	Convoluted name for punting with insured deposits; a zero-sum game played by banks out of desperation. Can turn positive when betting against central bank supporting unsustainable exchange rates. Governments oddly unconcerned about the contingent liability on their public finances.
Systemic Risk	As fearsome as the big bad wolf. The threat can now be posed by a single hedge fund. Great excuse for central bankers to open all available sluice gates.
Too Big to Fail	The modern definition of virtually any bank.

Source: Financial Times, December 27, 1998, p. 10.

| CASE STUDY | Whatever Happened at Barings? The Lure of Derivatives and Collapse |

This case was written by Professor Paul Stonham, EAP—European School of Management, Oxford, as the basis for class discussion rather than to illustrate either effective or ineffective handling of a management situation. This case was compiled from published sources.

Summary

On 27 February 1995, Barings, one of the UK's oldest merchant banks and a well-known name, was placed in administration following the disclosure that one of its Singapore traders, Nick Leeson, had accumulated losses of over £800 million on trading futures and options contracts.

... [T]his Case Study considers the scale of this disaster, placing it in the perspective of similar banking losses of recent years, as well as the damage that was caused to creditors. It reviews features of futures and options—the main financial products used in Leeson's authorised operations as well as the kind of risks that are encountered. It also considers Barings' ill-fated corporate strategy since the 1980s.

Run Up to the Collapse

Late on Thursday, 23 February 1995, a man was seen hurriedly leaving his office, Ocean Towers, the gleaming, glass-fronted headquarters of Baring Futures (Singapore) (BFS), in Raffles Place, the heart of Singapore's business district. This was Nick Leeson, general manager of Baring Futures and the company's senior floor trader on the Singapore International Monetary Exchange (SIMEX). He was never to return.

That evening, he and his wife Lisa drove to Kuala Lumpur, then flew to Kota Kinabalu. The following Wednesday, he flew alone to Frankfurt where German police took him into custody on the grounds of criminal charges notified to them by the Singapore Government.

Earlier, in the small hours of Friday 24 February, following growing suspicions, several senior Baring staff visited the offices of BFS and, after inspecting documents, were unable to obtain a reconciliation of BFS's cash position, detected a large fraudulent receivable, and found a concealed account listing massive losses mainly on futures contracts traded on SIMEX and Japanese stock exchanges.

This information was fed to an emergency meeting at the headquarters of the Barings Group in London on Thursday evening local time (London GMT is eight hours behind Singapore). At that meeting, Tony Gamby, Settlements Director of Baring Investment Bank and a director of Baring Broth-

(continued)

ers and Co Ltd (effectively the merchant bank and corporate finance advisory arm), was reported as saying that alarm bells were ringing.[1]

With colleagues, Gamby flew to Singapore the next day and all through Saturday, local time, worked on papers in the BFS offices. He was forced to confirm to HQ that BFS was apparently insolvent; the profits that Leeson had previously reported in 1993 and 1994 were illusory and, worse, the losses which were found could not be debited to client accounts, they were entirely to Barings' account.

In London, on Friday, local time, the directors of the parent company, Barings plc, allowed the Barings Group to continue trading, but notified the Bank of England (the supervisory authority) of apparent insolvency as the result of fraud. Over that weekend, the Bank of England failed to secure financial support from the international banking community and decided not to rescue Barings with tax-payers' money. Barings plc and most of its subsidiary companies were placed in administration with Ernst and Young. In Singapore, on Monday 27 February, SIMEX obtained approval from the Singapore High Court to appoint Price Waterhouse as judicial managers of BFS, and the company ceased trading.

Early Press Comment

This was a major shock to the international financial community and, predictably, made headlines in the world's Press. Even at this early stage, several *betes noires* were aired alongside comment on the immediate effects of the collapse, like the inherent risk of financial derivatives trading and the lack of proper regulation by trading markets and official regulators. These were to be explored in detail as the months went by.

In the UK, the Sunday newspapers were the first to break the news to the general public, following news agency reports on Sunday 26 February. A heading in the *Sunday Times* screamed,

> "Queen's bank near collapse in £400m loss. Bank desperate to find buyer after losing $600m in derivatives trading."

The "Queen's bank" was a reference to the fact that the Queen was a depository client of the merchant bank. £400m was an early, and much understated, calculation of the cumulative loss.

By Monday 27 February, all the UK newspapers had the story. The *Financial Times*, under the banner,

> "Barings forced to cease trading,"

said,

> "Barings, the UK merchant banking group, was last night placed in administration owing more than £500m on financial derivatives contracts after the Bank of England failed to organise a rescue by other banks."

The estimate of the loss had increased. Then, on Thursday 28 February, the *FT* along with other newspapers began more detailed analysis of the collapse under the heading,

(continued)

"The box that can never be shut,"

an apparent reference to the Bank of England's alleged inability to control the "Pandora's box" of financial derivatives and the exposure to risk that they can entail. The newspaper went on to say,

> "At the close of business on Friday, Barings enjoyed a reputation as one of the best managed of Britain's second-tier merchant banking groups. Before the markets had re-opened on Monday morning, the oldest name in British banking (founded 1762) had been reduced to beggary."

In fact, the accolade to Barings was unjustified. Later inquiry found the banking group's management of its securities business lax and confused, a factor contributing to the demise of BFS and the whole group, as important as the local wild trading and deceptive accounting which had taken place in Singapore.

What Exactly Was the Scale of the Disaster?

Although first estimates varied widely, by 28 February the British Press was talking in terms of £700m losses. There were reasons for this imprecision apart from the fact that a full investigation had not yet taken place. First, was the devious and untrustworthy nature of the accounts being kept by BFS, and second, the losses had resulted from one-way (unmatched) bets on futures contracts which still had open positions (had not been sold in this case) and on which the losses were increasing daily.

Eventually, a committee of inquiry (the Board of Banking Supervision) which reported to the House of Commons on 18 July 1995, calculated cumulative trading losses incurred by Leeson to amount of £827m on 27 February 1995 when trading ceased, and £927m when additional expenses to close out (sell), foreign exchange losses through revaluations, and SIMEX costs for taking over and closing remaining positions, were added in.

The immediate damage to markets (foreign exchange and stock markets) was less than might have been expected—mostly resulting from falls in confidence. The Pound dropped by about three pfennig to DM2.302, more than a pfennig below the previous record low of DM2.3125 reached in February 1993 after leaving the Exchange Rate Mechanism. The Tokyo Stock Exchange Index (Nikkei 225) fell 1,000 points, a slump of 5 percent on 27 February when markets re-opened, but finished that day down 3.8 percent at the close of trading. The London Stock Exchange Index (FTSE 100) lost only 12.4 points on 28 February to close at 3,025.3.

Neither was there "systemic" damage to the banking system. Partly this was because, in international terms, Barings was a "tiddler," a tiny player in international banking in comparison with the huge American and Swiss banks. Barings' £354m plus capital resources (assets £5.9 billion) were dwarfed by banks whose resources ran into several billions. Midland Global Markets, for instance, which is owned by HSBC Holding, has capital resources of £11.7 billion (assets £201 billion), and is the tenth most active derivatives trader; Barclays de Zoete Wedd (BZW), owned by Barclays

(continued)

Bank, is one of the top 15 global derivatives operators, and has capital resources of £10.5 billion (assets £166 billion).

To place Barings' loss in a wider perspective, Barings' loss would have wiped out Barclays' 1993 profits of £664m, of which £501m came from BZW, but not its 1994 profits of around £2 billion. In 1993, Midland made £844m in profits, of which £585m came from its derivatives arm. It is interesting to note that in 1994, Midland's derivatives trading contributed just £33m to group profits of £905m. The bank attributed the £552m drop to "losses from dealing in derivatives on the bond market." In other words, the Midland profit shortfall was more than half the loss that caused Barings to collapse, but there was much less agonizing over the reduced Midland profit position, and less recriminatory comment on the riskiness of derivatives.

However, as far as Barings was concerned, the losses were catastrophic—£827m in relation to shareholders' funds of £354m. There was much speculation in the business Press and in the days following the collapse about which creditors of Barings would suffer. Although BFS had incurred one-way losses on futures contracts traded on SIMEX and the Osaka Exchanges, because of the system of "margining" (daily installments of money paid to the Clearing House on falling market values of the contracts), SIMEX was owed only a few days' unpaid margins.

The problem was not that the counterparties to the BFS contracts (in effect the Clearing Houses) would not be paid the increased value of their contracts due to their more successful price forecasting, it was that BFS had been trading "for the house" (proprietary trading), that is to say, with its own money, not as an agent on behalf of client corporations paying margin with their funds. The £827m cumulative payments had been funded by Barings London either directly with cash or by borrowing (apart from some dishonest funding by Leeson).

There was therefore much newspaper speculation about which creditors of Barings would lose money. For example, there appeared to be some 3,000 depositors of Baring Brothers Bank with around £2.5 billion at risk. These included local councils, pension funds, banks, charities and building societies.

There were four "main arms" to the Barings group—Baring Asset Management (managing £27 billion in funds), Baring Brothers and Co (the merchant bank), Baring Securities, and Baring Investment Management. The last subsidiary managed investment funds for charities, pension funds and wealthy individuals, and was the only arm not placed in administration—it continued trading. Although the fund management side of Barings was "ringfenced" (its assets held separately from Baring Brothers Bank), unfortunately around £633m of cash was deposited in Baring Brothers Bank, and was therefore at risk. Similarly, offshore funds and investment funds of Barings were "ring-fenced," but had cash on deposit with the separate banking arm.

Among other major creditors were holders of Baring Brothers' 9.25 percent Perpetual Subordinated Notes, issued in January 1994 (bond-holders) which initially drew in £100m of bond-holders' money. In 14 months, these lost 100 percent of their value. Barings plc's share capital was privately subscribed by senior managers and the owners, and this was also at

(continued)

risk. Fifteen Japanese banks had a total of £425m of assets in Baring Securities (Japan); about £312m was likely to be written off as bad assets. Finally, a number of Japanese banks lent money to BFS in the form of government bonds to cover margin payments lodged with the Osaka Securities Exchange to the value of around £390m. There was great uncertainty about whether these would be repaid.

Did Barings Increase Its Risk Through Trading Derivatives?

There has been a catalogue of disasters arising from derivatives trading by banks and corporations in recent years, some of them, like Barings, large enough to have very damaging consequences. The list includes London-based food and drink manufacturer Allied Lyons in early 1991 ($220m loss on foreign exchange options), Nippon Steel Chemical in 1993 ($128m), Showa Shell Sekiyu in 1993 ($1.05 billion), Kashima Oil in 1994 ($1.45 billion on foreign exchange losses), the US washing powder and consumer goods company Procter and Gamble in 1993 (around $423m on interest rate swaps), Chile's State-owned copper company, Codelco in 1994 ($207m on copper futures trading), the German industrial company, Metallgesellschaft in 1993 ($660m on mismatches between its derivatives hedges and long-term oil contracts with customers), Japan's twelfth-largest commercial bank, Daiwa Bank, in its New York Office in 1995 ($1.1 billion on unauthorised bond and possible derivatives trading), and the Finnish bank Postipankk in 1995 ($100m).

Yet, these derivatives-related trading losses should be put into wider perspective before it is thought that derivative financial products are inherently dangerous.

While it is true that the volumes and value of futures, options and swaps contracts traded have increased astronomically in recent years, the amount of capital at risk in derivatives transactions is far less than the face value of these contracts. For example, some 153m contracts were traded on the London International Financial Futures Exchange (LIFFE) in 1993 compared with only 241,881 in 1982, the market's first year of trading. In 1994, the volume increased by another 50 percent on the four US exchanges—the Chicago Board of Trade, the Chicago Mercantile Exchange, the Chicago Board Options Exchange and the New York Mercantile Exchange—and volumes of futures and options increased 26 percent in 1994 to reach a total of 658.5m. Yet a 1994 Survey conducted by Arthur Andersen of the riskiest derivative transactions—privately-negotiated over-the-counter (OTC) transactions—showed that of the total notional value of swaps (principal amounts of contracts) of $8,133 billion, the cost of replacing the cashflows in these contracts was a mere one percent to two percent of the notional value. The International Swaps and Derivatives Association (ISDA) always boasts of the size and value of derivatives business, but this has led to confusion arising from using notional amounts to describe the amount of risk assume by market participants. It is because derivatives contracts are *leveraged*—buy-

(continued)

ers incur only a small cost of the principal sum in acquiring the contract, and most contracts are closed out before maturity.

A further report[2] by the Economist Intelligence Unit indicates that international companies are making rapidly growing use of derivatives despite the well-publicised corporate collapses, including Barings. From responses of 100 international companies, 95 percent reported a continuing favourable attitude to derivatives, with 52 percent regarding derivatives as "an essential and regularly utilised tool."

On the other hand, Touche Ross published a study[3] in 1995 of the use and control of derivatives by 26 companies in the London FTSE 100 Index. Touche Ross found that, despite knowledge of corporate losses from derivatives trading, only 65 percent of the companies surveyed had a written policy on the use of derivatives, and in many of these, the policies were inadequate. Only 50 percent said their policies specified the types of derivatives allowed, and 50 percent had policies which imposed limits on the volume and principal amounts of derivatives transacted. Only 58 percent of companies calculated the market value of their derivatives on a frequent basis. However, less than 10 percent reported that derivatives were used for speculative purposes.

Another point places the drama of derivatives into better perspective. Whilst the lightning speed with which an ancient but small British establishment bank's collapse from reckless futures trading is rightly frightening, the scale of this demise is small beside other banking losses in the cash markets. Barings cost the British taxpayer nothing, yet Credit Lyonnais, the French State-owned bank, had accumulated losses of FFr13.3 billion (£1.9 billion) by early 1995 from bad loans and poor investments (all in traditional, non-derivative-linked banking business). These were not only large losses, but they were illiquid in terms of laying them off compared with derivative risks on exchanges. All of the international banking community's losses on overseas investments and property in the 80s, and bonds in the 90s, dwarf derivatives' losses. Banks have not found it difficult to lose huge sums of money without going anywhere near derivatives.

Was Barings' Overall Corporate Strategy Ill-Fated?

Aside from the question of whether derivatives are inherently dangerous (to which the simplistic answer is that as well-managed insurance instruments, they are not), it may properly be asked if the Baring Group's corporate strategy was well-considered in the years running up to 1995.

Barings was an illustrious name. In 1818, the French Foreign Minister, Duc de Richelieu said, "There are six great powers in Europe: England, France, Prussia, Austria, Russia and Baring Brothers." This accolade did not apply so well eighty years later when Barings had to be rescued by the Bank of England for huge non-performing loans in Argentina.

From then on, however, Barings continued in traditional merchant banking, building up a reputation based on corporate finance, strong investment management, and the trading it did for one of the best client lists in London

(continued)

including the Royal Family. But by the time of "Big Bang" in London in 1987, it was in danger of being side-lined. Unlike its rivals, it did not attempt to create an integrated investment bank as others did following "Big Bang."

Up to 1984, Baring Brothers and Company (BB and Co) was a merchant bank specialising in corporate finance and debt trading. In 1984 it acquired the stockholding business of a small stockbroking company, Henderson Crosthwaite, a company with a staff of 15 based in London, Hong Kong and Tokyo. BB and Co then established Baring Securities Limited (BSL), as a separately (and liberally) managed business within the group. The head of BSL came from Henderson Crosthwaite, Christopher Heath. In the 1980s he was very successful, enjoying the fruits of the 1980s Tokyo Stock Market boom, and specialised in Japanese equity warrants—bonds sold with warrants exercisable into shares. Heath briefly earned notoriety when he was identified as Britain's highest-paid employee, earning £2.6m annually. At one point, in 1985, Barings bought Heath a £5m Asian securities business to develop which quickly returned £150m. Such was the expansion of the securities side of the business, and the growth of business in emerging markets, that Barings decided to consolidate BB and Co and BSL, the banking and securities side of its operations, for Bank of England reporting purposes. Between 1992 and 1995, Barings instigated a major internal reconstruction and management reorganization designed to combine BB and Co and BSL into a new and integrated structure, Baring Investment Bank (BIB). This reorganization had not been completed by the time of the collapse. Derivatives trading was, of course, part of BSL.

The success of Christopher Heath in the 80s (he resigned in 1993), contributing a disproportionate share of Barings' overall profits, proved to be a blessing and a curse. Heath's strength lay in understanding the securities markets in the Far East, and he paid less attention to client positions than the traditional merchant banking style would have done. There were definite problems of culture difference between the two sides of the group—stockholders versus bankers—mainly in terms of perception and management of risk, and also in technical understanding. Ironically, Heath departed after anxieties about the risk positions he was developing, although he never entered into unmatched derivatives trades like Leeson, even when doing proprietary business.

But growth became addictive, and after the departure of Heath, Barings still sought the high returns it had previously enjoyed from emerging markets and the new financial products, like equity warrants which had proved so profitable in the past. The gap between BB and Co and BSL seemed as big as ever, though. One former staff member is quoted as saying:

> "The distance between 8, Bishopsgate (the banking office) and 1, American Square (the securities office) was a few hundred yards and 150 years."

It was into this confused culture with its mixed reporting lines that Leeson took up his appointment in Singapore (in March 1992) to "head up the SIMEX operation and also act as floor manager."

In general terms, Barings fell into the same trap as in the 80s as did many other financial services organizations. World-wide banking profits were being

(continued)

eroded in their traditional lines of business, like lending at interest, by "disintermediation"—the growth of securities business like commercial paper at the expense of bank loans. Increased competition and technological innovation narrowed their margins further so that the banks were forced either to reinvent themselves or go out of business. A major new strategy was to push into new markets, like derivatives and new financial products, and to engage in proprietary trading on these and existing capital markets. Until its collapse, bank proprietary trading in bonds proved very profitable.

This was probably a mistake for a bank with shareholders' funds (in 1994) at only £354m. Such a narrow capital base was insufficient to run proprietary trading positions, especially in trades where the returns were leveraged and the risk high and complex to understand. Most dangerous of all, the experience of Christopher Heath and later from Leeson was that it seemed possible to make large profits from derivatives on what appeared to be a risk-free basis. But this trading everywhere was conducted by people who were able to profit from fast-moving markets, not by those schooled in the meticulous internal controls associated with traditional banking.

Ironically, by 1995, Barings was enjoying modest success in its merchant banking business and corporate finance. Among purely UK merchant banks it handled the largest number of acquisitions in Europe in 1994 after S G Warburg. Among all banks it was sixth advising on 29 transactions with a combined value of £8.7 billion—three times the 1993 value. In 1995 it was adviser to the pharmaceutical company Wellcome in the UK's largest-ever takeover by Glaxo. Other corporate advice included the giant 1994 flotation of 3i and Lloyds Bank's bid for the Cheltenham and Gloucester Building Society. In all in 1994, it advised 70 quoted corporate clients increasing the 1994 fee and commission income by 47 percent over the previous year.

Barings Securities also did well in other respects. In 1994 and 1995, it was a leading equity broker in Asia and Latin America; in fact, one-third of the company's employees of 4,000 staff were in emerging market countries. Emerging markets were also a specialty of Barings' third leg, Baring Asset Management, which had over £30 billion in funds under management.

None of this relatively profitable business was, however, able to save Barings from the debacle in the Far East.

Futures and Options in Risk Management

The derivatives which Leeson traded in the Far East were of the simplest type—futures and options. All derivative financial contracts are tradeable instruments whose value reflects, at least partially, that of the underlying asset—in Leeson's case equities, bonds and currencies—but also interest rates and commodities can be involved. Future contracts are agreements to buy or sell these assets at an agreed future date and price. Options are agreements that give the buyer the right—but not the obligation—to buy or sell an asset at or by an agreed future date. Both futures and options can be traded on official exchanges or over-the-counter (OTC).

(continued)

Futures and options evolved as instruments to manage (hedge) risk. With recent liberalization of exchange rates and increased volatility in currency markets, their use became more widespread, and the volume and value of contracts traded rocketed. Similarly, with greater freedom on capital markets and increased international borrowing and lending, the opportunities to lower costs of borrowing and to stabilise interest rate risk similarly became more available.

But all of this activity can legitimately be called "hedging" or insurance. With fine business margins, particularly internationally, it is important to safeguard those margins against external movements in currency prices and interest rates. The use of financial futures and options can offset that risk sometimes completely.

The principle is very simple—the hedger (bank, pension fund, corporate treasurer, etc.) takes a position in future contracts (buys or sells) that is equal and opposite to an existing or anticipated position in the cash market. The hedger "locks in" to currency prices or interest rates which he regards as acceptable and therefore guarantees them. Unfortunately, it means that the benefit of any favourable move in prices or rates is foregone. So, for instance, a long (buy) hedge in interest rates can be used to protect against exposure to falling interest rates or protect the return from a planned investment by buying futures contracts. Conversely, a short (sell) hedge can be used to protect against exposure to rising interest rates. Futures and options are normally dealt with on official exchanges like the Tokyo Stock Exchange and are standardised contracts so that the only variable is price. An example is the 10-year Japanese Government Bond (JGB) Future traded on the Tokyo Stock Exchange, one of the three main instruments traded by Leeson. It has the characteristics shown in [Table 1].

Futures contracts can also be used to hedge investment portfolios against future unfavourable movements in share prices. And this was another instrument traded by Leeson. A stock index futures contract is one in which the underlying asset is a specific stock index (like the Nikkei 225 stock index). An investor or portfolio manager who buys a stock index futures contract agrees to buy the stock index, and conversely, the seller of a stock index futures contract agrees to sell the stock index. The value of a stock index futures contract is the product of the futures price and the futures contract multiple. For the Nikkei 225 stock average future on SIMEX, the multiple is 500. Therefore, put another way, a stock index future is a contract to buy or sell the face value of the underlying stock index, where the face value is the value of the index multiplied by a specified amount.

The advantages of stock index futures to hedgers are important:

1. They allow investors to participate in a stock market without actually buying and selling the shares themselves.

2. The margining system allows this participation without the commitment of very large amounts of capital.

3. Buying and selling futures positions costs much less than buying and selling shares.

(continued)

The Tokyo Stock Exchange JGB Futures Contract	
Trading Unit	Standardized 6% 10-year JGB with a face value of ¥100m
Minimum Price Movement	1/100 point
Tick Size and Value	¥10,000
Contract Months	March, June, Sept. and Dec. Cycle (5 contract months at all times)
Last Day Trading	Ninth business day prior to each delivery date
Initial Margin Requirements	2% of nominal transaction value for members. The higher of 3% of nominal transaction value or ¥6m for clients (of which at least one-third must be cash)

4. Positions can be closed out quickly.

However, the overwhelming bulk of deals in derivatives markets like futures and options by volume and value is undertaken by traders (speculators) not hedgers, and are unconnected with underlying cash or trade transactions. Some of this speculation is risk-controlled but other forms can be very risky indeed. Whilst traders clearly add much-needed liquidity to derivatives markets, they can incur considerable risk themselves. In trading futures contracts, there are generally thought to be three trading strategies, in increasing order of risk:

1. Arbitrage trading—turning a profit from the simultaneous purchase and sale of futures contracts and cash instruments on the same or different exchanges where there is a temporary price mismatch.

2. Spread trading—taking a view on the way price differences between different future contracts will trend.

3. Position trading—making one-way bets on changes in interest rates or currency rates by buying or selling futures contracts.

Two features of financial futures and options contracts are especially relevant for trading—leverage and the margining system. It was also these features that caused particular problems for Leeson.

An example of the extreme effects of leverage is given by Derek Ross.[4] A trader wishing to establish a long position of $1 million in Eurodollar time deposit rates, could buy one futures contract on the London International Financial Futures Exchange (LIFFE), and he would be asked by LIFFE to deposit just $750 as the initial margin. If the futures price rose by 50 basis

(continued)

points (0.5 percent), since the value of each point is officially $25, he would show a profit of $1,250 (50 × $25) or nearly 100 percent return on his original investment. If, however, the rates had gone the other way, he would stand to lose nearly 100 percent of his original investment.

The margining system has been established by official exchanges like LIFFE and SIMEX to avoid or at least reduce counterparty risk on futures and options. Margins are "good faith" money. The initial margin on the Osaka Stock Exchange for the Nikkei 225 average future is 10 percent of the transaction value. On other exchanges the percentage of initial margin can be much lower. A speculator could bet on a rise in prices in the British gilt market through buying long gilt futures contracts on LIFFE. He could achieve a position of £1m in gilts for an outlay of just £20,000, and this initial margin could be deposited in interest-bearing securities rather than cash—a gearing of 50 times. It is the margin system that gives rise to the (unlimited) potential for gain and loss on a levered basis. But it is also this leverage possibility that reduces the cost of reducing price risk for hedgers. Although the exchange clearing house could not suffer large losses because of each day's marking to market in cash, an investor can lose large (levered) sums of money through a steady stream of margin calls.

For exchange-traded options, the buyer has no margin requirements because he pays the option price in full—it is the maximum amount he can lose. The option writer (seller) takes on all the risk of the position of the underlying asset; he is required to put up the option price received as margin and is usually also required to deposit additional margin as the position is marked to market daily. This gives rise to different risk/reward characteristics of options and futures. Futures provide a symmetrical risk/reward relationship—buyers and sellers lose/gain equally when the price of the future changes. The most the buyer of an option can lose is his option price; but the writer's downside risk is unlimited.

Leeson's Legitimate Business

Nick Leeson was authorised to conduct both proprietary and client account trading on Far Eastern exchanges, on behalf of other Barings companies, specifically, Baring Securities Limited (Singapore), Baring Securities (London) Limited, Baring Securities (Japan), Baring Securities Hong Kong Limited and Banque Nationale de Paris (Japan). He dealt in six main financial futures and some options on them, as follows:

1. the Nikkei 225 contract traded on SIMEX in Singapore;
2. the Nikkei 225 contract traded on OSE in Japan;
3. the 10-year JGB contract traded on SIMEX in Singapore;
4. the 10-year JGB contract traded on TSE in Japan;
5. the 3-month Euroyen contract traded on SIMEX in Singapore;
6. the 3-month Euroyen contract traded on TIFFE (Tokyo Financial Futures Exchange) in Japan.

(continued)

Around 1993, arbitrage business began to be an important part of Baring's Far Eastern operations. Initially this took the form of cash/futures arbitrage in Tokyo, and soon after the rapid build-up of arbitrage between SIMEX and OSE on Nikkei 225 futures contracts. The Barings' management called this authorised business "switching" although it would normally be known as a form of inter-exchange arbitrage. Leeson would buy and sell Nikkei 225 futures contracts simultaneously on SIMEX and OSE, benefitting from small differences in identical contracts—buying at the cheaper price and selling at the higher. These opportunities existed because OSE and SIMEX have different market conditions—OSE has local business, SIMEX mostly "off-shore" business, and OSE, being electronic, conducts business more slowly than SIMEX.

Leeson also "switched" JGB futures contracts on SIMEX and TSE. This arbitrage market provided good opportunities since the JGB market was rather volatile. He also did arbitrage business on SIMEX and TIFFE Euroyen contracts, although the opportunities here were limited.

Arbitrage business can generate only very small profits on large volumes of contracts traded. Even then, there is a built-in limit to the amount of profits that can be generated since, if orders for large quantities are placed on two exchanges, the price differences tend to diminish.[5]

As well as exploiting price differences in this way, Leeson could match client orders on SIMEX when liquidity was not available to execute it immediately, taking the other side and laying off the risk with the equivalent number of contracts on the more liquid OSE. He could therefore proprietary trade by "riding on the back" of large client buy orders for SIMEX Nikkei contracts, hoping to benefit from the markets being moved favourably. If the markets moved unfavourably, he could arbitrage between OSE and SIMEX. SIMEX later reported that this may have constituted the offence of "bucketing" under the Futures Trading Act.

Theoretically, arbitrage is risk-free since orders are matched, but timing differences between exchanges give rise to some risk of prices moving unfavourably. For this reason, Leeson was allowed to take unhedged positions on the following number of contracts during a single day: 200 OSE Nikkei contracts, 100 TSE JGB contracts and 500 Euroyen contracts. All open positions on the contracts had to be closed out at the end of a day's trading.

Leeson was not authorised to undertake proprietary trading in options; therefore no gross limits were set.

The products and kind of client/proprietary operations described above were all authorised by Barings HQ and supposedly subject to the Group's various levels of management control. However, even before Barings' collapse, there were curious features of Leeson's operations.

First, his supposedly low-risk arbitraging with Nikkei 225 and JGB futures produced apparently large returns, quite out of proportion to the type of business involved, even if the number of contracts traded was very large. From accounts disclosed for 1994 (later found to contain false reporting), Leeson's "switching" business contributed £28.5m to the Barings Group operating profits, about 8 percent of total profits, and nearly as great as the

(continued)

Banking Group's operating profit (£36.9m). Of this switching activity, £23.4m was generated solely from JGB arbitrage.

The second curious feature was the continuing call by BFS on the rest of the Group for funds for margin payments. The transfer of funds was unremitting and in the end, cumulatively enormous. [Table 2] shows the build-up.

By 24 February 1995, this cumulative funding represented well over the reported capital of the Barings Group. This astonishing situation was allowed to develop as the result of no reconciliation of the funding with client records. But even common sense would have been enough to make anyone realise that, if indeed Leeson's arbitrage was successful, and making real profits, then margin cash should have been *received* in large amount, not paid. Such receipts of margin would have been used for calls. A stream of margin calls building up to stratospheric cumulative sums could only have meant the contracts were losing value for Leeson as they were daily marked to market.

Third, Leeson was building up substantial long positions on SIMEX and short positions on TSE. Because BSF had continued to pay margin calls, the exchanges were satisfied. There was no apparent attempt by the Barings Group or the exchanges themselves to investigate the size of the open positions which resulted, although it must be said that Leeson was concealing the true size of these positions and even fraudulently computing margin payments to SIMEX. It was common knowledge among SIMEX, OSE and TSE traders in the first two months of 1995 that BFS had enormous open positions in the exchanges. Since also most participants in the exchanges were known to each other, and no-one seemed to know the clients on whose behalf BFS was acting, it did not seem a poor guess to assume there were proprietary and unmatched trades.

To give some idea of BFS's huge participation on SIMEX, in the months of January and February 1995, BFS was the largest trader holding between 12 and 8 percent of SIMEX volume. In 1993 it ranked 9th and in 1992, 26th. In December 1994 it held about 2 percent of outstanding contracts on Nikkei 225 futures traded on SIMEX, and in January 1995, 34 percent. In January 1993 it held 1 percent of outstanding contracts of Nikkei 225 options traded on SIMEX, and in January 1995, 35 percent.

Margin Payments to BSF from the Rest of the Barings Group			
Company	1 Jan 1994 £ millions	31 Dec 1993 £ millions	24 Feb 1995 £ millions
BSLL	7	13	105
BSL	33	142	337
BSJ	(1)	66	300
Total	39	221	742

Source: Board of Banking Supervision Inquiry, 1995. Inquiry team based on analysis prepared by Barings.

(continued)

The three warning signals described briefly above are ones which might have appealed to a simple common sense view of derivatives hedging and trading as perceived by anyone concerned with these markets and contracts. In fact, there was in place a range of controls internal and external to Barings and available to the regulatory and supervisory authorities which could have picked up more precise and factual information even though concealment was taking place.... These "common sense" warning signals should have alerted controllers and supervisors that Leeson's operations were not normal. It could, of course, have been possible that he was transacting authorised trades, but had simply exceeded his trading limits. But this could still not have accounted for the kind of warning signals of excess described above....

---

[1]*Report of the Board of Banking Supervision Inquiry into the Circumstances of the Collapse of Barings,* London, HMSO, 18 July 1995.
[2]*Strategic Derivatives: Successful Corporate Practices for Today's Global Marketplace,* Economic Intelligence Unit, London, 1995.
[3]*The Corporate Use of Derivatives,* Sarah Welch, Touche Ross, London, 1995.
[4]Derek Ross, *International Treasury Management,* 2nd edition, Woodhead Faulkner, Cambridge, 1990.
[5]*Baring Futures (Singapore) Pte Ltd., Investigation Pursuant to Section 231 of the Companies Act (Chapter 50). The Report of the Inspectors Appointed by the Minister for Finance*, Singapore, MOF, 6 September 1995.

Questions

1. Is lending to a company in Thailand more risky than lending to a company in Belgium? Why or why not?
2. What are the key elements of country risk?
3. What do you consider the most important variables in assessing country risk?
4. It is sometimes said that dictators make better debtors than democrats. Should bankers prefer lending to dictators or democrats? Why?
5. What do you think are the five riskiest countries in the world today? Why?
6. Using no more than ten variables, construct a simple model to measure country risk. Do you weight all variables equally? What are the constraints to your model? Under what circumstances do you expect it to perform well?
7. Who was to blame for the Latin American debt crisis of the 1980s? To what extent should greedy bankers bear responsibility for what happened?
8. Who was to blame for the Asian contagion of 1997–98? To what extent do you blame greedy bankers for this crisis?
9. What are the similarities between the Latin American debt crisis of the 1980s and Asian contagion of 1997–98? What are the differences? Do you think that bankers learned from their mistakes in Latin America? How likely do you think another international financial crisis similar to those two is in the future?
10. What are hedge funds? Explain the interplay between bankers and hedge funds.
11. Suppose you were a banker in the mid–1990s. Would you have extended credit to LTCM? Why or why not? Would you have participated in its bailout?

Suggested Readings

There is an embarrassment of riches available to the reader interested in learning more about the various financial crises that commenced in August 1982. A brief sampling follows.

Claudon, Michael P., editor. *World Debt Crisis: International Lending on Trial.* Cambridge, Mass.: Ballinger Publishing Company, 1986. Focuses on IMF and World Bank strategies for dealing with the Latin American debt crisis, as well as the role played by banks in creating the preconditions and deepening the crisis.

Clifford, Mark L., and Pete Engardio. *Meltdown: Asia's Boom, Bust, and Beyond.* New York: Prentice Hall Press, 2000. An accurate, journalistic depiction of Asia's 1997 economic collapse, emphasizing factors beyond the traditional boom and bust cycle.

Darity, William A. *The Loan-Pushers: The Role of Commercial Banks in the International Debt Crisis.* Cambridge, Mass.: Ballinger Publishing Company, 1988. Presents an interesting viewpoint on causes of the debt crisis and anticrisis management. Focus on how financing mechanisms and capital market developments created the setting for the debt crisis.

Eichengreen, Barry, and Peter H. Lindert. *The International Debt Crisis in Historical Perspective.* Cambridge, Mass.: MIT Press, 1989. Takes an economic history approach to Latin American debt crisis, drawing parallels between previous debt crises and the 1980s crisis.

Hunter, William C., George G. Kaufman, Thomas H. Krueger. *The Asian Financial Crisis: Origins, Implications, and Solutions.* Boston Kluwer Academic Press, 1999. Thorough and intelligent examination of the Asian crisis.

MacDonald, Scott, Margie Lindsay, and David L. Crum, editors. *The Global Debt Crisis: Forecasting for the Future.* London: Francis Pinter, 1990. Takes a regional view of 1980s debt crisis, drawing lessons for future crisis avoidance and management.

MacDonald, Scott, Jane Hughes, and Uwe Bott. *The Latin American Debt Crisis in the 1990s.* New York: Praeger, 1991. Focuses on prospects for Latin America following the "lost decade" of the 1980s.

Miller, Morris. *Coping Is Not Enough!: The International Debt Crisis and the Roles of the World Bank and IMF.* Homewood, Ill.: Dow Jones-Irwin, 1986. Management of the Latin American debt crisis, including analysis of the World Bank and IMF scenarios developed for addressing the crisis.

Roubini, Nouriel. Asian Financial Crisis website, at www.stern.nyu.edu/~nroubini/asia/AsiaHomepage.html. NYU's Professor Roubini developed this website to collect information and analyses of the Asian financial crisis in 1997–98. It is an essential site for anyone interested in this topic, providing a broad range of up-to-date academic and business-related analysis. A must!

Sachs, Jeffrey. *New Approaches to the Latin American Debt Crisis.* Princeton, N.J.: Princeton University Press, 1989. Another must; provides a critical view on the anticrisis policies adopted by Latin American governments from an important analyst of the period.

Watkins, Alfred J. *Till Debt Do Us Part: Who Wins, Who Loses, and Who Pays for the International Debt Crisis.* Washington, D.C.: University Press of America, 1986. Emphasis on major macro and psychological causes of the crisis; easy reading style. Discusses why banks were so eager to lend, including an estimate of the costs of the crisis for the banks.

In addition, the following books are focused specifically on country risk analysis.

Palmer, Howard. *Bank Risk Analysis in Emerging Markets*. London: Euromoney Publications, 1992.

Rogers, Jerry, editor. *Global Risk Assessments: Issues, Concepts, and Applications*. Riverside, Calif.: Global Risk Assessments, 1997.

Solberg, Ronald, editor. *Country Risk Analysis: A Handbook*. New York: Routledge, 1992.

Websites

www.prsgroup.com	Political Risk Services
www.emergingeconomies.net/ countryrisk/html	Country risk analysis of emerging market countries
www.grai.com/links.htm	More than 100 links for international economic, political, and business research
www.stern.nyu.edu/~nroubini/asia/ Asiahomepage.html	Asian financial crises
www.moodys.com	Sovereign debt ratings
www.ratings.com	Standard & Poor's ratings
www.imf.org	International Monetary Fund
www.worldbank.org	World Bank
www.ebrd.com	European Bank for Reconstruction and Development
www.asiandevbank.org	Asian Development Bank
www.iadb.org	Inter-American Development Bank

Notes

1. Martin Wolf, "On Sovereign Bankruptcies," *Financial Times*, May 5, 1995.

2. Martin Beckman, *Crashes: Why They Happen—What to Do* (London: Grafton Books, 1988).

3. Political Risk Services, *The Handbook of Country and Political Risk Analysis* (Syracuse, N.Y.: Political Risk Services, 1998).

4. Martin Wolf, "On Sovereign Bankruptcies."

5. Scott B. MacDonald, Jane Hughes, and Uwe Bott, *Latin American Debt in the 1990s: Lessons From the Past and Forecasts for the Future* (New York: Praeger, 1991).

6. Raul L. Madrid, *Over-exposed: U.S. Banks Confront the Third World Debt Crisis* (Washington, D.C.: Investors Responsibility Research Center, 1990).

7. Ibid.

8. Darren McDermott, "Citibank Uses Latin Lessons in Asia," *Wall Street Journal*, December 29, 1997, p. A6.

9. Bank for International Settlements, *Consolidated International Banking Statistics for End–1997* (Basel, Switzerland: May 1998), at www.bis.org.

10. "Regulating Capital Flows," Editorial, *Financial Times*, March 25, 1998, p. 33.

11. Janet Yellen, "Lessons from the Asian Crisis" (Council on Foreign Relations, April 15, 1998), available at www.whitehouse.gov.

12. Edmund L. Andrews, "Study Shows How World Banks Panicked Over Asian Trouble," *New York Times*, September 3, 1998, p. C1.

13. Sharon R. King, "Quick Action by US Banks Limits Damage," *New York Times*, September 3, 1998, p. C5.

14. Louis Uchitelle, "Helping Hand Replaces Hands-Off Role in Asia," *New York Times*, January 1, 1998, p. D1.

15. David Wessel and Bob Davis, "Currency Controls Are Getting a Hearing Amid Asian Crisis," *Wall Street Journal*, September 4, 1998.

CHAPTER 15

EMERGING TRENDS IN GLOBAL BANKING

The field of international banking in the early twenty-first century is confronted by a number of difficult questions. Will banks survive? Will nonbank financial institutions dominate what has traditionally been defined as international banking? How will people bank? Indeed, will the continuing onslaught of new technology, much of it linked to the Internet, make the banker obsolete?

In banking mythology, "the good old days" were a time when any self-respecting banker could reasonably expect to be on the golf course by 3:00 in the afternoon. (This was the old 3–6–3 rule: Borrow at 3 percent, lend at 6 percent, and tee off by 3 P.M.!) Thanks to deregulation, globalization, and increasing competition from nonbank sources of capital, those days are long over. The questions above reflect that. As we have recorded throughout this book, international banking has evolved into a fiercely competitive arena, requiring a mix of technical, financial, and managerial skills that was unheard of barely a decade ago. Business now runs for twenty-four hours around the planet, and 365 days a year. The disappearance of "easy" profits (based on lending) has spurred bankers to move more aggressively into the higher-risk, higher-stakes frontiers of international finance (based on fee income). The danger lies in being left behind, which in turn carries with it the risk of declining market share, reduced profitability, and ultimately being bought out as part of an ongoing wave of consolidation throughout the field of financial services. Above all, the new parameters of international banking in the early twenty-first century are defined by an almost relentless push to disintermediation, that is, the erosion of the traditional middleman role played by the banker.

The New Challenges

Although technological change is usually mentioned as a major force sweeping through the banking industry, it is impossible to overstate just how far-reaching it has become. Consider the following:

- Checks have declined in use: in Finland 82 percent of all transactions between banks and their customers in 1998 arrived in electronic form.
- One out of every ten Japanese aged twenty has taken advantage of Internet-based banking services. In an IBM Japan poll conducted in early 2000, a total

of 10.7 percent of respondents said that they have used such web services for checking deposits and withdrawals from their accounts as well as sending interbank remittances.

• Almost half of Canadians say they will likely use the Internet for banking in the next three years, while the majority expects banks to improve services with new technology.[1]

• In Turkey, the commercial banks and the conglomerates that own them are among the biggest investors in the Internet. As one observer noted: "Spurred by a combination of fierce competition and explosive growth in Internet use, Turkish banks are trying to slash costs by shifting more customers away from branches."[2]

While the traditional business of providing loans continues, it is far less attractive than it was—especially considering the wide range of challenges. It is certainly far less attractive than fee-income business. Thus, for international banks to survive, they must more fully embrace fee-income businesses, many of which have long been the domain of investment banking, and many of which require skills that may not be well developed among traditional bankers.

Business cultures differ for commercial and investment banks, complicating this shift to a more complete embrace of fee-income business. Transitions from one to another have not always been successful. Indeed, some banks, stung by volatility in international financial markets, have retreated from the international arena due to heavy losses incurred in failed ventures.

At the same time that commercial banks are moving into investment bank areas (the differences between the two are rapidly blurring), banks are increasingly being challenged by nonbank financial institutions even in their own backyards. These institutions come in a wide range of shapes and sizes. They include multibillion-dollar government-sponsored enterprises, such as the Federal Home Loan Mortgage Corporation (FHLMC or Freddie Mac) and the Federal National Mortgage Association (FNMA or Fannie Mae). In the U.S. mortgage market in 1999, commercial banks accounted for the largest percentage of market share, but with only 27 percent of the total market; nonbank financial institutions claimed much of the rest. As Table 15.1 amply demonstrates, the field for mortgage lending is highly competitive.

Other nonbank financial institutions competing in lending include finance companies, providing commercial and corporate credit. These include such institutions as Heller Financial, Finova, and Household International. Even old-economy manufacturing companies such as Ford and GE provide credit and an array of financial services. And this is not limited to the United States. In Japan, the commercial banks are facing competition from the postal bank system, the Yucho, and from a growing range of newcomers, including nonbanks such as Sony and Softbank (an Internet company) and convenience stores with ATMs.[3]

All of this calls into question the durability of old banking models. In the United States, Glass-Steagall has finally been overturned, and commercial banks now have the option to function as investment banks. In Japan, the traditional main bank system is giving way to a more competitive system, and consolidation is rapidly occurring.

TABLE 15.1 U.S. Mortgage Market 1999

Commercial Banks	27%
Fannie Mae & Freddie Mac	17
Thrifts	16
Life Insurance	8
Foreign Investors	7
Pension Funds	6
Credit Unions	3
Private Individuals	3
Other[1]	13
Total	100%

[1] Other includes Federal Home Loan Banks, Mutual Funds, REITs, MBS dealers inventory, and other mortgage debt holders not elsewhere classified.

Regulatory changes extend well beyond these obvious areas, further complicating the task of bank management. In the international arena, the proliferating financial crises in 1997–98, and the evidence of contagion across financial markets to a degree previously undreamed of, have magnified the role of multilateral institutions such as the IMF and the World Bank. Increasingly, the IMF is coming to play a policing role in international financial markets, pressuring debtor countries to enact responsible policies, and pressuring the lenders to participate more actively in the restructuring process. Moreover, these realignments in the supervisory and regulatory arenas may be only the tip of the iceberg with regard to global regulations for international banks. In the area of money laundering, for example, regulators from around the world are striving to work together to supplement or replace the existing patchwork of enforcement with a global, streamlined standard that will present new challenges for global banks.

The European Challenge

In Europe, the traditional universal bank model is under considerable pressure to change.[4] The previous business model of providing all services under one roof (a financial supermarket) has prevented many European banks from developing the highly specialized expertise needed to compete in global financial markets. In many cases, organizational structures have been overly bureaucratic. This is making it difficult for many European banks to attract and keep the high-priced expertise needed to compete in head-to-head competition with U.S. investment houses such as Merrill Lynch, Goldman Sachs, and Morgan Stanley. It also means that European universal banks are forced to consider downsizing large personnel rolls, shedding numerous branches, and seeking to buy the right talent, be it through mergers and acquisitions or by hiring individuals. Such drastic actions as firing redundant personnel or trimming staff by streamlining operations and augmenting technology often collide with government policies seeking to reduce unemployment. And depending on the country, government opposition to large-scale firings can brake restructurings.

As banks outside Europe, like the Hong Kong Shanghai Bank (HSBC), purchase European banks and make inroads into local markets, they put even greater pressure on the large surviving banks. Institutions such as the Dutch houses (ING and ABN Amro), the Swiss houses (Credit Suisse First Boston, and Union Bank of Switzerland [UBS]), the German banks (Deutsche Bank, Dresdner, Commerzbank), and their French and Italian counterparts must scramble to consolidate, streamline, and reduce their linkages to the retail world. They must pursue fee-income business more rigorously and hence deal with competition in the world of disintermediation. That shift will not be easy, and over time we will observe winners and losers in the process.

Dealing with the Ugly Word—Disintermediation

Disintermediation is clearly the major force shaping the new world of international banking. This is evident in one of the areas where international banking is moving most aggressively—the new European currency, the euro. The demise of foreign exchange trading among European currencies during the 1990s removed an important source of easy profits for many bank traders. In 1991, the fabled speculator George Soros made a cool $1.0 billion speculating against the pound sterling (he is alternately known as the man who broke the pound or the man who mugged the Bank of England). By the end of the decade, even though the pound had not joined in the euro scheme, this sort of trading had become extremely difficult.[5] As intra-European trading dwindled and disappeared in the 1990s (see Figure 15.1), bankers increasingly turned their attention to trading in the more "exotic" currencies of emerging markets, where illiquid, inefficient markets offered both more opportunity and more risk.

The advent of the euro threatens bank profits in other ways as well. It is another dimension of disintermediation. The whole point of the euro is to eliminate inefficiencies and to improve competitiveness within Europe. From the bank's point of view, though, inefficiencies are often just another word for profit opportunity based on arbitrage. Banks profit from inefficiencies, by earning high transaction fees and higher margins than would be expected in an efficient, transparent market.

The euro is just one example of a major trend threatening to overtake the world's banks. Financial deregulation and technological advances worldwide are creating a conundrum in which banks are losing their competitive edge. Put simply, the basic activity of bankers—taking deposits and making loans—is imperiled as customers increasingly turn to capital markets, the Internet, and other nonbank financial institutions for their needs. In a 1999 survey of international banking, *The Economist* warned: "All over the world, banks' traditional business of taking deposits and lending out the proceeds is in terminal decline. The ugly word for this is 'disintermediation.'"[6] This is evident in Figure 15.2, which depicts the essen-

HSBC ON THE ACQUISITION TRIAL:
VIVE LA (CREDIT COMMERCIAL DE) FRANCE

Allerton G. Smith and Justin J. H. Kim

O n April 3rd, HSBC Holdings Plc announced an 11 billion euro ($11.5 billion) offer for Credit Commercial de France (CCF), one of the most profitable and creditworthy banks in France, with $69.3 billion in assets and 650 branches at year-end 1999. HSBC has planned to finance the acquisition through issuing $3 billion in Tier 1 preference shares, up to $3 billion in ordinary common stock, about $4 billion in existing cash reserves, and up to $1.5 billion from Tier 2 capital.

We believe the CCF acquisition is a positive credit event for HSBC, despite the short-term decline in capitalization and large goodwill associated with the transaction. HSBC's Tier 1 ratio will fall from 8.5% at year-end 1999 to around 7% following the acquisition. However, management estimates that the ratio will improve to around 8% by the end of the year due to strong earnings retention. Despite the change in capitalization, ratios still compare favorably to its peers. All of the major rating agencies, including Moody's, S&P, and FitchIBCA, affirmed the ratings of HSBC Holdings following the announcement of the acquisition....

The acquisition of CCF will provide the HSBC group a significant foothold in the Euro zone. Specifically, it will strengthen HSBC's presence in the European retail banking and asset management market, in addition to strengthening its investment banking capabilities. Furthermore, the latest acquisition will further diversify group exposure away from Asia (specifically Hong Kong) and increase proportion of earnings generated in the developed markets.

Hong Kong Shanghai Bank's Global Preserve (US$ millions)					
	Pretax Profit	Percent of Total	Total Assets	Percent of Total	Net Loan Pro-visions	Percent of Total
Europe	$3,322	41.6%	$211,222	37.7%	$ 438	21.1%
Hong Kong	3,054	38.3	165,420	29.6	585	28.2
North America	959	12.0	110,120	19.7	108	5.2
Rest of Asia	329	4.1	55,291	9.9	809	39.0
Latin America	318	4.0	17,181	3.1	133	6.4
Group Total	$7,982	100%	$559,234	100%	$2,073	99.9%

Source: Donaldson, Lufkin & Jenrette High Grade Credit Research.

Source: Bank Notes. Donaldson, Lufkin & Jenrette High Grade Credit Research, April 4, 2000.

FIGURE 15.1 Falling Cross-Border Banking Revenues
(payments in US$ billions)

Sources: Data from George Graham, "Banks Face Falling Cross-Border Payments," *Financial Times,* September 8, 1999, p. 2.

FIGURE 15.2 Announcements in International Bank Credit
and Securities Markets (US$ billions)

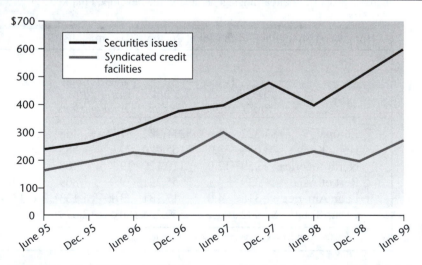

Sources: Bank of England; Capital DATA; Euroclear; ISMA; Thompson Financial Services; Bank of International Settlements. Available at www.bis.org.

TABLE 15.2 Banking Top Ten: World Internet League, 1999

Citibank
ForeningsSparbanken
Meritanordbanker
SEB
Union Bank of Switzerland
Wells Fargo
Net Bank
Egg
Credit Suisse Group
Commerzbank

Sources: IBM; Interbrand 1999, as quoted in the *Financial Times,* July 13, 1999, pg. 8.

tially flat trend of syndicated loan markets in 1995–99, compared with the steeply rising trend of securities issues.

In addition, the Internet poses an increasing threat to traditional banking. Prudential's web-based Egg, an Internet bank, for example, took in nearly $10 billion in deposits in its first six months of operation. By late 1999 it had become the only UK company to appear on a list of the global top ten online banks. (See Table 15.2.) Egg is planning to expand further; its ultimate goal is to become a web-based financial superpower. The Internet may be more of a threat to the financial services industry than to other industries, because financial services can be provided and delivered electronically at much lower cost than in the past. Thus Internet banking may be more than a challenge to traditional banking; rather, it may be poised to change the very nature of the industry to its core.[7]

But it is not only European banks that have come under pressure from the changes hitting the global banking system. U.S. banks are also under pressure from technology-driven disintermediation as well. One example of how technology helps customers bypass banks is Instinet, which has become an integral part of trading in the "fourth market" in the U.S. stock market. The fourth market is a market for institutional investors in which large blocks of stock, both listed and unlisted, trade in privately negotiated transactions unassisted by broker-dealers. The main facilitator of these transactions is the Instinet service, a privately operated computerized system. Institutional investors subscribing to the service can enter bids and offers and trade directly with other institutions, thus eliminating the need for the intermediary.

The most obvious and immediate impact of the disintermediation trend is increasing pressure on banks' margins (the difference between the banks' cost of funds and the interest rates that they can charge their borrowers, akin to gross profit for a manufacturing company). According to *The Economist* in its 1999 survey, in the United States margins for big money-center banks have plunged from 3 percentage points in the 1970s to perhaps 1.25 percentage points by 1998; in Germany, margins are down to just over 1 percentage point. That trend is expected to continue.[8]

BANK CREDIT RATINGS LIKELY TO CHANGE MORE QUICKLY

James Mackintosh

E uropean banks could see their credit ratings rise and fall more rapidly as a result of Internet competition, increasing the volatility of their bonds, according to Moody's Investors Service, the credit rating agency.

Moody's yesterday said it would put more weight on "intangibles" such as the board's Internet strategy and the strength of the brand when assessing a bank's creditworthiness.

Samuel Theodore, banking global coordinator at the agency, said there would be no short-term changes in ratings unless it found a bank with a "visibly inappropriate" Internet strategy.

"We believe that any bank not focusing on a competitive strategy for the Internet age does so at its peril," he said....

Source: Financial Times, February 8, 2000, p. 9.

Facing up to these challenges will require bankers to reinvent themselves. In the early twenty-first century, bank executives are intensively seeking out new strategies to help them position and grow their businesses in the face of new realities. Several strategic options have materialized:

- *Cost reduction.* The big American banks have been trailblazers in this area and have met with some success. Still, bringing down costs does not enhance revenue streams.

- *Retreat from international markets.* In the wake of the Asia/Russia crisis of 1997–98, some banks retreated to their home markets to lick their wounds and reflect on the perils of globalization.

- *New revenue sources.* Bankers are actively exploring alternative sources of revenue to the traditional lines, such as asset management. Off–balance sheet activities, which bring in fee income but do not put the bank's own capital at risk, are especially popular.

- *Investment banking.* Some banks are opting to follow their clients into the capital markets, which means that commercial bankers will reinvent themselves as investment bankers.

- *Riskier lending.* Inevitably, one result of the trend toward lower returns has been an increased willingness to lend to weaker borrowers. This is especially worrisome in light of the Asia/Russia crisis, which raised serious questions about banks' ability to manage their risks. This concern can also be extended to credit cards. Competition in the credit card business between bank and non-bank financial institutions is intense, and it is likely to remain that way. One result is an ongoing quest for new customers, a trend that will increasingly take the lender to the ranks of the less-than-creditworthy.

Retreat from International Markets

A number of banks are choosing to retreat from globalization and return to their home bases in the wake of serious losses suffered in 1997–98. In particular, banks are effecting huge cuts and restructuring in their emerging markets business. Bank executives around the world have announced that they will trim their international operations and focus their efforts on areas where they have the best position. Bank-Boston, for example, decided in 1999 to close down some Asian offices in countries where the bank did not enjoy a competitive advantage (e.g., Japan, the Philippines, and Taiwan).

BankAmerica, too, is retreating from overseas markets after suffering an embarrassing $433 million in trading losses during the second and third quarters of 1998, and establishing a $500 million reserve against other potential losses overseas. In the fourth quarter it slashed its loan and trading exposure to the highest-risk markets by 10 percent and announced plans to sell off its consumer banking operations in Taiwan, Singapore, and India. Moreover, bank officials add that they plan to slim down the bank's emerging market exposure by an additional 50 percent over the medium term. They will refocus the bank on its activities in the U.S. market, where it is a leader in consumer and commercial banking, to shield it from further turmoil in overseas markets.[9]

In Japan, where losses stemming from the turmoil of 1997–98 were much greater than in the United States, the retreat from overseas markets is correspondingly bigger. Japanese banks and brokers scrambled to build overseas empires in the 1980s, but they have been seriously buffeted since then. The Japanese banks encountered great difficulty meeting international capital adequacy standards under the Basel Accord of 1988. During the 1990s, increasing pressure to write off bad loans and to write down the value of shares that they held in other companies eroded their capital bases. (Japan's banks have at least $600 billion in problem loans on their books, and as Figure 15.3 illustrates, major banks operated in the

---

NOMURA STEERS CLEAR OF GLOBAL RISK AFTER RECORD LOSSES

Gillian Tett

Nomura Securities, Japan's largest broker, will refrain from competing in risky global business for the next couple of years following record losses in fiscal 1998, Junichi Ujiie, Nomura's president, has admitted.

It is the latest in a series of retrenchments by a group that a decade ago seemed poised to become a big player in global investment banking, with ambitions in the U.S. and Europe.

Nomura had concluded that its credit rating was too low to allow the bank to enter capital-intensive overseas operations, said Mr. Ujiie....

Source: Financial Times, July 1, 1999, p. 1.

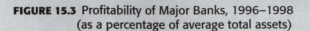

FIGURE 15.3 Profitability of Major Banks, 1996–1998 (as a percentage of average total assets)

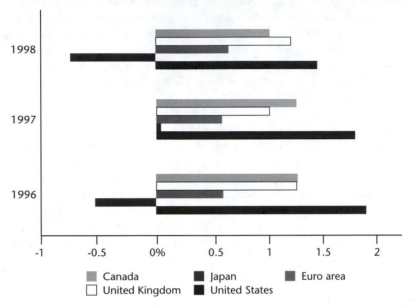

Source: Fitch IBCA, available at www.bis.org.

red during 1996 and 1998.) As a result, Japanese financial institutions are in a substantial retreat from global markets. The exodus includes some of the most prestigious names in Japanese banking. Daiwa announced that it would close *all* of its overseas branches and subsidiaries, as part of a plan to withdraw from all overseas business in order to avoid having to meet international capital adequacy standards.

European banks, too, have had to rethink their globalization policies, as prospects for the European banking sector have deteriorated. Reeling from the emerging markets turmoil in 1997–98, weak trading profits, and forecasts of slower economic growth in core areas, European banks are retrenching dramatically in the emerging markets area. For example, at the Credit Suisse annual meeting with analysts in 1998, company executives reportedly acknowledged that their diversification strategy had yet to achieve its goal of generating profits and protecting the bank from major losses.[10] Credit Suisse lost around $1 billion in Russia in 1998, a devastating blow to an august institution.

While there is a march out of globalization in the banking industry, not all banks are opting out. Capital flows between countries, especially to and from emerging markets, are notably cyclical in nature. International bankers often have short memories (many were relending to Latin America before the debt crisis had really ended!), and they tend to follow the herd when entering into and retreating from international markets. Thus, many banks are proceeding with globalization. Emerging markets rebounded in 1999 and 2000, providing large profits for those, like Credit Suisse, that remained in the game. Deutsche Bank went ahead with its merger with the U.S. Bankers Trust. At the same time, Barclays Bank is restructuring, with an eventual downsizing of 6,000 employees, largely targeted at its retail operations in the UK rather than at its capital markets operations. Other banks such as Citibank and HSBC have clearly underscored their ongoing commitment to remaining global players. Moreover, Econ 101 reminds us that as some institutions exit from the international banking arena, profit margins will increase for those remaining in the business—eventually luring more players back into international banking. Clearly, this is a cyclical process.

The Lure of Investment Banking

As numerous bankers retreat from emerging markets, many are drawn to investment banking. This indeed is one result of disintermediation. Over the past decade many bankers—motivated by commercial logic—tried to bridge the gap between commercial and investment banking, but remarkably few have succeeded, and cautionary tales abound.[11] The size of Union Bank of Switzerland's (UBS) exposure to Long-Term Capital Management (LTCM), for example, raised anew questions about the wisdom of a big commercial bank moving into investment banking.

It is, in fact, difficult to successfully merge the worlds of commercial and investment banking. The business cultures are alarmingly far apart. Commercial bankers tend to be a conservative bunch, priding themselves on their ability to assess creditworthiness and to manage risk. To many commercial bankers, investment bankers are quick-thinking, risk-taking cowboys (and cowgirls). Commercial bankers have trouble integrating with their more highly paid, more aggressive brethren at investment banks. It is difficult for them to develop "the risk-taking, quick decisionmaking culture needed to succeed in the business."[12]

Building an investment banking capability, whether it is through acquisition or through internal development, is an expensive proposition. Investment banking talent does not come cheaply. The bank must hire a phalanx of (very!) highly paid traders and deal makers, while opening technologically advanced offices in some of the world's most expensive real estate locations. Yet the potential rewards are too alluring to ignore. Thus some European banks are determined to regain the investment banking business that they have lost over the past decade to their giant Wall Street competitors. U.S. banks now dominate most core areas of European corporate finance, such as mergers and acquisitions. In fact, the record pace of M&A business in Europe during 1998 produced a windfall in fees for the deal makers, especially the two leading institutions—Morgan Stanley and Goldman Sachs. This was an immensely profitable year for investment bankers in Europe.

Consolidation—Bigger and Better?

Despite the challenges, it is evident that banks will continue to maneuver for more of the lucrative investment banking business in global markets, as a reaction to their shrinking traditional base. Banks have also reacted to the latest threats by embarking on an unprecedented wave of consolidations around the world. As Figures 15.4 and 15.5 demonstrate, while the number of M&A transactions in banking declined in 1997–98, the dollar value of these transactions soared.

FIGURE 15.4 Merger and Acquisition Activity in the Banking Sector: Number of Transactions

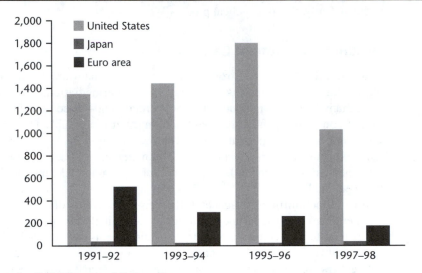

Source: Securities Data Company, available at www.bis.org.

FIGURE 15.5 Merger and Acquisition Activity in the Banking Sector: Value of Transactions (US$ billions)

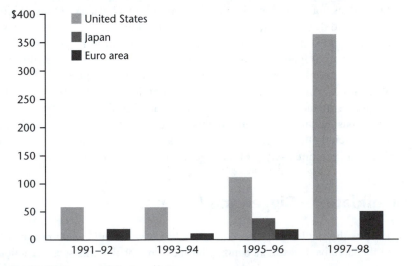

Source: Securities Data Company, available at www.bis.org.

DEUTSCHE GETS BANKERS TRUST FOR $10 BILLION

Edmund L. Andrews

Deutsche Bank formally announced today its plan for a $10.1 billion takeover of the Bankers Trust Corporation and said that the acquisition would result in the elimination of 5,500 jobs, mostly in New York and London....

The purchase of Bankers Trust would be the largest foreign takeover of an American bank and would vault Deutsche Bank over UBS A.G. of Switzerland and the new Citigroup as the world's biggest bank in assets. The deal is the most vivid illustration yet of how banking has become more global, and it may be a precursor for cross-border deals by others....

Source: New York Times, December 1, 1998, p. C1.

In the latest chapter of the race to become the biggest bank in the world, several months after the Deutsche Bank–Bankers Trust announcement, Banque Nationale de Paris (BNP) made an unexpected $37 billion takeover bid to acquire two of its biggest French rivals, Societe Generale and Paribas, which had themselves just agreed to merge! Not to be outdone, Deutsche Bank quickly let it be known that it was amassing a $3.4 billion war chest for acquisitions within Europe's rapidly consolidating bank industry. (The French deal ultimately dwindled to a merger of BNP and Paribas.) Then, three of Japan's biggest banks announced plans to join together to create the world's largest banking institution. As Table 15.3 indicates, the identity of the world's biggest banks has changed radically over the past decade. Perhaps the most striking change is the change in Japanese banking over the past decade; in 1989 they accounted for seven of the top ten banks, including the top six, whereas in 1999 there were only three Japanese banks in the top ten.

As measured by assets, the new Dai-Ichi Kangyo/Fuji/Industrial Bank will be the world's first trillion-dollar bank. Even if this merger collapses, it is only a matter of time before another merger creates a bank that large. (It is difficult to conceive of a bank so large; its assets would be equal the gross national product of China, the world's seventh largest economy.) Many observers believe that European banks face a period of consolidation that will eventually leave just five to ten megabanks on the continent, down from around forty at present. Certainly, the process of consolidation is already in motion in Spain, Italy, France, and Scandinavia.

The question is, though: Will this mania for mergers help banks cope with the challenges that they face in the new millennium? How big should a bank be? Bank consolidations undoubtedly yield returns by eliminating weak competitors and by streamlining operations. To the extent that overbranching and overstaffing are still a problem in the eurozone banking market, the merger and consolidation process can only help. However, there is also no good reason to assume that bigger is better in the banking world. Indeed, in 1989 Japanese banks accounted for seven of the world's ten biggest lenders—but they were never very profitable, and by the

TABLE 15.3 The Biggest Banks in the World: Now vs. Ten Years Ago, Ranked by Assets (US$ billions)

Now		*Then*	
Rank/Bank	*Assets*	*Rank/Bank*	*Assets*
1. Dai Ichi Kangyo/Fuji/ Industrial Bank	$1,321	1. Dai-Ichi Kangyo	$271
		2. Sumitomo	251
2. Deutsche Bank-BT	866	3. Fuji	244
3. Sumitomo/Sakura	864	4. Mitsubishi	228
4. BNP/Paribas	755	5. Sanwa	218
5. UBS	687	6. Ind. B. of Japan	216
6. Citigroup	669	7. Credit Agricole	214
7. Bank of America	618	8. Citicorp	198
8. Bank of Tokyo/ Mitsubishi	580	9. Norinchukin	187
		10. BNP	183
9. HSBC	554		
10. Bayerische Hypound Vereinsbank	541		

Sources: *Wall Street Journal,* March 11, 1999; *New York Times,* October 15, 1999.

N.B.: By the time you are reading this book, this table will be hopelessly outdated—a statement in itself about the fast pace of consolidation in the banking industry!

end of the 1990s a number were threatening to collapse under the weight of massive bad loans.

There is some reason to believe that, in fact, smaller banks are more efficient and more productive than their larger brethren. One study suggests that that the most efficient and profitable banks are those with $1–10 billion in assets; contrast this with Citigroup's $700 billion in assets. *The Economist* notes:

> *Mergers seem one way to make the banks' growth prospects look better. Yet expansion does not solve the problem. Huge, broadly diversified banks are not, on average, any more profitable than less far-flung ones. Economies of scale often taper off quickly with size; although costs are proportionately lower at banks with $10 billion in assets than at banks with $1 billion in assets, growing to $50 billion or $100 billion has typically offered few further gains. Nor does a ubiquitous branch network seem to improve profitability. Most troubling of all, the economies of scope that are meant to come from bringing a variety of financial firms together have proved elusive.*[13]

Similarly, a 1999 Bank for International Settlements study finds that the recent wave of consolidation and restructuring in the global banking industry has not been matched by improvements in bank profitability. During 1996–98, the return on assets of the banking systems fell in twelve out of sixteen countries surveyed; net interest rate margins fell in all but two countries. The BIS observes, "Organizational problems are systematically underestimated and acquirers tend to overpay for targets."[14]

Banks hope to create value through mergers by achieving that much-vaunted state of grace known as cross-selling. Cross-selling is the "Holy Grail" of financial service mergers. It simply means that the bank persuades customers who are already buying one product to buy another, and another, and another. Citigroup, for example, aims to double its 1997 earnings over the next five years, largely by cross-selling its financial products on the wholesale side and by becoming a one-stop shop for consumer banking products.[15] (And as Table 15.4 reveals, Citibank is generally considered one of the world's best banks.) The only problem, though, is that bankers have not yet proved their ability to cross-sell. During the 1980s several attempts at creating financial supermarkets foundered on precisely this weakness.

Finally, the merger of two huge financial institutions (or more) is often a dicey proposition. "Banks rarely blend well," writes one observer. "The best investment banks have such strong cultures they are sometimes compared to cults. Their most important assets are not loans and custody accounts but traders and deal makers—assets that, as the industry saying goes, walk out the front door each night."[16] The recent history of banking is littered with the corpses of bad deals that went awry because the cultures did not mesh. In spring 2000, for example, plans to create the world's biggest bank in terms of assets collapsed in a burst of acrimony between participants Deutsche Bank and Dresdner Bank.

A Winning Strategy

It is not clear, then, that mergers and consolidations will be the magic elixir that will enable banks to compete successfully in the new century. The Asian crisis of 1997–98 raised questions about banks' ability to manage risk in the new international environment. Furthermore, it underscored the gap between the

TABLE 15.4 *Euromoney's* Pick of the World's Best Banks, 1998–1999

Euromoney *Awards for Excellence*

	1998	1999
Best Bank	Citibank	Chase
Best Foreign-Exchange Bank	Citibank	Citigroup
Best Emerging Market Bank	Citibank	Citigroup
Best Global Investment Bank	Merrill Lynch	Morgan Stanley
Best Research	Merrill Lynch	Merrill Lynch
Best Underwriter of Emerging Market Debt	Goldman Sachs	JP Morgan
Most Improved Bank	Chase Manhattan	Deutsche Bank
Best at Syndicated Loans	Chase Manhattan	Chase
Best at Project Finance	Chase Manhattan	Citigroup

Source: *Euromoney*, July 1998, p. 74, and July 1999, p. 56.

MERGER MANIA, SOBERING STATISTICS

If there is a buzzword in banking right now, it is "big." The industry's future, goes an old mantra that is back in fashion, will belong to the superleague of behemoths, with fingers in banking, broking and insurance, that is emerging from the current wave of financial mergers. Some small banks may survive as niche operators. Middling ones, on the other hand, must either find partners or expect to be driven out of business. The bosses of financial institutions that have recently struck giant deals—such as Citicorp's John Reed and Travelers' Sandy Weill—have by and large been hailed as visionaries.

Their vision may be less sharp than it seems. In an index compiled for Strategic Finance, a corporate cousin of *The Economist,* Andersen Consulting has broken down costs and revenues on a customer-by-customer basis at a selection of banks in the United States that serve both individuals and small businesses. It has found that since 1995 the small banks in the group have consistently operated more efficiently per customer than their much larger competitors....

Fair enough, the biggest banks might reply, but our scale helps us to reap more profit from each customer by cross-selling products between our various businesses and rationalizing technology. Not so. On profits per customer, the numbers were closer, but the bigger banks still did worse than smaller rivals. And the small banks' higher profits came despite lower turnover per customer....

Source: The Economist, June 20, 1998, p. 89.

better-managed firms with coherent, disciplined strategies—and the others. The renowned economist Henry Kaufman wrote in 1999, "The ability of senior managers to manage leading financial institutions is being strained by the complexities of modern financial markets." He points out that the huge diversity of new financial instruments, as well as the new importance of different financial players, such as hedge funds, creates a new and more difficult playing field. This is not, he opines, "a financial world that helped nurture effective management control at the senior level."[17]

Yet the complexity of risks and opportunities facing international bankers requires senior managers who can handle the bank's far-flung, often highly complicated, operations with an unprecedented degree of creativity and flexibility. Banks with winning strategies will probably have a massive cushion of capital to enable them to ride out tough times; earnings diversification in terms of both geography and business segments; market leadership in their chosen business; and expense efficiencies.[18] It is far from clear that the winning banks will be those that leap into investment banking and international expansions. Within the U.S. market, for example, the regional and emerging national banks such as BancOne have

---

AWARDS FOR EXCELLENCE: BEST IN THE WORLD

Best Bank: Citibank

This may be the last year it is possible to give just one best bank award. Banking is changing so fast, and banks' strategies for coping are so different, that straightforward comparisons are becoming harder and harder to make.

Contenders for this award this year fall into four groups: those trying to become global providers of wholesale banking services; those trying to become global consumer banks; those with the infrastructure to offer operating and transaction services globally; and those aiming to create global asset-management businesses. Outside these groups are specialists—Bankers Trust and Nomura for example—and the national and regional institutions whose future looks less certain....

This year's best bank, Citibank, just outpoints Chase. It is leader in two of these global businesses and a contender in the others. Its strategy, becoming a leading local provider of basic commercial and retail banking services in its 98 country network, wins it dozens of our country awards, our foreign exchange, securitization and transaction processing awards, and gives it top three status in syndicated lending, project finance and trade finance....

Source: Euromoney, July 1998, p. 74.

---

been among the best performers over the past decade. In Europe, the same strategy has benefited Lloyds Bank, which stayed with its home market while competitors such as NatWest first strayed into, then retreated from, international investment banking. By the same token, the low-glamour segment of retail banking (while highly competitive in many countries) has proved its potential to be solidly and reliably profitable, rescuing many banks from the impact of their ill-advised forays into emerging markets.

The bottom line: Glamour and size may not be critical to the success of global banks. Faced with an unprecedented series of threats and opportunities, bankers are scrambling to position themselves for the world of the twenty-first century. The winners and losers are yet to be named, but the race is on.

ING and Global Financial Integration

Ivey

David Conklin and Yury Boshyk prepared this case with the assistance of Greg Kudar and Marc Trudeau solely to provide material for class discussion. The authors do not intend to illustrate either effective or ineffective handling of a managerial situation. The authors may have disguised certain names and other identifying information to protect confidentiality.

    Ivey Management Services prohibits any form of reproduction, storage or transmittal without its written permission. This material is not covered under authorization from CanCopy or any reproduction rights organization. To order copies or request permission to reproduce materials, contact Ivey Publishing, Ivey Management Services, c/o Richard Ivey School of Business, The University of Western Ontario, London, Ontario, Canada, N6A 3K7; phone (519) 661-3208; fax (519) 661-3882; e-mail cases@ivey.uwo.ca.

The Challenges and Opportunities of the Twenty-First Century

Centered in the Netherlands, the ING Group's strategy had developed on the basis of European insurance and retail banking. Yet, by 1999, ING operated in 55 countries and had more than 50,000 employees and US$350 billion in assets. Over many decades, ING had built a global insurance business with holdings in more than 40 insurance operations, and it had recently sought to create a global banking business. The global banking vehicle, ING Barings, was created by the 1997 merger of three organizations that had offered different products and operated independently: Barings Securities, ING Bank International and ING Capital. Barings Securities was a global brokering business; ING Bank International focused on bond trading, trade finance and payment services; ING Capital traded emerging market debt. Approximately 75 per cent of ING's profits originated in its insurance activities, while 25 per cent originated in its banking activities. Global financial integration was bringing with it both threats and challenges, and as it entered the twenty-first century, ING faced a series of difficult issues.

    The creation of a single currency in Europe was posing new challenges for all of Europe's banks. In recent decades, the role of banks within the financial system had developed very differently in Europe compared with the U.S. Many observers felt that European unification would compel European banks to shift to the U.S. model. This could require major changes in ING's European strategy. At the same time, European integration would inevitably create new opportunities for ING, as it could participate in mergers and acquisitions, as well as the shift from traditional banking to other forms of financial services, particularly investment banking.

(continued)

ING made newspaper headlines throughout the world when it took over Barings in 1995. Singapore-based rogue trader Nick Leeson's foray into derivatives had destroyed Barings, and ING stepped in to create, it was hoped, a turnaround in Barings' fortunes. Barings had extensive operations with over 8,000 jobs in emerging markets and an active investment banking business. However, the first three years following the takeover presented a series of financial setbacks, and in the third quarter of 1998, ING Barings lost US$168.5 million, much of it as a result of losses in emerging markets. As one observer summarized the situation in February 1999, "The question remained whether ING's takeover of Barings, which it rescued from bankruptcy after Nick Leeson ran up huge derivatives losses, was a whim that went wrong."[2] Some observers concluded that "the market would like to see ING quit investment banking altogether."[3]

The Asian financial crisis had been followed by crises in Russia and Brazil, and many other emerging markets seemed vulnerable, raising serious concerns about banking in emerging markets. Yet the international financial crisis was creating new opportunities, with the elimination in many countries of foreign ownership restrictions in banking, and with many governments hoping that foreign banks would be able to bring new efficiency and competitiveness to financial systems that were a major cause of their country's economic difficulties.

Over the past few years, some countries had seen a dramatic increase in electronic banking. Financial institutions that operated through an extensive network of retail branches experienced high operating costs that were vulnerable to the inexpensive transactions that could now be conducted electronically. In many countries, the use of home computers had become commonplace, enabling the average person to participate easily in electronic banking. ING had pioneered expansion into new markets on the basis of low-cost electronic banking. As it entered the twenty-first century, ING faced the question whether its strategy should place even more emphasis on expansion through electronic banking.

European Integration

Impacts on the Financial Sector

Many predicted that the European Monetary Union (EMU) would dramatically alter the banking industry. Banks derived their profits largely from interest income, as opposed to U.S. banks, which gained a larger percentage of their profits from trading income, such as dealing in swaps and derivatives. The shift to a single currency would expose the banks to far more competition, both from banks in other countries, and also from other types of financial institutions. It was expected that free capital movements would inevitably squeeze the interest rate spreads that banks enjoyed, and, hence, their profits. Nout Wellink told Reuters in an interview:

> EMU is likely to act as a catalyst to reinforce already prevailing trends in the banking industry. It will put more pressure on profits, it will reinforce pressure on reducing excessive capacity, it will lead to increased

(continued)

internationalisation as well as increasing consolidation and mergers and acquisitions.[4]

Many observers warned that the European financial systems were fragile, being dominated by banks, over half of which were government-owned and subsidized, and that seemed to have built up substantial bad loan portfolios. Furthermore, this environment had not only fostered inefficiency but had also created unfair advantages for certain banks. In particular, subsidies to the German state-owned Landesbanks were seen as inappropriate and unfair in the new competitive environment. As an *Economist* review stated:

> As markets become more competitive, banks have much to lose from even the slightest disadvantage. Accusations fly that, like the Japanese in the 1980s, the Germans hope to use regulatory tricks to support their banks and to strengthen Frankfurt's pretensions to become Europe's leading financial centre.
>
> The Landesbanks attract criticism on two main grounds: that the state has provided them with capital on subsidized terms, and that they benefit unfairly from an implicit public guarantee that allows them to raise capital cheaply. All of which, say commercial bankers, distorts markets and stymies much-needed consolidation among Germany's 3,400 banks. These privileges caused little fuss so long as the Landesbanks kept off commercial rivals' turf and stuck to their job as bankers to Germany's state-owned savings banks and to its 16 states. But in recent years several have started to compete aggressively with private-sector banks for corporate clients both at home and abroad. Olivier Szwarcberg of Barclays Capital reckons that, at the most pushy Landesbanks, commercial assets now outweigh those linked to traditional business.
>
> The benefits of a state guarantee are obvious. The Landesbanks generally carry the same credit rating (usually, the top one, AAA) as the state that backs them, despite operating on wafer-thin margins and making an average return on equity of only five per cent. Credit-rating agencies, such as Moody's, usually give them a lower financial-strength rating, which strips out external support and reflects banks' intrinsic creditworthiness.... By one estimate, it costs the biggest Landesbanks 15 basis points (hundredths of a percentage point) less than their healthier private competitors to raise money. An internal study by the European Commission says the advantage is even bigger, at DM250m–500m for every DM100 billion ($55 billion) borrowed. As private banks' ratings have fallen (Deutsche Bank was downgraded by two notches earlier this month) they have become more agitated—and, as the Landesbanks have spread their wings overseas, so have foreign competitors.[5]

European financial systems had grown up in a protected environment. European integration would dramatically change this. For example, "The vast majority of European savings remain trapped within their domestic financial systems, re-tracing patterns from the days of exchange controls. These have remained in place thanks to oligopolistic banking systems, underdeveloped private pensions, and protectionist taxes and regulations."[6]

Observers pointed to the effects that EMU would have on capital markets. These included:

(continued)

- A transfer of capital market services from domestic providers to global investment banks.
- A shift in focus from markets to products.
- A broadening of their investor base.
- Greater market efficiency due to elimination of tax and regulatory barriers to drive diversification of European investment portfolios.
- The disappearance of price and information advantages for domestic banks.
- The loss of foreign exchange business, and so the search for credit and/or restructuring risk to compensate.[7]

However, a number of obstacles remained before complete European financial integration:

> Different national regulations will continue to hamper the complete integration of financial markets in Europe and that the low stock market capitalization of European firms is likely to guarantee the predominance of the U.S. stock market—at least over the medium term.[8]

Changes in European Financial Regulations

Throughout Europe, each country had given birth to a number of banks that concentrated their activities within that particular country, and where these activities were regulated by the government of that particular country. Integration of all these financial markets would require changes in the regulatory structure. If a Spanish bank were to be regulated solely by the government of Spain, would this not place individuals and corporations in other countries at risk? Anyone in the U.K. doing business with a Spanish bank could have no assurance that this bank was subject to the same regulations as a U.K. bank. Yet the creation of a single regulatory structure for the banks would be such a huge change that many opposed the concept. As the following quotation indicates, this dilemma had perplexed Europe for two decades:

> The European Union has spent a good part of the past two decades trying to reconcile the claims of national regulators and global financial markets. It has tried two different approaches. The first is dear to EU bureaucrats' hearts: harmonisation. If national regulators harmonise their rules and standards, banks and exchanges can expect the same regulatory treatment wherever they offer their services in Europe. That keeps regulators happy too: their standards apply everywhere. One product of this approach, for instance, is Europe's capital-adequacy directive, which applies common European standards to the amount of capital banks and brokers must have.
>
> The second tack the EU tried was mutual recognition of each other's regulatory regimes (and differences). Thus, the EU's second banking directive granted banks a "single passport" so that they can offer their services throughout the EU without incurring regulations from lots of different jurisdictions. That led to the development of distinctions between a "home" regulator, who keeps an eye on the soundness of the bank, and a "host" regulator, who is concerned only with the bank's business practices. Host regulators must recognize the competence of home regulators.

(continued)

With the benefit of hindsight, it seems clear that harmonisation, although quite useful in some areas—such as aligning accounting and disclosure standards—holds limited appeal. European countries have found it difficult to agree on common standards. Sometimes there is no single "correct" standard on which to agree. Some of the common rules on which the EU did reach agreement quickly went stale. For instance, at precisely the time when the capital-adequacy directive came into force in 1996, regulators were busy amending an international accord on bank capital to allow banks more freedom to judge their own risks (and hence capital requirements). The EU directive had to go straight back to the drawing board.[9]

By 1998, the issue of creating an appropriate regulatory structure had become a major focus for the European Commission, as EU leaders at their June meeting in Cardiff asked the commission to submit a proposal for action. In response to this mandate, the European Commission developed an agenda for consultation that focused on several key questions:

- What can be done to make the financial services market function more effectively in Europe?
- How can the interests of consumer protection be best reconciled with the functioning of an internal market?
- How can the capital and financial markets in Europe be operated most efficiently in the wake of EMU?
- How can the current gap be filled on EU-level regulation for pensions?
- What changes are most needed to adapt financial reporting?[10]

Changing the Basel Accord

At the same time, international negotiations were being held in regard to capital requirements for financial institutions. The Basel Accord of 1988 had specified a target of eight percent as a level of capital that must be set aside against their loans in order to ensure a minimum level of safety for depositors and that would, it was hoped, prevent financial catastrophes. By 1999, many felt that this target should be raised and that it should be differentiated in accordance with the nature of each bank's assets. International differences of opinion had developed in this regard. In particular, German banks felt that the eight per cent capital-adequacy ratio was unduly high for their property loans, which had traditionally been a very safe portfolio. Banks in other nations were reluctant to accept the German position in view of the traditional volatility of real estate prices, and in view of the competitive advantage this would give the German banks. How these negotiations might affect market opportunities and competitiveness within Europe was unclear. As a 1999 *Economist* article noted:

As the years have passed since the accord was agreed in 1988, its terms have come to seem ever more arbitrary and capricious. The amount of capital it demands often conflicts with banks' own assessment of asset riskiness. Securitisation has made it easy to shed assets

(continued)

that seem to require too much capital, which has contributed to a general deterioration in the quality of banks' balance-sheets. Bill McDonough, president of the Federal Reserve Bank of New York, who became chairman of the Basel committee last year, has therefore been trying hard to get it to revise the accord to reflect more closely bank assets' true riskiness....

Yet the revised accord is being held up by Germany. The Germans are insisting that their banks should be allowed to put aside against commercial mortgages an amount of capital that most other regulators, and America's in particular, think inappropriately meager. On the liability side, they also insist that banks which buy *Pfandbriefe,* bonds issued by German mortgage banks, should continue to set aside only a minimal amount of capital, meaning that the mortgage banks get much cheaper funding than do their rivals. A third, simmering, problem, is the complaint that German regulators allow the country's banks to issue a form of subordinated debt to bolster core capital that other regulators last year agreed not to countenance.

The Germans are not entirely without a case. Commercial-property lending, for example, has indeed been less risky historically in Germany than it has been in other countries. But regulators in any country can always point to specific, less risky elements in their banking systems. Simple rules demand compromise and consistency. And a level playing-field demands an end to special subsidies.[11]

The basic concepts involved in calculating risk were also being challenged as the Basel Accord modification was debated. A key question was how many categories should be established for risk and the degree to which these different categories should have different reserve ratios. Related to this was the question of whose corporate risk ratings should be used for corporate loans. For example, U.S. banks might have an advantage since a higher percentage of companies in the U.S. had credit ratings than was true in Europe.

[Table 1] shows how the eight percent reserve ratio could be modified in accordance with various risk categories.[12] The chart presents percentages of the standard eight percent ratio. For example, a 20 percent rating means a 1.6 per cent capital requirement.

Economic Prospects for Europe

Many observers believed the creation of EMU would be a major stimulus for economic growth and, hence, would create exciting new opportunities for banks operating in Europe:

EMU will create an area whose economic potential will be comparable to that of the United States. Structural changes will occur primarily in financial markets. The present segmentation will be overcome in many respects and the European financial market will become truly integrated. The implied greater competition between banks and financial systems in general will lead to efficiency gains in terms of resource allocation and ultimately stimulate investment and job creation.[13]

(continued)

TABLE 1 Basel Balance: Proposed Weightings, %

Claim	AAA AA–	A+ to A–	BBB+ to BBB–	BB+ to B–	Below to B–	Unrated
Sovereigns	0	20	50	100	150	100
Banks: Option 1[1]	20	50	100	100	150	100
Banks: Option 2[2]	20	50[3]	50[3]	100[3]	150	50[3]
Corporates	20	100	100	100	150	100

Source: Basel Committee on Banking Supervision.

[1]Based on risk weighting of sovereign in which the bank is incorporated.

[2] Based on the risk assessment of the individual bank.

[3]Claims on banks of a short original maturity, e.g., less than six months, would receive a weighting that is one category more favorable.

ING shared this optimistic view:

> They see corporate finance in Europe booming as companies become more acquisitive and raise money through the capital markets rather than through house banks. They want to target their efforts on growth sectors such as telecommunications and media…
>
> The bank is placing much of its hope on what it argues is the comparatively virgin territory of the European corporate sector. Explains Robins: "We believe that the cake is going to be growing very rapidly in Europe in the coming years because of the likely explosion of activity in cross-border mergers and acquisitions and the development of an equity culture with the consequent explosion of business in equity markets." Tilmant believes a boom in corporate finance, as opposed to lending, is imminent. "The market worldwide is moving in the direction of more and more disintermediation. U.S. companies fund themselves through the markets—bond or equity—rather than only through bank loans, and we believe this will accelerate in Europe because of the impact of the euro."[14]

In 1997, the report of the executive board of ING clearly stated this optimism:

> Because of the substantially enlarged market that will be created, EMU will provide opportunities for expansion on a European scale. The advent of the euro will also create many openings for new products and markets. The NN Euro Fund, the Euro Plus Fund and the Euro Single-Premium Policy are examples of new products for personal customers in the euro market. Customer information is provided via the ING Eurodesk and other channels.[15]

Some academics remained pessimistic about the future growth in Europe, suggesting that the traditional forces of government regulation and ownership, expensive social security systems and high taxes would place a

(continued)

growing burden on all European countries, thereby constricting financial opportunities. David Smith, for example, pointed to this possibility:

> What if, as Walter Eltis suggests, Europe, particularly those parts of it participating in the single currency, are condemned to a future in which cyclical upturns have little effect on high unemployment levels but each downturn produces a further rise in the jobless total? In my book *Euro-futures* I sketched out a scenario, "the dark ages," in which this would happen, with an initial rise in emu unemployment to an average of 15 per cent, disguising rates in the most depressed regions of 30 to 40 per cent. Looking further ahead, it was possible to see the average unemployment rate climbing to 20 to 30 per cent, with rates in the worst-hit regions reaching 50 to 60 per cent. Inevitably, if such a scenario came about there would be a dangerous rise in social tensions. But there would also be other responses. Peter Jay, in his Darlington economics lecture, envisaged a situation in which, in such circumstances, there would be a forced increase in geographical mobility, not of the kind where workers would seek opportunities elsewhere to better their living standards, but, instead, something like a mass migration of economic refugees.[16]

The EMU would create one of the largest government bond markets in the world, since all new issues of government bonds would be in euro. Nevertheless, each member state would issue its own bonds, and so the market would assess the risk of default for each member state. Consequently, yield differences would remain, and investors would have to study carefully each country's fiscal policies. Of course, the Europe Stability Pact pledged each member to constrain its fiscal policy within specified targets, namely deficits equal to three percent of GDP and debt equal to 60 percent of GDP. A crucial question was whether these targets could be met by all member states on an ongoing basis.

Some commentators suggested that the default risk for any member would have an impact on the strength of the euro:

> Sharing a single currency means that all countries issue their debt denominated in it and consequently when one country threatens to default the others may be called upon to "bail it out." Why? There is a common concern for the reputation of the currency—in other words lenders may require a higher interest rate from all if one debt-issuer defaults, because lenders have inadequate information to distinguish between borrowers in fine detail.[17]

Coping with the Threat of U.S. Banks

It was not clear whether a European bank would be capable of taking advantage of the new opportunities. Instead, it might be U.S. banks that would come to dominate the European financial landscape. The European banks had been protected by national barriers and these would disappear with EMU, exposing them to a degree of competition far greater than they had previously experienced. For many banks, EMU could bring dire threats rather than opportunities. A study by Andersen Consulting analyzed this situation:

(continued)

It finds that the performance gap in financial services is widening. A minority of organizations are generating high returns to their shareholders, and fewer still are combining shareholder return with high revenue growth. A worrying fact for institutions that have been protected by national entry barriers is that firms in more competitive, deregulated markets perform far better for their shareholders, in general, than the firms in the more tightly regulated markets.... If those institutions are performing badly already, they could really suffer when they have to start competing in an open market—a case of competition acting as a kill-or-cure remedy.[18]

The Andersen study suggested three alternative paths to success. First, what it referred to as "optimizers" would dispose of low-margin businesses, eliminating certain products and customers, and focusing on cost reduction. A second group of "consolidators" would achieve cost savings through mergers and acquisitions. Third, "innovators" would identify new trends in customer preferences and market conditions, creating new products to fit these changing circumstances:

To carve a niche in the new European financial services industry, companies will have to decide quickly what their route to value is going to be. The removal of market barriers with the arrival of the euro will create unprecedented opportunities for companies that have the strategic vision to respond. Those that want to stand still may not have any future at all.[19]

The May 1999 issue of *Euromoney* presented ING's decisions in regard to selecting a market niche:

ING is initially setting its sights on selling corporate advice to the 2,000 borrowing customers of the parent bank, where it already has a foot in the door. ING Baring's corporate and investment finance department is analysing these clients according to size and activities. They tend to have a market cap of $300 million to $3 billion and Le May believes that "middle-size" companies are a more natural hunting ground for us. The top 200 European companies are over-banked and have good relationships with top banks. They are also very sophisticated and do a lot of the business themselves, so we can add less value than for smaller companies. The sort of companies we want to service would be off the radar screen for the big American firms.

ING Barings is unlikely to aim for a role in major privatizations, saying it would be a "waste of energy," and Robins rules out completely any claim to want to compete with the global bulge bracket. "We are not setting ourselves up, nor do we have any ambition, to compete with Goldman Sachs, Merrill Lynch or Morgan Stanley."

Market observers argue, however, that the industry is increasingly excluding those outside the bulge-bracket on the basis of the cost of capital. The flow of deals through the largest firms means they have to wait much less time to offload positions than do smaller firms such ING.

One banker who used to worked [sic] for Barings has doubts about the new style. "I wish Robins well," he says. "They may make a success of a small-companies strategy but the economics of that business are pretty unattractive."[20]

(continued)

Emerging Markets

Many believed that globalization of trade and investment depended upon the globalization of financial markets and perhaps even of financial institutions themselves. This set of relationships was seen as crucial for successful economic growth in the less-developed countries:

> The financial markets are something like the flywheels of globalisation. Free capital movements and efficient financial markets greatly facilitate direct investment. They provide the basis for transactions and for the safety of payment flows, which are the financial equivalent of real integration.
>
> The global financial markets promote and strengthen market structures. They also make it possible for investment in emerging economies to be funded privately, rather than officially, today on a much greater scale than previously. Capital is allocated today, more than it used to be, in accordance with economic, rather than political, criteria. Conversely, the integration of the emerging economies into the global financial markets provides new investment outlets for savings. This must also be seen against the backdrop of the ageing [sic] populations in most industrialised countries. They in particular must accumulate and invest capital today so as to be able to maintain their relative standard of living in the future, too.
>
> And the global capital markets have assumed a role which is bearing fruit in the disciplining of national policies. They offer opportunities, but also pose a risk, to countries which fail to follow the economic constraints. Nowadays they are an effective part of the checks and balances.[21]

Faced with these apparent realities, ING, in 1997, was determined to expand in emerging markets far beyond the Barings structure that it had acquired in 1995. The report of the executive board emphasized that it intended to maintain a leading position in emerging markets:

> ING is internationally recognised as a specialist in corporate and investment banking, life insurance and asset management in emerging markets. ING Barings intends to selectively expand its corporate and investment banking activities in countries with sufficient growth potential. New greenfields were set up in 1997 in Romania, the Philippines and, in cooperation with a local partner, in Indonesia. In Mexico, ING has formed a joint venture with Bital, a local bank, to address the privatised pension market. Furthermore, commercial banking activities (banking products for personal customers and small and medium-sized enterprises) were launched and existing operations were expanded in several countries. Adding banking products to the range offered by insurance greenfields can provide a useful stimulus for these young businesses. In addition, asset management activities were initiated in several emerging markets.[22]

In 1997, The *Economist* issued an article entitled " A Survey of Banking in Emerging Markets" in which it presented a very cautious analysis of such opportunities, giving its survey the title, "Fragile, Handle with Care":

(continued)

Since 1980 more than 100 developing countries have suffered some kind of serious banking-sector crisis.... Many bank-watchers worry that, on the evidence of the past few years, things are getting worse. In Africa, banking systems have been going down the tubes at the rate of two a year.... In Eastern Europe, banks in almost every country have run into trouble as they swapped communism for capitalism.... Banks in Latin America have been just as accident-prone.... Japan's banks have become mired in bad loans. Once-invincible bankers in other Asian countries have been caught out by falling markets, and we are starting to pay the price for a long lending binge. Decades of protectionism, corruption and lax regulation are taking their toll.[23]

This survey emphasized that banks played an even more important role in emerging markets than they did in the advanced countries, since they remained the main source of finance. Alternative financial institutions had not yet been developed. Yet their deposits as a percentage of GDP, often below 50 per cent, were far less than the percentages in advanced countries where this ratio might approach 100 per cent. From this perspective, emerging market banks had been inept at mobilizing savings and at being an efficient conduit for financial transactions. *The Economist* article suggested that since "they [knew] little about their borrowers, and [had] poor credit-assessment skills, emerging-market banks typically [needed] wide spreads to maintain quite low profitability."[24]

The Economist Survey pointed to four potential dangers for banks in emerging markets:

1. Macroeconomic volatility seemed to be inevitable, and this would continue to present banks with the difficulty of evaluating loan proposals and the recurrence of serious corporate bad debt problems.

2. The political and business culture in emerging markets would continue to create pressure for "connected" lending to the employees or owners of banks, to political figures and to companies with which they were linked.

3. The political environment would be subject to ongoing changes that would impact the fortunes of the banks.

4. Financial liberalization would create significant changes as new institutions entered the marketplace.

In regard to regulatory solutions to these dangers, *The Economist* argued that three major gaps would continue to exist:

1. The problems of regulating large financial industrial groups.

2. The increasing use of derivatives.

3. The possibility of evading domestic restrictions through offshore operations, particularly using customized derivative contracts in offshore markets and hiding bad loans offshore.

Shortly after this survey was published, Asia, Latin America and Russia experienced a new round of financial crises. The Asian foreign exchange cri-

(continued)

sis dramatically altered the country risks and competitive advantage in Asia. Although strengthening the export sectors, the currency devaluations severely damaged both the import sectors and businesses serving the domestic market.

Some argued that the Asian economy had been hurt by the IMF's efforts. Since the IMF insisted upon a considerable tightening of monetary and fiscal policy as a condition for its loans, the effects of these measures worsened the financial crisis and heightened economic recession. The IMF rescue packages may have stabilized foreign exchange rates in the short term, but they severely damaged domestic businesses that suddenly confronted a tight monetary policy and high interest rates. Furthermore, this process inflicted major harm on low-income families experiencing unemployment.

While foreign exchange volatility was reduced, the country risk for potential investors might actually have increased. The Indonesian currency board debate illustrated this dilemma. Some argued that the Indonesian rupiah should be pegged at a certain fixed exchange rate to the U.S. dollar. An independent currency board would supervise the money supply with the sole objective of maintaining this fixed rate. The money supply would be backed by reserves of dollars and expanded only in accordance with the rate of foreign currency inflows. Such a commitment might, at times, require extremely high interest rates to attract the capital inflows that would support the fixed rate. Even the IMF had argued that a currency board approach could create economic devastation in a future exchange crisis and that some future exchange rate flexibility would be necessary.

Further, the Asian crisis had created a new risk of heightened foreign exchange volatility for some countries. Exchange rates were maintained at unrealistically high levels as a result of considerable inflows of foreign capital. Now, the optimism of the foreign investor had been replaced by caution. In the future, capital flows would be much more sensitive to changes in each country's financial system and general economic conditions than they had been in the past. Future surges in capital flows activity might translate into increased volatility of foreign exchange rates for some countries.

For financial institutions everywhere, an ongoing challenge was that the time profile of liabilities was not the same as that of assets. Banks borrowed short-term from depositors and lent long-term. This exposed the banks to the risks that fixed assets might fall quickly in price and that depositors might make sudden withdrawals. Further to the non-performing loan problem, Asian banks had been confronted with dramatic reductions in land and stock prices. Bank loans made on the security of real estate and stocks suddenly were at a major risk of default, further exacerbating the effects of the financial crisis overall.

The insurance sector also faced problems caused by the difference in time profile of assets and liabilities. In Japan, insurance companies had based their premium schedules on expectations that they would be able to earn reasonable rates of return. However, over the past decade, Japanese interest rates and returns on equity had been far below the levels necessary to earn the expected returns. Consequently, the Japanese insurance sector faced new solvency risks—a problem that might add a new dimension to the Asian financial crisis.

(continued)

In Latin America as well, the risk of foreign exchange rate movements had become a paramount consideration, as had the risk that the government might simply lack the economic capacity to repay loans. The devaluation cycle remained a key economic risk in Latin America. Many Latin American countries had been experiencing ongoing fiscal deficits and money supply growth that exceeded that of each of the United States, Canada and Western Europe. Consequently, inflation rates remained high. And the realities of exchange rates meant that devaluation crises would appear from time to time. A devaluation in the exchange rate of one country automatically created pressure for devaluation in other countries' exchange rates. The 1999 Brazilian devaluation increased the Brazilian prices of imports from Argentina, and decreased the Argentinean prices of imports from Brazil with the result that the Argentine currency encountered severe downward pressure as the Argentinean balance of trade deteriorated. Competitive domino devaluation pressures were intensified because of the reliance of Latin American countries on primary product exports with their price volatility.

With the fall of communism in Russia, a new free market economy emerged. A lack of understanding of the mechanics of capitalism and unrealistically high expectations severely threatened successful growth as the economy struggled to free itself from old, inefficient, yet comfortable ways.

Modest GDP growth in 1997 soon turned to recession in 1998 as budget deficits increased due to falling revenues. Many strange actions on the part of Boris Yeltsin reduced investor confidence and foreign direct investment started to wane or leave. In March 1998, Yeltsin fired his prime minister, Viktor Chernomyrdin, and installed a young, inexperienced Sergei Kiriyenko who was not supported by the state duma. As the value of the ruble slid, the Central Bank raised its interest rates to 150 per cent.

In July 1998, the IMF announced it would provide a bail-out package worth US$22.6 billion provided the Russian government instituted strong reforms such as revenue collection. The duma then amended the government's reforms and reduced the planned revenues by two-thirds. On August 14, 1998, Yeltsin boldly announced that there would be no devaluation of the ruble, as many economists suggested should happen. Three days later, the government announced that it would allow the ruble to devalue, and it would be forced to default on and restructure its government debt. In addition, it imposed a 90-day ban on the payment of external debt. Analysts predicted that the currency would devalue by as much as 50 per cent by the end of 1998, inflation would average 45 per cent, and the economy would contract by three per cent for the year. Millions of rubles were printed to meet short-term commitments. Finally, Yeltsin replaced Kiriyenko, after five months in office, with former prime minister Chernomyrdin.

The repercussions of the crisis in Russia's economy were described by *The Economist Intelligence Unit*'s third quarter, 1998 report on Russia:

> In abandoning its defence of the ruble and the preservation of price stability, Russia has reversed its main economic achievement since the transition process began. The devaluation and accompanying default on

(continued)

domestic government and certain external obligations will have profound adverse effect not only on the Russian economy and the standard of living of the Russian population, but will also have wide-reaching political ramifications for the government, the presidency and the wider polity.[25]

Faced with its disastrous losses in the context of the Asian financial crisis and the consequent Latin American devaluations and recessions, and faced with the Russian default on government bonds, ING now had to decide whether emerging markets really did offer opportunities in the twenty-first century.

Euromoney was extremely negative in its evaluation: "If one institution best demonstrates the effects of the Asian and Russian crises on a bank, ING Barings is it. It's a salutary tale of billion dollar losses, of individuals left to go their own way at the expense of group strategy, of management failures."[26]

ING was not alone in this dilemma. Barclays Bank PLC had also announced a US$400 million write off in Russian ruble bonds in 1998. Perhaps these losses were simply "business as usual" in the global financial markets. If so, how should global financial institutions cope with these emerging market risks?

Electronic Banking

The Internet was playing an increasingly important role in the financial and insurance services landscape—ING faced the problem of how to incorporate Internet banking into its global financial strategy. Perhaps this was the ideal vehicle to create a global retail banking business. Perhaps the Internet could form an important component of future insurance sales and also banking for small and medium-sized companies. Canada was a new market that could be viewed as an experiment in this regard.

There was extensive debate about the impact of technology, especially the Internet, on banking and the financial services sector. The WTO suggested that technology would allow banks to lower costs and increase revenues while delivering higher levels of service, resulting in higher profits:

> Potential cost savings in the financial services sector are enormous: while the administrative (marginal) costs of clearing average US$1.20, and for a debit or credit card payment US$0.40–US$0.60, the transaction costs for an Internet payment can be as low as one cent.... The full cost of an Internet transaction (US$0.13) is only half the cost of PC-based banking and one-eighth the cost of transaction made over a bank counter.[27]

Yet despite the higher revenues and lower costs, the WTO warned that lower barriers to entry and increased competition could commoditize parts of the financial services sector.

> For established providers, technology is a double-edged sword. While it offers new opportunities to serve consumers better, it can give advantage to new competitors and threaten existing franchises. This is especially true for institutions with legacy technology and

(continued)

distribution systems requiring complex and costly re-engineering or replacement.[28]

Others agreed with Bill Gates, who declared that banks were dinosaurs destined to suffer from lower margins, greater competition, commoditization and eventual replacement by other technological solutions such as e-money and financial management software.[29]

According to a study by Ernst & Young, there were five leading-edge technologies that would alter the finance sector: Internet, PC banking, smart cards, data warehousing and document imaging.[30] The common link between these technologies was that they relied on efficient, low cost telecommunication infrastructure and the willingness of consumers to adopt new technologies.

Given that Canadian consumers had shown an eagerness to adopt new financial technologies, such as debit cards, the question facing Canadian finance firms was whether the regulatory environment would allow them to invest in new technologies. There was evidence that Canadian banks were spending less than U.S. banks on new technology, which suggested that there were policy or regulatory barriers to technological investments in Canada.[31]

The Canadian finance sector was small by world standards, both in terms of the size of its overall market and the relative size of its financial institutions.[32] Moreover, Canadian banks and other financial services companies were less efficient and less profitable by world standards.

> Compared to the best operating companies, Canada's banks lack a true performance ethic. Their cost efficiency, while collectively competitive, lags the leading performers in the United States and the United Kingdom…. Moreover, though their risk management skills are conventional and sound, the banks' legacy technology inhibits both rapid product innovation and more efficient processes overall.[33]

In Canada, the result was a tremendous concentration of banking services into the Schedule I banks, which commanded 86 per cent of total domestic bank sector assets (and most of this 86 per cent is under the control of the Big 5 banks).[34] This concentration had resulted in limited competition, which made banks less efficient and raised prices for users of banking services, making the Canadian finance sector, and all companies that used it, less competitive relative to the rest of the world.

In most industries, underperforming firms were threatened by new, more innovative and efficient competitors. However, in 1997, the record of new entry in the Canadian banking sector was very poor—there had only been two new Schedule I banks since 1987, compared with 207 new banks in the U.S.[35] In many smaller countries, foreign competition was used to maintain competition and innovation in sectors that were underdeveloped. However, regulations in Canada had prevented foreign competitors from entering the market as full-fledged equals of the Canadian banks.

(continued)

Canadian Regulatory Perspectives

Until 1980, foreign competitors were strictly forbidden from entering Canada. After 1980, foreign banks were allowed in, provided they met certain criteria. The number of foreign banks in Canada peaked in 1987 at 59, but had declined to only 42 in 1999.[36] These foreign competitors, while not a threat to the big banks in terms of deposit-taking or wealth management, were extremely important for business customers as these competitors tended to target specific clients (Wells Fargo) or communities (Hongkong Bank of Canada).[37]

New legislation advanced by the Department of Finance, passed in June 1999, allowed foreign banks to operate branches in Canada without incorporation. However, there was still no allowance for providing banking services without a branch network. The laws in this regard were developed at a time when it was not possible to conduct banking without a physical presence. As a result, the regulations were not only confusing, but penalized foreign banks. A prominent example was Well Fargo bank, which sought to use its marketing expertise to extend credit to Canadian small businesses, an underserviced market according to many critics of the Canadian big banks. The bank required no physical presence in Canada, and, therefore, was not entitled to incorporate in Canada.

In order to meet Canadian regulations where possible, Wells Fargo held discussions with the Canadian banking regulator, Office of the Superintendent of Financial Institutions (OSFI). The outcome of these discussions was that technically the Wells Fargo direct mail campaign did not qualify as "banking business," despite the fact that it would in fact be lending to small Canadian companies. As a result, Wells Fargo agreed to meet certain requirements recommended by OSFI. Wells Fargo would have to mail its material from the U.S., locate its call centre outside Canada and arrange for cheques drawn on its correspondent Canadian bank to be mailed to the U.S. and trucked back to the Canadian bank. The end result was that Wells Fargo incurred extra costs and Canadians lost jobs from the mailing and call centre activities.

The dearth of new entrants into the banking sector was also the result of the dominance of the Canadian banks in terms of their extensive branch network (over 8,000 branches across Canada). In addition, Canadians were reluctant to try new competitors, especially unknown foreign banks.

While foreign competition had received attention from policymakers, branch closures had received significant attention from the general public. Combined with the need to cut costs in order to be more competitive internationally, pursuing customers by alternative channels such as electronic banking had created a redundancy in the 8,000 branches currently operating in Canada. Many of these branches were in rural areas with declining populations, which could be equally well-served with appropriate technologies. Unfortunately, the affected constituents were most often seniors or individuals with lower incomes—two cohorts that were unlikely to use the Internet

(continued)

and related e-banking technologies. The result had been well-publicized outcries over branch closures, which had reached the ears of politicians. Criticism of banks over branch closures had been exacerbated by concerns regarding bank service to Canadians with below-average incomes (a high-cost, low-margin clientele).

With respect to foreign entry, the McKay Report and Department of Finance report recommended that the criteria for foreign entry be made less stringent, particularly in regard to capital requirements. The implications of technology were far-reaching for regulators, for two primary reasons.

First, regulators had no way to prohibit foreign banks from accessing domestic customers when solicitation and transactions were conducted by electronic means such as the Internet. This, in turn, had important implications, especially for Canadians who put their savings in potentially unhealthy foreign banks, as they might not have legal recourse in Canadian courts to retrieve their money in case of a bank closure. Electronic financial transactions could also facilitate money laundering and tax evasion, making it almost impossible for governments to trace profits flowing across the Internet.

Second, the fact that Canadian customers could deal with U.S. or other foreign financial firms meant that the Bank of Canada might lose some control over monetary policy.[38] For example, though it could restrict credit in the domestic marketplace (either through interest rate hikes or moral suasion with the big banks who conducted most of the lending), if Canadian borrowers could easily and cheaply access credit abroad, how could the Bank of Canada control money supply or interest rates domestically?

A final concern with respect to electronic banking, insurance and investment services was how to regulate the workers in those sectors. Currently, all levels of Canadian government had rules governing investment dealers, mutual fund sales staff and insurance brokers/sellers.[39] The laws governing these individuals were not designed with e-commerce in mind such that selling these items over the Internet had created a policy vacuum. While all laws applied to e-commerce, they were likely unenforceable.

In this context, ING decided to enter the Canadian banking business on the basis of electronic banking as opposed to the expense of setting up a physical branch network. It decided to offer simple financial products, such as no-fee savings accounts, guaranteed investment certificates and registered retirement savings plans that offered a higher interest rate than rival banks, and to offer personal loans of up to $50,000 at lower interest rates than rival banks.

> ING Group NV, one of the largest financial services organization in the world, is aggressively positioning its Canadian business to take advantage of consumers' willingness to make bank deposits and buy insurance over toll-free telephone lines. The company has built the second-largest property and casualty insurance group in Canada with $1.3 billion in annual premiums. ING's assets in Canada total $4 billion. With the deep financial pockets of its Dutch parent available, the

(continued)

Canadian operations have staying power, marketing muscle and ambition. To date, ING has acquired six companies, established an electronic bank, become a major seller of life insurance, bought a mutual fund dealer and developed a network of about 7,500 brokers to sell the company's products. "We are diversifying beyond core insurance and developing a number of different distribution systems to deliver an array of financial services and products to the consumer," said Yves Brouillette, president of ING Canada Inc., a Montreal-based holding company for the insurance operations. "The goal is to be a major integrated financial services player," he said.[40]

The very difficult Canadian regulatory environment posed a variety of obstacles for ING's electronic banking experiment. Furthermore, the relatively very large Canadian banks quickly responded with their own electronic banking programs, creating intense competition. ING faced the problem of how to evaluate this experiment and whether to extend the concept globally. At the same time, ING faced the question of how best to integrate its various financial services, particularly the insurance business, into the electronic banking structure.

Challenges in the Twenty-First Century Environment of Business

For the financial services industry, the twenty-first century would be very different from the twentieth century. Several basic forces were already seriously impacting this sector in the 1990s. For ING, an analysis of these forces would be a crucial step in developing appropriate strategy.

---

[1]This case has been written on the basis of published sources only. Consequently, the interpretation and perspectives presented in this case are not necessarily those of The ING Group or any of its employees.

[2]Karen Iley, *Reuters,* Amsterdam, February 11, 1999.

[3]Karen Iley, *Reuters,* Amsterdam, February 9, 1999.

[4]*Reuters,* Amsterdam, January 11, 1999.

[5]"Germany's Protective Wings," *The Economist,* May 22, 1999, 81.

[6]"The Euro: Remaking Europe's Financial Markets," *Mondag Business Reading,* Credit Suisse First Boston, July 1, 1998.

[7]Ibid.

[8]British Management Data Foundation, "The International Role of the Euro," in Helmut Schieber Deutsche Bundesbank, Frankfurt, September 21, 1998: http:/www.euro-know.org/speeches/Paperschieber1.html.

[9]"Border Control (Survey 11 of 12)," *The Economist,* U.S. ed., May 9, 1998.

[10]"Financial Services: First Hearing on the Future 'Framework for Action,'" *European Report,* September 16, 1998.

[11]"German Banks under Fire," *The Economist,* May 22, 1999, 20.

[12]"Banking Regulation: Growing Basel," *The Economist,* June 5, 1999, 70.

[13]http://europa.eu.int/euro/html/
page-dossier5.html?dossier = 100&lang = 5&page2&nav = 5, May 13, 1999.

[14]"One Last Push from the Trenches," *Euromoney,* May 1999, 36, 41.

[15]ING DIRECT Corporate Profile, August 1998, 27.

[16]David Smith, *Will Europe Work? http://www.euro.euro-know.org/articles/wew.html,* July 18, 1999.

(continued)

[17]Patrick Minford, *Editor's Guide,* 1999: *http://www.euro-know.org/biblio.html* (annual guide).

[18]"UK: EMU, Bank Strategy, Find Your Niche and Stick to It," *Reuters,* 10/08/98.

[19]Ibid.

[20]"One Last Push from the Trenches," *Euromoney,* May 1999, 41.

[21]Professor Dr h. c. Hans Tietmeyer, president of the Deutsche Bundeskbank, "Financial and Monetary Integration: Benefits, Opportunities and Pitfalls," the 1998 Mais Lecture delivered at the City University Business School in London on May 18,1998: *http://www.euro-know.org/speeches/text1.html.*

[22]ING Direct Corporate Profile, August 1998, 24.

[23]"A Survey of Banking in Emerging Marketing," *The Economist,* April 12, 1997, 5, 26.

[24]Ibid., 7.

[25]Country Report, Russia, *EIU,* 1998.

[26]"One Last Push from the Trenches," *Euromoney,* May 1999, 41.

[27]"Electronic Commerce and the Role of the WTO," *World Trade Organization,* 1999, 29–30.

[28]"Change, Challenge Opportunity: Report of the Task Force on the Future of the Canadian Financial Services Sector," September 1998, 27. Hereafter referred to as the McKay Report.

[29]"Survey of International Banking," *The Economist,* April 17, 1999, 32.

[30]"Canadian Financial Institutions and Their Adoption of New Technologies," Ernst & Young, research paper prepared for the *Task Force on the Future of the Canadian Financial Services Sector,* 1998, 5.

[31]See McKay Report, 28.

[32]"The Changing Landscape for Canadian Financial Services: New Forces, New Competitors, New Choices," *McKinsey & Co.,* 1998, 11–12.

[33]Ibid., 54.

[34]Ibid., 13.

[35]"Reforming Canada's Financial Services Sector: A Framework for the Future," *Department of Finance,* 1999, chap. 3, p. 1.

[36]"Reforming Canada's Financial Services Sector: A Framework for the Future," *Department of Finance,* 1999, chap. 3, p. 12.

[37]"The Changing Landscape for Canadian Financial Services: New Forces, New Competitors, New Choices, *McKinsey & Co.,* 1998, 13.

[38]See "Electronic Commerce and the Role of the WTO," *World Trade Organization,* 1998, 42.

[39]See McKay Report, chap. 7, and "Canadian Financial Institutions and Their Adoption of New Technologies," Ernst & Young, research paper prepared for the Task Force on the Future of the Canadian Financial Services Sector, 1998, 28–30 for a discussion regarding financial intermediaries and licensing.

[40]Dennis Slocum, "Canada: Aggressive ING Rings Up Growing Sales in Canada—Phone Is Key to Dutch Financial Giant's Strategy," *Globe and Mail,* 02/12/97.

Questions

1. What are the competitive threats facing international bankers at the dawn of the millennium?
2. Is Internet banking a threat or an opportunity to traditional banks?
3. Which banks do you think will be best positioned to deal with the threats outlined in Questions 1 and 2? Why?
4. What strategies are banks employing to deal with competitive threats? Do you think these strategies will be successful?
5. Explain the appeal of cross-selling.
6. What skills do you think a good commercial banker should have? Investment banker? Why might it be difficult to merge the two under one roof?

7. In what ways do you think the euro will affect international banks? How should bankers position themselves to benefit from the advent of the euro?
8. Should governments take any steps to help their banks compete in the global arena? Why or why not?
9. Is there an optimal size for a bank? What advantages does a big bank enjoy over its smaller competitors? Disadvantages?
10. Consider Table 15.3, the list of the world's biggest banks. Now go to the Internet and construct a list of the world's biggest banks today. How has this list changed, and why?

Notes

1. Dao Thu Hien, "Half of Canadians Say They Will Bank via the Internet by 2003," *Bloomberg*, April 18, 2000, at www.bloomberg.com.
2. Leyla Boulton, "Banks in Control of Turkey's Internet Explosion," *Financial Times*, March 13, 2000, p. 23.
3. "As Banking Services Spread, New Entries Need Close Watch," *Asahi Shimbun* (Tokyo), May 2, 2000.
4. For an excellent summation of this argument see Roy Smith and Ingo Walter, "The Death of Universal Banks," *Financial Times*, March 14, 2000, p. 7.
5. On April 28, 2000, George Soros announced a reorganization of his hedge funds, which were hit hard by losses in Internet stocks earlier in the month. In a letter to shareholders Soros commented that one of the problems facing hedge funds (as well as banks) in making such speculative plays was that there was greater scrutiny of the big players and big bets. As he stated of the problems facing his former flagship fund: "Quantum fund is far too big and its activities too closely watched to be able to operate successfully in this environment." *Source:* George Soros letter, April 28, 2000, at cnnfn.com/2000/04/28/mutualfunds/soros/letter.htm.
6. "On a Wing and a Prayer," *The Economist*, Supplement: A Survey of International Banking, April 7, 1999, p. 4.
7. James Mackintosh, "Internet Brands Set to Shake Up the Banking Sector," *Financial Times*, July 13, 1999, p. 8.
8. "On a Wing and a Prayer," p. 4.
9. Rich Brooks, "BankAmerica Retreats from Overseas Markets," *Wall Street Journal*, January 22, 1999, p. A2.
10. Christopher Rhoads, "European Banks Rethink Globalization," *Wall Street Journal*, October 5, 1998, p. A23.
11. "Commercial Propositions," *The Economist*, December 5, 1998, p. 84.
12. "On a Wing and a Prayer," p. 23.
13. "The Trials of Megabanks," *The Economist*, October 31, 1998, p. 23.
14. William Hall and Andrew Balls, "Bank Consolidation Fails to Boost Profitability," *Financial Times*, August 23, 1999.

15. John Authers, "Cross-Selling's Elusive Charms," *Financial Times*, November 16, 1998, p. 21.

16. Joseph Kahn, "One Big Bite After the Other Leads to Indigestion for Banks," *New York Times*, November 27, 1998, p. C1.

17. Henry Kaufman, "Too Much on Their Plate," *Financial Times*, February 4, 1999, p. 24.

18. Peter Lee, "Banking Crisis: Ways to Recover," *Euromoney*, November 1998, p. 30.

African Development Bank (AFDB): A multilateral development bank, created in 1964 by an agreement among a large number of African countries and nonregional countries, such as the United States, France, Germany, Italy, and other European nations. The bank provides long-term development loans, mainly for agriculture and capital improvement projects. In the mid–1990s the AFDB underwent a number of reforms to improve its performance and effectiveness.

Agency: An integral part of the parent bank, falling somewhere in between the branch and the rep office; agencies may perform more functions than a rep office, but not all of the functions of a full branch.

American Bankers Association (ABA): A national trade association of commercial banks in the United States, organized in 1875. The majority of U.S. banks are members of the association, which sponsors conferences and seminars, and promotes professional development in banking through its banking schools and the ABA educational arm, the American Institute of Banking. The ABA also represents the banking industry before Congress and federal regulatory agencies.

American Depositary Receipt (ADR): A negotiable certificate issued by a U.S. bank for shares of stock issued by a foreign corporation. The securities are held in a custodial account, either at the issuing bank or at an agent bank. ADRs are registered with the Securities and Exchange Commission. They provide the holder with the same benefits of ownership as shareholders. ADRs are priced in dollars and traded on stock exchanges and over the counter in the same fashion as U.S.-issued securities.

American option: An option that can be exercised at any time on or before the expiration date. [6*]

American Stock Exchange (AMEX): The third largest stock exchange in the United States in terms of trading volume. The AMEX lists securities of more small to medium-sized companies than the New York Stock Exchange, and it handles options trading for a sizable number of New York Stock Exchange listed companies. Furthermore, the AMEX handles a large volume of foreign securities traded in the United States.

Arbitrage: Profit making by purchasing a security, currency, or commodity at a low price in one market and simultaneously selling it in another market at a higher price. Alternatively, an arbitrageur borrows in one market and lends in another. The effect is to reduce price differences between markets.

Asian Development Bank (ADB): A multilateral development bank focused on Asia. It was organized in 1966 and lends economic assistance and technical support to developing countries in Asia. The ADB includes members from both within the region and outside, including the United States. It lends capital assistance through the Asian Development Fund, a soft loan window established in 1973. It is supported by member contributions and transfers from its own capital.

Ask price: The price at which a security or commodity is quoted or offered for sale. [7]

Bank crash: This is a failure of a financial institution (usually a deposit-taking institution) caused by a number of factors. As such, the banking system may reach such a condition that it is unable to provide payments or allocate credit, its traditional role. In a broader sense in which banks also play an important role in securities markets, a bank crisis can also result in a lack of liquidity for the buying and selling of bonds, stocks, and other financial instruments. Bank crashes can also be accompanied by runs, in which depositors appear at the bank and demand their money. The reserves in the banking system are quickly drained. This in turn results in an effort to restore reserves, in which the banks may call loans, refuse to extend new credit, or sell assets. This leaves the authorities in the difficult position of either having to close the bank that has had the run and is threatened by a crash or providing the bank with a line of credit as well as visible support for the institution in an effort to restore public confidence.

Bankers acceptance (BA): A time draft drawn on and accepted by a bank, the customary means of making payment for merchandise sold in import-export transactions and a source of financing used extensively in international trade. The BA has the credit strength of a bank behind it, and so it usually is considered a money market instrument.

Basel Agreement: The agreement on risk-based capital adequacy standards for commercial banks reached by central banking authorities from the United States, Western Europe, and Japan. It was finalized in July 1988, at the Bank for International Settlements in Basel, Switzerland. The Federal Reserve Board's final risk-based capital regulations are based on this agreement. Regulations that have been or will be issued

---

Superscript numbers refer to glossary term sources listed on page 462.

by other U.S. federal banking regulators and by banking regulators in Western Europe and Japan are based on the Basel Agreement. [7]

Basis point: One hundredth of a percentage point (0.01%) of yield on a bond or note. For example, a yield of 8 percent is 800 basis points. Basis points are useful for measuring small changes in interest rates. [7]

Bid price: The price offered for a security or commodity by a prospective buyer; the price at which a security or commodity is wanted, and subject to immediate acceptance, unless otherwise stated, for the amount specified. [7]

BIS: Bank for International Settlements. An international bank originally established in 1930 as a financial institution to coordinate the payment of war reparations among European central banks. It was hoped that the BIS, with headquarters in Basel, would develop into a European central bank, but many of its functions were taken over by the IMF after World War II. Since then the BIS has fulfilled several roles, including acting as a trustee and agent for various international groups such as the OECD, European Monetary Agreement, and so on. The frequent meetings of the BIS directors have been a useful means of cooperation among central banks, especially in combating short-term speculative monetary movements. Since 1986 the BIS has acted as a clearing house for interbank transactions in the form of European Currency Units. The BIS also sets capital adequacy ratios for banks in European countries. The original members were France, Belgium, West Germany, Italy, and the UK, but now most European central banks are represented as well as the United States, Canada, and Japan. [1]

Bond: A bond is an IOU issued by a borrower to a lender. They usually assume the form of fixed-interest securities issued by governments, local authorities or companies. Bonds come in many forms – with fixed or floating rates of interest, callable or uncallable, and secured or unsecured.

Branch: A branch office is an integral part of the parent bank, and acts as a full legal and functional arm of the head office.

Bridge financing: Bridge financing refers to a loan taken on a short term to bridge the gap between the purchase of one asset and the sale of another.

Bulge bracket: This refers to large investment banks, usually the major institutions that compose Wall Street and dominate the securities industry.

Call option: The right, but not the obligation, to buy a financial asset or instrument such as stock or foreign exchange.

Call risk: The risk that a bond might be called before maturity and an investor might be unable to reinvest his or her principal at a comparable rate of return.

Cash management: The art of managing cash balances in order to minimize non-productive cash levels while at the same time maintaining a prudent level of liquidity within the corporate treasury.

Certificate of deposit (CD): A receipt for the deposit of funds in a bank of which there are two classes, demand and time. Demand certificates of deposit are payable on demand, and time certificates of deposit are payable on a specified date upon proper endorsement. [4]

Clearing banks: These banks in the UK dominate the provision of financial services and play a significant role as international bankers. Products offered encompass documentary credits, bills, export finance, corporate finance, foreign exchange, and advisory services.

Clearing House Interbank Payments System (CHIPS): A computerized funds transfer system for international dollar payments linking major U.S. and foreign banks with offices in New York City. Funds transfers through CHIPS, operated by the New York Clearing House Association, account for 90 percent of all interbank dollar payments relating to international trade. Final settlement occurs through adjustments in special account balances at the Federal Reserve Bank of New York. Since 1981, settlement has occurred at the close of each business day when CHIPS members send and receive payments from other U.S. banks through the Federal Reserve's Federal Wire (Fedwire), the Fed's electronic funds transfer and securities transfer network.

Club deals: A joint loan put together by a small group of banks for a single borrower, in contrast to a syndication that may involve dozens, even hundreds, of banks making a joint loan to a single borrower.

Commercial paper: A short-term IOU, or unsecured money market obligation, issued by prime-rated commercial firms and financial companies, with maturities from 2 to 270 days. The most active market is in issues maturing in less than 30 days. Commercial paper is, in effect, a promissory note of the issuer used to finance current obligations. It is a negotiable instrument as defined by the Uniform Commercial Code. Interest rates on commercial paper are lower than bank loan rates, which makes the commercial paper market an attractive alternative to issuers.

Consortium bank: A group of banks joining together to form a consortium bank, aimed at promoting a common objective or engaging in a project of benefit to all the members.

Contagion: Contagion is the ability of a financial crisis in one country to spread into the financial system of another country. An example of this was the Asian financial crisis of 1997–98, which began in Thailand and soon spread to Indonesia, Korea, and Hong Kong and eventually to Russia and Brazil.

Controlled disbursement: A cash management service offered by banks, based on the use of a corporate zero balance account housed at a banking affiliate. Customers' checks clear through normal banking channels to the banking affiliate and are processed for posting to the customers' accounts. The service provides the customer with early morning notification of the clearings that will be posted so that the customer can fund the same amount, enabling optimal use of any excess funds at a customer's investment account.

Correspondent banking: A system of interbank relationships in which a bank sells services to other financial institutions. The institution providing the services is the correspondent bank or upstream correspondent. The institution buying the services is the respondent bank or downstream correspondent. Services provided by correspondent banks include check collection, data processing, federal funds trading, securities safekeeping, purchase or sale of securities, loans to directors and officers, international transactions, investment banking advice on mergers and acquisitions, loan participation, and many others. [7]

Country risk: The risk that most or all economic agents (including the government) in a particular country will for some common reason become unable or unwilling to fulfill international financial obligations. Country risks include those arising from social, political, or economic changes in a foreign country to which domestic banks extend loans that can lead to repudiation of the debt, delayed payments, or controls on foreign exchange transfers. [7]

Covered interest arbitrage: The process necessary to maintain the spot and forward exchange markets in the state of equilibrium described by interest rate parity.

Credit risk: The risk due to default or failure by a borrower or counterparty to fulfill its contractual obligation.

Cross-border lending: This occurs when a loan is made to a borrower in a country other than the lender's residence, and is denominated in a currency other than that of the borrower's currency. For example, a loan made by Deutsche Bank in London to a manufacturer in Mexico City and denominated in dollars is a cross-border loan.

Cross-border risk: Potential losses arising from the bank's operations in overseas markets.

Currency swap: A foreign exchange agreement between two parties to exchange a given amount of one currency for another and, after a period of time, to give back the original amounts swapped.

Derivatives: An asset or security whose value is derived from some other financial instrument in a contractual manner. The value of the underlying financial instrument at a particular point of time in the future establishes the payoff to the derivative product. [7]

Discount: This term has many meanings. In foreign exchange (FX) markets, it refers to the difference between the spot price and forward price of a currency. If a currency is trading at a discount in forward markets, then it is less expensive on the forward market than on the spot market.

Disintermediation: Movement of funds from low-yielding accounts at traditional banking institutions to higher-yielding investments in the general market—for example, withdrawal of funds from a passbook savings account paying $5\frac{1}{2}$ percent to buy a Treasury bill paying 10 percent. [2]

Due diligence: Due diligence is an independent review of the current financial state and future prospects of a company in anticipation of a major investment of venture capital or a stock or bond issuance.

Duration gap analysis: A method of examining the sensitivity of the market value of the bank's net worth to changes in interest rates. This is based on the concept of duration, which measures the average lifetime of a security's stream of payments.

Equity: Equity usually refers to ownership via stock in a company. A more precise definition equates equity to total assets less total liabilities.

Eurobond: Bond denominated in U.S. dollars or other currencies and sold to investors outside the home country of the currency. The bonds are usually issued by large multilateral underwriting groups composed of banks and issuing houses from many countries. An example of a eurobond transaction might be a dollar-denominated bond issued by a Belgian corporation through an underwriting group composed of the overseas affiliate of a New York investment bank, a bank in Japan, and a group of British merchant banks. The eurobond market is an important source of capital for multinational corporations and sovereign borrowers, including the governments of emerging market countries.

Eurocurrency: Currencies held outside their home country; thus, eurodollars are dollars on deposit outside their home country, mainly in Europe.

Eurodollar: U.S. currency held in banks outside the United States, mainly in Europe, and commonly used for settling international transactions. Some securities are issued in eurodollars—that is, with a promise to pay interest in dollars deposited in foreign bank accounts. [2]

European Economic Area (EEA): The extension of most of the elements of the EC 1992 single European market to the seven member countries of the European Free Trade Agreement (EFTA). [6]

European option: An option that can only be exercised at maturity. [6]

Exchange rate mechanism (ERM): Mechanism intended to reduce exchange rate fluctuations and to establish a zone of monetary stability in Europe through a multilateral system of fixed but adjustable exchange rates. [6]

Exercise price: See *Strike price.*

Floor value: The lowest price that a purchaser can receive for his or her financial instrument if he or she purchases an option.

Flight capital: Flight capital refers to the movement of capital out of one country and to another or others due to political or economic reasons as well as for better investment opportunities. Flight capital is a difficult issue in international finance as it is often hard to distinguish between it and foreign investment.

Foreign exchange or currency risk: This refers to the risk that can be incurred when loans are made across national borders and involve more than one currency. Any transaction involving more than one currency stands this risk. Simply stated, the value of a deal or loan can suddenly change if one of the currencies involved makes a rapid shift in valuation.

Forward: A cash contract by which two parties agree to the exchange of an asset to be delivered by the seller to the buyer at some specified future date, with the price agreed upon at the onset of the contract. [7]

Funding risk: This refers to the threat of insufficient liquidity on the part of the bank for normal operating requirements. This could mean, for example, that the bank has a shortfall in deposits and other funds and is unable to provide capital for its operations, such as making new loans.

Futures: Contracts with standardized provisions, leaving variable only price and delivery month, dealt in on the contract markets. [7]

Giro: An electronic payment system that is widely used in Europe and Japan for consumer bill payments. In contrast to the check system in the United States, which is a debit-based system, giros are credit transfers. In giro systems, a payment order automatically transfers funds from the consumer's account to the creditor's account and notifies the creditor when the transfer is made. Multiple payments from a single giro are also possible.

Glass-Steagall Act: Refers to the Banking Act of 1933, or occasionally, to that portion of the Banking Act that prohibited commercial banks from engaging in investment banking activities in the United States; largely repealed in 1999. [6]

Global custody: The business of processing trades and keeping shares safe on behalf of fund managers around the world.

Hedge fund: Speculative mutual fund or limited partnership, formed with the intention of taking aggressive and usually unhedged positions in a wide range of instruments and derivatives. [5]

Hedging: An action taken to reduce risk or market exposure. Reduced to its simplest terms, a form of insurance used among traders or dealers in commodities, foreign exchange, or securities, to prevent loss through price fluctuations. It is not speculation, but the avoidance of speculation. [7]

Herstatt risk: See *Settlement risk.*

Interest rate risk: The risk that earnings and returns will fluctuate in line with interest rates.

Intermediary role: This is the role middleman banks have played throughout history, from the traditional middleman role between borrowers and lenders to the more complex intermediation as risk managers.

Intermediation: The act of standing between two parties to facilitate transaction. This is the traditional function of banks, which has been eroded in recent years. [5]

International Bank for Reconstruction and Development (IBRD): Organization set up by the Bretton Woods Agreement of 1944 to help finance the reconstruction of Europe and Asia after World War II. That task accomplished, the World Bank, as IBRD is commonly known, turned to financing commercial and infrastructure projects, mostly in developing nations. It does not compete with commercial banks, but it may participate in a loan set up by a commercial bank. World Bank loans must be backed by the government in the borrowing country. [2]

International Monetary Fund (IMF): The IMF is an organization of countries that seeks to promote international monetary cooperation and to facilitate the expansion of trade, thus contributing to increased employment and improved economic conditions in all member countries. To achieve its purposes, the fund has a code of economic behavior of its members, makes financing available to members in balance-of-payments difficulties, and provides them with technical assistance to improve their economic management. As of 1992, the fund had 173 member countries, accounting for four-fifths of total world production and 90 percent of world trade. The Articles of Agreement on the IMF were formulated at the United Nations Monetary and Financial Conference held in Bretton Woods, New Hampshire, July 1–22, 1945, and came into force on December 27, 1945. [7]

Intrinsic value: The value of an option if it were to be immediately exercised.

Investment bank: A bank whose function is the provision of long-term equity and loan finance for industrial and other companies, particularly new securities. Investment banks are also involved in leasing, mergers and acquisitions advice, and financial engineering.

Legislative risk: The risk that a change in law might adversely affect a security.

Letter of credit: An instrument drawn by a bank, known as the credit-issuing bank (and eventually the drawee bank), on behalf of one of its customers (or on behalf of a customer of one of its domestic correspondents), known as the principal (who guarantees payment to the credit-issuing bank), authorizing another bank at home or abroad, known as the credit-notifying or negotiating bank (and usually the payer bank), to make payments or accept drafts drawn by a fourth party, known as the beneficiary, when such beneficiary has complied with the stipulations contained in the letter. [7]

LIBOR: London Interbank Offered Rate. The rate at which banks in London place eurocurrencies and/or eurodollars with each other. Since the LIBOR is a prime bankers' rate, it is often used in international banking as a basic rate, for example, "LIBOR plus $\frac{1}{8}$ of 1 percent," in referring to an interest rate negotiated. [7]

Liquidity risk: The risk that sufficient cash flows will not be available to meet the bank's financial commitments at some point in time.

Market or price risk: The risk that a bank may incur losses due to market or price fluctuations in well-defined markets.

Merchant banks: Commercial and investment banks found in European countries. Merchant banks frequently lend, borrow, underwrite, deal in securities, and provide other banking services. Certain aspects of merchant banking were prohibited for U.S. banks by the Glass-Steagall Act. However, U.S. banks are allowed to act as merchant banks in foreign countries with regulatory approval. [7]

Mezzanine bracket: Members of a securities underwriting group whose participations are of such a size as to place them in the tier just below that of the largest participants. In the newspaper tombstone announcing the new securities offering, the underwriters are listed in alphabetical groups: first the lead underwriters, then the mezzanine bracket, and then the remaining participants.

Money laundering: Money laundering is the act of transforming profits earned from a criminal activity into legal profits. This is often linked to international drug trafficking, which generates large amounts of profits. It can also be linked to tax evasion.

Money market funds: Mutual funds whose primary objective is to make higher-interest securities available to the average investor who wants immediate income and high investment safety; also called liquid asset or cash funds. [7]

Moral hazard: This refers to the situation that arises when one party to an agreement has an incentive to behave opportunistically in a way that undercuts the interests of the other party. In lending, a moral hazard is more likely to occur when the borrower has an incentive to conceal information or act in a way that is detrimental to the lender's interests or when conditions are such that banks are apt to avoid the proper due diligence in the belief that governments will cover or pay for their mistakes.

Note Issuance Facility (NIF): A credit facility provided by a bank or group of banks under which the borrower may issue short-term Euro-notes (notes sold in the euromarket) over a given time period. The underwriting banks are committed to either purchase unsold notes or to provide guarantees that the notes will be repaid.

Offer price: The price at which the owner of a security, financial instrument, or other asset is willing to sell. This is also called the asked price. This differs from the bid price, the price a buyer is willing to pay.

Operating risk: See *Operational risk.*

Operational risk: Potential losses due to a breakdown in information, communication, transaction processing, settlement systems and procedures, fraud by employees or outsiders, or unauthorized transactions by employees.

Option: The right, but not the obligation, to buy and/or sell specified securities or commodities in specified amounts, at specified prices, and for a specified duration of time. Since consideration passes for such options, they are legally binding contracts for their duration. [7]

Payment risk: See *Settlement risk.*

Performance letter of credit: A standby letter of credit issued by a bank that guarantees the bank will pay to the beneficiary an agreed sum if the bank's client does not perform a contractual obligation. [5]

Political risk: The risk that political factors might impair a borrower's ability to service its debt.

Premium: This term has four meanings:

1. The percentage of price that a security commands over its face value.
2. The annual (or less frequent) sum paid by an insured party on an insurance policy.
3. The price paid on an option contract or other privilege. [7]
4. The difference between the spot price and forward price in foreign exchange (FX) markets. If the forward price is at a premium, then the currency is more expensive in forward markets than in spot markets.

Primary market making: This is the first market in which a security trades as opposed to the secondary market, where aged or seasoned securities are allowed to trade. Aging or seasoning refers to the time between issuance and when the bonds or shares are permitted to trade in the secondary market.

Private banking: Banking services, including lending and investment management, for wealthy individuals. Private banking primarily is a credit-based service, and it is less dependent on accepting deposits than retail banking.

Project finance: A type of finance in which the debt is to be serviced by cash flows attributable to the project itself, rather than by the project's "sponsors" (those who are involved in an entrepreneurial and ownership position). The borrower is the project itself.

Proprietary trading: Trading activities in which the bank's traders take a position on the direction of foreign currency or other traded instruments, putting the bank's own capital at risk in an attempt to profit from price fluctuations.

Purchasing power parity: A theory postulating that, under perfect conditions, exchange rates adjust for inflation differentials between countries.

Put option: The right, but not the obligation, to sell a financial asset or instrument, such as stock or foreign exchange.

Regulatory forbearance: The putting off of tough actions on the part of regulators in the hope that a bank will recover on its own. One of the risks is that if regulators wait too long, the crisis can spin out of control and become even more difficult to remedy.

Representative office: An office established by a parent bank in an overseas location with very limited functions. The rep office cannot accept deposits or make loans, so it functions primarily to assess business opportunities in a new market.

Revolving credit: A commitment by a bank to lend to a customer under predefined terms; open-end credit. The commitments generally contain covenants allowing the bank to refuse to lend if there has been a material adverse change in the borrower's financial condition. [7]

Risk management: Control of the exposures intrinsic to banking. Because banks are institutions actively engaged in profit maximization, they face the risks inherent in any such activities. It is a banker's job to manage risk, not avoid it. Banks have complicated models constructed to help the management of risk.

Run: A run is an unexpectedly large series of withdrawals at a bank, which can threaten the solvency of the institution. Runs can start because of well-publicized news about a particular bank, the passage of new laws, or rumors pertaining to the health of the bank.

Security: Instrument that signifies an ownership position in a corporation (a stock), a creditor relationship with a corporation or governmental body (a bond), or rights to ownership such as those represented by an option, subscription right, or subscription warrant. [2]

Settlement risk: Sometimes called Herstatt risk, this refers to the risk that banks may incur if they pay out, or settle, their side of a foreign exchange (FX) contract before the counterparty settles up.

Smurfing: This is a term used in money laundering. Named after small blue cartoon characters, Smurfs are individuals who help move the funds from one institution to another or from one country to another. A smurfing operation will involve a major coordinator or a "Papa Smurf", who will direct his smurfs to make multiple deposits at a large number of banks, usually in numbers just below local reporting requirements.

Sovereign debt: Any debt reflecting the understanding that such debt is backed by the full faith and credit of that particular country's government and is thus regarded as the highest creditworthiness from that country, above corporate debt.

Sovereign risk: The risk that the government as a borrower may prove to be uncreditworthy.

Speculation: Taking on risk in anticipation of a gain.

Spot market: In foreign exchange (FX) markets, a trade for current value at current prices.

Spread: This term has six meanings:
1. The difference between the bid and asked prices of a security. This difference may be "narrow" or "wide," depending on the supply and demand of the particular issue and the activity of its market.
2. The difference between the public offering price fixed for a new issue and the net proceeds to the issuer, constituting the underwriters' compensation and any expenses of issuance borne by agreement of the issuer. The underwriting spread is compensation for underwriting risks assumed in the "firm" and

"standby" types of underwriting, and is compensation for preparation of the issue for market and for distributional expenses and services.

3. A combination of a put and a call by which the purchaser has the privilege of "putting" at one price, or "calling" at another price, the specified security within the contract period. A straddle is similar to a spread except that the put and call prices are the same.
4. In commodity futures trading, the difference between two delivery months, whether in the same market or in different markets.
5. In arbitrage operations in foreign exchange, the difference in rates between two markets, which difference is larger than normal.
6. The yield rate minus the cost of funds. [7]

Standby letter of credit: Any letter of credit that represents an obligation to the beneficiary on the part of the issuer:

1. To repay money borrowed by, advanced to, or for the account of the account party.
2. To make payment on account of any indebtedness undertaken by the account party.
3. To make payment on account of any default by the account party in the performance of an obligation.

Stress testing: A method used to measure market risk in abnormal market conditions. This technique relies on computer modeling of different scenarios, and computation of the results of those scenarios on a bank's portfolio.

Strike price: Also referred to as exercise price, the price at which the option may be exercised.

Subordinated loan: A loan junior in claim on assets to other debt—that is, repayable only after other debts with a higher claim have been satisfied. [2]

Subsidiary: In international banking, a separate legal entity from the parent bank, organized under the laws and regulated by the authorities of the host country. It may engage in full banking activities as permitted by host country regulations.

Suspicious transactions: This refers to any transactions conducted at a bank or financial institution that arouse the suspicion of the banker as to the point of origination of the funds. Suspicious transactions include such things as a deposit made just below the $10,000 currency transaction reporting limit (in the United States), an excessive cash flow from a business in an area which is economically depressed, or someone showing up at the bank with large amounts of cash. Simply stated, it is anything that raises any questions out of the ordinary in terms of the origin of the money, especially if it is thought to have come from criminal activities.

Swap: This term has many meanings. In FX markets, it refers to the simultaneous purchase and sale of foreign currency for two different value dates, with the same counterparty. In the derivatives market, it refers to an agreement to exchange one security for another. Two parties to a swap agree that for a certain period they will exchange regular payments.

Swap rate: With regard to forward foreign currency quotes, the swap rate refers to the points added to or subtracted from the spot rate to find the forward rate.

SWIFT: The Society for Worldwide Interbank Financial Telecommunications, a cooperative company that transmits financial messages, payments orders, foreign exchange confirmations, and securities deliveries to nearly 7,000 financial institutions on the network, located in 190 countries. SWIFT's global network carried more than 1 billion messages in 1999, with an average daily value of over $5 trillion.

Syndicated loans: Loans participated in by multiple banks and other institutions where the overall credit involved exceeds an individual lender's legal lending or other limits. One bank in the syndicate usually acts as agent for the other institutions. [7]

Systemic risk: This refers to a situation in which the entire banking system comes under acute stress, usually beginning with the collapse of or major problems in one institution. In a sense, cumulative losses will occur from an event that ignites a series of successive losses along a chain of institutions or markets.

Time value: The difference between the option premium and its intrinsic value.

To mark its book to market: This refers to the practice of investment banks in marking the value of their books at the close of business each day, be it in bonds or equities. This practice, also known as marking-to-market, means taking the value of the security from the opening of the market to the closing. It provides an accurate idea of the value of the trading book and helps measure profits and losses, as well as signaling potential risk trends.

Tombstones: Term used for financial advertising listing acquisitions, new securities for sale, with the banks managing the deal listed. The actual term tombstone refers to the fact that like tombstones for the dead, the amount of information is very basic.

"Too big to fail" doctrine: Refers to a particular bank regarded as having substantial problems that may threaten its solvency, but that is also one of the largest banks in the financial system. A failure by that institution could have considerable repercussions on the rest of the economy, including a drastic reduction in the money supply of the national economy with significant negative effects on economic activity. Moreover, a massive bank failure could raise the cost of credit intermediation and reduce demand, cooling economic growth. The ultimate fear is that the failure of a large bank could cause a financial black hole, capable of sucking in other banks and businesses that have credit and debt relations with the bank.

Transfer risk: The risk that a commercial borrower will be unable to service its debt because the government restricts access to foreign exchange.

Transparency: In financial transactions, this refers to the provision of clear, credible information to all parties involved.

Treasury bills: Debt obligations of the U.S. government that mature in one year or less. All bills are sold at discount, so that the return to the investor is the difference between the purchase price of the bill and its face or par value. [7]

Universal banking: The ability of a bank to offer the full range of financial services, including commercial banking as well as securities issuance and trading and the selling of insurance products, all under one roof. Europe is regarded as the home of universal banking, though the model is now used in varying degrees around the globe.

Underwriting: Underwriting is defined as the providing of long-term equity and debt finance for corporations and governments, largely through the issuance of new securities to the public. It is important to note that it can also refer to the detailed credit analysis preceding the granting of a loan, based on credit information obtained from the borrower and considering such things as employment history, salary and financial statements.

Value at Risk (VAR): A method used to assess market risk in everyday, normal market conditions. VAR methodology allows banks to measure statistically probable losses that their trading portfolios could incur over a certain period of time. From a given set of inputs, the bank calculates the maximum loss, or VAR, that it might experience to a given level of probability.

Venture capital: Venture capital is capital used for start-up businesses. It is regarded as being used for high-risk business ventures.

Willful negligence: Often related to the issue of money laundering, willful negligence is the intentional failure to comply to the law. Sometimes referred to as "turning a blind eye," it is regarded by most law enforcement agencies as a criminal act with severe penalties.

World Trade Organization (WTO): The world trading system founded at the Uruguay round of the General Agreement on Tariffs and Trade (GATT) in 1994, to supersede GATT and to implement the measures agreed on at the Uruguay round by 2002. WTO's aims are to continue the work of GATT in furthering the liberalization of international trade. WTO has wider and more permanent powers than GATT and extends its jurisdiction into such aspects of trading as intellectual property rights. The highest authority of WTO is the Ministerial Conference, held at least every two years. WTO has ninety-seven member states and a further thirty-two GATT contracting parties. [1]

Yen bond: Any bond denominated in yen, usually issued in the Japanese money market. There are several types of yen bonds. If issued in the euromarket, it is called a euroyen issue. Yen-denominated bonds issued in Japan to non-Japanese investors are priced by the major Japanese securities firms, and they are known as Samurai bonds.

Zero balance accounts: A type of account whose end-of-day target balance is zero, enabling all funds to be swept into overnight interest-bearing accounts. This is a standard cash management tool offered by banks.

---

[1] Butler, B., D. Butler, and A. Isaac, A. *A Dictionary of Finance and Banking,* Second Edition. Oxford: Oxford University Press, 1997.

[2] Downes, J., and Jordan E. Goodman. *Dictionary of Finance and Investment Terms,* Second Edition. New York: Barron's, 1987.

[3] Fitch, Thomas. *Dictionary of Banking Terms.* New York: Barron's Educational Series, Inc., 1997.

[4] Garcia, F. L. *Encyclopedia of Banking and Finance,* Sixth Edition. Boston: The Bankers Publishing Company, 1962.

[5] Mahony, Stephen. *The Financial Times A–Z of International Finance.* London: FT Pitman Publishing, 1997.

[6] Newman, P., M. Milgate, and J. Eatwell. *The New Palgrave Dictionary of Money and Finance.* London: The Macmillan Press Limited, 1992.

[7] Woelfel, Charles J. *Encyclopedia of Banking and Finance,* Tenth Edition. Chicago: Fitzroy Dearborn, 1994.

SELECTED BIBLIOGRAPHY

Articles and Monographs

Ali, Nazim. "Islamic Banking: Points of Law." The Banker, February 1999, p. 67.

Aliber, R. Z. "International Banking: A Survey." *Journal of Money, Credit and Banking,* 16, No. 2 (1984), pp. 661–695.

Andelman, David. "The Drug Money Maze." *Foreign Affairs,* July/August 1994, p. 94.

Andrews, Edmund L. "Study Shows How World Banks Panicked Over Asian Trouble." *New York Times,* September 3, 1998, p. C1.

"As Banking Services Spread, New Entries Need Close Watch." *Asahi Shimbun* (Tokyo), May 2, 2000.

"Asian Banks: Diminishing Returns." *The Economist,* April 29, 2000, pp. 73–74.

Atkins, Ralph, and Tasso Enzweiler. "German Reform May 'Weaken Corporate Culture.'" *Financial Times,* April 14, 2000, p. 18.

Authers, John. "Cross-Selling's Elusive Charms." *Financial Times,* November 16, 1998, p. 21.

Bank for International Settlements, *Consolidated International Banking Statistics for End–1997.* Basel, Switzerland: May 1998. Available at www.bis.org.

"Banks in Trouble: The Bigger They Are." *The Economist,* October 28, 2000, pp. 65–67.

Barboza, David, and Jeff Gerth. "On Regulating Derivatives." *New York Times,* December 15, 1998, p. C1.

Basel Committee on Banking Supervision. *Enhancing Bank Transparency.* Basel, Switzerland: Basel Committee on Banking Supervision, September 1, 1999.

Baums, T. "The German Banking System and Its Impact on Corporate Finance and Governance." In M. Aoki and H. Patrick, editors, *The Japanese Main Bank System.* Oxford: Oxford University Press, 1994.

Bench, Robert. "The Role of Regulation and Supervision in the Global Banking System." In William H. Baughn, Thomas I. Storrs, and Charles E. Walker, editors, *The Bankers Handbook,* p. 1187. Homewood, Ill.: Dow Jones Irwin, 1988.

Berg, Sigbjorn Atle. "The Banking Crises in the Scandinavian Countries." In *Bank Structure and Competition 1993.* Chicago: Federal Reserve Bank of Chicago, 1993.

———. "Bank Failures in Scandinavia." In Gerard Carpio Jr., William C. Hunter, George G. Kaufman, and Danny M. Leipziger, editors, *Preventing Bank Crises: Lessons from Recent Global Bank Failures,* p. 198. Washington, D.C.: The World Bank, 1998.

BIS Quarterly Review, February 2000. Available at www.bis.org.

Black, F., and M. Scholes. "The Pricing of Options and Corporate Liabilities." *Journal of Political Economy,* June 1973.

Bokhari, Farhan. "Islamic Banking Survey." *Financial Times,* October 27, 2000.

Borish, Michael, and Fernando Montes-Negret. "Restructuring Distressed Banks in Transition Economies: Lessons from Central Europe and Ukraine." In Gerard Carpio Jr., William C. Hunter, George G. Kaufman, and Danny M. Leipziger, editors, *Preventing Bank Crises: Lessons from Recent Global Bank Failures,* p. 69. Washington, D.C.: The World Bank, 1998.

Boulton, Leyla. "Banks in Control of Turkey's Internet Explosion." *Financial Times,* March 13, 2000, p. 23.

———. "On Target for an Economic Turnaround." *Turkey: Banking and Investment, Financial Times* Survey, November 20, 2000, p. 1.

Brooks, Rich. "BankAmerica Retreats from Overseas Markets." *Wall Street Journal,* January 22, 1999, p. A2.

Buckley, Neil. "Fortis Lifts Merger Benefit Estimates." *Financial Times,* November 22, 1999, p. 25.

Bureau of International Narcotics and Law Enforcement Affairs, U.S. Department of State. *International Narcotics Control Strategy Report, 1997.* Washington, D.C.: U.S. Department of State, March 1998.

Cable, J. R. "Capital Market Information and Industrial Performance: The Role of West German Banks." *Economic Journal,* 95 (1985), pp. 118–132.

Chernow, Ron. "The End of 'High' Finance." *Wall Street Journal,* September 14, 2000, p. 26.

"Commercial Propositions." *The Economist,* December 5, 1998, p. 84.

Cramb, Gordon. "ABN Amro Will Seek Clients via Online Banking." *Financial Times,* July 19, 2000, p. 28.

Crooks, Ed. "Islands Look to E-commerce Boost." *Financial Times,* July 27, 2000, p. 10.

Cunningham, Andrew, and Elisabeth Jadison-Moore. *Analysing the Creditworthiness of Islamic Financial Institutions.* Moody's Investors Service, November 1999.

Czech National Bank. *Report on Banking Supervision in the Czech Republic.* Prague: Czech National Bank, December 1999.

The Economist Intelligence Unit, *India/Nepal Country Profile 1997–98.* London: The Economist Intelligence Unit, 1997.

Edwards, Burt. "The History and Future of Credit." In Burt Edwards, editor, *Credit Management Handbook,* pp. 3–14. Aldershot, UK: Gower, 1997.

Financial Action Task Force. *Financial Action Task Force on Money Laundering: Review to Identify Non-cooperation Countries or Territories: Increasing the Worldwide Effectiveness of Anti–Money Laundering Measures.* Paris: Financial Action Task Force, June 22, 2000.

Francis, Roger. "US Banks and the Credit Market Meltdown." *IBJ Research* (Tokyo), November 2, 2000.

Frydman, Roman, Andrzej Rapaczynski, and Joel Turkewitz. "Transition to a Private Property Regime in the Czech Republic and Hungary." In Wing Thye Woo, Stephen Parker, and Jeffrey Sachs, editors, *Economies in Transition: Comparing Asia and Europe,* p. 75. Cambridge, Mass.: The MIT Press, 1997.

Fuerbinger, Jonathan. "The Wounds Haven't Healed in Emerging Markets Debt." *New York Times,* November 28, 1999, p. 7.

"Global Custody." *Financial Times* Survey, July 14, 2000, p. 1.

Gonnelli, Adam. *The Basics of Foreign Trade and Exchange.* New York: Federal Reserve Bank of New York, Public Information Department, 1993.

Grandin, Elisabeth. "France, Bank System Report." *Standard & Poor's,* October 1997, p. 2.

Hall, William. "Liechtenstein Fund Inflow Hit." *Financial Times,* July 27, 2000, p. 3.

Hall, William, and Andrew Balls. "Bank Consolidation Fails to Boost Profitability." *Financial Times,* August 23, 1999.

Hien, Dao Thu. "Half of Canadians Say They Will Bank via the Internet by 2003." *Bloomberg,* April 18, 2000, available at www.bloomberg.com.

Holland, Kelley, Linda Himelstein, and Zachary Schiller. "The Bankers Trust Tapes." *Business Week,* October 16, 1995, p. 106.

Innocenti, Nicol Degli. "Reeling in South Africa's Loan Sharks." *Financial Times,* July 19, 2000, p. 5.

"International Project Finance." *Financial Times* Survey, December 3, 1996, p. 51.

James, Canute. "Antigua to Act on Money Laundering." *Financial Times,* April 13, 1999, p. 8.

"Japanese Banks Racing into Vietnam." *Nikkei Weekly,* December 9, 1996, p. 10.

Kahn, Joseph. "One Big Bite After the Other Leads to Indigestion for Banks." *New York Times,* November 27, 1998, p. C1.

Kane, Edward J. "No Room for Weak Links in the Chain of Deposit Insurance Reform." *Journal of Financial Services Research,* 1 (September 1987), pp. 77–111.

Kapstein, Ethan B. "Global Rules for Global Finance." *Current History,* November 1998, p. 355.

Kaufman, George G. "Bank Failures, Systemic Risk, and Bank Regulation." *Cato Journal,* 16, no. 1 (Spring/Summer 1996), pp. 325–359.

———. "Bank Fragility: Perception and Historical Evidence." Chicago University Working Paper No. 96-6, 1996.

Kaufman, Henry. "Too Much on Their Plate." *Financial Times,* February 4, 1999, p. 24.

King, Sharon R. "Quick Action by US Banks Limits Damage." *New York Times,* September 3, 1998, p. C5.

Labate, John, Gary Silverman, Joshua Chaffin, and Elizabeth Wine. "Blow to CSFB as Key Banker Defects to Rival." *Financial Times,* November 22, 2000, p. 17.

Lee, Peter. "Banking Crisis: Ways to Recover." *Euromoney,* November 1998, p. 30.

Linnell, Ian. "Bank Industry Risk Analysis, United Kingdom." *Standard & Poor's,* April 1996, pp. 3–4,

Lissakers, Karin. "The Role of the International Monetary Fund." In Gerard Carpio Jr., William C. Hunter, George G. Kaufman, and Danny M. Leipziger, editors, *Preventing Bank Crises: Lessons from Recent Global Bank Failures,* p. 28. Washington, D.C.: The World Bank, 1998.

Lopez, Robert S. "The Dawn of Medieval Banking." In the Center for Medieval and Renaissance Studies, University of California, Los Angeles, editors, *The Dawn of Modern Banking,* p. 2. New Haven, Conn.: Yale University Press, 1979.

The Luxembourg Bankers' Association. "Banking in Luxembourg: Facts and Figures, June 1998."

MacDonald, Scott B. "The Significance of Disclosure and Transparency in Thailand's 1997 Economic Crisis." *Asian Survey,* July 1998.

———. "Thunder in the Andes: Ecuador's Political and Economic Crises." *CSIS Hemisphere 2000,* Series VIII, Issue 9 (May 10, 2000).

———. "The Return of Hong Kong: Riding the New Economy?" *FinanceAsia.Com,* June 2, 2000.

MacDonald, Scott B., and Bruce Zagaris. "Caribbean Offshore Financial Centers: The Bahamas, the British Dependencies, and the Netherlands Antilles and Aruba." In Scott B. MacDonald and Bruce Zagaris, editors, *International Handbook on Drug Control,* pp. 137–156 (Westport, Conn.: Greenwood Press, 1992).

Mackintosh, James. "Internet Brands Set to Shake Up the Banking Sector." *Financial Times,* July 13, 1999, p. 8.

Maingot, Anthony P. "The Offshore Caribbean." In Anthony Payne and Paul Sutton, editors, *Modern Caribbean Politics,* p. 263. Baltimore: The Johns Hopkins University Press, 1993.

Mainlander, Christopher. *Reshaping North American Banking: The Transforming Effects of Regional Market and Policy Shifts.* Washington, D.C.: CSIS Policy Papers on the Americas, July 1999.

Major, Tony. "WestLB Split May Provide Model for German Banking." *Financial Times,* November 10, 2000, p. 20.

Major, Tony, and Eric Frey. "HVB to Take Over Bank Austria." *Financial Times,* July 24, 2000, p. 22.

Major, Tony, and Rolf Lebert. "Commerzbank in Talks to Strengthen European Alliances." *Financial Times,* August 17, 2000, p. 18.

McCawley, Tom. "Bank Bali Faces Decision on Recapitalisation Scheme." *Financial Times,* July 19, 2000, p. 4.

McDermott, Darren. "Citibank Uses Latin Lessons in Asia." *Wall Street Journal,* December 29, 1997, p. A6.

Merchant, Khozem, and Angus Donald. "New Delhi to Cut Stake in State-Owned Banks." *Financial Times,* November 17, 2000, p. 8.

Moody's Investors Service. *India: Banking Systems Outlook.* New York: Moody's Investors Service, November 1998.

Murphy, Dan. "Banking: Paper Tiger." *Far Eastern Economic Review,* April 22, 1999, p. 68.

Murray, Matt. "Derivatives: A Mixed Bag for U.S. Banks." *Wall Street Journal,* September 29, 1998, p. C1.

O'Brien, Kevin. "Germany's Banking Bonanza." *Bloomberg Markets,* December 2000, p. 46.

"On a Wing and a Prayer." *The Economist,* Supplement: A Survey of International Banking, April 7, 1999, p. 4.

Paritate Bank's website. At www.paritate.lv.aboutparitate.htm.

Pauly, M. "The Economics of Moral Hazard." *American Economic Review,* 58, no. 1 (1968), pp. 31–58.

Peel, Michael. "Crackdown May Hold Upside for Offshore Centers." *Financial Times,* July, 28, 2000, p. 11.

Radelet, Steven. "From Boom to Bust: Indonesia's Implosion." *Harvard Asia Pacific Review,* Winter 1998–99, pp. 65–66.

"Regulating Capital Flows" (editorial). *Financial Times,* March 25, 1998, p. 33.

Rhoads, Christopher. "European Banks Rethink Globalization." *Wall Street Journal,* October 5, 1998, p. A23.

Roubini, Nouriel. Asian Financial Crisis website. At www.stern.nyu.edu/~nroubini/asia/AsiaHomepage.html.
Saigol, Lina, and Peter Thal Larsen. "UK Banks in Talks Over Possible $32 bn Merger." *Financial Times,* November 3, 2000, p. 17.
Sassen, Saskia. "Global Financial Centers." *Foreign Affairs,* January/February 1999.
Shirreff, David. "FX: Plotting the Death of Settlement Risk." *Euromoney,* May 1998, pp. 70–72.
Siems, Thomas F. "10 Myths About Financial Derivatives." Case Policy Analysis no. 283, September 11, 1997, available at www.cato.org/pubs.
Sikora, Peter. "Bank Profit Pressure to Prevail in India in the New Milennium." *Standard & Poor's Credit Week,* May 3, 2000, p .18.
Smith, Roy, and Ingo Walter. "The Death of Universal Banks." *Financial Times,* March 14, 2000, p. 7.
Soros, George. Letter of April 28, 2000. At cnnfn.com/2000/04/28/mutualfunds/soros/letter.htm.
Spencer, Jeffrey, and Goergie Bennett. *Landesbank Handbook—Gotterdammerung: Twilight of the Guarantees?* London: Merrill Lynch High Grade Research, October 11, 2000.
Sprong, Kenneth, and Richard J. Sullivan. "The Outlook for the U.S. Banking Industry: What Does the Experience of the 1980s and 1990s Tell Us? *Federal Reserve Bank of Kansas City Economic Review,* 84, no. 4 (fourth quarter 1999), pp. 65–83.
Sunami, Miho, and Koyo Ozeki. "Japanese Banks Growing Threat to Credit Position of Regional Banks." *Merrill Lynch Fixed Income Research* (Tokyo), November 9, 2000, p. 2.
SWIFT website. At www.swift.com.
Tan, Charles X. "Banking System Outlook: China—The Start of a Long March." *Moody's Investor Service,* August 1999, p. 9.
Ter Wengel, Jan. "International Trade in Banking Services." *Journal of International Money and Finance,* 14, no. 1 (1995), p. 47.
Thackray, John. "Whatever Happened to the Hedge Funds?" *Institutional Investor,* May 1977, pp. 71–74.
Thomas, Richard. "Russia's Banks: A New Beginning or a Dead End? *Standard & Poor's Credit Week,* January 19, 2000, p. 10.
Timewell, Stephen, "Going Global." *The Banker,* February 1999, p. 40.
"The Trials of Megabanks." *The Economist,* October 31, 1998, p. 23.
Uchitelle, Louis. "Helping Hand Replaces Hands-Off Role in Asia." *New York Times,* January 1, 1998, p. D1.
Walter, Ingo. "Project Finance: The Lender's Perspective." In David W. Pearce, Horse Siebert, and Ingo Walter, editors, *Risk and the Political Economy of Resource Development.* London: Macmillan Press, 1984.
Warde, Ibrahim. "Crony Capitalism: LTCM, a Hedge Fund Above Suspicion." *Le Monde Diplomatique,* November 1998, available at www.monde-diplomatique.fr/en/ 1998/11/04warde2.
Waters, Richard. "Putting Back the Trust into BT." *Financial Times,* May 13, 1996, p. 19.
Wessel, David, and Bob Davis. "Currency Controls Are Getting a Hearing Amid Asian Crisis." *Wall Street Journal,* September 4, 1998.
White, E. H. "Before the Glass-Steagall Act: An Analysis of the Investment Banking Activities of National Banks." *Explorations in Economic History,* 23 (1986), pp. 33–55.
Willman, John. "Five Banks Link Up in Web Venture." *Financial Times,* July 28, 2000, p. 16.
———. "Banking on Borrowed Time." *Financial Times,* November 6, 2000, p. 20.
Wolf, Martin. "On Sovereign Bankruptcies." *Financial Times,* May 5, 1995.
World Bank. *Global Development Finance: Analysis and Summary Tables.* Washington, D.C.: The World Bank, 1998.
World Trade Organization website. At www.wto.org.
Wrong, Michela. "Between the Devil and the Deep Blue Sea." *Financial Times,* July 27, 2000, p. 10.
Yellen, Janet. "Lessons from the Asian Crisis." Council on Foreign Relations, April 15, 1998, available at www.whitehouse.gov.
Zagaris, Bruce. "Money Laundering: An International Control Problem." In Scott B. MacDonald and Bruce Zagaris, editors, *International Handbook on Drug Control,* p. 29. Westport, Conn.: Greenwood Press, 1992.
Zagaris, Bruce, and Scott B. MacDonald. "Money Laundering, Financial Fraud and Technology: The Perils of an Instantaneous Economy." *George Washington Journal of International Law and Economics,* 26, no. 1 (1992), pp. 61–107.
Zlotnik, Michael. "Germany: Bank System Report." *Standard & Poor's,* August 1997, p. 10.

Books

Arditti, Fred D. *Derivatives.* Boston: Harvard Business School Press, 1996.
Banks, Erik. *The Rise and Fall of the Merchant Banks.* London: Kogan Page Ltd., 1999.
Beckman, Martin. *Crashes: Why They Happen—What to Do.* London: Grafton Books, 1988.
Brady, Rose. *Kapitalizm: Russia's Struggle to Free Its Economy.* New Haven, Conn.: Yale University Press, 1999.
Bruck, Connie. *The Predators' Ball: The Insider Story of Drexel Burnham and the Rise of the Junk Bond Raiders.* New York: Penguin Books, 1989.
Butler, Brian, David Butler, and Alan Isaacs, editors. *Oxford Dictionary of Finance and Banking: From International to Personal Finance.* New York: Oxford University Press, 1997.
Calomoris, Charles W. *The Postmodern Bank Safety Net: Lessons from Developed and Developing Economies.* Washington, D.C.: AEI Press, 1997.
Canals, Jordi. *Universal Banking: International Comparisons and Theoretical Perspectives.* New York: Oxford University Press, 1997.
Carpio, Gerard, Jr., William C. Hunter, George G. Kaufman, and Danny M. Leipziger, editors. *Preventing Bank Crises: Lessons from Recent Global Bank Failures.* Washington, D.C.: The World Bank, 1998.
Chancellor, Edward. *Devil Take the Hindmost: A History of Financial Speculation.* New York: Farrar, Straus, and Garoux, 1999.

Chernow, Ron. *The Death of the Banker: The Decline and Fall of the Great Financial Dynasties and the Triumph of the Small Investor.* New York: Vintage Books, 1997.

Claudon, Michael P., editor. *World Debt Crisis: International Lending on Trial.* Cambridge, Mass.: Ballinger Publishing Company, 1986.

Clifford, Mark L., and Pete Engardio. *Meltdown: Asia's Boom, Bust, and Beyond.* New York: Prentice Hall Press, 2000.

Crane, D. B., et al.*The Global Financial System.* Boston: Harvard Business School Press, 1995.

Darity, William A. *The Loan-Pushers: The Role of Commercial Banks in the International Debt Crisis.* Cambridge, Mass.: Ballinger Publishing Company, 1988.

Date, R. *International Banking Deregulation.* Oxford: Blackwell, 1993.

Dewatipont, M., and J. Tirole. *The Prudential Regulation of Banks.* Cambridge, Mass: The MIT Press, 1994.

Diamond, Walter. *Tax Havens of the World, Volume 1.* New York: Matthew Bender, 1974–1983.

Edwards, Burt, editor. *Credit Management Handbook.* Aldershot, UK: Gower, 1997.

Eichengreen, Barry, and Peter H. Lindert. *The International Debt Crisis in Historical Perspective.* Cambridge, Mass.: The MIT Press, 1989.

Eiteman, David K., Arthur I. Stonehill, and Michael H. Moffett. *Multinational Business Finance,* Eighth Edition. Reading, Mass.: Addison Wesley Publishing Company, 1998.

Endlich, Lisa. *Goldman Sachs: The Culture of Success.* New York: Simon & Schuster, 1999.

Federal Deposit Insurance Corporation. *History of the Eighties—Lessons for the Future.* Volume I: *An Examination of the Banking Crises of the 1980s and Early 1990s.* Washington, D.C.: Federal Deposit Insurance Corporation, 2000.

Fitch, Thomas. *Dictionary of Banking Terms.* New York: Barron's Educational Series, 1997.

Geisst, Charles R. *Wall Street: A History.* New York: Oxford University Press, 1997.

Germain, Randall. *The International Organization of Credit.* Cambridge, UK: Cambridge University Press, 1997.

Goldstein, Morris, and Philip Turner. *Banking Crises in Emerging Economies: Origins and Policy Options.* Basel, Switzerland: Bank for International Settlements, 1996.

Gup, Benton E. *Bank Failures in the Major Trading Countries of the World: Causes and Remedies.* Westport, Conn.: Quorum Books, 1998.

Gustafson, Thane. *Capitalism Russian-Style.* New York: Cambridge University Press, 1999.

Hamilton, Adrian. *The Financial Revolution.* New York: The Free Press, 1986.

Handelman, Stephen. *Comrade Criminal: Russia's New Mafiya.* New Haven, Conn.: Yale University Press, 1995.

Hayes, Declan. *Japan's Big Bang: The Deregulation and Revitalization of the Japanese Economy.* Boston: Tuttle Publishing, 2000.

Hayes, Samuel L., III, and Philip M. Hubbard. *Investment Banking: A Tale of Three Cities.* Boston: Harvard Business School Press, 1990.

Heffernan, Shelagh. *Modern Banking in Theory and Practice.* New York: John Wiley & Sons, 1996.

Higgins, J. Kevin. *The Bahamian Economy: An Analysis.* Nassau, The Bahamas: The Counsellors Ltd., 1994.

Hubbard, R. Glenn. *Money, the Financial System, and the Economy,* Third Edition. Reading, Mass.: Addison Wesley, 2000.

Hull, John C. *Options, Futures, and Other Derivatives,* Third Edition. Upper Saddle River, N.J.: Prentice Hall, 1997.

Hunter, William C., George G. Kaufman, and Thomas H. Krueger. *The Asian Financial Crisis: Origins, Implications, and Solutions.* Boston: Kluwer Academic Press, 1999.

International Monetary Fund. *International Capital Markets: Developments, Prospects, and Key Policy Issues.* Washington, D.C.: International Monetary Fund, November 1997.

Johnson, Hazel J. *The Banker's Guide to Investment Banking: Securities and Underwriting Activities in Commercial Banking.* Chicago: Irwin Publishers, 1996.

Jones, Geoffrey. *British Multinational Banking 1830–1990.* Oxford: Clarendon Press, 1993.

Jones, Michael Arthur. *Swiss Bank Accounts: A Personal Guide to Ownership Benefits and Use.* New York: Liberty Press Books, 1990.

Jorion, Philippe. *Value at Risk.* New York: McGraw Hill, 1997.

Kindleberger, Charles. *Manias, Panics and Crashes: A History of Financial Crashes.* New York: John Wiley & Sons, 1996.

Kolb, Robert W. *Financial Derivatives.* Malden, Mass.: Blackwell Publishers, 1997.

Krieger, Andrew, with Edward Claflin. *The Money Bazaar: Inside the Trillion Dollar World of Currency Trading.* New York: Times Books, 1992.

Kumar, Anjali, with Terry Chuppe and Paula Perttunen. *The Regulation of Non-bank Financial Institutions: The United States, the European Union and Other Countries.* Washington, D.C.: The World Bank, 1997.

Lederman, Jess, and Robert A. Klein, editors. *Hedge Funds: Investment and Portfolio Strategies for the Institutional Investor.* New York: McGraw-Hill, 1995.

Lindbeck, Assar, Per Molander, Torsten Persson, Olof Petersson, Agnar Sandmo, Birgitta Swedenborg, and Niels Thygesen. *Turning Sweden Around.* Cambridge, Mass.: The MIT Press, 1994.

Litan, R. E. *What Should Banks Do?* Washington, D.C.: The Brookings Institution, 1987.

Lowenstein, Roger. *When Genius Failed: The Rise and Fall of Long-Term Capital Management.* New York: Random House, 2000.

Luxembourg. Luxembourg: Editions Binsfeld, 1980.

MacDonald, Scott B., and Albert L. Gastmann. *Credit, Trust and Power: A History of Credit in the Western World and Its Role in Global Development and International Politics.* Rutgers, N.J.: Transaction, forthcoming in 2001.

MacDonald, Scott B., and Bruce Zagaris, editors. *International Handbook on Drug Control.* Westport, Conn.: Greenwood Press, 1992.

MacDonald, Scott B., Margie Lindsay, and David L. Crum, editors. *The Global Debt Crisis: Forecasting for the Future.* London: Francis Pinter, 1990.

MacDonald, Scott B., Jane Hughes, and Uwe Bott, editors. *The Latin American Debt Crisis in the 1990s.* New York: Praeger, 1991.

Madrid, Raul L. *Over-exposed: U.S. Banks Confront the Third World Debt Crisis.* Washington, D.C.: Investors Responsibility Research Center, 1990.

Marshall, John E., and M. E. Ellis. *Investment Banking and Brokerage: The New Rules of the Game.* New York: McGraw Hill, 1993.

Miller, Morris. *Coping Is Not Enough!: The International Debt Crisis and the Roles of the World Bank and IMF.* Homewood, Ill.: Dow Jones-Irwin, 1986.

Mishkin, Frederic S., and Stanley G. Eakins. *Financial Markets and Institutions,* Third Edition. Reading, Mass.: Addison Wesley, 2000.

Organization for Economic Cooperation and Development (OECD). *OECD Economic Outlook 1998.* Paris: OECD, 1998.

——. *Belgium/Luxembourg: OCED Economic Survey 1999.* Paris: OECD, 1999.

——. *Mexico: OECD Economic Survey 1999.* Paris: OECD, 1999.

——. *Slovak Republic: OECD Economic Survey 1999.* Paris: OCED, 1999.

——. *OECD Economic Outlook June 2000.* Paris: OECD, 2000.

——. *Towards Global Tax Co-operation, Report to the 2000 Ministerial Council Meeting and Recommendations by the Committee on Fiscal Affairs: Progress in Identifying and Eliminating Harmful Tax Practices.* Paris: OECD, 2000.

Orsingher, Roger. *Banks of the World.* New York: Walker and Company, 1967.

Palmer, Howard. *Bank Risk Analysis in Emerging Markets.* London: Euromoney Publications, 1992.

Park, Yoon S., and Jack Zwick. *International Banking in Theory and Practice.* Reading, Mass.: Addison-Wesley Publishing, 1985.

Partnoy, Frank. *F.I.A.S.C.O.: Blood in the Water on Wall Street.* New York: W. W. Norton & Company, 1997.

Pass, C., B. Lowes, L. Davies, and S. J. Kronish. *The Harper Collins Dictionary of Economics.* New York: Harper Perennial, 1991.

Patrick, H., and Yoon Park, editors. *The Financial Development of Japan, Korea, and Taiwan: Growth, Repression and Liberalization.* New York: Oxford University Press, 1994.

Permanent Subcommittee on Investigations of the Committee on Governmental Affairs, U.S. Senate. *Crime and Secrecy: The Use of Offshore Banks and Companies.* Washington, D.C.: U.S. Government Printing Office, 1985.

Political Risk Services. *The Handbook of Country and Political Risk Analysis.* Syracuse, N.Y.: Political Risk Services, 1998.

Powis, Robert E. *The Money Launderers: Lessons from the Drug War—How Billions of Illegal Dollars Are Washed Through Banks and Businesses.* Chicago: Probus Publishing Company, 1992.

Robinson, Jeffery. *The Laundrymen: Inside the World's Third Largest Business.* London: Pocket Books, 1998.

Sachs, Jeffrey. *New Approaches to the Latin American Debt Crisis.* Princeton, N.J.: Princeton University Press, 1989.

Smith, Roy C., and Ingo Walter. *Global Banking.* New York: Oxford University Press, 1997.

Smithson, Charles W., Clifford W. Smith Jr., and Wilford D. Sykes. *Managing Financial Risk: A Guide to Derivative Products, Financial Engineering and Value Maximization.* New York: McGraw Hill, 1995.

Solberg, Ronald, editor. *Country Risk Analysis: A Handbook.* New York: Routledge, 1992.

Solnik, Bruno. *International Investments.* Reading, Mass: Addison-Wesley, 2000.

Strause, Jean, *Morgan: American Financier.* New York: Random House, 1999.

Tamaki, Norio. *Japanese Banking: A History, 1859–1959.* New York: Cambridge University Press, 1995.

Truell, Peter, and Larry Gurwin. *False Profits: The Inside Story of BCCI, the World's Most Corrupt Financial Empire.* New York: Houghton Mifflin, 1992.

United Nations. *World Economic and Social Survey 1999: Trends and Policies in the World Economy.* New York: United Nations, 1999.

U.S. Department of State, Bureau of Narcotics Affairs. *International Narcotics Control Enforcement Report 1997.* Washington, D.C.: U.S. Department of State, 1997.

Walter, Ingo. *The Secret Money Market: Inside the Dark World of Tax Evasion, Financial Fraud, Insider Trading, Money Laundering and Capital Flight.* New York: Harper Collins, 1990.

Warburton, Peter. *Debt and Delusion: Central Bank Follies that Threaten Economic Disaster.* London: Penguin Press, 1999.

Watkins, Alfred J. *Till Debt Do Us Part: Who Wins, Who Loses, and Who Pays for the International Debt Crisis.* Washington, D.C.: University Press of America, 1986.

Wicker, Elmus. *Banking Panics of the Gilded Age.* New York: Cambridge University Press, 2000.

The World Bank. *Entering the Twenty-First Century: World Bank Development Report 1999/2000.* New York: Oxford University Press, 2000.

INDEX

Note: Page numbers followed by the letters *f* and *t* indicate figures and tables, respectively.

Credits

Page 12, from *The Wall Street Journal*, © 2000 by Dow Jones & Co., Inc. Reprinted with permission of Dow Jones & Co., Inc. via Copyright Clearance Center Inc. Page 33, Reprinted with permission. © The Economist Newspaper Group, Inc. Further reproduction prohibited. www.economist.com. Page 44, from *The Wall Street Journal*, © 1997 by Dow Jones & Co., Inc. Reprinted with permission of Dow Jones & Co., Inc. via Copyright Clearance Center, Inc. Page 47, Reprinted with permission. © *The Financial Times,* March 13, 1995. Page 57, © 1998 by the New York Times Co. Reprinted by permission. Page 89, © Institutional Investor, Inc. Reprinted with permission. Page 90, Reprinted with permission. © *The Financial Times,* March 2, 2001. Page 99, Reprinted with permission. © *The Financial Times*, March 27, 1999. Page 102, © Institutional Investor, Inc. Reprinted with permission. Page 108, Reprinted with permission. © *The Financial Times*, January 22, 1999. Page 139, from *The Asian Wall Street Journal, © 1999 by Dow Jones & Co., Inc. Reprinted with permission of Dow Jones & Co., Inc. via Copyright Clearance Center, Inc. Page 142, Reprinted with permission.* © *The Financial Times,* March 1, 1999. Page 154, from RIDING THE BULL by Paul Stiles, © 1998 by Paul Stiles. Used by permission of Times Books of Random House, Inc. Page 161, *CNN Financial,* September 12, 2000, at http://cnnfn.cnn.com/2000/09/12/deals/dresdner. Page 170, Charles P. Wallace, *Fortune*, © 1998 Time, Inc. All rights reserved. Page 176, Reprinted with permission. © *The Financial Times*, October 27, 1999. Page 179, Reprinted courtesy of *The Boston Globe*. Page 184, Reprinted with permission. © *The Financial Times*, October 21, 1999. Page 199, Reprinted with permission. © *The Financial Times*, October 28, 1997. Page 205, Reprinted with permission. © *The Financial Times,* June 2, 2000. Page 209, © 1998, 1995 Addison-Wesley Publishing Company, Inc. Reprinted with permission of Addison Wesley Longman. Page 211, © 1998, 1995 Addison-Wesley Publishing Company, Inc. Reprinted with permission of Addison Wesley Longman. Page 218-219, Reprinted with permission. © *The Financial Times*, November 2, 1999 Page 231, Reprinted with permission of Cambridge University Press. Page 232, © 1999 by the New York Times Co. Reprinted by permission. Page 236, Reprinted with permission. © *The Financial Times*, August 23, 1998. Page 240, Reprinted with permission. © *The Financial Times,* July 6, 2000. Page 245, Reprinted with permission. © *The Financial Times,* March 23, 1999. Page 247-248, from WHEN GENIUS FAILED, by Roger Lowenstein, © 2000 by Roger Lowenstein. Used by permission of Random House, Inc. Page 249, © 1999 by the New York Times Co. Reprinted by permission. Page 250, Reprinted with permission. © *The Financial Times*, December 4, 2000. Page 255, The Economist Newspaper Group, Inc. Reprinted with permission. Further reproduction prohibited. www.economist.com. Page 256, Reprinted with permission. © *The Financial Times*, April 12, 1999. Page 298, © 1999 by the New York Times Co. Reprinted by permission. Page 300-301, © 2000 Addison Wesley Longman Inc. Reprinted by permission of Addison Wesley Longman. Page 302, Reprinted with permission of The MacGraw-Hill Companies. Page 303, Reprinted with permission of The MacGraw-Hill Companies. Page 306, Reprinted with permission. The Economist Newpapers, Inc. Further reproduction prohibited. www.economist.com. Page 311, Reprinted with permission. © *The Financial Times*, January 7, 2000, Page 312, Reprinted with permission. © *The Financial Times*, February 3, 1998. Page 318, © 1999 by Nancy Birdsall and Devesh Kapur. Reprinted by permission. Page 320, Reprinted courtesy of *The Boston Globe*. Page 327-328, Reprinted with permission. © *The Financial Times*, April 19, 1999. Page 351, from *The Wall Street Journal*, © 1998 by Dow Jones & Co., Inc. Reprinted with permission of Dow Jones and Co., Inc. via Copyright Clearance Center, Inc. Page 354-355, © 2000 Addison Wesley Longman Inc. Reprinted by permission of Pearson Education Inc. Page 357 & 358, © 2000, 1997, 1995, 1994 Addison Wesley Publishing Company Inc. Reprinted by permission of Addison Wesley Longman. Page 360, Reprinted with permission. © *The Financial Times*, June 19, 2000. Page 362-363, © 2000 Addison Wesley Longman Inc. Reprinted by permission of Pearson Education Inc. Page 363, © 1998 by The New York Times Co. Reprinted by permission. Page 364, Reprinted with permission. © *The Financial Times*, March 20, 1998. Page 364-365, © *The Financial Times*, May 24, 1993. Page 369, from *The Wall Street Journal*, © 1999 by Dow Jones & Co., Inc. Reprinted with permission of Dow Jones & Co., Inc. via Copyright Clearance Center, Inc. Page 378-379, Reprinted with permission. © The Economist Newspaper Group, Inc. Further reproduction prohibited. www.economist.com Page 386, © 1998 by The New York Times Co. Reprinted by permission. Page 390 (top), Reprinted by permission. © *The Financial Times*, September 9, 1999; (bottom) Reprinted by permission. © *The Financial Times*, August 28, 1998. Page 392, from *The Wall Street Journal*, © 1998 by Dow Jones & Co., Inc. Reprinted with permission of Dow Jones & Co., Inc. via Copyright Clearance Center Inc. Page 393, Reprinted with permission. © *The Financial Times*, September 25, 1998. Page 424, Reprinted by permission. © *The Financial Times*, February 8, 2000. Page 425, Reprinted by permission. © *The Financial Times*, July 1, 1999. Page 429, © 1998 by The New York Times Co. Reprinted by permission. Page 432, Reprinted with permission. © The Economist Newspaper Group, Inc. Further reproduction prohibited. www.economist.com.